THE QUIET PINT

The Daily Telegraph

THE QUIET PINT

A GUIDE TO PUBS WITH NO PIPED MUSIC

SIXTH EDITION

Compiled and Edited by
DEREK and JOSEPHINE DEMPSTER

AURUM PRESS

This edition first published 2004 by Aurum Press Ltd
25 Bedford Avenue, London WC1B 3AT

A catalogue record for this book is available from the
British Library.

ISBN 1 85410 996 0

1 3 5 7 9 8 6 4 2
2004 2006 2008 2007 2005

Design by Don Macpherson

Typeset by M Rules

Cover design by Mark Latter at Vivid Design

Cover photograph by John Blay

Printed in Great Britain by Bookmarque Ltd, Croydon

Contents

vii Introduction
xi The Pipedown Campaign
xiii J.D. Wetherspoon
1 Quiet Pint Areas

ENGLAND

2 Bedfordshire & Cambridgeshire
16 Berkshire
26 Buckinghamshire
Cambridgeshire see Bedfordshire
36 Cheshire
Cleveland see Northumbria
44 Cornwall
58 Cumbria
72 Derbyshire & Staffordshire
86 Devon
110 Dorset
Durham see Northumbria
122 Essex
136 Gloucestershire
Greater Manchester see Lancashire
156 Hampshire
172 Hereford, Shropshire & Worcestershire
192 Hertfordshire
200 Kent
216 Lancashire, Greater Manchester & Merseyside
230 Leicestershire, Lincolnshire & Nottinghamshire
Lincolnshire see Leicestershire
Merseyside see Lancashire
246 Midlands (Northamptonshire, Warwickshire & West Midlands)
260 Norfolk
Northamptonshire see Midlands
Northumberland see Northumbria
272 Northumbria (Cleveland, Durham, Northumberland, Tyne & Wear)

Nottinghamshire see Leicestershire
284 Oxfordshire
Shropshire see Hereford
300 Somerset
Staffordshire see Derbyshire
320 Suffolk
338 Surrey
350 Sussex, East & West
Tyne & Wear see Northumbria
Warwickshire see Midlands
West Midlands see Midlands
376 Wiltshire
Worcestershire see Hereford
390 Yorkshire, North, West & South

LONDON
418 London Pubs by Postal District

452 **SCOTLAND**

474 **WALES**

494 Northern Ireland (Wetherspoon only)

495 Wetherspoon at the Airports

497 Pub nomination forms

499 Index

PLEASE NOTE.
A 'Q' symbol on the maps means QUIET pubs – fully described within a county.
'B' stands for BEST OF THE REST: worthwhile – some outstanding – pubs with
very quiet music, briefly described at the end of each county section.
'W' shows location of Wetherspoon pubs – some fully described, the rest listed
at the end of each section.

Introduction

When *The Quiet Pint* was launched in 1995, music in many pubs had already crossed the border from being tolerable to being unbearable. Since then piped music has spread, notwithstanding the efforts of the Pipedown Campaign, the United Kingdom Noise Association and other anti-muzac groups. You notice this when you look forward to visiting a pub that was wonderful last time you dropped by and find it is now no longer the same. The building might not have changed, but the ambience has; the natural buzz of customers – if they're still there – chatting against a background of clinking glasses is now louder, attempting to prevail over the coarse cacophony they call pop music.

Unaccountably, there's a dearth of music-free pubs in some counties. They're candidates for an interesting sociological study. For a long time Surrey was among them. But this year, what was a musically challenged Surrey has surprisingly delivered a number of new pubs to *The Quiet Pint*. There was a reversal in Berkshire! Yorkshire is such a big county it was inevitable that some gems, with a tremendous help from two of our enthusiastic readers, have found their way into this edition.

Much has gone on in the licensing trade since the last edition of *The Quiet Pint*. Pub groups have moved around like pieces on a chess board in a seemingly endless game run by banks and accountants. This frequently means a change of policy and one more pub dropped from the guide. We have unfortunately lost a number of establishments during the last two years: some for the obvious reason – the introduction of piped music; others seem to have lost the will to live and didn't come up to scratch. Some, known in the past for the excellence of their food, have been taken over by new owners who unfortunately lack the culinary expertise, musical understanding and flair of their predecessors. I'm always surprised how many unsuitable people take on the lease of a tied pub and wonder at the stupidity of brewers and pub groups when they engage inappropriate couples to manage an outstanding village pub and allow it to be run into the ground.

With food representing over 60% of a pub's turnover, the best pubs are as good as some of the nation's finest restaurants. Others, not so ambitious, serve some interesting dishes, while a great number are content to offer 'fill-a-gap-fare'. We have made a point of not recommending the quality of food unless we have an indication from those able to give a considered opinion that it is right to do so. '*Experientia docet*' was the maxim on my old school's coat of arms. Experience has indeed taught us to know when a pub is buying in ready meals from specialist caterers or actually preparing locally produced ingredients in their own kitchens. We let you know what you can expect on a menu and with experience you too will be able to interpret the dishes on offer and have a very good idea as to whether there is a skilled hand in the kitchen, or that hand has perfected moving a ready-prepared dish from the freezer to the microwave. You would hardly credit some publicans with ever thinking of deep-frying Brie – now overtaken by a Caesar salad, braised lamb shanks and grain mustard mash. But think on this: that sleight-of-hand from freezer to microwave is infinitely preferable to the standard of cooking you still find in some pubs where a toasted cheese sandwich is the most edible thing you can choose from the menu.

A long menu is suspect; a short menu with that '*je ne sais quoi*', making it just that little bit different, will indicate that someone in the kitchen is giving what they serve some serious thought and you are the one to benefit. Over the last few years more and more pubs have become concerned with the quality and freshness of the ingredients coming into their kitchens; they are making a tremendous effort to source the best local produce. Cheese, lamb, beef, venison, locally shot game, fresh fish, fruit and vegetables and even local wines are being used to create some exciting menus.

Wine lists are as varied as the food on offer. More than ever you will find a carefully chosen selection. Some pubs have a cellar that would be the envy of many. Gone are the dark days when wine from the Antipodes would be jokingly labelled Bondi Bleach and Kanga Rouge. Unless you are very lucky though, it's not as easy to find a palatable red wine by the glass as it is to find a good white wine. Qualilty is however improving and we hope it continues to do so.

As for the beer, we rely on CAMRA and several of our very knowledgeable readers for guidance and pass on their recommendations. Some names appear time and again, but new, local, interesting ales from the small breweries find their way into many of our pubs.

Compiling a pub guide makes you realize that one man's meat is another man's poison. It's often necessary to make a judgement on a pub that's been both recommended and brick-batted. In the course of surveying the field for this edition, we visited a pub twice in a month; the first lunch we had there was very good, the second, a disappointment. Nothing at the pub had apparently changed; same hands in the kitchen, same behind the bar, all of which goes to show that recommendations can be deceptive and that it is rare to find that everything is on the button every time you visit.

Our aim has always been to find worthwhile piped-music free pubs with that little something that makes them more interesting. Some are a beer-lover's heaven, a few serve food that would rival the best anywhere, others are just good, reliable pubs that appeal. To some a filled roll would be taking catering a step too far: crisps and nuts are what you get and if you're really lucky a pickled egg. Horses for courses: these pubs are for the serious beer-drinkers – which prompts this recently found statistic: in every second of every hour in

1983, Britons drank 350 pints of beer. In 2002 the amount had dropped to 330 pints a second! Does this tell you anything?

It is difficult when you publish every other year to include prices. They can change so much during that time. If the menus look a little more exciting than usual, expect to pay for the quality. The price of a pint varies too and we have had complaints about a pint of shandy in one pub. Of complaints there is a limit to what we can do. On prices, really nothing at all except make a comment when writing about the pub. When music is introduced we judge that on what type it is and how loud, If it passes our criteria, it is listed in the Best of the Rest. Badly run establishments with rude, indifferent staff, are never given a second chance, they are taken out. Fortunately there are not many. As for smoking and smoky pubs, more and more have big smoke-free areas; some are becoming totally non-smoking.

The pubs listed in *The Quiet Pint* are varied. We hope there's something in the book to meet everyone's taste. We know there are plenty more out there waiting to be discovered. We are lucky to have a dedicated set of readers whose ferreting will no doubt find them; without their enthusiasm we would have difficulty compiling this book. Year after year they keep us informed about what is going on in their own parishes – and often on their business or holiday travels. They deserve a million thanks.

Derek and Josephine Dempster

Pipedown:
The Campaign for Freedom from Piped Music

By Nigel Rodgers, National Secretary

If all the impartial opinion polls are to be believed, piped music comes top of the list of things most hated in pubs and similar places. Yet piped music in pubs represents the triumph of the music industry's spin doctors over both good commercial and common sense.

The Campaign for Freedom from Piped Music was founded eleven years ago to fight the colonization of pubs, restaurants, hotels, cafés and other places by those spin doctors, so I was delighted when Derek and Josephine Dempster started *The Quiet Pint*, as it was obvious that such a guide was badly needed and that it would strengthen the Pipedown Campaign's armoury. What I did not anticipate was that the book would be so entertaining and informative. Far from being dryly factual, it is crammed with fascinating details of a pub's history, architecture and locality, as well as information about whether it has rooms and if dogs and/or children are welcome, and also how you can get to it – even if it has a resident ghost! This new edition is even better and more detailed that the first five.

Pipedown itself does not solely campaign against pubs playing piped music (which means of course music of any type piped or relayed around a room where people have not asked for it and may not want it). We fight piped music in shops, hotels, restaurants, bus and railway stations, airports, hospitals and swimming pools. If needed we will fight it on the beaches! We have had major successes – persuading Gatwick Airport and Tesco supermarkets to drop their piped music, for example – but the fight is far from won. Currently we are opposing plans to introduce piped television onto every train, so creating what many would feel is hell on wheels. If you would like to join us (the subscription is £15 a year) or would just like more information, please send an SAE to Pipedown, PO Box 1722, Salisbury SP4 7US, or look at our website www.pipedown.info/

J.D. Wetherspoon

We've changed the way we list the pubs in J.D. Wetherspoon plc's growing empire. Instead of grouping them in one long list, we have placed them in the relevant county sections within the body of the book rather than tucked away at the end.

Tucked suggests cosy and cosy they're not; big, big and bigger is the thought. As you know, Wetherspoon specializes in converting redundant high-street buildings into successful and popular pubs; all have a character of their own and one thing you can be sure of is that they are nearly always where you want them. When, in the middle of the afternoon, everything else in the town is closed, there is tremendous comfort in knowing that a Wetherspoon is open just for you.

Always reliable, dependable and good value, they stand alone. They don't even try to compete with a well-managed, atmospheric old town pub, they fill a totally different niche – and do it extremely well.

In the last edition we mentioned the other branch on the Wetherspoon tree, Lloyd's No 1 – but these are not for followers of *The Quiet Pint*: they have piped music. Since then a new bough has grown – Wetherspoon Lodges, where you can stay – but just so you know, some of these beds have a musical accompaniment.

Tim Martin, Chairman of Wetherspoon plc, writes:

What could be more perfect than enjoying a pint of beer in a pub? Pubs appeal to people of all ages and classes and are truly an important aspect of English heritage and culture. With almost 60,000 pubs in the UK, there is plenty of choice for everyone.

At Wetherspoon we pride ourselves on offering good quality pubs with the emphasis on an excellent choice of drink and food in comfortable, quality surroundings. Just as important to both us and our customers is the complete absence of music and other background noise in our 600 Wetherspoon outlets across the UK.

Since the first Wetherspoon opened in 1979 the company has followed its music-free policy – with the exception of the few Lloyds No 1 branches.

We are not against music in pubs; indeed live music is often the making of a pub. However, piped music can be both intrusive and annoying. The pubs listed in *The Quiet Pint* allow people to enjoy their time in a pub without having to listen to annoying piped and background music. This is something both I and Wetherspoon wholeheartedly support.

Enjoy the book.

QUIET PINT Areas

J·D·WETHERSPOON

SCOTLAND

NORTHUMBRIA

CUMBRIA

YORKSHIRE

LANCASHIRE, MANCHESTER & MERSEYSIDE

CHESHIRE

LEICESTER, LINCOLNSHIRE & NOTTINGHAMSHIRE

STAFFORDSHIRE & DERBYSHIRE

HEREFORDSHIRE, SHROPSHIRE & WORCESTERSHIRE

NORFOLK

WALES

MIDLANDS

CAMBRIDGESHIRE & BEDFORDSHIRE

SUFFOLK

GLOUCESTERSHIRE

OXFORDSHIRE

BUCKINGHAMSHIRE

HERTFORDSHIRE

ESSEX

LONDON

BERKSHIRE

SURREY

KENT

WILTSHIRE

HAMPSHIRE

SUSSEX

SOMERSET

DEVON

DORSET

CORNWALL

2

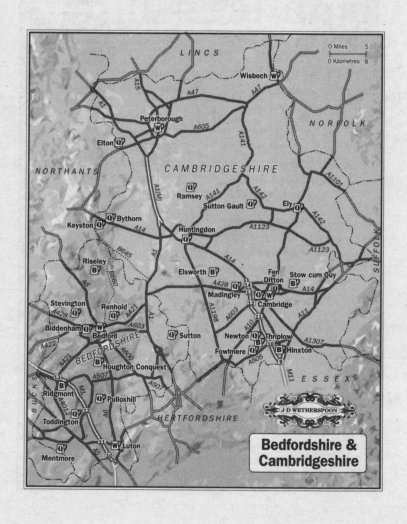

Bedfordshire & Cambridgeshire

Biddenham

Three Tuns ☽ 01234 354847
57 Main Road, Biddenham, Beds MK40 4BD
Greene King. Kevin Bolwell, tenant

West of Bedford, off the A428, along a lane that swings off the main road through the village and back again. Biddenham is a quiet village with some delightful colourwashed cottages, some of which, like the Three Tuns, are thatched. Popular and busy, it is well beamed inside with carpets on the floor, paintings and photographs on the walls, two fires, darts and skittles in the public bar – and no fruit machine. There are lots of interesting things on the menu from home-made soup of the day, egg mayonnaise and prawns, single and double-decker sandwiches and ploughman's to steak and kidney pie, braised beef in Guinness with horseradish mash, home-made lasagne, a choice of steaks, casseroles and, on Sunday, a highly praised roast lunch. Children's meals and some home-made puds too. Greene King IPA, Abbot, Ruddles, the occasional guest beer and a short, well-chosen wine list. Outside there are seats on the terrace and plenty of room for everyone in the large, enclosed garden. An extension is planned to give them double the dining space they have now.

OPEN: 11.30–2.30, 6–11. Sun 12–3, 7–10.30. Food served 12–2, 6.30–9 (except Sun eve).
Real Ale. Children and dogs welcome. Car park. Wheelchair access.
Cards: all except Amex.

Bythorn

White Hart ☽ 01832 710226
Bythorn, nr Huntingdon, Cambs PE28 0QN
Free House. Bill Bennett, licensee

Friendly and informal with comfortable furnishings and a cosy fire, the White Hart's focus is very much on inventive food in its restaurant, Bennett's Bistro, though there is always a warm welcome if you just want to lean on the bar with a pint of well-kept ale, or something from the good-value wine list. Food is served in the bar as well as the restaurant and no-smoking dining room, and the menus in this 17th-century pub are creative and popular: home-made soups, ploughman's, duck-liver terrine, fresh scallops, venison casserole, game in season, loin of pork in orange sauce, steaks and home-made puddings. Big Sunday lunches. Greene King IPA, Abbot ales, Everards Tiger, Guinness and lagers. Wines by the glass. Seats and tables in the garden.

OPEN: 11–3, 6–11. Closed Sun eve and all day Mon.
Real Ale. Restaurant. No-smoking dining room.
Children welcome. No dogs.
Occasional Morris dancers.

Cambridge

Champion of the Thames ① 01223 352043
68 King Street, Cambridge CB1 1LN
Greene King. Catherine Dixon, licensee

A traditional pub in the centre of town, this is a small, cosy local with interesting etched windows, panelled bars and old benches. Atmospheric and friendly. Decorated with boat-race prints and pictures of Cambridge, the two bars quickly fill up with university dons, students, businessmen and anyone else wanting to enjoy a quiet pint in this old place. There's a new licensee since our last edition and new regime; no food now, not a crumb, but you can still enjoy the well-kept Greene King IPA and Abbot.

OPEN: 11–11.
Real Ale.
No children. Dogs: yes, if the landlady likes the look of you.

Cambridge Blue ① 01223 361382
85–87 Gwydir Street, Cambridge CB1 2LG (side street off Mill Road)
Free House. Chris Lloyd, licensee
e-mail: c.lloyd13@ntlworld.com

In an attractive back street, this late Victorian pub among the terraced houses is straightforward and uncomplicated; oars and rowing photographs for you to admire on the walls and daily papers and local magazines to read while you enjoy your drink. The whole of the pub is a no-smoking, no-mobile phone area. The pub serves generous helpings of good traditional food in the dining conservatory: farmhouse paté, toasted ciabatta rolls, sausage mash and onion gravy, baked potatoes, hot Texas chilli, salads and other cold dishes from the cold cabinet, daily specials too. Roast lunch with all the trimmings on Sunday. On the first Tuesday evening of each month they hold a speciality night when food from a particular region or country is featured. Seven real ales from small local brewers as well as Guinness, Aspal Cider, Cassels Cider and wines by the glass or bottle. One of the joys of this pub is its unexpectedly large garden.

OPEN: 12–2.30, 5.30–11. Sat 12–3, 6–11. Sun 12–3, 6–10.30.
Real Ale.
Children in conservatory area. Dogs on leads. Wheelchair access (not WC).
Cards: Delta, MasterCard, Switch, Visa, Visa Debit.

Eagle ① 01223 505020
Bene't Street, Cambridge CB2 3QN
Greene King. Sian Crowther, manager

Originally known as the Eagle and Child (or the Bird and Baby?), this handsome, lively, rambling pub was once a very important coaching inn between Cambridge and London. It's wonderfully old, still with much of the original 17th-century pine panelling, contemporary fireplaces, wall paintings and mullioned windows. Another historically important feature, totally divorced from its great age, is the names of British and American airmen written on the never to be redecorated 'R.A.F. ceiling' in lipstick, candle smoke or whatever else came to hand during World War II. On the menu is a simple, well-cooked range of bar food – ploughman's, a choice of fillings for the baguettes and jacket potatoes, sausage, egg and chips, home-made pie of the day, grilled salmon steak with a hollandaise sauce, warm chicken and bacon salad, tagliatelle verdi with wild mushrooms, steaks and a choice of fish; chef's specials too. Lunch and dinner menus served in any of the five bar areas. Greene King ales on hand pump. The wine list – mulled wine at Christmas – includes champagnes by the glass. There are seats and tables in the cobbled, galleried yard.

OPEN: 11–11. Food 12–2.30, 5.30–8.45 (not Fri, Sat or Sun eves).
Real Ale.
Children only in courtyard. No dogs, except guide dogs. Wheelchair access.
Cards: most accepted, however, only debit cards for drinks if not eating.

Free Press ① 01223 368337
Prospect Row, Cambridge CB1 1QU
Greene King. Donna & Martin Thornton, tenants

In a picturesque street, this pub was named after a local temperance newspaper that, unsurprisingly, was a convincing failure. Perhaps they opened the pub to commemorate the newspaper's demise! Certainly the decor in this place – the best of back-street pubs – celebrates its printing connection. Totally non-smoking, the Free Press is building a reputation for serving good home-made food: tomato and roasted pepper soup or Tuscan bean soup, both with crusty bread, filled, toasted ciabatta bread, hot, home-made Scotch eggs with salad, stuffed sweet peppers with a hot chilli sauce, ploughman's and delicious puds. The menu changes daily. Ales change regularly too and there is range of malt whiskies and a good wine list. Seats in the small, sunny, sheltered terrace where honeysuckle and roses flourish.

OPEN: 12–2.30, 6–11.
Real Ale.
Children welcome. Dogs on leads. Wheelchair access (not WC).
Cards: Maestro, MasterCard, Solo, Visa, Visa Electron.

Elton

Black Horse ① 01832 280240
14 Overend, Elton, Peterborough, Cambs PE8 6RU
Free House. John Clennell, licensee

A very handsome stone building with grounds overlooking Elton Hall park, another 'Cromwell was here' area, with, as usual, devastating results. All that remained of the 15th-century Elton Hall after the Civil War was the gatehouse and the crypt of the old building; the hall you see today is 17th century, the same date as the Black Horse. This comfortable, welcoming pub has a big log fire in the bar and several dining areas with plenty of room in which to sit and sample something from the menu. At lunchtime there will be soup of the day, well-filled sandwiches, baguettes with hot or cold fillings, home-made pie of the day, salads and filled jacket potatoes. In the evening there could be mussels in cream and garlic, Caesar salad, pan-fried wild goose breast with pear and ginger chutney, fillet of sea bass with king prawns and hollandaise sauce or game pie. There is also a vegetarian menu. Ales are Bass, Nethergate Suffolk County, Everards Tiger and Caledonian Deuchars. The wine list is comprehensive. Plenty of room in the extensive, sheltered grounds.

OPEN: 12–3, 6–11.
Real Ale. Restaurant.
Children and dogs welcome. Car park.
All cards.

Ely

Prince Albert ① 01353 663494
62 Silver Street, Ely, Cambs CB7 4JF
Greene King. E. M. Hunt, tenant

Near the cathedral, this is a classic, well-cared-for two-bar pub with a friendly, enthusiastic landlord. Outside is an attractive garden, window boxes and hanging baskets. Lunchtime food only; menus change according to the seasons so there will be good-value home-cooked hot dishes, pies, soups, quiches and a variety of freshly made sandwiches, including their 'famous egg and bacon chin dribbler' to go with the beer. No food Sunday. Greene King IPA, Abbot Ale, Mild, seasonal ales and two guest beers. Seats in the lovely garden.

OPEN: 11–4, 6–11. Sun 12–4, 7–11.
Real Ale.
Children in garden only. Dogs on leads. Wheelchair access (not WC).

Fen Ditton

Ancient Shepherds ① 01223 293290
High Street, Fen Ditton, Cambs CB5 8ST
Pubmaster. John Harrington, tenant

A charming 16th-century pub named after the 'Ancient Order of Shepherders' – who used to meet here many years ago. The interior is warm and welcoming with a small bar, lounge and no-smoking, but musical, dining room. The menu is quite traditional with the addition of a few, more exciting, daily specials. Bar food includes filled baguettes, ploughman's, steak and ale pie, and fish specials on the daily blackboard. Menus change regularly. Beers are Greene King IPA, Adnams Bitter and an occasional guest. There is a new seating area in the garden.

OPEN: 12–3, 6–11.
Real Ale.
No children. Dogs welcome in bar and garden. Car park. Wheelchair access.
N.B. May be classical music playing during quiet early evenings.

Fowlmere

Chequers ① 01763 208369
High Street, Fowlmere, Cambs SG8 7SR
Free House. Norman Rushton, licensee

A 16th-century pub with a very chequered past! Soon after it was built it was used as a coffin stop – a chapel of rest between London and Cambridge – then as a stopping place for post-chaise passengers. Samuel Pepys spent the night here on 24 February 1660 on his way to Cambridge. In 1675 it was renovated by the Thrist family – which is probably the date of the priest hole above the bar – and a few centuries later was a favourite with pilots stationed at Fowlmere aerodrome during the First and Second World Wars. Now a very civilized dining pub, it has an open fire in the comfortable bar where you can indulge in something from the interesting menus served either here, in the no-smoking conservatory, or the galleried restaurant: among other dishes on the menu could be home-made soup of the day, a traditional French country pork and duck paté served with salad leaves and an apricot chutney, grilled brochette of king prawns served with basil aioli mayonnaise and Thai dipping sauce and, for a main course, grilled halibut steak served on a creamed orange and green-peppercorn fish sauce with mangetout and Irish champ potatoes, Portuguese-style fillet of pork with baby scallops, chorizo sausage, spiced with chillies, parsley and garlic served with lemon jasmine rice and a lambs lettuce salad or a grilled Dover sole. Lots more chef's specials, vegetarian dishes, cheeses and home-made puddings too; the blackboard menu changes daily. Roast sirloin of English beef served Sunday lunchtime. Wide range of wines by the glass; Adnams Bitter and a good choice of malt whiskies, ports and brandies. Seats in the pretty, flowery garden. The chequers on the inn sign represent on one side the USAAF 339 Fighter Group and on the other 19 Squadron of the RAF.

OPEN: 12–2.30, 6–11.
Real Ale. Restaurant.
Children welcome – if parents are well behaved! No dogs. Wheelchair access (not WC).
Cards: Amex, Delta, MasterCard, Switch, Visa.

Huntingdon

Old Bridge Hotel ① 01480 424300 Fax: 01480 411017
1 High Street, Huntingdon, PE29 3TQ
Free House. Martin Lee, chef/patron
e-mail: oldbridge@huntsbridge.co.uk

On the edge of town what was, years ago, a private bank has metamorphosed into this handsome, classy, creeper-covered hotel overlooking the river Great Ouse. You can have everything here: a mooring on the river, a drink in the panelled bar, or something from the imaginative menu in the no-smoking restaurant or terrace room, or a proper tea in the very elegant lounge; you can stay the night, or just sit, enjoy the appealing gardens and watch the river flow by. While the regularly changing menus have an international influence, many of the ingredients are locally sourced. There could be wonderful soups and hot or cold sandwiches, peppered tuna and salmon sushi with wasabi, pickled ginger, soy, coriander and cress salad, risotto of the day with parmesan, braised pork with gnocchi, roast sweet potato, spinach and sage, Caesar salad with bacon and quails eggs, roast fillet of Aberdeenshire beef with shallot purée, rösti potato, grilled leeks and girolle mushrooms. A daily choice of fresh fish from Cornwall and very good puds. During the week there is a bargain lunch, £12 for two courses. Adnams Bitter, and changing guest beers, champagne and an excellent, wide-ranging wine list.

OPEN: 11–11. Sun 12–10.30.
Real Ale. Restaurant.
Children in lounge area and restaurant. Dogs allowed in bar. Car park. 24 bedrooms – all en suite. Fishing.
Cards: Amex, Delta, Diners, MasterCard, Switch, Visa.
N.B. Music once a month on themed evenings.

Keyston

Pheasant ① 01832 710241 Fax: 01832 710464
Village Loop Road, Keyston, nr Bythorn, Cambs PE18 0RE
Free House. Clive Dixon, licensee

An immaculately kept, large, white-painted, thatched inn, run by the same group as the Old Bridge Hotel at Huntingdon. Heavily beamed inside, it has one room divided into two distinct areas. The food here is really something else. The monthly changing menus, serving both the casual and the more formal sides of the pub, include fresh fish and game in season and an extensive list of starters, light snacks and blackboard specials: leek and potato soup with crème fraiche, salad of baby leeks, mozzarella, radish, shaved fennel and piquillo peppers, Parma ham with rocket and parmesan, fish cakes on buttered spinach, poached and grilled guinea fowl with mashed potato, buttered cabbage and foie gras sauce, chunky pork sausage on mashed potato with onion and thyme sauce; European farmhouse cheeses and wonderful puds. Adnams Bitter and three changing guest beers. An individual wine list; 20 house wines, all available by the glass. Tables outside.

OPEN: 12–3, 6–11.
Real Ale. Restaurant with a no-smoking area.
Children welcome. Dogs in bar. Wheelchair access (not WC).
Cards: Amex, Delta, Diners, Mastercard, Switch, Visa.

Madingley

Three Horseshoes ① 01954 210221 Fax: 01954 212043
High Street, Madingley, Cambs CB3 8AB
Free House. R. Stokes & John Hoskins, licensees

Looking very much a pub from the outside, this is, however, more an informal restaurant, though pints are still served in the busy bar. Whitewashed and thatched, it's a delightful place with a very combustible past, having caught fire three times. Like the Pheasant at Keyston and the Old Bridge Hotel at Huntingdon, it's a member of the Huntsbridge Group – lucky Cambridgeshire. Here the emphasis is on Mediterranean-style food, both in the very elegant conservatory and the bar. Home-made soup, toasted bread with the new season's Tuscan olive oil, baked aubergine with tomato, mozzarella and pesto, fillet of beef marinated in thyme, garlic and Chianti with a red onion tarte tatin, tomato and basil tart, and lots more. Interesting cheeses and good puddings. The majority of the customers are very serious about their wine; they appreciate the enviable, imaginative, wide-ranging wine list. Adnams Best and three guest beers are on hand pump. Tables in the flowery garden during the summer.

OPEN: 11.30–2.30, 6–11.
Real Ale. Restaurant (closed Sun eve).
Children welcome. No dogs. Wheelchair access (not WC).
Cards: Amex, Delta, Diners, MasterCard, Switch, Visa.

Mentmore

Stag ① 01296 668423
The Green, Mentmore, Beds LU7 0QF
Charles Wells. Michael & Jenny Tuckwood, licensees

The Stag is very near the county border, and in spite of where other guides want to put it the licensees are sure, and so is the map, that they are in Bedfordshire. A solid, impressive stone building whose fortunes have changed for the better over the last few years. Now it's that desirable combination of successful village pub and well-regarded restaurant where they serve some creative food. The simpler bar menu will have well-filled sandwiches, seasonal salads, the Stag's spicy sausage and mash, maybe spiced pork spare ribs with sweet chilli sauce, breast of pigeon and partridge on sauté bubble and squeak with a rich red wine jus and roasted shallots or smoked salmon and scrambled eggs. More-ish puds and British cheeses. Menus are seasonal and change regularly. Beers are Charles Wells Eagle and Bombardier with Adnams as the guest. Wide-ranging list of wines, most of them by the glass. Seats at the front of the pub among the flowers and in the garden at the back.

OPEN: 12–3, 6–11. Sat & Sun 11–11.
Real Ale. Restaurant.
Children and dogs welcome. Car park. Wheelchair access.
Cards: Connect, Delta, MasterCard, Switch, Visa.
N.B. Very quiet classical or jazz only in restaurant.

Newton

Queens Head ① 01223 870436
Fowlmere Road, Newton, nr Cambridge, Cambs CB2 5BG
Free House. David & Juliet Short, licensees

Without doubt a hugely popular village inn. Locals, students and dons all pile into the small, beamed saloon bar or the larger, simply furnished Victorian public bar of this charming 17th-century pub. Good, simple bar food complements the fine ales and country wines. During the week there is a wide choice of sandwiches, all cut to order, home-made soup (a firm favourite), along with the roast beef or smoked ham sandwiches, or platter of mixed cheeses. Evenings and Sunday lunchtime there is a selection of cold meats and cheeses served with brown bread and butter. Adnams Bitter and Broadside and Regatta with Adnams Fishermans Ale in winter – all tapped from the cask. Organic apple juice, freshly squeezed orange juice and farm cider. Seats at the front of the pub or on the green. The painting of the goose on the pub sign is of poor Belinda, one-time keeper of the car park, now in residence in the public bar – stuffed.

OPEN: 11.30–2.30, 6–11. Sun 12–2.30, 7–10.30.
Real Ale.
Children in games room and dogs on leads if well behaved (in both cases). Wheelchair access into pub only.
No cards.

Pulloxhill

Cross Keys ① 01525 712442
High Street, Pulloxhill, Beds MK45 5HB
Charles Wells. Peter & Sheila Meads, tenants

Perhaps it was a minor skirmish during the Civil War that left the ghost of a Cavalier to stalk the pub by night, as no major battle took place near this little village. Maybe a lost soul found this typical English country pub and stayed. Outside, it's white-painted and flower-bedecked; inside, heavily beamed with large log-filled fireplaces. There is a limited lunchtime bar snack menu; also satisfying soups, egg mayonnaise, trout with salad, fresh mushrooms in garlic butter, chicken Kiev, mixed grill, grilled steaks, poached salmon fillet in a white wine sauce, haddock in a cheese and prawn sauce, ploughman's, salads, vegetarian dishes and a children's menu; daily specials too. During the week they serve a very reasonable, three-course lunchtime menu for the retired. A comprehensive wine list, Charles Wells and Adnams ales. Serious jazz sessions on Sunday nights.

OPEN: 11–3, 6–11.
Real Ale. Restaurant. Specially priced lunches for senior citizens Monday–Friday.
Children in own room. No dogs. Wheelchair access.
Cards: Access, Switch, Visa.
Jazz every Sunday eve.

Ramsey

Jolly Sailor ① 01487 813388
43 Great Whyte, Ramsey, Cambs PE26 1HH
Pubmaster. Michael Rogers, licensee

You might not immediately think of the middle of Cambridgeshire as having anything to do with jolly sailors, but there is a river, the Great Whyte, flowing under the road, and you can even moor your boat on the nearby High Lode about five minutes away. So even though Ramsey is an ancient market town on the edge of the Fens it is really quite nautical. This is a jolly and cosy Grade II building, with no food – well, a crisp and a nut if you're peckish – but plenty of beer: Adnams Broadside and Bitter, Charles Wells Bombardier, Guest Session Bitter and a weekend guest beer and a garden in which to sit and enjoy them.

OPEN: 11–3, 5.30–11. Sat 11–3, 6–11. Sun 12–3, 7–10.30.
Real Ale.
Children in one bar. Dogs on leads.
N.B. Two bars are quiet, the back bar has music.

Stevington

Red Lion ① 01234 824138
1 Park Road, Stevington, Bedford MK43 7QD
Greene King. Geoff & Karen Gallimore, tenants

There are remains of an old mill on the circular walk that leads to this comfortable village pub where you'll get a short, satisfying, traditional menu that offers freshly filled baguettes, salads, filled jacket potatoes, all-day breakfasts, steak and ale pie, vegetable lasagne, filled Yorkshire puddings, breaded cod and chips and some home-made daily specials. The same menu, with the addition of a choice of steaks, features in the evening. There are always a few gluten-free and vegetarian dishes on the menu. The ales are Greene King IPA and Abbot. Outside, the sheltered garden has picnic tables and two pétanque pistes for the slightly more energetic.

OPEN: 12–2.30, 5–11. All day Sat and Sun. No food Mon.
Real Ale.
Children welcome. Dogs on leads. Two double bedrooms.

Sutton

John O'Gaunt Inn ① 01767 260377
30 High Street, Sutton, Sandy, Beds SG19 2ND
Greene King. Les Ivall, tenant

By no means just a pub, the John O'Gaunt has an investment club, two quiz teams, a golf society and serious boules players in the local league. The pink-washed, 18th-century building is in a pleasant village near a 13th-century packhorse bridge and ford which, since the weather pattern lurches between drought and excessive rain, could be full of water; or maybe not. With plenty of beams inside, the bar is no-smoking and so is part of the lounge. Well-kept ales and an extensive bar menu offering, among other things, home-made soup, sandwiches and baguettes, filled jacket potatoes, toasted sandwiches, shepherd's pie, steak and kidney pudding, Moroccan lamb tagine with couscous, fisherman's pie, tuna and pasta bake, Balti and vegetarian dishes and daily specials. Well-kept Greene King IPA and Abbot ales, plus guests such as Gales HSB, draught Bass or Old Bailey. Skittles are played in the public bar – the pub is in the local league – and during the summer the local Morris Men occasionally entertain you in the large garden. The John O'Gaunt was voted the East Bedfordshire community pub of the year.

OPEN: 12–3, 7–11.
Real Ale.
Well-behaved children over 14 welcome. Dogs in public bar.
Folk music sessions on the third Friday of the month.

Sutton Gault

Anchor Inn ① 01353 778537
Bury Lane, Sutton Gault, Cambs CB6 2BD Fax: 01353 776180
Free House. Robin Moore, licensee
e-mail: anchorinnsg@aol.com

This 17th-century place, on the banks of the New Bedford River, also known as the 'Hundred-Foot Drain' – well named, as it is ruler straight – offers really interesting, innovative food. More an informal restaurant combined with a very good pub, inside are four heavily beamed rooms with sturdy pine tables and chairs, old settles and big log fires. Cooking is the best of modern British with a touch of Mediterranean; dish of olives, wonderful soups, home-cured gravadlax with dill mayonnaise, king prawn spring roll, watercress and sesame seed salad, orange and chilli dipping sauce, local sausage and mash with onion gravy and green beans, smoked haddock ramekin, with spinach, egg in a saffron cream sauce, roast breast of corn-fed chicken on a bed of wild mushroom risotto with a sauté of green beans and Italian ham with basil dressing. Seafood and specials on the blackboard, British cheeses, desirable puddings and a good-value wine list. Not forgetting the beers: Hampshire King Alfred, Black Sheep Bitter, City of Cambridge Hobsons choice and Hoegaarden. You can sit in the garden or watch the wildlife from the river bank.

OPEN: 12–3, 7–11 (Sat 6.30–11).
Real Ale. Restaurant.
Children welcome. No dogs. Car park. Wheelchair access to all parts of the pub.
Bedrooms.
Cards: Amex, Delta, MasterCard, Switch, Visa.

Toddington

Sow & Pigs ① 01525 873089
19 Church Square, Toddington, nr Dunstable, Beds LU5 6AA
Greene King. Roger Martin, licensee

At first glance a traditional, two-bar Victorian commercial pub with a friendly landlord serving very well-kept beer – but it is a pub with a difference, for it has a theme: pigs – some even flying. It's one of the more eccentric pubs, with not many concessions to comfort in the minute public bar, nor in the lounge either, but you do have a fire to sit by, old books to read and an unusual collection of furniture to sit on from where you can order freshly made soup, filled rolls or something from the cold table to go with seasonal guest beers and ales from Greene King.

OPEN: 11–11. Sun 12–10.30.
Real Ale.
Children welcome. Dogs on leads.
Occasional musical evenings. They have a function room which is used more and more for parties (maximum 28) where they put on quite a spread – but this doesn't interfere with the pub, where you will still be well looked after.

BEST OF THE REST

Elsworth, Cambs
George & Dragon ① 01954 267236
41 Boxworth Road, CB3 8JQ
This well-kept, well-run pub in a pretty village just outside Cambridge serves interesting food. There's one menu for three different dining areas: bar snacks – soup, sandwiches, ploughman's – that sort of thing – and pork ribs in a barbecue sauce, salmon topped with prawn and anchovy butter, mixed grill and daily specials. Greene King and Ruddles County, decent wine. Children: if they're eating.
Open: 11–3, 6–11. Sun 12–3 only.

Hinxton, Cambs
Red Lion ① 01799 530601
High Street, CB10 1QY
Pink and 16th century. Changing, really imaginative chef's specials in either the spacious bar (with parrot accompaniment) or the smart restaurant (without). Adnams, Greene

King and guest ales. Wines from Adnams – with their wine merchant hat on. Children over 10 in eating areas.
Open: 11–2.30, 6–11. Sun 12–2.30, 7–10.30.

Houghton Conquest, Beds
Knife & Cleaver ☎ 01234 740387
The Grove, MK45 3LA
Opposite the medieval parish church, this is a panelled, polished. comfortable, attractive and stylish, 16th-century inn where the food is really very good. Dishes of the day on the blackboard, a wonderful choice of fish in the restaurant. More of a restaurant than a pub, but it still has a bar with Bass and Batemans XB on hand pump, a great number of malt whiskies and some good wines. Children in eating areas. Wheelchair access (not WC). Bedrooms.
Open: 12–2.30, 6.30–11. Closed Sun eve.

Ridgmont, Beds
Rose & Crown ☎ 01525 280245
89 High Street, MK43 0TY
Once part of the Duke of Bedford's estate and handy for a little refreshment if you are planning to visit Woburn Abbey, this is a 17th-century pub with a lovely sunny garden, serving traditional, home-made pub food, real ale from Charles Wells and a guest. If you're interested, there is room outside to park your caravan. Children in restaurant. Wheelchair access.
Open: 10.30–2.30 (Sat 12–3), 6–11. Sun 12–3, 7–10.30.

Riseley, Beds
Fox & Hounds ☎ 01234 708240
High Street, MK44 1DT
Outside heating on the terrace will keep you cosy if you can't force your way into this busy pub. If you do, you can relax in the comfortable, heavily beamed, lounge bar. This is a well-run, accommodating place where they serve some rather good steaks – their speciality – and imaginative specials, as well as the more usual pub food. Charles Wells range of beers, some guests and good wines. Children and dogs welcome.
Open: 11.30–2.30, 6.30–11. Sun 12–3, 7–10.30.

Stow Cum Quy, Cambs
White Swan ☎ 01233 811821
11 Main Street, CB5 9AB
East of Cambridge, off the A45, among the village cottages, this is a friendly local serving very well-kept beer and some better than average food. On two levels, the lower bar, which is no-smoking, is used mainly as a restaurant though you can eat anywhere in the pub. Our reporter tells us there were 'large servings of excellent food and welcoming staff. We shall return'. Too late to make a main entry in this edition, but be assured that the only music comes from the chef's radio in the kitchen, just audible through the open door. This is a jolly place, full of people enjoying the food and choice of beer: Adnams Bitter, Greene King IPA, Woodfordes Wherry and a guest. Children and dogs welcome. Most cards accepted.
Open: 11–3, 6–11. Sun 12–3, 7–10.30

Thriplow, Cambs

Green Man ① 01763 208855
Lower Street, SG8 7RJ
Tastefully decorated and full of collectors' bits and pieces; the surroundings are certainly not dull. Good, filling, classic bar food to go with quietly playing classical music. Evening menu jumps up a notch or two. Timothy Taylors Landlord, about four guests from smaller breweries and some interesting wines. Children over 5 in eating area.
Open: 12–2.30, 6–11. Closed Tues.

Wetherspoon in Bedfordshire and Cambridgeshire

Bedfordshire

Bedford – Banker's Draft, 115 High Street
① 01234 342931
Bedford – Pilgrim's Progress, Midland Road
① 01234 363751
Luton – White House, 1 Bridge Street
① 01582 454608

Cambridgeshire

Cambridge – Regal, 38–39 St Andrews Street
① 01223 366459
Peterborough – College Arms, 40 The Broadway
① 01733 319745
Wisbech – Wheatsheaf Inn, 18–22 Church Terrace
① 01945 469890

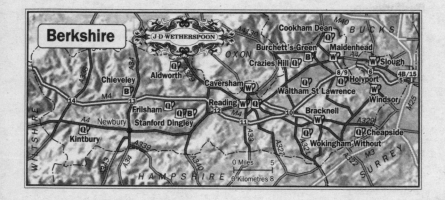

Berkshire

Aldworth

Bell ① 01635 578272
Aldworth, nr Reading RG8 9SE
Free House. H. E. Macaulay, licensee

Close to the Ridgeway, the prehistoric track that crosses the sweeping landscape of the Berkshire Downs, this totally unspoilt, unchanging 14th-century pub is hugely popular with locals, walkers and cyclists. In the same family for over two hundred years, it's a little treasure, heavily beamed, with panelled walls, traditional furnishings, old bread ovens and a stone-floored tap room. There's no bar counter, just a hatch into the tiny bar through which you are served. The bar menu lists hot crusty rolls filled with ham, cheese, ox tongue, corned beef, smoked salmon, salt beef, Devon crab, or spicy prawns; a nice crisp salad tossed in a garlic mayonnaise; ploughman's; and home-made soup during the winter. Ales are West Berks Ol' Tyler, Dark Mild and a monthly guest from the brewery, also Arkells BBB and Kingsdown. Wines from Berry Bros. A good claret and a house medium-dry white always on offer by the glass. Seats in the attractive garden next to the cricket pitch.

OPEN: 11–3, 6–11. Closed Mon except bank holidays.
Real Ale.
Well-behaved children in tap room. Dogs on leads. Wheelchair access (not WC).
No cards.
Occasional Morris dancing.

Bracknell

Old Manor ① 01344 304490
Grenville Place, High Street, Bracknell RG12 1BP
Wetherspoon.

On an island, seemingly surrounded by endlessly busy roads, the Old Manor is now a busy town-centre pub, but it has a forgotten past. During renovations several years ago some interesting escape tunnels and hidey-holes dating back to the Reformation were found, but where they led, nobody knows. Some ancient beams are left inside, otherwise all has changed. Now there is a large drinking area, a third of which is no smoking, where you can sample something from a choice of five or six reasonably priced beers plus a changing guest from one of the smaller breweries. As in all Wetherspoon establishments, the food is good and reliable.

OPEN: 11–11.
Real Ale.
No children. No dogs. Wheelchair access.

Cheapside

Thatched Tavern ☏ 01344 620874
Cheapside Road, Cheapside, Ascot SL5 7QG
4cInns. Caroline Burke, manager

It probably was once thatched, but there is not a straw to be seen on the roof now. Things have moved on a bit though; it has recently been extended and brought up to date without losing its character. This fine old place still has its low ceilings, beams, polished flagstone floors, an inglenook fireplace and an air of well-being. With rather smart dining rooms, it is hugely popular and now leans more towards dining than drinking. Food ranges from home-made soup to steak and kidney pudding, local game, wild salmon, fish (various) and vegetarian dishes. Proper puds too. Courage Best, Fullers London Pride and Brakspears Bitter and an interesting wine list. Seats outside on the sheltered lawn. Parking is tricky, so instead of starting your walk from here make it the stopping-off place – there is a car park about a mile away!

OPEN: 12–11. Bar meals and snacks lunchtime only.
Real Ale. Restaurant.
Children, not in the bar. Dogs welcome. The mile-away car park gets very full.

Cookham Dean

Jolly Farmer ☏ 01628 482905
Church Road, Cookham Dean SL6 9PD
Free House. David Kelsey, licensee

A village consortium owns the pub and maintains a close eye on what is going on, keeping tradition alive. You are in an area with a surfeit of Cookhams: Cookham, Cookham Rise, then Cookham Dean and the Jolly Farmer: one on the river, the others in its embrace. It's a small 18th-century pub on the other side of the village green, with cosy rooms with fires, a charming dining room and a bar. Good, filling lunchtime bar food: sandwiches, wraps, beef and Guinness pie, ham, egg and chips, and in the evening pan-fried scallops and smoked bacon salad, duck breast with a Victoria plum sauce, steaks or a mushroom stroganoff with a timbale of rice among other dishes. Well-kept Brakspear, Courage Best and guest beers. Lots of room in the big garden.

OPEN: 11.30–3, 5.30–11.
Real Ale. Dining room.
Children away from bar. Well-behaved dogs allowed. Wheelchair access.

Crazies Hill

Horns ① 01189 401416
Crazies Hill, Wargrave RG10 8LY
Brakspears. Andy Hearn, tenant, Sarah Folley, manager
e-mail: thehorns@aol.com

North of Twyford, off the A4, then just follow the signposts. There have been some changes since our last edition, with the addition of a new garden bar which leads into the recently landscaped garden. The original bar is in the oldest part of the building – once a Tudor hunting lodge – and the old barn is used as a restaurant, painted white, with timbers outside, beams inside, big open fires and those essential stags' antlers strategically placed. On the varied and imaginative menu is a wide selection of dishes: pancakes filled with leeks, walnuts and Roquefort cheese, field mushrooms topped with Provençale vegetables and goat's cheese on a bed of lettuce, warm salad with bacon, mushrooms, avocado and Stilton served with 'the Horns' salad dressing, pan-fried calves liver with black pudding, spring onion mash and onion gravy, beef, mushroom and Guinness pie under a puff pastry lid and 'fresh fish of the day' on the specials board. There are vegetarian dishes and a selection of puds and cheeses, and home-made soup and filled baguettes for the less hungry. Sunday lunch is comprehensive: a choice of roasts, fresh fish or just a bar snack. Meals are served in the restaurant every weekday evening. Brakspears ales and lots of malt whiskies. Good choice of wines. Lucky them: the pub has a big garden of several acres.

OPEN: 11–2.30, 6–11. No food Sun eve.
Real Ale. Brasserie meals Fri and Sat eves: must book.
Children at lunchtime only. Doubtful about dogs – you have to ask. Wheelchair access.
Cards: Delta, Diners, MasterCard, Switch, Visa.

Frilsham

Pot Kiln ① 01635 201366
Frilsham, nr Hermitage RG18 0XX
Free House. Philip Gent, licensee

A solid, brick building down a narrow country lane, looking more like a farmhouse than a pub, the Pot Kiln is popular with locals and passing ramblers. It's not the easiest place to find, particularly if you approach it from the wrong direction, the very indirect 'country' route, when it seems to get further away, not nearer. When you do arrive you will find a counter to lean on in the small, basic public bar – you can bring the dog in here – otherwise service is through a hatch in the tiny entrance hall. Plenty of room though, in the main room. Good fires to keep the customers warm in winter and a simple bar menu to sustain them. Home-made soup, lots of fillings for the rolls, ploughman's, venison and red wine casserole, smoky fisherman's crumble (haddock and mixed fish with a crumble topping served with fresh vegetables), sausages in a beer and onion gravy and daily specials. There is a separate evening menu. Ales include Morlands Original and Arkells

BBB. There is also Brick Kiln ale and Gold Star, a beer brewed with local honey for the Pot Kiln at the back of the pub. Tables in the big, sheltered garden. Good walks nearby.

OPEN: 12–2.30, 6.30–11. Closed Tues lunchtimes and no food Tues eves.
Limited food Sun.
Real Ale.
Children in back room. Dogs on leads. Wheelchair access (not WC).
Cards: Amex, Electron, JCB, Maestro, MasterCard, Solo, Switch and Visa.
Live music first Sun of month.

Holyport

Belgian Arms ① 01628 634468
Holyport Street, Holyport, Maidenhead SL6 2JR
Brakspear. Alfred Morgan, tenant

You can just spot the pub sign among the foliage on the front of the pub, which is painted – the bits you can see – bright white under a tiled roof. Near the village pond, the pub looks wonderful when the wisteria is out and the garden is in full flower. It's dimly lit and atmospheric inside, with illustrations of Belgian army uniforms and other military prints adorning the low-ceilinged bar. A friendly, busy place with a dining area in the airy conservatory. Traditional bar food includes sandwiches, plain and toasted, pizzas with various toppings, ham and eggs and daily specials; Sunday lunches too. Brakspears ales and several malt whiskies are available. Seats in the garden overlook the pond and village green.

OPEN: 11– 3, 5.30–11 (Sat 6–11). No food Sun eve.
Real Ale.
Children in conservatory. Dogs on leads. Wheelchair access (not WC). Cards: all credit cards.

Kintbury

Dundas Arms ① 01488 658263
53 Station Road, Kintbury, nr Newbury RG17 9UT
Free House. David A. Dalzell Piper, licensee
e-mail: info@dundasarms.co.uk
www.dundasarms.co.uk

You really couldn't get much nearer to the Kennet and Avon canal without being in the water. In an area of outstanding natural beauty, this is an appealing 18th-century pub in a wonderful position, hugely popular during the summer when you have a grandstand view from the terrace and dining room of passing horse-drawn canal barges. As a commemorative gesture, the pub was named after Lord Dundas, who opened the canal in 1810. Inside is bright and colourful, the cooking skilled and enthusiastic. The luncheon menu and à la carte dinner could list home-cured gravadlax with a mustard and dill sauce, grilled scallops with black pasta and saffron sauce, baked sea bass fillets, roast breast of duck with cider and apple sauce and of course delicious puddings and a selection of British cheeses. However, you can eat less ambitiously in the small bar: home-potted

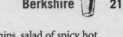

shrimps, fresh dressed crab salad, home-baked ham, egg and chips, salad of spicy hot chicken with guacamole, steaks and a choice of seasonal fish. A wide variety of wines from the cellar. Butts Barbus Barbus and Morland Original are the permanent ales; Butcombe Bitter, Adnams and West Berkshire Brewery Good Old Boy are the guests.

OPEN: 11–2.30, 6–11.
Real Ale. Restaurant.
Children to stay. No dogs. Car park. Wheelchair access (not WC). Five bedrooms.
Cards: Amex, Delta, MasterCard, Switch, Visa.

___

Reading

Sweeney & Todd ① 01189 586466
10 Castle Street (off St Mary's Butts) Reading RG1 7RD
Free House. Mrs June Hayward, licensee

Go to the back of the baker's shop – which also sells a range of pies to take away – up the couple of steps behind the counter and into a railway-carriage-shaped room with lots of booths, bare boards on the floor, a busy bar and proper waitresses. All with more than a hint of a bar contemporary with its inspiration, the notorious Fleet Street barber who had a predilection for pies with more macabre ingredients. There is an extensive, satisfying menu: soup, smoked oysters with French bread and salad, quiche, cold meats with salad, roast dishes, casseroles and hot home-made pies with adventurous fillings. Puddings to finish. Always exceptionally busy at lunchtimes during the week. Wadworths 6X, Adnams Bitter, Badger Tanglefoot and a guest beer.

OPEN: 11–11. Closed all day Sun. Breakfast served 8.30–10.30 a.m.
Real Ale.
Children welcome. No dogs.

___

Slough

Moon & Spoon ① 01753 531650
86 High Street, Slough SL1 1EL
Wetherspoon.

The bigger, the better; by now you all know that size is everything to Wetherspoons. Originally a building society, now a big pub with a giant 'spoon man' to welcome you. Always five very reasonably priced beers; always a good reliable menu with daily specials; always a no-smoking area, and this Wetherspoon has real draught cider.

OPEN: 10.30–11. Sun 12–10.30.
Real Ale.
No children. No dogs. Wheelchair access to all areas.

Stanford Dingley

Old Boot Inn ☎ 01189 744292
Stanford Dingley RG7 6LT
Free House. John Haley, licensee

This is a delightful, white-painted 18th-century pub in a glorious area, yards from the quietly flowing River Pang, a combination of a popular dining pub and local which appeals to everyone. Inside there is plenty of room for the regulars in the beamed bars, and to make sure you don't forget the name, a giant boot is next to the fireplace – holding the fire irons. The restaurant extends into the no-smoking conservatory. From the bar menu you can have home-made soup as well as filled baguettes, ploughman's, duck liver paté, home-cured gravadlax, calves' liver and bacon with mushrooms in a red wine sauce, home-made lasagne, fish cakes, steaks, salads and some comforting puds. The à la carte menu is constantly changing and there is a daily fresh fish board. Beers are draught Bass and something from Brakspear, Youngs and the West Berks brewery. Over 40 bottles on the wine list, about six by the glass.

OPEN: 11–3, 6–11.
Real Ale. Restaurant.
Children welcome, dogs too. Car park. Wheelchair access (not WC).
Cards: Delta, MasterCard, Switch, Visa.

Waltham St Lawrence

Bell ☎ 01189 341788
The Street, Waltham St Lawrence RG10 0JJ
Free House. Ian Glenister, licensee

A very attractive, historic building in the middle of the village, the 16th-century Bell, an important Wealden hall house, was bequeathed to the village in 1608 by Ralph Newbery, the rent from the house to be used for the poor and needy of the parish. It wasn't until 1723 that a building 'known as The Bell' was used as licensed premises for the grand rent of £8 per annum. Black and white, beamed, panelled and popular, altered little externally over the years, it is a very handsome building. Inside the attractive bars are good log fires to keep you warm, and when the weather improves you can sit in the appealing garden. Home-made soups and a wide selection of traditional dishes, bar snacks and daily specials. They have their own beer, Waltham St Lawrence No 1, brewed exclusively for the pub; four other pumps have rotating guests. An extended range of whiskies and malts. Voted CAMRA pub for Reading, Berkshire and the South Central region

OPEN: 11.30–3, 5–11. Sun 12–10.30. No bar food Sun eve.
Real Ale.
Children welcome in eating areas. Dogs in bar.
All major cards accepted.

Wokingham Without

Crooked Billet ➀ 01189 780438
Honey Hill, Wokingham Without RG40 3BJ
Brakspear. Rodney MacManus, manager

Quieter during the week, frantically busy at weekends. On the very outskirts of
Wokingham, a charming, 18th-century, weatherboarded pub with a grade II listing. Inside
are low beamed ceilings, real fires, a little snug, a small no-smoking restaurant and a
wonderful bar girl who has been working here for over 25 years. A little refurbishment has
been taking place since our last edition so everything should have been gently brought
into the 21st century. Plenty of choice from any of the menus – restaurant, bar menu or
the two specials boards – which can be eaten anywhere in the pub, there are no
restrictions. Generous servings and lots to choose from – anything from soup to a T-bone
steak, home-made pies, curries, pastas, various fish dishes, vegetarian meals and puds.
Brakspears range of ales, and one guest. Seats in the garden.

OPEN: 11–11. Sun 12–10.30.
Real Ale. Restaurant.
Children in restaurant and garden. Dogs in bar and garden. Ample car parking. Wheelchair
access.

BEST OF THE REST

Burchetts Green
Crown ➀ 01628 822844
Burchetts Green SL6 6QZ
Off the A4, this well-liked place has a small bar serving snacks and light lunches, also a
bigger bar-cum-dining room. The blackboard menu changes twice a day and dishes range
from the usual pub favourites to chicken in a wine sauce or poached fillet of salmon.
Greene King, Bass and a decent selection of wines. Children allowed in restaurant.
Open: 12–2.30, 6–11.

Chievely
Blue Boar ➀ 01635 248236
North Heath, Wantage Road, Chievely RG20 8UE
Difficult to find, but console yourself that it is only two miles from junction 13 off the M4,
so can't be that far away. A 'Cromwell was here in 1644' pub, with views over the
surrounding country, this rambling 17th-century thatched inn serves better than average
bar food to go with Fullers London Pride and Wadworths 6X. Having found it, you can
stay the night too. Bedrooms.
Open: 11–3, 6–11.

Stanford Dingley
Bull ➀ 01189 744409
Stanford Dingley RG7 6LS
Go through Bradfield to find the 15th-century Bull, now extended, changed around and
opened up. Straightforward bar food: soups, sandwiches, filled baked potatoes – that sort

of thing – as well as daily specials. Seats at the front and the side garden of this old pub. On summer Saturdays it's a meeting place for classic cars and motorbikes. Brakspears Bitter and something from the West Berkshire Brewery. Children in restaurant. Bedrooms. Open: 12–3, 6–11 (Sat 7–11).

Wetherspoon in Berkshire

Bracknell – Old Manor, Church Road
☎ 01344 304490
Caversham – Baron Cadogan, Prospect Street
☎ 01189 470626
Maidenhead – Greyhound, 92–96 Queen Street
☎ 01628 779410
Reading – Back of Beyond, 104–108 Kings Road
☎ 01189 595906
Reading – Hope Tap, 99–105 Friar Street
☎ 01189 582266
Reading – Monks Retreat, 163 Friar Street
☎ 01189 507592
Slough – Moon and Spoon, 86 High Street
☎ 01753 531650
Windsor – Windlesora, 17 William Street
☎ 01753 754050

Buckinghamshire

Amersham

Kings Arms ① 01494 726333
30 High Street, Old Amersham HP7 0DJ
Free House. John Jennison, licensee
e-mail: info@kingsarmsamersham.co.uk

The High Street of the old town is a wonderful mix of Georgian and Elizabethan architecture, charming cottages, cobbled courtyards and this imposing, black-and-white half-timbered old inn. Built as two separate timber-framed open hall houses circa 1450, it has a wealth of beams, supporting timbers, inglenook fireplaces and lots of those little nooks and crannies you get in a converted 15th-century building. Over the years it has been altered, added to and improved in virtually every century since it was built, including this one. Inside are comfortable bars, a restaurant and private dining rooms; from the bar menu there could be soup of the day, chunky sandwiches or baguettes, filled jacket potatoes, hot paninis with different fillings, sausage and mash with onion gravy, steak and Guinness pie, a choice of salads and daily specials on the blackboard. If you want to dine in style you can order three courses from the restaurant table d'hôte menu which changes every four to five weeks or the à la carte which changes every month. Ind Coope Burton, Rebellion IPA and two weekly guest ales. Wines by the glass. Seats in the flowery courtyard or on the lawn.

OPEN: 11–11. Sun 12–10.30.
Real Ale. Restaurant (closed Sun eve and all day Mon).
Children welcome; they have their own area. Dogs on leads. Car park. Wheelchair access (not WC).
Cards: Amex, MasterCard, Visa.

Beaconsfield

Greyhound ① 01494 673823
33 Windsor End, Beaconsfield HP9 2JN
Free House. Maggie Miller, licensee

This largely unspoilt small 16th-century pub has low ceilings, beams, open fires and loads of atmosphere. In the older part of Beaconsfield, opposite the parish church among the cottages and 17th-century houses, the Greyhound, originally a drovers' pub, is near the old coaching road. Just two bars and a dining room where they serve reliable food – ranging from sandwiches to elaborate fish, steak and chicken dishes, home-made pies and a daily changing blackboard menu. Courage Best and Fullers London Pride; two guest ales change weekly. Seats in the garden. Good walks are not far away.

OPEN: 11–3, 5–11.30.
Real Ale.
No children. No dogs. Wheelchair access (not WC).

Bledlow

Lions of Bledlow ① 01844 343345
Church End, Bledlow HP27 9PE
Free House. Mark McKeown, licensee

In this village of Georgian houses and cottages the Lyde stream flows beside the unspoilt 13th-century church, and from Bledlow Ridge above you can see over hills, fields and woods. If you're in your walking boots this pub is hard to miss. All the best-used tracks seem to end up here, making it an ideal place to start or finish a long walk. The beamed, rambling, 16th-century pub has a large bar, settles to settle in, log fires, views from the windows and a dining room. In summer you can relax on the sheltered terrace and admire the scene; in winter, warm up by the huge fire in the comfortable beamed bar. On the menu are home-made soups, lots of fillings for the baguettes, ploughman's, salads, oriental prawns in filo pastry with cajun dip, lasagne served with garlic bread and salad, steak and Guinness pie, Mediterranean vegetables in a tomato and white wine sauce served with rice; fish dishes and daily specials are on the blackboard. Brakspear, Courage Best, Marstons Pedigree, Wadworths 6X ales on hand pump and one guest beer.

OPEN: 11.30–3, 6–11. Sun 12–3, 7–10.30.
Real Ale. No-smoking dining room.
Children if well supervised. Dogs very welcome; water and biscuits for them. Car park.
Cards: Amex, Delta, Diners, MasterCard, Switch, Visa.

Chenies

Red Lion ① 01923 282722
Chenies Village, Rickmansworth WD3 6ED
Free House. Heather & Mike Norris, FBII, owners/licensees

On a corner site, towards the outskirts of a picturesque estate village, this is a very appealing flower-trimmed, bay-windowed pub. There is a small, cosy snug towards the back behind the large main bar that, along with the small dining area, was the original 17th-century cottage around which the present pub was built. They serve a varied selection of very popular home-cooked bar food which could include soup of the day, hot or cold fillings for the French sticks or wholemeal baps, lots of interesting fillings for the jacket potatoes, a three-cheese paté with olives served with a salad, smoked haddock bake with a cream, egg and basil sauce topped with tomatoes, mixed seafood and ratatouille gratin, the special 'Chenies Pies' – with different fillings – oven-baked lamb with a ginger wine jus, also rump steaks cooked however you like them. All dishes come with fresh vegetables, but no chips. Daily specials from the blackboard. Wadworths 6X, Vales Best Bitter, Lions Pride, brewed for the pub by The Rebellion Beer Co, and a guest beer from Rebellion. They have a comprehensive wine list and five white and five red by the glass. If you want a little culture, Chenies Manor House – a Tudor manor built by the Earl of Bedford in 1526 and still with its original Tudor garden – is not far away.

OPEN: 11–2.30, 5.30–11.
Real Ale.
No children. Dogs on leads. Car park. Wheelchair access.
Cards: Amex, Delta, Diners, MasterCard, Switch, Visa.

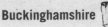

Coleshill

Red Lion ① 01494 727020
Village Road, Coleshill HP7 0LN
Alehouse Company. Christine & John Ullman, lease

Just an old-fashioned village local about two miles from Amersham. Not a typical-looking pub, more 1930s villa, but it is the focus of local events and hugely popular with all age groups for its well-kept beers and reliable bar food: freshly made sandwiches, ploughman's, salads (smoked salmon with scrambled eggs is a favourite), real ham – off the bone, also daily seasonal specials such as braised pheasant, oxtail in winter, cold salmon with prawns and salad, and warm crab tartlets with avocado salad in summer. There is a choice of roasts on Sundays. Good selection of puddings. Greene King IPA, Brakspear and Rebellion ales. A selection of wines by the glass. Tables at the front of the pub in summer and barbecues in the garden at the back.

OPEN: 11–3.30, 5.30–11. Sat 11–11. No food Sun eve.
Real Ale.
Children welcome. Dogs on leads. Wheelchair access (not WC).

Forty Green

Royal Standard of England ① 01494 673382
Forty Green, nr Beaconsfield HP9 1XT
Free House. Cyril & Carol Cain, licensees

A very ancient building with an interior full of interesting decorative objects and architectural details; splendid, carved oak panelling, magnificent oak beams, old stained glass and big fireplaces with roaring log fires in winter. Very much a 'Charles II was here' place – he hid in the pub's rafters to escape the Parliamentarians after the Battle of Worcester in 1651. Once Charles was back on the throne he granted special permission for the name to be changed to The Royal Standard of England in gratitude for their help in ensuring his safety; the name is exclusive to the pub. There is a wonderful choice of food, from home-made soup, exciting fillings for the sandwiches and ploughman's to crispy roast duck with damson sauce, lamb slow-cooked in mild ale and mead, skate with black butter sauce, and for vegetarians a wild mushroom, celeriac and squash roulade, chicken, leek and mushroom pie, beef and Owd Roger ale pie, sweet potato, spinach and rosemary bake topped with parmesan, and daily specials too. A good selection of cheeses, chutney made to a centuries-old secret recipe, and various continental breads. Marstons Pedigree, Morlands Old Speckled Hen, Brakspears and regular local guest beers. Good choice of malt and Irish whiskies; also fruit wines and a decent wine list. Lots of seats in the garden.

OPEN: 11–3, 5.30–11. Sun 12–3 (or later), 7–10.30. No food Sun eve.
Real Ale.
Children in three special areas. Dogs in garden only. Wheelchair access.
Cards: MasterCard and Visa.

Frieth

Prince Albert ① 01494 881683
Moors End, nr Henley-on-Thames RG9 6PX
Brakspear. Daniel Newman, licensee

Behind the village, along a quiet country lane in lovely countryside, surrounded by attractive woodland and lots of wonderful walks, is this small, white-painted 18th-century pub. There's not a great deal of room inside, so all is very cosy and intimate with low beams, fires to warm you and local guides to read while you wait. The menu on the blackboard lists the usual bar food: sandwiches with different fillings, ploughman's, salads, sausage and mash and daily specials. Brakspears Bitter and Special on hand pump. Good choice of wines and decent whiskies. Seats at the front of the pub and in the flowery garden at the side.

OPEN: 12–3, 5.30–11.
Real Ale.
Children welcome. Dogs on leads. Wheelchair access (not WC).

Great Hampden

Hampden Arms ① 01494 488255
Great Hampden, nr Great Missenden HP16 9RQ
Free House. Louise & Constantine Lucas, licensees

This small timbered pub in a large garden near the Icknield Way is a favourite with those valiant walkers wanting a little rest and refreshment. Inside, there are just two cosy beamed rooms, one with the bar; you can eat and drink in both – if you can find a space. Standing room only in summer; you must book if you want to sit and eat inside. Outside there are lots of tables, so if you hit a busy period, just hope the weather is fine. Lots of dishes to choose from the printed or blackboard menu – something for everyone – plus a range of starters, snacks and vegetarian as well as specials. Abundance all round. Adnams, Brakspears, Addlestones draught cider and a small wine list.

OPEN: 12–3, 6–11. Sun 12–3, 7–10.30.
Real Ale.
Children welcome. Dogs on leads – ask first. Car park. Wheelchair access.
Cards: Amex, Delta, Diners, MasterCard, Switch, Visa.

Great Kingshill

Red Lion ① 01494 711262
Missenden Rd, Great Kingshill, High Wycombe HP15 6EB
Pubmaster. Pepe Rivero-Cabrera, tenant

North of High Wycombe, the Red Lion might look like a pub and indeed it does sell beer; you are more than welcome to sit down to have a pint – or a glass of wine. But this is really more of a restaurant; all the tables are set for dining. Quieter during the day, very busy in the evening. There are some classic meat dishes – tournedos Rossini, lamb cutlets

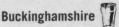

and beef stroganoff – but their speciality is fresh fish and shellfish – all sorts, and lots of it, from cream of lobster bisque and fresh sardines to skate: calamares alla Romana, coquille St Jacques, fillets of smoked trout, grilled sea bream and Dover sole, halibut au gratin, prawn and mushroom crepes, grilled fillet of turbot or fillets of sole bonne femme, lobster, baby crayfish and smoked salmon salad; lots more on the menu and you can even order a takeaway traditional paella. Even the chips are properly made. Benskins and Tetleys ales and wines by the glass.

OPEN: 12–2, 6–10. Closed Sun eve and all day Mon.
Restaurant.
Children welcome. No dogs.
Cards: all except Amex and Diners.

Hedgerley

White Horse ① 01753 643225
Village Lane, Hedgerley Village, nr Slough SL2 3UY
Free House. Kevin Brooker & Dot Hobbs, licensees

This is a charming, 15th-century, family-run village pub serving some worthwhile lunchtime food and excellent beer. At the end of the village, it is a typical country local with an original flagstone-floored small public bar with a big inglenook fireplace and a larger-beamed lounge bar. On the food front, the cold bar menu has a refrigerated tray that keeps the salads fresh; hot food could include steak and mushroom pie, chilli, home-made fish cakes, quiches and some chicken dishes. The menu frequently changes. Always seven ales available; they change too from day to day. Lovely views from the big garden. Good walks nearby. Beer festivals in the garden during the spring bank holiday.

OPEN: 11–3, 5.30–11. Sun 12–10.30. Lunchtime food only.
Real Ale.
Children allowed in the garden. Dogs in public bar and garden. Car park.

Little Missenden

Crown ① 01494 862571
Little Missenden, nr Amersham HP7 0RD
Free House. Trevor How, licensee

Truly a family pub; the How family have celebrated a century in this unspoilt 17th-century converted cottage. This village on the river Misbourne has retained its charm, unlike its greater namesake further up the road. Inside, the bar is decorated with old farm implements and serves simple home-made food at lunchtime: sandwiches, ploughman's, steak and kidney pies, salads – that sort of thing. Hook Norton Best Bitter, Adnams and one weekly changing guest beer. Seats in the sheltered garden through which the River Misbourne runs (except in a drought), eventually flowing into Shardloes Lake.

OPEN: 11–2.30, 6–11. Sun 12–2.30, 7–10.30. No food Sun.
Real Ale.
No children. Dogs on leads.

Swan Bottom

Old Swan at Swan Bottom ① 01494 837239
Swan Bottom, The Lee, Gt Missenden HP16 9NU
Free House. Mr & Mrs S. C. Michaelson-Yeates. licensees
e-mail: myoldswan@aol.com

Off the A413 Great Missenden to Wendover, find The Lee first if you're using an ordinary map, and the tiny hamlet of Swan Bottom is just north of the village along a single-track road. Among the Chiltern hills, in two acres of garden, the 16th-century Old Swan is a well-loved local pub with tremendous appeal. Inside are 'mind your head' beams, sensible stone floors, open fires and a small cosy restaurant serving some worthwhile food. Be assured that they know what they're doing in the kitchen; Sean, the licensee, was a chef at both the Savoy and the Grosvenor House. From the daily changing menu there could be home-made leek and potato soup, smoked fish platter, home-made potted shrimps with salad, sausage and mash with onion gravy, large fillet of cod roasted in olive oil and rock salt on a bed of creamed potato and leaf spinach, grilled steaks served with a mushroom and red wine sauce or a pan-fried breast of duckling on spicy oriental noodles with a honey, plum glaze. More-ish puds too. Beers are Brakspear, Adnams and London Pride. There is a short wine list, some by the glass. The pub is also a film star with bit parts in The Midsomer Murders and Noel's House Party.

OPEN: Tues–Fri 12–3, 6–11. Sat 12–11. Sun 12–7. Closed Mon.
Real Ale.
Children and dogs welcome. Car park. Wheelchair access.
Cards: MasterCard, Switch, Visa.

West Wycombe

George & Dragon ① 01494 464414
High Street, West Wycombe HP14 3AB
Unique. Philip and Cass Todd, lease
e-mail: enq@george-and-dragon.co.uk

The early Georgian frontage on this handsome, substantial building on the old London to Oxford road hides a much earlier structure – or so the old timbers at the back of the inn would indicate. Part of an historic village full of 15th- and 18th-century houses that has been owned by the National Trust since 1934, the inn was extended and modernised in 1720; you walk through a cobbled archway to an entrance leading to atmospheric rooms full of huge beams, walls slightly off the vertical, big log fires and the ghost of a servant girl said to haunt the staircase. From the rambling, comfortable bar they serve well-prepared food: home-made soup, ploughman's, wild boar and apple sausages with mash in a cider gravy, steak and onion toastie in ciabatta, lamb and spinach curry with rice, Cajun chicken wings served with home-baked roll, a choice of fillings for the ciabatta roll or tortilla wrap and home-made puddings. There is a separate evening restaurant menu. The beers are Charles Wells Bombardier, Adnams Broadside and Courage Best. As the owners have opened a wine shop on the premises you can expect a choice wine list, all by the glass. Interesting walks close by.

OPEN: 11–2.30, 5.30–11. Sat 11–11.

Real Ale. Restaurant.
Children in own room. Dogs on leads. Car park. Wheelchair access to the pub difficult –
lots of cobbles – but possible. Accommodation.
Cards: Amex, Delta, Diners, MasterCard, Switch, Visa.

Wheeler End

Chequers ① 01494 883070
Bullocks Farm Lane, Wheeler End, High Wycombe HP14 3NH
Fullers. S. Warner & A. Kaiser, licensees

South of the M40, on the edge of Wheeler End Common, west of Marlow, white painted and
unspoilt, very rural, friendly and welcoming. Over 300 years old, the Chequers is a pleasing
village pub in well-kept gardens. Inside, the cosy bar has a large inglenook fireplace with a big
winter log fire which leads through to the no-smoking restaurant. The bar snack menu is
available lunchtimes only: soup of the day, traditional fish soup with garlic croutons, seared
scallop and king prawn salad, venison pie, wild boar and apple sausages on a scallion mash
with red wine jus, hot and cold filled baguettes, freshly made plain and toasted sandwiches,
mussels cooked in cumin, ginger, white wine and cream, Thai fishcakes, warm avocado and
smoked bacon salad, and from the main menu, roast salmon supreme and king prawns in a
lobster and tarragon sauce, haunch of venison braised in red wine and junipers or roast West
Wycombe partridge on a bed of savoy cabbage and pancetta with cranberry game jus and
fondant potatoes. There is also an à la carte menu and Sunday roast lunch. Fullers range of
ales, and a good selection of wines. Plenty of walks nearby.

OPEN: 11–3, 5.30–11. Sun 12–10.30.
Real Ale.
Children welcome. Dogs on leads in bar.
Cards: all major cards except Amex and Diners.

BEST OF THE REST

Easington
Mole & Chicken ① 01844 208387
Easington HP18 9EY
You come – through rolling Buckinghamshire countryside, north of Long Crendon, along
Carters Lane and Chilton Road – to a very pretty pub that leans hard towards being a
restaurant but, as they serve beer and cider in the bar, it is still a pub – with a difference. The
dishes you choose are from an à la carte menu – no bar snacks – and what you get has
distanced itself from the average pub menu. How about grilled crostini of smoked salmon,
trout and halibut over cream cheese with basil oil, or chicken breast basted in mixed herbs
stuffed with cream cheese and wrapped in smoked bacon and puff pastry with a smoked
cheddar and spring onion sauce? Try to leave plenty of room for scrummy puds. Greene King
IPA, Morlands Old Speckled Hen and Strongbow cider. Children welcome. Wheelchair access
(not WC).
Open: 12–3, 6–12. Sun 11–9.

Moulsoe

Carrington Arms ① 01908 218050
Cranfield Road MK16 0HB

An imposing building, originally built to house Lord Carrington's estate manager, it's now a small, grade II listed hotel, well known for its steaks and fresh fish – all displayed for you to choose. Sold by weight, you can pick and mix and watch it cooked in front of you. Real ales, good wine list and champagne by the glass. Children allowed. Bedrooms.
Open: 11–2.30, 6–11.

Newton Longville

Crooked Billet ① 01908 373936
2 Westbrook End, Newton Longville MK17 0DF

Still very much the traditional thatched village pub with an interior to match, but here you can sample some fantastic cooking that has nothing at all in common with your average pub grub. From the changing bar menu there could be slow-roasted ham hock terrine with apple and cider jelly, Cornish crab and English Oagleshield cheese tart with rocket salad, crayfish linguini, and a Billet ploughman's – ham, chicken and pork pie, Montgomery cheddar, corn beef mash and pickles; or roasted pork belly, crackling, savora mustard mash and gravy. Lots more, delicious puds, English cheeses and an exciting, inventive restaurant menu. About 300 wines on the list – all by the glass and plenty of beer: Greene King IPA, Abbott, Old Speckled Hen, Wychwood Hobgoblin, Castle Eden Nimmos, Everards Tiger and Batemans XXXB. No children. No dogs. Car park. Wheelchair access. Cards: Amex, Delta, JCB, MasterCard, Switch, Visa.
Open: Mon 5.30–11. Tues–Sat 12–2.30, 5.30–11. Sun 12–4, 7–10.30.

Prestwood

Polecat Inn ① 01494 862253
170 Wycombe Road, Prestwood HP16 0HJ

A lovely pub in a lovely garden, very food-oriented with some interesting dishes on the menu: leek and potato soufflé baked in filo served on mixed leaves with chive sour cream and a fillet of beef Wellington for a main course. Lots more; delights await. Beers are Marstons Pedigree, Theakstons Best, Ruddles County, Wadworths 6X and Morlands Old Speckled Hen. About a dozen wines by the glass. Children in bar eating area. Dogs welcome. Wheelchair access.
Open: 11.30–3, 6–11. Closed Sun eve.

Thornborough

Lone Tree ① 01280 812334
Bletchley Road, Thornborough MK18 2DZ

Just off the busy A421 (which has been straightened, so the pub's not quite on the road), the Lone Tree is all alone, but certainly not forgotten. The tree, after which it was named, has been gone since the 1920s, but the pub flourishes. Small, well kept, well polished and hugely popular. They serve decent food, unusual real ales and some unusual English cheeses. Good wine list, farm ciders and country wines. Children, if eating. Dogs – ask first. Wheelchair access.
Open: 12–3, 6–11.

Waddesdon

Five Arrows ① 01296 651727
High Street, Waddesdon HP18 0JE

Built in the late 19th century as part of the Rothschild estate, now a rather smart, comfortable, small hotel with a good bar and a restaurant serving interesting, stylish food. Adnams Bitter, Fullers London Pride, a really good wine list, champagne by the glass and anything else you might want – within reason. From here you are poised for a visit to Waddesdon Manor, the Five Arrows' impressive neighbour. Children welcome. Wheelchair access. Bedrooms.

Open: 11.30–11. Sun 12–10.30. No bar snacks on Sundays.

Wetherspoon in Buckinghamshire

Chesham – Last Post, 77 The Broadway
① 01494 785622
High Wycombe – Falcon, 9 Cornmarket
① 01494 538610
Milton Keynes – Wetherspoons, 201 Midsummer Boulevard, Bouverie Square
① 01908 606074
Milton Keynes – Moon under the Water, Xscape, Avebury Boulevard
① 01908 528854

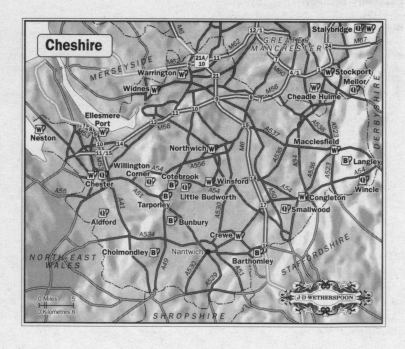

Cheshire

MERSEYSIDE

GREATER MANCHESTER

DERBYSHIRE

STAFFORDSHIRE

SHROPSHIRE

NORTH EAST WALES

Stalybridge
Warrington
Widnes
Stockport
Mellor
Cheadle Hulme
Ellesmere Port
Neston
Macclesfield
Northwich
Langley
Willington Corner
Cotebrook
Winsford
Wincle
Chester
Little Budworth
Congleton
Tarporley
Smallwood
Aldford
Bunbury
Crewe
Cholmondley
Nantwich
Barthomley

J·D·WETHERSPOON

0 Miles 5
0 Kilometres 8

Cheshire

Aldford

Grosvenor Arms ① 01244 620228
Chester Road, Aldford CH3 6HJ
Brunning & Price. Gary Kidd, licensee
e-mail: grosvenorarms@brunningandprice.co.uk

A large, very dignified, Victorian brick building with a touch of the local vernacular on the top floor, a part of the Grosvenor estate. Inside it has the feel of an elegant country house: spacious, comfortable seating areas, a library and smart, flowery, no-smoking conservatory. Don't feel overwhelmed; there is a bar serving very well-kept beer where you can also order a sandwich with distinction: egg and bacon mayonnaise on sun-dried tomato bread, rare roast beef with horseradish or farmhouse cheddar and chutney. From the imaginative menu a black pudding and chorizo fritter with apple sauce, potted ham hock with piccalilli and salad, Caesar salad, roasted peppers with a couscous and Mediterranean vegetable stuffing glazed with mozzarella and herb oil, salmon fishcakes with tomato and spring onion salad and lemon mayonnaise, braised shoulder of lamb with tomato and mint sauce, maybe passion fruit cheesecake to finish. Robinsons Best and Flowers IPA are the beers, plus guests; there are over 100 single malts, 30 Bourbons and 25 Irish whiskies which could keep you happily occupied for a considerable time, as well as a wide-ranging, good, reasonably priced wine list, many by the glass. Outside is an attractive terrace and garden leading onto the village green.

OPEN: 11.30–11. Sun 12–10.30.
Real Ale.
Children welcome. Dogs in one bar only. Car park. Wheelchair access.
Cards: Amex, Delta, MasterCard, Switch, Visa.

Chester

Albion ① 01244 340345
Park Street (off Newgate), Chester CH1 1RN
Pubmaster. Michael Mercer, licensee
e-mail: mike@albioninn.freeserve.co.uk

Still a pub, but a bit of a showcase too for the landlord's fascination with the First World War. Tucked beneath one of the old city walls the Victorian Albion, friendly and unchanging, has an amazing collection of memorabilia and contemporary pictures – as well as a number of artifacts from the 40s and 50s, all displayed in the Edwardian-style rooms. An interesting choice of bar food and an inventive, changing menu. From the 'Trench Rations' there could be lamb's liver and smoked bacon with onions in a rich cider gravy, Penrith Cumberland sausages with apple sauce, McSween's award-winning haggis and tatties, Staffordshire oatcakes with a broccoli and cheese filling, an individual cottage pie with a crisp leek and cheese crust served with pickled red cabbage, filled butties (doorstep size), daily specials and home-made puddings on the blackboard. Timothy Taylors Landlord, Cains Bitter and a Jennings Cumberland guest beer, large selection of malt whiskies and a short wine list – nothing French.

OPEN: 11.30–3, 5.30–11. Fri 11–11.
Real Ale.
Children not encouraged. Dogs welcome.

Old Harker's Arms ① 01244 344525
1 Russell Street, Chester CH3 5AL
Brunning & Price. Barbie Hill & Catryn Devaney, lease
e-mail: harkersarms@brunningandprice.co.uk

You could never be bored here. What was, until the middle of the 1980s, an unused Victorian canal warehouse, is now a very spacious, successful pub. A big space divided up into different areas; high ceilings, solid pillars and plenty of wall space, most of it covered with pictures, prints and information that would take you a week to look at, soft leather seating and solid old furniture. A well-run place serving pub grub with a difference: soup of the day, ploughman's, hot and toasted sandwiches, smoked trout fillet on rocket leaves and cherry tomatoes, black olive, anchovy and caper tapenade with toasted French bread, minute steak on toasted bread with horseradish mayonnaise, Harker's Caesar salad, steak, ale and mushroom pie, oven-baked spinach, mushroom, cranberry and puff pastry parcel served with carrot and parsnip mash and leek and mushroom sauce, rib-eye steak with sauté mushrooms, spring onions, chips and salad; fish and vegetarian choices. Daily papers to read if you're kept waiting, and plenty of things to drink: Boddingtons, Thwaites ales and six changing guests, eight cask beers always on; 27 malt whiskies and a good wine list, all available by the glass. No music, no fruit machines, no pool table – just a friendly, jolly pub, with a view of the watery activity on the canal.

OPEN: 11.30–11. Sun 12–10.30.
Real Ale.
Children before 7pm. No dogs. Car parking after 5.30 and all weekends and bank holidays. Wheelchair access.
Cards: Amex, MasterCard, Visa.

Little Budworth

Shrewsbury Arms ① 01829 760240
Chester Road, Little Budworth, nr Tarporley CW6 9EY
Robinsons. Tim Gandy, tenant
e-mail: tim@gandyt-fsnet.co.uk

On the outskirts of the village, what was once a quiet 16th-century farmhouse, and during the mid-19th century a beer house with a rackety, lively past, is now an appealing, popular pub. Inside are framed articles reporting the days when, as a beer house very near the racecourse, the pub's cellars became a hiding place for the local bookmakers escaping indignant Irish navvies who had foolishly bet, and lost, their wages at the local races. Now in less fraught times this is a friendly, relaxed place serving better than average pub food. On the 'Cheshire Fine Food Trail', the menu includes several vegetarian choices, fresh fish and many specials: chicken tikka masala, peppered pork, good steaks, duckling à l'orange and of course bar snacks and freshly made soup, egg mayonnaise, steak casserole and cottage pie. The only 'real' ale is Robinsons Best Bitter, but they keep other Robinsons seasonal ales too. Short, wide-ranging wine list. You are very near good local walks – the Whitegate Way and Delamere Forest – also the interesting Winsford Salt mines, and if you're so inclined, Oulton Park motor racing circuit.

OPEN: 11.30–2.30, 6–11. Sun 12–2.30. 7–10.30.
Real Ale. As they are busy, it is advisable to book for meals at weekends.
Children welcome, so are dogs. Car park. Wheelchair access.
Cards: MasterCard, Switch, Visa.

Mellor

Oddfellows Arms ① 0161 449 7826
73 Moor End Road, Mellor, nr Stockport SK6 5PT
Free House. Robert Cloughley, licensee

Difficult to miss as this is a substantial structure – all three floors of it: a fine, 300-year-old building with a handsome, traditional bar on the ground floor and no-smoking restaurant and smaller dining room on the first floor. Known locally for its fish dishes – there is usually a choice of eight including a Catalan dish – Zarzuela – which has salmon, cod, halibut and swordfish in a rich, garlicky tomato and spiced stew topped with clams, black tiger prawns, whole langoustine and mussels, with plenty of bread to mop up the juices – as well as a roast of the day and a good choice of bar food, all prepared 'in pub': soup, mussel chowder, filo-wrapped Thai spiced prawns with plum sauce, Catalan cassoulet, pork Schnitzel and cabbage, also sirloin or fillet steaks, a selection of spicy dishes, hot sandwiches and paninis, traditional sandwiches, salads or something from the specials board. The restaurant is no smoking and there are some tables outside. Adnams Best, Marstons Bitter, Pedigree and a rotating guest beer.

OPEN: 12–3, 5.30–11 (Sun 7–10.30).
Real Ale. Restaurant Tues–Sat eves and Sun lunchtime.
Children until 8.30pm. Wheelchair access into bar only.
Cards: all major credit cards except Amex.

Smallwood

Blue Bell Inn ① 01477 500262
Spen Green, Smallwood, nr Congleton CW11 2XA
Pubmaster. Barrie & Sandra Sheehan, tenants
e-mail: barriesandra@bluebellinn.fsnet.co.uk

Only three miles from Congleton and Alsager, the 16th-century Blue Bell is a gem of a pub with beamed bars and three big log fires – just as you imagine it ought to be. Using local produce whenever possible, bar food, available every lunchtime, is seasonal; in winter there will always be soup, regular and toasted sandwiches, home-made pies, filled baguettes, all-day breakfast, filled jacket potatoes and a bowl of chunky chips. In summer, lots of salads on the menu. Sunday roast – advisable to book. Beers are Greenalls Bitter,

Bass, Fullers London Pride and one weekly guest. Keg beers too. Outside is a picturesque garden.

OPEN: 12–3, 5.30–11 (Sat 6–11, Sun 7–10.30). Closed Mon lunchtimes. Food served Tues–Sun lunchtimes only.
Real Ale.
Children welcome. Dogs on leads.

Stalybridge

Stalybridge Station Buffet Bar ① 0161 303 0007
Stalybridge Station, Rassbotham Street, Stalybridge SK15 1RF
Free House. Sylvia Wood & John Hesketh, licensees
www.buffetbar.co.uk

Nostalgia is fully catered for in this old Victorian station buffet. All the original fittings are still here: coal fire, railway memorabilia, photos of the glory of steam and the working station as well as a conservatory and the important bar where you are still able to get a drink. Enthusiasts meet here, enthuse together and enjoy a beer. There are newspapers and magazines to read and seats on the platform where you can sip your freshly made tea or coffee. Home-cooked food: sandwiches, ploughman's and two or three daily specials. Boddingtons beer, Flowers IPA, Wadworths 6X and constantly changing guests – over 4500 in six years – increasing all the time. Traditional scrumpy or perry available too. Regular beer festivals with jazz on the platform. On Monday evenings there is a not too serious quiz night.

OPEN: 11–11. Sun 12–10.30.
Real Ale.
Children welcome. Dogs too. Car park. Wheelchair access.
Folk music on Saturday nights.

Willington

Boot Inn ① 01829 751375
Boothsdale, Willington, nr Tarporley CW6 0NH
Tied to Nomura. Michael Gollins, licensee

In the shelter of a hill in Cat Lane, the Boot, known locally as the Cat, is a charming pub in glorious countryside. What was originally an attractive collection of cottages and a beer house has over the years been gathered up and turned into this delightful inn. Inside are some fine old beams, quarry-tiled floors and big fires. On 'Cheshire's Fine Food Trail', the Boot's menu is served in either the bar or restaurant: home-made soup, anchovy bake, devilled kidneys in a port-wine sauce, warm smoked trout, traditional steak and kidney cooked in ale, escalopes of chicken, calves' liver, bacon and onions, steaks, salad platters, filled warm baguettes or even a freshly made sandwich; specials and vegetarian dishes too. Traditional roast on Sundays. Greenalls, Bass Cains, Flowers IPA, the local Weetwood ales and regular guests. Over 35 malt whiskies and a good wine list. A booklet detailing six circular walks from the Boot is available in the pub. Tables on the west-facing terrace with views towards the Welsh hills.

OPEN: 11–3, 6–11. Sat 11–11 Sun 12–10.30.
Real Ale. Restaurant.
Children with well-behaved parents. Dogs in garden only. Car park.

Wincle

Ship ① 01260 227217
Wincle, nr Macclesfield SK11 0QE
Free House. Giles Meadows, licensee

In a wonderfully remote community close to the River Dane, and down the hill at Danebridge, is the comfortable old Ship. It's on the very edge of the county, surrounded by excellent walks, and many a footpath ends close to this 16th-century stone pub – as do the walkers. Inside, in the two delightfully traditional rooms, they offer a good range of bar food, from soup and lunchtime sandwiches to roast lamb and steaks with regularly changing specials on the blackboard menu. Titanic Bitter from Burslem and changing guests – Timothy Taylors Landlord is the most regular guest but about 100 different ales per year. The wine list has been extended and includes specialist wines at sensible prices.

OPEN: 12–3, 7–11. Closed Mon.
Real Ale.
Well-behaved children in family room. Dogs on leads. Car park. Wheelchair access (not WC).
Cards: Delta, MasterCard, Switch, Visa.

BEST OF THE REST

Barthomley
White Lion ① 01270 882242
Barthomley, nr Crewe CW2 5PG
First licensed in 1614: very traditional, black and white and thatched. Opposite is the 15th-century village church which was the centre of a little local fracas during the Civil War. Ghosts may roam, but not during lunch. Smartened up but still wonderfully beamed, panelled and full of atmosphere. Reasonably priced bar food: soups, cheese and onion oatcakes, ham or cheese ploughman's and daily specials. Burtonwood Bitter and Top Hat plus a guest. Sunday roast lunch – do book. Children away from main bar. Dogs on leads. Open: 11.30–11.

Bunbury
Dysart Arms ① 01829 260183
Bowes Gate Road, Bunbury CW6 9PH
Sister pub to the Aldford Arms the mid-Georgian Dysart Arms unfortunately does have very quiet music. It's opposite the church, in a lovely garden, with a handsome, heavily timbered, listed interior. Interesting dishes on the menu include freshly prepared soup, a choice of four cheeses for the ploughman's, open sandwiches too and roasted red peppers filled with cherry tomatoes and goat's cheese, chicken liver paté with piccalilli and for a

main course roasted artichoke, black olive and pearl barley cakes on creamed leeks, pan-fried chicken breast with garlic potatoes, fine beans, babycorn and a red pepper dressing, good puds and changing English – and Irish farmhouse – cheeses. Concise wine list and a number of beers; Timothy Taylors Landlord, Thwaites, Weetwood Eastgate, Hanby Drawwell, Rudgate Viking and whatever takes their fancy. Children under 10 until 6 o'clock. Dogs welcome – in bar. Car park. Wheelchair access. Cards: Delta, MasterCard, Switch, Visa.
Open: 11.30–11. Sun 12–10.30.

Cholmondeley
Cholmondeley Arms ① 01829 720 300
Cholmondeley ST14 8HN
Easy enough to find as the Cholmondeley Arms, opposite the gates of Cholmondeley Castle, was cleverly created in the late 1980s out of what was the village school. As you would expect, it is spacious inside, still with classroom-size rooms, big windows, high ceilings and a great fire-place. They are very serious about the food here. The interesting menu could list flat mushrooms stuffed with spinach and grilled with hollandaise, pheasant and pickled walnut terrine witrh Cumberland jelly, and among the main courses could be a leek and cheddar soufflé with salad, rack of lamb with rosemary gravy, four seasons salad with prawns, eggs, crispy bacon with croutons, Cholmondeley steak and kidney pie and some really good home-made puds. Banks' ales, Marstons Pedigree, Adnams and something from Westwood – a very local Cheshire brewery – and a well-chosen wine list. Seats in the garden and on the terrace. Children welcome, so are dogs. Car park. Wheelchair access. Bedrooms in the old school house. Cards: most, except Amex and Diners.
Open: 11–3, 6.30–11

Cotebrook
Fox & Barrel ① 01829 760529
Forest Road, Cotebrook, Tarporley CW6 9DZ
North-east of Tarporley in the quiet Cheshire countryside, this is a desirable pub serving some really good food. Inside, the bar has a huge log fire and there is an atmospheric, candle-lit dining room. From the changing menus, as well as chef's home-made soup, well-filled sandwiches, baguettes and a choice of ploughman's, there could be a bowl of Bantry Bay mussels, warm salad of shredded duck, bacon, toasted pine kernels and croutons, beef bourguignon, steak, ale and mushroom pie, or a fillet of Scottish salmon on a bed of braised leeks and sliced new potatoes with a pink peppercorn, chive and white wine butter sauce. Beers are draught Bass. John Smiths Cask, Marstons Pedigree and Jennings Cumberland Ale; there is a wide-ranging wine list. Children welcome. No dogs. Car park. Cards: all except Diners.
Open: Mon-Fri 12–3, 5.30–11. Sat 12–11. Sun 12–10.30.

Langley
Leathers Smithy ① 01260 252313
Clarke Lane, Langley SK11 0NE
If you're a walker, you probably know this place; if you're not – well here it is: not far from Macclesfield Forest, and the wild moorland beyond, Teggs Nose country park and the Ridgegate Reservoir. A well-run, cosy old pub serving good-value, interesting bar food to go with the Marstons Pedigree, Courage Directors and RCH Pitchfork, cider and a choice of Irish or Scotch whiskies. No food Monday evening.
Open: 12–3, 7–11.

Tarporley

Rising Sun ☺ 01829 732423
38 High Street, Tarporley CW6 0DX
In a tiny village full of interesting architecture, including what was once a medieval church – now largely rebuilt. Much in demand, the jolly, friendly Rising Sun looks very pretty when the flowers are in bloom. They serve traditional bar food: sandwiches, toasties, filled jacket potatoes, lasagne and home-made pies as well as a restaurant menu. Robinsons range of ales. Children in eating area. No children under 12 in evening. Open: 11.30–3.30, 5.30–11. Open all day Sat and bank holidays.

Wetherspoon in Cheshire

Cheadle Hume – King's Hall, 13 Station Road
☺ 0161 485 1555
Chester – Wetherspoons, 78–92 Foregate Street
☺ 01244 312281
Congleton – Counting House, 18 Swan Bank
☺ 01260 272654
Crewe – Gaffer's Row, 48 Victoria Street
☺ 01270 503820
Ellesmere Port – Wheatsheaf, 43 Overpool Road
☺ 0151 356 7454
Macclesfield – Society Rooms, Park Lane
☺ 01625 507320
Neston – Lodestar, Brook Street
☺ 0151 353 0485
Northwich – Penny Black, 110 Witton Street
☺ 01606 42029
Stalybridge – Society Rooms, Grosvenor Street
☺ 0161 338 9740
Stockport – Calverts Court, Saint Petersgate
☺ 0161 474 6750
Warrington – Friar Pinkeph, 4 Barbauld Street, Friars Gate
☺ 01925 237320
Widnes – Premier, 93–99 Albert Road
☺ 0151 4224920
Winsford – Queens Arms, Dean Drive
☺ 01606 595350

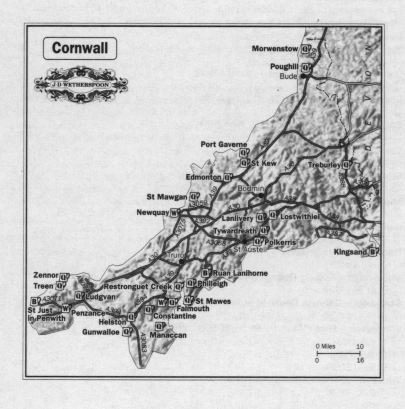

Cornwall

J·D·WETHERSPOON

Morwenstow
Poughill
Bude

Port Gaverne
St Kew
Edmonton
Treburley
Bodmin
St Mawgan
Newquay
Lanlivery
Lostwithiel
Tywardreath
Polkerris
St Austell
Truro
Kingsand
Ruan Lanihorne
Zennor
Restronguet Creek
Philleigh
Treen
Ludgvan
St Mawes
St Just
in Penwith
Penzance
Falmouth
Helston
Constantine
Gunwalloe
Manaccan

0 Miles 10
0 16

Cornwall

Constantine

Trengilly Wartha ① 01326 340332
Nancenoy Constantine, nr Helston TR11 5RP
Free House. Nigel Logan & Michael Maguire, licensees
e-mail: reception@trengilly.co.uk

Inside this delightful 18th-century pub you'll find a low-beamed main bar, a lounge, an eating area off the bar and a no-smoking family conservatory; picnic tables outside. The pub serves a good selection of home-made bar food: soups and risotto, chicken liver and port paté with home-made chutney and toasted brioche or half a dozen Helford oysters. Perennial favourites are leek and cheese soufflé, crab cakes, Tregilly sausages, braised ham hock, tagliatelle with smoked trout, a traditional Cornish pasty as well as various ploughman's with home-made pickles, salads, steaks and daily specials from the blackboard, which usually features a number of fish dishes. Don't forget the delicious puds. There is also an imaginative restaurant menu. Exmoor Ale, Cotleigh, Tawny and Sharp's Doom Bar Ale; other guests from small independent breweries. Ciders, a big selection of malt whiskies, and choice of wines – by the bottle or glass. This is a breathtakingly beautiful area: you are near one of several creeks of the Helford River that wander inland between lovely wooded banks. On the other side of the river is Frenchman's Creek, immortalised by Daphne du Maurier, now managed by the National Trust.

OPEN: 11–2.30, 6–11 (6.30–11 in winter).
Real Ale. Restaurant.
Children welcome. Dogs on leads. Car park. Wheelchair access (not WC). Bedrooms.
Cards: Amex, Delta, Diners, MasterCard, Switch.

Edmonton

Quarryman ① 01208 816444
Edmonton, nr Wadebridge PL27 7JA
Free House. Terry & Wendy de Villiers Kuun, licensees

The village is a little west of Wadebridge – the old port at the head of the Camel estuary – and the Quarryman, part of a rebuilt courtyard that was originally used as quarrymen's quarters during the 19th century, is a friendly pub, bistro and holiday complex. Inside are one bar and three separate drinking areas – one of which is no smoking – where they serve good, sustaining bar food: sandwiches, filled ciabattas, garlic mushrooms in a cream sauce, lasagne, home-made pies, Aberdeen Angus steaks (their speciality), lamb shanks, local game (when available), vegetarian cannelloni, lots of fresh, locally caught fish and daily specials. Sharp's Eden Ale, Skinner's Knocker and Coastliner, also guest beers. Handy for the Camel trail; there's also a good walk from Wadebridge to Padstow along a path that follows the abandoned railway line. Other good walks too, and you're near the County Showground.

OPEN: 12–11.
Real Ale. Restaurant. Food served 12–2.30, 6–9.
Children in eating area. Dogs on leads. Wheelchair access (not WC).
Cards: MasterCard, Switch, Visa.

_____

Falmouth

Seven Stars ① 01326 312111
1 The Moor, Falmouth TR11 3QA
Free House. The Rev. Barrington Bennetts, licensee

A wonderfully quiet, historically interesting and unchanging town centre pub, built in 1660 with a Grade II* rating – making it one of the county's treasures. Owned by the landlord's family since 1873, this is an entertaining place with an amusing man of the cloth behind the bar and chatty locals. Just one, long room with a snug behind. No food except crisps and nuts. Refreshment of the liquid kind only; draught Bass and Sharp's from the cask and guest beers. Tables on the forecourt. On The Moor is a monument celebrating the 150 years that the 'Falmouth packets' – fast, light ships, privately owned but contracted to the Post Office – delivered the mail to Europe and as far away as the West Indies.

OPEN: 11–3, 6–11.
Real Ale.
No children. Dogs in the back bar. Wheelchair access (not WC).

_____

Gunwalloe

Halzephron ① 01326 240406
Gunwalloe, Helston TR12 7QB
Free House. Angela Thomas, licensee
e-mail: halzephroninn@gunwalloe1.fsnet.co.uk

Close to dramatic cliffs, small fishing villages and Church Cove. A hugely popular place during the season, not only for the well-kept beers but food which is way above the usual. The Cornish name 'Halzephron' means 'hell cliffs', aptly named as this area had more than a nodding acquaintance with the smuggling and wrecking that went on in the past; a smugglers' shaft connected to an underground tunnel still exists. Most of the wood you see in this 500-year-old stone pub comes from ships wrecked in the local waters. There is one menu for both bar and no-smoking restaurant which ranges from the usual pub favourites to home-cooked dishes from the daily changing specials board: celeriac and potato soup, paté of the day with a toasted brioche, Cornish smoked fish selection with salad garnish, prawn salad platter, a choice of ploughman's and from the specials board, beef stroganoff with a timbale of rice, a ragout of lamb with redcurrant, rosemary and vegetables, or pan-fried sea bass and tiger prawns with chorizo sausage, artichokes, fennel capers, olives and cherry tomatoes or roasted saddle of rabbit with mushrooms and herbs, wrapped in parma ham, served on spinach with a filo basket of wild mushrooms. Food here is creative and tempting. The beers are Helzephron Gold, brewed for the pub by Organic Brewhouse at Helston, with a guest and an interesting wine list. Seats outside on the terrace and in the garden. Next to National Trust land, the pub has wonderful views across Mount's Bay towards Penzance and Land's End.

OPEN: 11.30–3, 6–11 (6.30–11 in winter).
Real Ale. Restaurant. Food served until 2 p.m. and 9 p.m. (9.30 in summer holidays).
Children in family room and if over 8 in restaurant. Must book. No dogs. Car park.
Wheelchair access possible but not easy. Two en-suite double rooms.
Cards: Amex, Delta, MasterCard, Switch, Visa.

Helston

Blue Anchor ① 01326 562821
50 Coinage Hall Street, Helston TR13 8EL
Free House. Kim Corbett & Simon Stone, licensees

This street has a close association with the Cornish tin mines; it was here, early in their history, that the local miners brought their tin to be weighed in Coinage Hall, and they later received their wages in this old pub. The thatched Blue Anchor was originally a monk's rest house, becoming licensed during the 15th century. The monks started brewing ale here about 500 years ago so there is every possibility that this is the oldest brewery in the country. Locally very popular. Inside are flagstones, low beams and a big inglenook, two bars and a family room. No food except lunch on Sunday. Ales here are in-house so to speak: Blue Anchor, Best, Spingo Special and Extra Special. Beware the strong own-brew Spingo Ale! You are allowed to see around the brewery some lunchtimes – by arrangement of course.

OPEN: All day.
Real Ale.
Children in family room. Dogs on leads.
Live music at weekends.

Lanlivery

Crown Inn ① 01208 872707
Lanlivery, nr Bodmin PL31 30BT
Free House. Ros & Dave Williams, licensees

Steeped in history, with beams, slate floors and a priest hole in the chimney, this 12th-century longhouse opposite the church must be one of the oldest buildings in Cornwall and in its long life it has somehow managed to gather a couple of friendly ghosts along the way. In the large bar, the food includes a variety of bar snacks: home-made soup, sandwiches, ploughman's, pasties and salads; mushrooms in a creamy garlic sauce, locally caught scallops sautéed in garlic, tomatoes and herbs with salad and melba toast, steak in a rich white wine sauce flavoured with shallots, mushrooms, brandy and tarragon; also chef's specials from the blackboard which change twice a day. The à la carte menu in the restaurant always has fresh fish and shellfish – the straight-out-of-the-sea-into-the-kitchen sort – and a comprehensive vegetarian menu. The vegetables are all freshly steamed and the bread rolls are made in the pub. All Sharp's ales at the moment. Picnic tables in the garden. Lovely views. Lanlivery is just off the Lostwithiel road, about five miles from the Eden Project, and on the Saintsway, an ancient path which goes from coast to coast.

OPEN: 11–3, 6–11.
Real Ale. Restaurant.
Children welcome. Dogs too. Wheelchair access. Two double en-suite bedrooms with their own gardens.
Cards: most cards.

Lostwithiel

Royal Oak Inn ① 01208 872552
Duke Street, Lostwithiel PL22 0AG
Free House. Malcolm & Eileen Hine, licensees

A well-run old pub in the centre of this pleasant market town on the river Fowey. Inside are a comfortable lounge bar, restaurant and a more lively, but noisy, beamed and flagstone-floored public bar. They serve a good choice of food from either the printed menu or the blackboard: French onion soup, stuffed mushrooms, smoked fish platter, salmon steak poached in a dill and cucumber sauce, steak, kidney and ale pie, salads, vegetarian options and fruit pies for puds, not forgetting the clotted cream. At least six real ales including Fullers London Pride, Marstons Pedigree, draught Bass, guest beers from the smaller breweries and lots of unusual bottled beers. Seats on the terrace. Very handy for the Eden Project about five miles away.

OPEN: 11–11. Sun 12–10.30.
Real Ale. Restaurant.
Children welcome. Dogs on leads. Car park. En-suite bedrooms.
Cards: Amex, Delta, Diners, MasterCard, Switch, Visa.
N.B. Jukebox in public bar.

Ludgvan

White Hart ① 01736 740574
Churchtown, Ludgvan, nr Penzance TR20 8EY
Inn Partnership. Dennis Churchill, tenant

If you're looking for an unchanging, old-fashioned, period pub, then this is it. The 14th-century White Hart's small beamed rooms are full of interesting objects; pictures and photographs on the wall, rugs on the floor, fine old seats and tables, wood-burning stoves to keep you warm and beer served from barrels at the back of the bar. They serve good, reasonably priced bar food: sandwiches, home-made soup, real Cornish pasties, salads, omelettes, steaks, daily specials and fresh fish. There is a no-smoking section in the eating area. Flowers IPA and Marstons Pedigree from the barrel, plus one guest ale during the season.

OPEN: 11–2.30, 6–11. No food Mon eve Oct–May.
Real Ale. Restaurant.
Children in restaurant. Dogs on leads. The church and pub share the car park.

Manaccan

New Inn ① 01326 231323
Manaccan, Helston TR12 6AJ
Pubmaster. Penny Williams, licensee

Between the delightfully picturesque creek-side village of Helford (no cars allowed in the summer) and the small hamlet of Carne at the head of Gillan harbour you can find this small, friendly, old-fashioned, cob-built thatched village pub. From the comfortable, beamed bar they offer a prodigious range of sandwiches, ploughman's, fresh fish of course, steak in ale pie, and daily specials too. There is a separate evening menu and they do a popular Sunday lunch. Flowers IPA from a barrel behind the bar, Castle Eden, Wadworths 6X and a guest beer. An attractive garden at the rear takes the overflow.

OPEN: 12–3, 6–11.
Real Ale.
Children, if very well behaved. Dogs welcome.

Morwenstow

Bush Inn ① 01288 331242
Morwenstow, nr Bude EX23 9SR
Free House. Mrs B. Moore, licensee.

Only ten minutes' walk from the cliffs, the south-west coast path and the Norman church that clings to the side of a coastal combe in a parish renowned during the early 19th century as being full of 'smugglers, wreckers and dissenters'. The Bush is surrounded by windswept fields and isolated farms on one side, cliffs and the sea on the other. This remote village is in an area now owned and protected by the National Trust. As a monastic rest-house, thought to date back to the 10th century, the inn joins those listed as one of the oldest in Britain. Quiet and unchanging; in the bar are old settles, flagstones, beams and a big stone fireplace. Lunchtime bar food only: home-made soup and a home-made stew in winter. You will also find pasties, ploughman's and daily specials. Beers include St Austell HSB on hand pump and guests. Draught Guinness and cider. Seats outside in the courtyard. There is a ship's figurehead from the wrecked Caledonia in the graveyard, surrounded by the graves of unknown men who drowned in the ferocious storms that blow up in this part of Cornwall.

OPEN: 12–3, 7–11. Closed Mon Oct–Apr except bank holidays.
Real Ale. Lunchtime food only (not Sun).
No children. No dogs.

Philleigh

Roseland ① 01872 580254
Philleigh TR2 5NB
Free House. Colin Phillips, licensee
www.roseland-inn.co.uk

A narrow lane connects the rest of Cornwall with this tiny village on the Roseland Peninsula and its whitewashed, slate-roofed 16th-century pub. Inside, one low-ceilinged bar serves two rooms and there is a separate dining room. Big fires in winter; in summer there is a sunny, flowery courtyard for you to enjoy. Home-made, much appreciated food, includes chicken liver paté with red onion marmalade, toast and salad, locally smoked fish platter with salad and a lemon and cracked pepper mayonnaise, ploughman's, sandwiches and ciabattas also freshly baked, real Cornish pasties, bangers and mash served with onion gravy and, as you would guess, a number of fish dishes. A greater selection of fish finds its way onto the summer menus. Greenalls Bitter, Morlands Old Speckled Hen, Marstons Pedigree and draught Bass. Farm cider in summer; a good range of malt whiskies. Short, reasonable wine list, some by the glass. Certainly no musak, no jukebox or one-armed bandits, but they do entertain the local rugby club – singers all – and the choir practises here a couple of times a week.

OPEN: 11–3, 6–11 (winter 11.30–3, 6.30–11).
Real Ale.
Children welcome. Dogs on leads. Car park. Wheelchair access.
Cards: MasterCard, Switch, Visa.

Polkerris

Rashleigh Inn ① 01726 813991
Polkerris, Par PL24 2TL
Free House. Jon & Samantha Spode, licensees
e-mail: jonspode@aol.com

In this small hamlet tucked between wooded slopes, the Rashleigh, known, unsurprisingly, as 'The Inn on the Beach', is in a prime position on the edge of the sea wall, overlooking the sandy beach which is sheltered by a wonderful, curving, stone breakwater. It was once the local coastguard station; and the main bar is in what was the boathouse. Inside, the stone walls, beams and open fires make it very appealing. Lots of local produce is used in the menus: West Country cheeses, locally grown vegetables, clotted cream, smoked produce from the local smokery; the fish is very local too, much of it from the bay: lobster, john dory, Dover and lemon sole and plaice. From the bar menu: freshly made soup, sandwiches, open sandwiches, smoked duck and avocado salad, ploughman's and trawlerman's – hot smoked salmon, trout and mackerel fillets with horseradish cream, seafood pie, or home-made seafood cocottes, steak 'plate' pie, home-made beef curry or home-cooked honey glazed ham. Vegetarian dishes and a children's menu. Daily specials on the blackboard. There is an à la carte menu in the dining room every evening except Sunday. Timothy Taylors Landlord, Sharps Doom Bar, Rashleigh Bitter and two or three guests. Comprehensive wine list. Seats at the front of the pub face south-west so get the best of the sun and wonderful sunsets.

OPEN: 11–11. Sun 12–10.30.
Real Ale
Children welcome. No dogs. Car park – limited but local car park too. Wheelchair access.
Cards: all except Amex and Diners.

Portgaverne

Port Gaverne Inn ☎ 01208 880293
Portgaverne PL29 3SQ
Free House. Graham Sylvester, licensee

At the top of a narrow inlet between sheltering cliffs, what was a flourishing port and fishing village in the 19th century is now a delightful place to stay. This handsome 300-year-old pub overlooks the sea, and inside are flagstones, beams, big log fires, local artists' paintings on the walls and comfortable bars serving a good choice of bar food: home-made crab soup, freshly filled sandwiches, ploughman's with Cornish cheeses, ham and eggs, seafood pie, steak and ale pie, wonderful fish dishes – grilled Dover sole with herb butter, pan-fried goujons of monkfish with a tomato, garlic and basil sauce – and daily specials. Sunday lunch. Sharp's Doom Bar and Bass. A good-size wine list and malt whiskies. If you're feeling energetic you can walk over the headland to Port Isaac, and, from the top of the cliffs, if the weather is favourable, see Tintagel.

OPEN: 11–11. Sun 12–10.30. Closed early Jan to mid Feb.
Real Ale. No-smoking restaurant.
Children in restaurant. Dogs on leads. Parking can be difficult.

Poughill

Preston Gate Inn ☎ 01288 354017
Poughill, nr Bude EX23 9ET
Free House. N. Rice, licensee

Surrounded by things to do and places to see. Hugely popular during the season; two miles inland from Bude, that surfers' paradise, and a short distance from exhilarating walks along the cliffs on the north coast path – the cliffs now managed by the National Trust. Lunchtimes are busy here, especially in summer. Locals join the visitors in the evening. Popular bar food could include marinated mussels, Oriental crab cakes, fisherman's platter, ham, egg and chips, chicken Kiev with mushrooms, grilled plaice, basket meals, ploughman's, lunchtime sandwiches and of course, daily specials off the blackboard. Marstons, Flowers IPA, Boddingtons and Hoegarden white beer. Water for the dog. Seats on the terrace.

OPEN: 12–2.30, 6.30-ish–11.
Real Ale.
No small children. Love dogs. Car park. Wheelchair access.
No cards.

Restronguet Creek

Pandora ☉ 01326 372678
Restronguet Creek, Mylor Bridge, nr Falmouth TR11 5ST
St Austell. John Milan, tenant.

The Pandora is named after HMS *Pandora*, which was sent to the Pacific in 1789 to capture the *Bounty* mutineers. This very pretty whitewashed, 13th-century thatched pub is in the wonderfully sheltered Restronguet Creek off the Carrick Roads, a haven for small boats and yachts. With a very high spring tide, the Pandora isn't so much near the water as almost in it. There is a pontoon where you can tie up under the eyes of a lively audience who, drinks in hand, could be trying to be helpful. Inside this charming place are showers for visiting yachtsmen and no fewer than three bars, a no-smoking restaurant above the pub and two no-smoking areas. Bar food includes home-made soup, rich chicken liver paté served with garlic bread, Mediterranean fish stew, crab cakes, Mylor Bridge sausages with Cornish apple chutney, huntsman's platter with ham and paté and a fisherman's platter with smoked salmon, crab and prawns, lots of local fish, and daily specials. There is an evening à la carte menu when you could have local Helford mussels (when available) steamed in white wine and flavoured with herbs, breast of chicken stuffed with wild mushrooms, sage and bacon in a Marsala sauce, roast rack of lamb in a port and rosemary sauce and lots more fish. St Austell's ales and Bass on hand pump. Malt whiskies and a large selection of wines. If you are coming by road remember parking can be a bit tight at the height of summer.

OPEN: 11–11.
Real Ale. Food until 9.30 p.m. in summer; restaurant open all year.
Children in eating area. Dogs on leads. Car park. Wheelchair access.
Cards: Delta, MasterCard, Solo, Switch, Visa.

St Kew

St Kew Inn ☉ 01208 841259
St Kew, nr Wadebridge PL30 3HB
St Austell. Des & Ginny Weston, tenants

In this village north of Wadebridge, found among a tangle of country lanes, is the impressive, stone-built, 15th-century St Kew Inn. Next to the parish church, the inn has high ceilinged bars and two dining rooms, both with very extensive menus which could offer home-made soup, sandwiches, seafood lasagne, beef in Guinness with herb dumplings, fish and chips, steaks and king prawns in garlic and a children's menu, also roasts on Sunday. The beers are St Austell Tinners, Hicks, Cornish Cream, Duchy served from casks behind the counter and one guest in summer. Outside is a large garden. You always needed some form of transport to get here as you can see from the spacious stable yard – now the pub's car park.

OPEN: 11–2.30, 6–11. July & Aug 11–11.
Real Ale. Restaurant.
Children (well behaved, allowed in restaurant and own room – none under 14 in bar; none under 6 in eves). No dogs.

St Mawes

Rising Sun ① 01326 270233 Fax: 01326 270198
The Square, St Mawes, nr Truro TR2 5DJ
St Austell. R.J. Milan, tenant

For anyone who loves boats the sheltered harbour of St Mawes on the Cornish Riviera is full of them – a forest of masts in the season. This delightful town, a short ferry ride from Falmouth, is on a peninsula between Carrick Roads and the Percuil river. Just across the road from the harbour wall is the small, elegant, beautifully cared-for Rising Sun where the cooking is exceptional; from the daily changing dinner menu there could be a mushroom and fennel soup, white crabmeat tart, hot and cold salmon collection and for a main course, roast halibut fillet served with crème fraiche and cucumber, chilli and ginger salsa, game pie – venison, pheasant, partridge cooked in red wine with apple and sage topped with puff pastry or fillet steak in sherry and cream; raspberry oatmeal meringue or spiced chocolate and pear roulade to finish. The blackboard in the bar lists more simple snacks such as open sandwiches or cottage pie. The well-thought-out menus go with the well-kept St Austell's range of ales and good wine list, about 18 by the glass. Seats on the sunny terrace facing the harbour.

OPEN: 11–11.
Real Ale. Restaurant.
Children welcome. Dogs too. Car park. Wheelchair access. Classy en-suite bedrooms.
Cards: Amex, Delta, Diners, MasterCard, Switch, Visa.

St Mawgan

Falcon Inn ① 01637 860225
St Mawgan, Newquay TR8 4EP
St Austell. Andy and Helen Banks, tenants
e-mail: enquiries@falconinn.net

Two miles inland, in a village tucked into a wooded valley, this is an attractive, wisteria-covered 16th-century inn serving a menu that specialises in fish, most of it straight off the local boats. It has a comfortable, carpeted bar with a wonderful log fire and a slate-floored no-smoking dining room where you can enjoy something from the main menu or the changing specials board. There are always at least four fish dishes, which could include Isles of Scilly scallops grilled in the shell with lime and coriander, Fowey river mussels with local mead and cream, sea bream with hazelnuts and scallions, Cornish smoked salmon and Greenland prawns. And if you're not into fish, there's diced local lamb cooked in a spicy Moroccan sauce, red Thai chicken curry or a 12oz West Country sirloin steak, vegetarian dishes and local ice cream, home-made apple pie, tangy lemon cheesecake and local cheeses. There is a very strong 'buy local' policy. Outside is a cobbled courtyard at the front and an award-winning garden at the back, with a children's play area. The village – and the pub – is in the Vale of Lanherne conservation area.

OPEN: 11–3, 6–11. Sun 12–3, 7–10.30.
Real Ale.
Children welcome, dogs too. Car park. Wheelchair access.
Cards: All except Amex.

Treburley

Springer Spaniel ➀ 01579 370424
Treburley, nr Launceston PL15 9NS
Wagtail Inns Ltd. Andy Brotheridge, manager

A handsome, white-painted roadside pub. Inside a simple bar leads to another, more comfortably furnished room, with settles by the wood-burning stove, wall benches and rustic tables, and to a beamed, no-smoking restaurant. Using fresh ingredients – most of the salads, herbs and vegetables are locally sourced – the imaginative menu is available in both bar and restaurant: pan-seared scallops with garlic and lemon, smoked duck with melon and raspberry dressing or a speciality Cornish crab pasty for a light snack. More substantial dishes are listed on the main menu or the daily changing blackboards; fillet of sea bass with roast pepper butter, rack of lamb with a mustard and herb crust with redcurrant and mint dressing and other dishes featuring Cornish produce. Wonderful puds. Sharp's Doom Bar, Eden Ale, Cornish Coaster and Springer Ale, brewed especially for the pub. Well-chosen wine list (seven by the glass) to go with the good food.

OPEN: 11–3, 5.30–11.
Real Ale. No-smoking restaurant.
Children welcome. Dogs on leads. Car park. Wheelchair access (not WC).
Cards: Delta, MasterCard, Switch, Visa.

Treen

Gurnard's Head Hotel ➀ 01736 796928
Treen, Zennor, St Ives TR26 3DE
Free House. Ray & Joy Kell, licensees
e-mail: enquiries@gurnardshead.free-online.co.uk

Surrounded by wild moorland and impressive coastal views. Close to the route of the North Coast Path – which makes a slight kink to Gurnard's Head – this is a solidly built, traditional Cornish country pub in the hamlet of Treen above the rocky promontory on the spectacular Atlantic coast between St Ives and St Just. Inside are a large, welcoming, cosy bar and dining room. Not surprisingly, as the sea is on the doorstep so to speak, the emphasis is on fish. The same menu, available in both the bar and dining room, always has some favourites such as their own Cornish seafood broth, the catch of the day, a 'walkers platter' – for encouragement – maybe Cornish crab claws with a garlic mayonnaise, Moroccan-style grey mullet fillet, sautéed duck breast with pine nuts and balsamic jus; more basically, sandwiches or ham, egg and chips. Evenings there could be a trio of Cornish fish, rillettes of pork, supreme of chicken Normandy style, or Aberdeen Angus steak, delicious puds and daily specials on the blackboard. Flowers Original, Skinner's Cornish Knocker ale and Fullers London Pride. Short wine list.

OPEN: 11–3, 6–11. Sun 12–4, 7–10.30.
Real Ale.
Children welcome, dogs too. Car park. Wheelchair access. Bedrooms.
Cards: Amex, MasterCard, Switch, Visa.
N.B. Wednesday and Friday nights are live music at 'The Gurnard's'.

Tywardreath

New Inn ① 01726 813901
Fore Street, Tywardreath PL24 2QP
St Austell. Mr & Mrs Hill, licensees

The only pub in this small village, it's architecturally a classical Georgian building of stone under a slate roof, built by the mine owners in the 18th century. It still has sash windows and a simple, pillared porch. Inside is just one bar and a family area. A basic bar menu is served at lunchtime but you're really here for the beer; people come from miles around for the draught Bass tapped straight from the barrel. Other beers are St Austell XXXX Mild, Tinners and the seasonal Winter Warmer. Local cider. Seats at the front of the pub and in the secluded garden. You are near a safe beach at Par Sands.

OPEN: 12–3, 6–11. Sat 11–11. Sun 12–4, 7–10.30.
Real Ale.
Children welcome. Dogs on leads. Small car park. Three bedrooms.

Zennor

Tinners Arms ① 01736 796927
Zennor TR26 3BY
Free House. David Care, licensee

In a tiny village at the end of the St Ives to Zennor coastal walk. You are in the very heart of the mining area; disused mines are all around and this pub used to be the tin miners' local – there is an image of a miner over the door. It was built of local granite 400 years ago on the site of the 12th-century hostelry that housed masons working on the local church. Continuing the tradition of feeding and watering the populace, this comfortable old pub offers good simple bar food: smoked mackerel, lasagne, ploughman's, chicken and ham pie and some vegetarian dishes. The menu changes with the season. Sharp's ales from the barrel – as well as Sharp's Special during the winter and Cornish Coaster in the summer. Opposite are the roughcast walls of St Senara's church where you can see the famous 'mermaid chair' and learn the legend of the choirboy lured to the beach, never to be seen again.

OPEN: 11–3, 6.30–11. Summer 11–11.
Real Ale.
Children, but not in main bar. Dogs on leads.
N.B. Occasional Classic FM.

BEST OF THE REST

Kingsand
Halfway House ① 01752 822279
Fore Street PL10 1NA

This pub marks the official border between the two very attractive conservation villages of Kingsand and Cawsand. The Cornwall South Coast path passes both these villages, so if you're thinking of stopping off, wander down the hilly streets towards the harbour and Cawsand where you'll find a warm welcome at the Halfway House. Here they serve some interesting bar food: fish soup, chicken supreme with wild mushrooms, venison casserole with port and Guinness, filled baguettes and of course a ploughman's to go with the Boddingtons, Sharps and Bass. Decent wines. Children welcome. Bedrooms.
Open: 12–3, 6.30–11.

Ruan Lanihorne
Kings Head ① 01852 501263
Ruan Lanihorne TR2 5NX

It is here that the River Ruan meets the Fal, and you'll find this beamed and comfortable pub opposite the village church. They serve a good choice of bar food including home-made soup, potted shrimps, fillet steak, vegetarian dishes and daily specials. Wine by the bottle, carafe or glass, and Hardy and Sharps ales. Views of the Fal estuary from the sunny garden. Children in family room.
Open: 12–2.30, 7–10.30. Closed Mon from Sept to Easter.

St Just in Penwith
Star ① 01736 788767
1 Fore Street TR19 7LL

A small coastal pub, unchanged for years. The L-shaped bar, with its mining memorabilia, reminds the visitor that you are in what was once a prosperous tin-mining area. Food is served all day, but only pasties and rolls between 3 and 6, otherwise soups, pasties, local sea food, fresh crab sandwiches (when there is fresh crab), home-made pies, good bacon sandwiches and daily specials. St Austell ales from the cask. Mulled wine in winter, cider in summer. Seats on the pretty back terrace. Children in snug, dogs on leads. Wheelchair access. Bedrooms.
Open: 11–11.

Wetherspoon in Cornwall

Falmouth – Packet Station, 4 The Moor
① 01326 310110
Newquay – Towan Blystra, Cliff Road
① 01637 852970
Penzance – Tremenheere, 4–8 Market Place
① 01736 335350

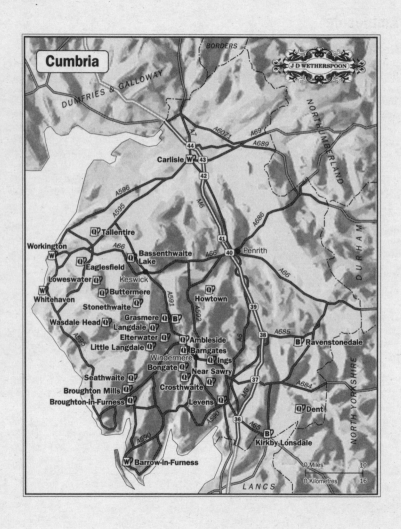

Cumbria

J·D·WETHERSPOON

BORDERS

DUMFRIES & GALLOWAY

NORTHUMBERLAND

Carlisle

Workington

Tallentire

Bassenthwaite Lake

Eaglesfield

Loweswater

Keswick

Whitehaven

Buttermere

Penrith

Stonethwaite

Howtown

Wasdale Head

Grasmere

Langdale

Elterwater

Ambleside

Little Langdale

Barngates

Windermere

Ravenstonedale

Bongate

Ings

Near Sawry

Seathwaite

Crosthwaite

Broughton Mills

Levens

Broughton-in-Furness

Dent

DURHAM

NORTH YORKSHIRE

Kirkby Lonsdale

Barrow-in-Furness

LANCS

0 Miles 10
0 Kilometres 16

Cumbria

Ambleside

Golden Rule ① 015394 32257
Smithy Brow, Ambleside LA22 9AS
Robinsons. John Lockley, tenant

You get used to everything being on a slope in the Lake District and the Golden Rule doesn't disappoint. Once inside though, everything straightens up to go with the golden rule above the bar. This is an area really geared to the tourist, climber and gentler walker; and here they welcome you all – and your dog. Go towards Kirkstone Pass, north of Ambleside, to find this unchanging, welcoming place, a friendly local waiting to serve you the perfect pint. Bar snacks are just that, only filled rolls, a pork pie or scotch egg to fill a gap, but you will find Hartleys XB, Robinsons Hatters Mild, Stockport Bitter, Best Bitter Cumbria Way and Fredericks on hand pump. Seats outside in the secluded, flowery yard.

OPEN: 11–11.
Real Ale.
Children welcome until 9 p.m. Dogs on leads. Parking very difficult. Wheelchair access and to ladies' loo, not gent's.

Barngates

Drunken Duck ① 015394 36347
Barngates, Ambleside LA22 0NG (off B5286 Hawkshead to Ambleside road)
Free House. Stephanie Barton, licensee
e-mail: info@drunkenduckinn.co.uk

Somewhere that manages to be all things to all people. Here you can stay in stylish rooms, dine extremely well, lean on the bar at lunchtime with a pint of their very own beer before choosing something from the imaginative bar menu and last, but not least, sit and appreciate the view over magnificent scenery, some of it belonging to the Drunken Duck. No newcomer this; travellers have been dropping in to enjoy the hospitality for over 400 years. Full of atmosphere, warm and inviting, the pub is beamed, cosy with good winter fires, and with walls so covered with pictures and interesting bits and pieces that it would take you a week to finish looking. They take their drink and food very seriously here. At lunchtime there are lots of fillings – hot and cold – for the sandwiches, game pie with roast vegetables and red wine jus, baked aubergine with pesto, roast flat mushrooms and grilled goat's cheese, red onion and blue cheese tartlet with new potatoes and herb salad and sautéed Thai chicken strips with Caesar salad. The evening menus go up a notch or two and include lots of delicious puddings and local cheeses. The home of Barngates Brewery, they serve their own Cracker Ale and Chesters Strong, Ugly and Tag Lag; also Jennings Best Bitter, Theakstons Old Peculier, Yates, and other guest beers. Over 60 malt whiskies. Seats on the veranda, which has opulent hanging baskets in summer, and views towards Lake Windermere.

OPEN: 11.30–11.
Real Ale. Restaurant.
Children in eating area. Dogs on leads. Car park. Wheelchair access. Very stylish bedrooms include two suites across the courtyard.
Cards: Amex, Delta, MasterCard, Switch, Visa.
N.B. Sometimes background music in restaurant.

Bassenthwaite Lake

Pheasant ➀ 017687 76234
Bassenthwaite Lake, nr Cockermouth CA13 9YE
Free House. Matthew Wylie, licensee

At the quieter, northern end of the Lake District, and set in its own gardens and woodland between the lakes and the fells, the whitewashed Pheasant is a large, solid, very comfortable Cumbrian inn. Beams, settles, log fires and antiques abound creating a very welcoming atmosphere. The polished pubby bar quickly fills up at lunchtime for the home-made soup, cheese or meat platter, potted Silloth shrimps, Cumberland sausages, Cumberland pork and ham pie, smoked local trout, local lamb and much more; there is an à la carte menu in the no-smoking restaurant and you can take proper tea in the elegant lounge. Theakstons Best, Jennings Cumberland and Bass on hand pump. Wines by the glass and half bottle and a choice of whiskies. Walks lead from the garden into the surrounding woodland.

OPEN: 11.30–2.30, 5.30–10.30 (Fri & Sat 5.30–11). Sun 12–2.30, 6–10.30.
Real Ale. Restaurant.
Children in eating area. Dogs in bar only. Wheelchair access. Bedrooms – quite a lot.

Bongate

Royal Oak Inn ➀ 01768 351463
Bongate, Appleby-in-Westmoreland CA16 6UN
Mortal Man Inns. Tim Collins, manager
e-mail: m.m.royaloak@btinternet.com

Between the Lake District and the Pennines, past rolling sheep pastures and near the River Eden's gently wooded valleys. The Royal Oak, opposite Bongate's old church, is a fine, white-painted old coaching inn. Full of atmosphere, it has beautifully cared-for beamed and panelled rooms where you can enjoy a well-kept pint and choose a dish from the creative menu: home-baked bread to go with the soup, home-cooked ham and beef to go in the sandwiches, potted shrimps, Royal Oak smokie – a selection of home-smoked morsels served with a cranberry and orange relish – filled crêpes, beef in ale, fillet of codling baked with a herb crust, pork fillet in cream and Madeira sauce, more fresh fish, steaks, vegetarian dishes, daily specials and good puds. A children's menu too. There is a restaurant, and no-smoking dining room. Ten beers are kept on hand pump; guests include interesting beers from lesser-known small breweries in the north of England and

Scotland. They have an extensive wine list. In summer there are seats among the flower-filled tubs at the front of this attractive old place. Lots of lovely walks nearby; Appleby is one of the stops on the Settle–Carlisle Railway which is well worth a trip.

OPEN: 11–11. Sun 12–10.30.
Real Ale. No-smoking dining room.
Well-behaved children welcome. Dogs in bar. Wheelchair access (not WC). Nine bedrooms, all en suite.

Broughton-in-Furness

Manor Arms ① 01229 716286
The Square, Broughton-in-Furness LA20 6HY
Free House. David Varty, licensee

From Broughton, the river Duddon widens into a broad estuary southwards to the sea. On the southern edge of the lovely Duddon Valley, and overlooking the estuary, the town is ideally placed for trips to the western lakes of the Lake District. Broughton is a handsome town with a delightful Georgian square and the popular Manor Arms, a good-looking, white-painted, three-storey Georgian building – just the place for an excellent pint of beer in the comfortable bar warmed by two blazing fires. A favourite with CAMRA members so you know the beers are perfectly kept. And there's quite a choice: always a minimum of eight beers on hand pump, including two or three guests, currently Yates Bitter, Timothy Taylors Landlord and Coniston Bluebird. Food is limited to snacks: toasties, sausages and a pot of home-made soup kept hot in the bar when the weather turns chilly. A centre for walks in contrasting landscapes; south-east for woodland, rocks and rushing water; north-west for fell walking and views towards the high peaks.

OPEN: 12–11.
Real Ale.
Children welcome. Dogs welcome too. En-suite bedrooms.
Cards: all major cards except Amex.

Broughton Mills

Blacksmiths Arms ① 01229 716824
Broughton Mills, Broughton-in-Furness LA20 6AX
Free House. Margaret Blackburn, licensee ·
e-mail: blacksmithsarms@aol.com

A delightful, very attractive, late 16th-century pub with tremendous character; open fires – one an impressive range – in the three rooms keep you warm; beams and uneven flagstones reflect its age. A full 'traditional English' menu is on offer seven days a week, as well as sandwiches and ploughman's, battered Lancashire cheese, Blacksmith's steak pie in a suet pastry, Lancashire black pudding – pan fried and served with a cranberry sauce – steaks in different sauces (devilled, Stilton or pepper) and an extensive specials board with salmon terrine, local roast pork tenderloin, Westmoreland hot pot, a venison casserole using local game and local Herdwick lamb dishes; all you need to sustain you. Jennings range of ales and local guests. This is a very special place – the only pub in Cumbria listed on CAMRA's National Inventory as having an interior of outstanding heritage interest. Do go and see it. Seats among the flowers at the front of the pub.

OPEN: 12–2.30 (not Mon), 5–11. Sat & Sun 12–11. Summer opening: 12–11.
Real Ale. Children's menu.
Children welcome. Dogs too. Car park.
Cards: Delta, Maestro, MasterCard, Switch, Visa.

Buttermere

Bridge Hotel ① 017687 70252
Buttermere CA13 9UZ
Free House. Peter McGuire, managing director
e-mail: enquiries@bridge-hotel.com

By a small stone bridge between Buttermere and Crummock Water, what was just a small coaching inn during the 18th century has, over the years, been greatly extended and improved, resulting in the appealing, handsome place you see today. Inside are friendly beamed bars, comfortable lounges, open fires and an elegant dining room. There is even a smart, stone-floored walkers' bar – which is where you will be with your muddy boots. Soaked to the skin? Worry not. Help is at hand; the Bridge Hotel even has a drying room! The selection of bar food from the walkers' snack corner ranges from simple soups, sandwiches and ploughman's to puff-pastry ricotta cheese and spinach parcels, Cumberland hotpot, chicken breast cooked in herbs and garlic, grilled chicken supreme, spicy fruit lamb curry, chef's daily specials and vegetarian dishes. Sunday roast. There is a table d'hôte menu which changes daily; you could choose poached Borrowdale trout with hot caper butter, prime sirloin chargrilled to order, and lots more. Black Sheep Best Bitter and a summer guest beer. Wines by the glass and a selection of malt whiskies. Seats outside on the terrace and wonderful views and walks.

OPEN: 10.30–11. Food served 12–9.30.
Real Ale. Evening restaurant.
Children welcome. Dogs on terrace and sometimes they can stay. Twenty-two bedrooms and self-catering apartments.
Cards: Access, Switch, Visa.

Crosthwaite

Punch Bowl Inn ① 015395 68237 Fax: 015395 68875
Crosthwaite LA8 8HR
Free House. Steven Doherty, licensee
e-mail: enquiries@punchbowl.fsnet.co.uk

This is very much a place working on two fronts: a successful pub with a restaurant serving some seriously good food. Next to the church, this solidly built, 17th-century coaching inn looks like a pub and still sells beer, but the food is the thing. Inside is relaxed, informal and spacious, with low ceilings, beams and open fires. Something from the creative menu is available in both the bar and the dining room. If you're lunching during the week you will appreciate the very reasonably priced two-course lunch. There could be pea and ham soup, venison terrine with rhubarb chutney, warm new potato salad with rollmop herrings, braised local beef with rich braising juices, chargrilled fillet of tuna on pesto mash or roast breast of duck on mashed potato with petit pois à la française. Delicious puds and British cheeses too. The menu ratchets up a notch for dinner. A good, short wine list includes half bottles and some by the glass. Beers: Theakstons Best, Jennings Cumberland, Black Sheep and Morlands Old Speckled Hen. Tables on the terrace which has views over the Lyth valley.

OPEN: 11–11. Sun 12–3. Closed Sun eve and all day Mon.
Real ale. Restaurant.
Children welcome. Car park. Bedrooms – all en suite.
Cards: MasterCard, Switch, Visa.

Dent

Sun Inn ① 01539 625208
Main Street, Dent, Sedbergh LA10 5QL (off A683)
Own Brew. Martin Stafford, licensee

This is a very picturesque village in the lovely Dentdale overlooking the River Dee, very popular with tourists. On the cobbled main street you'll find the Sun, unpretentious, beamed and comfortable, and very serious about its beer. And just up the road is the Dent Brewery, providing the Sun with Bitter, Ramsbottom, T'Owd Tup beers and Kamikaze strong ale, which lives up to its name. The home-cooked bar food includes the stalwarts, also pasties, chicken curry, lasagne, chilli, steak and kidney pie, Cumberland sausage, salads and specials. Seats outside in summer.

OPEN: 11–11. Sun 12–10.30. Winter weekdays 11–2.30, 7–11.
Real Ale.
Children welcome until 9 p.m. Dogs on leads. Bedrooms. Wheelchair access into pub and, if you're a gent, to the W.C.
N.B. Jukebox in the separate pool room.

Elterwater

Britannia Inn ① 01539 437210
Elterwater, Ambleside LA22 9HP
Free House. Claire Woodhead & Chris Jones, licensees
e-mail: info@britinn.co.uk

Facing the pretty village green, the 500-year-old Britannia is a traditional Cumbrian inn. In one of the most attractive areas of the Lake District, many of the customers are walkers appreciating the fine ales and hearty food. The whitewashed inn has small, friendly bars with beams and log fires where they serve a wide-ranging menu which always features the local Langdale Herdwick lamb, served as either a rack of lamb, a leg, or braised – all very popular; also the usual favourites: soups, filled baps, baked potatoes, ploughman's, home-made Cumberland paté, home-made Langdale pie – chicken, lamb, ham and vegetables in a cream sauce with a pastry topping – and daily specials. Good breakfasts, afternoon teas too. Well-kept Jennings Bitter, Coniston Bluebird and Timothy Taylors Landlord, plus guest ales and a good wine list which includes fruit wines. Lots of garden chairs and tables on the attractive terrace in front of the pub so you can admire the view.

OPEN: 11–11.
Real Ale. No-smoking dining room.
Children and dogs welcome. Nine guest bedrooms.
Cards: Amex, Delta, MasterCard, Switch, Visa.

Grasmere

Dove & Olive Branch ① 015394 35592
Wordsworth Hotel, Grasmere LA22 9SW
Free House. J. G. van Stipriaan, manager
e-mail: enquiry@wordsworth-grasmere.co.uk

If you're on the tourist trail you really can't miss this place, since St Oswald's churchyard is where the poet William Wordsworth is buried. From the churchyard you will be able to see the smart Wordsworth Hotel; the Dove & Olive Branch is its 'in-house pub'. On the menu are tasty bar snacks, home-made salmon cakes, filled rustic rolls, freshly cooked fish and chips, ploughman's and daily specials served in both the bar and the conservatory. Well-kept Tetley Cask Smooth-Flow, Jennings Cask Cumberland Ale and one guest beer.

OPEN: 11–3, 6–11.
Real Ale.
Children welcome, but no infants. No dogs. Wheelchair access. Bedrooms in the Wordsworth Hotel.

Howtown

Howtown Hotel ① 017684 86514
Howtown, Ullswater CA10 2ND
Free House. Mrs Jacqui Baldry and son David, licensees

Very much a summer place; closed in winter. You'll find it on a narrow lane along the sheltered southern shore of Ullswater, which runs through seven miles of breathtaking scenery. The Howtown is in a quiet little village surrounded by the drama of the Lakes – sweeping tree-clad lower slopes above which are tree-less crags and fells where you will find every type of walk from the gentle to the very difficult. The walkers' bar at the back of the hotel is a favourite meeting place for those still in their boots; the rest are in the hotel bar, a delightfully old-fashioned place serving freshly filled sandwiches, good filling lunches and all the usual things you get from a welcoming hotel – coffee and afternoon tea. No real ale, only a keg beer, but you can get a decent glass of wine. The hotel is along a narrow lane and there is no car park, but I'm sure there is somewhere to leave the car or you can walk, bike or sail in.

OPEN: 11–11. Closed from beginning of November to end of March.
No children. No dogs. Wheelchair access, but not into the public bar.

Ings

Watermill Inn ① 01539 821309
Ings, nr Stavely, Kendal LA8 9PY (east of Windermere)
Free House. Alan & Brian Coulthwaite, MBII, licensees
www.watermill-inn.demon.co.uk

Near the church, what was a redundant, stone-built wood mill is now an ivy-covered, comfortable, family-run inn. There are a few ecclesiastical touches in the bar – made out of church pews – where they serve bar favourites and the constantly changing chef's specials featured on the blackboard. Among the dishes there could be a gamekeeper's casserole, pan-fried pheasant breast stuffed with apricot and sausage meat, grilled Scottish salmon finished with fresh hollandaise sauce, brie and fresh coriander wrapped in filo pastry, deep fried and served with a red onion marmalade sauce and lots more fish, steaks and other good things on the menu. Up to 16 real ales on hand pump, among them Black Sheep Special, Coniston Bluebird, Theakstons Old Peculier and Hawkshead Best, also farmhouse scrumpy and Erdinger Weibbier plus continental and English bottled beers. There is a viewing area into the cellar so you can keep an eye on the beer. The River Gowan, which used to power the old mill, runs through the grounds. Seats in the sunny beer garden.

OPEN: 12–11.
Real Ale.
Children in lounge. Dogs on leads in bar. Wheelchair access. Seven bedrooms.
Cards: Electron, MasterCard, Switch, Visa.

Langdale

Old Dungeon Ghyll ① 015394 37272
Gt Langdale, Ambleside LA22 9JY
Free House. Neil Walmsley, licensee

Surrounded by serious hiking country, this old hotel echoes with the sound of walking boots. The road ends at the hotel and campsite opposite, which has been owned by the National Trust since the early 1900s. In the hotel the Hikers' Bar, with wooden floors, wooden benches and big, warming fire, is fairly basic and well able to cope with damp, exhausted hikers. Here you can get a pint of perfectly kept, refreshing beer to go with good, hearty home-cooked meals and snacks – soups, sandwiches, Cumberland sausages, chicken dishes, local trout, steaks, etc. The hotel serves a four-course dinner in the no-smoking restaurant. Jennings Cumberland, Theakstons XB, Old Peculier and Yates Bitter plus some guest beers. You'll certainly need your walking boots to climb the steep path that leads you to the spectacular Dungeon Ghyll waterfall – after which the hotel was named – which drops into an abyss 100 feet below. The campsite gets very jolly and busy at weekends.

OPEN: 11–11.
Real Ale. Evening restaurant.
Children welcome. Dogs on leads. Bedrooms.
Occasional live music.

Levens

Hare & Hounds ① 015395 60408
Causeway End, Levens, Kendal LA8 8PN
Pubmaster. Colin Burrow, licensee

On the edge of the Lyth Valley, in a village near the mud flats of the Kent estuary which attracts a huge number of seabirds – it's an ornithologist's heaven. The mostly Georgian Hare and Hounds is known for serving good, uncomplicated, reliable food: plain or toasted lunchtime sandwiches, home-made soup of the day, garlic mushrooms, potted shrimps, black pudding served with tomatoes, mushrooms and onions, lasagne, Cumberland sausage, gammon steak, chicken Kiev, filled jacket potatoes and at least three vegetarian dishes. The home-made daily changing specials board features dishes using fresh, local produce and usually includes Ann's renowned, home-made Cumbrian hot pot. Flowers IPA, Theakstons and a regular guest ale, Guinness and a good selection of malt whiskies. Seats on the terrace with views of the estuary. You are not too far from Sizergh Castle and its wonderful gardens and the amazing topiary gardens at Levens Hall.

OPEN: 11.30–3, 6–11.
Real Ale. Dining room.
Children welcome. Dogs in bar only. Car park. Wheelchair access.
N.B. Music in pool room well away from the bar and dining area.

Little Langdale

Three Shires Inn ① 015394 37215
Little Langdale, Ambleside LA22 9NZ
Free House. Ian Stephenson, licensee
e-mail: enquiry@threeshiresinn.co.uk

In the Little Langdale valley, a few miles west of Ambleside, this attractive 19th-century inn was built near to where the three shires of Cumberland, Westmoreland and Lancashire meet, close to the Lake District's most difficult road between the high passes of Wrynose and Hardknott. Inside is a slate-floored, beamed bar, where you can enjoy a bar snack or a more substantial dish of home-cured marinated salmon in a sweet dill and whisky sauce, rich chicken-liver parfait with Cumberland sauce, marinated venison, pan fried and served with a port and Stilton sauce, locally made Cumberland sausage with onion rings and home-made chutney, the popular beef and ale pie, vegetarian dishes or something from the specials board. All dishes are cooked to order from fresh ingredients. Jennings Cumberland Ale, Old Man Ale, Coniston, Jennings Best Bitter, Hawkshead Best as a guest and an extensive wine list. Glorious views from the seats under the veranda at the front of the hotel; seats also in the stream-side garden. Lots of walks.

OPEN: 11–11. (N.B. Restricted opening hours in Dec and Jan and no evening meals during those months.)
Real Ale. Restaurant. Packed lunches provided.
Children until 9 p.m. Dogs in bar. Car park. Wheelchair access. En-suite bedrooms.
Cards: MasterCard, Switch, Visa, Visa Debit.

Loweswater

Kirkstile Inn ① 01900 85219
Loweswater, Cockermouth CA13 0RU
Free House. Roger & Helen Humphreys, licensees
e-mail: info@kirkstile.com

In the western Lakes, this is a typical Cumbrian inn near Crummock Water. Outside are peaks, fells and woods, spectacular countryside – and the Cumbrian weather. So if you want to dry off after a wet walk, this is the place to be; another pub with a drying room. Opposite the church, this attractive, white-painted, slate-roofed inn is not only ready to look after you if you're soaked to the skin, but however you arrive. Inside, a warm, beamed bar serves good sustaining food. Freshly baked rolls served with the home-made soup of the day, chicken liver paté served with home-made Cumberland sauce and crostini, filled baguettes and baked potatoes, Navarin of lamb, steak, mushroom and pink peppercorn pie and local Cumberland sausages, also vegetarian dishes. Lots of home-made daily specials from the blackboard – starters, main courses, puddings and a cheese and wine selection. Jennings Bitter, Yates Bitter and Melbreak Bitter – brewed on the premises – draught Guinness, Coniston Blue Bird, 16 malt whiskies and 18 different wines. Seats on the enclosed veranda from where you can admire the view.

OPEN: 11–11.
Real Ale. Dining room (piped music in here Thurs, Fri and Sat).
Children welcome. Dogs on leads. Car park. Bedrooms are geared up to hikers as well as the non-energetic.

Near Sawrey

Tower Bank Arms ① 015394 36334
Near Sawrey, Hawkshead LA22 0LF
Free House. Philip Broadley, licensee
e-mail: sales@towerbankarms.fsnet.co.uk

This is the small country inn described in *The Tale of Jemima Puddleduck*, next to the author Beatrix Potter's Hill Top Farm and between the medieval village of Hawkshead and western end of Lake Windermere. In lovely, gentle countryside, the Tower Bank Arms is in the right place to greet you after you have made the long journey around the lake. It's a friendly and very busy old place with a comfortable beamed bar and winter log fires, where they serve traditional bar food of home-made soup, filled rolls, a choice of ploughman's, potted shrimps, home-made cheese flan, Lakeland game pie (turkey, venison and hare), breaded Whitby seafood platter with tartare sauce, salads, something for the vegetarian and a pudding or two. There is a changing specials board and more substantial dishes are available during the evening. Theakstons ales, guest beers – many of them local – Belgian fruit beers and a good selection of malt whiskies. There are seats outside and good walks nearby. Thimble Hall, in the centre of Hawkshead, houses an exhibition of Beatrix Potter's life and work.

OPEN: 11–3, 5.30–11 (6–11 in winter).
Real Ale. Restaurant. N.B. Tapes played here in evening.
Children lunchtime only. Dogs on leads. Car park. Wheelchair access (not WC). Bedrooms.
Cards: Amex, JCB, MasterCard, Switch, Visa.

Seathwaite

Newfield Inn ➀ 01229 716208
Seathwaite, Duddon Valley, Broughton-in-Furness LA20 6ED
Free House. Paul Batten, licensee

The road through the valley follows the river, where you will find delightful stretches of little waterfalls among the grassy slopes. This old Lakeland pub in the Duddon Valley – one of Wordsworth's favourite places – is very popular with fell walkers and climbers who might take some solace when they come in from a dampish hike over the fells to discover that this Seathwaite is not the wettest place in Britain – only the second wettest. The wettest is another Seathwaite, further north, near Borrowdale! An interesting slate floor in the main bar shows different levels of volcanic activity, and legend has it that the old beams in the pub came from ships broken up after the Spanish Armada. Homely bar food of soups, filled rolls and jacket potatoes, deep fried whitebait, free-range egg and chips, home-made steak pie, Cumberland sausages, home-cooked gammon and grilled steaks, plus three vegetarian dishes, and good puds; the full menu is served all day. Apart from the ham and gammon, all the meat is very local. Always four hand-pulled ales which include Jennings, Coniston and others from local breweries. Interesting selection of malt whiskies. Tables in the garden, from where you can admire the dramatic scenery.

OPEN: 11–11.
Real Ale. Restaurant. Food served 12–9 all year.
Children welcome if well behaved. Dogs on leads.
Wheelchair access (not WC). Self-catering flats available.
Cards: all debit cards. Not Amex.
Radio 2 on in one room. Very occasional folk music.

Stonethwaite

Langstrath Country Inn ➀ 01768 777239
Stonethwaite, Borrowdale, Keswick CA12 5XG
Free House. Gary & Donna Macrae, licensees
e-mail: info@thelangstrath.com

A solid, 16th-century inn in a quiet hamlet surrounded by the magnificent Borrowdale fells. You are in serious walking country; the Coast to Coast and the Cumbrian Way Walk virtually pass the door. Here you can recover from your exertions, warm yourself by the fire, enjoy something from the menu or stay the night. In the cosy bar, with views over the fells, you can have a light lunch which could include home-made country soup, smoked Borrowdale trout paté, Stonethwaite spiced black pudding with a mild curry sauce, slow roasted local lamb, wild boar and duckling pie, Newlands valley steaks or home-made vegetable pie as well as a selection of home-made puddings. Beers are Jennings Black Sheep, Coniston Bluebird and guests. Something for everyone on the wine list. Seats outside from where you can appreciate your surroundings.

OPEN: 11–11. Restricted opening hours during Dec & Jan.
Real Ale.
No children. No dogs. Car park. Wheelchair access. Nine en-suite bedrooms.
Cards: MasterCard, Switch, Visa.

Wasdale Head

Wasdale Head Inn ① 01946 726229
Gosforth, Seascale CA20 1EX (north-east of Wastwater)
Free House. Howard Christie, licensee
e-mail: wasdaleheadinn@msn.com

You're on the valley bottom between three major peaks, Pillar, Great Gable and Scafell Pike, and at the head of the dramatic Wastwater – the deepest lake in England. Bleak and magnificent, this is one of the most remote places in the Lake District, approximately nine miles from the nearest habitation; just a collection of sheep pastures and an inn. But what a welcome for the weary traveller or climber. A wonderfully sturdy, handsome three-storey building with comfortable bars decorated with climbing photographs, where they serve a good selection of well-prepared, hearty bar food ranging from home-made soups, vegetable curry and the popular beef in ale pie to local lamb casserole. On the evening menu: chicken and bacon terrine with a lightly spiced pear chutney, pan-fried strips of peppered duck on a Caesar salad with garlic croutons and for a main course, red mullet fillets on a pea purée finished with a red pepper coulis or chicken breast on a sweet potato mash with an artichoke and white wine sauce, good puds too. Well-kept ales: up to nine – all local – two very local as they now brew their own. Others could include Jennings Cumberland, Yates Bitter, Hesket Newmarket and Dents Ramsbottom on hand pump. Dramatic scenery. No need to say there are wonderful walks round here because that is probably why you are here anyway.

OPEN: 11–11 (Jan & Feb 11–10).
Real Ale. Restaurant.
Children and dogs welcome – both on leads. Wheelchair access. Twelve bedrooms and seven self-catering apartments. Camping site.
Cards: all major credit cards.

BEST OF THE REST

Grasmere
Travellers Rest ① 015394 35604
Grasmere LA22 9RR
A 16th-century former coaching inn tucked into the rolling hills in the heart of the Lake District, about half a mile north of Grasmere. There are wonderful views, a welcoming landlord and plenty of good things on the menu: home-made soup, honey-baked ham,

steak and kidney pie and daily specials. Jennings range of ales and Marstons Pedigree. Children welcome, dogs too. Wheelchair access (not WC). Bedrooms.
Open: 11–11.

Kirkby Lonsdale
Snooty Fox ① 01524 271308
Main Street, Kirkby Lonsdale LA6 2AH
In one of the most beautiful towns in south Cumbria, the imposing, Jacobean, white-painted Snooty Fox serves a good, varied menu – everything freshly prepared: home-made soups, filled baguettes, pan-fried lamb's kidneys flamed with sherry served in a filo nest, twice-baked three-cheese souffle with garlic cream, vegetarian dishes and lunchtime daily specials on the blackboard. Hartleys XB, Theakstons Best and Timothy Taylors Landlord on hand pump. New World wines. Children welcome. Wheelchair access (not WC). Bedrooms.
Open: 11–11.

Ravenstonedale
Fat Lamb Country Inn ① 015396 23242
Crossbank, CA17 4LL
Off the A683, between the Lake District and the Yorkshire Dales, this is a rather remote, attractive, stone-built 17th-century inn, situated in the most glorious countryside; a nature reserve of wetlands and meadows is just beyond the back garden. Well-chosen dishes on the menu include local trout. Boddingtons beer. You can also stay. Children welcome. Wheelchair access.
Open: 12–11.30.

Wetherspoon in Cumbria

Barrow in Furness – Furness Railway, Abbey Road
① 01229 820818
Carlisle – Woodrow Wilson, 48 Butchergate
① 01228 819942
Whitehaven – Bransty Arch, Bransty Row
① 01946 517640
Workington – Henry Bessemer, New Oxford Street
① 01900 734650

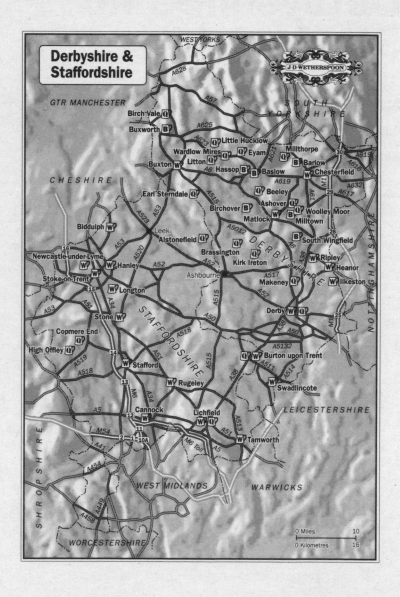

Derbyshire & Staffordshire

J·D·WETHERSPOON

WEST YORKS

GTR MANCHESTER

SOUTH YORKSHIRE

Birch Vale

Buxworth

Little Hucklow

Wardlow Mires

Eyam

Millthorpe

Litton

Barlow

Buxton

Hassop

Baslow

Chesterfield

Beeley

Earl Sterndale

Ashover

Birchover

Woolley Moor

Matlock

Milltown

CHESHIRE

Biddulph

Leek

South Wingfield

Alstonefield

Brassington

Ripley

Newcastle-under-Lyme

Kirk Ireton

Heanor

Hanley

Ashbourne

Ilkeston

Stoke-on-Trent

Makeney

Longton

Derby

Stone

DERBYSHIRE

Copmere End

STAFFORDSHIRE

High Offley

Burton upon Trent

Stafford

Rugeley

Swadlincote

Cannock

LEICESTERSHIRE

Lichfield

Tamworth

NOTTINGHAMSHIRE

SHROPSHIRE

WEST MIDLANDS

WARWICKS

WORCESTERSHIRE

| 0 Miles | 10 |
| 0 Kilometres | 16 |

Derbyshire and Staffordshire

Alstonefield

George ① 01335 310205
Alstonefield, Ashbourne, Derbyshire DE6 2FX
Burtonwood. Richard & Sue Grandjean, licensees

On the edge of Dovedale, a beautiful stretch of the River Dove which tumbles through a dramatic tree-lined gorge known as Little Switzerland. In this small village between Ashbourne and Buxton, among the glories of the Peak District and some of the best and varied walking country, the beamed, traditional, 17th-century George is reputed to have the smallest bar in the county. Undeterred, the customers manage to force their way in to choose something from a good selection of hearty bar food: home-made soup, paté, ham or cheese ploughman's, different fillings for the sandwiches, meat and potato pie, lasagne, quiche, plus about eight home-made puds; daily specials and puddings are shown on wall in the passage. Burtonwoods range of ales. Children have a separate room and there are seats in the garden.

OPEN: 11–3, 6–11. Sat 11–11. Sun 12–10.30.
Real Ale. No-smoking restaurant.
Children welcome. No dogs. Wheelchair access from the rear car park.
Cards: MasterCard, Switch, Visa.

Ashover

Crispin Inn ① 01246 590591
Church Street, Ashover, Derbyshire S45 0AB
Mansfield. David Spittal, tenant
e-mail: davidspittal@btclick.com

In the Derwent valley and surrounded by some quite spectacular scenery where wooded valleys open up into rolling stone-walled fields, the Crispin, off the A632 between Matlock and Chesterfield, is one of the oldest inns in the area with a beamed lounge bar and dining room dating back to the mid-15th century. Whatever age, this is a popular local, serving traditional pub food and a very reasonable three-course Sunday lunch to go with the Mansfield ales: Riding Bitter, Mansfield Mild and Pedigree.

OPEN: Mon, Wed & Fri 12–3. Sat 12–11. Sun 12–10.30.
Real Ale.
Children welcome. Dogs allowed in bar. Car park. Wheelchair access. Bedrooms; four with TV.

Beeley

Devonshire Arms ① 01629 733259
Beeley, nr Matlock, Derbyshire DE4 2NR
Free House. J. A. Grosvenor, MBII, licensee

Well, you really couldn't ask for better neighbours! During the 18th century three separate cottages were converted and quickly became a prosperous coaching inn on the Matlock to Bakewell road; it's now a popular, charming, beautifully kept village inn at the gateway to Chatsworth House. Full of character, the Devonshire Arms caters for locals and visitors to Chatsworth and the Derbyshire Peak District. They offer an interesting bar menu that ranges from soup of the day, hot or cold fillings for the baguettes, ploughman's, vegetarian dishes and various salads to devilled whitebait, pan-fried mushrooms in garlic served on a bed of roquette leaves, duck and fig terrine, smoked haddock rarebit, breast of chicken in a wine and Stilton sauce, braised knuckle of lamb in a rosemary sauce or steak au poivre. Friday night is fish night so you could start with a seafood taster platter or a well-dressed crab and tuna niçoise, maybe grilled halibut in orange and lemon butter as a main course. Specials on the blackboard, also a wide range of home-made puds. Sunday mornings they serve a 'Victorian breakfast', with Bucks Fizz, from 10 a.m. until noon, for which you must book. Theakstons XB, Old Peculier, Black Sheep Best, Special and a guest beer. About 30 single malt whiskies and a short wine list. At the southern end of Chatsworth Park, this is an outstanding area for walking and cycling.

OPEN: 11–11. Food served every day 12–9.30.
Real Ale. No-smoking restaurant.
Children welcome – upstairs family room. No dogs. Wheelchair access (not WC).
Cards: Amex, MasterCard, Visa.

Birch Vale

Waltzing Weasel ① 01663 743402 (also Fax)
New Mills Road, Birch Vale, Derbyshire SK22 1BT
Free House. Michael Atkinson, licensee
e-mail. w-weasel@zen.co.uk

Solidly comfortable, the stone-built Weasel has well-decorated bars, open fires and interesting pieces of furniture, antique settles, tables and decent prints taking the edge off the usual pub furnishings. Still a pub with room for an elbow on the bar, though food's the thing – English with more than a touch of Italy. They serve new and exciting vegetarian dishes, peasant casseroles and stews (at least one a day); food with a definite Italian accent. From the bar menu, marinated anchovies or black olive paté as a starter, then maybe pizza, seafood tart, sea trout, Moroccan vegetable casserole or marinated, then roast leg of lamb Italian style. Beers are Marstons Pedigree and Best, wines are mainly French with a soupçon from the New World. It's amazing what you learn in such a tremendously enjoyable place; peaceful enough for one of our readers to overhear a learned discourse on science and religion by visiting academics enjoying a pint. You are high on the hill, so outside is a pretty garden and terrace with a view. This is an area of spectacular Derbyshire countryside and the crowning glory of the Peak District – Kinder Scout – all 2088ft of it.

OPEN: 12–3, 5.30–11.
Real Ale. Restaurant.
Children welcome. Wheelchair access (not WC). Car park. Bedrooms (all en suite).
Cards: Amex, Delta, MasterCard, Switch, Visa.

Brassington

Ye Olde Gate ① 01629 540448
Well Street, Brassington, Derbyshire DE4 4HJ (north-east of Ashbourne)
Wolverhampton & Dudley. Paul Burlinson, tenant

Another ghostly pub! But this unknown ghost, nearly three hundred years younger than the pub, has become a film star, having featured in TV's 'Heart of the Country' programme. This tremendously atmospheric place has slowly changed with the centuries but the heart of Ye Olde Gate is genuinely olde, dating back to the early 17th century. Stone walls, beams, a panelled dining room, log fires, cosy, timeless furnishings; all primped, polished and looking their best. Bar food changes by the day, but baguettes with varied and interesting fillings are available at lunchtime as well as home-made curries, Cajun chicken, seafood dishes, roasts, steaks and good puds. No-smoking dining room. Marstons Pedigree and guest beers, plus lots of malt whiskies. Seats in the sheltered garden. There have not only been ghostly happenings here but historical ones too, as during the Civil War the panelled dining room was used as a temporary hospital.

OPEN: 12–2.30 (Sat 12–3), 6–11. No food Mon or Sun eve.
Real Ale. Summer barbecue.
Children over 10 in dining room. Dogs on leads. Wheelchair access.
Cards: MasterCard, Switch, Visa.

Burton-upon-Trent

Burton Bridge Inn ① 01283 536596
24 Bridge Street, Burton-upon-Trent, Staffs DE14 1SY
Own Brew. Kevin & Jan McDonald, tenants.

Lots of bits and pieces here relate to the brewing industry – notices, awards and brewing memorabilia are all displayed in the front bar. Not surprising really, as beer is brewed on site and this 17th-century inn is the brewery tap. So popular has it become that a new room gives a greater bar area; oak panelled with a feature fireplace, it looks out onto the brewery. With more space in the pub, one room is now totally non smoking. If you're getting a bit peckish the lunch menu lists quite a range of bar snacks: filled cobs and filled oatcakes, giant Yorkshire puddings with various fillings, hot bacon and egg rolls, toasties and ploughman's. A function room – and skittle alley which seems to be booked months ahead – is available for private parties. Burton Bridge Bitter, XL Bitter, Porter and Festival plus seasonal varieties. Selection of malt whiskies and fruit wines.

OPEN: 11.30–2.15, 5–11. Sun 12–2, 7–10.30.
Real Ale. No food Sun.
Children over 10 in eating area. Dogs on leads. No cards.

Cop Mere End

Star ① 01785 850279
Cop Mere End, Eccleshall, Staffs SP21 6EW
Free House. Mike Davis, licensee

West of Eccleshall, this classic, traditional, two-room country pub opposite Cop Mere Pool – a big lake, well used by the Star's fishing club – is friendly and welcoming, a great favourite with walkers and the local cycling club. It's known for well-presented, freshly made food – well-filled sandwiches, ploughman's, a large selection of fish dishes and steaks, and a popular roast for Sunday lunch. Draught Bass and always a guest ale. Lovely garden to sit in.

OPEN: 12–3, 7–11. Sat 12–11. No food Sun eve or Mon.
Real Ale.
Children welcome. No dogs. Car park.

Derby

The Flower Pot ① 01332 204955
25 King Street, Derby DE1 3DZ
Free House. Michael John Evans, licensee

At the centre of things, not far from the cathedral and shopping centre, this is a mecca for those serious about their beer; regular beer festivals take place and guest beers change all the time. You won't get bored in the early 18th-century Flower Pot, which is larger than it looks from the frontage. It has a small library – mostly of books donated by the customers – with which you can while away the time, or you can study the history of old Derby from interesting photographs in the back bar. Last but not least, there is a wide choice of hearty bar food to accompany the beer: sandwich platters served with salad and spicy potatoes, filled jacket potatoes, home-made soup, lots of meat and fish dishes, a selection of vegetarian meals and some bar snacks such as chip butties and cheese burgers. Fruit crumble or bread and butter pudding are among the puds. Sunday lunches too. Hartington Bitter, Bass and Marstons Pedigree are the regular ales; there are also guest beers and quite a selection of malt whiskies. Small walled garden at the back of the pub.

OPEN: 11–11.
Real Ale.
Children welcome until 7.30. Dogs on leads.

The Smithfield ① 01332 370429
Meadow Road, Derby DE1 2BH
Free House. Roger Myring, licensee

Close to the centre, but on the opposite side of the River Derwent and downriver from the old cattle market, this riverside pub offers a warm welcome. Beer is very important here; the Smithfield keeps ten ales on hand pump including draught Bass, Marstons Pedigree and beers from Derbyshire breweries. A good selection of basic bar food is served. Seats in the large garden by the river and on the new terrace at the water's edge.

OPEN: 11–11. Sun 12–10.30. No food Sun.
Real Ale.
Children welcome until 9. Dogs on leads. Large car park.

Ye Olde Dolphin ① 01332 267711
6/7 Queen Street, Derby DE1 3DL
Enterprise Inns. James Harris, tenant

Close to the cathedral and the pedestrianised area of a city that can trace its origins back to the Norman Conquest, this timbered 16th-century inn is a traditional pub, the oldest in the city. Two doors lead into four beamed, panelled and cosy rooms serving familiar pub food: soup of the day, lots of fillings for the baps, sautéed mushrooms in a creamy black-pepper sauce topped with melted cheese, filled jacket potatoes, sandwich platter with salad, fries and home-made coleslaw, grills, lambs liver and onions, steak and kidney pudding, vegetarian dishes and more. Sunday carvery. Beers are Black Sheep, Greene King Abbot, Marstons Pedigree, Adnams, Bass, Worthington, Caledonian Deuchars and three weekly changing guests. Seats in the garden.

OPEN: 10.30–11. Sun 12–10.30.
Real Ale. Restaurant. Sunday carvery 12–6.
Children welcome. No dogs. The Dolphin organizes a monthly ghost night for which you must book – they sell out very quickly.

Earl Sterndale

Quiet Woman ① 01298 83211
Earl Sterndale, nr Buxton, Derbyshire SK17 0BU
Free House. Ken Mellor, licensee

Opposite the village church and green and amid some of the prettiest countryside in the Peak District. Nine walks start or end here and walkers always get a warm welcome at this unchanging and uncomplicated village local with a beamed and tile-floored room, well-scrubbed tables and a good fire. The menu has got even shorter now; only local pork pies to keep your strength up for the next few miles. The well-kept ales are Marstons Pedigree, Bitter, Mansfields Dark Mild, Everards Tiger Bitter and guest ales: Adnams, Hartington Ales, Slaters, Stonehenge and Timothy Taylors Landlord. The large garden has a picnic area and donkeys, geese, pigs, hens, ducks and turkeys – for you to admire, not for lunch! But you can buy free-range eggs, also postcards of the pub and pub sign. There is parking for three touring caravans, also a large park for caravettes and somewhere to pitch your tent.

OPEN: Moveable hours – usually 12–3, 7–11.
Real Ale.
Children welcome. No dogs.

Eyam

Miners Arms ① 01433 630853
Water Lane, Eyam, Derbyshire S32 5RG
New Century Inns. John & Michele Hunt, tenants

The scenery surrounding this very famous plague village is magnificent and very popular with walkers and hikers. The Miners Arms, built in 1630 – 35 years before the village was struck by the plague and lost most of its population – has three comfortable, beamed rooms where they serve a very good choice of home-made dishes, many prepared from local seasonal produce. Bar lunches, which change daily, might include home-made soups, crispy roast duck, Cumberland sausages in onion gravy, steak and ale pie, chicken breasts in cream and Parmesan sauce, braised beef, quiche, ploughman's, sandwiches and a selection of home-made puds. There is also a separate evening à la carte menu and a traditional roast on Sunday. Stones ales, Bass and one guest. Seats outside the front of the inn and in the courtyard at the back. The village church of St Lawrence is partly a museum dedicated to the plague's victims and the story of the village.

OPEN: 12–11.
Real Ale. Evening restaurant.
Children welcome until 9. Wheelchair access. Bedrooms – and dogs can stay as well.
Cards: all credit and debit cards except Amex and Diners.

High Offley

Anchor ① 01785 284569
Peggs Lane, Old Lea, High Offley, Staffs ST20 0NG
Free House. Mrs Olive Cliff, licensee

On the canal, the Anchor, run by the same family for over 100 years, is a two-bar pub with a gift shop selling painted canal-ware, a beer garden to sit in on sunny days – they won the 'Stafford in Bloom' garden competition 2003 – and a camping site. Built during the late 19th century, this is a little treasure of a pub, unchanged and delightful. You can get here in various ways, but the easiest is by water. Clutching a canal map, the pub is alongside bridge 42 on the Shropshire Union canal. The alternative is to walk along the towpath; you can obviously get here by car but you will have to ask directions. It is worth it. Simple snacks usually available to go with the perfectly kept Wadworths 6X, Marstons Pedigree, Owd Roger and the real ciders brought up from the cellar.

OPEN: 12–3, 7–11.
Real Ale.
No children. Dogs on leads. Wheelchair access to WCs; two steps into pub. Touring caravan site, camping and caravans to rent.

Kirk Ireton

Barley Mow ① 01335 370306
Main Street, Kirk Ireton, Ashbourne, Derbyshire DE6 3JP
Free House. Mary Short, licensee

Converted years ago from a gabled, Jacobean farmhouse, the Barley Mow is largely unspoilt and has a character all its own. Inside, one room leads into another, all with tiled or wood floors, mullioned windows, panelling, antique settles and open fires. The small cosy bar serves only filled rolls at lunchtime. Evening meals are prepared, but you have to be a resident. Well-kept beers from the cask: Hook Norton Old Hooky, Pedigree, Hartington IPA and weekly changing guests. Thatchers draught cider and a speciality single apple cider in the bottle, Carlsberg Export lager. Seats in the garden and at the front of the pub. The old stables have been transformed into the village post office.

OPEN: 12–2, 7–11.
Real Ale.
Children welcome by arrangement. Dogs on leads. Wheelchair access. Bedrooms (5 en suite).

Lichfield

Queens Head ① 01543 410932
Queen Street, Lichfield, Staffs WS13 6QD
Marstons. Roy Harvey, tenant
e-mail: queen2@queen2.worldline.co.uk

Lichfield is a delightful, small cathedral city. A short walk from the city centre will bring you to the Queens Head, a true local with a simple, well-kept interior. Known for its ales, it also has a wonderful choice of over 20 different cheeses; and patés, breads and pickles to go with them; ample helpings, you don't go hungry here! Beers are Marstons Pedigree, Timothy Taylors Landlord and Adnams Southwold Bitter. Two regularly changing guests.

OPEN: 12–11. Sun 12–3, 7–10.30.
Real Ale.
No children. Dogs on leads.

Little Hucklow

Ye Olde Bulls Head ① 01298 871097
Little Hucklow, Tideswell, Derbyshire SK17 8RT
Free House. Julie Denton, licensee
www.yeolde-bullshead.co.uk

At first glance, this white-painted inn is not obviously 12th century, but it is, and the fifth oldest pub in England. An unspoilt pub in a small limestone village surrounded by sheep pastures, it has two bulls' heads outside on the signs and one inside on the wall. There are two welcoming beamed rooms with built-in settles, both with open fires and a collection of mugs, tankards and mementoes of the mining that used to take place in and around this old place. It's famous for continuing the tradition of serving huge, juicy, gammon steaks topped with either an egg or a slice of pineapple; but you can also choose home-made vegetable soup, hot 'n' spicy prawns, garlic mushrooms, steak plate pie, mixed grill platter, fresh deep-fried cod and vegetarian dishes. John Smiths and Tetleys beers plus a guest and a selection of malt whiskies. Seats in the garden, and lots of walks nearby.

OPEN: Mon–Thurs 6–11. Fri–Sun 12–3, 6–11.
Real Ale.
Children welcome. No dogs. Car park. Wheelchair access.
Cards: all major credit cards.

Litton

Red Lion Inn ① 01298 871458
The Green, Litton, nr Buxton, Derbyshire SK17 8QU
Free House. Michele & Terry Vernon, licensees
e-mail: redlioninn@littonvillage.fsnet.co.uk

In the glories of the Peak District, this popular 17th-century pub is on the edge of a pretty village green where the benches are handy as a summer overflow. Inside are three cosy, beamed rooms, each with an open fire, where walkers, dogs, muddy boots and all are more than welcome; you can't keep them away as they are surrounded by the most wonderful scenery and footpaths galore. When you arrive you will be well looked after; as they admit, this is no gastropub but an inn serving good, straightforward food. There is a basic bar menu of soup, steak and ale pie, steaks and sandwiches but the landlady's specials board could feature local rabbit casserole in cider, pork and apricot casserole, garlic and rosemary lamb, apple and blackberry crumble or Bakewell pudding to finish; local Hartington Stilton cheese too. Barnsley Bitter, Jennings Cumberland and one guest, maybe something from Black Sheep, Timothy Taylors or Shepherd Neame. A few wines by the glass. Orchids abound in the fields in spring; June is the famous well-dressing festival and at Christmas you are jollied along by the local brass band playing carols.

OPEN: Mon–Thurs 12–3, 6–11. Fri–Sun 12–11.
Real Ale.
No children. Dogs welcome. Car park. Two bedrooms. During 2004 there will be a cottage to let, sleeping four.
Cards: Switch, Visa.

Makeney

Hollybush Inn ① 01332 841729
Hollybush Lane, Makeney, Derbyshire DE56 0RX
Free House. John Bilbie, licensee

This is a 'Dick Turpin-was-here' pub. Quite probable, after all – he did travel around a bit! It's certainly old enough. Originally a farmhouse, the 17th-century Grade II Hollybush is an unchanging, unspoilt village pub with two bars and between them a cosy snug, all with beams, flagstone floors, panelling and roaring fires. The beer is brought up from the cellar in jugs, just as it used to be. They serve familiar pub food plus bar snacks. Five beers available: Marstons Pedigree, Ruddles County and guests. Regular beer festivals when there are plenty of new beers for you to try.

OPEN: Mon–Thurs 12–3, 4.30–11. Fri–Sun 12–11.
Real Ale.
Children allowed in back conservatory. Dogs on leads.

Millthorpe

Royal Oak ① 01142 890870
Millthorpe, Holmesfield, Dronfield, Derbyshire S18 7WJ
Free House. R. H. & E. Wills, licensees

Very close to the county border and the unfenced moors between Derbyshire and south Yorkshire. Walkers abound and are very welcome here, even their muddy boots are allowed into the bars. A friendly, stone-walled, 17th-century pub; inside the beams and good fires in the bar create a warm atmosphere. As well as the usual bar snacks of soup and ham, cheese and pork sandwiches, there might be fresh salmon pie, beef in red wine, pork steak with spring onions and ginger, meat and potato pie and some vegetarian dishes; bread and butter pudding, upside-down pudding or treacle tart to follow. Everything is home made in the pub. Real, freshly percolated coffee too. Tetley Cask, Tetley Smoothflow, Marstons Pedigree, Carlsberg Export, Castlemaine XXXX and a wide range of malt whiskies. Leg Over beer from the Dalehead Brewery, Harrogate is put on once every six weeks. There is a very pleasant garden and seats on the terrace.

OPEN: 11.30–2.30, 5.30–11.30, but closed all day Mon, Tues & Wed lunchtimes, and Sun eve.
Real Ale.
Children in garden. Dogs, not at meal times.

Stafford

Picture House ① 01785 222941
Bridge Street, Stafford ST16 2HL
Wetherspoon.

The ornate, contemporary plasterwork from the listed art-deco cinema is still in situ. The bar is on stage, the stalls and circle are organized seating areas and there are old film posters for you to admire. You will be as well looked after here as you invariably are at all Wetherspoon establishments. There is something for everyone on the menus from light bites, filled baps and jacket potatoes, wraps, salad bowls, to main meals, steaks and vegetarian meals. Egon Ronay works with Wetherspoon helping to maintain quality and variety. Beers are consistently cheaper, wines are sourced from all over the world – something for everyone. Unusually for a converted cinema, they have an outside drinking area.

OPEN: 11–11.
Real Ale.
No children. No dogs. Wheelchair access.

Wardlow Mires

Three Stags Heads ✆ 01298 872268
Wardlow Mires, Tideswell, Derbyshire SK17 8RW
Free House. Geoff & Pat Fuller, licensees

This is very much a Friday night and weekend place as they close during the week, unless during summer weekday evenings they find thirsty people gathering, hoping to be let in. When open you'll find a small, cosy, very unspoilt, 17th-century village pub with flagstone floors for the walking boots and muddy dogs, where they serve good, sustaining bar food. The menu ranges from home-made soups to seasonal game (grouse, pheasant, pigeon, duck, rabbit and hare), cottage pie, chicken chorizo, potato and bacon omelettes and vegetarian dishes – it all depends on what is available and what inspires the cook. Home-cooked food on home-made plates – there is a pottery in the barn. The ales are from the Abbeydale Brewery in Sheffield: Matins, Best Bitter, Absolution – and Black Lurcher, which is exclusive to the pub. A number of continental and British bottled beers. Lots of local dogs enjoy the fire – their owners too – and there is an interesting mummified cat well out of harm's way – in a case.

OPEN: Fri 7–11. Sat, Sun and bank holidays 12–11.
Real Ale.
Children until 8.30. Dogs on leads.
Live music Sat eve.

Woolley Moor

White Horse ✆ 01246 590319
Badger Lane, Woolley Moor, Derbyshire DE5 6FG
Free House. Charlotte Adshead & Keith Hurst, licensees

Between Matlock and Clay Cross, this handsome old stone coaching inn overlooks the Amber Valley and the Ogston reservoir which is fed by the Amber river. Off the beaten track, high in the Dales in lovely rural surroundings, this is a lively, busy pub where they serve some interesting bar food, way above the norm. From the bar menu are sandwiches – hot or cold and served with either a side salad or salad and chips, toasted paninis, game and ale pie, Manhattan mussel chowder, trio of local sausages with onion gravy, poached salmon and prawn salad, vegetarian dishes and lots more. There is also a restaurant menu in the no-smoking conservatory. Much of the food is from very local sources: butcher, baker and an enthusiastic vegetable grower. They hold a beer carnival weekend. Draught Bass, and four guest beers all on hand pump, which change weekly. Excellent walks nearby and you can hire a local guide. They have their own boules piste if you feel energetic, and an adventure playground for lively children. Sometimes there may be classical music playing in the lounge bar, but there are plenty of opportunities to get away from it if you want to.

OPEN: 12–2, 6–9. Sun 12–7.
Real Ale. Restaurant (possibly classical music in here).
Children in eating area or restaurant. Dogs in public bar. Wheelchair access.
Cards: all major cards.

BEST OF THE REST

Barlow, Derbyshire
Trout ① 01142 890893
Valley Road, Common Side, Barlow S18 7SL
If first impressions don't inspire, what goes on inside will. North-west of Chesterfield, this is one of those places that can be all things to all people. A typical pubby bar on one side serves Bass, Boddingtons and Marstons Pedigree, as well as something from the menu; on the other is a popular restaurant serving good home-made food. Children allowed in restaurant.
Open: 12–3, 6–11.

Baslow, Derbyshire
Cavendish ① 01246 582311
Baslow DE4 1SP
A plain, solid stone building outside, classy and desirable inside. Sitting on and overlooking the Chatsworth estate, this hotel – really an inn – is a lovely place to be. You can eat informally – comparatively speaking – in the conservatory, or in the dining room. Interesting food, beautifully served in wonderful surroundings. Children welcome. No dogs.
Open: hotel hours.

Birchover, Derbyshire
Druid Inn ① 01629 650302
Main Street, Birchover DE4 2BL
Between Matlock and Bakewell, this is a creeper-covered old stone pub in a glorious part of the Peak District. Lots of walkers end up here to enjoy rest and recuperation and prepare for the onward march. Beers are Marstons Pedigree, Morlands Old Speckled Hen, Mansfield Bitter and Druid, brewed for the pub. But if you're here to eat, and most are, there is a wide choice of imaginative dishes on the changing blackboard menu; the best of English cooking with a touch of the Far East. Children until 8 p.m. No dogs. Wheelchair access (not WC).
Open: 12–3, 7–11.

Buxworth, Derbyshire
Navigation ① 01663 732072
Silkhill, Buxworth SK23 7NL
As you might guess from the name, this is an 18th-century canal pub on the restored Buxworth arm of the Peak Forest Canal. Bits and pieces decorating the interior celebrate the past glories of the canal age. Flagstone floors, warm fires and good wholesome food – home-made soup, Cumberland sausages, bubble and squeak, that sort of thing – to go with the Marstons Pedigree, Timothy Taylors Landlord, Websters Yorkshire and a couple of guests. Children allowed. Bedrooms.
Open: 11–11.

Hassop, Derbyshire
Eyre Arms ① 01629 640390
Hassop DE45 1NS
North of Bakewell, this is an unspoilt, creeper-covered village pub; certainly here at the time of the Civil War as a ghostly Cavalier soldier has taken up residence. Known for serving popular food and some interesting blackboard specials. Well-kept ales but don't

ask for a little taste of a new beer – they have been known to refuse. Children in eating area of bar. No dogs. Wheelchair access.
Open: 11–3, 6.30–11

Milltown, Derbyshire

Miners Arms ① 01246 590218
Oakstedge Lane, Milltown S45 0HA
Not far from Ashover, in a lovely part of Derbyshire. Good walks take you past grass-covered and landscaped old mine workings, remains of the area's industrial past. It's wise to book if you want to eat in the evening as this is a popular place serving good-value, above average food. Regularly changing ales and some decent wines. Children welcome.
Open: 12–3, 7–11. Closed Mon and Tues.

South Wingfield, Derbyshire

Old Yew Tree Inn ① 01773 833763
Manor Road, South Wingfield DE55 7NA
You need to know that this pub is only open weekday evenings, from 5 p.m., and at weekends. In a village six miles from Matlock, the stone-built, 16th-century Yew Tree serves traditional pub food: home-made soup, salads, sandwiches, plain or toasted, vegetable lasagne, chicken Kiev, grills, a 'Yew Tree Mighty Grill', steak au poivre and three different sizes of steak. Roast lunch on Sunday. Marstons Pedigree always on tap, so to speak, but Greene King Abbot and Fullers London Pride are popular. Children welcome. No dogs. Wheelchair access (not WC).
Open: Mon–Fri 5–11. Sat 12–3, 6.30–11. Sun 12–4, 7–10.30.

Wetherspoon in Derbyshire and Staffordshire

Derbyshire

Buxton – Wye Bridge House, Fairfield Road
① 01298 709324
Chesterfield – Portland Hotel (a Wetherspoon Lodge), West Bars
① 01246 293600
Chesterfield – Spa Lane Vaults, 34 St Mary's Gate
① 01246 245410
Derby – Babington Arms, 11–13 Babington Lane
① 01132 383647
Derby – Standing Order, 28–32 Irongate
① 01322 207591
Heanor – Red Lion, Derby Road
① 01773 533767
Ilkeston – Observatory, 14a Market Place
① 0115 932 8040
Matlock – Crown, Crown Square
① 01629 580991
Ripley – Red Lion, Market Place
① 01773 512875
Swadlincote – Sir Nigel Gresley, Market Street
① 01283 227560

Staffordshire

Biddulf – Bradley Green, 68 High Street
① 01782 375500
Burton-upon-Trent – Lord Burton, 154 High Street
① 01283 517587
Cannock – Linford Arms, 79 High Green
① 01543 469360
Hanley – Reginald Mitchell, Tontine Street
① 01782 281082
Lichfield – Acorn Inn, 12–18 Tamworth Street
① 01543 263400
Longton – Last Post, Transport Lane
① 01782 594060
Newcastle-under-Lyme – Arnold Machin, 37 Ironmarket
① 01782 557840
Rugeley – Plaza, Horsefair
① 0188 958 6831
Stafford – Picture House, Bridge Street
① 01785 222941
Stoke on Trent – Wheatsheaf, 84–92 Church Street
① 01782 747462
Stone – Poste of Stone, 1 Granville Square
① 01785 827920
Tamworth – Bolebridge, 8 Bolebridge Street
① 01827 317510

Lundy Island

Devon

SOMERSET

Barnstaple

Molland

Sheepwash

Iddesleigh

Tiverton

Forches Corner

Broadhembury

27 M5

28

Stockland

Crediton

Broadclyst

Newton St Cyres

Whimple

Colyton

Sticklepath

Woodbury

Salterton

Sidford

Drewsteignton

Exeter

Branscombe

29

30

31

Topsham

Lydford

Chagford

Doddiscombsleigh

Lower Ashton

Lustleigh

Haytor Vale

Exmouth

Widecombe in the Moor

Newton Abbot

Buckland Monachorum

Hoine

Stokenteignhead

Lutton

Woodland

Torquay

Hemerdon

Rattery

Paignton

Plymouth

Dartington

Brixham

Harberton

Noss Mayo

Tuckenhay

Holbeton

Dartmouth

Blackawton

Kingston

Stokenham

Bantham

South Pool

0 Miles   10
0 Kilometres   16

J·D·WETHERSPOON

Devon

Barnstaple

Panniers ① 01271 329720
33 Boutport Street, Barnstaple EX31 1RX
Wetherspoon.

Every week the local farmers and market gardeners bring their produce to sell at the lively and colourful Pannier Market. The town itself is steeped in history. From Saxon times a thriving wool trade and sheltered moorings on the River Taw helped it develop into what was a bustling port – now but a memory. The Panniers, converted from two redundant shops into the popular pub you see today, has the added bonus of a well-designed outside eating area. As with all Wetherspoon establishments, reliability is the key. Something for everyone on the reasonably priced menu, beer that is consistently cheaper than anywhere else and whatever else you want to drink available from the bar.

OPEN: 11–11
Real Ale.
No children. No dogs. Wheelchair access.

Blackawton

George Inn ① 01803 712342
Main Street, Blackawton, nr Totnes TQ9 7BG
Free House. Vic Hall & Ruth Coe, licensees
e-mail: george@barncourt.com

Drive along deep-sided Devon lanes to this attractive, quiet village west of Dartmouth and the George, an old traditional local. Two hop-hung beamed bars with comfortable furnishings and a lounge with a fire and a view. An interesting pub serving a variety of home-made bar food: garlic mushrooms with bacon and cream, freshly made pizzas, curries, dishes cooked in a skillet and vegetarian dishes – fish and steaks on the blackboard. Teignworthy Spring Tide, guests and a huge range of bottled and draught Belgian beers, some of these very strong. Beers are always changing and they also have regular small beer festivals, so you'll have to go to see what is on offer. Picnic tables in the garden with uninterrupted views to the south-west.

OPEN: 12–2.30, 6–11. Sun 12–3, 7–10.30. Summer 11–11 (Sun 12–10.30).
Real Ale. Children in eating area. Dogs on leads. Bedrooms.
Cards: all cards accepted.
Occasional live music sessions.

Branscombe

Fountain Head ① 01297 680359
Branscombe, nr Seaton EX12 3BG
Free House. Mrs Catherine Luxton, licensee

This delightfully traditional pub expanded into what was the old blacksmith's shop next door. So, blacksmiths' tools are on show and, as you would expect, there is a really good fire in the hearth. Reputedly haunted by a previous landlord (keeping his eye on the beer sales no doubt), the Fountain, near the partly Norman church – which has an unusual three-decker pulpit – is in a village of cob and thatch houses. Unsurprisingly, being near the sea, there are fishy things on the bar menu – cockles, mussels and crab sandwiches as well as home-made lasagne, cottage pie, salads and occasionally fried sardines and salmon steaks with fresh herbs as daily specials. Friday is fish and chip night; speciality food nights at other times. Mrs Luxton's husband runs his own brewery a mile away and the Own Brew beers include Branoc, Jolly Geff, Hells Bells in the winter, Yo Ho Ho brewed for Christmas and Summa' That during the summer. Farm cider. Seats outside on the terrace. A jolly beer festival is held over three days in mid-summer: barbecues, Morris men, over 30 ales, farm ciders – a really good time is had by all.

OPEN: 11.30–2.30, 6.30–11. Winter 11.30–2, 7–11.
Real Ale.
Children – in own room at lunchtimes; if over 10, in eating area in evening. Dogs on leads – biscuits for them. Two self-catering cottages.

Mason's Arms ① 01297 680300
Main Street, Branscombe, nr Seaton EX12 3DJ
Free House. Murray Inglis & Tim Manktelow-Gray, licensees
e-mail: reception@masonsarms.co.uk

In a hidden valley between Sidmouth and Seaton, the Mason's Arms has, for over 700 years, been at the lower end of this quiet village. What was once just a simple cider house has expanded into neighbouring cottages and become the place you see today. Outside, an abundance of thatch: thatched roof, thatched umbrellas over the tables and thatched hats over the doors. Inside is, as you would hope, rambling, beamed, stone walled and slate floored. The bar has a roaring log fire, complete with a spit that is regularly used for roasting beef, lamb, pork, sometimes goose and very occasionally, a whole shark. The menu offers dishes from Italy, France and South America. Bar food could include Branscombe crab bisque, ceviche of Lyme Bay mackerel, monkfish and king prawn salad, tagine of lamb shank with apricots and dates, half a roasted duck, steak and kidney pudding, steaks and grilled fish, mullet, sea bass, plaice or whatever is available. The changing bar specials board lists some vegetarian dishes too. On Sundays there is a full menu. Part of the restaurant is no smoking and there is a no-smoking bar in place of the top dining room. Always three ales on permanently: Otter Bitter, Bass and Dartmoor, plus two guest beers. Eighty wines on the list, 18 by the glass. Twenty whiskies; a beer festival in July and a whisky festival in December. The wine list is mainly French; six white and six red by the glass. Last but not least, two draught ciders and in summer a local farmhouse cider.

OPEN: 11–11. Winter 11–3, 6–11.
Real Ale. Restaurant.
Well-behaved children may be allowed, away from bar. Dogs on leads. Car park.
Wheelchair access. Bedrooms – lots, some in the cottages opposite.
Cards: Delta, MasterCard, Switch, Visa.

Broadclyst

Red Lion ① 01392 461271
Broadclyst, nr Exeter EX5 3EL
Free House. Fiona Conway, licensee

A pub and peaceful village largely owned by the National Trust – part of the Trust's 6000-acre Killerton House estate. In an unrivalled position on the green, the Red Lion has a heavily beamed, flagstoned bar where they serve a good traditional snack menu and interesting specials. New regime here; new chef too, so there's a changed menu, more extensive and featuring a greater number of fish dishes. Bass, Eldridge Pope Royal Oak, Worthingtons Best, Wadworths 6X and a changing guest. Good range of house wines by the glass. Seats at the front of the pub, and in the garden.

OPEN: 11–11.
Real Ale. Restaurant.
Children in own room. Dogs on lead. Wheelchair access.
Cards: all major cards except Amex.

Broadhembury

Drewe Arms ① 01404 841267 Fax: 01404 841765
Broadhembury EX14 0NF
Free House. Nigel Burge, licensee

Between Cullompton and Honiton, this is an unspoilt country pub with a glorious garden. A 15th-century cob and thatch building looking its best; inside, cream-washed walls, flagstone floors, beamed ceilings, comfortable furnishings and decorative bits and pieces. They specialise in wonderful fish dishes – using crab, brill, red mullet, sea bass, salmon, langoustines and anything else that's fresh and available. Other than fish, there are some open sandwiches, a chicken dish or two, fillet of beef. But the emphasis is on fish. Beers are from the Otter range; there is a good wine list with about 12 by the glass.

OPEN: 11–3, 6–11. Sun 12–3.
Real Ale. Restaurant.
Children welcome in eating areas. Dogs – you have to ask. Car park. Wheelchair access.
Cards: Delta, MasterCard, Switch, Visa.

Buckland Monachorum

Drake Manor Inn ① 01822 853892
The Village, Buckland Monachorum, Yelverton PL20 7NA
Innspired. Mandy Robinson, licensee
e-mail: drakemanor@internet-today.co.uk

In the centre of the village, between the church and the stream, this is a long, low building with a prize-winning summer floral display. Inside are beamed bars, large inglenooks, wood-burning stoves and flagstones in the restaurant. Lots of games in the popular public bar and serious devotees of both the cryptic, and quick, *Daily Telegraph* crosswords. Filled, freshly baked baguettes and ploughman's are served at lunchtime only, otherwise you could start with crispy vegetable parcels, Oriental sesame chicken fillets, home-made Brie and broccoli filo parcels with a sweet pepper sauce, chicken supreme, steak and kidney pie, home-made lasagne, a choice of fish, salads and a specials board which could have a fresh crab starter, venison steak with forest fruits, port wine and rosemary, or monkfish with lemon grass, ginger and white wine. Beers are Sharps Doom Bar, Greene King Abbot and Courage Best. Wide-ranging wine list and a tremendous number of malts. Seats in the pretty side garden.

OPEN: 11.30–2.30, 6.30–11. Sat 11.30–3, 6.30–11. Sun 12–2, 7–10.30.
Real Ale. Restaurant.
Children and dogs welcome. Car park. Wheelchair access.
Cards: Amex, MasterCard, Solo, Switch, Visa.

Chagford

Ring O'Bells ① 01647 432466
44 The Square, Chagford TQ13 8AH
Free House. Gordon Adams & Sharon Wegener, licensees
e-mail: ringobellschagford.co.uk

On Dartmoor, by the Teign river and surrounded by woodland, is a village of Tudor and Georgian houses and among them the 17th-century Ring O' Bells. Very atmospheric inside with panelled walls, and a candle-lit dining room. Always sandwiches and ploughman's on the bar menu as well as dishes using as much local produce as possible: Devonshire mussels, roast Dartmoor lamb, pork and apple griddle cakes, deep-fried Brie wedges, Danish salad, sirloin steak with a fresh cream pepper sauce, mushroom risotto, vegetable lasagne and home-made puds. Beers are Exmoor Ale, Butcombe Bitter, St Austell HSD and Guinness. Short wine list. Seats in the sunny, sheltered garden.

OPEN: 11–3, 5–11. Sun 12–3, 5–10.30.
Real Ale.
Children in dining room. Dogs on leads. Free town car park very near. Wheelchair access.
Cards: all major cards except Amex.

Colyton

Kingfisher ① 01297 552476
Dolphin Street, Colyton EX13 6NA
Free House. Graeme & Cherry Sutherland, MBII, licensees

Narrow streets, hidden alleys, fine Georgian houses, small cottages and a handsome church: an attractive small town amid high-sided lanes and rolling countryside. The Kingfisher is an unchanging local with a comfortable bar and a family room. Hearty bar food and daily specials: ploughman's, hot or cold fillings for the baguettes, gammon steak with pineapple, whitebait, cheese and broccoli bake, salads, filled jacket potatoes, lunchtime sandwiches, evening steaks and home-made puddings. Badger Best, Tanglefoot and several guest beers on hand pump. An extension built onto the back of the pub is used as a no-smoking dining area and family room. Seats on the terrace overlooking the garden.

OPEN: 11–2.30, 6–11.
Real Ale.
Children in family area. Dogs on leads. Wheelchair access.
No cards.

Dartmouth

Windjammer ① 01803 832228
Victoria Road, Dartmouth TQ6 9RT
Free House. Mary Coombe & Andy Coombe, licensees

Opposite the old market hall, this is a straightforward town pub with just one bar – with a winter log fire – decorated with shipwright's tools, charts and other nautical memorabilia in a town synonymous with everything naval – a port since Roman times. Family run, the pub has a growing reputation for serving better than average bar food, much of the produce coming from the surrounding area. As well as sandwiches and filled baguettes, there are smoked fish and meats, West Country cheeses, local sausages and wines. From the light meal menu you could choose savoury stuffed mushrooms served with mango chutney, grilled garlic prawns served with crusty bread or deep-fried West Country cheeses served with home-made tomato and pepper ketchup, and for a main meal a mixed bean cassoulet with parsnip chips, breast of hickory smoked chicken, grilled with pineapple and hoi sin sauce or a loin of pork with honey and mustard sauce; the very local fish on the menu are caught in nearby Start Bay and vary according to the catch. Ales are the local Princetown Dartmoor IPA, draught Bass, a continually changing guest beer and Luscombe organic cider. Short, wide-ranging wine list.

OPEN: 11–3, 5.30–11. Sun 12–3, 6.30–10.30.
Real Ale.
No children. Dogs welcome. Wheelchair access with help – one step.
Cards: Maestro, MasterCard, Solo, Switch, Visa. Not Amex.

Doddiscombsleigh

Nobody Inn ☺ 01647 252394
Doddiscombsleigh, nr Exeter EX6 7PS
Free House. Nick Borst-Smith, MBII, licensee
e-mail: info@nobodyinn.co.uk

Turn left off the A38 at Haldon Racecourse (signposted Dunchideock) and follow the signs to Doddiscombsleigh. The hint that you're nearly there is an inn sign, probably hidden by foliage, near a notice saying 'Unsuitable for Motor Vehicles', ignore it and carry on – everyone else does. Low and white, and that's the pub, unchanging and very secluded. When you arrive, you could think 'this is just another village house with a front garden and gate', but once inside you'll find beams, dark, intimate corners, varied, well-thought-out bar food and a changing blackboard menu. Widely acclaimed for their imaginative dishes and specials. From the bar menu, French onion or 'Nobody' soup, smoked Dartmouth mackerel with horseradish sauce, gravadlax with crevette and garlic mayonnaise, brown shrimp, butter bean and borlotti bean salad, beef steak cooked in a Guinness and mushroom sauce, three-bean fritters with sweet chilli sauce and a variation on a ploughman's – a countryman's, with two or three local cheeses with tomato and apple chutney, apple, celery a small salad, fresh brown bread and local butter. But that's not all: if you are a cheese buff, you have about 40 to choose from, many from the county. It's not difficult to find a good wine to go with the cheese as there are between 700 and 800 bottles in the pub cellar – about 20 by the glass – and 250 different malt whiskies. Nobody's Beer (brewed by Branscombe), Teign Valley Tipple and other guest beers on hand pump or from the cask. Farm ciders. Seats outside from where you can look at the view and appreciate the peace and quiet.

OPEN: 12–2.30, 6–11.
Real Ale. Restaurant open evenings only (not Sun or Mon).
No children under 14. No dogs. Car park. Bedrooms.
Cards: Delta, MasterCard, Switch, Visa.

Drewsteignton

Drewe Arms ☺ 01647 281224
The Square, Drewsteignton EX6 6QN
Whitbread. Colin Sparks, tenant

Two unchanging small rooms at the front, one with a log fire, and a larger dining area at the back of this unspoilt ale house in a village high above the Teign valley. A picturesque, old thatched pub next to the church, which has hardly changed since the 19th century. The ales and draught ciders are still kept on racks in the tap room: Flowers IPA, Gales, Greene King and Morlands Old Speckled Hen. They serve a fairly traditional menu, with a few interesting additions; soup, sandwiches, ploughman's, fish dishes and daily specials on the blackboard.

OPEN: 11–3, 6–11. Sun 12–3, 7–10.30.
Real Ale. Restaurant.
Children welcome. Dogs on leads. Wheelchair access. Bedrooms.

Exeter

Imperial ① 01392 434050
New North Road, Exeter EX4 4HF
Wetherspoon.

There is a wonderful view across the city from the Imperial's huge, old orangery, originally built to house a collection of tropical plants. Now fully restored, it has become one of the Imperial's three bars. In its own private park, the Imperial – originally the old Imperial Hotel and before that a private house built at the beginning of the 19th century – is again a landmark in the city. Much of the original 'grand' decor, as befitted the building's standing in Exeter society, still exists. As you would expect, there are always six, reasonably priced, cask-conditioned ales for you to try. A full menu is available throughout the day, seven days a week. Tables in the courtyard and in the grounds.

OPEN: 11–11. Sun 12–10.30.
Real Ale.
No under 18s. No dogs. Wheelchair access.

Forches Corner, Clayhidon

Merry Harriers ① 01823 421270
Forches Corner, Clayhidon, nr Cullompton EX15 3TR
Free House. Barry & Christine Kift, owners/licensees
e-mail: themerryharriers@fsbdial.co.uk

It was here, in the 17th century, that they planned an ambush which resulted in some nasty fisticuffs during the failed Monmouth rebellion in 1685. Now, in quieter times the Merry Harriers is a place where you will eat rather well; where they serve some interesting, imaginative dishes. It is, however, still a pub with beams, an inglenook and a comfortable bar with a good, changing, bar menu: home-made soup and open sandwiches, fresh tomato and baby mozzarella salad drizzled with basil olive oil, Oriental King prawn tails with sweet chilli dipping sauce, pan-fried scallops with garlic and rosemary butter, local roast rump of beef with Yorkshire pudding and red wine gravy and wild venison braised in Exmoor ale with wild mushrooms. There is a more extensive evening menu; on Sunday a traditional roast. Beers are from Otter, Cotleigh, Exmoor, Bishops, Stonehenge, Wychwood, O'Hanlans, Wyre Piddle and Smiles. Local cider too. Wide-ranging wine list with about 10 by the glass. Seats outside on the terrace and in the sizable garden.

OPEN: 12–3, 7–11. Closed Sun eve and Mon.
Real Ale.
No children. Dogs welcome. Car park. Wheelchair access.
Cards: Delta, MasterCard, Switch, Visa.

Harberton

Church House Inn ① 01803 863707
Harberton, nr Totnes TQ9 7SF
Free House. David & Jennifer Wright, licensees

Built to house the workers who built the handsome church in the 12th century, it was owned and used by the church until the 1950s. Next door to the church and gloriously atmospheric, the inn, full of oak beams, has one of the oldest oak screens in the country, a huge inglenook fireplace of great antiquity and some very ancient glass – thought to be Tudor. Food here is up to the mark – a choice of 'little eats': devilled whitebait, mushrooms in garlic butter, their own chicken liver paté, ploughman's and various sandwiches; the lunchtime specials could include fillet of plaice marinated in white wine, garlic and lemon, steak and kidney pie, home-made soups, locally made sausages, curries and grills. Virtually all the vegetables are local and fresh; free-range eggs from the village, local pork and lamb – even the rabbits have a Devon accent. Draught Bass plus two weekly changing guest beers. Good selection of wines and farm cider.

OPEN: 12–3, 6–11. Closed Sun eve.
Real Ale. Restaurant.
Children in family room & eating area. Dogs on leads. Wheelchair access (not WC).
Bedrooms.
Cards: all major credit cards.
Morris dancers in summer.

Haytor Vale

Rock ① 01364 661305
Haytor Vale, nr Newton Abbot TQ13 9XP
Free House. Christopher Graves, licensee
e-mail: inn@rock-inn.co.uk

Being on the edge of the Dartmoor National Park you are surrounded by wonderful walking country, and also the great granite outcrops after which the pub was named. Built as a coaching inn over 200 years ago, the Rock is a friendly local serving a small, rural community. Inside are two panelled rooms, both with big log fires, a no-smoking dining area and a restaurant. Good choice of bar food: home-made soup, mussels in chilli, lemon and parsley, Dartmouth smoked salmon and prawns, interesting fillings for the sandwiches, local ham and rib of beef platter salad, fresh fish from Brixham, shank of lamb on spring onions with minted jus, chicken curry with mango chutney, steak and kidney suet pudding and daily specials. Also home-made puddings and a Sunday roast. Dartmoor Best and Morlands Old Speckled Hen on hand pump. Malt whiskies. You might like to know that this is another haunted pub; this ghost, by the name of Belinda, has been seen by several customers, but whether before or after hours hasn't been established! A pretty garden and an adjoining terrace are in high favour in summer.

OPEN: 11–3, 6–11. Sat 11–11.
Real Ale.
Children in eating area of bar. No dogs. Wheelchair access (not WC). Bedrooms.
Cards: Amex, Delta, Diners, MasterCard, Switch, Visa.

Hemerdon

Miners Arms ☎ 01752 343252
Hemerdon, nr Plymouth PL7 5BU
Free House. Hannah Drewitt, licensee

High on the hill, looking towards Plymouth, the only thing left to remember the closed tin mines are mementoes of the past and the name of the pub. The family who ran the pub since 1870 and who witnessed all the social changes in this part of the country have gone and a new era is about to begin. Still a friendly local on the edge of Dartmoor with flagstones underfoot and beams above, it is soon to change with the opening of the new garden restaurant extension in 2004 from a predominately drinking establishment serving just beer and fill-you-up-to-keep-you-going pub food to somewhere serving something more exciting than the usual, very traditional menu. Beers are well-kept draught Bass, Ushers, Boddingtons, Sutton XSB (a local brew) and one guest and they occasionally have a really local farm cider.

OPEN: 11–2.30, 5.30–11. Sun 12–3, 7–10.30.
Real Ale.
No children. Dogs welcome.

Holbeton

Mildmay Colours ☎ 01752 830248
Fore Street, Holbeton, Plymouth PL8 1NA
Free House. Louise Price, licensee
www.mildmay-colours.co.uk

Built during the 17th century as a small manor house, later licensed as the George, it was renamed in 1967 in memory of Anthony Mildmay, Lord Mildmay of Flete, a leading amateur rider who persuaded the late Queen Mother to buy her first steeplechaser. The sign is painted in his racing colours and inside the pub the pictures and prints lean heavily towards the world of racing. Built high above the street in a village that won 'Devon Village of the Year 2003', this is a very popular place. Bar food includes home-made soup, triple sandwiches, ploughman's, filled baked potatoes, tiger prawns wrapped in filo pastry with a salsa dip, home-made lasagne, local sausages and local ham, Mexican chicken enchilada and daily specials from the large blackboard. They have a popular curry night on Wednesdays, fish night on Fridays and a carvery Sunday lunchtime. The pub has a 'buy local' policy and tries to source all its food and real ales from Devon or Cornwall. The beers, brewed in Truro, are SP and Colours Best; they also have other guest beers. They hold an annual beer festival over the August Bank Holiday where you can try up to 10 real ales – all brewed in Devon or Cornwall. Plenty of tables outside at the front of the pub, and in the garden at the back.

OPEN: 11–3, 6–11 (occasionally all day in the summer).
Real Ale. Carvery restaurant for Sunday lunch.
Children welcome. Dogs on leads. Six en-suite bedrooms in the old brewery.
Cards: MasterCard, Solo, Switch, Visa.
N.B. Background music in restaurant only.

Holne

Church House ① 01364 631208
Holne, nr Ashburton TQ13 7SJ
Free House. Tony Skerritt, licensee
e-mail: tony@holne.net

You get to the 14th-century, white-painted, timbered Church House along winding country lanes on the wilder southern edge of Dartmoor. Both the pine-panelled bar and the comfortable, carpeted lounge have big, winter log fires. Two of the bars and the restaurant are no smoking. Only the best, fresh ingredients reach the kitchen: locally produced organic vegetables, some of them home-grown, fish from Brixham and carefully chosen local meat. Lunchtime snacks could include Greek salad with feta cheese, olives and red onion, home-cured gravadlax with sweet dill dressing, vegetable bruschetta – garlic and olive bread with chargrilled vegetables, melted mozzarella cheese, salad and herb pesto, West Country fish pie, Holne lamb hotpot, Dartmoor rabbit casserole and good puds. There are daily specials and a weekly changing à la carte menu in the bars and the restaurant. Butcombe Bitter, Ring of Bells and Summerskills, varying guest ales plus two lagers and Murphys. Local cider and a good choice of house wines, 14 by the glass. Lovely views over the moors from the front of the pub.

OPEN: 12–3, 7–11.
Real Ale. Restaurant.
Children and dogs welcome. Six letting bedrooms. Wheelchair access (not WC).
Cards: Delta, MasterCard, Switch, Visa.

Iddesleigh

Duke of York ① 01837 810253
Iddesleigh, Winkleigh EX19 8BG
Free House. Jamie Stuart & Pippa Hutchinson, licensees

Long, low and thatched, the 14th-century Duke of York, the best of country pubs, is full of character. A blazing log fire and an unpretentious, comfortable interior make it popular with locals and visitors. Home-made food is listed on the blackboard in the main bar: soup of the day, crab mayonnaise with salad, a Stilton and port or chicken liver paté, rollmop herrings with salad, fish of the day, fillet of salmon with a creamy dill sauce, beef and Guinness casserole, leg of lamb steak with minted gravy, steak and kidney pudding; always some vegetarian dishes and something interesting on the restaurant menu: roast quarter of duck in a port and orange sauce, fillet of beef medallions in red wine and mushrooms, a selection of four or five fish dishes and a variety of smoked seafood from Dartmouth. Locally made ice-creams. Cotleigh Tawny, Adnams Broadside and Sharps Doombar Bitter from the cask. Farm ciders and guest beers, a good number of New World wines, some by the glass and a pretty back garden to sit in.

OPEN: 11–11. Sun 12–10.30. Food served 11–10 every day.
Real Ale. Restaurant.
Children welcome. Dogs on leads. Limited wheelchair access. Bedrooms.
Cards: Delta, MasterCard, Switch, Visa.

Kingston

Dolphin Inn ① 01548 810314
Kingston, nr Bigbury TQ7 4QE
Ushers. Jan Male & Geoff Smith, tenants
e-mail: neil@dolphininn.freeserve.co.uk

The well-beamed, traditional interior of the 16th-century Dolphin reflects its age. Outside, gardens and an outstanding display of flowerpots compete with a very flowery village. The menus change with the seasons but there could be a tomato and basil soup, crab bake with brown bread, home-made pie of the day, home-cooked ham, freshly poached salmon, plaice fillets with a spinach and mushroom stuffing in a cream and wine sauce, grills, fisherman's pie, vegetarian meals or even a sandwich or ploughman's. Lots more fish on the daily specials board. Wash that down with Courage Best Bitter, Ushers Founders and Sharps Doom Bar Ale or even something from the wide-ranging wine list. Tables in the garden, where you can sit with your dog. Lovely walks along the river Erme or to the sandy beach at Wonwell where the river Erme reaches the sea.

OPEN 11–2.30, 6–11. Sun 12–3, 6–10.30.
Real Ale.
Children welcome. Dogs in garden only. Wheelchair access. Three en-suite bedrooms.
Cards: most accepted.

Lower Ashton

Manor Inn ① 01647 252304
Lower Ashton, Teign Valley, nr Exeter EX6 7QL
Free House. Clare & Geoff Mann, owners/licensees
e-mail: cms.mann@virgin.net

Looking its colourful best when the creeper changes colour in the autumn and with glorious views across the Teign Valley, this is a delightful old place in more ways than one. They are very serious about their ales and one room reflects this, with beer mats, brewery advertisements and of course the beer: Teignworth Reel Ale, RCH Pitchfork (a Somerset brewery), Princetown Jail Ale (a Taunton brewery), and regularly changing guest ales. They also recognize that you have to eat sometimes and there is a wide choice of food: home-made soup, sandwiches and ploughman's, filled jacket potatoes, tagliatelle bolognese, home-made 8oz beefburger, ratatouille topped with cheese, homecooked ham, vegetable bake, salads and a changing specials board which could feature roast duck breast served with a morello cherry sauce, lamb casseroled in red wine and mushrooms and salmon and prawn au gratin. There are always three special boards with at least three choices of vegetarian dishes, ten meat and eight fish – something for everyone. Picnic tables in the garden on the other side of the road.

OPEN: Tues–Fri 12–2, 6.30–11. Sat & Sun 12–2.30, 7–11 (7–10.30 Sun). Closed Mon except bank holidays.
Real Ale.
No children. Dogs welcome. Car park.
Cards: all except Amex.

Lundy Island

Marisco Tavern ① 01237 431831
Lundy Island, Bristol Channel, Bideford EX39 2LY
Free House. Paul Roberts, licensee
e-mail: general@lundyisland.co.uk

You probably know it already, but I'm going to tell you anyway that 'Lundy' comes from the old Norse word for puffin. Apt, as there are still puffins on this island, which is now owned by the National Trust, though Lundy, 12 miles off the north Devon coast, is managed by the Landmark Trust. The Marisco, a solid, stone building, is the only place on the sparsely populated island – out of season the population numbers about 20 residents, plus thousands of birds – where you can get a pint of beer and something to eat. In season, the 15,000 or so visitors each year make the inconvenience of living on an island worth the effort of it all. Breakfast, morning coffee, lunch, afternoon tea and dinner are served, light bar meals at lunchtime and a greater choice in the evening. The very traditional pub food includes something for everyone: home-made soup, filled baguettes, mushrooms au gratin, sweet and sour pork, chicken and black bean stir fry, steak and Lundy ale pie, omelettes, specials on the blackboard, children's meals and four vegetarian dishes. Two ales on hand pump – Bass and Exmoor Bitter (Lundy Experience), also Guinness, Celtic Smooth and lagers. Good wine list. Very dependent on the weather and what and who the boat brings in. Reaching Lundy takes about two hours by boat – in favourable conditions – from either Ilfracombe or Bideford. On Lundy there are lots of delightfully restored cottages and houses to stay in – all well managed and beautifully furnished by the Landmark Trust.

OPEN: 8.30–10 for breakfast. 12–2.30, 6–11 officially, but depends on boat arrivals. On boat days lunch is served until 30 mins before departure.
Real Ale.
Children welcome. No dogs.
Cards: MasterCard, Visa only.

Lustleigh

Cleave ① 01647 277223
Lustleigh, nr Newton Abbot TQ13 7TJ
Heavitree. Alison Perring, tenant

This is an attractive village of thatched and creeper-covered granite cottages nestling in the Dartmoor foothills. The 15th-century thatched Cleave, a 13th-century village church keeping a benevolent watch and an occasional cricket match on the village green complete the picture. As one of our readers wrote, 'a blissful place'. Inside, the low-ceilinged bar has a really huge inglenook fireplace. Bar meals are available at lunchtimes and evenings: home-made soups, deep-fried whitebait, chicken liver and brandy paté, tomato and mozzarella salad, hot cheese and onion flan, 'Cleave' steak, kidney and stout pie with a light puff pastry crust and local butcher's sausages with mash and onion gravy. From the specials board you could start with a smoked salmon and prawn parcel or deep fried brie with a sweet and sour sauce, and for a main course, pancakes filled with home-made ratatouille served with a creamy mushroom sauce or half a duckling roasted with honey and served with an orange and Grand Marnier sauce. Roast lunches on Sunday, a good short restaurant menu, home-made puddings too. Bass, Otter Ale and Greene King Abbot on hand pump. Farm ciders. Short wine list, many by the glass. Morning coffee.

OPEN: 11–3, 6–11. Summer 11–11.
Closed all day Monday from Oct to March.
Real Ale.
Children in no-smoking family area. Dogs on leads. Car park. Wheelchair access to pub and gents' W.C.
Cards: Delta, MasterCard, Switch, Visa.

Lutton

Mountain Inn ① 01752 837247
Old Church Lane, Lutton, nr Cornwood, Ivybridge PL21 9SA
Free House. Derek Wilson & Jo Dixon, licensees
e-mail: jod@mail.pml.ac.vic

The Mountain is a traditional village pub near the Wildlife Park on the edge of the Dartmoor National Park. Aptly named – it is up a steep hill – it serves some interesting beers to go with well-presented, traditional bar food: home-made leek and potato soup, lasagne, Cornish pasties, pies and seasonal specials such as beef in Guinness. The beers are Bass, Princetown and two changing guest beers; among them could be something from Badger, Cotleigh, Harviestoun, Charles Wells or the RCH brewery in Weston-super-Mare. Seats on the large terrace with views across the National Park.

OPEN: 11–3, 6–11.
Real Ale.
Children welcome. Dogs on leads. Car park. One step up for wheelchairs.
No cards.

Lydford

Castle Inn & Hotel ① 01822 820242
Lydford, nr Okehampton EX20 4BH
Heavitree. Richard Davis, manager

Easy to find – where else would the inn be but next to the dominating ruins of the 12th-century castle after which it was named? An enchanting, pink-washed building, with low-beamed bars, a no-smoking snug and dining room – which has a very early fireplace. There is a good choice of food from the daily changing blackboard menu to go with the Fullers London Pride and Morlands Old Speckled Hen on hand pump, wines by the glass.

Within walking distance, along a twisting path from the Castle Inn, is the dramatic Lydford Gorge and, at the southern end, the spectacular White Lady waterfall plunging down the cliffs into the River Lyd below.

OPEN: 12–11.
Real Ale. Restaurant.
Accompanied children in snug and lounge by day, in the restaurant in evening. Dogs on leads in bar areas. Car park. Wheelchair access (not WC). Nine individually designed bedrooms.
Cards: Delta, MasterCard, Switch, Visa.

Lydford

Dartmoor Inn at Lydford ➀ 01822 820221
Lydford, Okehampton EX20 4AY
Free House. Philip & Karen Burgess, owners/licensees
e-mail: karen@dartmoorinn.co.uk

On the River Lyd, near a spectacular walk alongside the rushing waters in the wooded Lydford Gorge, this is a pretty, secluded village on the western fringes of the Dartmoor National Park. The Dartmoor itself is a beautifully restored 16th century coaching inn. The interior is a delight, all very comfortable and done with tremendous style; with flowers on the tables, small, intimate dining areas and a big winter fire in the inviting bar. Here you can relax before choosing something from the tempting bar menu. Always a bowl of soup as well as fish and chips with a green mayonnaise, omelette with creamed smoked salmon, chicken liver paté with toast, farmhouse sausages with mustard mash, pan-fried lamb's liver and kidneys with onions or a chargrilled fillet steak with onion rings and maris piper chips. From the restaurant a casserole of Cornish sea bass, scallops and john dory with ginger and green onions and, to finish, a rich hot chocolate pudding with a chocolate sauce and clotted cream. There is also a vegetarian menu, a two- or three-course set lunch and more-ish puds. Dartmoor Best, Bass and London Pride beers and a well-chosen wine list. Seats on the terrace and in the garden.

OPEN: Tues–Sat 11.30–3, 6–11. Sun 12–2.30. Closed Sun eve & Mon.
Real Ale. Restaurant. Food served 12–2.30, 6.30–9.30.
Children welcome, dogs too. Car park. Wheelchair access. Bedrooms from Easter 2004.
Cards: all major cards.

Molland

The London Inn ➀ 01769 550269
Molland, South Molton EX36 3NG
Free House. Michael Short, licensee

Near the river Yeo, this is hilly, farming country on the edge of Exmoor. The thatched 15th-century London Inn is still largely unspoilt, though the interior has been rearranged over the years. The dining room is where the original inn used to be and the bar is in the old brewhouse. The food is good value and ranges from bar snacks to full meals in the dining room. Bar snacks could include savoury pancakes and Welsh rarebit topped with bacon and mushrooms; specials are on the blackboard but from the weekly changing evening menu you could choose a crispy salad with bacon, red peppers and croutons, or Somerset pork tenderloin in a cider cream sauce. Well-kept Cotleigh and Exmoor Ale from casks behind the bar. Sunny garden to sit in. Next to the pub, the village church has links to the legend of Lorna Doone, and a wonderfully complete Georgian interior, including a three-decker pulpit – well worth seeing.

OPEN: Coffee from 11. Bar opens 11.30–2.30, 6–11. Sun 12–2.30, 7–10.30.
Real Ale. Dining Room.
Children welcome. Dogs too. Car park. Wheelchair access. Bed and breakfast accommodation.

Newton St Cyres

Beer Engine ① 01392 851282
Newton St Cyres, Exeter EX5 5AX
Own Brew. Peter Hawksley, FBII, licensee

Built as a railway hotel in the mid 19th century, this is now a well-known brewery and pub where all the beers have a railway theme. Not many trains pass through but the past is remembered in the names they give their beers: Rail Ale, Piston Bitter, Sleeper (obviously rather strong) and occasionally a special brew. You can see through to the brewery from the Boiler Room Bar and tours can be arranged. Reasonably priced bar meals include cod and parsley pie, speciality sausages, lasagne, casseroles, a selection of fresh fish, at least three vegetarian dishes and a vegetarian soup. Roast lunches every Sunday. Rumour has it that there is a female ghost walking the pub, but as the only people who have seen it are the chaps who have had a few beers, it could be a case of a vivid imagination and a few pints of the strong ale! There are tables in the large sunny garden and glorious summer floral displays

OPEN: 11–11. Sun 12–10.30.
Real Ale. You can take home up to 20 litres of beer from the brewery.
Children in eating area. Dogs on leads.
Wheelchair access difficult but possible.

Noss Mayo

Ship Inn ① 01752 872387
Noss Mayo, South Devon PL8 1EW
Free House. Bruce & Lesley Brunning, owners/licensees
e-mail: ship@nossmayo.com

At high tide you can sail right in – with permission – but when the tide is out it really is out – out of sight, and then you are high and dry. On the very edge of the creek, in a village surrounded by National Trust woodland, the Ship has been restored to its former glory to be a proper, village inn. Inside, old furniture on wooden floors, log fires, pictures to look at, bookcases full of books and newspapers to read. The Galley, Bridge and Met Office on the first floor are no-smoking areas. From the daily changing menu, served throughout the pub, there could be smoked Shetland salmon with mustard mayonnaise, button mushrooms in a garlic and chive sauce on granary toast, smooth liver paté with red onion marmalade and brioche and for a main course, roast fillet of wild sea bass served on sun-blushed tomato and spring onion mash, salmon cod and prawn cassoulet served on seafood pasta, medallions of pork tenderloin served on roast vegetables with a Calvados sauce, steaks with herb butter, fries and side salad, Cornish crab salad as well as sandwiches and ploughman's with local cheeses. Summerskills Tamar, Shepherd Neame Spitfire, Dartmoor IPA and West Country Gold are the beers. Something for everyone on the wine list. Views over the creek from the sunny rooms and the tables on the forecourt.

OPEN: 12–11.
Real Ale.
Children welcome until 7.30 p.m. Dogs on leads. Car park – this depends on the tide too! Wheelchair access.
Cards: all except Amex.

Rattery

Church House ① 01364 642220
Rattery, South Brent TQ10 9LD
Free House. Ray Hardy, licensee

There are huge beams inside Church House holding up this listed building, which dates back to the early 11th century. Thought to be the oldest pub in Devon, it has a beamed open bar, large fireplaces, a cosy snug and no-smoking dining room. Obviously a building with strong ecclesiastical roots, it's said to be connected to the church by a tunnel. The range of bar food available includes freshly made soup, filled baguettes, ploughman's, plain and toasted sandwiches, devilled whitebait, creamy coconut chicken curry, steak and kidney pie, fisherman's pie, fresh salmon fillet with white wine, tarragon and cream sauce, chicken in a whisky and cream sauce, grills, vegetarian dishes and a children's menu. Furgusons Dartmoor Best, Abbott Ale, Marstons Pedigree and a guest beer on hand pump. Range of old malt whiskies. Farm cider. Between 50 and 60 wines to choose from. Seats in the beer garden. Lovely views of the wooded countryside from the pub.

OPEN: 11–2.30, 6–11.
Real Ale.
Children welcome. Dogs on leads. Wheelchair access with help.
Cards: most accepted but not Amex.

Sheepwash

Half Moon ① 01409 231376
Sheepwash, nr Hatherleigh, N. Devon EX21 5NE
Free House. Nathan & Lee Adey, licensees
e-mail: lee@halfmoon.demon.co.uk

Between Hatherleigh and Holsworthy, the long, white-painted Half Moon has ten miles of fishing rights for salmon, sea and brown trout on the nearby River Torridge. A thriving fishermen's pub and hotel, totally geared up for all eventualities: a rod room, somewhere to dry yourself when you fall in, and a tackle shop where you can buy all those bits and pieces you thought you had packed. Fishing pictures to encourage you and a big log fire in the beamed bar to warm you. Bar snacks at lunchtime are all you could wish for: home-made soup, sandwiches, hot home-made pasties, home-cured ham salad, two cheese ploughman's, home-made cottage pie and filled jacket potatoes. Dinner at night includes pork Normandy, beef medallions, steaks and fresh fish. Courage Best, Ruddles Best and one locally brewed ale as a guest on hand pump. Selection of malt whiskies. Impressive wine list.

OPEN: 11.30–2.30, 6–11.
Real Ale. Evening restaurant. Snacks at lunchtime.
Children lunchtime only. Dogs on leads in bar. Wheelchair access. 14 bedrooms en suite.

South Pool

Mill Brook ① 01548 531581
South Pool, Kingsbridge TQ7 2RW
Free House. Peter Evans & Claire Starkey, licensees

A pretty village of colour-washed cottages at the head of a natural creek off the Kingsbridge estuary. Banks of mud at low tide but at high tide you can virtually sail straight in and order drinks – very popular with the local sailors and visiting yachtsmen. Inside is a charming, comfortable bar with lots of fresh flowers on the tables where they serve good, dependable bar food such as soup, home-made paté, smoked salmon, ploughman's, a variety of sandwiches – including their popular crab sandwiches – salads, cottage pie, home-made fisherman's pie, Cumberland sausages and mash and lasagne. Daily specials too. Fullers London Pride, Bass and Wadworths 6X plus a guest ale on hand pump and farm ciders. Seats on the delightful terrace at the back of the pub by the old mill stream and at the front – both covered and with heaters.

OPEN: Summer 11–3, 5.30–11 or longer. Winter 11.30–2.30, 6.30–11, all approx.
Real Ale.
Children in family room. No dogs. Wheelchair access difficult.

Sticklepath

Devonshire Inn ① 01837 840626
Sticklepath, Okehampton EX20 2NW
Free House. John & Ann Verner-Jeffreys, licensees

Until 1960, they used to make tools for Devon's farmers and miners next door in Finch's Foundry, now a museum run by the National Trust where you can still see the three huge water wheels that drove the forges, grindstones and polishing wheels. The Devonshire, a friendly, popular, 17th-century thatched local has a low-beamed, slate-floored bar with comfortable furnishings, a small cosy snug, big log fires in winter and something to read if you're waiting. The food is reasonably priced and freshly cooked to order; they also cater for small dinner parties on request. Booked meals only on Sunday and in the evening. Real ales include St Austell's Tinners, Bass and some guest beers. Farm cider.

OPEN: 11–3, 5–11. Fri, Sat & summer weekdays 11–11. Sun 12–3, 7–10.30.
Real Ale.
Children under control. Dogs always welcome. Wheelchair access (not WC). Bed and breakfast available – for dogs too.

Stokenham

Tradesman's Arms ① 01548 580313
Stokenham, Kingsbridge TQ7 2SZ
Free House. Nick & Rebecca Abbott, licensees

Between Dartmouth and Kingsbridge, this pretty thatched, 15th-century pub has a heavily beamed bar warmed by a wood-burning stove and, off to one side, a no-smoking room. All the tables can be reserved (very advisable at the weekend), but if you just want a drink you are very welcome to come and lean on the bar. Food is the thing though – interesting and creative. For starters you can choose soup of the day, mussels steamed with garlic, white wine and cream, goat's cheese, tomato and pine nut salad, three-fish terrine, and for a main course, pan-fried turbot with Parisienne potatoes and a coconut curry sauce, fillet of Devon beef, saddle of monkfish, wild mushroom tagliatelle and saffron cream of Barbary duck breast, cream cabbage and pancetta redcurrant jus. Always three draught beers and an extensive wine list. Heron Valley cider and a fine range of malts.

OPEN: 11–3, 6–11 (Sat 6.30–11). Sun 12–3, 7–10.30.
Real Ale.
Children welcome. Dogs in bar. Car park. Wheelchair access (not WC).
Cards: Delta, JCB, MasterCard, Switch, Visa.

Topsham

Bridge Inn ① 01392 873862
Bridge Hill, Topsham EX3 0PQ
Free House. Mrs C. Cheffers-Heard, licensee
www.cheffers.co.uk

An enchanting town, a bustling port until the 17th century, between the tidal rivers Exe and Clyst. The handsome 16th-century pink-washed, Grade II Bridge Inn – with even earlier foundations – has been in the same family for five generations. This is an unspoilt gem of a pub with panelled walls, log fire and sizeable settles. Traditional pub food only – three different ploughman's – including smoked chicken, home-made winter soup, sandwiches and hot meat and potato pasties – but lots of different beers. Years ago they used to brew their own; now they try different ones, but Blackawton West Country Gold,

Exe Valley, Otter and Branscombe ales, also O'Hanlons Port Stout are permanent and many other West Country ales are guests.

OPEN: 12–2. 6–10.30 (Fri & Sat 6–11, Sun 7–10.30).
Real Ale.
Children welcome. Dogs in the tap room.

Torquay

Crown & Sceptre ☎ 01803 328290
2 Petitor Road, St Marychurch, Torquay TQ1 4QA
I. P. L. Co. R.D. Wheeler, licensee

Originally an 18th-century coaching inn, this is now a friendly two-bar local serving exceptionally good beer in an exceptional town. Subtropical trees and a mild climate make Torquay the nearest thing we have to the French Riviera. At the Crown & Sceptre they serve sustaining pub fare, ranging from plain or toasted sandwiches, ploughman's, pasties, ham, egg and chips, seafood platter, filled jacket potatoes to daily specials. Courage Best Bitter and Directors, Youngs Special, Morlands Old Speckled Hen, Fullers London Pride, Marstons Pedigree and two different guest ales every week.

OPEN: 11–3, 5.30–11.
Real Ale.
No children. Dogs welcome.
N.B. Live music – folk and jazz – Tues and Sun eves.

Tuckenhay

Maltsters Arms ☎ 01803 732350
Tuckenhay, nr Totnes TQ9 7EQ
Free House. Denise & Quentin Thwaites, licensees
e-mail: pub@tuckenhay.demon.co.uk

Its position is unrivalled, overlooking the lovely, wooded Bow creek off the River Dart – very appealing to sailors who can moor here, and everyone else, however they arrive. Inside the 18th-century Maltsters Arms is a narrow bar linking a snug and dining area. The bar menu offers plenty of choice and variety; as well as ploughman's, double-decker sandwiches and home-made soups, there could be clams and mussels in cream and vanilla, smoked salmon, mackerel and trout with dill mayonaise, chicken and spinach curry with spring roll, chargrilled lamb steak with gooseberry and mint jelly, steak, kidney and Guiness pie, fish from Brixham harbour and dishes using locally caught, and raised, game – both the lunch and evening menus change daily. Princetown Dartmoor IPA, changing guests, many local, and a good wine list. You can sit by the creek and watch all the comings and goings. Moorings for your boat. Barbecues at the weekend.

OPEN: 11–11. Christmas Day, bar only 12–2.
Real Ale.
Children in certain rooms. Dogs on leads. Wheelchair access (not WC). Bedrooms overlook the river.
Cards: MasterCard, Switch, Visa.
Live music first and third Friday of each month.

Widecombe-in-the-Moor

Rugglestone Inn ☽ 01364 621327
Widecombe-in-the-Moor, S. Devon TQ13 7TF
Free House. Diane & Rod Williams, licensees

In a fold of hills, Widecombe is the capital of the moor. Uncle Tom Cobleigh and the well-known song Widecombe Fair made this tourist village famous and the fair is still held on the second Tuesday in September. The 'Rugglestone', after which the pub is named, is a huge granite stone on the moor, south of the village. On a lane just outside the village, the pub is a favourite stopping place for the locals, walkers and anyone enjoying the glories of Dartmoor. Very unspoilt with stone floors in the small beamed rooms – just the thing for all those walking boots – and open fires. Menus are listed on the blackboards and change regularly; all very traditional 'English' cooking now. Beer is served through a hatch: draught Bass, Butcombe Bitter and St Austell Dartmoor Best. Plenty of room and shelter for children in the garden on the other side of the stream.

OPEN: 11.30–3, 6.30–11.
Real Ale.
Children welcome except in public bar. Dogs welcome too. Wheelchair access (not WC). No cards.

Whimple

New Fountain Inn ☽ 01404 822350
Church Road, Whimple, Exeter EX5 2TA
Free House. Paul Mallett, licensee

This is cider country and the village is the original home of Whiteway's cider. Next door to the village museum, the New Fountain is cosy and welcoming; they serve good-value food to go with the local beer: freshly made sandwiches, ploughman's, garlic mushrooms, chef's choice of paté, whitebait, home-made steak and kidney pie, locally cooked ham, mini steak in a crusty roll with onions and mushrooms, home-made chicken curry and daily specials such as a Dartmouth smoked chicken and seafood platter. Three vegetarian dishes always available. The steaks on the evening menu come from West Country herds. Whenever possible all produce is locally sourced. Teignworthy Reel Ale, O'Hanlons beers and a keg cider, Pheasant Plucker, from Bristol. Seats in the beer garden.

OPEN: 12–2.30, 6.30–11.
Real Ale.
Children welcome. Dogs too. Car park. Wheelchair access (not WC).
Cards: Electron, JCB, Maestro, MasterCard, Solo, Switch, Visa.

Woodland

Rising Sun ① 01364 652544
Woodland, Ashburton TQ13 7JT
Free House. Heather Humphries, licensee
e-mail: mail@risingsunwoodland.co.uk

Between Torbay and Dartmoor, look out for the pub's very own signpost; you will see it deep in the Devon countryside between the A38 and the A381. Well worth finding for the comfortable, welcoming, beamed interior where they provide some really good bar snacks, including home-made pies (which you can also order to take home), soup, local sausages, local venison and home-made chutney to go with the ploughman's. Scrummy home-made puds. More choices on the changing blackboard menu. Roast lunch Sunday. Princetown Jail Ale and maybe two guests. A couple of family areas in the pub, and a play area in the garden so you can park the little darlings.

OPEN: 11–3, 6–11. Sun 12–3.30, 7–10.30.
Real Ale. Restaurant.
Children in eating areas and restaurant. Dogs on leads.
Bedrooms.

BEST OF THE REST

Bantham
Sloop Inn ① 01548 560489/560215
Bantham, nr Kingsbridge TQ7 3AJ
The Sloop is in a naturally beautiful area, very near the coastal path and sandy beaches. This interesting old smuggling inn was once owned by a famous smuggler, John Whiddon. Traditional pub grub on the bar menu, also a variety of fishy things – all very fresh: sea bass, monkfish, lobster – also local steaks and good home-made puddings. Draught Bass, Ushers Best and bottled beers. Comprehensive wine list and lots of malt whiskies. Children, dogs and wheelchairs can all get in.
Open: 11–2.30, 6–11. Sun 12–2.30, 7–10.30.

Dartington
Cott Inn ① 01803 863777
Dartington TQ9 6HE
Whitewashed stone, touches of black, and a great deal of thatch: the 14th-century Cott – first licensed in 1320 – looks, and is, solid and prosperous. Pretty as a picture outside; inside are beams, flagstone floors, big fireplaces and lots of room. At lunchtime there is a choice of salads, cold meats, Dart salmon, quiches, etc. Otherwise you could have a

country terrine with Cumberland sauce, tenderloin of pork with bacon, mushrooms, green peppers in a mustard sauce; menus change daily. Otter ales, Wadworths 6X and an interesting wide-ranging wine list. Children, dogs on leads. Bedrooms. Wheelchair access into pub, but not bedrooms.
Open: 11–2.30, 5.30–11.

Sidford
Blue Ball ① 01395 514062
Sidford EX10 9QL
North of Sidmouth, the Blue Ball is big, thatched and family friendly. Beamed and comfortable, it serves a fairly traditional pub menu of sandwiches, ploughman's, locally made sausages, fresh fish, steak pie and daily specials. Boddingtons, Flowers, Otter and a guest beer, all well kept, and a changing choice of wines. Children in restaurant and family room. Play area outside. Bedrooms.
Open: 10.30–11. Sun 12–10.30.

Stockland
Kings Arms ① 01404 881361
Stockland EX14 9BS
Off the Chard to Honiton road, this 16th-century, white-painted thatched inn has an interesting interior: beams, a medieval oak screen and a huge stone fireplace big enough to take half a tree. A well-used bar for the locals, otherwise they concentrate on some seriously good food: king prawn thermidor, pigeon rossini, lamb Siciliano, prawn curry, steak au poivre and more-ish puds. Note: there are no Sunday, or evening, bar snacks. Courage Directors, John Smiths, Otter and Exmoor ale. Good wine list, some by the glass, and farm ciders. Children if eating, dogs in bar. Wheelchair access. Bedrooms.
Open: 12–3, 6–11.

Stokeinteignhead
Church House ① 01626 872475
Stokeinteignhead TQ12 4QA
A really old – well, most of it – thatched pub in an unspoilt village north of Torquay. Some interesting additions (seafood pancakes, chargrilled chicken, breast of duck) to the usual menu to go with the Bass, Flowers and Wadworths. Farm ciders too. Children welcome.
Open: 11–3, 5.30–11. Sun 12–3, 6.30–10.30.

Woodbury Salterton
Diggers Rest ① 01395 232375
Woodbury Salterton, nr Exeter EX5 1PQ
e-mail: bar@diggersrest.co.uk
A huge amount of work has been completed by the new owners to bring this lovely old pub up to scratch. Everything that needed renewing, improving and rebuilding has been done without taking away the charm of this heavily beamed, thatched, 14th-century village pub. All is as it should be with open fires, old polished tables, comfortable chairs and sofas. Tremendously popular at lunchtime when they serve a variety of bar food including a pot of mixed olives to nibble on, home-made soup, sandwiches and filled baguettes, warm red onion and Parmesan tart, crudités and chargrilled pitta bread, roast chicken, blue cheese and apple salad and lots more. Local produce whenever possible; always fresh vegetables and home-made puddings. London Pride, Otter Ale and Bitter.

Interesting wines with bin ends on the blackboard. Outside are lots of seats on the re-developed, secluded terrace. Well-behaved children in family area. No dogs.
Open: 11–2.30, 6.30–11.

Wetherspoon in Devon

Barnstaple – Panniers, 33–34 Boutport Street
℧ 01271 329720
Brixham – Vigilance, 4 Bolton Street
℧ 01803 850489
Crediton – General Sir Redvers Buller, 37 High Street
℧ 01363 774381
Exeter – Imperial, New North Road
℧ 01392 43405
Exmouth – Powder Monkey, 2–2a The Parade
℧ 01395 280090
Newton Abbot – Richard Hopkins, 34–42 Queen Street
℧ 01626 323930
Paignton – Isaac Merritt, 54–58 Torquay Road
℧ 01803 556066
Plymouth – Britannia Inn, 1 Wolsey Road, Milehouse
℧ 01752 607596
Plymouth – Gog & Magog, Southside Street
℧ 01752 264160
Plymouth – Mannamead, 61–63 Mutley Plain
℧ 01752 825610
Plymouth – Union Rooms, 19 Union Street
℧ 01752 254520
Tiverton – White Ball Inn, Bridge Street
℧ 01884 251525
Torquay – London Inn, 15–16 The Strand
℧ 01803 380003

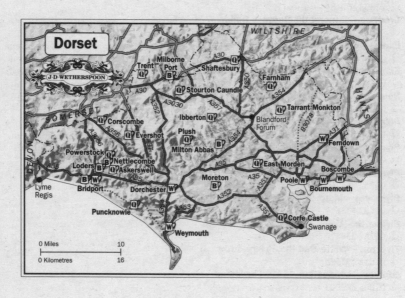

Dorset

Askerswell

Spyway Inn ① 01308 485250
Askerswell, nr Bridport DT2 9EP
Free House. Kevin Wilkes, licensee

Above the village, this old inn, reputedly a haunt of smugglers when smuggling was rife in Dorset, has a pretty, south-facing garden with a wonderful vista over glorious countryside towards the coast. It's an area full of panoramic views; the steep lane next to the pub leads to Eggardon Hill, all 827 feet of it, which has an Iron Age hill fort and Bronze Age barrows at the summit. Inside the beamed, rambling Spyway Inn is a fine collection of decorative rural objects. From the printed menu there is soup of the day, home-cooked ham and other fillings for the baguettes or baps, ploughman's, filled jacket potatoes from the bar or steak, ale and mushroom pudding, sausage and mash, wild boar sausages, grilled salmon fillet, honey roast duck, steaks and much more from the main menu. Well-kept Adnams Southwold Bitter, Greene King Abbot, Branscombe Vale's Branoc and a summer guest beer. Wines by the glass, country wines and a large selection of malt whiskies.

OPEN: 11–2.30, 6–11. Sun 12–3. Closed Sun eve and all day Mon.
Real Ale.
Children allowed in restaurant. Dogs in garden only – on leads. Wheelchair access (not WC).

Bournemouth

Moon in the Square ① 01202 314940
4–8 Exeter Road, Bournemouth BH2 5AD
Wetherspoon.

Large and thriving, this pub is on two floors – the top one totally non-smoking. Unusually for a town-centre pub, it also has an outside drinking area, where you can smoke. As with all Wetherspoon outlets there will be five or six cask ales and a big selection of guest beers from the smaller breweries. One beer will be considerably cheaper than elsewhere. Consistently reliable bar food: ploughman's, filled jacket potatoes or baps, different burgers, a vegetarian dish, haddock and chips, bangers and mash – that sort of thing.

OPEN: 10.30–11. Sun 12–10.30.
Real Ale.
No children. No dogs.

Corfe Castle

Fox Inn ① 01929 480449
West Street, Corfe Castle BH20 5HD
Free House. Miss A. Brown & Graham White, licensees

Besieged by Cromwell during the Civil War, the remains of Corfe Castle, high on the hill, overlook the village. Inevitably, much of the stone from the castle ruins found its way into the walls of the local buildings. The Fox is a very old, unchanging place; ancient architectural remains found within the pub have been incorporated in the changes made over the years, including a very ancient fireplace; there's also a well, now with a glass cover, which was found during restoration work. The pub serves a traditional bar menu plus daily specials; vegetarian dishes always available. Sunday roasts in winter. Morlands Old Speckled Hen, Marstons Pedigree, Youngs Special, Fullers London Pride, Greene King Abbot, Wadworths 6X and Burton Ale. Outside, the dramatic castle ruins are part of the scenery from the mature, sheltered and sunny garden of the old inn. Good walking country.

OPEN: 11–3, 6–11. Winter 11–2.30, 6.30–11.
Real Ale.
Children in the garden only. Dogs welcome. Cards: all major cards accepted.

Corscombe

Fox Inn ① 01935 891330
Corscombe DT2 0NS (off A356 south of Crewkerne towards Dorchester, take the left turn to Corscombe & Halstock, NOT the one just to Corscombe. Pub at bottom of hill)
Free House. Clive Webb owner, Peter Rice, licensee
e-mail: dine@fox-inn.co.uk

When you look at the Fox for the first time it seems the most perfect country pub, and you won't be disappointed. Everything radiates a general air of well-being. The thatched, cream-painted building has thatched hats over the doors, climbing roses and hanging baskets on the walls. Inside is just as atmospheric, with flagstones, beams, inglenook fireplaces and comfortable furnishings. Good things are happening in the kitchen too, and the food is all you could wish for: seafood risotto with mussels and prawns, French beans with bacon, garlic and olive oil, mushroom- and bacon-filled filo baskets, medallions of tuna au poivre, herb-crusted fillets of brill with red pesto, rabbit braised with mustard, cream and rosemary, Moroccan leg of lamb tagine, braised venison with wild mushrooms, thyme and red wine, beef braised with bacon, mushrooms and red wine, Burmese beef curry, imaginative vegetarian dishes and desirable puddings. All vegetables are freshly cooked. Exmoor Ale, Exmoor Fox and Fullers London Pride beers. Good, well-chosen wine list – only house wines by the glass; home-made damson vodka, sloe gin and elderflower cordial. Tables outside and by the stream; there is also a conservatory full of flowers and a really large oak table.

OPEN: 12–2.45, 7–11-ish.
Real Ale. Restaurant.
Well-behaved children. No dogs. Car park. Wheelchair access (not WC). Four bedrooms.
Cards: Amex, Delta, MasterCard, Switch, Visa.

East Morden

Cock & Bottle ☎ 01929 459238
East Morden, nr Wareham BH20 7DL
Badger. Pete Meadley, licensee

An original cob-walled longhouse is incorporated in this cosy, welcoming pub, which is over 300 years old. Though it's close to the road there are wonderfully open views over fields from the back. The rambling beamed interior has good winter fires, several dining areas – one no-smoking – and a public bar with music. Food is plentiful and varied, ranging from interesting bar snacks and meals – with a good choice of fish and game – to dishes with an international bias: crab and ginger tartlet, roast partridge wrapped in bacon with port wine, ragout of seafood with white wine sauce. Always very busy, so you should book if you want to eat. Badger Dorset Best, Tanglefoot and King and Barnes Sussex. Short wine list, some by the glass. Outside there are seats on the terrace and in the beer garden with views across the open country.

OPEN: 11–2.30, 6–11. Sun 12–3, 7–10.30.
Real Ale. Restaurant.
Children welcome. Dogs too. Car park. Wheelchair access.
Cards: Delta, MasterCard, Switch, Visa.

Evershot

Acorn Inn ☎ 01935 83228
Fore Street, Evershot, Dorchester DT2 0JW
Free House, Todd & Louise Moffat, licensees

Deep in Hardy country and surrounded by gentle Dorset hills, the Acorn, in a delightfully unchanging village, features in Thomas Hardy's novel *Tess of the d'Urbervilles*. Beamed, polished and handsome, this comfortable 16th-century inn is everything it should be. They serve a more traditional bar menu than did the previous regime, with soup, sandwiches, salmon fishcakes, a pasta dish and home-made steak and kidney pie, that sort of thing. A greater choice is available in the restaurant. Butcombe Bitter is the beer and you'll find a comprehensive wine list. A small garden to sit in and lots of good walks in the

surrounding area. Midway between Yeovil and Dorchester, so it's not far from the Fleet Air Arm museum at Yeovilton and the Thomas Hardy museum in Dorchester.

OPEN: 11.30–2.30, 6.30–11.
Real Ale.
Children welcome. Dogs too. Car park. Wheelchair access (not WC). Nine classy bedrooms – all en suite. Well-behaved dogs can bring their suitcases too.
Cards: Amex, Delta, MasterCard, Switch, Visa.

Farnham

Museum Inn ① 01725 516261
Farnham, nr Blandford Forum DT11 8DE
Free House. Mark Stephenson & Vicky Elliot, licensees
e-mail: enquiries@museuminn.co.uk

This partly thatched, 17th-century inn on the Dorset-Wiltshire border is at the heart of Cranborne Chase. The Museum is that very desirable mix of traditional local pub and country-house hotel where they serve some very, very good food. Inside there is a spacious flagstone-floored bar – with an inglenook fireplace – leading to the other areas, including the dining room. Menus change daily, but there could be bubble and squeak, poached free-range egg and hollandaise as a starter, as well as guinea fowl and wild mushroom terrine, sultana toast and spice apples, mushroom and artichoke soup with parmesan shavings and for a main course, a bouillabaisse made with sea bass, scallops and salmon with croutes and parmesan, Scotch fillet of beef roasted with bacon and wild mushrooms, slow-braised lamb casserole, shallot dumplings, aubergines, mint and tomatoes and really yummy puds such as apple and hazelnut crumble with vanilla ice cream or lemon cheesecake with lemon macaroons to finish. A roast beef sandwich or smoked ham and Gruyère toastie if you just want a quick snack. The produce used in the kitchens is local, traceable, traditionally grown and reared. Bread is baked every day and they make all the pickles, chutneys and marmalade. Three ales on tap from the smaller breweries such as Exmoor or Ringwood. Eight wines by the glass from an encompassing list.

OPEN: 12–3, 6–11. Sat 12–11. Sun 12–10.30.
Real Ale. Restaurant, only open Fri and Sat eves and Sun lunchtime.
Children over 8. Dogs welcome. Car park.

Ibberton

Crown ① 01258 817448
Church Lane, Ibberton, nr Blandford DE11 0EN
Free House. John Wild, licensee

Small and idyllic, a 16th-century pub in the heart of the well-wooded and beautiful Blackmoor Vale watered by the Stour and Lydden rivers. Inside are flagstone floors, a big inglenook fireplace and historic photographs of times past. Traditional bar food ranges from soup and sandwiches to pies, chicken dishes, fresh fish and grills. They serve local

Burrow Hill cider, very well-kept Butcombe Bitter and a changing guest. Seats in the attractive garden which has its own small stream.

OPEN: 11–2, 7–11 (summer 5.30–11).
Real Ale.
Children welcome. No dogs. Car park. Wheelchair access (not WC).

Plush

Brace of Pheasants ☏ 01300 348357
Plush, Dorchester DT2 7RQ
Free House. Toby & Suzie Albu, licensees

Yes, pheasants are on the menu at the right time of year, and a stuffed brace of them are permanent residents welcoming you into the pub. Plush, the hamlet, Plush the brook – and plush the inn, brightly white and thatched. Inside, this 16th-century building is beamed, polished and traditionally furnished with an eclectic collection of paintings, ceramics and country tools. Big log fires in winter; sometimes in summer too. Good, popular bar food with creative 'extras': toasted focaccia sandwiches, salmon fishcakes, wild game terrine with red onion marmalade and the pub's signature dish 'Brace of Bangers' – two large venison sausages with mash – is always on the menu. From the seasonally changing menu there could be roasted partridge with a cep and polenta mash, pan-fried fillet of cod with roasted cherry tomatoes, calves' liver and bacon and a specials board with more exciting dishes. Delicious puds and popular Sunday roasts. Both the restaurant and family room are no smoking. Very well-kept beers, maybe Fullers London Pride, Bass, Ringwood Best and a guest available at peak times. All served straight from the cask. A good, international wine list with eight available by the glass. Lovely walks in real 'Hardy' country.

OPEN: 12–3, 7–11. Closed Mon.
Real Ale. No-smoking restaurant.
Children welcome. Dogs on leads. Wheelchair access (not WC).
Cards: Delta, MasterCard, Switch, Visa.

Powerstock

Three Horseshoes ☏ 01308 485328
Powerstock DT6 3TF
Palmers. Andy & Marie Preece, tenants

You are surrounded by glorious countryside, and from the large pub garden there are fine views across rolling fields towards the sea. Next to the church, the old stone-built Three Horseshoes was rebuilt in 1906 after a damaging fire. Inside this popular local is one bar and an attractive, panelled, no-smoking restaurant. It's a busy, friendly place that uses as much local produce as possible. On the lunch menu will be home-made soup, Blue Vinny ploughman's, wild boar sausages and mash; venison, lamb shanks, steaks and a choice of fish in the evening. Home-made puds. Good, short, wine list; six by the glass. The ales are Bridport Bitter and Palmers IPA. Seats in the garden.

OPEN: 11–3, 6.30–11.
Real Ale. Restaurant.
Children in restaurant and garden. Dogs welcome. Car park. Wheelchair access.
Bedrooms.
Cards: MasterCard, Switch, Visa.

Puncknowle

Crown Inn ① 01308 897711
Church Street, Puncknowle, nr Dorchester, DT2 9BN
Palmers. Mike Lawless, tenant
e-mail: thecrowninn@puncknowle48.fsnet.co.uk

Opposite the church in a quiet village full of honey-coloured stone houses, this beamed and spacious well-run 16th-century thatched inn offers a wide choice of well-prepared food: home-made soup, freshly made sandwiches, ploughman's, filled jacket potatoes, smoked peppered mackerel, gammon steak topped with pineapple, chicken Kiev, whole trout topped with toasted almonds, pork and apple casserole cooked in cider, as well as home-cooked steak and kidney pie cooked in Guinness, vegetarian dishes, grills and more besides. Children's portions and a traditional Sunday lunch. Palmers Copper, IPA and Tally Ho!, when available, 200 (the Anniversary Ale), and a selection of country wines. Seats in the big garden where they sometime erect a marquee for large functions. Outside bars. Delightful area with lots of walks. You are about two miles inland from Chesil Beach – that 10-mile long strip of banked shingle fringing the Dorset coast.

OPEN: 11–2.30, 7–11.
Real Ale.
Children welcome in the family room. Dogs on leads in the public bar, and to stay.
Wheelchair access. Bedrooms.
Once a month, during the summer, the Wessex Military Band gives a Sunday lunchtime concert.

Shaftesbury

Ye Olde Two Brewers ① 01747 854211
24 St James Street, Shaftesbury SP7 8HE
Enterprise Inns. Tracy & Harvey Jones, lease

From the top of the incredibly steep, cobbled Gold Hill – famous if you're old enough to remember it as the street in the Hovis advert – you have a view over the roofs of thatched and stone cottages towards the Blackmoor Vale and the Stour. Somewhere among the roofs is this pub, easily found as the name is painted on the tiles! When you get there, you'll find a large, open-plan, comfortable, carpeted bar with several different drinking areas. New licensees now, but there is still something for everyone on the menu which lists soup, sandwiches, ploughman's, steak and ale pie – traditional pub food and a vegetarian dish or two. Good puds. Well-kept Fullers London Pride, Green King, Courage Directors and frequent guests. From the front door of the pub you look directly at the hill site of the ruined abbey, founded in AD 880 by King Alfred the Great. Wonderful views from the garden too.

OPEN: 11–3, 6–11. Sun 12–3, 7–10.30.
Real Ale.
Children welcome. No dogs. Wheelchair access (not WC).

Stourton Caundle

Trooper Inn ① 01963 362405
Stourton Caundle, nr Sturminster Newton, DT10 2JW
Free House. Richard Soar, licensee

Not only a pub but a small private museum as well, the Trooper has a fascinating collection of old country tools and artifacts on the bar walls and more in the skittle alley. In an attractive village, deep in the Dorset countryside, this two-bar, stone-built inn is between Stalbridge and Sherborne. A traditional lunchtime bar menu is served to go with Cottages Champflower, Hampshires King Alfred, Oakhill Best, Otter Bitter and something from the Exmoor brewery. Evening meals by arrangement. Various traditional ciders – Thatchers or Burrow Hill. Tables at the front of the pub and a small beer garden.

OPEN: 12–2.30 (not Mon), 7–11.
Real Ale.
Children and dogs welcome. Wheelchairs difficult (not WC). Bed and breakfast available.

Tarrant Monkton

Langton Arms ① 01258 830225
Tarrant Monkton, nr Blandford DT11 8RX
Free House. Mrs Barbara Cossins, owner/licensee
e-mail: info@thelangtonarms.co.uk

Near the church, in a delightful hamlet, the 300-year-old thatched Langton Arms looks the perfect village pub. Outside there are flowers around the door, inside there are beams, an inglenook fireplace, good food and well-kept beers – all you could possibly want. You have a wide choice from the menus and blackboard specials: filled baguettes, ploughman's, baked potatoes, lasagne, liver and bacon, fillet of salmon, wild boar sausages, pot roast rabbit, fish and chips or a lamb and rosemary stew. Home-made chutney to go with the ploughman's and home-made puddings to finish. There is a no-smoking dining room in a converted stable where they hold the occasional themed evenings. A changing number of wines by the glass and ever-changing beers that could include Flashmans Clout, Smiles Best and Ringwood Fortyniner ales. Seats and play area in the garden. Good walks nearby. Annual beer festival.

OPEN: 11–11. Sun 12–10.30.
Real Ale. Restaurant.
Children welcome. Dogs on leads. Bedrooms. Car park. Wheelchair access.
Cards: MasterCard, Switch, Visa.
N.B. Jukebox in the snug and background music in restaurant, but bar quiet.

Trent

Rose & Crown ☏ 01935 850776
Trent, nr Sherborne DT9 4SL
Free House. Ian Phillips, licensee
e-mail: ian@roseandcrowntrent.fsnet.co.uk

With roses around the door, the unspoilt, partly thatched Rose and Crown is a 15th-century pub with an 18th-century addition. Inside is one big bar leading to smaller rooms and distributed among these are beams, flagstone floors and three open fires. A dining room/conservatory is at the back. You are spoilt for choice on the food front as you can order something from the bar, from the full menu or from the daily specials. From the bar there are lunchtime salads, various fillings for the ciabattas, steak and kidney pie, scampi and chips, home-cooked ham, egg and chips, ploughman's or a chicken or prawn curry. Among the dishes on the full menu will be Dorset farmhouse paté with home-made chutney, Cornish mussels in white wine and cream liquor and, for a main course, seafood mornay, pan-fried chicken on a bed of creamed leeks, pasta carbonara in a cream sauce or fillet of beef in a red wine and mushroom sauce; puds from the board and interesting cheeses, some of them local. Shepherd Neame Spitfire and three varying guest ales. Lovely views from the large garden. Swings and slides in the hope that children will stay outside.

OPEN: 12–3, 7–11. Closed Sun eve and Mon.
Real Ale. Conservatory/restaurant.
Children preferably in garden but there is a special room. Dogs welcome. Wheelchair access. Bed and breakfast.
Cards: all major cards except Amex.

BEST OF THE REST

Bridport
George ☏ 01308 423187
4 South Street, Bridport DT6 3NQ
This ancient town was once famous for its now defunct rope-making industry, something that could account for the exceptionally wide streets which were needed by the rope-makers. Handsome, busy and well run, the George is opposite the Georgian Guildhall. They serve everything from morning coffee to better than average home-made dishes, fresh fish and a choice of English cheeses. Palmers ales as well as decent wines. Children in family room.
Open: 11–11 (earlier for coffee).

Loders
Loders Arms ☏ 01308 422431
Loders DT6 3SA
When you think of Dorset, this is the sort of village that comes to mind. Deep in the country north of Bridport, it's full of thatched stone cottages as well as the attractive, appealing, well-run Loders Arms. Here they serve traditional bar food as well as some inspired options and home-made puddings. Palmers ales. Children and dogs welcome – in certain areas. Wheelchair access. Two bedrooms.
Open: 11.30–3, 6–11. Sun 12–10.30.

Milborne Port

Queens Head ① 01963 250314

High Street, Milborne Port, nr Sherborne DT9 5DQ

Not what it seems; this early Georgian building is basically Elizabethan and Milborne Port has nothing to do with the sea – no whiff of ozone here! The pub serves a traditional menu and specials on the blackboard. On Mondays there is a two-course meal for £5.25; Tuesdays you get a free bottle of wine if the order is over £18.50; Wednesday evening is curry night; on Thursdays you can have two steaks for the price of one! Ales include the regulars – Fullers London Pride, Butcombe Bitter and Old Speckled Hen – and there are two different ciders to choose from. Children welcome. Dogs in public bar – with the music. Wheelchair access (not WC).

Open: 11–2.30, 5.30–11. Sat & Sun 11–11.

Milton Abbas

Hambro Arms ① 01258 880233

Milton Abbas DT11 0BP

The Earl of Dorchester built this village of whitewashed thatched cottages in the 1770s. At its heart is the Hambro Arms, serving familiar bar snacks, a selection of hot dishes, as well as daily specials from the blackboard and a choice of fresh fish. On Sundays, there is a popular lunchtime carvery. Boddingtons and Flowers Original ales. Seats outside on the terrace. No children or dogs.

Open: 11–3, 6.30–11.

N.B. There is a jukebox in the pool room which you can sometimes hear.

Moreton

Frampton Arms ① 01305 852253

Moreton, nr Dorchester DT2 8BB

T. E. Lawrence is buried in Moreton churchyard and inside the church are some wonderful etchings by Lawrence Whistler. The Frampton Arms has a quiet lunchtime restaurant and a charming conservatory. On the menu are home-made soups, freshly filled sandwiches, casseroles, seafood and fish specialities, also a small selection of daily specials and vegetarian dishes on the blackboard. Boddingtons and Flowers IPA and a short wine list. Music in evenings. Children welcome. Dogs in public bar.

Open: 11–2.30, 6–11.

Nettlecombe

Marquis of Lorne ① 01308 485236

Nettlecombe DT6 3SY

In a peaceful setting on a narrow country lane off the Bridport to Beaminster road, what started out as a 16th-century farmhouse is now a well-run, busy pub. It offers a wide choice of dishes from the bar menu, much of it home-made, including interesting soups, fresh fish and daily specials. Palmers range of ales and a good wine list. Big, pretty garden and lovely views. Children welcome. Bedrooms.

Open: 11–2.30, 6–11

Wetherspoon in Dorset

Boscombe – Sir Percy Florence Shelley, 673–675 Christchurch Road
① 01202 300197
Bournemouth – Moon in the Square, 4–6 Exeter Road
① 01202 314940
Bridport – Greyhound, 2 East Street
① 01308 421905
Dorchester – Royal Oak, High Street West
① 01305 755910
Ferndown – Night Jar, 94 Victoria Road
① 01202 855572
Poole – Lord Wimbourne, 59 Lagland Street
① 01202 493290
Weymouth – Swan, 41–43 St Thomas Street
① 01305 750231

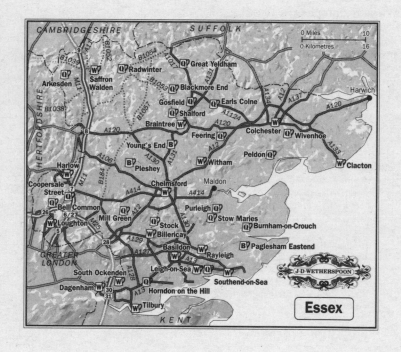

Essex

Arkesden

Axe and Compasses ① 01799 550272
Arkesden CB11 4EX
Greene King. Themis & Diana Christou, lease
www.axeandcompasses.co.uk

You really can't miss it; the flowering tubs and hanging baskets rival the local plant centre. Where the flowers stop, the pub stops. You certainly relax at the Axe, a spacious, 17th-century, mostly thatched pub that has been added to over the years. Set in the middle of a pretty village of thatched cottages, some of whose owners have to cross the 'occasional stream' – probably a raging torrent in times of high rainfall – by their own footbridges. Inside, the Axe is a basic, traditional bar, with a more comfortable lounge and a restaurant. Meals are served in both the bar and restaurant: home-made soup, breaded brie with Cumberland sauce, grilled sardines, and well-filled sandwiches, supreme of chicken with port and Stilton, medallions of monkfish in a prawn, lemon and parsley butter sauce, sirloin steak Diane, pan fried with mushrooms, shallots, red wine and brandy, noisettes of lamb, served with a mint and red wine gravy, a choice of fresh fish, some vegetarian dishes, scrummy puds and daily specials. Greene King beers and a very good wine list. Seats on the terrace among the hanging baskets.

OPEN: 11–2.30, 6–11.
Real Ale: Cask Marque award. Restaurant.
Children in eating areas. No dogs. Car park.
Cards: Delta, MasterCard, Switch, Visa.

Bell Common

Forest Gate Inn ① 01992 573312
111 Bell Common, Epping Forest CM16 4DZ
Free House. Stokes family, owners/licensees

As the name suggests, this inn is alongside what used to be one of the original gates into the forest. Covering 6000 acres, Epping is one of the oldest forests in Europe, full of wild flowers, ancient oaks and beeches. Crossed by tracks, bridleways and paths it is a delightful place to spend the day, and the 19th-century Forest Gate Inn is waiting to refresh you. Sustaining food is always available, also draught Adnams and Ridleys ales. Soak up the sun sitting on the small green in front of the pub.

OPEN: 10–2.30, 5.30–11.
Real Ale.
Well-behaved children and dogs allowed. They can just force a wheelchair in (not WC)!

Blackmore End

Bull ① 01371 851037
Blackmore End, nr Braintree CM7 4DD
Free House. Allan Weir, licensee

In a quiet village surrounded by the gentle Essex countryside, the 17th-century timbered Bull, a straightforward-looking pub with a jolly interior, has a reputation for creative menus, good wines and well-kept beer. People flock here to sample something from the regularly changing menu. If you want a quick snack you will find the usual sandwiches, ploughman's, salads, interesting home-made soups and patés. The dining end of the pub has an à la carte menu – available in the bar – and the choice of more dishes on the changing blackboard menus, maybe fillet of steak in a port sauce, venison cutlet in a red wine sauce, lamb baked with herbs and with a redcurrant sauce, all served with fresh vegetables, delicious home-made puds too. Adnams, Greene King IPA and a guest beer. A selection of European and New World wines.

OPEN: 12–3, 6–11. Sat & Sun 12–11.
Real Ale. Restaurant.
Children in eating area of bar. No dogs.

Burnham-on-Crouch

Olde White Harte ① 01621 782106
The Quay, Burnham-on-Crouch CM0 8AS
Free House. John Lewis, licensee

The River Crouch runs deep inland providing sheltered moorings for yachts at Burnham, a popular yachting centre since the end of the 19th century. A walk along the Quay, which passes busy yacht builders and chandlers, is the most interesting way to get from one end of town to the other. On the Quay is the elegant 17th-century Olde White Harte, which also backs onto the largely Georgian High Street. You can't quite sail into the hotel, but it does have its own jetty so, when the tide is high, and if the moorings allow, you can get really close, and believe me, this is one of the places everyone gets really close to during Burnham week. This is the sailing highlight of the east coast, when everyone who is anyone in sailing is in town. Enjoy a drink on the jetty, or inside among the beams in the comfortable bar. The bar menu has something for everyone; the restaurant has an à la carte menu. Bar food varies daily, but there could be roast pork, liver Lyonnaise, pan-fried skate, locally caught cod, grilled plaice or steak and kidney pie. Specials change weekly: fresh asparagus tips, poached salmon in a mushroom, chive and cider sauce, or duck à l'orange. Adnams Bitter, Crouch Vale IPA and a good wine list.

OPEN: 11–11. Sun 12–10.30.
Real Ale. Restaurant.
Children if well behaved. Dogs on leads. Car park. Wheelchair access (not WC). Eleven bedrooms en suite, eight others.
Cards: all except Amex and Diners.

Coopersale Common

Theydon Oak ① 01992 572618
Coopersale Common, Epping CM16 7QJ
Free House. John Paget, owner/licensee

Looking at a map you will see Coopersale Common is south of North Weald airfield and
north of where the M11 crosses the M25 – east of Epping. Weatherboarded and hung
about with flowery baskets, inside is a long bar, beamed and cosy, as well as a restaurant.
Traditional menu ranging from sandwiches to fresh fish and daily specials. Sunday roasts.
Green King IPA, Blacksheep Bitter and Whitbread Best. Comprehensive selection of Old
and New World wines. Seats on the terrace and in the garden.

OPEN: 11–3, 6–11. Sun 12–4, 7–10.30.
Real Ale. Restaurant.
Children welcome in restaurant only. No dogs. Car park. Wheelchair access (not WC).
No cards.

Dagenham

Lord Denman ① 020 8984 8590
270–2 Heathway, Dagenham RM10 8QS
Wetherspoon.

Another large space converted into a successful and always popular Wetherspoon outlet,
named after the first Lord Denman, Lord Chief Justice of England, who lived in Dagenham
from 1850 to 1852. A bust of Lord Denman has a prominent place in the bar and photos of
local boys who made a name for themselves in the world are on the walls. A reasonably
priced, reliable and varied menu and always six real ales, one of which is invariably cheaper
than elsewhere. On two levels, they have a special stairlift for wheelchairs. Seats in the garden.

OPEN: 11–11.
Real Ale.
No children. No dogs. Wheelchair access to all parts.

Earls Colne

Bird in Hand ① 01787 222557
Coggeshall Road, Earls Colne, Colchester CO6 2JX
Ridleys. Colin & Lesley Eldred, lease

During the last war you couldn't have chosen a more vulnerable place to have a pub – at
the end of a runway used by the U.S. Army Air Corps from 1942 to 1944. It's between the
villages of Earls Colne and Coggeshall – that was the safe bit – and without casting
aspersions on our American friends' flying ability, they felt it circumspect to remove the
roof. It's now restored to its full height, and you can see the 'before and after' photographs
displayed in the saloon bar. There is a full, traditional pub menu of favourite dishes –
some of which are home-made, and these, understandably, are the most popular, and

could be a steak and mushroom pie, beef lasagne or chicken curry. Six different fillings for the potatoes. Basket meals; specials on certain days. Ridleys range of ales; draught and bottled. Seats in the large garden.

OPEN: 12–2, 6–11. Sun 7–10.30.
Real Ale.
No children under 14. Dogs: perhaps. Wheelchair access.

Feering

Sun Inn ① 01376 570442
Feering Hill, Feering, nr Colchester CO5 9NH
Free House. Charles & Kim Scicluna, licensees

If you are into the more unusual beers, then this is the place to be. This timbered, 16th-century building has plenty of beams inside, some heavily carved, which relate to the history of the pub, thought to be part of an Elizabethan mansion, and now a jolly, easy-going place with no pretensions. Bar food is plentiful and varied with no surprises: home-made soup, sandwiches, ploughman's, garlic mushrooms, spicy creole beef on rice, roast beef or lamb, steak and kidney pie, lots more and plenty of puddings. Beers do vary; about 20 on the go but no regulars. They could come from Adnams, Mauldons, Nethergate, Archers, Cottage, Charles Wells, Fullers, Brains and Batemans among others. Seats on the terrace and in the attractive garden.

OPEN: 12–3, 6–11.
Real Ale.
Well-behaved children welcome. Dogs too. Car park.
No cards.

Gosfield

Green Man ① 01787 472746
The Street, Gosfield CO9 1TP
Greene King. Mr & Mrs Richard Parker, lease

About four miles north of Braintree on the main road through the village, the Green Man (in pagan times a symbol of fertility) is, confusingly, prettily pink washed. The ambience is warm, the service friendly and the food imaginative. Inside are two small bars, a dining room and separate function room. As well as bar snacks, there is an exceptional lunchtime cold table and a full à la carte menu lunchtimes and evenings. Always lots of interesting things on the blackboard menu: home-made soups and curries, fresh fish, lamb chops, steak and kidney pudding and home-made puddings. Good, reasonably priced wine list. Greene King IPA and Abbot on hand pump.

OPEN: 11–3, 6.30–11 (Sun 7–10.30).
Real Ale. Restaurant (no food and no restaurant Sun eves).
Well-behaved children in eating area. Dogs if very restrained. Wheelchair access.
Cards: Amex, Delta, MasterCard, Switch, Visa.
N.B. Jukebox in public bar.

Great Yeldham

White Hart ① 01787 237250
Poole Street, Great Yeldham, Halstead CO9 4HJ
Free House. John Dicken, manager
e-mail: reservations@whitehartyeldham.co.uk

On the edge of the village, the pub's large gardens still run down to the River Colne, but it was unfortunate that in the last floods, the river decided to run up to, and into the pub, a wonderful, Grade I*, early 16th-century, half-timbered inn now restored to its former glory. Inside are some very low-beamed ceilings, panelling and big log fires. Add the interesting menus and all in all it's a very desirable place. There's always a warm welcome if you just want a beer and a snack, but the culinary delights in the no-smoking restaurant might tempt you to stay longer. From the snack menu you could have home-made soup which varies with the season, a sandwich of honey-roast ham and cheddar with home-made crisps, the White Hart ploughman's (honey-glazed ham, Montgomery cheddar, sausage roll, hovis rolls, chutney and plum tomato salad), beef pie with creamy mash and buttered cabbage or Thai-style chicken curry with cardamom rice. The full menu offers grilled goat's cheese with spiced figs, red onion and walnuts, crispy bacon, caramelised onion and pigeon crostini with a garlic crouton salad, roasted cod with a pesto crust, Mediterranean vegetables and salsa verde, or pork tenderloin on sweet potato and bacon mash with roasted leeks and mushroom cream, chocolate and pecan nut tart with crème fraiche to finish, other delicious puds and a selection of cheeses. The à la carte menu changes about every two weeks. Monday to Friday there is a good value prix fixe: £10.50 for two courses, £14.50 for three. An extensive wine list; some wines by the glass. Two or three ales on permanently and guests including seasonal and speciality ales from regional brewers.

OPEN: 11–3, 6–11. Sun 12–3, 7–10.30.
Real Ale. Restaurant (not Sun eve).
Children welcome. Dogs in garden only. Car park. Wheelchair access.
Cards: Amex, Delta, Diners, MasterCard, Switch, Visa.

Horndon on the Hill

Bell Inn ① 01375 642463
High Road, Horndon on the Hill SS17 8LD
Free House. John Vereker, CMBII, licensee
e-mail: info@bell-inn.co.uk

Handsome, cream washed and flower bedecked, this is a delightful 15th-century coaching inn. Inside are beams, flagstone floors, fires, settles and enthusiastic, friendly staff. There's one bar in the Bell for drinks and snacks, another for restaurant customers. There is an extensive, changing blackboard menu; celeriac soup with tarragon and chestnut ravioli, poached mackerel in fennel oil with creamed corn and chorizo risotto, Parma ham and sweetcorn baji with goat's cheese Chantilly, celeriac and clam salsa, grilled rib eye of beef with hoi sin, plum sauce and prawn cracker and Guinness-battered sea bass with confit cabbage, mussels and parsley sauce. Home-made puddings as well. Good selection of wines, many by the glass or half bottle. The landlord has produced notes on what to drink with what; you can buy wine from him too. Draught Bass and Greene King IPA on hand pump, plus weekly changing guest beers such as Crouch Vale Brewers Gold. Seats outside in the courtyard.

OPEN: 11–2.30 (Sat 11–3), 6–11. Closed all bank holidays.
Real Ale. Restaurant.
Children in eating area. Dogs on leads. Car park. Wheelchair access. Fourteen en-suite bedrooms.
Cards: Amex, Delta, MasterCard, Switch, Visa.

Leigh-on-Sea

Crooked Billet ① 01702 714854
51 High Street, Leigh-on-Sea SS9 2EP
Six Continents. Wayne Bowes, manager

It is the railway line that has helped keep Leigh, now part of Southend, much as it was. Luckily, the narrow high street still has its old fisherman's cottages; there is a sailing club, boat builders, cockle boats and a small sandy beach with a slipway. With sea views and by the sea wall, the characterful 16th-century Crooked Billet, once the haunt of smugglers, is flourishing. From the lounge bar you can sit and look out to sea, warmed by a solid fuel stove, and think about what you would like to try from the choice of four or more different beers from the barrel. A beer festival is held annually when more than 30 beers are served. Bar food consists of home-made soups, freshly baked baguettes, ploughman's, hot and cold sandwiches and filled jacket potatoes. A seafood platter is a speciality of the house, but there are also daily specials and some vegetarian dishes. The pretty hanging baskets and window boxes feature during the summer on the big terrace, from where you can enjoy a view of the working harbour.

OPEN: 12–11. Lunchtime meals and snacks only. No food Sun.
Real Ale.
No children. No dogs. Occasional live music events.
Cards: all credit cards.

Mill Green

Viper ① 01277 352010
Mill Green, nr Ingatestone CM4 0PS
Free House. Roger & Sharon Beard, licensees
e-mail: beard@theviperpub.com

On a quiet country road, in a delightful wooded setting, this unchanging little pub has been run by the same family since 1938. The 15th-century building is nearly hidden by wonderful floral displays, with a large, flowery garden. Inside are four rooms, two with carpets, two without (for those still in their walking boots). The food is simple but varied, bar food of the fill-a-gap variety: soup, sandwiches, ploughman's, chillis and weekend 'real-ale' sausages – that sort of thing. Between three and four weekly changing beers from the smaller, less-well-known breweries. Seats outside in the attractive garden.

OPEN: 12–3, 6–11. Sun 12–3-ish, 7–10.30.
Real Ale. Lunchtime snacks.
Dogs on leads. Wheelchair access difficult.

Peldon

Peldon Rose ① 01206 735248
Mersea Road, Peldon, Colchester CO5 7QJ
Lay & Wheeler Bars. John Riddleston, licensee, and Alex Scarfe, manager

Headline news in 1884 when an earthquake had its epicentre at the front of the pub and gave it a bit of a fright; nothing in this 600-year-old pub is quite as horizontal or vertical as it once was. If you turn off the main road on the way to Mersea you will find the aptly named, rose-pink Peldon Rose. Inside are two heavily beamed bars with crooked doors, uneven floors and a big log fire to make you welcome. All the food is prepared and cooked 'in-house': sandwiches and light snacks are available all day until 4.30, otherwise the varied menu includes a lot of fresh, local fish, and vegetarian dishes. On Sundays there is roast sirloin of beef and home-made puddings. Daily cream teas in summer. Adnams, Greene King and Fullers London Pride beers. The owners are wine merchants so you can be sure there will be some good names on the list. Seats in the spacious garden – with pond – in the summer.

OPEN: 11–11. Sun 12–10.30.
Real Ale. Restaurant. No-smoking conservatory.
Children welcome away from bar. Dogs on leads. Wheelchair access. Three en-suite bedrooms.
Cards: all accepted.

Purleigh

Bell ① 01621 828348
The Street, Purleigh CM3 6QJ
Free House. B. Mott, licensee

Next to the church, the Bell is an interesting old pub; rambling, beamed and very cosy when there is a good log fire in the inglenook – just what you want when the sea mist rolls in on an easterly wind. The village, south of Maldon, is equidistant from two rivers, the Crouch and the Blackwater, with sheltered moorings and sailors on all sides. The highlight of the east-coast yachting calendar takes place at Burnham on Crouch at the end of August and the famous sailing barge races on the Blackwater during July. Good, home-made lunchtime food: sandwiches, ploughman's, filled jacket potatoes, a plate of smoked ham with pickle, home-made pies, omelettes, sausage egg and chips, cheese or prawn salad to go with the Adnams Bitter, Ridleys IPA and a guest beer. Seats outside and views towards the Blackwater.

OPEN: 11–3, 6–11. Sun 12–3, 7–10.30.
Real Ale.
Children not encouraged, but over 14 allowed with an adult. Dogs on leads.
Cards: most cards accepted.

Radwinter

Plough Inn ① 01799 599222
Sampford Road, Radwinter, Saffron Walden CB10 2TL
Free House. Derek Clarke, licensee

On high ground, just east of the village, the 17th-century, white-painted, weatherboarded Plough has westerly views over open farmland towards Saffron Walden. It's a friendly, sociable place with an open-plan, beamed bar where they serve lunchtime snacks and a new no-smoking restaurant – McAllisters – for the main meals. The traditional bar menu will include ploughman's, freshly cut sandwiches, filled jacket potatoes, pasta dishes and daily specials. From the restaurant menu there could be home-made soup of the day, coarse pork terrine with the Plough's own cranberry jelly, smoked trout fillets with mixed leaf salad and for a main course, spinach roulade with cream cheese and oven-roasted red peppers, medallions of pork with caramelised apples, fresh cider sauce and mashed potato, fillet of smoked haddock cooked in a paper parcel with saffron, white wine with bay leeks, rump or fillet steak with different sauces, a choice of fish and home-made puds to finish. Everything is freshly prepared using as much local produce as possible. An ever-changing range of ales from Greene King IPA, Hook Norton, Batemans, Brakspear, Timothy Taylor, Nethergate, Crouch Vale, Dark Horse, Smiles and whatever else they can get hold of. Keg ciders and draught scrumpy in the summer. Interesting wine list. Seats on the lawn and on the clematis-covered patio.

OPEN: 11.30–3, 6.30–11. Sun 12–4, 7–10.30.
Real Ale.
Children and dogs welcome if both on their best behaviour. Car park. Wheelchair access throughout.
Cards: all major cards except Amex.

Shalford

George ① 01371 850207
The Street, Shalford CM7 5HH
Free House. Wendy Buckman, licensee

Surrounded by the scenery that Constable loved and painted, this part of Essex has wide-open skies and winding river valleys. The George, in a pretty village by the River Pant, dates back to the 15th century. Heavily timbered inside with low beams and a huge log-filled inglenook fireplace, it's a friendly old place serving plenty of pub favourites, written up on the blackboards – something for everyone. Adnams Broadside, Greene King IPA, Caffreys and an occasional guest beer. Outside there are tables on the large terrace.

OPEN: 12–3.30, 6.30–11. Closed Sun eves.
Real Ale. Restaurant.
Children if eating only. No dogs.
Cards: all major cards.

Stock

Hoop ① 01277 841137
21 High Street, Stock, Ingatestone CM4 9BD
Free House. Albert Kitchin, licensee

Four hundred and fifty years old and nothing much changes in this popular pub. In the cosy, friendly bar you can try something from the range of six changing beers. Ever changing they are too; as, on average, 500 different ales are brought into the pub over a year, some on hand pump, some straight from the cask. The pub also provides a good selection of dishes – at least two fresh fish dishes from Tuesday to Saturday and five or six other specials, such as braised steak and dumplings, braised oxtail, lamb and barley stew, also soups, omelettes, ploughman's, sandwiches, filled jacket potatoes, fish pie with trout and prawns, chicken and ham pie and hotpots. The range of ales, including some from the tiny independent breweries, is so extensive it is best to go and see what's on offer. Each year about 150 ales feature in the May beer festival, which lasts for about ten days. They also have farm cider, wines by the glass and mulled wine in winter. Seats outside, either in the pretty garden or in the pagoda-like extension which has a bar and about 40 seats.

OPEN: 11–11. Food served Mon–Thurs 11–2.30, 6–9; Fri & Sat 11–9; Sun 12–8.
Real Ale.
Children in garden. Dogs on leads.
Cards: MasterCard, Switch, Visa.

Stow Maries

Prince of Wales ① 01621 828971
Woodham Road, Stow Maries CM3 6SA
Free House. Rob Walster, licensee

A small marsh pub with cosy, beamed rooms, the Prince of Wales is part of a restored group of weatherboarded buildings which includes an old Victorian bakery; still baking bread and pizzas. On the main road from Basildon to Burnham-on-Crouch, it's a beer taster's heaven, run by a real-ale fanatic who changes his selection of beers every week. To go with the beers, they serve a good selection of home-made bar food which includes a choice of fish – some more exotic than others – pizzas on winter Thursdays, and comforting puds. There is an ever-changing range of five or six beers, a selection of

Belgian beers, malt whiskies and a farm cider. The beer is very special here; the landlord searches out the more unusual brews for the benefit of his customers and his beer festivals.

OPEN: 11–11. Sun 12–10.30.
Real Ale.
Children – maybe. Dogs very welcome. Car park.

Wivenhoe

Rose and Crown ① 01206 826371
The Quay, Wivenhoe, nr Colchester CO7 9BX
Punch Retail. Martyn Daley, licensee

The Rose and Crown is at the bottom of a steep street of old houses that leads to the old Quay where the smacks and barges used to tie up. It's quieter now – the ship builders who were here since Elizabethan times have gone and the fishing boats have virtually disappeared, but the Rose and Crown is still an important part of the scenery, as it has been for the last 250 years. So if you're in a boat and aiming for the Rose and Crown, you need to be on the Colne river, sailing in the direction of Colchester. It's only a small place with low beams, log fire, nautical pictures and tables outside on the quayside, where you can enjoy your drink and watch the nautical comings and goings when the tide is in – lots of mud and feeding wildfowl when it's not. In the last few years it has had a new kitchen, cellar and back bar. So a traditional bar menu is served every day now: filled baguettes, wraps and ciabattas, soup, steak and ale pie, sausage and mash, grills and specials on the blackboard. On Sunday there is a roast lunch. Adnams, Greene King Abbot, IPA, mild and Bass. Small, interesting wine list – some by the glass. You can catch a ferry from Wivenhoe to Fingeringhoe, depending on the tide.

OPEN: 11–11. Sun 12–10.30.
Real Ale.
Children welcome until 6 p.m. Dogs with well-behaved owners.

BEST OF THE REST

Paglesham Eastend
Plough & Sail ① 01702 258242
Paglesham Eastend SS4 2EQ
Don't be put off when you get to Churchend, Eastend's a bit further on down the winding road, as remote as you can get; next stop, along a rough track, is the river Roach. If you're a sailor you know the pub is here, if you're not, now is the chance to be adventurous. It's old, weatherboarded, charming and delightfully cosy, ready to withstand the cold east winds straight off the sea. You will find familiar bar food and some creative daily specials. Lots of fish – and oysters when available – as the oyster beds are very near. Greene King beer and a guest. Children welcome in eating area.
Open: 11.30–3, 6.30–11. Sun 12–10.30.

Pleshey
White Horse ① 01245 237281
Pleshey, Chelmsford CM3 1HA
A 15th-century beamed and timbered pub with later additions. They offer an extensive bar menu listing ploughman's, filled jacket potatoes, huffers (a local bread roll) with a variety of fillings, fish dishes, steak and something for the vegetarian. A full à la carte menu is provided in the no-smoking restaurant. Nethergate Best, Tolly Original and regularly changing guest beers which could include Crouch Vale and Ridleys. There is an extensive list of wines from various parts of the world. Seats on the terrace and in the garden during the summer. Children welcome. No dogs.
Open: 11–3, 7–11.

Young's End
Green Dragon ① 01245 361030
Upper London Road, Young's End CM7 8QN
On the road between Braintree and Chelmsford, here's a neat, double-fronted, white-painted pub, serving much appreciated food. The restaurant is in the big, brick-built barn alongside the pub. Menus are more imaginative than usual, with fish dishes something of a speciality. Greene King ales and a guest. Children over 10 welcome.
Open: 12–3, 5.30–11. Sat & Sun 11–11.

Wetherspoon in Essex

Basildon – Moon on the Square, 15 Market Square
① 01268 520360
Billericay – Blue Boar, 39 High Street
① 01227 655552
Braintree – Wetherspoons, Fairfield Road
① 01376 550255
Chelmsford – Globe, 65 Rainsford Road
① 01245 261263
Chelmsford – Ivory Peg, 4–7 New London Road
① 01245 253130
Clacton – Moon and Starfish, Marine Parade East
① 01255 222998
Colchester – Playhouse, St John's Street
① 01206 571003
Dagenham – Lord Denman, 270–2 Heathway
① 020 8984 8590
Harlow – William Aylmer, Aylmer House, Kitson Way
① 01279 620630
Leigh-on-Sea – Elms, 60 London Road
① 01702 74687
Rayleigh – Roebuck, 138 High Street
① 01268 748430
Saffron Walden – Temeraire, 55 High Street
① 01799 516975
South Ockenden – Moon Under Water, Broxburn Drive
① 01708 855245
Southend-on-Sea – Last Post, Weston Road
① 01702 431682

Tilbury – Anchor, Civic Square
01375 850560
Witham – Battesford Court, 100 Newland Street
01376 504080
Witham – Little Elms, Dorothy Sayers Drive
01376 510483

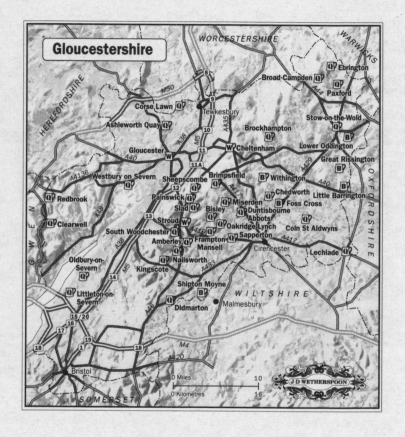

Gloucestershire

WORCESTERSHIRE

WARWICKS

HEREFORDSHIRE

M50

Ebrington

Broad-Campden

Paxford

Corse Lawn

Tewkesbury

Stow-on-the-Wold

Ashleworth Quay

Brockhampton

Lower Oddington

Gloucester

Cheltenham

Great Rissington

OXFORDSHIRE

Westbury on Severn

Sheepscombe

Brimpsfield

Withington

Redbrook

Painswick

Chedworth

Little Barrington

Miserden

Foss Cross

Slad

Bisley

Duntisbourne

Clearwell

Stroud

Abbots

South Woodchester

Oakridge Lynch

Coln St Aldwyns

Sapperton

Amberley

Frampton

Mansell

Cirencester

Lechlade

Nailsworth

Oldbury-on-Severn

Kingscote

Shipton Moyne

WILTSHIRE

Littleton-on-Severn

Didmarton

Malmesbury

Bristol

M4

M50

A420

SOMERSET

0 Miles   10

0 Kilometres 16

J.D.WETHERSPOON

Gloucestershire

Amberley

Black Horse ① 01453 872556
Littleworth, Amberley, Stroud GL5 5AD
Free House. Patrick O'Flynn, licensee
e-mail: oflynn@aol.com

A straightforward friendly local with two bars, a welcoming fire, papers to read,
conservatory, no-smoking family room and a permanent barbecue area for those sultry
summer days. They serve a reasonably priced, traditional pub menu: soup, ploughman's,
sandwiches, Mexican dishes, pasta, steaks, fresh fish and seafood; fish and chips on Fridays.
Tetleys Bitter, Smooth, Archers Best, Golden, Fullers London Pride, Wickwars Brand Oak
Bitter and Black Rat Cider and guest beers. Seating on the terrace and in the large, pretty
garden, with spectacular views over the Stroud valley. If you want a bracing walk you are
close to 600 acres of National Trust land at Minchinhampton Common.

OPEN: 12–11.
Real Ale.
Children welcome. Dogs on leads.

Ashleworth Quay

Boat Inn ① 01452 700272
Ashleworth Quay GL19 4HZ
Free House. Ron, Elizabeth & Louise Nicholls, licensees

In an enviable position on the banks of the River Severn, this is a celebrated place in more
ways than one. Not only was this small 15th-century pub granted a licence during the
reign of Charles II, it has been run by the same family from that time. So over the
centuries they've had more practice than most in the art of being the perfect landlords.
Inside are two timeless, simply furnished rooms and a small back tap room with a couple
of settles and casks of ale. Lunchtime there are locally baked rolls filled with proper ham
or mature cheddar, served with home-made pickle. Beers include RCH Pitchfork, Arkells
3B, something from Wye Valley and various others. Westons Farm cider. Seats in the
flowery sunny courtyard.

OPEN: 11–2.30, 6–11 (winter 7–11). Closed Mon & Wed lunchtimes Oct–Apr.
Real Ale.
Children welcome. No dogs in the pub.

Bisley

Bear Inn ➁ 01452 770265
George Street, Bisley GL6 7BD
Pubmaster. S. N. Evans, MBII, tenant

The Bear is a delight to see: an attractive 16th-century inn, parts of which date back to the 14th century. A handsome colonnaded front supports an upper storey under which is a small flagstoned sitting area. In a charming village, high in the Cotswolds – apparently known as 'Bisley-God-Help-Us' when the winter wind blows – the Bear is there for shelter and comfort. All is as it should be inside this lovely old place which has two secret passages and a priest's hole to add to the atmosphere. Menus change daily, using fresh local produce; you'll find home-made soup, Caesar salad, prawns in lemon and garlic butter, lots of fillings for the baguettes, sautéed potatoes and onions on a bed of lettuce with additions such as chicken and bacon or sausages and coarse-grained mustard, a rabbit and vegetable pie, chicken and pasta baked in a tomato, rosemary and garlic sauce topped with cheese, white fish and prawns casseroled in cider and topped with potato and cheese, vegetable pasties, home-made burgers and other dishes. The daily specials – selection of local cheeses and home-made puds – are listed on the blackboard. Flowers IPA, Tetley Cask, Charles Wells Bombardier and Marstons Pedigree on hand pump. Seats in the garden too.

OPEN: 11–3, 6–11. No food Sun eve.
Real Ale.
Children in own room. Dogs on leads.
Cards: Mastercard, Solo, Switch, Visa.
Irish folk music first Thursday of every month.

Brimpsfield

Golden Heart ➁ 01242 870261
Nettleton Bottom, Brimpsfield, Birdlip GL4 8LA
Free House. Catherine Stevens, licensee

Here is everything you could possibly want in a country pub: an unspoilt interior, exceptional food and well-kept beers. This beamed, extended 16th-century country inn has low ceilings, a huge inglenook fireplace and traditional furnishings. You are going to find some interesting dishes on the menu: salmon mousse with hot buttered toast, chicken, apricot and bacon terrine, hot artichoke dip with tortilla chips, baked ham hock with parsley sauce, Hungarian beef goulash, Thai red chicken curry, maybe medallions of ostrich rump with black pepper and cognac. If you just want a snack there are well-filled sandwiches and jacket potatoes, ploughman's and salads. Timothy Taylors Landlord, Bass, Marstons Pedigree on hand pump, or from the barrel, as well as Murphys and Guinness. Beer festivals are held over the May and August bank holidays. Guest barrels behind the bar are changing all the time. A well-chosen, wide-ranging wine list. Scrumpy and wine by the glass. Seats outside on a sunny terrace.

OPEN: 11–2.30, 6–11. Fri–Sun 11–11.
Real Ale.
Children welcome in their own room. Dogs on leads.

Broad Campden

Bakers Arms ① 01386 840515
Broad Campden, nr Chipping Campden GL55 6UR
Free House. Ray & Sally Mayo, licensees

There are many things to tempt you to the creeper-covered Bakers Arms. It used to be the local bakery and there is an early photograph in the bar showing it in its heyday. Now you come to enjoy the atmosphere of what is a traditional pub interior, with a big fire, well-kept, ever-changing beers and reasonably priced bar food. The bar menu includes soups, paté, ploughman's, a very popular cottage pie, giant Yorkshire puddings with a choice of fillings, smoked haddock bake, lamb's liver, bacon and onions, beef bourguignon, lasagne verdi, chicken curry and savoury suet pudding of the day. Vegetarian dishes and daily specials are on the blackboard; these can include peppered pork, duck breast, lamb shank or coq au vin; fruit crumbles and other favourites for afters. Ales change all the time but five usually on hand pump, mainly from independent breweries such as Donnington, Hook Norton, Stanway Bitter, Timothy Taylors Landlord and Charles Wells Bombardier. Seats outside on the sunny terrace where you are surrounded by some wonderful walks in marvellous countryside.

OPEN: April–Oct 11–11. Nov–March 11.30–2.30, 6–11. (Sun 12–3, 7–10.30.)
Real Ale. New dining room.
Children welcome. No dogs in pub. Wheelchair access.
Folk night third Tuesday of month.

Brockhampton

Craven Arms ① 01242 820410
Brockhampton, nr Cheltenham GL54 5XH
Free House. Dale Campbell, licensee

In a rather upmarket village a couple of miles north of the A436, this is a rambling, 17th-century village pub with flagstone floors, stone walls, low beams and the essential log fire. Deservedly, a popular lunchtime meeting place. They serve a wide choice of good-value, wholesome, home-made food in attractive surroundings. Invariably ploughman's, as well as steak, kidney and ale pies, smoked salmon, crab fishcakes, home-made paté with a home-made chutney, steaks, a chicken dish or two and vegetarian options. Sunday roasts.

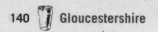

Ales are Wadworths 6X, Hook Norton Best Bitter, Butcombe Bitter, Goff's Jouster, Fullers London Pride, draught Bass and guest ale. There are plenty of seats in the big garden.

OPEN: 11–3, 6–11. Sun 12–3, 7–10.30.
Real Ale. Restaurant.
Children in eating area of bar or restaurant. Dogs welcome, under control.
Cards: all major cards except Amex and Diners.

Chedworth

Seven Tuns ① 01285 720242
Chedworth, Cheltenham GL54 4AE
Smiles. Alex Davenport Jones, licensee

This is an area surrounded by good walks and interesting places to see, close to the well-preserved Roman villa at Chedworth – a particularly desirable house at the time, with underfloor heating, two types of bath and a water shrine constantly topped up by an ancient spring. Keeping up the watery theme, this attractive 17th-century pub – once used by Cromwell's troops – has a working water wheel in the garden. Always welcoming to families, walkers and dogs, the Seven Tuns is hugely popular, especially in the summer walking season; big log fires and good, well-presented food keep up the appeal in winter. The menu changes daily, and everything is freshly cooked; they specialise in steaks and fish, but there is a popular bar menu as well. Sunday roasts. Smiles Best and Bitter from the Bristol Brewery, one guest and Guinness on draught. Skittle alley and games room to hire if you're so inclined. Plenty of tables outside.

OPEN: 11–11.
Real Ale.
Children and dogs welcome.
Cards: all credit cards accepted.
N.B. Music in public bar.

Clearwell

Wyndham Arms ① 01594 833666
Clearwell, nr Coleford GL16 8JT
Free House. Nigel Stanley, licensee

You are spoilt for choice in this area as to what to do and what to see; local attractions abound. So what better than to use the attractive, whitewashed Wyndham Arms as your base? Standing in its own grounds in the middle of the village, this 600-year-old charming small hotel with beams, oak floors and open fires has a wonderfully atmospheric interior. Here you are surrounded by the most glorious countryside: the Royal Forest of Dean, Symond's Yat and the Wye valley. Interesting architectural buildings surround you, and below ground are the Clearwell caves, an amenity for mining and caving enthusiasts, geologists, historians and sightseers. The Wyndham Arms serves not only a restorative pint of draught Bass or glass of well-chosen wine, but also an excellent choice of bar snacks and starters: home-made soup, thinly sliced marinated salmon with a dressing of mustard, dill and honey, brandied chicken liver parfait with gherkin salsa and toasted brioche, smoked haddock and spring onion fishcakes with lime mayonnaise and for a main course, medallions of pork with a compote of apples on creamy mash with a cider sauce, roast rump of lamb on olive mash with a rosemary jus, baked breast of free-range organic chicken with a wild mushroom sauce, and chef's specials too. There is a very reasonable two- and three-course table d'hôte lunch and dinner menu. Most of the vegetables, fruit and herbs are locally grown. All food is cooked to order, so expect a little delay. Delicious ice-creams and puds to finish. Seats outside on the terrace during the summer. Bass and beers from the Freeminer range on hand pump, a good wine list and an excellent choice of malt whiskies.

OPEN: 11–11.
Restaurant.
Children welcome. Dogs on leads. Car park. Good wheelchair access. Eighteen rooms.
Cards: Delta, MasterCard, Switch, Visa.

Coln St Aldwyns

New Inn at Coln ① 01285 750651
Coln St Aldwyns, nr Cirencester GL7 5AN
Free House. Angela Kimmet, licensee

There is everything you could possibly want in this very handsome, creeper-covered, Elizabethan coaching inn. Not only is there a comfortable beamed bar – with log fire – where they serve well-kept ales and something from the impressive bar menu, but if you want to stay the night there are some really classy bedrooms. On the Courtyard bar menu you will find at lunchtime filled sandwiches, baguettes and ciabattas, and dishes such as tiger prawns wrapped in filo pastry with chilli jelly, New Inn fishcakes with aioli dressing and fresh leaves, a salad of langoustines, Cornish crab with a dill mayonnaise, Caesar salad with smoked chicken, Parma ham wrapped chicken breast, with saffron crushed potatoes, olives and red wine, braised shank of lamb, sun-dried tomato, new potato and a port jus, warm poached salmon or pan-fried chicken livers and crispy bacon with mixed leaves. Chocolate and rum cheesecake with a dark chocolate sauce and raspberry coulis to finish; selection of cheeses too. If after all that you want more excitement, you might catch sight of the resident ghost; jangling keys herald his arrival. Hook Norton, Butcombe, Wadworths 6X ales and other guest beers on hand pump. A round-the-world wine list, about eight by the glass. Seats in the garden. The walk along the river to Bibury is not to be missed.

OPEN: 11–11.
Real Ale. Restaurant.
No children under 10 in restaurant. Dogs on leads. Car park. Wheelchair access. En-suite bedrooms.
Cards: Amex, Delta, MasterCard, Switch, Visa.

Corse Lawn

Corse Lawn Hotel ① 01452 780771
Corse Lawn, nr Tewkesbury GL19 4LZ
Free House. Denis Hine, licensee
e-mail: enquiries@corselawn.com

This fine, early 18th-century building replaced a burnt-down Tudor inn. It was built as a coaching inn, and the old 'coach wash' at the front of the hotel has been retained as an unusual ornamental pond, and the name, Corse Lawn, comes from the wide, mile-long green each side of the road. The relaxed and welcoming hotel serves an eclectic menu in the bar/bistro that mainly reflects the nationality of the owner – M. Hine is French. Dishes could include Mediterranean fish soup, terrine of chicken with lemon, basil and garlic, bruschetta of grilled vegetables with parmesan and mozzarella and baked queen scallops with Provençale stuffing; for a main course grilled sea bass fillet with cauliflower cream and caper dressing, pigeon breasts with red wine, red cabbage and black sausage, haunch of venison with a port sauce, creamed cabbage and chestnuts, fillet steak with red wine sauce and salsa verde, crisp asparagus pancake with an artichoke sauce and lots more; fish and shellfish are a speciality here. There are also sandwiches, baguettes, omelettes, creative vegetarian dishes and good puddings. Worthington Best and Caffreys. Hine cognac and over 300 wines.

OPEN: 12–2, 6–11.
Children welcome. Dogs on leads. Car park. Wheelchair access. Nineteen rooms – all en suite.
Cards: Amex, Delta, Diners, MasterCard, Switch, Visa.

Didmarton

Kings Arms ① 01454 238245
The Street, Didmarton GL9 1DT
Free House. Zoe Coombs, licensee
e-mail: kingsarms@didmartin.freeserve.co.uk

Nothing overly exciting to look at from the outside, but inside the 17th-century Kings Arms is a fine, restored, traditional Cotswold inn. The well-beamed, comfortable interior has painted panelling, a stone fireplace, garlands of hops, and, more importantly, the added bonus of menus featuring good food: home-made soup, smoked meats and poultry, locally caught game, vegetarian dishes and home-made puds. The menu is available in the restaurant, conference room and front bar. Beers are Uley's Bitter, plus two guests. They have an interesting wine list, which includes champagnes – a few by the glass – chosen by their own wine specialist. A true local; everyone comes here, including crowds during

Badminton week when there's standing room only. Large garden with a boules pitch. Close to the year-round delights of the Westonbirt Arboretum.

OPEN: 12–3, 6–11 (Sun 7–10.30).
Real Ale. Restaurant.
Well-behaved children welcome. Dogs on leads. Car park. Wheelchair access (not WC).
Bedrooms. Three self-contained holiday cottages.
Cards: all cards except Amex and Diners.
N.B. There may be a CD playing in the back bar.

Duntisbourne Abbots

Five Mile House ① 01285 821432
Old Gloucester Road, Upper Duntisbourne Abbots GL7 7JR
Free House. Jo Carrier, licensee

One of a group of Duntisbournes on the river Dunt, a river lazily meandering past (down the village street in the case of Duntisbourne Leer) two villages and two hamlets. You are deep in the Cotswolds, in a valley off Ermine Street, the main Roman road from London to Wales. Five Mile House is a very special place, beautifully restored and with a small bar that has a listed interior. No wonder they are very firm as to where you eat and drink: no crumbs in this bar if you please! Drinkers do their serious drinking on one side; anyone can eat on the other. You can do both only in the tap room. The restaurant is smart and there is a no-smoking cellar bar – which you can hire. Specials on the blackboard and a good choice of lunchtime bar snacks, home-made soups, open sandwiches, ploughman's, home-cooked gammon and in the evening, stuffed shoulder of lamb, steaks, chicken in a cream sauce, nice puds and a good, varied wine list. Donningtons BB, Youngs PA, Timothy Taylors landlord and rotating guest ales.

OPEN: 12–3, 6–11.
Real Ale. Restaurant. There is a marquee in the summer for larger functions.
Children: not in bar. Dogs on leads. Car park. Wheelchair access (not WC).
Cards: no charge cards.

Ebrington

Ebrington Arms ① 01386 593223
Ebrington, nr Chipping Campden GL55 6NH
Free House. Barry Leach & Nick Hurt, licensees

Unchanging for years, but now there is a new regime and things have moved on in the best possible way. A mid 18th-century village pub, newly refurbished. A favourite stopping-off place for hearty walkers, the flagstones underfoot take the walking boots without protest. Inside is a beamed, stone walled, flagstoned bar and a new dining room with handsome fireplaces. The display of fine trophies bears witness to an enthusiasm for dominoes – on the whole, a nice quiet game. However, tension increases on match days. If you are short-sighted remember to bring your glasses as the extensive menu is written on the beams of the bar where you will find traditional bar food as well as 'modern English and French'

dishes. Hook Norton Best, Donnington SBA and guest beers on hand pump. Farm cider.
Seats outside on the sheltered terrace.

OPEN: 11–2.30, 6–11. Sun 12–4, 7–10.30.
Real Ale. Restaurant.
Children in eating area. Dogs on leads – not when food is served.
Cards: all major cards accepted.

Frampton Mansell

The White Horse ① 01285 760960
Cirencester Road, Frampton Mansell GL6 8HZ
Free House. Shaun & Emma Davis, licensees

In the lovely Golden Valley between Sapperton and Chalford, what was, at the beginning
of this century, an empty, unloved old place, is now a thriving pub and restaurant. Here is
the best of both worlds: an attractive, very comfortable bar – where you can come for just
a drink and chat – combined with a hugely popular restaurant serving some really
worthwhile food. For a starter from the daily changing menu you could have curried
parsnip soup, hot cheese fritters with an onion cream sauce, stuffed beef escalopes with
tarragon and parma ham with tomato chutney and brandy cream sauce; and for a main
course, red mullet fillets with a pineapple and chilli relish, coriander and lemon dressing,
roast rib of beef with Yorkshire pudding, roast potatoes and pan gravy, pan-fried calves'
liver with mashed potato and bacon and puy lentil jus or smoked cheddar and red pepper
filo parcel with rocket, black olive and parmesan salad; lemon possit with spun sugar, or
chocolate, banana and coffee steamed pudding with chocolate sauce and clotted cream to
finish. Hook Norton, Uley Best and Arkells Summer Ales, Guinness, John Smiths and
Strongbow cider. Carefully chosen, very interesting wine list, six by the glass. Seats in the
large, attractive garden.

OPEN: 11–3, 6–11.
Real Ale. Restaurant.
Children welcome, so are dogs. Car park.
Cards: all except Amex.

Kingscote

Hunters Hall ① 01453 860393
Kingscote, Tetbury GL8 8XZ
Old English Inns. Miss Stephanie Ward, tenant
e-mail: huntershall.kingscote@oldenglishinns.co.uk

This is all things to all people; a place for everyone. Outside, a striking, creeper-covered
16th-century inn; inside, full of character, are beams, flagstone floors, stone walls, open
fires, three bars and a no-smoking dining room. Very family minded; there is a no-
smoking family gallery above the bars and the garden is planned for children. The back
public bar has a pool table, darts and jukebox. The interesting bar food menu changes
daily; there will be a cold buffet in the dining room at weekends, otherwise, as well as
sandwiches and ploughman's, dishes range from seafood chowder infused with dill, home-

cured gravadlax, Hunters Hall chicken and duck liver paté with pear and onion chutney, grilled lemon and garlic chicken salad to fillet of cod on a bed of Mediterranean vegetables, braised lamb shank on a bed of creamed potato, beef lasagne and a steak, kidney and local beer pie. Also à la carte and table d'hôte menus; three roasts on Sundays. As they say, 'traditional English cuisine with a continental flair'. Beers are Greene King IPA, Abbott, Ruddles Best, Uley Hogs Head. Wines by the glass, and a selection of malt whiskies. A summer barbecue in the children-oriented garden.

OPEN: 11–11. No bar food Sun.
Real Ale. Restaurant.
Children welcome. Dogs on leads. Wheelchair access to pub and bedrooms. Twelve en-suite bedrooms in what was once the stables and smithy.
Cards: all cards.
N.B. Music (very low) in restaurant.

Lechlade

Trout Inn ① 01367 252313
Lechlade on Thames GL7 3HA
Nomura. Bob & Penny Warren, lease

A handsome Georgian building in a town that takes its name from the Leach river, which joins the young Thames just below St John's bridge. At such an important watery meeting place it is not surprising that the pub leans towards a piscatorial theme; it has fishing rights too. Built on 13th-century foundations, the old pub has two pleasant, low-beamed bars and an extra outside bar that functions during the summer. There are dependable menus in both restaurant and bar: home-made soups, paté, salmon, steaks, locally produced sausages, daily specials and home-made puds. John Smiths Yorkshire and Courage Best ales, Smiles Best and Bass are the changing guests. Aunt Sally has replaced boules. On a warm day you can sit in the big garden or on the river bank.

OPEN: 10–3, 6–11 (all day summer Sat).
Real Ale. Dining room with no-smoking area.
Children in eating area of bar. Dogs on leads (not in dining or children's room). Wheelchair access.
Piano music on Friday and Saturday evenings.

Littleton-on-Severn

White Hart ① 01454 412275
Littleton-on-Severn BS12 1NR
Youngs. Howard & Liz Turner, licensees

Originally a 16th-century farmhouse, the pub has kept much of its character. Inside are three rooms plus family room with flagstones, tiles, a truly handsome fireplace, hops on the beams and a country pub ambience. It's near the Severn river and the bridge; occasionally, depending on the rainfall, a little too near! There is a wide choice of bar food ranging from home-made soup, filled crusty rolls, ploughman's, steak and kidney pie, fish pie, vegetarian dishes to special seafood and game dishes – all at pub prices – and daily

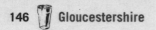

specials. Smiles range of ales and two guests, one of which is Wadworths 6X. The others change regularly. Seats at the front in the pretty, cottagey garden and on the terrace at the back of the pub. On a clear day you get a good view of Wales and the Welsh mountains.

OPEN: 12–2.30, 6–11.
Real Ale.
Children in the garden room. Dogs on leads. Four en-suite bedrooms in the converted barn.

Miserden

Carpenter's Arms ① 01285 821283
Miserden GL6 7JA
Free House. Johnny Johnston, FBII, licensee
e-mail: bleninns@clara.net

On the great estate of Miserden Park, with its Elizabethan mansion and idyllic gardens, this estate village, near the delightful Duntisbourne villages, is largely unspoilt. The 18th-century Carpenter's Arms has just two bar areas, two fires and a no-smoking dining room. The old carpenters' workshop is still in existence but not as part of the pub. The bar menu could list soup of the day, filled rolls and jacket potatoes, four different ploughman's, crispy whitebait, creamy mushroom stroganoff with rice, spinach and ricotta tortellini in a creamy white wine sauce with garlic bread and pie of the day as well as something from the daily changing specials board: pork, apple and cider casserole, diced venison in port and red wine, leek and parmesan quiche, Miserden lamb sausages with mustard mash and onion gravy, honey-roast ham with egg and chips or baked trout and almonds. The beers are Greene King IPA, Wadworths 6X, a guest and there is a short wine list, some by the glass. Tables in the garden.

OPEN: 11–3, 6–11.
Real Ale.
Children welcome until 8.30 p.m. Dogs in bars. Car park.
Cards: Amex, MasterCard, Switch, Visa.

Nailsworth

Weighbridge Inn ① 01453 832520
Longfords, Minchinhampton GL6 9AL
Free House. Simon Hudson, licensee
e-mail: enquiries@2in1pub.co.uk

During the 19th century, the landlord of this pub led a frantically busy life: he was not only responsible for the pub itself, but also for manning the Weighbridge, after which the pub was named. Before that he was kept busy with traders passing the inn on the old packhorse route to Bristol – now a footpath and bridleway – and everyone using the old turnpike road. This is a very historic place as parts of the original building on the site date back to 1220 and a stone or two will surely be in the fabric of this inn. Inside are three traditionally furnished rooms housing an interesting collection of country artifacts. No restaurant food, just good, seasonal pub grub. Filled baguettes and baked potatoes, salads, two-in-one pie – a speciality of the house – half cauliflower cheese and the other half a filling of your choice from the menu, topped with a short pastry crust. A mini version of the same is also on offer – so you can leave room for a pudding – also bangers and mash, moussaka, cottage pie, spinach and mushroom lasagne, those comforting puddings and a selection of English cheeses. The guest ales change frequently but there will be something from the local Uley range of beers and Wadworths 6X. A good number of wines by the glass or bottle. Seats outside in the sheltered garden.

OPEN: 12–11. Food served 12–9.30 every day.
Real Ale.
Children in rooms away from bar. Dogs on leads. Wheelchair access – disabled loos.
Cards: all cards except Amex.

Oakridge Lynch

Butchers Arms ① 01285 760371
Oakridge Lynch, nr Stroud GL6 7NZ
Free House. Peter & Brian Coupe, licensees

High on the hill, with a view over the village to the valley below, this is not the easiest pub to find, but there's no better place to be on a summer's day. With a good map – and watching out for the pub's signpost on the main road – wander the steep, overgrown, highsided lanes until you find the village. The Butchers Arms serves good-value home-cooked food, including bar snacks and daily specials. They serve a three-course Sunday lunch – for which you must book. Archers Best, Wickwar Bob, Youngs Bitter and Greene King Abbot ale are among the ales kept. Plenty of room to park in the detached car park and there are seats in the garden from where you can gaze at the view. Not far from good walks along the old Thames and Severn canal.

OPEN: 11–3, 6–11. Sun 12–3, 7–10.30. No food Sun eve or Mon.
Real Ale.
Children in anteroom and restaurant only. Dogs on leads.

Oldbury on Severn

Anchor Inn ① 01454 413331
Church Road, Oldbury on Severn, South Glos BS12 1QA
Free House, Michael Dowdeswell & Alex de la Torre, licensees

The river is just fields away from this lovely country pub, a great favourite with a path opposite that will take you down to the water's edge. The summer floral displays will catch your eye; flowers hang from everywhere and behind all the opulence is the pub. It's comfortably furnished, with old beams, winter fires, and window seats. You can eat in either lounge, bar or no-smoking dining room. One menu throughout the pub offers a mix of traditional English with the best of continental cuisine. Local meat, fruit and vegetables – all the produce is as fresh as can be. They have delicious ways with potatoes but there are no chips; however, on offer are 14 different salads, a leek and potato bake, Oldbury chicken – chicken breast cooked in apple juice with brandy, cream and mushrooms – locally reared pork and garlic sausages cooked on a charcoal grill, Yorkshire pudding with a generous filling, or there's fresh salmon in a cream and wine sauce and Caribbean pork cooked with ground coconut, ginger, mango, raisin, pineapple and lime juice. Amazing puds and home-made ice cream. Theakstons Best Bitter, Old Peculier, draught Bass, Butcombe Bitter, John Smith, Guinness and three different lagers. Over 75 malt whiskies, an extensive wine list, Frobishers fresh fruit juices and lots of sparkling water. Large garden at the back of the pub. Surrounded by attractive walks.

OPEN: 11.30–2.30, 6.30–11. Sat 11.30–11. Sun 12–10.30.
Real Ale. Dining room.
Children welcome in dining room and garden only. Dogs on leads – not in dining room. Car park. Wheelchair access and disabled W.C.
Cards: MasterCard, Visa.

Painswick

Royal Oak Inn ☾ 01452 813129
St Mary's Street, Painswick GL6 6QG
Blenheim Inns. Alan & Carol Harris, managers

In the conservation area of Painswick, one of the loveliest towns in the Cotswolds, the Royal Oak is a handsome, stone-built, town pub. Parts of the pub date back to the 16th century, but the facade, as with much of the town, is a century or so later. Inside are two bars, with good fires, which have remained largely unchanged over the years, and where you can order something from the menu; filled sandwiches, jacket potatoes, toasted panini and ploughman's on the snack menu or you could have chicken liver paté with toast, cauliflower cheese with jacket potato and bacon, gammon steak with egg or pineapple, home-made fishcakes, roast fillet of salmon with hollandaise sauce, grilled steaks, vegetarian dishes and seasonal dishes from the specials board. Beers are Hook Norton Best, Wadworths 6X, Flowers Original and guests. European and New World wines on the list. Outside is a sunny courtyard – heated in the cooler weather. The church of St Mary isn't up to much – this is one that Cromwell certainly knocked about a bit – but the setting and the churchyard with the clipped yews and handsome tombs is well worth a visit.

OPEN: 11–3, 5–11.
Real Ale.
Children and dogs welcome. Wheelchair access.
Cards: all accepted.

Paxford

Churchill Arms ☾ 01386 594000 Fax: 01386 594005
Paxford, nr Chipping Campden GL55 6XH
Free House. Leo Brooke-Little, licensee
www.thechurchillarms.com

Simply furnished with an unpretentious interior, flagstone floors, tongue and groove on the walls, low ceilings, a good fire in the snug, and plenty of tables, this is a pub where you can experience some really imaginative cooking. There is a daily changing blackboard with, normally, a selection of six starters: saffron-marinated mackerel with cucumber sauce, chicken cooked in herbs and olive oil with asparagus, aubergine and tomato dressing, pan-fried scallops, spring onion mash and crisp pancetta. For a main course, john dory with red wine risotto, capers, spring onions in olive oil and tapenade, loin of rabbit filled with spiced aubergine, lentils and mustard dressing or brill with creamed leeks, beurre blanc and smoked salmon. Always some inventive puds to follow. Menus are constantly changing. Arkells BBB, Hook Norton Best and a guest, all on hand pump. Reasonable wine list, about nine by the glass.

OPEN: 11.30–3, 6–11. Sun 12–3, 6.30–10.30.
Real Ale.
Children not in bar. Dogs in garden only. Wheelchair access (not WC). Four bedrooms – all en-suite.
Cards: MasterCard, Switch, Visa.

Redbrook

Boat Inn ① 01600 712615
Lone Lane, Redbrook, Penallt, Monmouth, Gwent, S. Wales NP23 4AJ
Free House. Donald & Pat Ellis, licensees

A favourite stopping place for serious walkers and anyone else nearby. The Boat is on the Welsh side of the River Wye, but the car park is in Gloucestershire, but as the car park is bigger than the pub, that's the county we are putting it in! A pleasing, genial atmosphere in the bar where there is a roaring fire and they serve good, familiar bar food. Mushrooms in garlic butter with salad garnish, potato wedges and dips, ploughman's, the house dish of Panhaggerty, steak and Guinness pie, filled baked potatoes, hot chicken Caesar salad, lamb in olive oil, lemon, red wine and sugar served with a Greek salad, vegetarian dishes and specials and puddings on the blackboard. There are seats in the steep garden from where you can watch the river. Up to ten ales from casks behind the counter, Wadworths 6X, Wye Valley Butty Bach and Greene King and others according to availability; they change all the time. A 30-yard footbridge across the Wye connects the pub to its Gloucestershire car park.

OPEN: 11–11. Sun 12–10.30.
Real Ale.
Children welcome, so are dogs.
Live music Tues and Fri eves.

Sapperton

Bell Inn ① 01285 760298
Sapperton, Cirencester GL7 6LE
Free House. Paul Davidson & Pat Lejeune, licensees

The Frome river winds its way past this lovely village at the head of the Golden valley where the 18th-century Bell, 'done up' and looking its best, has three comfortable rooms, flagstones on the floor, log fires, newspapers to read and dishes to savour. Very interesting things are going on in the food line: seared Scottish scallops with orange chutney,

Vietnamese chicken noodle salad, charcuterie plate with marinated vegetables and mountain gorgonzola, ploughman's lunch of three West Country cheeses, apple, celery and old spot chutney, wild mushroom risotto with truffle oil, chargrilled loin chop of Middle White pork with cider apple mash, roasted cod with green olive and garden herb crust, breast of free-range chicken, coriander and goat's cheese pesto with roasted peppers and to finish, home-made puddings. Fresh fish and specials will be on the boards. Uley Old Spot, Hook Norton and others – all on hand pump as well as scrumpy cider. A considerable number of wines by the glass from a wide-ranging wine list. Tables at the front of the pub and in the garden at the back. It is here in 1789 that the two-and-a-half-mile Sapperton Tunnel was cut through the hill to link the Thames and Severn rivers. Now restored, the eastern entrance is well worth a visit.

OPEN: 11–2.30, 6.30–11.
Real Ale.
Children and dogs welcome (no children under 10 in the evenings). Wheelchair access.
Cards: MasterCard, Visa.

Daneway Inn ① 01285 760297
Sapperton, Cirencester GL7 6LN
Wadworth. Liz & Richard Goodfellow, licensees.

This quiet local, in lovely wooded surroundings, is at the western end of the tunnel that takes the canal under the A419. The old Daneway, built to house workers constructing the canal in the 18th century, will, with the imminent restoration of the canal, be just as important again. It might not be housing the workers this time but it will be helping to keep them fed and happy. The pub has an unpretentious interior except for an amazingly grand fireplace in the lounge bar which came out of the long-since-demolished manor house. Lunchtime bar food varies from filled hot baps, baked potatoes and ploughman's to lasagne verdi, gammon steak with egg or pineapple, Cumberland sausage and chips, beef in ale pie and steaks; additional dishes are on the evening menu. Wadworths 6X, Henry's Original IPA, plus seasonal ales and Westons Old Rosie cider from the cask. Tables in the pretty garden overlook the canal and the river valley.

OPEN: 11–3, 6.30–11. Sun 12–3, 7.30–10.30.
Real Ale.
Children in no-smoking family room. No dogs.
Cards: JCB, Maestro, MasterCard, Solo. Switch, Visa, Visa Electron.

Sheepscombe

Butchers Arms ① 01452 812113
Sheepscombe, nr Painswick GL6 7RH
Free House. Johnny Johnston, FBII & Hilary Johnston, MBII, licensees
e-mail: bleninns@clara.net

Nothing could be better than a pint of beer – or whatever you fancy – a sunny day and a seat on the sloping grass to admire the wonderful, panoramic views over the Stroud valley. The 17th-century Butchers Arms has a timeless atmosphere, bay windows to sit in, huge winter log fires, walls covered with old pictures and prints, no fruit machines or jukebox, just happy, chatting customers. Plenty of choice on the daily changing boards – home-made soup of the day, smoked haddock and prawn pancake with salad, breast of chicken marinated in cajun spices served with fries and salad, pork escalope marinated in cranberries with Worcestershire sauce, spinach and ricotta cannelloni with salad, filled jacket potatoes, filled rolls, ploughman's and daily specials from the blackboard and home-made puds. Hook Norton Best, Wye Valley Dorothy Goodbody and changing guest beers. Farm ciders, local fruit juices, original lemonade and ginger beer and a good wine list.

OPEN: 11–11. Sun 12–10.30. Winter 11–2.30, 6.30–11.
Real Ale. No-smoking restaurant.
Children in eating areas. No dogs. Wheelchair access into pub and restaurant.
Cards: Amex, Diners, JCB, MasterCard, Switch, Visa.

Slad

Woolpack ① 01452 813429
Slad, nr Stroud GL6 7QA
Free House. Richard Bolton & Daniel Chadwick, licensees

This was the late Laurie Lee's local; a popular 16th-century pub, clinging to the side of the hill with stunning views across the lush Slad valley to the woods opposite. Immortalised in his book *Cider with Rosie*, the valley is a mecca for walkers, most of whom reach this pub. Carefully restored over the last few years, it serves reasonably priced home-made bar food, all local, home-made and organic; as they say: ' nothing fancy, but very traditional, sandwiches, baguettes, steaks, faggots, home-made hot dishes, a lot of fish during the summer, that sort of thing'. Worth a trip for Uley's locally brewed Old Spot, Bitter and Pig's Ear; always four or five ales and three or four draught ciders.

OPEN: 12–2.30, 6–11. Sun 7–10.30.
Real Ale.
Children welcome. Dogs on leads. Wheelchair access (not WC).
Cards: all major cards accepted.

South Woodchester

Ram Inn ① 01453 873329
Station Road, South Woodchester, nr Stroud GL5 5EL
Free House. Tim Mullen, licensee
e-mail: drink@raminn.com

Another pub with spectacular views. From the front you look over the Woodchester valley, Gloucestershire at its most attractive. The stone-built, 17th-century Ram is warmed in winter with no fewer than three fires. In the traditionally furnished, beamed bar they serve an interesting, reasonably priced menu including the usual sandwiches and ploughman's, maybe spinach roulade with a cream-cheese and smoked-salmon filling, plaice with a prawn and mushroom stuffing, Italian beef casserole, spicy pork loin with a brandy and apricot sauce, fillet of steak with a cream and pepper sauce, venison in red wine and always fresh vegetables. The well-kept ales change frequently but there are usually eight or nine on hand pump; serious beer drinkers flock here.

OPEN: 11–11. Sun 12–10.30.
Real Ale. Restaurant.
Children welcome. Dogs on leads. Wheelchair access (not WC).
Cards: MasterCard, Switch, Visa.

Stow-on-the-Wold

Eagle and Child ① 01451 830670
Digbeth Street, Stow-on-the-Wold GL54 1BN
Free House. Alan & Georgina Thompson, licensees
www.theroyalisthotel.co.uk

As they poured their first pint in these premises in AD 947, you can safely assume that this is the oldest pub in the country. But it was closed for several years – so perhaps the lack of continuity negates the claim. Whatever the case, this is a seriously good place, and very, very old. The pub, part of the rather smart hotel next door, has stone walls, flagstones on the floor, a small bar and a dining conservatory. What they serve is several notches above good pub food – dishes with a little excitement. There will always be the favourites, battered fish with chips, steak in ale pie, local sausages with onion gravy; then there will be a leap forward to pan-fried sea bream with saffron risotto or crab and brie omelette. To end your meal you can sample some English farmhouse cheeses. Hook Norton Best Bitter is always on as well as one guest beer. Short wine list, all available by the glass.

OPEN: 11–11. Sun 12–10.30. Winter 12–11.
Real Ale.
Children and dogs welcome. Wheelchair access. Bedrooms in the hotel.
Cards: Amex, Delta, MasterCard, Switch, Visa.

Westbury-on-Severn

Red Lion ① 01452 760221
Westbury-on-Severn GL14 1PA
Free House. John Bolton, licensee

A half-timbered, rambling, corner pub, half on a busy road and the other half on a quiet lane leading to the river. Who knows how the craze started, but the Red Lion has a definite baseball theme, with a large collection of caps hanging on the beams, brought by customers and friends from all over the world. A well-run, fine pub serving an extensive menu: soup, filled baguettes, moussaka and chilli con carne from the bar, also spicy Thai fish cakes, country paté, lamb braised in red wine, redcurrant sauce and garnished with button mushrooms and onions, fisherman's crumble or breast of chicken sliced and laid on a bed of red, yellow, orange and green peppers marinated in basil, pesto and garlic, vegetarian dishes – and lots of puds. Always four real ales and a good selection of malt whiskies, South African and New World wines. Seats in the garden.

OPEN: 11–2.30, 7–11.
Real Ale.
Children welcome. No dogs. Car park. Four en-suite bedrooms. Good English breakfasts.

BEST OF THE REST

Foss Cross
Hare & Hounds ① 01285 720288
Foss Cross GL54 4NN
On the A429 south of Fossbridge and north of Cirencester, this lovely old place is cosy and full of beams with three large, log-burning fireplaces. Seriously good dishes on the menu, such as salmon and potato terrine on a warm bed of pickled cucumber with a dill cream sauce or a fillet of beef wellington with a rich port jus; daily specials too: filled ciabattas if you just want a snack. Arkells 2B and 3B, ciders and a short wine list. Children and dogs welcome. Wheelchair access.
Open: 11–3, 6–11.

Great Rissington
Lamb ① 01451 820388
Great Rissington GL54 2LP
Between Oxford and Cheltenham, west of Burford and past Great Barrington. Overlooking the Windrush valley, this is a smartened-up, 17th-century pub. You can stay here and eat well. Lots of home-made dishes on a traditional bar menu; even more served in the restaurant. Fullers London Pride, Wadworths 6X, Ruddles and a good wine list. Children and dogs welcome. An interesting walk from here to Bourton-on-the-Water.
Open: 11.30–2.30, 6.30–11.

Little Barrington
Inn for all Seasons ① 01451 844324
Little Barrington, nr Burford OX18 4TN
If you are on your way to the Cheltenham races you might like to know that this handsome creeper-covered 17th-century coaching inn has enough room for you to park your helicopter, so avoiding all the traffic jams. Inside is a welcoming, traditional bar with a log fire, magazines to read and comfortable chairs to loll in. What you will definitely want to know is that the food here is worth a detour. They specialise in fish but also have a clever, inventive, non-fishy menu. Wadworths 6X, something from Wychwood and an impressive wine list. Children are welcome and there are bedrooms if you want to spend the night.
Open: 11–2.30, 6–11.

Lower Oddington
Fox ① 01451 870555
Lower Oddington GL56 0UR
Honey-coloured and creeper-covered stone walls make this an attractive village pub – inside and out – where they also serve some very good food. Menus change monthly but typically there could be watercress soup, beef stew with parsley dumplings, a warm

chicken, bacon and avocado salad – that sort of thing. Badger Tanglefoot, Hook Norton Best, Marstons Pedigree, changing guests and a really good wine list. A very popular place. You can take the children – on their best behaviour – and you can stay.
Open: 12–3, 6.30–11.

Shipton Moyne
Cat & Custard Pot ☺ 01666 880249
The Street, Shipton Moyne, nr Tetbury GL8 8PN
A pub with a faithful local following. Traditional pub food and plenty of it; friendly service and conversation, welcoming fire and a satisfying menu which includes the Cat and Custard Pot classics: sausage and mash with onion gravy, Wiltshire ham, egg and chips and an all-day breakfast. Ales are Wadworths 6X, Fullers, Bass, Worthington, Guinness and a short wine list. Dogs, children and wheelchairs all find their way in.
Open: 11–3, 6–11.

Withington
Mill Inn ☺ 01242 890204
Withington GL54 4BE
You will probably be exploring the Gloucestershire lanes if you land up here, and it will be well worth it. This inn is in a lovely place, standing alone in a little wooded valley with its very own river running through the garden. They serve good traditional bar food: ploughman's, vegetarian lasagne, roast beef and Yorkshire pudding, daily specials too. Sam Smiths range of ales. Children welcome. Bedrooms.
Open: 11.30–3, 6–11.

Wetherspoon in Gloucestershire

Cheltenham – Moon under Water, 16–28 Bath Road
☺ 01242 583945
Gloucester – Regal, 33 St Aldate Street, Kings Square
☺ 01452 332344
Stroud – Lord John, 15–17 Russell Street
☺ 01453 767610

Hampshire

J·D·WETHERSPOON

BERKSHIRE

WILTSHIRE

Tangley
Ashmansworth
Basingstoke
Fleet
Clanville
Andover
Crondall
Well
Longstock
Bentworth
Broughton
Aresford
Priors Dean
Winchester
Ovington
Steep
East Tytherley
Cheriton
Whitsbury
Rockbourne
Upham
Droxford
Damerham
Dundridge
Hambledon
Shirley
Southampton
Cosham
Havant
Emsworth
Ringwood
Titchfield
Fareham
Langstone
Bransgore
Boldre
Gosport
Portsmouth
Lymington
Cowes
Ryde
Freshwater
Newport
ISLE OF
WIGHT
Bonchurch

DORSET
WEST SUSSEX
SURREY

0 Miles   10
0 Kilometres   16

Hampshire

Alresford

Globe on the Lake ☎ 01962 732294
The Soke, Broad Street, Alresford SO24 9DB
Free House. Marc & Emma Duveen Conway, licensees
e-mail: duveen-conway@supanet.com

Confusingly there are two Alresfords, Old Alresford on one side of the River Arle and the newer town on the other. This fine old pub, between the two, has its own lakeside garden and dining room and garden rooms looking over Alresford Pond. Broad Street, which leads to the lake, is lined with Georgian houses. The Globe has been renovated and structurally improved to put its best face forward for another successful century. From the daily changing menu you could have a Stilton and leek soup or a smoked salmon and prawn paté, spinach and brie flan with salad, local smoked trout, peppered sirloin steak with French fries and delicious puds to follow. Brakspear Bitter, Courage Best, Directors and Wadworths 6X are the beers. Well-chosen, reasonably priced wine list, many by the glass. Lots of room to sit outside and appreciate the watery surroundings, teeming with wildlife.

OPEN: 11–3, 6–11. Summer Sat & Sun 11–11. Winter Sun 12–8.
Real Ale.
Children in garden, garden room and dining room until 7.30. Dogs on leads in garden.
Wheelchair access from garden.
Cards: Amex, Delta, MasterCard, Switch, Visa.

Ashmansworth

Plough ☎ 01635 253047
Ashmansworth, nr Newbury, Berks RG20 9SL
Free House. Oliver Davis, licensee

A small, simple place, built of brick and flint in 1778 and totally without pretensions. For all its long life the Plough has been primarily just a beer house, with only one quarry-tiled bar – there were once two, but they were knocked through. The bottles and the cheery landlord face you as you come in. South of Newbury – hence the Berks address – and south of Highclere Castle, the pub is too small to do much with food, but there is soup, sandwiches, jumbo pork and leek sausages and ploughman's – familiar bar favourites to go with the beer. Archers Village, Best and Golden, served from the barrel. Seats in the small side garden.

OPEN: 12–2, 6–11. Sun 12–3, 7–10.30. Closed Mon and Tues lunch.
Real Ale.
Children at lunchtime and until 8 p.m if well behaved. Dogs welcome. Small car park.
Wheelchair access (not WC).

Bentworth

Sun Inn ① 01420 562338
Bentworth, nr Alton GU34 5JT (at Sun Hill off A339 from Alton)
Free House. Mary Holmes, licensee

Down a narrow country lane south of the village, this is a pub with special appeal in winter. On a dreary day there is nothing quite so inviting as walking into a pub to find big log fires in equally big fireplaces. A cosy, friendly place with an unspoilt interior, the Sun not only has a good choice of real ales but also some worthwhile dishes on the blackboard menu: daily specials could be watercress or asparagus soup, a choice of pasta dishes, steak and kidney pie, venison in Guinness, liver and bacon, Somerset pork, sweet and sour chicken, as well as sandwiches, ploughman's, filled baked potatoes, ham and eggs, salads and home-made puddings. Eight real ales vary and could include Fullers London Pride, Bunce's Pigswill, Badger Best, Youngs Special. Gales country wines. When summer comes, there are tables outside amongst the flowering tubs.

OPEN: 12–3, 6–11. Sun 12–10.30.
Real Ale.
Children in garden room. Dogs on leads. Wheelchair access.
Occasional Morris dancers.

Boldre

Red Lion ① 01590 673177
Ropehill, Boldre, nr Lymington SO41 8NE
Eldridge Pope. Vince Kernick, lease

On the southern extremity of the New Forest, this pub is a riot of colour in summer; not only are there flower-filled tubs, but hanging baskets and window boxes create an award-winning floral display. Inside this fine black and white 17th-century pub is an interesting collection of all those artifacts you associate with past country life – a man-trap anyone? – displayed around its four well-beamed rooms. They serve a wide choice of better than usual bar food: home-made soup, fish cakes in a white wine and cream sauce, liver and bacon, beef and mushroom pie, excellent ploughman's and triple-decker sandwiches, some vegetarian dishes and quite a choice of puddings and daily specials; menus change daily. Bass and Flowers IPA ales. Wines by the glass. Seats in the attractive garden. Good nearby walks across the nature reserve.

OPEN: 11–11. Sun 12–10.30.
Real Ale. Restaurant.
No children under 14 inside pub. No dogs. Wheelchair access.
Cards: most cards, not Amex.

Bransgore

Three Tuns ① 01425 672232
Ringwood Road, Bransgore, nr Christchurch BH23 8JH
Whitbread. Steve Biss, lease
e-mail: stevebiss@aol.com

With fresh flowers inside and out, this picturesque 17th-century thatched pub with an eye-catching floral display is on the south-western edge of the New Forest. During the cooler months a cheery fire welcomes you in the beamed bar and the snug. Here you will find a varied and interesting choice of dishes listed on the blackboard: home-made soups, savoury choux stuffed with Stilton served on a red pepper, tomato and rosemary coulis, home-made venison terrine, filo wrap filled with wild mushrooms, asparagus, baby spinach and savoury rice served with a sweet chilli dressing, braised Scotch beef and kidney in a rich stout, mushroom and herb jus with a pastry case, whole fresh brill – puddings too. The restaurant has been extended – eating here is popular. Ringwood Fortyniner and Best, Timothy Taylors Landlord and Deuchars IPA. Good range of wines by the glass. Lots of room to sit outside.

OPEN: 11–2.30, 6–11. Sun 12–3, 7–10.30.
Real Ale. Restaurant.
No children. Dogs on leads. Car park. Wheelchair access.

Broughton

Tally Ho! ① 01794 301280
High Street, Broughton, nr Stockbridge SO20 8AA
Free House. Trevor Draycott & Patricia Witts, licensees

Broughton is one of four enchanting villages on the Wallop Brook which runs into the River Test at Horsebridge, off the tourist route but a favourite stopping place for walkers on the long distance Clarendon Way. Opposite the 13th-century church, among the timbered village houses, is the comfortable and well-restored Tally Ho! Here they serve reliable, home-made bar snacks and a wide variety of daily specials including vegetarian dishes. The ales change frequently so there will always be something new. There is a lovely, colourful, walled garden at the back of the pub. A mile away is the Roman road that linked Winchester and Salisbury and, slightly nearer, a 17th-century dovecote in the churchyard.

OPEN: 12–3, 7–11. Sat 12–11. Sun 12–4, 7–10.30. No food Sun eve or all day Tues.
Real Ale.
Children welcome. Dogs on leads. Wheelchair access at the back.

Cheriton

Flower Pots ① 01962 771318
Cheriton, Alresford SO24 0QQ
Own Brew. Joanna & Patricia Bartlett, licensees

What else would you call a pub that was bought by a retired gardener but Flower Pots – an inspired choice and it's the only one we know of. The names of the beers from its own brewery, the Cheriton Brewhouse, which started production in 1993, lean towards the horticultural too. On the edge of a pretty village, this small, brick-built pub has two little rooms where they serve good-value bar food: well-filled jacket potatoes, sandwiches – plain and toasted – seven different fillings for the large baps, five varieties of ploughman's and a number of hotpots: lamb and apricot, chilli con carne, beef and spicy mixed bean. The reasonably priced beers are Cheriton Best, Village Elder, Diggers Gold and Pots' Ale. Seats outside at the front and the back of the pub take the overflow from this popular place which gets even busier when they host a beer festival on August bank holiday.

OPEN: 12–2.30, 6–11. Sun 12–3, 7–10.30. No food Sun eves or Bank Holiday Mon eves.
Real Ale.
No children. Dogs on leads. Car park. Wheelchair access (not WC). Bedrooms.
No cards.

Damerham

Compasses Inn ① 01725 518231
Damerham, nr Fordingbridge SP6 3HQ
Free House. James Kidd, licensee

A notice on the pub door reads: 'Clean wellies, boots and dogs are allowed in the public bar'. At least you know where to go! An attractive old coaching inn with two bars – a public and lounge – both with good winter fires. Well-thought-out menus: the emphasis is on fresh, local produce, and they have something for everyone in both the bar and dining room: soup of the day, ploughman's with home-made pickles from the bar, and from the specials board there could be john dory and salmon with an orange salsa, pork tenderloin with prunes in a white wine sauce, king prawns, mussels and pasta with herbs, garlic and cream or a gammon and leek pie and home-made puds to follow. They have their own Compasses Ale, Ringwood Best, Wadworths 6X, Hop Back Summer Lightning and frequently changing guest beers. Varied selection of wines, many from the New World, and 120 malt whiskies. The pub is recommended by the British Cheese Board for the excellence of its cheeses. Delightful gardens with views of the surrounding countryside.

OPEN 11–3, 6–11. Sat 11–11. Sun 12–10.30.
Real Ale.
Children welcome. Dogs in public bar – juke box in here. Six en-suite bedrooms. All disabled facilities. Award-winning toilets here; they have won the Loo of the Year award for several years running!

Dundridge

Hampshire Bowman ① 01489 892940
Dundridge Lane, Bishops Waltham SO32 1GD
Free House. Heather Seymour, proprietor

Near Bishops Waltham, but you need to ask directions, or have a map at the ready, as it is not the easiest place to find. Tucked away in a small hamlet down a single-track lane in splendid walking country, it's a mid-Victorian pub in a position to take full advantage of spectacular sunsets. A friendly, cosy old place that welcomes everyone – children, walkers, dogs and local eccentrics – it's also the headquarters of the Portuguese sardine racing club! They serve good wholesome bar food: well-filled sandwiches and baguettes, jacket potatoes, ploughman's, pies, chicken breasts wrapped in bacon with mushroom and Stilton sauce, local trout with spring onions and ginger, venison steak with port and orange, wild mushroom stroganoff and choice of puds. Cheriton Pots Ale, Ringwood 49er and four constantly changing guests. Seats in the garden from where you can appreciate the view.

OPEN: Mon–Thurs 12–3, 6–11. Fri–Sun 12–11.
Real Ale. Restaurant.
Children and dogs welcome. Car park.
Cards: Electron, JCB, Maestro, MasterCard, Switch, Visa.

East Tytherley

Star Inn ① 01794 340225
East Tytherley, nr Romsey SO51 0LW
Free House. Paul & Sarah Bingham, licensees

You can stay, and you can eat well. On a quiet lane, overlooking the village cricket field, the Star is a welcoming place with big log fires in the bar, a separate no-smoking bar and restaurant. Everything is prepared 'in house' so you must be patient. The restaurant and bar menus are interchangeable; there could be home-made soup, seared scallops with smoked salmon kedgeree and cream sauce, marinated chicken supreme with light curry seasoning and saffron rice, pan-fried calves' liver and ostrich set on creamy mash with red onion confit, grilled fillets of sea bass on braised fennel and asparagus with a langoustine jus, battered cod and chips, steak, kidney and Guinness pie, something from the specials board, always a choice of vegetarian dishes and good, proper puds. Ringwood Best beer and one guest. Seats in the garden, where there is a children's play area.

OPEN: 11–2.30, 6–11. Sun 12–3, 7–10.30. Closed Mon except bank holidays.
Real Ale. Restaurant.
Children welcome – under control. Dogs allowed. Bedrooms.
Cards: all major cards except Amex and Diners.

Emsworth

Kings Arms ① 01243 374941
19 Havant Road, Emsworth PO10 7JD
Gales. Adrian & Penny White, tenants

If you want a brisk walk after a good lunch you are quite close to the Sussex Border Path, but if it's only a quick saunter you're after, it's a short step to the big mill pond and its resident ducks and swans. On the Havant road (A259) westward out of Emsworth, the black-and-white Kings Arms is unmissable in the growing season; the flowers are splendid. If it is very quiet, the landlord will sometimes put on a little light classical music to take the edge off the early morning silence, but it quickly fades out as the customers move in. Just one bar with a no-smoking area; ploughman's, salads, steaks, etc. on the bar menu; home-made fish pie, a halibut, cod and prawn bake, pork and prune casserole, or Burgundy beef, home-made vegetarian dishes, also daily specials and puddings on the blackboard. A selection of wines by the glass and the bottle. Well-kept Gales beers and guest ales. Gales country wines. Outside there is a prize-winning garden.

OPEN: 11–2.30, 5.15–11. Sun 12–2.30, 7–10.30.
Real Ale.
No children in bar. Well-behaved dogs on leads. Wheelchair access (not WC).
Cards: Connect, MasterCard, Switch, Visa.

Hambledon

Vine ① 02392 632419
West Street, Hambledon PO7 4RW
Free House. Peter Lane, licensee

In a pretty village, surrounded by good walking country, near the South Downs Way, this is a traditional, 16th-century country pub with beams, panelling, open fires and a welcoming landlord. Interestingly, one fire is open on both sides and heats two rooms; very economic. There is also a no-smoking restaurant area. They serve good, creative dishes: lamb with fresh coriander, rib-eye steak with bacon, mushrooms and tomatoes, boeuf bourguignon, fresh fish and a popular steak and kidney pie; menus change regularly. Beers are Timothy Taylors Landlord, Ringwood Best Bitter, Gales Butser and Butcombe Bitter. European and New World wines – the house wine is Chilean. Seats in the garden. Obviously no music, except the landlord's rendition of 'Show me the way to go home' when he is desperate to get the customers to drink up and go!

OPEN: 11.30–3, 6–11. Sun 12–4, 7–10.30.
Real Ale.
Children over 14. Dogs welcome if they get on with resident pug. Wheelchair access (not WC).
Cards: all except Amex and Diners.

Langstone

Royal Oak ☾ 02392 483125
19 Langstone High Street, Langstone, Havant PO9 1RY
Whitbread. Chris Ford, manager
e-mail: royaloak.langstone@laurelpubco.com

Particularly warm and comfortable in winter, the 16th-century Royal Oak is appealing in all seasons. From this tiny village, on the edge of a natural harbour and conservation area, there are views over the huge marshy expanse towards Chichester and Hayling Island, which divides the tidal waters of both harbours. At high tide only a low wall stands between the Royal Oak and the water. The pub serves a traditional range of bar and restaurant dishes: well-filled sandwiches and wraps, Brie and bacon quiche, spinach and mushroom cannelloni, creamy four-cheese, four-herb risotto, chicken Caesar salad, slow-cooked Welsh lamb, gammon steak, baked salmon fillet with lemon butter, steak and ale pie with mustard puff pastry, farm-assured Cumberland sausages and something from the two daily specials boards. Flowers Original, Gales HSB and draught Bass are on permanently, Wadworths 6X, Fullers London Pride, Ringwood Best and others are guests. Short wine list, most by the glass. Seats at the front of the pub – from where you can watch the nautical comings or goings, or, at low tide, the feeding waders – and in the garden behind.

OPEN: 11–11.
Real Ale.
Children in eating areas. Dogs on leads in part of pub.

Ovington

Bush Inn ☾ 01962 732764
Ovington, nr Alresford SO24 ORE
Wadworths. Nick & Cath Young, managers/licensees
e-mail: thebushinn@wadworth.co.uk

South of Alresford the 400-year-old Bush is in an area hugely popular with walkers and cyclists. The village is on the south side of the fast-flowing River Itchen where it is joined by two other streams – the Arle and the Candover. Noted as an excellent trout stream, the Itchen also has some wonderful riverside paths. Inside the low-ceilinged, traditionally furnished Bush are three comfortable rooms with good winter fires. Better than average, regularly changing bar food is readily available, and the blackboard lists a short, more adventurous choice of dishes. From the menu there could be soup of the day, Thai-spiced crab cake with rocket salad and a chilli peanut dressing, Loch Fyne smoked salmon and prawn roulade, queen scallops in the shell with garlic butter and crispy garlic breadcrumbs, and for a main course, home-made beef and ale pie, or beef lasagne, chargrilled rib-eye steak with a garlic and anchovy butter, venison steak with spiced red cabbage in a whisky and sherry vinegar sauce or a baked sea bass fillet with dill and chives

on plum tomatoes, also home-made puds. Wadworths range of ales plus seasonal beers. Various country wines. Seats overlooking the river and, naturally enough, lovely walks.

OPEN: 11–2.30, 6–11.
Real Ale.
Children in eating area lunchtimes only. Dogs on leads. Limited wheelchair access.

Priors Dean

White Horse Inn ① 01420 588387
Known as The Pub with No Name.
Priors Dean, nr Petersfield GU32 1DA (clutching a good map, you go up a track past East Tilstead/Privett crossroads, between Petersfield and Winchester)
Gales. Georgie & Paul Stuart, tenants

The pub sign blew out of the frame over thirty years ago and nobody bothered to put it back so now you know why there is an abandoned frame and the White Horse is known to everyone as The Pub with No Name. High on the Downs with an all-round view of the surrounding country, this 17th-century farmhouse is simple and traditional – a country pub that hasn't changed for decades. Menus vary with the seasons – as do the specialities – and everything is cooked to order. There are bar snacks – you can always get sandwiches, soup (in winter made on the Aga), and ploughman's – and there is an à la carte menu. Ballards Best, Courage Best and Directors, No Name Best, No Name Strong, Fuggles, Bass, Theakstons Old Peculier, Gales Festival Mild, Butser and IPA are among the ales on offer, plus guest ales. A considerable number of country wines, including wine from a local vineyard. There are occasional visits from those wonderful old steam road rollers and the pub is a meeting point for vintage cars and motorbikes. If you want to pitch your tent, you can do that too.

OPEN: 12–3, 6–11 (Sun 7–10.30).
Real Ale.
Children allowed in restaurant. Well-behaved dogs on leads. Wheelchair access.

Rockbourne

Rose & Thistle ① 01725 518236
Rockbourne, Fordingbridge SP6 3NL
Free House. Tim Norfolk, licensee
e-mail: enquiries@roseandthistle.co.uk

The timeless, thatched, 16th-century Rose and Thistle is in a charming village north-west of Fordingbridge. Small bridges cross the chalk stream that flows through the village, giving access to the houses on the north side. On the border of three counties, Hampshire, Dorset and Wiltshire, the village, with its thatched cottages and Tudor and Georgian houses, is a mix of centuries. Inside the beamed pub, the welcoming bar has the ambience you would expect. There is a short, well-chosen menu of freshly prepared food. Lunchtime favourites include home-made soup, scrambled eggs with smoked salmon, a cheese, ham or rare roast beef ploughman's, bacon and mushrooms on toast and local sausages and mustard mash. In the evening there are more substantial dishes such as fillet steak with a port and Stilton sauce, roast rack of lamb with redcurrant sauce or a venison steak with a red onion and raisin relish. There will always be fish, as well as a daily pasta dish and specials on the blackboard. Maybe seafood tagliatelle, roasted cod with lemon and black pepper crust or john dory stuffed with lime and coriander butter. Fullers London Pride and Strongs Best Bitter are on permanently, Hopback Brewery beers are the guests. Wide-ranging wine list, ten by the glass. This is a lovely area, a favoured place; certainly the Romans thought so, as over 50 years ago a substantial Roman villa was excavated east of the village. A museum on the site contains all the fascinating objects found there.

OPEN: 11–3, 6–11. Sun 12–3, 7–10.30.
Real Ale. Restaurant.
Children welcome, dogs too. Car park. Wheelchair access (not WC).
Cards: Delta, MasterCard, Switch, Visa.
N.B. Classical music sometimes on in bar.

Steep

Harrow Inn ① 01730 262685
Steep, Petersfield GU32 2DA
Free House. Ellen McCutcheon, licensee

Steep it is too; drive along a winding road north of Petersfield and you will find the pub sitting firmly on a ledge in the fold of a hill. It's slightly difficult to find: aim for the village of Sheet, turn left at the church, follow the sign to Steep and the Harrow is on the other side of the bypass bridge. Beside a winding stream, the narrow, tile-hung inn, parts of which are 16th century, has been lovingly tended by the McCutcheon family since the 1920s. Beamed and panelled, hung with hops and dried flowers, it has old oak benches in the public bar and a big inglenook fireplace. Beer is served through a hatch from the barrels behind. Generous portions of the home-cooked ham (cooked by the landlady), scotch eggs, soups, salads and, an added bonus, treacle and bakewell tart to follow. A hundred years of ale accounts have been kept by the pub; now the beers are: Ringwood Best, Cheriton Pots, Diggers Gold and Ballards Trotton beers. Country wines. Tables in the wild garden.

OPEN: 12–2.30 (Sat 11–3), 6–11. Sun 12–3, 7–10.30. Closed Sun eve Oct–Apr.
Real Ale.
No children. Dogs on leads. Always help for the wheelchair.

Tangley

Cricketers Arms ① 01264 730283
Tangley, Andover SP11 0SH
Free House. Edward Simpson, licensee

On the edge of the village, this old drover's inn is close to the borders of three counties: Berkshire, Hampshire and Wiltshire. Not only does it have a wonderful cricketing sign outside but the pub is full of cricketing memorabilia. Full of atmosphere, the front bar has a tiled floor, low beams, a huge inglenook fireplace and casks of ale on racks behind the bar. The bar food is well-cooked, traditional pub food at its best; they bake their own bread and well fill the rolls, which they call dustbin lids! And provide the customers with what they want: sausage and mash, ham and eggs and salmon fishcakes as well as a choice of fish and different casseroles. Cheriton Brewhouse Pots Ale, Hampshire Ironside and others from local micro-breweries. Wide-ranging wine list. Tables on the terrace.

OPEN: 11–3, 6–11.30.
Real Ale.
Children and dogs welcome. Car park. Wheelchair access. Ten en-suite bedrooms.
Cards: MasterCard, Visa.

Titchfield

Fishermans Rest ① 01329 845065
Mill Lane, Titchfield PO15 5RA
Laurel Pub Company. Teresa Gisborne, licensee

Position is the thing, and this pub is on the banks of the River Meon opposite the remains of Place House, previously Titchfield Abbey. Inside are comfortable, flagstone-floored bars with two log fires, papers to read and fishing bits and pieces on the walls for you to admire. The food is as you would expect: a good choice of familiar, freshly prepared dishes including ever-popular filled baked potatoes, fish and chips, steak and kidney pie. Daily specials are listed on the blackboard. Wadworths 6X, Flowers Original, Gales HSB, Bass and Boddingtons. Wines by the glass. Seats in the large, waterside garden.

OPEN: 11–11. Sun 12–10.30.
Real Ale.
Children allowed in the no-smoking area. Dogs welcome.

Upham

Brushmakers Arms ① 01489 860231
Shoe Lane, Upham, nr Bishops Waltham SO32 1JJ (village signposted from Winchester)
Free House. Tony Mottram, licensee

There are two Uphams in this part of Hampshire – the other one is Lower – literally, nearer to Winchester. In lovely countryside between Bishops Waltham and Winchester, this is a welcoming local with a comfortable, good-sized bar divided by a wood-burning stove in a central fireplace and a small snug; naturally there are brushes for most occasions hanging around the pub. Better than average choice of bar food and a Sunday roast; the menus are all on blackboards now, so things are constantly changing but there will always be four or five vegetarian dishes. Bass, Ringwood and Charles Wells Bombardier plus regular guest beers to wash it all down. A choice of malt whiskies, Addlestone cider and country wines. Seats outside on the terrace and the lawn.

OPEN: 11–3, 5.45–11. Sun 12–3, 7–10.30.
Real Ale.
Children welcome away from bar. Dogs on leads. Wheelchair access (not WC).

Well

Chequers Inn ① 01256 862605
Well, Odiham RG29 1TL
Hall & Woodhouse. Clare Baumann & Kieran Marshall, licensees

This charming 17th-century village pub is deep in the Hampshire countryside. Outside, at the front, is an attractive vine-covered terrace; inside it is beamed and panelled with shelves of books to read if you are waiting for someone and a log fire to sit by. The menu chalked on the blackboard in the bar is enterprising, changes daily and is cooked to order. Always some traditional bar snacks, otherwise it's whatever inspires the chef. Sunday roasts. Badgers Best, Fursty Ferret and Tanglefoot are the ales. Good range of wine.

OPEN: 11–3, 6–11. Sun 12–3.30, 7–10.30.
Real Ale. Restaurant. Food is served until 8.30 p.m Sun eve.
Dogs welcome – on leads.

Whitsbury

Cartwheel ① 01725 518362
Whitsbury Road, nr Fordingbridge SP6 3PQ
Free House. Patrick Lewis, licensee

In the scale of things this is quite a youthful place, only getting a licence in the 1920s. A listed, slate-roofed, tile-hung building, early last century it was a shop and wheelwrights – long since gone. Slightly difficult to find, along twisting country lanes between Salisbury and Fordingbridge, it's a pleasant, beamy country pub serving good imaginative food: freshly filled sandwiches, ploughman's, steaks, salads, local trout and daily specials. There are usually about six ales on offer which are continually changing, so what is here today may not be there next week – you'll have to go and see what they've got. Good-size garden with children's play area and summer barbecue.

OPEN: 11–2.30, 6–11. Sun 12–3, 7–10.30.
Real Ale. Restaurant.
Children in eating areas. Dogs welcome. Car park.

Winchester

Wykeham Arms ① 01962 853834
75 Kingsgate Street, Winchester SO23 9PE
Gales. Peter & Kate Miller, managers

A handsome, classy place tucked away down narrow streets near the school and Cathedral, the Wykeham Arms is beautifully run, with high standards in every department. Six rooms radiate from a central bar (where the serious drinking goes on), full of interesting furniture, bits and pieces, tankards by the score and anything else they find to create an appealing ambience. There is plenty of space for you to sample the extremely popular bar food; the lunchtime menu is changed daily and you should get there early to avoid disappointment as all Winchester seems to beat a path to the door. From the menu there could be cream of carrot and coriander soup, pork, Stilton and walnut terrine, fillet of beef carpaccio with wild roquette and parmesan shavings dressed with balsamic syrup and, for a main course, pan-roasted rack of Hampshire down lamb on ratatouille with garlic roasted potatoes and fresh asparagus finished in a rosemary jus, oven-baked breast of free-range chicken on celeriac gratin, with braised leeks and sweet potato coated in a red wine sauce or a fillet of smoked haddock on bacon and leek risotto, buttered spinach and broccoli in a classic hollandaise sauce. Specials will be on the blackboard. There is also an award-winning, very interesting restaurant menu as well as an impressive wine list. Several no-smoking areas. Draught Bass and Gales range of ales. Seats on the terrace and small lawn.

OPEN: 11–11. No snacks Sun.
Real Ale. Evening restaurant.
No children. Dogs on leads. Car park. Fourteen en-suite bedrooms.
Cards: Amex, MasterCard, Switch, Visa.

Isle of Wight

Bonchurch Inn ① 01983 852611
The Shute, Bonchurch, Ventnor, Isle of Wight PO38 1NU
Free House. Ulisse & Aline Besozzi, licensees
e-mail: bonchurchinn@ aol.com

Everything seems to be on a steep slope in this part of the Island and the inn is no exception. Tucked into the hill, in a delightful village with its own beach, this is one of the prettiest areas and the Bonchurch Inn is a delight. Inside the owners have created a remarkably old-style English pub full of interesting junk – statues, pottery and all sorts of other stuff that fills up any odd space. Even the floors have a history, having come from a ship's deck, and as for the chairs, they're from an ocean liner! As well as the traditional English pub fare you'll find several Italian specialities in the Italian restaurant and on the wide-ranging bar snack menu: tagliatelle carbonara, seafood risotto, risotto Milanese and home-made lasagne, as well as plaice with a prawn sauce, king prawns provençale with rice, chicken Cordon Bleu or grilled fillet steak. Good, small wine list, also Courage Directors and local beers. Ruddles is the summer beer.

OPEN: 11–3, 6.30–11. Sun 12–3, 7–10.30.
Real Ale. Italian restaurant.
Children welcome. Dogs in public bar. Car park. Wheelchair access. Self-catering holiday flat.
Cards: all credit cards.

S. Fowler & Co
41–43 Union Street, Ryde, Isle of Wight ① 01983 812112
Wetherspoon.

Always aware of the importance of local traditions and social history, Wetherspoon kept the name of the well-known shop and just changed the fittings: clothes rails and haberdashery out, beer pumps and kitchens in. As usual it looks wonderful; they have done the old place proud. Ryde is a hugely popular resort; the building of the pier in 1813 was the start of a love affair with tourists which has continued to this day. Here, as with all Wetherspoon's pubs, you will get a very reasonably priced pint of beer (they say about 30 per cent less than in other places). No wonder all the customers are happy. Seasonally changing menus and always a big no-smoking area.

OPEN: 11–11.
Real Ale.
No children. No dogs.

BEST OF THE REST

Clanville
Red Lion Country Inn ① 01264 771007
Clanville, nr Andover SP11 9HN
A large car park and a helicopter landing pad: what more could you want? That said, they welcome you however you arrive – by bike if you wish. What was once a modest brick and flint coaching inn has been hugely extended. Lots of rooms for lots of functions and different menus in different places: 'light bites' and daily specials in the bar and à la carte menu in the bistro. They also serve a traditional Sunday lunch. Fullers London Pride, Brakspear ales and whatever else you could ever want. Children and dogs welcome. All disabled facilities.
Open: 11–3, 6–11.

Crondall
Plume of Feathers ① 01252 850245
The Borough, Crondall GU10 5NT
A 500-year-old pub on the remains of a late 11th-century building mentioned in the Domesday book, this is an attractive old place, beamed and full of character; you will be well looked after here. They serve good, familiar bar food: home-made soup, ploughman's, baguettes, steak sandwiches, lasagne, terrines, fresh fish, steak, ale and mushroom pie, also game in season from the specials board. Ruddles Best, Greene King range, Charles Wells Bombardier as a guest and a choice of wines. Children, dogs and wheelchairs – all welcome.
Open: 11–3, 6–11. Sun 12–10.30.

Droxford
White Horse Inn ① 01489 877490
South Hill, Droxford SO32 3PB
With quiet areas and noisy bits, the 17th-century White Horse is a bit of a mixture; a quiet, beamed lounge bar and no-smoking restaurant, but a public bar with games, jukebox and music. A varied bar menu offers a home-made soup, filled French sticks, locally smoked salmon paté, steak pie cooked in Guinness, fish pie and various game pies. Fruit pies and crumbles to finish. Morlands Old Speckled Hen, Flowers Original, Burton Bridge, Guinness, also Morlands IPA, Kaliber and White Label bitter. Children in family room and restaurant. Dogs firmly under control. Bedrooms.
Open: 11–11.

Longstock

Peat Spade ① 01264 810612

Longstock, nr Stockbridge SO20 6DR

An elegant, warm and comfortable pub in a pretty village, the Peat Spade, an inn since the middle of the 19th century, has grown from somewhere serving 'luncheons and teas' to a place offering a wide range of freshly prepared dishes streets ahead of the usual pub food. From the regularly changing menu: salad of smoked eel and smoked mackerel, rillette of duck with apple chutney, breast of Gressingham duck with damson sauce, home-made ravioli of mushrooms, cream cheese and smoked baby tomatoes, home-made faggots and mash and well-filled sandwiches. Carefully selected wine list. Ringwood Best, 49er, Hampshire King Alfred or Strong ales. Lovely garden and terrace which you share with some Scottish Grey chickens. (We have had a complaint about the exorbitant price of a pint of shandy here – £2.85, and quite how this is justified we don't know. The price in Wetherspoons is £1.40. So watch what you drink.) Children and dogs welcome. Wheelchair access. Two bedrooms.

Open: 11.30–3, 6–11. Closed Sun eve & Mon.

Isle of Wight

Red Lion ① 01983 754925

Church Place, Freshwater, Isle of Wight PO40 9BP

Next to the church, near the River Yar and the causeway, the Red Lion is extremely popular during the season – particularly weekends. Really old, this comfortable pub serves an interesting, varied menu to go with Flowers Original, Fullers London Pride, Wadworths 6X and a local guest beer. Decent wine list; about 15 by the glass. Good walks nearby. Children over 10 allowed in.

Open: 11.30–3, 5.30–11.

Wetherspoon in Hampshire

Andover – John Russell Fox, 10 High Street
01264 320920
Basingstoke – Maidenhead Inn, 17 Winchester Street
01256 316030
Cosham – First Post, 42 High Street
01705 210331
Fareham – Lord Arthur Lee, 100–108 West Street
01329 280447
Fleet – Prince Arthur, 238 Fleet Road
01252 622660
Gosport – Star, 28–29 High Street
023 9251 2130
Havant – Parchment Makers, 1 Park Road North
01705 474023
Portsmouth – Isambard Kingdom Brunel, 2 Guildhall Walk
01705 295112
Portsmouth – John Jaques, 72–82 Fratton Road
023 9277 97420
Portsmouth – Sir John Baker, 80 London Road, Northend
023 9262 7960
Shirley – Bright Water Inn, 370–372 Shirley Road
023 8077 6717
Southampton – Giddy Bridge, 12–18 London Road
01703 336346
Southampton – Standing Order, 30 High Street
01703 222121
Winchester – Old Goal House, 11 Jewry Street
01962 850095
Isle of Wight – S. Fowler & Co, 41–43 Union Street, Ryde
01983 812112

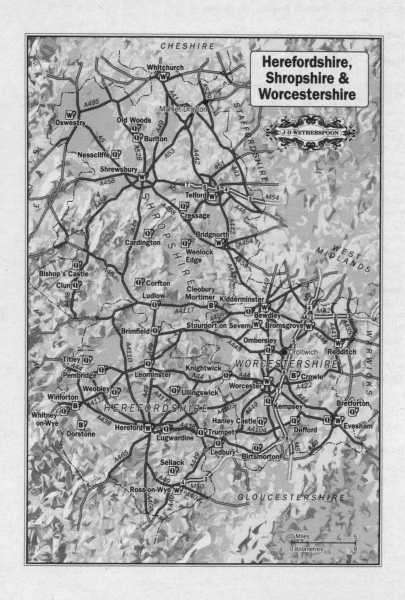

Herefordshire, Shropshire and Worcestershire

Bewdley

Little Pack Horse ① 01299 403762
31 High Street, Bewdley, Worcs DY12 2DH
Inspired Pubs plc. Michael Gaunt, licensee
e-mail: littlepackhorse@aol.com

Being in the middle of an old town clinging to the hillside on the west bank of the River Severn is probably enough to allow the Little Pack Horse some cheerful eccentricity. Low-beamed, well-timbered and cosy, the pub, home to the famous 'Desperate Dan Pie', has great appeal. The pies have inventive fillings, otherwise the food leaps from a traditional pub menu – sandwiches, filled baguettes and jacket potatoes, sausage and mash, that sort of thing, to the more exotic – sautéed native mussels in a garlic and cream sauce, oriental tiger prawn chow mein, fresh roasted tuna steak on a niçoise salad, half roast Cajun chicken, as well as about five vegetarian dishes and satisfying puds. Greene King IPA and a guest ale. On the fringe of Wyre forest – the remains of a Royal hunting ground – and near a three-mile-long nature trail. Note: there is no nearby parking.

OPEN: 12–3, 6–11. Sat 11–11. Sun 11–10.30.
Real Ale.
Children in back bar or stable room.
Cards: MasterCard, Visa, Switch, Solo, Electron.

Birtsmorton

Farmers Arms ① 01684 833308
Birts Street, Birtsmorton, nr Malvern WR13 6AP
Free House. Jill & Julie Moore, licensees
e-mail: farmersarmsbirtsmorton@yahoo.co.uk

A welcoming black and white timbered pub with a low-beamed, rambling interior and traditional furnishing; a favourite local. Well cared for and ably run by a mother and daughter team. On the menu is a good range of familiar bar food including sandwiches, ploughman's, salads, steak and kidney pie, mixed grill, steaks and good puddings. Well-kept Hook Norton Old Hooky and guest beers on hand pump. Seats in the garden during summer. Many good walks nearby.

OPEN: 11–2 (Sat 11–3), 6–10.
Real Ale.
Children welcome. Dogs on leads. Wheelchair access.

Bishop's Castle

Three Tuns ☎ 01588 638797
Salop Street, Bishop's Castle, Shropshire SY9 5BW
Free House. Janet Cross, licensee

Wonderful news: the brewery is brewing again. We thought that three hundred and fifty years of brewing at the Three Tuns had come to a halt but they are back in business. The Victorian building, on the site of the original 17th-century brewery, has been taken over by the John Robert Brewing Co. and has been fully restored. The inn and the black and white malt store are probably contemporary with the granting of its licence in 1642. Inside, the plainly furnished pub reflects its age, retaining many original features including heavy oak beams and a good Jacobean staircase. The changing blackboard menu includes traditional dishes with an emphasis on local produce. The Three Tuns popular fish soup, a number of fish, vegetarian dishes and interesting pub specials such as beef in ale – all freshly prepared. The original XXX Bitter is back on pump; the other beers include Remergence and Castle Steamer. There is an interesting small wine list. In July they hold a summer beer festival. Seats on the terrace and in the sheltered summery garden. Lovely walking country.

OPEN: 11.30–11.
Real Ale. Dining room.
Children welcome if well behaved. Dogs in bar and snug. En-suite rooms available in the converted stable block.
Occasionally there is live music in the Victorian Assembly Room attached to the pub.

Bretforton

Fleece ☎ 01386 831173
The Cross, Bretforton, nr Evesham, Worcs WR11 5JE
Third Room Ltd Small Pubs Group. Nigel Smith, licensee
e-mail: nigel@thefleeceinn.co.uk

A treasure not to be missed, the Fleece is a unique, living museum full of the most wonderful family collection of antique furniture, pewter, china, ornaments and artifacts: a timeless interior still with witch's marks on the flagstones in front of the fireplace. Five hundred years of a family's life remains, much as it was when it was given to the National Trust on the death of Miss Taplin in 1977. A medieval farmhouse, the Fleece only became an inn during the 19th century. During its long life it has been added to and extended and these alterations can be seen by the changes in the timber framing at the front of the pub. Once completely thatched, the roof is now a mixture of thatch and stone. Beer was brewed in the back kitchen well into the 19th century. It seems a bit mundane to talk about food and beer, but special as this place is, it is still the village local and as such provides good ales and an equally good choice of generous, varying bar food; a full menu is served both at lunchtime and in the evening. Hook Norton, Uley Old Spot, Pig's Ear, Ansells Bitter and two guests. Country wines and farm ciders. Seats outside in the orchard.

OPEN: 11–3, 5.30–11. Sat 11–11. Sun 12–10.30. (June–September Mon–Sat open 11–11.)
Real Ale.
Children welcome. No dogs when food is served; in garden the rest of the time.
Occasional live entertainment and lots of summer 'events'. Visiting Morris men and silver band.

Brimfield

Roebuck Inn ☾ 01584 711230
Brimfield, nr Ludlow, Shropshire SY8 4NE
Free House. Peter & Julie Jenkins, licensees
e-mail: peter@theroebuckinn.com

A fine old 16th-century pub on the borders of three counties: Hereford, Worcester and Shropshire. A complete all-rounder, it has an atmospheric bar with beams and panelling, an exceptionally well-regarded restaurant, and classy accommodation. This is a well-loved, lively local serving really good home-made food; the choice is considerable. There is something for everyone: 'soup of the moment', lemon spiced gravadlax, crab ravioli, quails eggs, figs and balsamic salad, pan-seared scallops, roast chicken breast served with a sauce of caramelised button onions, smoked bacon and red wine, their famous fish pie, tenderloin of pork stuffed with wild mushrooms, coated with a garlic and herb crust served with a grain mustard sauce, fillet of wild venison, prime fillet steak in a red wine and shallot jus and a fantastic choice of puddings. An even more extensive menu features in the restaurant. Woods ales, Tetleys Cask and a weekly guest. Local ciders and some half bottles of wine from a wine list featuring French and New World wines.

OPEN: 12–2.30, 7–11.
Real Ale. Restaurant – two AA rosettes.
Children welcome. Dogs in the snug bar. Car park. Wheelchair access (not WC).
Bedrooms – four AA diamonds.
Cards: Delta, MasterCard, Switch, Visa.
N.B. Occasional CD in front bar.

Bromsgrove

Golden Cross Hotel ☾ 01527 870005
20 High Street, Bromsgrove, Worcs B61 8HH
Wetherspoon.

What was an old, run-down commercial hotel has been knocked about and transformed into a busy, popular pub – improving the local area and livening things up a bit. Standards are high, the beer is a reasonable price, facilities are good and the food is reliable. The menus throughout the Wetherspoon chain change three times a year but there will always be some daily specials on offer. As for the beers: six regulars, including Courage Directors,

Theakstons Best & XB, Youngers Scotch Bitter, Banks Mild, Morlands Old Speckled Hen and guest ales. The new long bar has 21 hand pumps! They drink a lot of beer here.

OPEN: 11–11. Sun 12–10.30.
Real Ale.
No children. No dogs. All wheelchair facilities.

Burlton

Burlton Inn ① 01939 270284
Burlton, nr Shrewsbury, Shropshire SY4 5TB
Free House. Ann & Gerry Bean, licensees
e-mail: bean@burltoninn.co.uk

On the road, and unmissable, this pub is in the front row for prizes for its displays of hanging baskets and tubs of flowers. Behind the eye-catching show is the family-run, comfortable and stylish Burlton. There is room inside for you to sit and appreciate the well-kept beers but much of the space is taken up by diners. They serve interesting, home-cooked food seven days a week; anything from a light snack to a four-course meal. Always filled rolls, sandwiches, ploughman's and specials from the blackboard; you could start with a platter of Scottish smoked salmon, New Zealand mussels, giant king prawns with a piquant mayonnaise or garlic bread topped with red onion and melted cheddar and as a main course, grilled field mushrooms topped with pesto and Parmesan crumb served with a garlic croute, steak, kidney and beer pie or cider chicken tagliatelle, more fish and steaks too. Always four real ales: Banks's Bitter and Camerons Strong Arm the regulars. Short wine list, some by the glass. Seats outside on the terrace and in the lovely garden.

OPEN: 11–3, 6–11. Sun 12–3, 7–10.30. Mon lunchtime: only soup, rolls or ploughman's.
Real Ale.
Children welcome. Dogs on leads. Car park. Wheelchair access. There is an annexe with six en-suite bedrooms, one with disabled facilities.
Cards: Delta, MasterCard, Switch, Visa.

Cardington

Royal Oak ① 01694 771266
Cardington, nr Church Stretton, Shropshire SY6 7JZ
Free House. Mike Carter, licensee

Tucked behind the church in this quiet village, the charming creeper-covered 15th-century Royal Oak is reputed to be the oldest pub in Shropshire. Inside it has a rambling, well-beamed bar with a good log fire in the inglenook fireplace, where they serve reliable bar food at lunchtime including ploughman's, soups and filled baguettes, traditional Shropshire Fidget, steak and onion and chicken and vegetable pies – all freshly baked – steaks, mixed grill and specials on the board. Bass, Hobsons and Woods Parish Bitter. About a mile from the pub is Caer Caradoc, 1500ft high, where, so it is said, the British chieftain Caractacus made his last stand against the Romans in AD 50 – you can walk up there too, stand and admire the view. Tables on the terrace at the front of the pub with views over the glorious undulating countryside.

OPEN: 12–3, 7–11 (Fri 6–11). Closed Mon except bank holidays.
Real Ale.
Children welcome. No dogs.

Clun

Sun Inn ① 01588 640559
10 High Street, Clun, Craven Arms, Shropshire SY7 8JB
Free House. Mr & Mrs Osborne, licensees

Clun, in the impressive Clun river valley, is one of the most ancient settlements in the country, inhabited since the Bronze Age. Drive along high-hedged lanes to Clun village and the very ancient Sun at Clun. It is not obvious from the outside but this is a 15th-century, cruck-framed building full of beams, huge flagstones and equally huge fireplaces; the atmosphere is wonderful. Food is plentiful and good, much of the produce locally sourced. The bar menu lists some familiar dishes: home-made cottage pie, steak and kidney pudding, lasagne and daily specials, vegetarian options too. Beers are Banks, Hobsons and a guest. Close to the Shropshire border, Clun is dominated by the ruins of the 12th-century castle built by the Normans to keep out the troublesome Welsh. Unbelievably there are 95 rights of the way in the parish; the Clun Valley is the most wonderful area for walking, with Clun forest, Long Mynd, the surrounding hills and the rest.

OPEN: 12–3. 5–11 (Sun 7–11). Closed Wed lunchtimes.
Real Ale. Restaurant.
Children allowed only when dining. Dogs on leads. Car park. Bedrooms.
Cards: Switch, Visa. No Amex or Diners.

Corfton

Sun Inn ① 01584 861239
Corfton, nr Craven Arms, Shropshire SY7 9DF
Free House. Teresa & Norman Pearce, licensees
e-mail: normanspride@aol.com

'Normans Pride' is one of the pub's ales brewed behind the pub in their own microbrewery – Corvedale Brewery. At quiet times, if you ask nicely, a tour can be arranged. This is an old pub, licensed in 1613 and thought to be the oldest licensed premises in Corvedale. There is a regularly changing selection of dishes: the popular lamb Shrewsbury and Shrewsbury stew as well as gammon, various steaks and fish dishes, a vegetarian menu and somewhere there is a pudding menu too. Eggs are free range, vegetables from local growers and meat from the local butcher. Four real ales from the pub's own brewery are permanent, but approximately 1200 guest ales have been tried. Seats in the garden. They hold small beer festivals with 15-plus ales to try at Easter and the

August Bank Holiday. Ales produced on the premises are bottled and are available as a souvenir.

OPEN: 12–2.30, 6–11. Sun 12–3, 7–10.30.
Real Ale.
Children welcome. Dogs on leads in front bar. Wheelchair ramps to all parts of pub. Disabled toilets. They have won the 'Open to All' award for services to the disabled.
Cards: All except American Express.
N.B. Music in the public bar. Lounge and dining area quiet.

Cressage

Riverside Inn at Cound ① 01952 510900
Cressage, nr Shrewsbury, Shropshire SY4 1DB
Free House. Peter Stanford Davis, licensee

This is an appealing stretch of the River Severn; and if you are staying, you can fish for free. Open fires, beams and flagstone floors in this well-run, renovated, 17th-century coaching inn. Everything goes on here; you can stay, get married and have a mini-conference – they have two executive rooms – and eat well. The menu ranges from home-made soups, filled baguettes, chicken breasts in a mushroom and cream sauce to fillet steak. Delicious puds to follow. Interesting wine list, Marstons Best and Pedigree plus some weekly changing guests. Seats in the garden from where you can appreciate the charms of the river.

OPEN: 11–11. Winter Sun 12–3, 7–10.30.
Real Ale.
Children welcome. Dogs on leads. Bedrooms.
N.B. Music in the tiny reception area, but not throughout the pub.

Defford

The Cider House (Monkey) ① 01386 750234
Woodmancote, Defford, Worcester WR8 9BW (no pub sign, the last cottage after Oak Public House)
Free House. Graham Collins, licensee

Nothing much changes. Run by one family for over 150 years, this is a traditional cider house but with no obvious sign. It could be just any pretty black and white cottage at the end of a row of cottages, except for a notice near the door saying they sell cider and tobacco. The cider is kept in barrels from which they fill a jug they pass through a hatch and fill a mug – an experience not to be missed. Simple and totally unspoilt, it is one of only a few of these unique places left in the country. Beer is available – in a can; nuts and crisps to sustain you. However, there is nothing to stop you bringing your own picnic to enjoy with the cider.

OPEN: 11–2.30, 6–10.30 (Fri & Sat 6–11). Closed Mon eve, all day Tues and Wed & Thurs lunchtime.
Cider.
No food. No dogs. Wheelchair access.

Evesham

Evesham Hotel ① 01386 765566
Coopers Lane, off Waterside, Evesham, Worcs WR11 1DA
Free House. John Jenkinson, licensee
e-mail: reception@eveshamhotel.com

Evesham, a market town on the River Avon, is in the centre of a famous fruit-growing district, and in spring is surrounded by fields of blossom. The Evesham, originally just a 16th-century farmhouse, is not so much a pub but a well-known hotel – with a welcoming bar – in lovely grounds. As our informant says, 'The owner is a little eccentric but charming, and certainly aims for, and achieves, the highest standards in food and service. The slightly quirky menu gives a full description of the dishes, leaving you in no doubt as to what you'll be getting.' Well, this is what it could be, from the 'un-mucked about food' menu: home-made soup of the day, Scottish smoked salmon with fresh lime and brown bread and butter, Dover sole, salmon steak grilled or poached and pork escalope pan fried with apple. You could also sample the reasonably priced, substantial buffet lunch or, from the daily changing menus, a fricassée of seafood, oriental lamb served with long-grain and wild rice in an oyster mushroom sauce or cider-baked rabbit. Many more imaginative dishes, delicious puddings and a good cheese selection. A fascinating, amusingly described list of the more unusual alcoholic drinks available, as well as an extensive wine list. Something for absolutely everyone.

OPEN: hotel hours.
Only keg beer. No-smoking restaurant. Mobile phones are forbidden in all public rooms.
Children and dogs can stay. Car park. Wheelchair access.
Cards: Amex, Diners, MasterCard.

Hanley Castle

Three Kings ① 01684 592686
Hanley Castle, Worcester WR8 0BL (north of Upton upon Severn off B4211)
Free House. Mrs Sheila Roberts, licensee

The same family have been running this well-loved old place for over 90 years, and nothing much has changed. Attractively timbered, with a really big inglenook, the 15th-century building has several small rooms, including a tap room, each with its own atmosphere. Always a good choice of bar snacks ranging from soups and sandwiches, to ploughman's and omelettes. Gammon and egg and a toasted bacon and mushroom sandwich are the most popular items. Specials, which can take half an hour to prepare, include grilled trout and steaks. Beer is served through a hatch and includes Thwaites and

Butcombe Bitter plus three guest beers. Over 50 malt whiskies and one farm cider. Seats at the front of the pub overlook the village green. In November they hold an annual beer festival.

OPEN: 12–3, 7–11 (roughly!). No food Sun eves.
Real Ale.
Children in family room. Dogs, do ask. One letting bedroom.
Live music Sun and some Sat eves.

Kempsey

Walter de Cantelupe Inn ① 01905 820572
34 Main Road, Kempsey, Worcs WR5 3NA
Free House. Martin Lloyd Morris, manager/owner

Just south of Worcester and a short walk from the River Severn is this pub with an unforgettable name. During the 13th century, a local man, Walter de Cantelupe, commemorated in the name of the pub, became Bishop of Worcester. The compact, informal and unassuming inn makes a point of using, where possible, locally produced vegetables, meat and cheese to create a reasonably priced, well-chosen menu which includes their very own speciality – mushrooms in a cream sauce with brioche. Home-made soup, usually vegetarian, smoked Scottish salmon cornets filled with prawns, grilled gammon, wild mushroom and fennel stroganoff, chicken breast stuffed with Stilton, wrapped in smoked bacon and covered in a mushroom and Calvados sauce, baked sea bass fillet, freshly filled sandwiches, curry, steaks and other dishes. During the six-week asparagus season they have a special menu featuring locally grown asparagus. A favourite pudding is a banana-filled pancake served with toffee sauce and crème fraiche. Quality wines by the glass; they hold regular free tasting sessions. Very well-kept Everards Beacon, Timothy Taylors Landlord, King's Shilling from the Droitwich brewery Cannon Royall, and a guest ale, usually from one of the smaller breweries. Seats in the flowery hidden garden.

OPEN: 12–2.30, 6–11. Sun 12–3, 7–10.30. Closed all day Mon.
Real Ale.
Children lunchtime & until 8.15 p.m. Well-behaved dogs allowed. Car park. Wheelchair access (not WC). Three bedrooms.
Cards: Amex, Delta, MasterCard, Switch, Visa.

Knightwick

Talbot Inn ① 01886 821235
Knightwick, nr Worcester WR6 5PH (at Knightsford Bridge off A44 Worcester–Bromyard)
Free House. Ann & Wizz Clift, licensees
e-mail: admin@the-talbot.co.uk

Local hops are used to brew their very own beer, most of the vegetables for the kitchen are home-grown, happy hens at the back lay the eggs and local farmers supply what they can to fill the gaps. As much as possible is locally sourced. This is an efficient 'we know where it comes from' supply line, mostly from within the Teme Valley area – organic if possible. A comfortable, 15th-century coaching inn, the Talbot has a reputation for serving imaginative, well-cooked food, well-kept ales (their own) and good wines. A daily changing menu for both bar and restaurant features interesting and adventurous dishes. From the bar menu you could choose fresh crab blinis with garlic mayonnaise, smoked salmon with salmon ceviche, carrot and fennel soup, meat balls with rice and tomato, chicken and leek casserole or salmon kedgeree with stir-fried spinach. From the main menu there could be stuffed pork loin, shellfish pasta or pot roast grouse. Proper puddings too, such as sticky date and toffee pudding, Malvern apple pudding or lemon meringue pie. Sunday roast. Their own-brew beers are: 'This', 'That', 'T-other' and 'Wot' – all on hand pump. Good wine list and wines by the glass. Seats outside and opposite the pub. Lots of walks nearby. (For the last three years the Talbot were winners of 'Tastes of Worcestershire' in the public house/inn category.)

OPEN: 11–11.
Real Ale. Restaurant.
Children in eating area until 7.30. Dogs: ask first. Car park. Wheelchair access is just possible. Bedrooms.
Cards: Amex, Delta, MasterCard, Switch, Visa.
A Teme Valley Farmer's Market is held on the second Sunday of every month at the pub. Morris dancers winter Wed.
N.B. Juke box in the back bar.

Ledbury

Feathers Hotel ① 01531 635266
High Street, Ledbury, Herefordshire HR8 1DS
Free House. D.M. Elliston, licensee
e-mail: mary@feathers-ledbury.co.uk

Close to the impressive, chestnut-pillared 17th-century market hall and surrounded by narrow lanes full of half-timbered buildings, the handsome, 16th-century Feathers is a wonderful example of timber-framed building. Locals and visitors make for the big, beamed bar and the Fuggles Brasserie – the name of a local hop – where they can choose something from the menu: chargrilled vegetable terrine with mixed leaves, warm salad of button mushrooms and smoked bacon with hazelnut dressing, baked cod fillet with white wine, tomato and basil, chive fishcakes with French fries, tournedos of Herefordshire beef fillet with thyme, wild mushrooms, burgundy and glazed shallots or tenderloin of pork with fresh sage, Marsala and lemon jus. Lots of fish, sea bass, hake, tuna, Cornish plaice or lemon sole, vegetarian dishes and imaginative home-made puddings. There is also an elegant restaurant (Quills), and they serve tea in the lounge. Three-course Sunday lunch. Fullers London Pride, Worthington BB and Bass on hand pump plus two guest beers. Large wine list and choice of malt whiskies and farm ciders. There are seats outside on the flowery terrace.

OPEN: 11–11.
Real Ale. Restaurant.
Children in eating area. Dogs on leads. Wheelchair access (not WC). Bedrooms.
Cards: Delta, Mastercard, Switch, Visa.

Leominster

Grape Vaults ① 01568 611404
Broad Street, Leominster, Herefordshire HR6 8BS
Free House. Philip & Julie Saxon, licensees

Among Broad Street's fine Georgian buildings is the restored Grape Vaults, a small 17th-century pub with much to recommend it. No fruit machines, computer games or jukebox, just the murmur of satisfied customers and the clink of glasses. All the advantages of an English country inn, but in town. There is a wide-ranging bar menu of home-cooked food and specials to go with the Marstons Pedigree, Banks Original and Bitter and the two daily changing guests.

OPEN: 11–3, 5–11. Sun 12–3, 7–10.30.
Real Ale.
No children. Dogs on leads. Wheelchair access just possible.

Ludlow

Unicorn ① 01584 873555
Corve Street, Ludlow, Shropshire SY8 1DU
Free House. Mike & Rita Knox, licensees

The Unicorn is on the banks of the small, willow-fringed River Corve which eventually merges with the much larger River Teme in Ludlow, a town full of architectural treasures and dominated by the remains of an 11th-century castle. Near the centre of town is the half-timbered 17th-century Unicorn. Inside are beams, oak panelling and fires in the inglenook – everything you would hope to see. There are two dining areas in the pub, one with a view over the flood meadows on the other side of the river. Above average bar food with daily specials on the blackboard – ham served with a parsley sauce, black pudding with a cider and mustard sauce – always some vegetarian dishes. Chicken wrapped in bacon in a cream and mushroom sauce is on the restaurant menu as well as half a chicken roasted in ginger wine and apple sauce, fillet of cod with crab and prawn bisque and lots more well-thought-out, well-cooked dishes. Beers are draught Bass, Hancocks HB, Timothy Taylors Landlord and two guests which change twice a month. Seats on the terrace of this attractive old place with views over the Corve river.

OPEN: 12–2.30, 6–11. Sun 12 until empty, 7–10.30.
Real Ale. Restaurant.
Children welcome. Dogs on leads. Wheelchair access to the back of the pub.

Lugwardine

Crown & Anchor ① 01432 851303
Cotts Lane, Lugwardine, Hereford HR1 4AB (off A438 east of Hereford)
Free House. Nick & Julie Squire, licensees

Two miles from the centre of Hereford, this small 16th-century black and white building used to be a favourite haunt of bargees on the nearby River Lugg, but the opening of the

Gloucester to Hereford canal in 1845 led to a decline in fortunes – now very much revived. Inside the pub are comfortable, beamed rooms, a huge log fire and one family room. They offer a good variety of traditional bar food, blackboard specials and well-kept ales. Plenty to choose from in the bar: avocado and prawns with fresh green herb mayonnaise, garlic mushrooms, spiced chicken wings with tomato and garlic sauce, Poacher's pie (flaked salmon in cream sauce with potato and cheese topping), chicken with lemon and sweet pepper sauce, roast guinea fowl with apple and walnut stuffing, game sausages in Madeira wine with button onions and mushrooms, pot roast partridge with brandy, white wine and parsnip purée, grills, vegetarian dishes, vegan dishes and either a ploughman's (cheese pickle and crusty bread) or a squire's lunch (a selection of cold meats, salad, pickle and crusty bread). More salads, children's menu and puddings. A daily changing specials board too. Worthington BB, Butcombe Bitter, Timothy Taylors Landlord and a weekly changing guest beer all on hand pump. A range of wines. Seats in the delightful garden.

OPEN: 11.30–11. Sandwiches are served Mon to Sat lunchtime only.
Real Ale.
Children welcome. Dogs on leads. Wheelchair access.

Nesscliffe

Old Three Pigeons ① 01743 741279
Nesscliffe, nr Shrewsbury, Shropshire SY4 1DB
Free House. Mike Brooks, licensee

On the Shrewsbury to Oswestry road, this stone-built 17th-century pub was constructed as economically as possible, using secondhand ship's timbers – floated up the Severn perhaps, and hauled onto site. Things have certainly moved on a bit over the centuries. Now they have pieces of military hardware dotted around, all for hire – a Russian tank anyone? – not the first thing you associate with a pub. More understandably, a collection of feathered friends are out at the back, some of which lay eggs. However, inside this well-used, well-liked old place it is quite traditional; two bars, log fires and a good-size restaurant serving food that is just that little bit different. Inspiration changes all the time – so does the menu. Everything is written on the huge blackboard where you'll find lots of fresh fish and locally raised meat, all cooked to order. Three weekly changing ales and a good wine list, some by the glass.

OPEN: 11.30–3, 6–11. Sun 12–10.30. Closed winter Mon & Tues.
Real Ale. Restaurant.
Children welcome. No dogs. Wheelchair access.

Old Woods

Romping Cat ① 01939 290273
Old Woods, Shrewsbury, Shropshire SY4 3AX
Free House. Mr G. Simcox, licensee

Keen beer drinkers come for miles to this pub in a small hamlet about five miles north-west of Shrewsbury. They are only here for the beer as they don't do food. Just one room with an open fire and a snug, both very cosy and decorated with a collection of framed prints and photographs. On hand pump, the ales could be Boddingtons, London Pride and a choice from four guest beers – they change all the time.

OPEN: 12–2.30, 6–11 (Sat 7–11, Sun 7–10.30). Closed Mon, Wed & Fri lunchtimes.
Real Ale. No food.
Children welcome. Dogs too.

Ombersley

Kings Arms ① 01905 620142
Main Road, Ombersley, Droitwich, Worcs WR9 0EW
Free House. David Pendry, licensee
e-mail: kaombersley@btconnect.com

No music and no machines either in this rambling old place, just handsome beamed rooms with lots of nooks and crannies and good log fires in the inglenook fireplaces. A 16th-century black and white inn with a definite lean away from the vertical, and tremendous charm; big, beamed and aptly named. Charles II supposedly took refuge here after his defeat at the Battle of Worcester in 1651; he probably did too as someone bothered to put his coat of arms on the ceiling in one of the rooms. Plenty of choice from the changing menus; these could include buttered prawns with warm potato salad, roasted lemon chicken risotto, Mediterranean fish stew and for a main course, chargrilled fillet of English beef on watercress and garlic mash with rich red wine sauce, roast rack of English lamb on mint salsa with lyonnise potatoes, local sausages of the day with mash and onion gravy, and a seafood platter or paella for two. Fish from the daily changing blackboard, puddings and English cheeses. Draught Banks's Bitter, Marstons Pedigree, Hook Norton Old Hooky and Riding Bitter. A range of malt and Irish whiskies and a good wine list, a dozen by the glass. Tables in the walled garden among the summer flowers.

OPEN: 11–2.45, 5.30–11. Sat 12–10.30.
Real Ale.
Children, not after 8.30 p.m. No dogs. Car park. Wheelchair access.
Cards: Delta, MasterCard, Switch, Visa.

Pembridge

New Inn ① 01544 388427
Market Square, Pembridge, Hereford HR6 9DZ
Free House. Jane Melvin, licensee

The most wonderful black and white inn, a traditional place with all you would expect from a building this old. Contemporary with the Market Hall and the church, in a tiny medieval village of half-timbered houses, the 14th-century 'new' inn is a delight; flagstones and heavily beamed bars inside – with not a right angle between them – and a fireplace big enough for half a tree. Well-chosen home-cooked food: smoked haddock and spring onion fishcakes, croissant filled with hot garlic mushrooms, Herefordshire beef casserole with horseradish dumplings, chicken, leek and cider pie, seafood stew and crusty bread, different variations on a ploughman's, filled jacket potatoes, hot and cold fillings for the crusty bread sandwiches and interesting puddings. Fullers London Pride, Dunn Ploughman Kingdom

Bitter, Woods Shropshire Lad and Black Sheep beers. New World wines and a considerable range of malt whiskies. Tables outside with views towards the church. The separate bell tower, with arrow slits, was used as a refuge during the Welsh border wars.

OPEN: 11–3, 6–11 (winter 6.30–11).
Real Ale. Restaurant (not Sun eve).
Children in eating area until 9 p.m. No dogs. Car park. Wheelchair access (not WC).
Bedrooms.
Cards: MasterCard, Switch, Visa.

Sellack

Lough Pool Inn ☎ 01989 730236
Sellack, nr Ross-on-Wye, Hereford HR9 6LX
Free House. Stephen Bull, owner/licensee

North of Ross-on-Wye, deep in some of the best countryside, this black and white 17th-century pub is full of character. Glorious hanging baskets outside, beams, flagstone floors and inglenook fireplaces inside – just as it should be. With a professional chef running the pub you can be sure that the bar menu is better than average and includes some interesting dishes and imaginative daily specials. From the menu there could be Piedmontese peppers baked with tomatoes, garlic and anchovies, ham and guinea fowl terrine with quince chutney and brioche, haggis fritters with beetroot relish, a plate of cured and smoked fish with celeriac, apple and poppy-seed salad and for a main course, roast saddle of Kentchurch venison with red cabbage and juniper, risotto of wild mushrooms and spinach with chargrilled artichokes, chargrilled liver and bacon with crispy onion rings, sage and lemon butter or Brixham whiting in beer batter, tartare sauce and chips; yummy puds such as lemon and polenta cake with maple syrup and clotted cream or rum and vanilla pannacotta with shortbread, home-made ice creams and British farmhouse cheeses with home-made walnut and raisin bread. Everything that should be freshly cooked is, so be prepared to wait a bit. Local farm ciders, Wye Valley Butty Bach, Theakstons, something from the local Spinning Dog Brewery, John Smiths cask, a guest and a good, reasonably priced wine list. Seats outside in the pretty garden with far-reaching views.

OPEN: 11.30–2.30, 6.30–11. During the winter closed Sun eve and all day Monday.
Real Ale. Restaurant.
Children and well-behaved dogs welcome. Car park. Wheelchair access (not WC).
Cards: Delta, MasterCard, Switch, Visa.

Titley

Stagg Inn ☎ 01544 230221
Kington, Titley, Herefordshire HR5 3RL
Free House. Steve & Nicola Reynolds, licensees
e-mail: reservations@thestagg.co.uk

Surrounded by some lovely countryside, the attractive small village of Titley is between Kington and Presteigne. The Stagg is not only the local pub but a pub where the emphasis is on serving fantastic food in appealing surroundings. However, it is still a pub, and there will be a place in the cosy bar if you just want to join the locals for a pint of their well-kept ale. But many of the customers will be making their way to the dining rooms – must book – for an experience not to be missed. Many of the ingredients used to create the menus are locally sourced: organic meat and dairy produce, fish from Cornwall, fruit and vegetables from local growers, cheese from small producers, elderflowers and sloes from the hedgerows and anything else local and edible able to find its way into the kitchen. You may not be able to afford Le Gavroche, but this is the next best thing – Steve Reynolds trained with the Roux brothers. You can choose one of ten local cheeses for the ploughman's or a salmon and cod cake with tomato butter, pigeon breast with fig and port sauce, wild mushroom and leek tart and for a main course, venison fillet, celeriac gratin and purée, rack of Marches lamb with potatoes baked in lamb stock with shallot purée, Herefordshire rump steak with pepper sauce, Gressingham duck breast with poached pear and perry, fish and specials on the blackboard and some very desirable puddings. Hobsons Best and Town Crier beers plus various guests, local cider and perry. Eight house wines from a list of over 100, mainly French wines. There are new gardens to appreciate. You are surrounded by wonderful walking country, and if you're a doggy person the pub dog would probably like a walk too.

OPEN: 12–3, 6.30–11. Closed Sun eve and all day Mon, also first two weeks of November.
Real Ale. Restaurant.
Children welcome. Dogs in bar. Car park. Two en-suite bedrooms.
Cards: Delta, MasterCard, Switch, Visa.

Trumpet

Verzons ① 01531 670531
Hereford Road, Trumpet, nr Ledbury, Herefordshire HR8 2PZ
Free House. David Roberts, licensee
e-mail: info@theverzons.co.uk

What was once an important Georgian country house set in four acres of grounds has been carefully converted to become the hotel you see today. The Hop bar keeps in touch with its local, rural past – hops, farming implements, Hereford cattle, apple orchards – and is where the locals and everyone else meet for a drink and something from the bar menu. As well as home-made soup, sandwiches and more-ish puddings there is a daily specials board with perhaps casserole of Gloucester Old Spot pork sausages, sage and cider champ, bacon, mushroom and spring onion potato skins topped with cheese, rib-eye steak au poivre, roast rack of lamb with spicy couscous and minted apricot sauce, four-cheese macaroni gratin and roasted monkfish fillet orientale. There is also a more formal restaurant. Beers are Hook Norton, Bass and Spitfire; the wine list is all embracing. From the Garden Room restaurant you have views of the Malvern Hills.

OPEN: 11–11. Sun 12–3, 7–10.30.
Real Ale.
Children welcome. Dogs by arrangement. Car park. Wheelchair access. Eight en-suite bedrooms.
Cards: all except Diners.

Ullingswick

Three Crowns Inn ☎ 01432 820279
Ullingswick, Herefordshire HR1 3JQ
Free House. Brent Castle, licensee
e-mail: info@threecrownsinn.com

At least 300 years old, a building that started out as it meant to go on; one of the county's few remaining, original, public houses. On the road to Little Cowarne, about a mile from the village, you'll find this unassuming, simple brick and timber building. Inside is as you would hope it to be; full of atmosphere, hops on the beams, big fire in the grate, all primped and polished, and blackboards listing the delights to come. All you hear is the happy hum of a pub doing everything as it should be done and better than most – an ideal combination of good pub and good restaurant. All the vegetables are organic, either from local growers or out of the pub garden, fish from Cornwall, and other supplies as local as they can be. Jon Howe is the busy chap in the kitchen creating all the delights. For a starter from the daily changing menu you could have: fish soup with rouille and croutons, charcuterie plate with artichokes and green bean salad, grilled mackerel with lime and dahl or moules marinière; for a main course, roast rack of Marches lamb with tartlet of root vegetables and wild mushrooms, pavé of seabass with saffron mash, fennel and lava bread sauce, pot roast mallard with confit leg, beetroot risotto and honey parsnip, maybe glazed lemon tart or nougat and chocolate parfait to follow. Always some additions to the lunchtime menu, vegetarian dishes too, interesting cheeses and more delicious puds. They do a reasonably priced two- and three-course lunch. Hobsons Best ale and one or two local guests. Interesting, wide-ranging wine list, house wines by the glass, one local cider and a choice of malts and brandies.

OPEN: 12–2.30, 7–11. Closed Mon. Set lunch menu not available on Sun.
Real Ale.
Children – yes, but no special room. No dogs. Car park. Wheelchair access.
Cards: Delta, Electron, JCB, MasterCard, Maestro, Solo, Switch, Visa.

Wenlock Edge

Wenlock Edge Inn ☎ 01746 785678
Hilltop, Wenlock Edge, Shropshire TF13 6DJ
Free House. Dave Morgan, licensee
www.wenlockedgeinn.co.uk

High on Wenlock Edge there are fine views towards the Welsh mountains to the west and across the Shropshire countryside to the south. The pub is a good base if you are thinking of a bracing walk on the Edge, a limestone ridge which runs for 16 straight miles. The Georgian stone cottages which became the pub in 1925 have a friendly, welcoming atmosphere. Inside are a bar, lounge with inglenook, restaurant and conservatory. With the new owners there will be a change in the style of cooking; dishes are listed on the blackboard, and there could be soups, marinated Orkney herrings, spicy prawns, smoked salmon with herbed cheese. Popular pies include venison, rich beef and vegetable, farmhouse chicken and savoury flans. Also salmon baked with peppers, prawn and salmon gratin, a chicken and duck dish, ham served with interesting sauces; at least one roast is served at weekends and there are some imaginative vegetarian dishes. Children's menu too. Two locally brewed ales plus one guest and they serve their own porter. Selection of malt whiskies and wines by the glass.

OPEN: 12–3, 7–11. Closed all day Mon.
Real Ale. Restaurant.
Children in restaurant only (not under 10 after 8 p.m.). Dogs on leads in bar. Car park. Three bedrooms.
Cards: Amex, Delta, MasterCard, Switch, Visa.
On the second Monday of the month there are storytelling evenings when a local group swaps stories, tall and taller, from 'the Edge'. There is a Festival of the Edge every July.

Weobley

Salutation Inn ① 01544 318443
Market Pitch, Weobley, Hereford HR4 8SJ
Free House. Dr Mike Tai, licensee

This ancient village, full of black and white timbered buildings, looks so perfect that someone likened it to a film set. Not to be outdone, the black and white Salutation is one of the best examples of an age-old country inn. Old, but not the oldest in the village and the bits that matter are firmly in the 21st century. Heavily beamed, it has a comfortable bar and big log fire; a popular local, just the place to meet for just a drink and a chat or something from the bar menu. If you just want a quickie snack they have soup, sandwiches and a variety of salads, local ham and lamb. Seasonal specials, vegetarian dishes and interesting puds to finish. They serve a very popular three-course lunch on Sundays. Wye Valley Butty Bach, Flowers IPA and Shepherd Neame Bishops Finger, Westons cider and a guest ale. Over 120 different wines and 20 malt whiskies. Seats on the terrace at the back of the pub.

OPEN: 11–11.
Real Ale. Restaurant.
Children in eating areas. No dogs. Wheelchair access to eating area only.
N.B. Jukebox in public bar.

Whitney-on-Wye

Rydspence Inn ① 01497 831262
Whitney-on-Wye, Hereford HR3 6EU (one mile west of village on A438)
Free House. Peter & Pamela Glover, licensees
e-mail: info@rydspence-inn.co.uk

Overlooking the Wye valley and Black Mountains, this is a very handsome, spacious building in its own delightful grounds. Originally built as a manor house, the stream in the garden is the boundary between England and Wales. Before the railway age, the timbered Rydspence was an assembly point for drovers en route to the English market towns, even as far as London. The 140 acres surrounding the inn were divided up into penny, ha'penny and farthing fields, so if you didn't have many animals for overnight grazing, a farthing field would do. Inside are two bars, one in the heavily beamed, 16th-century end of the building with a big log fire; both serve bar meals lunchtime and evenings. There is also a very attractive, formal restaurant. Everything beautifully kept and cared for. From the bar menu you could choose ploughman's platters with crusty bread, grilled sardines, Szechuan chicken noodles, Mediterranean vegetables in a puff pastry case, braised liver in onion gravy, steak and kidney pie, chef's hot and spicy curry, grills, vegetarian dishes – and more – everything freshly prepared. Good selection of home-made ice creams and sorbets. Robinsons Best Bitter and draught Bass. Interesting wine list. Local cider. Seats on the sunny terrace and in the large garden.

OPEN: 11–2.30, 7–11.
Real Ale. Restaurant.
Children welcome. No dogs. Car park. Wheelchair access (not WC). Bedrooms.
Cards: Amex, MasterCard, Switch, Visa.

BEST OF THE REST

Cleobury Mortimer, Shropshire
Kings Arms ① 01299 270252
Church Street, Cleobury Mortimer DY14 8BS
An ancient market town between Ludlow and Bewdley, full of half-timbered and 18th-century buildings. The formal Georgian frontage of the Kings Arms hides a far older building. They serve traditional bar food and daily specials to go with the Hobsons Best ale. Children welcome. Bedrooms.
Open: 11.30–11.

Crowle, Worcestershire
Old Chequers Inn ① 01905 381275
Crowle Green, Crowle, nr Worcester WR7 4AA
Fed up with the M5? On the top of the hill, just outside Crowle, only a couple of miles from the motorway, this is just the place to make for. Four hundred years old but brought firmly up to date, inside it has beams, a spacious bar and tables in an extension. Here you will do rather well choosing something from either the regular menu or the daily changing specials. There could be home-made paté with apricot chutney, pancakes filled with chicken, mushroom, bacon and sweetcorn in a cheese sauce, prawn and haddock smokies. poached halibut with a chervil and tomato hollandaise, roast duck with a sticky plum sauce, or from the specials board a pot roast poussin with peas, shallots and garlic sausage, or Chinese-style beef casserole with rice and prawn crackers. Beers are Banks Bitter, and various guests. Well-chosen wine list. No children or dogs. Car park. Wheelchair access.
Cards: Amex, MasterCard, Visa.
Open: 12–2, 7–11. Closed Sun eve.

Dorstone, Herefordshire
The Pandy ① 01981 550273
Dorstone, nr Hay-on-Wye HR3 6AN
Another 'Cromwell was here' pub. Well, I hope he had time to appreciate the surrounding scenery. You are in the outstandingly beautiful Golden Valley where the River Dore winds between the villages of Dorstone and Pontrilas. Parts of the Pandy are thought to date back to 1185, which would make it the oldest inn in Herefordshire. Stout beams everywhere and a big welcoming fire in a fireplace built to accommodate half a tree. Substantial bar food listed on the blackboard menu: soups, sandwiches, filled pancakes,

steak and kidney pie, steaks from a local supplier and Welsh lamb from the hills. Roast Sunday lunch, Sunday evenings – curry night. Bass, Wye Valley HPA and lots of malt whiskies. Children welcome, so are dogs but only in garden.
Open: 12–3, 6–11. Sat 12–11. Closed Mon lunchtime.

Winforton, Hereford
Sun Inn ☎ 01544 327677
Winforton HR3 6EA
At the centre of a quiet village of black and white houses in unspoilt Welsh border country, the whitewashed Sun is very old, with a rustic interior of stone walls and beams; the cooking however is very up to date. Their award-winning ploughman's comes with home-made pickles, chutneys and a choice of local cheeses. Other dishes could be fennel, leek and parsnip soup, caramelised onion tart with chilli and balsamic dressing, roast Welsh marches lamb with hedgerow jus or rib-eye of local beef with a Stilton sauce. Daily specials and delicious puds. Flowers, Hook Norton, Jennings and Felinfoel Double Dragon beers, ciders and a sizable wine list. Children welcome. No dogs. Wheelchair access (not WC). Bedrooms.
Open: 11–3, 6.15–11.

Wetherspoon in Herefordshire, Worcestershire and Shropshire

Herefordshire

Hereford – Kings Fee, 49–53 Commercial Road
☎ 01432 373240
Ross on Wye – Mail Rooms, Gloucester Road
☎ 01989 760920

Worcestershire

Bromsgrove – Golden Cross Hotel, 20 High Street
☎ 01527 870005
Evesham – Old Swanne Inn, 66 High Street
☎ 01386 442650
Kidderminster – Hare and Hounds, Stourbridge Road
☎ 01562 753897
Kidderminster – Penny Black, 16–18 Bull Ring
☎ 01562 861041
Redditch – Rising Sun, Unit 4, Alcester Place
☎ 01527 62452
Stourport on Severn – Ye Olde Crown Inn, 9 Bridge Street
☎ 01299 855693
Worcester – Postal Order, 18 Forgate Street
☎ 01905 22373

Shropshire

Bridgnorth – Jewel of the Severn, 80–81 High Street
☎ 01746 711980
Oswestry – Wilfred Owen, Willow Street
☎ 01691 684910
Shrewsbury – Shrewsbury Hotel (a Wetherspoon Lodge), Bridge Place
☎ 01743 236203
Telford – Church Wicketts, Church Road
☎ 01952 506825
Whitchurch – Red Lyon, 46 High Street
☎ 01948 667846

Hertfordshire

J·D·WETHERSPOON

CAMBRIDGESHIRE

BEDFORDSHIRE

ESSEX

BUCKINGHAMSHIRE

Letchworth
Hitchin
Nuthampstead
St Ippollitts
Stevenage
Ayot St Lawrence
Watton at Stone
Bishop's Stortford
Sawbridgeworth
Marsworth
Ware
High Wych
Tring
Aldbury
Hertford
Berkhamsted
St Albans
Hemel Hempstead
Potters Crouch
Cheshunt
Bovingdon Green
Potters Bar
Waltham Cross
Flaunden
Borehamwood
Rickmansworth
Watford

GREATER LONDON

0 Miles   10
0 Kilometres   16

Hertfordshire

Aldbury

Valiant Trooper ① 01442 851203
Trooper Road, Aldbury, nr Tring HP23 5RW
Free House. Tim O'Gorman, licensee

East of Tring, a pub in a pretty village in the Chiltern Hills very near the Ridgeway Path
and the National Trust's Ashridge Estate – six square miles of woods and commons
leading to Ivinghoe Beacon. This is a much filmed, picture-postcard village, with a green
that still has a duck pond, whipping post and stocks – they knew how to control the local
drunks in the 19th century! The friendly, welcoming Georgian Valiant Trooper was here
long before that, a place with lots of character: low ceilings, beams and flagstone floors.
They serve a short, uncomplicated menu in the bars – filled baguettes, baked potatoes,
ploughman's, that sort of thing – or the blackboard specials, which could be roast sea bass
with garlic prawns, chicken stir-fry, venison and wild boar sausages and fresh fish – a
choice of three or four; everything home cooked using fresh ingredients – no chips; always
some vegetarian options. There is also a restaurant in the old stable block where there is a
more wide-ranging menu. Morrells Oxford Blue, Fullers London Pride and Becks plus
three weekly changing guest beers. Strongbow and Scrumpy Jack ciders. Around 20 wines
on the list. Charming, cottagey garden to sit in.

OPEN: 11–11. Sun 12–10.30. No food Sun or Mon eves.
Real Ale. Restaurant.
Children in one room at lunchtime. Dogs on leads.
Cards: all except Amex and Diners.

Bovingdon Green

Royal Oak ① 01442 832126
Bovingdon Green, Bovingdon HP3 0LZ
Punch. Jemma Whitman, lease
e-mail: bovingdonoak@aol.com

From the outside, a 'between the wars' village pub which has been extensively refurbished,
the interior looking, so our informant said, like an officers' mess. Well, he was in the RAF,
and it does have connections with the Americans who were stationed at Bovingdon during
the war. Now it's all very comfortable inside and you can eat rather well. From the snack
bar menu you could have beef and ale pie, sausage and mash, baguettes with hot fillings,
beer-battered cod, sandwiches, ploughman's and as a 'light bite' prawns and smoked
salmon salad, carbonara, spicy avocado and bacon salad; or for a main course lamb's liver,
bacon and onions, lamb noisette, filled steak or darne of salmon. Vegetarian dishes too.

Beers are London Pride, Adnams Bitter, Greene King IPA, Shepherd Neame Spitfire and there is a short wine list. Seats in the really big garden.

OPEN: 11.30–3, 6–11. Sat 11.30–11. Sun 12–10.30.
Real Ale.
Children and dogs welcome. Car park.
Cards: all cards accepted.

Flaunden

Bricklayers Arms ① 01442 833322
Hogpits Bottom, Flaunden HP3 0PH
Free House. Alvin Michaels, licensee

Outside the village and near woodland walks, this appealing 18th-century country pub has low beams, timbered walls and log fires and is tremendously popular, filled to overflowing at weekends. The generous bar food, served throughout the day until 6.30, ranges from soups and well-filled sandwiches to mussels marinated with chilli, garlic, red peppers and sautéed in a rich tomato sauce, crispy squid with aioli, millefeuille of wild mushrooms with a red wine jus, roast sea bass with grilled asparagus and tomato butter, fresh fish of the day, steaks with different sauces, specials and more-ish puds. The bar specials change daily and there is a creative evening à la carte menu in the restaurant. Well-kept Marstons Pedigree, Fullers London Pride, Ringwood Old Thumper and five guest beers. Good selection of wines. Seats in the lovely cottagey garden. Good walks nearby.

OPEN: 12–11.
Real Ale. Restaurant.
Children in restaurant. Dogs on leads. Wheelchair access (not WC).
Cards: all major credit cards.

Hertford

White Horse ① 01992 501950
33 Castle Street, Hertford SG14 1HH
Fullers. Nigel Crofts, lease

Near the old castle, this small timber-framed, old-fashioned local should be on every beer-lover's list. They usually have about 10 real ales on the go, many from the smaller breweries, and for those of you who want something else to try, a selection of country fruit wines. The 14th-century (in parts) beamed and timbered White Horse is a popular, traditional pub – no frills here – serving straightforward pub food every lunchtime: filled baguettes, seafood pie, or their very own, 'cheesey-hammy-eggy'. Very busy at weekends. Upstairs is an antique bar billiards table and a no-smoking area, where supervised children are allowed; somewhere to sit outside too.

OPEN: Mon–Thurs 12–2.30, 5.30–11. Fri–Sun 12–11. Food served 12–2 daily, 1–3 on Sun.
Real Ale.
Children welcome upstairs. Dogs on leads. Wheelchair access (not WC).
Cards: all major credit cards.

High Wych

Rising Sun ① 01279 724099
High Wych, nr Sawbridgeworth CM21 0HZ
Free House. Stephen Prior, licensee

An unspoilt village pub with chatty, friendly locals, run by the Prior family since 1929. The Rising Sun is one of those pubs that belongs to different periods; bits have been added over the years resulting in a classic layout of small public bar, saloon bar (fire in here) and tap room (without carpet). No food – a crisp and nut place this – just beers. But they do want you to concentrate on the matter in hand, the beer, so no communication with the outside world – mobile phones and pagers must be switched off! Well-kept Courage Best and a guest beer from one of the smaller breweries. Relax in the quiet garden at the back of the pub.

OPEN: 12–2.30 (Fri & Sat 12–3), 5–11.
Real Ale.
Children welcome in tap room. Dogs on leads.

Marsworth

Red Lion ① 01296 668366
Vicarage Road, Marsworth, nr Tring HP23 4LU
Free House. R. D. Brake, licensee

Long, low and partly thatched, the Red Lion is in the centre of the village, opposite the green where you will find the stocks – very useful for controlling excitable customers! Grade II listed, inside are three bars, public (with all the games), snug and lounge where they serve a traditional menu of various ploughman's, chicken combo – garlic mushrooms, potato wedges, breaded onion rings and chicken nuggets – spicy prawns, smoked mackerel, cod in batter, chilli con carne, Cumberland sausages, the popular home-cooked ham and egg, and specials on the board. Beers are Fullers London Pride, Vale Brewery Notley and one or two guests per week. Benches at the front of the pub facing the green and in the garden at the back.

OPEN: 11–3, 5–11 (Sat 6–11). Sun 12–3, 7–10.30.
Real Ale.
Children and dogs welcome. Car park. Wheelchair access.
Cards: MasterCard, Solo, Switch, Visa.

Nuthampstead

The Woodman ① 01763 848328
Nuthampstead, nr Royston SG8 8NB
Free House. Ian & Sandra Johnson, licensees
e-mail: woodman.inn@virgin.net

It's not obvious from the outside, but the Woodman is basically a 17th-century building. Thatched and weatherboarded in an individual way, it is full of character inside, with beams and open fires, also fascinating original photos and memorabilia of the USAF 398 Bomb Group. The Group flew Flying Fortresses out of Nuthampstead airfield and the Association regularly returns for a reunion. The memorial outside the Woodman commemorates those members of this group who lost their lives in the last war. From the bar, the menu includes basket meals, local ham and sausages and daily specials on the blackboard. An à la carte menu features in the recently extended restaurant and function room – mainly grills, steaks, salmon and chicken – traditional fare. Ales vary; usually four cask-conditioned ales are available. It is a favourite place for those pursuing country sports or just having an energetic walk.

OPEN: 11–11. Sun 12–4, 7–10.30.
Real Ale. Restaurant.
Children welcome. No dogs. Wheelchair access. Bedrooms.
Cards: Amex, MasterCard, Switch, Visa.

Potters Crouch

Holly Bush ① 01727 851792
Potters Crouch, St Albans AL2 3NN
Fuller, Smith & Turner. Ray Taylor, tenant

A short distance from St Albans, this white-painted and creeper-covered pub is a classy little place, all primped, polished and beautifully run, an early 18th-century building looking its best. As our impressed informant said, 'This should win the pleasantest pub competition.' Traditional, short bar menu at lunchtime only; never on Sunday. There is a Hollybush ploughman's, home-made chilli con carne, Ardennes paté served with a mixed salad and wholemeal toast, chicken and vegetable pasty, Hollybush burgers and platters – mixed, cheese, meat, French or fish – egg mayonnaise and toasted sandwiches. A Fullers pub, with very well-kept Fullers ales. There is a big, attractive garden to sit in.

OPEN: 11.30–2.30, 6–11. Sun 12–2.30, 7–10.30. No food Sun.
Real Ale.
Children in garden only. No dogs. Car park. Wheelchair access.
Cards: Delta, MasterCard, Switch, Visa.

St Albans

Rose & Crown ① 01727 851903
10 St Michael Street, St Albans AL3 4SG
Pubmaster. Ruth Courtney, tenant

You are in an important part of the city. It was here that the Romans established Verulamium on the river Ver; the pub car park was built over the gates of the old Roman town, and the 400-year-old, Grade II listed Rose and Crown was built in the shadow of the ninth-century abbey. Beamed and cosy inside, with big seasonal fires, 'this is', said our researcher, 'an excellent traditional English pub in all respects'. At lunchtime one area is set aside for non-smokers. For lunch there is soup and a wide variety of sandwiches, from the 'gourmet' Royalty version and double-deckers to the 'Serf' sandwiches with simpler fillings. There is also coarse liver paté with toast, broccoli and creamy cheese bake, lasagne, tuna with pasta, moussaka or vegetable stroganoff. Adnams, Tetleys, Courage Directors and Fullers London Pride, ciders, a choice of malt whiskies and a short wine list. Plenty of tables among the flowers in the quiet garden

OPEN: 11.30–3, 5.30–11. Sat 11.30–11. Sun 12–10.30. Food lunchtime only.
Real Ale.
Children in eating area. Dogs on leads. Car park. Wheelchair access.
Cards: all cards.

Lower Red Lion ② 01727 855669
34–36 Fishpool Street, St Albans AL3 4RX
Free House. Mary Hamilton & Alan Dean, licensees

A walk along Fishpool Street will take you past some of St Alban's medieval history hiding behind a Georgian frontage. Some of the town's inns are 15th century and many are built over medieval foundations. Far younger, though, is the white-walled 17th-century Lower Red Lion, built to provide accommodation for the many travellers on their way to and from London and the West Country. Well beamed and handsome, this old place still provides a bed for the night as well as serving decent home-cooked food at lunchtime and a choice of ale. Nine beers on hand pump, among them JHB from the Oakham brewery and Fullers London Pride as well as ever-changing guests from micro-breweries. Delightful, good-size garden for you to sit in. Beer festivals are held on the May Day and August Bank Holidays.

OPEN: 12–2.30 (Sat 12–3), 5.30–11. Food lunchtime only.
Real Ale.
No children under 14 years old. Dogs on leads but preferably in the evening when no food is served. Car park. Bedrooms.
Cards: MasterCard, Switch, Visa.

St Ippollitts

Greyhound ② 01462 440989
London Road, St Ippollitts SG4 7NL
Free House. Roy Pearce, FBII, owner/licensee
e-mail: greyhound@freenet.co.uk

This village takes its name from a Roman martyr, horse doctor and patron saint of the 14th-century church – St Hippolytus, which, in the way of the English, evolved into St Ippollitts. However, the Greyhound has absolutely nothing to do with horses. Set in attractive countryside south of Hitchin, this early 20th-century inn has one comfortable bar and a small dining room. They serve an extensive range of food including sandwiches, bar snacks, vegetarian dishes and daily specials. They will even cook something specially for you – give them a bit of notice though! Very popular Sunday lunches too. Adnams is

the beer, plus one guest. You are in good walking country, close to the north loop of the Chiltern Way.

OPEN: 11.30–2.30, 5–11.
Real Ale.
Children welcome. No dogs. En-suite bedrooms. Car park. Wheelchair access with assistance.
Cards: Amex, Delta, Electron, Solo, Switch.

Tring

Kings Arms ① 01442 823318
King Street, Tring HP23 6BE
Free House. John Francis, Victoria North & Thomas North, licensees
e-mail: ka@jsf.me.uk

In the older part of Tring, built early in the 19th century for the local John Brown's Brewery. The rather grand frontage belies the unpretentious interior but interestingly, they do have a unique feature – fireplaces beneath the windows. The food is all top quality (strictly no chips!) The cooking is adventurous and takes its inspiration from Asia to South America: jerk burgers – grilled minced beef with Caribbean jerk seasoning – Hungarian chicken goulash, Fabada Asturiana – a hearty casserole from northern Spain of ham, chorizo, salt pork, black pudding and white beans served with olive oil, toasted bread and Keralan country chicken, also filled baguettes, double-decker sandwiches and filled baked potatoes. Wadworths 6X and four regularly changing guests. No-smoking area and an enclosed, heated courtyard. Unfortunately the pub doesn't have a car park so parking can be quite a challenge.

OPEN: 12–2.30 (Sat 11.30–3), 7–11. Sun 12–4, 7–10.30.
Real Ale.
Children welcome. No dogs. Wheelchair access with help (not WC).
Cards: all accepted.

Watton at Stone

George & Dragon ① 01920 830285
High Street, Watton at Stone SG14 3TA
Greene King. Peter & Jessica Tatlow, lease

Between Stevenage and Hertford, the 16th-century George and Dragon is not to be missed; this is a very civilized, desirable place. Inside is as you would expect: beams, half-timbered walls, shining brass, interesting pieces of furniture and a reputation for good imaginative food. From the menu there could be a locally smoked salmon served on a celeriac and crème fraiche râpé, mini-fishcakes served with a cucumber, tomato, coriander, olive and red onion salsa, smoked chicken timbale, and for a main course, medley of seasonal fish, Moroccan-style lamb shank, tournedos of beef fillet on roasted flat mushroom and paté with a Rioja and rosemary sauce, filo pastry parcels filled with a Greek-style mince or an Aberdeen Angus sirloin steak. Light snacks include a 'Millionaires' Bun' – fillet steak in a roll – 'Billionaires' get twice as much steak! Pasta of the day, salads and well-filled sandwiches, home-made puddings and blackboard specials. Greene King IPA, Abbot and one guest, wide choice of wines and choice of malt whiskies. No-smoking area in restaurant.

OPEN: 11–2.30, 6–11. Sat & Sun 11–11.
Real Ale. Restaurant.
Children in family room and restaurant. No dogs.
Car park. Wheelchair access difficult but just possible.
Cards: all cards.

BEST OF THE REST

Ayot St Lawrence
Brocket Arms ☯ 01438 820250
Ayot St Lawrence AL6 9BT
Opposite the ruins of a medieval church, the 14th-century Brocket Arms is surrounded by timbered village cottages. The unchanging, well-beamed interior reflects its age. A popular bar menu includes soup, sandwiches, home-made curries, game pie and specials on the blackboard. Adnams Broadside, Greene King IPA and Fullers London Pride plus a guest ale and a short wine list. A suntrap of a garden has a children's play area. There is also a house ghost – a priest, who was tried and hanged in the pub during the Reformation.
Children welcome. Bedrooms.
Open: 11–11.

Wetherspoon in Hertfordshire

Berkhampstead – Crown, 145 High Street
☯ 01442 863993
Cheshunt – King James, 2–3 Lynton Parade, Turners Hill
☯ 01992 781250
Hemel Hempstead – Full House, 128 The Marlowes
☯ 01442 265512
Letchworth – Three Magnets, 18–20 Leys Avenue
☯ 01462 681093
Potters Bar – Admiral Byng, 186–192 Darkes Lane
☯ 01707 645484
St Albans – Cross Keys, 2 Chequer Street
☯ 01727 839917
Stevenage – Standard Bearer, Unit 1, The Plaza, New Town, Market Square
☯ 01438 731450
Stevenage – Standing Order, 33 High Street
☯ 01438 316972
Waltham Cross – Moon and Cross, 104–106 High Street
☯ 01992 700761

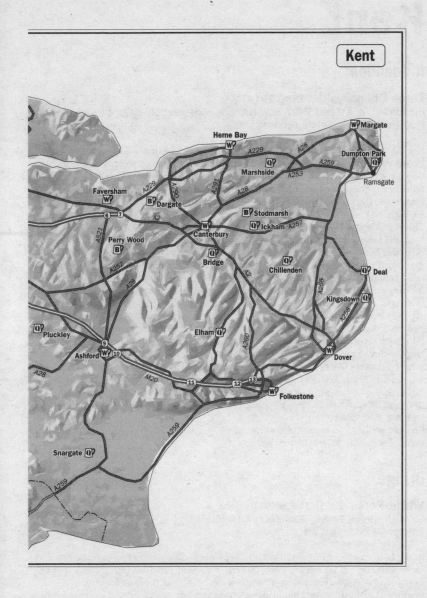

Kent

Kent

Biddenden

Three Chimneys ① 01580 291472
Biddenden, nr Ashford TN27 8LW HA (one mile west of village on A262)
Free House. Craig Smith, licensee

Not the easiest place to find even though it is on the Biddenden to Sissinghurst road. Unless you are keeping a careful eye out you can miss the pub completely as it is slightly below road level, on the right at a junction of three roads, a mile and a half west of Biddenden. The name Three Chimneys is a corruption of the French 'trois chemins' – three ways. During the Napoleonic Wars the French officers imprisoned in nearby Sissinghurst Castle were allowed out for a walk as far as the meeting of the three roads. This pub is a gem of a place; 15th century, rambling, with atmospheric, low-lit beamed bars, and huge log fires. Good imaginative food on offer; the blackboard menus change every day but there could be a garlic and chilli bruschetta topped with tomato and garlic, roasted aubergine and red peppers or Parma ham and mozzarella, marinated anchovy salad with black olives, parmesan croutons, roasted cherry tomatoes and a Caesar-style dressing or crab and salmon fishcakes with a Thai-style sweet and sour sauce; and for a main course, grilled British fillet steak, pan-fried fillets of seabass or wild boar and apple sausages topped with Three Chimneys' chutney on a bed of mash with a rich port jus; puddings change daily too. There is a restaurant and tables in the pretty garden which is filled with shrubs, roses and nut trees. The range of ales, tapped from behind the bar, could include Shepherd Neame Spitfire, Adnams Best, Harveys Best and maybe Woodfords Wherry, Harveys Old or Bishops Finger, a strong local cider, local wines and a varied wine list; mostly French. Wines by the glass and half bottles.

OPEN: 11.30–2.30, 6–11. Sun 12–2.30, 7–10.30.
Real Ale. Restaurant.
No children. Dogs on leads. Car park. Wheelchair access.
Cards: Delta, MasterCard, Switch, Visa.

Bridge

White Horse ① 01227 830249
53 High Street, Bridge, Canterbury CT4 5LA
Enterprise Inns. Alan Walton, lease

At the bottom of the hill, the White Horse – painted white – is the first pub you come to in the village if you are coming from Canterbury. A well-cared-for 16th-century building, inside are low beams, interesting carvings on the beam over the huge inglenook, photographs of the pub and old Bridge and a general air of well-being. Good food is high on the agenda here: the son of the house has come from being the chef in a Michelin-starred restaurant to take charge of the kitchen. All produce used is as local as can possibly be; they even get the nearby market garden to grow all their vegetables. From the changing brasserie menu there could be a smoked salmon, trout and eel salad with horseradish dressing, spicy crab cakes with a carrot, spring onions and mint salad, a 'posh' ploughman's with Stilton, Caerphilly and ham with chutney and salad, minted pea soup with a soft boiled quail's egg, Whitstable clams steamed in garlic, fennel and cider cream sauce, and, for a main course, roast chicken with garlic, lemon and sage jus and herbed couscous, green bean, pea, smoked bacon and herb tagliatelle, peppered rib-eye steak or fillet steak with salad and fries, and yummy puds. There is also a separate restaurant menu. Beers are Shepherd Neame Masterbrew, Old Speckled Hen, Wadworths 6X, Fullers London Pride and Greene King IPA. The wide-ranging wine list includes some surprises. Big garden beyond the car park.

OPEN: 11–3, 5–11. Sun 12–5.
Real Ale. Restaurant. If very busy on a Saturday night the brasserie will close at 7.30.
Children welcome, dogs too.
Car park. Cards: all except Diners.
N.B. Always musically quiet at lunchtime, very quiet jazz in evening.

Canterbury

Thomas Ingoldsby ① 01227 463339
5–9 Burgate, Canterbury CT1 2HG
Wetherspoon.

Close to the cathedral in an area of the city that was heavily bombed in the last war – all that was left was the tower of the church on the other side of the road. The miracle was that the cathedral survived destruction. The Thomas Ingoldsby, in the rebuilt area, is a big, airy place and tremendously popular. Lots of satisfying food on the menu and daily specials board. You're really spoilt for choice if you want a beer – about eight on the go – or you could have a glass of scrumpy or house wine. Wetherspoon establishments are never cosy and intimate, but they are friendly places; this one has a particularly nice atmosphere.

OPEN: 11–11.
Real Ale. Always a no-smoking area.
No children. No dogs. Disabled facilities.

Chiddingstone

Castle ① 01892 870247
Chiddingstone, nr Edenbridge TN8 7AH
Free House. Nigel Lucas, licensee
e-mail: info@castleinn.co.uk

The handsome Castle Inn, opposite the church, is among a row of spectacular timbered houses in what is considered to be one of the finest village streets in Kent. Originally a 15th-century house, this building, along with the rest of the fine, largely Tudor village, was bought by the National Trust in 1939 for £25,000. Understandably, the heavily beamed saloon and public bar can get very busy in summer. The food here is first class; an extensive 'Fireside Menu' is available in the saloon bar: home-made soup, a Caesar salad with croutons and Parmesan shavings, a tartlet of Camembert, lovage and tomato with basil and roquette pesto, wild mushroom and asparagus risotto or breast of organic chicken with sautéed chicken livers and French beans; scrummy puds too. Pub stalwarts are on the lunchtime bar menu: local sausages, a plate of smoked salmon, open sandwiches, a daily pasta (read the blackboard), lots of different salads and fillings for the jacket potatoes, ploughman's and of course daily specials. More elaborate two or three-course meals available in the restaurant, also an à la carte menu. Tea too. No cucumber sandwiches, but you'll find something desirable on the menu and the choice of teas ranges from rosehip to Darjeeling. The ales are Larkins Traditional (porter in winter), Harveys Best and a guest ale. There is an extensive wine list featuring wines from all over the world. Outside is a very pretty vine-hung courtyard, with tables and its own garden bar; beyond that a lovely garden. Not far from Hever Castle, Anne Boleyn's home.

OPEN: For coffee and soft drinks at 10.30, otherwise 11–11. On Sundays, 11.00 for coffee, otherwise 12–10.30.
Real Ale. Restaurant – closed Tues.
Children welcome. Dogs on leads.
Cards: Amex, Diners, Electron, MasterCard, Solo, Switch, Visa.

Chillenden

Griffins Head ➀ 01304 840325
Chillenden, nr Canterbury CT3 1PS (off Eastry to Nonington Road)
Shepherd Neame. Mark J. Copestake, tenant

Nothing much has changed since it was built, apart from the bar and the addition of a first floor. In fact this 13th-century Wealden hall house looks, from the outside, much as it has through the centuries, white with black beams, heavily beamed inside, rambling and with two big inglenook fireplaces. Only one bar serving three different areas and a dining room. Food is the usual pub food with the occasional highlight: very variable but the weekend summer barbecues are good, otherwise there could be home-made soup, chicken liver paté, beef stew, minute steak, grilled sea bass or seasonal game on offer. You also have a choice of champagnes and a list of bin ends on a blackboard. Shepherd Neame ales: Spitfire, Masterbrew, Best Bitter and Bishops Finger. Lots of picnic tables in the large garden; a barbecue in the middle of the car park is lit at weekends during the summer. On the first Sunday of every month the local vintage car enthusiasts meet and admire each others' vehicles.

OPEN: 11–11. No food Sun eve.
Real Ale.
No children. Dogs on leads. Car park.
Cards: Amex, Delta, MasterCard, Switch, Visa.
Annual jazz festival.

Chislehurst

Ramblers Rest ① 020 8467 1734
Mill Place, Chislehurst BR7 5ND
Scottish & Newcastle. Barter Inn has the holding tenancy.

Drive to the pub along a track off the Chislehurst to Bromley road (A222). Keep a sharp look out as you could easily miss the turning. Chislehurst is built around a large wooded common, home to the Chislehurst cricket ground and golf club. On the edge of the common is the pretty little 17th-century Ramblers Rest, a typical Kent building of white-painted weatherboard. Outside is bedecked with flowers in the summer; inside is a wealth of beams and a warm welcome. Familiar, well-tried bar food served at lunchtime only: steak and kidney pie, spaghetti bolognese, chilli, fisherman's pie, toasties, sandwiches, salads and ploughman's – that sort of thing. Courage ales plus guest beers. Seats in the secluded garden.

OPEN: 11–3, 5.30–11. Sat 11–11. Sun 12–10.30. No food evenings or Sunday.
Real Ale.
Children in eating area. Dogs on leads.
Cards: most major cards accepted – and you can get cashback!

Sydney Arms ① 020 8467 2025
Old Perry Street, Chislehurst BR7 6PL
Unique. Simon Grover & Andy Durton, licensees

In Old Perry Street, about a mile from the centre of Chislehurst, which contains some of the most historic buildings in the town, you'll find the handsome, Victorian Sydney Arms. Near to Scadbury National Park, part of the old Scadbury Manor which dated back to Saxon times, the Sydney Arms is a popular place with walkers and families. There is a large no-smoking area where they serve a well-liked, reasonably priced traditional menu of soup, filled rolls, ploughman's, wing of skate with a burnt butter sauce, poached salmon, steak and ale pie, T-bone steak and specials on the board. Always two, changing real ales which could be Charles Wells Bombardier and Fullers London Pride. Wines by the bottle or glass. Outside are seats in the large garden.

OPEN: 11–11. Sun 12–10.30.
Real Ale.
Children and dogs welcome. Car park. Wheelchair access (not WC).
Cards: all major credit cards.

Cobham

Darnley Arms ① 01474 814218
The Street, Cobham DA12 3BZ
Greene King. Trudie Mockrie, licensee

In a village high on a hill looking towards Gravesend, the 18th-century Darnley Arms was built on the foundations of an earlier 15th-century inn. Serious cricket fans will know this village, as Cobham Hall – once the residence of the Earls of Darnley, hence the name of the pub – was also the home of the Hon. Ivo Bligh, the 19th-century cricket captain of Cobham, Kent and England. Charles Dickens knew the village too and mentioned one of the old inns in *Pickwick Papers*. There is always a good range of bar food available: sandwiches, ploughman's, home-made pies, tiger prawns, various fish dishes, grills and daily specials. Steamed pudding or ice cream for afters. Greene King range of ales and a selection of wines and liqueurs.

OPEN: 11–3, 6–11. Closed Sun eve.
Real Ale.
Children if well behaved. No dogs.

___

Deal

Three Compasses ① 01304 374661
129 Beach Street, Deal CT14 6JS
Free House. K. & F. Mayr, owners/licensees

Deal isn't on the way to anywhere – except the sea. It luckily escaped becoming an important seaside resort during the 19th century, so most of the town is still as it was, mainly 18th century. Originally just a corner pub on the seafront, the Three Compasses is now a pub/restaurant but with very limited opening hours. A small, well-run, beautifully kept, smart restaurant and drinking area. If you only want a drink you are very welcome but there is only one beer, Ruddles County, plus Murphys Stout on hand pump – lagers too. But if you're here in the evening, you will want to eat. Home-made paté and toast to start, or some smoked salmon, different salads, oven-baked Kentish lamb in Madeira sauce, grilled fillet of turbot, fillet steak in a creamed brandy and pepper sauce or game in season – all served with potatoes and fresh vegetables. There is a very good wine list and excellent coffee. Bracing walks along the seafront or along the pier only a few hundred yards away.

OPEN: Wed–Sat 7–10.30. Sun 12–3. Closed Mon & Tues and all November. Food only in the evenings.
No children. No dogs.

___

Dover

Eight Bells ① 01304 205030
19 Cannon Street, Dover CT16 1BZ
Wetherspoon.

Wherever you are the Norman castle, high on the cliff, is keeping watch over the town. Dover, as the gateway to Europe, has had a long and eventful history and the Eight Bells, a redundant bingo hall, is surrounded by Dover's past and future. It is at the centre of things; only five minutes' walk from Dover Castle, Dover Museum, the medieval boat and the Roman Painted House. Always reliable food in these establishments, always a reasonably priced beer and usually about nine guest ales.

OPEN: 11–11.
Real Ale. No-smoking area.
No children. No dogs. Wheelchair facilities.

Dumpton Park

Brown Jug ① 01843 862788
204 Ramsgate Road, Dumpton Park, Broadstairs CT10 2EW
Thorley Taverns. Jennifer Skudder, tenant

An early 18th-century, flint pub with a giant brown jug above the door, this is a timeless place, with two small rooms at the front; in one, which could probably accommodate about ten people standing, is a very handsome carved settle. The other, larger room has some 18th-century fitted cupboards either side of the fireplace. A really small front bar, but the back room, with a fine collection of jugs, is quite spacious and leads out to the exuberant garden and pétanque pitch. They really are keen players; all playing in a local team. No food, just something to drink. Greene King cask ales, Whitbread Mild, Guinness and a good number of malt whiskies.

OPEN: 1–3, 6–11 (but fluid). Sat & Sun 11–11. If busy during the week, they stay open.
No children – no licence. Dogs on leads. Car park. Loos outside.

Elham

Rose and Crown ① 01303 840226
High Street, Elham CT4 6TD
Free House. Gerard McNicholas, licensee
e-mail: info@roseandcrown.co.uk

Partly 16th century, this was an important coaching inn between Canterbury and the coast, and has its own semi-believable legend: during the French Revolution, the man on whom the fictional Scarlet Pimpernel was based used to dine here while waiting for a fresh horse to take him to the coast to catch the boat to France. Horses out, beds in, as the stables are now six letting bedrooms. Inside the pub is a huge inglenook fireplace surrounded by comfortable sofas and chairs, a separate bar and restaurant. Traditional pub snacks are available, but the menu leans towards fish dishes. These are on the comprehensive, daily changing blackboard and could include baked sea bass, lemon sole, crab and salmon fishcakes with a fruit salsa, also home-made chicken liver paté, steak and kidney pudding, mussels in garlic, medallions of pork on a nest of wild mushrooms and chargrilled sirloin steak among other delights. Hopdaemon Brewery Golden Braid and Skrimshander IPA, Ruddles Best, Harveys Sussex and guest beers.

OPEN: 11–3, 6–11. Sun 12–3, 7–10.30.
Real Ale. No-smoking restaurant.
Children in eating areas. Dogs on leads. Car park. Wheelchair access (not WC). En-suite bedrooms.
Cards: MasterCard, Solo, Switch, Visa.

Fordcombe

Chafford Arms ① 01892 740267
Fordcombe, Tunbridge Wells TN3 0SA
Whitbread. Barrie Leppard, licensee

Outside this Victorian, tile-hung pub is the most wonderful floral display. Inside, a comfortable bar where you'll find an extensive bar menu which includes speciality fish dishes. As well as the home-made country soup, you could have calamares, Greenland prawns, local Weald-smoked trout, fresh Dover sole, home-made prawn provençale, king prawns cooked in garlic or chilli on a timbale of rice, farmhouse gammon steak, chicken Kiev, a selection of vegetarian dishes, ploughman's, sandwiches or a salad. The landlord has been running this pub for over 35 years, so there is a very steady, guiding hand on the beer pump serving the Larkins Traditional and Spitfire ales and choice of wines. Outside there is a large, award-winning garden, with lots of secluded areas in which to enjoy your drink.

OPEN: 11–3, 6.30–11. Sun 12–4, 7–10.30. No food Sun and Mon eves.
Real Ale.
Children welcome, well-behaved dogs as well. Wheelchair access to pub and elsewhere with help. Car park.
Cards: Delta, MasterCard, Switch, Visa.
N.B. Live jazz and Broadway standards third Sunday eve in the month.

Groombridge

Crown ① 01892 864742
10 The Walks, Groombridge TN3 9QH
Free House. Peter & Pauline Kilshaw, licensees

A 16th-century coaching inn on the edge of the village green with views towards the village below, which has a foot in two counties: the old, original village in Kent, the rest in Sussex. The Kent half includes the Crown and a charming terrace of tile-hung, 18th-century cottages. This old smuggling pub, which is mentioned in one of Sir Arthur Conan Doyle's novels, is full of beams, ancient timbers and an inglenook fireplace. There is a comprehensive menu; you could choose home-made soup, chicken liver paté with toast fingers, steak and Harvey's ale pie, chargrilled fillet of Scotch beef on a bed of spinach, some vegetarian dishes and daily specials on the blackboard. Harveys IPA, Courage Directors and Harveys Armada – but this selection changes two or three times a year – local farm cider and house wines by the glass. Seats on the sunny terrace in front of the pub. Groombridge Place is very near and well worth a visit.

OPEN: 11–3, 6–11. Sun 12–3, 7–10.30. No food Sun eves.
Real Ale. Restaurant (evenings).
Children in restaurant. Dogs on leads in bar only. Wheelchair access into pub just possible. Five en-suite bedrooms.
Cards: all major credit cards.
Endless Morris dancers!

Ickham

Duke William ① 01227 721308
The Street, Ickham, Canterbury CT3 1QP
Free House. Alistair & Carol McNeil, licensees

On the main village street, facing some 'executive homes' built on what used to be a huge, wonderfully empty space, the 17th-century Duke William – with 19th-century etched windows – is a lovely, jolly, friendly place. You step up from the street into the pub, where the bar counter faces you and divides the room. At the back, beyond the bar, is a dining area and conservatory – supervised by a very well-behaved, handsome, African Grey parrot – which in turn leads out into the garden. Food is always good here with something for everyone from home-made soup, imaginative fillings for the baguettes, ploughman's, steak and kidney pie, sausage and mash, salads, pasta with lots of different sauces, specials on the blackboard and a restaurant menu that goes up a gear. Beers are Adnams Bitter, Fullers London Pride, Shepherd Neame Masterbrew and a guest. There is a very wide-ranging wine list.

OPEN: 11–3, 6–11.
Real Ale.
Children welcome in conservatory. Dogs in bar.

Kingsdown

Zetland Arms ① 01304 364888
Wellington Parade, Kingsdown, Deal CT14 8AF (at the sea end of South & North Roads)
Unique Pub Co. T. J. Cobbett, licensee

Just an unchanging pub at the end of two unmade-up roads bordered by small fishermen's cottages. The fishermen moved out and the roads are still unmade and bumpier than ever, but the cottages have gone up-market, and well out of the price range of any fishermen. Position is the thing and the Zetland is in the right place to take full advantage of glorious summer days; it is virtually on the beach – well, where the pub stops, the pebbles begin and so does the car park – on the pebbles. When a north-easterly gale is blowing, you can watch the waves crashing against the sea defences from the safety of the bar. Nothing much to look at – weather-beaten is a good description. Just one bar with helpful, friendly staff. Food is traditional with dishes such as quiche, fish and chips, a pint of prawns, a huge dish of mussels cooked in wine and garlic (highly recommended), rib-eye steak, curries and crab or prawn sandwiches and a bowl of chips. Shepherd Neame Spitfire, Greene King IPA and Guinness on hand pump are among the ales. Carlsberg and Holstein lagers also on draught. Water for the dog. There is a path along the coast into Deal and, about a mile away, a wonderful walk over the cliffs to St Margaret's Bay. Seats outside the pub and on the sea wall.

OPEN: 11–3, 6–11. Sun 12–3, 7–10.30. Summer 11–11.
Real Ale.
Children welcome. Dogs on leads.

Marshside

Gate Inn ☎ 01227 860498
Boyden Gate, nr Marshside, Canterbury CT3 4EB (off A28 Canterbury–Margate road near Upstreet)
Shepherd Neame. Christopher Smith, tenant

Streams, apple trees, ducks, farmland and marshes. A very local local, this is an unspoilt country pub in a small hamlet with a very loyal following and a landlord who has been here for over 28 years. Inside are just two connecting rooms warmed by a big log fire in the central fireplace. The Gate has a thriving trade and offers a well-cooked, simple menu based, whenever possible, on fresh local produce. Sandwiches (they do a prize-winning black-pudding one), hot torpedoes (filled French bread), filled jacket potatoes, Gateburgers, lots of home-made pickles, spicy hotpots, 'mega' grills, a variety of 'ploughpersons', and light meals. At lunchtime the dining area is no-smoking. Shepherd Neame Masterbrew, Spitfire and seasonal ales tapped from the cask. In summer you can sit outside by the stream and feed the assortment of ducks and geese that have made their home there.

OPEN: 11–2.30 (Sat 11–3), 6–11. Sun 12–4, 7–10.30.
Real Ale.
Well-behaved children in eating area and family room. Dogs on leads.

Pluckley

Dering Arms ☎ 01233 840371
Pluckley, Ashford TN27 0RR
Free House. James Buss, licensee
e-mail: info@deringarms.com

This is a very scattered village but the tall, imposing, Dutch-gabled Dering Arms is easily found – by the railway station. Built as a hunting lodge for the local Dering family, this is not a cosy pub, more impressive; inside, the beamed main bar has high ceilings, stone floors and a huge fireplace; there is a smaller bar and more intimate restaurant serving some interesting food. The pub provides imaginative menus, using local ingredients where possible. Look for specials from the blackboard but dishes range from mussels in cider and cream sauce, potted shrimps, pasta with Stilton and basil sauce, whole crab salad, rack of lamb with herb crust, pheasant casserole with red-wine sauce, many more fish dishes such as potted crab, fillet of halibut and local trout, home-baked pies, steaks, selected cuts of pork and lamb to scrummy puds. Every meal is prepared to order. Gourmet evenings are held several times a year. Ales include specially brewed Dering ale and Goachers Maidstone ale. Extensive, wide-ranging wine list and local farm cider. Garden parties and musical evenings are sometimes held in the large garden. Telephone for details.

OPEN: 11–3, 6–11.
Real Ale. Restaurant (closed Sun eve and all day Mon).
Children in restaurant and eating area. Dogs on leads. Wheelchair access (not WC). Three bedrooms.
Cards: all except Diners.

Smarden

Chequers ① 01233 770217
The Street, Smarden, nr Ashford TN27 8QA
Free House. Charles Bullock, licensee

A small, delightful village with just one main street of half-timbered and weatherboarded houses. Along with nearby Tenterden and Cranbrook, Smarden was one of the centres of the Flemish cloth trade and much business was anticipated, which probably accounts for the surprisingly large church, known as 'the barn of Kent'; but in fact it didn't expand, staying just as it was. Three roads lead into Smarden, and as the Chequers takes up a biggish corner site, two of them nearly end up in the pub, the third in the churchyard. Part of the 14th-century pub used to be the village meeting place; it still is of course but in a totally different way. Comfortable and welcoming with lots of beams, two bars, two dining areas – one a no-smoking dining room – two open fires and a general air of prosperity. An extra dining area has been built at the back – timber-framed, with a lot of glass, it can be totally closed off or open to the terrace. A pub serving some really good food, but with plenty of local support for the beer. Daily specials on the blackboard could be tempura prawns with a sweet chilli dip, leek and potato soup, poached salmon with a wholegrain mustard sauce, home-made steak and kidney pudding, fillet or T-bone steak, also a reliable bar snack menu: a hotpot, something with pasta, fisherman's pie and a vegetarian dish or two. Always draught Bass, Harveys Best, maybe Hardy and Hansons Frolicking Farmer plus guests from microbreweries. A wide-ranging wine list to go with the good food. Outside the courtyard has seats for 40. The car park at the back of the pub has been enlarged; beyond that, well landscaped, grass, seats, and a pond with ducks.

OPEN: 10–3, 6–11. Sun 12–3, 7–10.30.
Real Ale. Restaurant.
Children if well behaved. Dogs on leads. Car park. Wheelchair access (not WC). Disabled loo in the village. Bedrooms.
Cards: Delta, MasterCard, Switch, Visa.

Snargate

Red Lion ①01797 344648
Snargate TN29 9UQ (on B2080 Brenzett–Appledore road)
Free House. Doris Jemison, licensee

Truly a family pub, run by the same family for ninety years; the last time anyone thought of modernising it was in 1890! The gaslight fittings are still there, and oil lamps that come into their own when they run out of candles. Electricity has however crept in but apart from that, nothing much has changed – not even the paint! A totally unspoilt, unchanging, timeless treasure a couple of miles from Brenzett. Opening hours are a little flexible. When you do get in, you walk straight into the bar, large enough to accommodate at least six people sitting down, and only a few more than that standing. This bar is also the passageway to the other two, equally small rooms. Time has stood still here; beers from the barrel, crisps from the box, maybe a nut to keep you going – and coal fires in winter. You come here for the experience and the good ale, not the comfort. Goachers Light Ale is on permanently, Rother Valley Level Best (brewed at Northiam) is the guest. Double Vision cider from Staplehurst.

OPEN: 12–3, 7–11 (roughly).
Real Ale.
No children. No dogs inside and heaven only knows where the loos are.

Stansted

Black Horse ① 01732 822355
Tumblefield Road, Stansted, nr West Kingsdown TN15 7PR
Free House. Ian Duncan, licensee
e-mail: lavraki@stanstedpub.freeserve.co.uk

A handsome, white-painted pub at the heart of the community in this downland village, high on the chalk downs about five miles from West Kingsdown. Food is filling pub favourites with a traditional roast on Sunday. On Tuesday to Saturday evenings excellent Thai food is served in the restaurant – subdued oriental music in here. Beers are Larkins, Youngs Special, two guests and two draught lagers. As this is a good walking area, you need to be well stoked up for the onward march. Outside, the large garden has a play area to keep the little darlings occupied. The second week in July they hold a Kent Fair Week on land belonging to the pub. The Fair promotes all Kent produce: wine, cheese, beer, fruit, vegetables – everything grown in Kent. During that week they also hold a vintage car rally.

OPEN: 10–11. Sun 12–10.30.
Real Ale. Thai restaurant with quiet music.
Children under control. Dogs on leads. Wheelchair access. Four en-suite bedrooms.
Cards: all major credit cards except Amex and Diners.
N.B. Live traditional Irish music every second Sunday in the month.

Staplehurst

Lord Raglan ① 01622 843747
Chart Hill Road, nr Staplehurst TN12 0DE
Free House. Andrew Hutchison, owner/licensee

Alone among the orchards, about a mile from Staplehurst, it's amazing how many people manage to find the Lord Raglan for lunch, so you can too. A country pub as you remember them; unspoilt, the oldest bit is 17th century, full of old beams and with open log fires. There is one long bar and a dining area, but you can eat wherever you can find a table. An unusual and interesting addition to the usual pub furniture is slumped in a chair by the door into the car park – a full-size model of a man dressed in 18th-century clothes! The bar menu offers various sandwiches and ploughman's and the regularly changing blackboard menu may list marinated herring fillet, smoked duck and orange salad, Mediterranean prawns, and for a main course, grilled lamb chops, poached salmon in a lemon and herb sauce, guinea fowl in red wine, shepherds pie and stir-fried beef and peppers. Home-made puds such as blackberry and apple crumble to finish. Harveys Best

Bitter, Goachers Light plus a guest beer – two in summer. As befits the area, there is an orchard garden.

OPEN: 12–3, 6–11. Closed Sun.
Real Ale. Dining room.
Children welcome. Dogs on leads. Car park. Wheelchair access.
Cards: MasterCard, Switch, Visa.

Tunbridge Wells

Opera House ① 01892 511770
48–60 Mount Pleasant Road, Royal Tunbridge Wells TN1 1RB
Wetherspoon.

The Opera House had become a bingo hall; it was a sorry sight and very unloved. Now it is rescued, restored and performing again. Go and gaze at the lovely interior, everything as it was in its heyday, then settle down to a cheaper-than-usual pint or something from the menu; these change twice a year and are standard throughout the chain. One thing worth noting is that they have a good selection of vegetarian dishes. Always about eight real ales on the go, cider, and anything else you want really, including a reasonably priced champagne.

OPEN: 11–11.
Real Ale.
No children. No dogs. All disabled facilities.

BEST OF THE REST

Dargate
Dove ① 01227 751360
Plum Pudding Lane, Dargate ME13 9HB
Signposted off the A299, between Whitstable and Faversham, the Dove is unspoilt in a very civilized way, just as a country pub should be, catering for thirsty locals and discerning travellers. Enjoyable, original, food – way above the usual – the sort of place to make a detour for. Shepherd Neame range of beers and a good wine list. Children and dogs welcome.
Open: 11.30–3, 6–11. Closed Mon lunchtimes.

Markbeech
Kentish Horse ① 01342 850493
Markbeech TN8 5NT
Drive along country lanes until you reach this tiny hamlet south of Edenbridge. There is only one Kentish Horse in the country and this is it; where it should be – in Kent. White painted and Victorian, it has just one long main bar with a log fire, the blackboard menus, and a smart dining room. Unpretentious but excellent quality home-made soups, local sausages, filo prawns, home-cooked ham, steak and ale pie, Thai red chicken; all cooked with care. Well kept Fullers London Pride, Harveys, Larkins, a guest and a modest wine list. Children welcome and dogs – in the bar.
Open: 12–11.

Perry Wood

Rose & Crown ① 01227 752214
Perry Wood, nr Selling ME13 9RY

In an area of narrow country lanes, the signposts tell you where you want to go, but actually getting there is something else entirely! So, out with the map to find this place; if Kent has a hinterland, then this is it. Once here it is a delight. The garden is lovely and if you have the dog with you the walks are wonderful. Inside is as you would expect a 16th-century pub to be. Traditional bar food with a few surprises. Local cider and four changing ales on hand pump. Children and dogs welcome.
Open: 11–3, 6–11.

Smarts Hill

Bottle House Inn ① 01892 870306
Coldharbour Road, Smarts Hill, nr Penshurst TN11 8ET

About a mile outside Penshurst, then follow the signs to this 15th-century pub. Inside it is a comfortable, well-beamed old place; outside you have views of the Kent countryside. Dishes are more imaginative than the usual pub food – lots of fresh fish and dishes such as fillet of beef Wellington. Harveys Best and Larkins beers, local cider and local wine. Children and dogs welcome.
Open: 11–3, 6–11.

Stodmarsh

Red Lion ① 01227 721339
Stodmarsh, nr Canterbury CT3 4BA

The pub has been prettily rebuilt on what were 15th-century remains (there are probably a couple of bricks and a beam or two left from the original). The Red Lion, at the heart of an appealing small village, is in a delightful valley about four miles from Canterbury. Well worth the journey for the friendly atmosphere, welcoming fire and good food. Menus change depending on what is available. Warming oxtail stew, rabbit pot au feu, roasted partridge or pan-fried kidneys could be on the winter menu. Greene King ales, guest ales on Thursdays, a good choice of wines – Mr Whigham used to be a wine merchant – and whatever else you could possibly want. The pub isn't that big and gets very busy towards the end of the week. Plenty of room in the garden if inside is a bit of a crush. Outside, ducks wander, hens lay and herbs grow. Children allowed. Dogs welcome. Car park. Three letting bedrooms. Cards: all except Amex and Harrods.
Open: 10.30–11. Sun 11–10.30.

Tunbridge Wells

Beacon ① 01892 524252
Tea Garden Lane, Tunbridge Wells TN3 9JH

Drive past Nevill Park towards Rustall Common to find Tea Garden Lane and the Beacon, a Victorian pub with the most wonderful views towards the west from the back terrace. Very popular for its extremely reasonable two-course lunches, or anything else you want from the bar menu: poached salmon salad, game terrine, braised rabbit or cod in batter – that sort of thing; cooking is inventive. Beers are Fullers London Pride, Harveys Best and Timothy Taylors Landlord. Children allowed in the eating areas.
Open: 11–11.

Wetherspoon in Kent

Ashford – County Hotel, 10 High Street
℡ 01233 646891
Canterbury – Thomas Ingoldsby, 5–9 Burgate
℡ 01227 463339
Canterbury – West Gate Inn, 1–3 North Lane
℡ 01227 464329
Dover – Eight Bells, 19 Cannon Street
℡ 01304 205030
Faversham – Leading Light, 20–22 Preston Street
℡ 01795 535075
Folkestone – Wetherspoons, 213 Rendezvous Street
℡ 01303 251154
Gravesend – Robert Pocock, 181–183 Windmill Street
℡ 01474 352765
Herne Bay – Saxon Shore, 78–80 Central Parade
℡ 01227 370316
Maidstone – Muggleton Inn, 8–9 High Street
℡ 01622 691527
Maidstone – Society Rooms, Brenchly House, Week Street
℡ 01622 350910
Margate – Mechanical Elephant, 28–30 Marine Terrace
℡ 01843 234100
Rochester – Golden Lion, 147–149 High Street
℡ 01634 880521
Sevenoaks – Sennockian, 139–141 High Street
℡ 01732 469010
Sittingbourne – Summoner, High Street
℡ 01795 410158
Tonbridge – Humphrey Bean, 94 High Street
℡ 01732 773850
Tunbridge Wells – Opera House, 88 Mount Pleasant Road
℡ 01892 511770

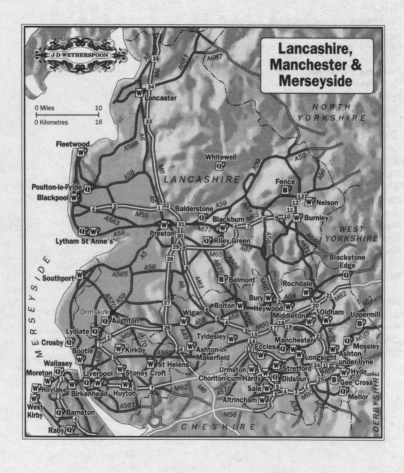

J·D·WETHERSPOON CO

Lancashire, Manchester & Merseyside

0 Miles 10
0 Kilometres 16

NORTH YORKSHIRE

LANCASHIRE

WEST YORKSHIRE

MERSEYSIDE

DERBYSHIRE

CHESHIRE

Lancaster
Fleetwood
Whitewell
Poulton-le-Fylde
Blackpool
Balderstone
Fence
Nelson
Blackburn
Burnley
Preston
Riley Green
Lytham St Anne's
Blackstone Edge
Southport
Belmont
Rochdale
Bury
Heywood
Ormskirk
Bolton
Middleton
Oldham
Uppermill
Aughton
Wigan
Lydiate
Tyldesley
Mossley
Crosby
Manchester
Ashton-under-Lyne
Bootle
Kirkby
Ashton-in-Makerfield
Eccles
Longsight
Wallasey
St Helens
Urmston
Stretford
Hyde
Moreton
Liverpool
Stoney Croft
Chorlton-cum-Hardy
Didsbury
Gee Cross
Hoylake
Birkenhead
Huyton
Sale
Mellor
West Kirby
Altrincham
Barnston
Raby

Lancashire, Manchester and Merseyside

Aughton

Dog & Gun Inn ① 01695 42330
233 Long Lane, Aughton, Ormskirk, Lancs L39 5BU
Burtonwood Brewery. Mrs Shirley Davies, tenant

The friendly mock-Tudor Dog and Gun has been ably run by the same landlady for over 30 years. South of Ormskirk, it's in a village surrounded by good farming country and, if you are looking for a little culture, the interesting Norman church with an early 18th-century sundial in the churchyard is well worth a visit. Seasonal hanging baskets and tubs of flowers put on a good display outside; in winter coal fires warm the lounge and snug. Not a TV or fruit machine in the place – no food either. There are a couple of benches among the flowers at the front of the pub where you can sit, admire the flowers and watch the world go by while clutching your pint of well-kept Burtonwood Mild, Bitter or Forshaws Bitter and munching a nut or two. Darts and quiz teams in the winter; bowls on the proper bowling green in the summer. Extra seats in the pub garden. (Confusingly there are two Aughtons in Lancashire; the other is further north beyond Blackpool.)

OPEN: Mon–Fri 5–11. Sat & Sun 12–2, 6–11.
Real Ale.
Quiet children welcome. No dogs. Car park. Wheelchair access.

Balderstone

Myerscough Hotel ① 01254 812222
Whalley Road, Balderstone, Blackburn, Lancs BB2 7LE (on A59)
Robinsons. Ian Riddock, licensee

This country pub is in the Ribble valley, away from main roads but only a few miles from the M6. So, if you're looking for a welcome break, swing off the motorway at Exit 31 and head for the A59 towards Clitheroe and Balderstone. Close to the British Aerospace plant, don't be surprised to see a Canberra bomber and Lightning fighter gate-guardians parked by the side of the road; the Myerscough is opposite the two jets. This friendly country pub is a favourite place for lunch during the week, particularly with businessmen and families. Spacious, comfortable bars – one is no-smoking – where they serve good traditional bar food. Robinsons ales and Hartleys XB plus a good selection of malt whiskies. Picnic tables and assorted livestock in the garden.

OPEN: 11.30–3, 5.30–11. Sun 12–10.30.
Real Ale.
Children in front room till 8.30 p.m. No dogs except guide dogs. Bedrooms.
Wednesday quiz night.

Barnston

Fox & Hounds ① 0151 648 7685
Barnston Village, Wirral CH61 1BW
Free House. Ralph Leech, licensee
www.the-fox-hounds.co.uk

Situated in one of the most attractive areas in the south Wirral peninsula, this early 20th-century pub was built to replace the original 18th-century Fox and Hounds (pictures of which can be seen in the bar). Inside is a traditional pub layout: comfortable lounge bar, separate entrance to the public bar and a small snug. They offer a good choice of home-cooked pub food, soup, open sandwiches, ploughman's (the lasagne, quiche and coronation chicken are very popular), lamb hotpot, country casserole, glazed supreme of salmon, well-filled baked potatoes, salads and changing specials from the blackboard – it all depends on what inspires the chef. Puds on the blackboard too. Sunday lunch always has four roasts and a fish dish. Theakstons Best, Old Peculier and Cool Cask, Websters Yorkshire, and two guests. The pub has a flowery courtyard, an outside bar and lovely garden, not to mention attractive surroundings and good walks.

OPEN: 11–11.
Real Ale.
Children welcome. Dogs on leads. Car park. Wheelchair access (not WC).

Blackstone Edge

White House ① 01706 378456
Blackstone Edge, Little Borough, Rochdale OL15 0LG
Free House. Neville Marney, licensee

This whole area is serious walking country; one way and another it has been since Roman times. The Roman road running across this lonely stretch of moorland – approached from Ripponden – is one of the best preserved in the country. If you're on the Pennine Way it crosses the road outside this windswept but welcoming old pub, which is over 1400ft up in the clouds. Inside, you'll find a good coal fire in the main bar and from another room you have far-reaching views over the moors. Daily specials, as well as generous portions of traditional bar food: soup of the day, sandwiches, garlic mushrooms, quiche, steak and kidney pie, sirloin garni and salads. Children's portions. Moorhouse Pendle Witches' Brew, Theakstons Best, Timothy Taylors Landlord, Black Sheep Bitter plus weekly changing guests. Farm ciders and several malt whiskies. Remove the muddy boots and leave them in the porch; only clean shoes or socks inside the bars.

OPEN: 11.30–3, 7–11. Sun 12–10.30.
Real Ale. Restaurant.
Children welcome. No dogs. Wheelchair access.

Crosby

Crow's Nest ① 0151 924 6953
63 Victoria Road, Crosby, Liverpool, Wirral L23 7XY
Scottish & Newcastle. David Hughes, licensee

A very serious drinking establishment – a 'behave yourself' sort of place where they keep a tight grip on things: a notice reads: 'No music, no pool, no fruit machines, no footballers and no food'. This is an interesting, listed town pub and popular local, with bar, snug and lounge, CAMRA's 'Pub of Excellence in North West' for 2002 and 2003. Beer aficionados all! So serious that you have to go early to try the guest beer before it runs out. Sales are booming – good traditional beer and conversation combine well, and it's frequented largely by professionals – teachers, barristers and the like. Five cask ales: Cains, Boddingtons, Theakstons and Greenalls and a daily changing guest, various lagers, stouts and cider. There is a garden ready to be enjoyed.

OPEN: 11.30–11.
Real Ale.
Children allowed if well behaved. No dogs.

Didsbury

Royal Oak ① 0161 434 4788
729 Wilmslow Road, Didsbury, Greater Manchester M20 0RH
Marstons. Robert & Hazel Long, managers
e-mail: srbrt@aol.com

Some refurbishment has gone on, but they still specialise in cheese. They are truly knowledgeable, and the selection is wonderful: usually 40 available, sometimes 100, depending on the time of year. For a lunch snack you can have any cheese from the many available, with a chunk of bread, a slice of paté, an olive or two and salad. What you don't finish, you can take home, doggy bags provided. If you're not into cheese, there are 10 different patés for you to choose from. Marstons Pedigree Bitter, Banks's Original and a guest beer, plus sherries and port from the barrel; delicious with cheese.

OPEN: 11–11. Lunchtime snacks only, not weekends or bank holidays.
Real Ale.
No children. No dogs.

Liverpool

Roscoe Head ① 0151 709 4365
24 Roscoe Street, Liverpool L1 2SX
Punch Taverns. Carol Ross, licensee

A very civilized Victorian town pub which is open all day. Unspoilt and quiet, with two parlours, a snug and bar; the larger of the two parlours used to house the famous tie collection but it all became too much. It was difficult to keep clean and the ties were starting to fall apart when washed, so the collection is no more. The plus side is that at least you know that the unusual club tie you might be wearing will stay around your neck and not end up on the pub wall. Food, which you can pre-order if you are pushed for time, is served at lunchtime only – reliable pub grub of filled baguettes, jacket potatoes, curries, steak pie, chicken pie, sausages – that sort of thing. Well-kept Ind Coope Burton, Jennings Bitter, Cumberland Ale, Tetleys Mild and Bitter and a weekly guest. Stella, Skol and Carlsberg Pilsner lagers. No outdoor drinking area. A place for animated conversation.

OPEN: 11.30–11. Sat 12–11.
Real Ale.
No children. No dogs.

Lydiate

Scotch Piper ① 0151 526 0503
Southport Road, Lydiate, Merseyside L31 4HD
Pyramid Pub Co. Fred & Anne-Marie Rigby, tenants

On the county border, on the northern edge of Merseyside near the Leeds/Liverpool canal, this ancient, thatched building is, one of our readers tells us, a gem of a pub. Reputed to be the oldest in Lancashire, legend has it that it was built around an oak tree in the 14th century, and was then, unsurprisingly, known as the Royal Oak. The name change came, so it is said, when a Highland piper from the 1745 rebellion sought refuge in the pub and married the innkeeper's daughter – always a good move. Having had a fairly combustible life the pub was carefully restored after its third fire in the mid-1980s to have three cosy rooms, fires – under control – low beams and a friendly, relaxed atmosphere. No food, just a crisp and nut to go with an excellent pint of Banks Bitter or Marstons Pedigree.

OPEN: 12–3, 5.30–11. Sat 12–11. Sun 12–10.30.
Real Ale.
No children. Dogs welcome. Car park. Wheelchair access (not WC).

Lytham

The Taps ① 01253 736226
12 Henry Street, Lytham, Lancs FY8 5LE
Laurel Pub Co. Ian Rigg, manager

Behind the Clifton Arms hotel, this is the place to be if your interest is beer, possibly the more unusual brews. The Victorian Taps has always existed for the true beer enthusiast. It's not far from the beach – a street away – so there's a seashore theme running through the pub (fish, boats and things) – but the real interest here is what is in the cellar. So far they've tried well over a thousand different varieties of ale, and no doubt ones they've missed will be tasted by the Taps' patrons in due course. From a choice of eight at a time, you take pot luck (if that's the expression with beer), as who knows what's on offer and when. There are also farm ciders and some country wines. A basic sort of place where they serve good traditional bar food with home-made daily specials.

OPEN: 11–11. Lunchtime meals & snacks, not Sunday.
Real Ale.
Children in eating area at mealtimes. No dogs.

Manchester

Circus Tavern ① 0161 236 5818
86 Portland Street, Manchester M1 4GX
Tetley Walker. Steven Campbell, licensee

An exceptional little place, with two minute rooms and a corridor between. This is, I'm sure, the smallest pub in Manchester. Well known for being miniature; a timeless treasure. Don't be put off by the fact that it looks closed: it isn't, but you might have to knock to be let in! So small there is room for only one beer – a well-kept Tetley Bitter. No room to cook – certainly nowhere to put a plate! So a bag of crisps and a nut, neither of which take up much space, is all you will get.

OPEN: 11–11.
Real Ale.
Children welcome. Dogs – yes, if well behaved and not too big!

Moon under Water ① 0161 834 5882
68–74 Deansgate, Manchester M3 2FN
Wetherspoon.

Built on the site of an old ABC cinema with three separate bars on two levels and a passenger lift – not many pubs have one of those – this is said to be the biggest 'pub' in the country; not what you would call intimate. Beer is cheap though. Situated in the heart of the city, decorations include pictures, photographs and, slightly unnervingly, sculptures of five Manchester celebrities. Keeping a watchful eye on what is going on, they have their own cinema seats on the first floor: Ena Sharples from Coronation Street, Sir Robert Peel,

Emmeline Pankhurst, Hattie Jacques and horror actor Christopher Lee. Always five or six real ales, a guest ale and anything else to drink you could want. Bar snacks, or a full menu if you're hungry. Good solid reliable fare, plus a daily special or two.

OPEN: 11–11.
Real Ale.
No children. No dogs.

Mellor

Devonshire Arms ① 0161 427 2563
Longhurst Lane, Mellor, nr Marple SK6 5PP
Robinsons. John Longworth, tenant

Confusingly there are two Mellors in Lancashire. You can be sure this is the one you want if you are very near the Cheshire border, between the A626 and the A6015 – the other is further north. Once you've got here you'll find the Devonshire Arms is a cheerful, friendly pub with a reputation for serving some above-average food. The constantly changing menu leans towards curries and spicy dishes, varied soups, steamed fresh mussels, chicken and peppers in spicy sauce, smoked sausage, vegetarian dishes, steaks and home-made puds. Robinsons ales including the occasional Robinsons Stockport's Arches ale, lots of malt whiskies and a good selection of wine.

OPEN: 12–3, 6–11. Sun 11–10.30.
Real Ale.
Well-behaved children in eating area. No dogs.
N.B. Live jazz every other Tuesday evening.

Oddfellows Arms ① 0161 449 7826
73 Moor End Road, Mellor, nr Marple SK6 5PT
Free House. Robert Cloughley, licensee

This splendid old country pub has everything you could hope for: low ceilings, flagstone floors, comfortable furnishings, good fires and, very importantly, really interesting dishes on the menu. The emphasis is on food, but the bar is there to lean on, the beer to be appreciated and the locals to chat to. But if you're tempted, there are good things on the bar menu: home-made soup, ploughman's, usually a good choice of fish served with imaginative sauces, curries, chicken in garlic and yoghurt, Moroccan lamb casserole, steaks and puddings. Upstairs is a no-smoking restaurant. Adnams and Marstons Pedigree are on permanently with one guest ale.

OPEN: 12–3, 5.30–11 (Sun 7–10.30).
Real Ale. Restaurant.
Children welcome. Dogs in bar. Wheelchair access into bar only.

Mossley

Tollemache Arms ① 01457 832354
415 Manchester Road, Mossley, Ashton-under-Lyne, Lancs OL5 9BG
Robinsons (Stockport). Lynn Kenworthy, licensee

Quiet and inviting, with not even a gaming machine – not even a till up to a few years
ago – this old roadside pub looks over the restored Huddersfield canal. A popular place
that draws to it an interesting cross section of the local populace. Inside is a small, cosy tap
room where you can play darts, dominoes and cards and, when you feel a bit peckish
you'll find a choice of bar snacks. No meals now; new licensee, new regime. Robinsons
range of ales.

OPEN: 12–11.
Real Ale.
Children welcome and dogs. Wheelchair access. One bedroom.

Poulton-le-Fylde

Thatched Public House ① 01253 891063
12 Ball Street, Poulton-le-Fylde, Lancs FY6 7BG
Scottish & Newcastle. Brian Ballentine, manager

A quiet, restful pub in more ways than one – no music and no children either, you are able
to contemplate your pint in peace. The name is a misnomer, as the thatch on this pub –
just off Market Square and next to the Norman Church – was taken off in 1906 and
replaced by tiles. Appealing to those of you who appreciate a good pint – no food to be
had – there is just one bar and four rooms where you can enjoy a drink and a few crisps
and nuts. No pool table, gaming machine with the sound turned off – this is a talking pub
and very busy serving well-kept Boddingtons Bitter, Theakston Cool Cask, Charles Wells
Bombardier and rotating guests.

OPEN: 11–11.
Real Ale.
No children. No dogs. All wheelchair facilities.

Raby

Wheatsheaf Inn ① 0151 336 3416
The Green, Rabymere Road, Raby, Wirral CH63 4JH
Free House. Thomas Charlesworth, licensee

The village is quiet and the pub, with a thatched roof, black timbers, whitewashed walls
and wonderful baskets of flowers, is very traditional. Tremendously popular and known
locally as 'The Thatch', it has a single bar with a big inglenook fireplace and, opposite, a
small snug. Lunchtime snacks: a huge variety of toasties, bacon baps and sandwiches – but
the toasties are the favourites. In the restaurant – called 'The Cowshed' – they serve far
more elaborate dishes: dressed Cornish crab, asparagus tartlet, poached chicken breast

wrapped in Parma ham served with a tomato and hollandaise sauce and vegetarian dishes, unfortunately with a musical accompaniment. There is a good choice of real ales: Thwaites Bitter, Theakstons Best and Old Peculier, Cains Bitter, Tetleys, Charles Wells Bombardier, Morlands Old Speckled Hen and guests. There are seats at the front of the pub so you can while away the time, admire the flowers and enjoy your drink.

OPEN: 11.30–11. Sun 12–10.30.
Real Ale. Restaurant open every evening except Sun and Mon – music in here.
Children at lunchtime only. Dogs in pub, not in restaurant. Car park. Ramp and disabled facilities for restaurant.

Riley Green

Royal Oak ① 01254 201445
Blackburn Old Road, Riley Green, Hoghton, nr Preston, Lancs PR5 0SL
Daniel Thwaites PLC, Blackburn. Eric & Trish Hargreaves, licensees

There's plenty to see and do here; it's near the towpath of the Leeds/Liverpool canal and a short walk from Hoghton Tower, a historic house rebuilt in the 17th century on a steep, wooded hill, and restored in the 19th. On a good day, the view from the hill is impressive. The Royal Oak, originally an important coaching inn, is a low-ceilinged country pub with stripped stone walls, beams, open fires, comfortable armchairs to lounge in and settles to sit in. Not a jukebox, radio, TV, pool table or gaming machine to be seen. Reliably good food is served every day. To start you could have home-made soup, black pudding slices with a wholegrain-mustard dip, home-baked cheese and onion pie, grilled gammon or grilled fillet steak, lasagne with garlic bread, freshly filled sandwiches, jacket potatoes, a ploughman's or something from the specials board such as a beef pot roast, casserole of lamb with Stilton dumplings or halibut with prawns and dill. Vegetarian dishes too, children's portions and a big selection of hot and cold puds. Very well-kept Thwaites Best Bitter, Mild, Lancaster Bomber and Thoroughbred on hand pump, also Thwaites Smooth, Guinness and Kingston Press cider; about three dozen single malt whiskies. The large garden looks towards Hoghton Tower. Very popular with walkers, especially at weekends.

OPEN: 11.30–3, 5.30–11. Sat 11.30–11. Sun 12–10.30.
Real Ale.
Children welcome – on leads until 9pm. Dogs too – no time limit. Two big car parks with CCTV. New loos.
Cards: All major credit cards except Amex.

Wallasey

Magazine Hotel ① 0151 637 3974
7 Magazine Brow, Wallasey, Merseyside CH45 1HP
Six Continents Retail. Martin Venables, manager

On the banks of the river Mersey, overlooking what was once the busiest shipping lane in Europe, the 18th-century Magazine was an inn during the days when sailing ships had to unload their gunpowder before being allowed to dock. The gunpowder was put into the magazine 50 yards away – which is why the pub is so named. Unfortunately the unloading of gunpowder ceased and the hotel trade died out, so the black and white Magazine survived by becoming a simple pub. Inside is one main bar and lots of small rooms full of beams and shiny brass where they serve home-made soups, steak and kidney pies, lasagne, mixed grills and daily specials. Food is served every lunchtime. Evenings are devoted to the serious drinker. Draught Bass, Stones Bitter and Worthington Clean Flow.

OPEN: 11–11. Sun 12–10.30. Food served Mon–Sat 12–2.30, Sun 1–4.
Real Ale.
Children allowed. Dogs in garden. Wheelchair access.

Whitewell

Inn at Whitewell ① 01200 448222
Whitewell, Forest of Bowland, Clitheroe, Lancs BB7 3AT
Free House. Richard Bowman, licensee

In the lovely wooded Hodder valley, this village of grey stone cottages is as perfect a place as you could wish, in one of the most attractive areas of the county. The 14th-century Inn at Whitewell, next to the village church and the river, is an inn of many parts: hotel, pub, wine merchant and art gallery. Lots of magazines and guide books to read and a piano to play to while away the time. Traditional, well-cooked bar food and a more adventurous selection from the restaurant menu. From the bar menu are interesting soups, open sandwiches, salads and ploughman's, poached salmon, the popular Whitewell gourmet fish pie, honey-glazed joints of chicken and lots more; specials of the day are on the blackboard. Grouse, partridge and pheasant in season. Home-made puds and a good cheese selection. The food is excellent. Marstons Pedigree, Timothy Taylors Landlord and Boddingtons ales. Extensive, interesting wine list. View of the river from the restaurant and the seats in the garden.

OPEN: 11–3, 6–11.
Real Ale. Restaurant (not Sun lunchtime).
Children welcome. Dogs on leads. Car park. Seventeen bedrooms.
Cards: Amex, Delta, Diners, MasterCard, Switch, Visa.

BEST OF THE REST

Belmont, Lancs
Black Dog ① 01204 811218
2–4 Church Street, Belmont BL7 8AB
This village is surrounded by moorland and in it is a delightful old farmhouse, now the pub. Inside are lots of cosy corners from where you can admire the interesting bits and pieces collected by the licensees over the years. Welcoming and very popular, they serve a good selection of filling bar food varying from home-made soup to pork in a Cumberland sauce. Holts range of beers. Walks onto the moors and a garden to sit in. Children welcome. Bedrooms.
Open: 12–4, 7–11.

Fence, Lancs
Forest ① 01282 613641
Cuckstool Lane, Fence BB12 9PA

Sturdy, stonebuilt and on a country lane just off the A6068 outside Fence, near the Forest of Pendle, the Forest is an acknowledged 'dining pub', which loosely translates into 'you eat very well here'. You can of course have a sandwich – it is after all a pub – but there could also be king prawns in filo pastry with a coriander and mint dressing, or pavé of Scottish salmon with a spring onion and dill velouté, home-made puds too. Ruddles and Theakstons Best plus a couple of guests and a good wine list. Weekends are busy; you need to book. Children welcome. No dogs. Wheelchair access.
Open: 12–11.

Gee Cross, Cheshire
Grapes Hotel ① 0161 3682614
Stockport Road, Gee Cross, Hyde SK14 5RU

Edwardian through and through, this is a gabled, bay-windowed building, with leaded lights, engraved Edwardian windows, four large carpeted rooms with red ceilings, brass light fittings, and tiles from bar top to floor. It's on the corner of a steep hill in the old village of Gee Cross, opposite an imposing Victorian-Gothic church. You'll find cheerful, friendly staff and customers and Robinsons traditional ales including Bitter and Best Mild. A bowling green is attached to the pub so you can while away the time encouraging the experts. No children. No dogs. Occasional stabling for your horse. Wheelchair access (not WC).
Open: 12–3, 5–11.

Uppermill, Lancs
Church Inn ① 01457 820902
Uppermill, Saddleworth OL3 6LW

Upper it is too. Find the village, then the turning to Saddleworth Church and keep on going – up! Alone except for the church, it's worth it for the eccentricity of the place. You also have views over the valley, their 'own brew' beer and a traditional menu – home-made soup, sandwiches, steak and ale pie and daily specials. Frequent Morris Dancers practising their steps – the head brewer is one of the dancers. Children welcome, and dogs.
Open: 12–11.

Wetherspoon in Lancashire, Greater Manchester and Merseyside

Lancashire

Ashton-in-Makerfield – Sir Thomas Gerard, Gerard Street
① 01942 713519
Ashton-under-Lyne – Ash Tree, 18 Wellington Road
① 0161 339 9670
Blackburn – Postal Order, 15 Darwen Street
① 01254 676400
Blackpool – Auctioneer, 235–237 Lytham Road
① 01942 713519
Burnley – Brun Lea, 31–39 Manchester Road
① 01282 463700
Fleetwood – Sir Thomas Drummond, London Street
① 01253 775020

Lancaster – Green Ayre, 63 North Road
℃ 01524 585240
Lancaster – Sir Richard Owen, 4 Spring Garden Street
℃ 01524 541500
Nelson – Station Hotel, Hibson Road
℃ 01282 877910
Preston – Greyfriar, 144 Friargate
℃ 01772 558542
St Annes on Sea – Trawl Boat Inn, 36–38 Wood Street
℃ 01253 783080

Greater Manchester

Altrincham – Unicorn, 1–7 Ashley Road
℃ 0161 926 4610
Bolton – Robert Shaw, Market Street, Westhoughton
℃ 01942 844110
Bolton – Spinning Mule, 1–2 Nelson Square
℃ 01204 533339
Bury – Robert Peel, 5–10 Market Place
℃ 0161 764 7287
Chorlton-cum-Hardy – Sedge Lynn, 21a Manchester Road
℃ 0161 860 0141
Eccles – Eccles Cross, 13 Regent Street
℃ 0161 788 0414
Heywood – Edwin Waugh, 10–12 Market Street
℃ 01706 621480
Hyde – Cotton Bale, 212–225 Market Place
℃ 0161 351 0380
Longsight – Sir Edwin Chadwick, 587 Stockport Road
℃ 0161 256 2806
Manchester – Moon under the Water, 68–74 Deansgate
℃ 0161 834 5882
Manchester – Paramount, 33–35 Oxford Street
℃ 0161 233 1820
Manchester – Waterhouse, 67–71 Princes Street
℃ 0161 200 5380
Manchester – Wetherspoons, 49A Piccadilly
℃ 0161 236 9206
Middleton – Harbord Harbord, 17–21 Long Street
℃ 0161 654 6226
Oldham – Up Steps Inn, 17–23 High Street
℃ 0161 627 5001
Rochdale – Regal Moon, The Butts
℃ 01706 654334
Sale – J P Joule, Northenden Road
℃ 0161 962 9889
Stretford – Bishop Blaize, 708 Chester Road
℃ 0161 873 8845
Tyldesley – George and Dragon, 185–187 Elliott Street
℃ 01942 897426

Urmston – Tim Bobbin, 41 Flixton Road
① 0161 749 8239
Wigan – Brocket Arms (also a Wetherspoon Lodge), Mesnes Road
① 01942 820372
Wigan – Moon under Water, 5–7a Market Place, The Wiend
① 01942 323437

Merseyside

Birkenhead – Brass Balance, 39–47 Argyle Street
① 0151 650 8950
Birkenhead – John Laird, Europa Centre
① 0151 650 0620
Bootle – Wild Rose, 2a & 1B Triad Centre, Stanley Road
① 0151 922 0828
Hoylake – Hoylake Lights, 52–54 Market Street
① 0151 632 1209
Huyton – Oak Tree, Liverpool Road
① 0151 482 1337
Kirkby – Gold Balance, 6–10 New Town Gardens
① 0151 548 7939
Liverpool – Picturedome, 286 Kensington
① 0151 261 2410
Liverpool – Raven, 72 Walton Vale
① 0151 524 1255
Liverpool – Thomas Frost, 177–187 Walton Road
① 0151 207 8210
Liverpool – Welkin, 7 Whitechapel
① 0151 243 1080
Liverpool – Wetherspoons, Units 1–3 Charlotte Row
① 0151 709 4802
Moreton – Mockbeggar Hall, 239–241 Hoylake Road
① 0151 678 5659
St Helens – Glass House, Market Street
① 01744 762310
Southport – Wetherspoons, 93–97 Lord Street
① 01704 530217
Stoney Croft – Wetherspoons, 694 Queens Drive
① 0151 220 2713
West Kirby – Dee Hotel, 44 Grange Road
① 0151 929 6300

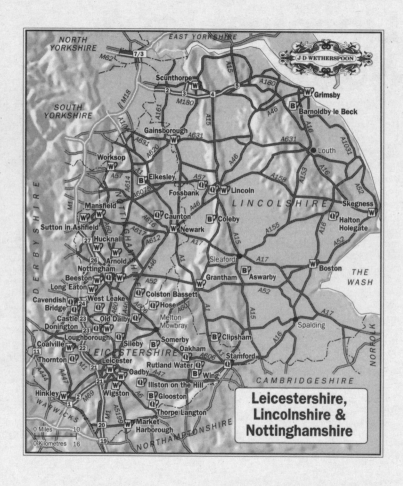

Leicestershire, Lincolnshire & Nottinghamshire

Leicestershire, Lincolnshire & Nottinghamshire

Castle Donington

Nags Head Inn ① 01332 850652
Hill Top, Castle Donington, Leics DE74 2PR
Wolverhampton & Dudley. Ian Davison, tenant
e-mail: idavison@aol.com

Close to East Midlands airport, the motor racing circuit and the county borders of
Derbyshire, Nottinghamshire and Leicestershire, the Nags Head has friendly staff and a
touch of elegance that give the old place a wonderful ambience. Gently colourwashed
inside, with beams and open fires, it seems to be in a food league of its own with
something for everyone on the blackboard: sandwiches are re-interpreted, baguettes and
ciabattas have imaginative fillings, and there's Lincolnshire sausages with mashed potato
and onion gravy, beef, mushroom and red wine casserole, monkfish with stir-fried oriental
vegetables, maybe fillet of beef in Cajun spices with tzatziki. Vegetarian dishes too. All the
more-ish puds are home-made: fruit crumbles, treacle tarts, that sort of thing. Beers are
Marstons Pedigree, Mansfield Bitter and Banks Mild; thirty wines on the list, six by the
glass.

OPEN: 11.30–2.30, 5.30–11. Sun 12–3, 7–10.30.
Real Ale. Restaurant. No food Sunday. Booking advisable for dinner. The pub is totally non-
smoking.
No children. Dogs in bar. Car park. Wheelchair access.
Cards: Amex, Delta, MasterCard, Switch, Visa.

Caunton

Caunton Beck ① 01636 636793
Main Street, Caunton, Newark, Notts NG23 6AB
Free House. Julie Allwood, licensee

Other pubs are open all day but, unlike the Caunton Beck, not usually in time to serve an
early breakfast. Over the years this 16th-century building has been restored and extended
using reclaimed materials and knowledgeable expertise to create the delightful place you
see today. Expertly run by the same people who run the Wig and Mitre in Lincoln, under
the low beams are scrubbed tables, country chairs, restful decor and daily papers to read.
Menus could offer smoked mussels or a lightly curried mussel soup, chicken liver paté

with chutney and toast, pan-fried breast of pheasant in a port sauce, baked fillet of cod with herb crumbs and butter sauce, and lots more. A good choice of cheeses and interesting puds; Blue Mountain coffee with home-made fudge or bitter chocolates. There is a viewing window into the original cellar where the cask-conditioned ales are racked up on two levels; Timothy Taylors, Adnams and Marstons Pedigree are the permanent beers. They also have a considerable wine list. Outside is a lawn, rose arbour and plenty of places to sit to enjoy your surroundings.

OPEN: 8 a.m.–11 p.m. every day and food served all day.
Real Ale. Restaurant.
Children welcome. Dogs not usually: but if you and your dog are very nice they might let you into the garden. Car park. Wheelchair access.

Cavendish Bridge

Old Crown ① 01332 792392
Cavendish Bridge, Leics DE72 2HL
Free House. Peter Morton-Harrison, licensee

South of the river Trent, this peaceful hamlet comprises just a whitewashed pub and a few houses. Admire the scenery, look the other way and you could be out in the country again having missed the pub. Older than it looks, it's been here since the 17th century, but everything else is bang up to date, especially the cooking. Substantial pub food of filled baguettes, fish and chips and vegetarian dishes. But it is the wildly imaginative specials that will catch your eye. Draught Bass and Marstons Pedigree and the regular beers, plus guests and usually something from the local Shardlow brewery set up in the old Cavendish stables across the river. Short wine list with a few by the glass.

OPEN: 11.30–3.30, 5–11.
Real Ale.
Children welcome. Dogs too. Car park. Wheelchair access.
Cards: Delta, MasterCard, Switch, Visa.

Colston Bassett

Martins Arms ① 01949 81361
School Lane, Colston Bassett, Notts NG12 3FD
Free House. Lynne Strafford Bryan & Salvatore Inguanta, licensees

The Vale of Belvoir is famous for its rich farmland, Stilton cheese and pork pies. The handsome 17th-century Martins Arms, opposite the Market Cross in the village, was originally a farmhouse where they brewed beer, only becoming a proper pub early in the 19th century. Things have moved on since then; you can stay the night, get married, have a conference or buy an antique. There is the feel of a smart country house, with a touch of bygone formality in the uniformed staff. The excellent bar menu includes speciality sandwiches that are offbeat and different: poached salmon, basil mayonnaise and pickled peppers, grilled chicken, watercress and plum tomatoes, bacon, lettuce and tomato – all on ciabatta bread, or if you don't want sandwiches there could be a classic Caesar salad with barbecued chicken strips, grilled tuna and salad niçoise or a ploughman's which would keep any ploughman going all day – Melton Mowbray Pork Pie, Colston Bassett Stilton or Cheddar, home-cured ham and pickles, slices of apple, roll and garnish – wonderful. Inventive vegetarian dishes, pasta dishes and for a main course, fillet of beef with braised cabbage or breast of guinea fowl with puy lentils, roasted garlic and baby onions are just a few examples from the menu. Lots more: daily specials on the blackboard, home-made puddings and proper coffee to finish. Restaurant menu too. Adnams, Timothy Taylors Landlord, Marstons Pedigree, Bass, Wadworth 6X, Black Cat Mild and Green King IPA are among the ales they keep. Interesting wine list, including champagnes and sparkling wines. Tables outside in the large garden with views over National Trust parkland.

OPEN: 12–3, 6–11 (Sun 7–10.30).
Real Ale. Restaurant (no food Sun eve).
Children in garden. No dogs. Car park. Wheelchair access. Two bedrooms.
Cards: All cards except Amex and Diners.

Fossebank

Pyewipe Inn ☼ 01522 528708
Fossebank, Saxilby Road, Lincoln LN1 2BG
Free House. Mr & Mrs R. L. Pickles, licensees
e-mail: robert@pyewipe-inn.co.uk

From the centre of Lincoln it's just a two-mile walk along the Fossedyke canal to the Pyewipe. This substantial three-storey, late-Georgian building was an ale house by the end of the 18th century and an inn by 1823. In four acres of grounds there is enough room to land your helicopter – and they do. Plenty of room inside too. The blackboard menus change daily and list some imaginative dishes; for a starter you could choose game paté with red wine jelly, smoked salmon and marlin or melon with ginger and white wine. For a main course, fillet of lamb with onion mash or guinea fowl in a port and cranberry sauce. The daily specials boards will list fresh fish, home-made puds and vegetarian dishes. The à la carte menu changes three times a year. Tetley, Greene King Abbots Ale, Bass, Flowers Original, Bass, Timothy Taylors Landlord and Wadworths 6X. Views towards Lincoln Cathedral, and boat trips to and from Lincoln land here at the Pyewipe.

OPEN: 11–11. Sun 12–10.30.
Real Ale.
Children welcome but not after 7 p.m. Dogs on leads. Car park. Wheelchair access.
Twenty bedrooms in a new, purpose-built lodge.
Cards: all major cards except Amex.
N.B. Quiet music in lounge.

Halton Holegate

Bell Inn ☼ 01790 753242
Firsby Road, Halton Holegate, Lincs PE23 5NY
Free House. John & Irene Clayton, licensees

From the village you have an uninterrupted view over the fens to Boston and the 'Boston Stump', the 272ft tower of St Botolph's Church about 15 miles away as the crow flies. The

16th-century Bell is another pub with a ghost, but not your usual ghost: this is a labrador dog whose history is unknown. Inside is one big bar with low-beamed ceilings and an inglenook fireplace. Interesting food is served in both bar and restaurant: home-made fish soup, seafood au gratin served in a scallop shell, sandwiches, salads, lots of steaks, chicken Kiev, the Bell special steak, onion and mushroom pie in a rich Madeira sauce, lots more and a vegetarian menu. Sunday roast. Batemans XB, Tetley Smooth Flow, Tom Woods Cask, Calders Premium Cream and occasional guests. Tables and chairs at the front of the pub. Several walks around the pub, one to the River Lymn.

OPEN: 12–3, 7–11.
Real Ale. Restaurant.
Children in restaurant. Dogs on leads. Car park.
Cards: Amex only.

Hose

Black Horse ① 01949 860336
21 Bolton Lane, Hose, nr Melton Mowbray, Leics LE14 4JE
Tynemill Group. Mike Aram, tenant

A traditional, timeless and busy village pub in the Vale of Belvoir. Inside are three rooms: an unspoilt flagstoned tap room, lounge-bar-cum-snug and small restaurant. The blackboard menu in the bar changes weekly but there could be melon, egg mayonnaise or prawn cocktail to start with, a range of steaks, the pub's very own way with a chicken – chicken breasts cooked in cornflakes with a sweet-and-sour sauce, rack of lamb with a redcurrant sauce, swordfish and a vegetarian dish or two. Six well-kept ales: draught Bass, Castlerocks Farriers Gold, a local bitter and two guests. Seats in the garden.

OPEN: 12–2.30, 6.30–11. Sun 12–3, 7–10.30.
Real Ale. Restaurant. No food Mon or Tues.
Children welcome. Dogs on leads. Car park. Wheelchair access.
N.B. Music in restaurant, not in bar.

Illston on the Hill

Fox & Goose ① 01162 596340
Main Street, Illston on the Hill, Leics LE7 9EG
Everards. George Bullers, tenant

This is an timeless, unchanging little pub full of things to look at and admire. Small, white-painted and delightfully quiet, the Fox and Goose is in a country village off the Market Harborough to Melton Mowbray road. You would come here for the beer and the freshly made sandwiches. Everards Beacon, Tiger, Old Original and always one guest beer as well as Guinness and Carling lager. Seats among the flowers at the front of the pub.

OPEN: 12–2.30, 5.30–11 (Sun 7–10.30). Closed winter lunchtimes Mon–Thurs.
Real Ale.
Children welcome. Dogs on leads. Holiday flat to let.

Lincoln

Victoria ① 01522 536048
6 Union Road, Lincoln LN1 3BJ
Tynemill. Neil Renshaw, manager

As you would expect from the name, it's Victorian – and to emphasize the point, there are pictures of Queen Victoria on the walls. Busy and unpretentious, this is a two-room, city pub by the West Gate of the Norman castle. Here you can expect some very good beer and to go with it good-value home-cooked food; nothing deep-fried, nor any chips. Usually a soup of the day, filled rolls, ploughman's, bacon butties, an all-day breakfast (Saturday only), curries, pies and stews. At least five guest beers available – always a dark mild – also draught Belgian beers and 10 bottled ones. They hold two yearly beer festivals: in June and December. The small beer garden is tucked under the Castle walls.

OPEN: 11–11. Sun 12–10.30.
Real Ale.
No children. Dogs on leads. Limited wheelchair access.
Cards: Electron, JCB, MasterCard, Solo, Switch, Visa.

Wig & Mitre ① 01522 535190
30–32 Steep Hill, Lincoln LN2 1LU
Free House. Toby Hope & Valerie Hope, licensees
e-mail: reservations@wigandmitre.co.uk

Steep Hill, which winds down from the Cathedral area, is full of medieval buildings, many two centuries older than the Wig & Mitre. However, this handsome 14th-century place is full of period features. On two levels: the bar on the ground floor, the restaurant above, with a view of the castle and cathedral. Food is served throughout the day from an early breakfast to tea or dinner in the evening. The interesting menu changes regularly but there will always be a 'daily fish' and possibly sun-dried tomato pasta with Parma ham, spring onions and Parmesan cheese; baked cheese soufflé or sirloin steak with cracked black peppercorns, brandy and cream, puddings and a piece of cheese too. Nothing is too much trouble. Wines (nearly 100 and many by the glass), ales and spirits are available from 11 in the morning until midnight. Morrels Varsity and Marstons Pedigree ales on hand pump, and as you would expect, freshly squeezed orange juice and coffee.

OPEN: 8 a.m.–midnight. Food served continuously.
Real Ale. Restaurant.
Children in eating area and restaurant. No dogs.
Cards: Amex, Delta, Diners, MasterCard, Switch, Visa.

Loughborough

Swan in the Rushes ① 01509 217014
21 The Rushes, Loughborough, Leics LE11 5BE
Free House. Ian Bogie, licensee

This plain, matter-of-fact sort of place is unmistakeably Victorian, a serious town pub. No frills, but with a reputation for simple, good quality, home-cooked bar food – filled baguettes, ploughman's and daily specials to go with the range of European bottled beers, whiskies and the nine or more beers on hand pump. These could include Archers Golden, Tetley Bitter, Castle Rock Gold and up to seven guests. There is also a changing selection of farm ciders. With all this on offer, it is not surprising the pub is very popular and can get crowded, but they are unfazed, invariably friendly and efficient. Lucky them – a city pub with a small beer garden.

OPEN: 11–11. Sun 12–10.30. No food Sat or Sun eve.
Real Ale.
Children in dining and the no-smoking room. Dogs on leads. Wheelchair access.
Jukebox in public bar. Folk music every two weeks.

Nottingham

Ye Olde Trip to Jerusalem ① 0115 9473171
Brewhouse Yard, Castle Road, Nottingham NE1 6AD
Hardy & Hansons. Karen Ratcliffe, manager
www.triptoJerusalem.com

Certainly something is very old in Brewhouse Yard. During the 12th century the Castle had a brewery here and somewhere, under the Olde Trip, are the remains of what would have been the oldest pub in England – 'The Pilgrim'. It was also here, in the 12th century, that the Crusaders met before sailing off for years of serious skirmishing. This old place was probably rebuilt on the site of the original inn sometime during the 17th century. Inside, the panelled rooms have alcoves cut into the rock and the cellars are in rock caves. Tunnels, staircases, hidden rooms are all hewn out of the sandstone below the castle. An impressive, part-panelled, part-rockface, high-ceilinged bar, is open upstairs every day and well worth seeing. Traditional, sustaining food in the stone-floored bar: steak and kidney pudding, garlic and herb chicken, filled giant Yorkshire puddings – that sort of thing, daily specials plus a good choice of vegetarian dishes. Marstons Pedigree and Hardy and Hansons 'cellarman's cask' range of ales which changes every two months. Seats outside in the courtyard.

OPEN: 11–11. Sun 12–10.30. Meals served 11–6 (Sun 12–6).
Real Ale.
Children until 6. No dogs. Wheelchair access (not WC).
Cards: Delta, MasterCard, Solo, Switch, Visa.

Oakham

Grainstore Brewery ① 01572 770065
Station Approach, Oakham, Rutland LE15 6RE
Own Brew. A. H. Davis. licensee

Next to the railway station, the Grainstore has been converted from a disused three-storey, Victorian grainstore into a tower brewhouse where, as they say, 'the raw materials start at the top and the finished beer comes out at the bottom, all through gravity'. Inside is, as you would expect, a converted industrial building: bare boards, timber ceilings and substantial iron pillars holding everything up. The bar has a cheerful, relaxed atmosphere with friendly, welcoming barmaids. Our informant was told that the part-time bar staff has included, very briefly, the Prince of Wales. Lunchtime food is served in both the bar and an upstairs room. The menu is traditional: soup, filled baguettes, ploughman's, steak and ale pie and specials. From the smallest county's largest brewery come Rutland Panther, Cooking Bitter, Triple B, Steamin' Billy Bitter and Ten Fifty. There is a takeaway service. Seats on the terrace.

OPEN: 11–2.30, 5–11. Fri & Sat 11–11. Sun 12–2.30, 7–10.30.
Real Ale.
No children. Dogs allowed in bar. Wheelchair access.

Old Dalby

Crown ① 01664 823134
Debdale Hill, Old Dalby, nr Melton Mowbray, Leics LE14 3LF
Free House. Alan Hale, licensee

Surrounded by plenty, the Crown is not far from Little Dalby, the birthplace of Stilton cheese, and Melton Mowbray, where the first pork pie was baked in 1850; both feature on the pub's menu. Creeper-covered and really quite stylish, the 16th-century Crown, a converted farmhouse, has comfortable, beamy rooms with open fires, all well kept and prosperous looking. The food on the daily menu is home made and could include a warm salad of smoked chicken, bacon and pear with blue cheese dressing, fresh linguini, potato cakes filled with Stilton or Cheddar cheese served with mango chutney. Also speciality sandwiches, filled ciabattas with a dressed salad and a venison sausage or two. The Crown ploughman's – Melton Mowbray pork pie, Colston Bassett Stilton or Cheddar, home-cured ham and pickles with slices of apple, wholemeal roll and garnish – should keep you quiet for a bit! Lots more, several vegetarian dishes, specials on the blackboard. Delicious puds. There is a separate menu in the no-smoking dining room. Ales are always changing, something from the Belvoir Brewery in a cask behind the bar and Courage Directors, Charles Wells Bombardier, Theakstons Old Peculier and Morlands Old Speckled Hen as guests. Choice of malt whiskies and a good wine list. Tables on the terrace overlook the large garden. There is also a pétanque pitch and a landlady who is a very skilled player. The Midshire Way Pennine walk nearby offers plenty of scope for healthy exercise.

OPEN: 12–3, 6–11.
Real Ale. Restaurant (not Sun eve).
Children over 10 in restaurant only. Dogs on leads welcome. Wheelchair access.

Rutland Water

Barnsdale Lodge Hotel ① 01572 724678
The Avenue, Rutland Water, nr Oakham, Rutland LE15 8AH
Free House. Robert Reid, owner/licensee
e-mail: barnsdale.lodge@btconnect.com

A substantial, restored stone farmhouse overlooking Rutland Water in the smallest county in England. There's lots to do near here, whether on or off the water: walking, birdwatching, sailing, windsurfing and cycling around the traffic-free shore. The famous gardens at Barnsdale are close, as are historic Oakham and Uppingham. In the hotel there is a welcoming bar and an elegant conservatory where they serve bar meals and snacks, also two dining rooms for more formal eating. Outside the gardens are lovely, and there are tables in the well-planted courtyard. You want for nothing; elevenses, lunches inside or out, afternoon tea and supper. They serve an interesting choice of food and have a good wine list. The beers are Grainstore Oakham Best, Ruddles Best and Marstons Pedigree. All rooms in the hotel have views over the surrounding countryside.

OPEN: All day; the bar is open until midnight for residents.
Children welcome, dogs too, except in main eating areas – guide dogs excepted. All wheelchair facilities.
N.B. A pianola plays in the bar area.

Sileby

White Swan ① 01509 814832
Swan Street, Sileby, Leics LE12 7NW
Free House. Bob & Theresa Miller, licensees

There's not only well-kept beer here but good-value home-cooked food too. Unusually, among the ancients, this bright and cheerful pub was built only in the 1930s. You can eat either in the attractive book-lined restaurant or in the bar. Lots of fillings for the baguettes, jacket potatoes and rolls, or you could choose a hot Mediterranean vegetable tartlet with a garlic and herb cream cheese topping, deep-fried prawns in garlic and herb breadcrumbs, baked chicken breast wrapped in bacon with home-made sausage, pan-fried sirloin steak in red wine, deep-fried lemon sole fillet in breadcrumbs with battered squid rings, or salmon and prawn pasta with a cream and cheese sauce. Ansells Bitter, Mansfield Cask, Banks Original, Fullers London Pride plus a guest. A glass or two of wine, a garden to sit in and a skittle alley to hire. They have their own dog, Leo; in his youth a past finalist in the UK's naughtiest dog competition, so they don't want any outside influences!

OPEN: 11.45–3, 7–11. No food Sun eve or all day Mon.
Real Ale. Restaurant.
Children welcome. No dogs. Car park. Wheelchair access.
Cards: All except Amex.

Stamford

George of Stamford ① 01780 750750
71 High Street, St Martins, Stamford, Lincs PE9 2LB
Free House. Ivo Vanocci & Chris Pitman, licensees
e-mail: reservations@georgehotelofstamford.com

Of considerable age, far older than the handsome Georgian façade, the George was built during the 16th century over the ruins of a Norman hospice and crypt, and these ancient remains are still visible under the present cocktail bar. Georgianised when coach travel between London and York was at its peak, it has two named bars – facing each other just inside the hotel – the waiting rooms for the 40 coaches that stopped here each day to change horses and allow the passengers some refreshment. The panelled York Bar serves quick, light snacks: soup of the day with Italian bread, Cheddar and Stilton platter with ciabatta, open toasted sandwich, lots of fillings for the ciabatta bread, or if you want to fill more than a corner, a Daniel Lambert sandwich – ciabatta bread, sirloin steak, fried onions, tomato and mushroom. The Garden Lounge menu, available all day, ranges from a warm salad of chicken strips, smoked bacon, avocado, spinach and cherry tomatoes to a Grand Brittany Platter which includes half lobster, crab langoustine, mussels, king prawns, oysters, clams, shell-on prawns and whelks. Much, much more, also a restaurant menu. Adnams ales, Ruddles, a guest ale, a considerable wine list from a substantial cellar – many by the glass – and all the other niceties you associate with a well-run establishment – freshly squeezed orange juice, good coffee and afternoon teas. An attractive cobbled courtyard at the rear of the creeper-covered George is filled with tables and chairs among flowering tubs and hanging baskets.

OPEN: 11–11.
Real Ale. Restaurants (two).
Children welcome. Dogs in garden. Wheelchair access. Bedrooms.
Cards: All major credit cards.

Thornton

Bricklayers Arms ① 01530 230808
Main Street, Thornton, Leics LE67 1AH
Everards. T. Swyer, tenant
e-mail: janeswyer5@hotmail.com

Here is an unspoilt, 16th-century village pub, still with a basic, stone-floored bar and more comfortable lounge, both with good open fires. No food is served on Monday, but there is a two-course special Tuesday, Wednesday and Thursday: mince and dumplings, toad in the hole, seven vegetables to choose from – no skimping on the portions here – and a pudding to follow. All home-cooked comfort food and it's very popular. Well-kept Everards Tiger, Beacon Bitter, Old Original and a guest beer. Seats in the large garden.

OPEN: 12–3, 6–11. Sat 12–11. Sun 12–10.30. No food Mon. Except on Sunday, the pub opens one hour earlier during the summer.
Real Ale.
Children welcome. Dogs on leads. Wheelchair access. N.B. Some major refurbishment is going on, with new loos etc.

Thorpe Langton

Bakers Arms ① 01858 545201
Main Street, Thorpe Langton, Leics LE16 7TS
Free House. Kate Hubbard, licensee & manager

The seriously good Baker's Arms has built up an excellent reputation for fine food in the last few years. A welcoming 16th-century thatched pub, it is more a place to eat than just to drink. There is a constantly changing menu – all on blackboards. You could start with a warm salad of new potatoes, black pudding and bacon or grilled goat's cheese with roast cherry tomatoes, and for a main course roast shank of lamb with cumin, honey and roast parsnips, or whole baked sea bass with mussels, leeks and saffron, and scrummy puds. It's wise to book a table. That said, they do still serve a pint or two: Tetleys ales and Guinness accompanied by a knowledgeable wine list, about six by the glass. The pub piano is brought to the fore on Friday evenings, so if you don't appreciate a little night music, you know when to avoid it. Picnic tables in the garden.

OPEN: Tues–Sat 6.30–11, also Sat & Sun 12–2. Closed Mon and Sun eve and weekday lunchtimes.
Real Ale.
No children under 12 – ever. No dogs. Car park. Wheelchair access (not WC).
Cards: Amex, Delta, MasterCard, Switch, Visa.

West Leake

Star Inn ① 01509 852233
Melton Lane, West Leake, nr Loughborough, Notts LE12 5RQ
Enterprise Inns. Edward Woolford, licensee

On the outskirts of the village, north of Loughborough, this lovely old coaching inn is full of character with a traditional, beamed bar, and a comfortably furnished, panelled dining area with open log fires. Food is home cooked and the menu changes daily, but there could be soup, mushrooms in cream and garlic sauce, paté, roast leg of pork, chicken chasseur and a choice of puddings. They have beers from many of the small breweries, currently something from Caledonian, Adnams, Robinsons, Charles Wells and Black Sheep, but these do change, and there is always draught Bass. Over a dozen malt whiskies. Seats and tables in the large garden. You are surrounded by beautiful countryside.

OPEN: 11–3, 6–11.
Real Ale.
Children in family room. Dogs on leads. Wheelchair access.
Cards: MasterCard, Solo, Switch, Visa.

BEST OF THE REST

Aswarby, Lincs
Tally Ho ① 01529 455205
Aswarby NG34 8SA
On the Peterborough to Lincoln road, this pub's in an enviable position, with apple trees to sit under and contented sheep in the park to look at. In what was originally a 17th-century farmhouse, they serve really good bar food and specials, also inspired dishes from the restaurant menu: chicken in a pepper and orange sauce, warm duck salad, pork with olives, beef fillets in a peppercorn sauce and delicious puds. Batemans, a guest and a good wine list. Children and dogs welcome. Bedrooms.
Open: 12–3, 6–11

Barnoldby-le-Beck, Lincs
Ship Inn ① 01472 822308
Main Road, Barnoldby-le-Beck, Grimsby DN37 0BG
Along a minor road off the A18, this is a cosy, welcoming country pub full of Victorian bric-a-brac, full of atmosphere with open fires in both the bar and restaurant. Known for its imaginative cooking, menus change regularly but for a starter there could be a seafood crêpe, Caesar salad, or chef's special paté and for a main course a Captain's mixed grill, Stilton chicken in a creamy leek sauce, fresh salmon fillet topped with prawns in puff pastry, Ship's special fish pie, vegetarian dishes and freshly filled sandwiches and baguettes. Beers are Timothy Taylors Landlord, Boddingtons and Black Sheep, Scrumpy Jack cider and a wide-ranging wine list. Dogs welcome. Wheelchair access. All major credit cards.
Open: 12–3, 6–11.

Clipsham, Rutland
Olive Branch ① 01780 410355
Main Street, Clipsham LE15 7SH
Only a cluster of cottages and a pub. The lucky locals have a little treasure on their doorstep that reopened in 1999. Here you will be looked after and fed extremely well. You can choose from either a short bar menu or the delights of the prix fixe lunch; beers are from the Grainstore Brewery in Oakham and other small, eastern breweries. Wine is taken very seriously here, reflected in the interesting offers on the wine-boards. Children welcome. Dogs in the bar. Wheelchair access.
Open: 12–3, 6–11. Sat 12–11. Sun 12–6.

Coleby, Lincs
Bell ① 01522 810240
3 Far Lane, Coleby LN5 0AH
This village south of Lincoln is fortunate to have the busy, comfortable, beamed and panelled 18th-century Bell and, more importantly, a creative chef in charge of the pub's kitchen. From the reasonably priced menu you could find crostini with garlic mushrooms, a lightly poached selection of fresh fish in a saffron sauce, Suffolk cured gammon with free-range eggs, daily specials and lots more – something for everyone. Thursday night is fish night. Flowers Original, Bass and Tetleys ales; Marstons is the guest. Range of malt whiskies and a short wine list. Seats in the garden. Children in eating areas. Dogs welcome. Bedrooms (3-crown rated by the English Tourist Board).
Open: 11.30–3, 5.30–11. Sun 12–10.30.

Elkesley, Notts
Robin Hood ① 01777 838259
High Street, Elkesley DN22 8AJ
Close to a 12th-century church, also close to the A1 – if you want to break your journey, here is a possible refuge. A friendly village pub with some better than usual offerings on the food front. From the constantly changing menu and specials board there could be home-made soup and well-filled sandwiches, ploughman's, also courgette, mushroom and cheese bake, chargrilled chicken with Mediterranean vegetables, duck breast on potato rösti with a port wine and cherry sauce. Wines to go with your meal as well as Boddingtons and a guest beer. Children in eating area of bar.
Open: 11.30–2.30, 6.30–11.

Glooston, Leics
Old Barn ① 01858 545215
Andrews Lane, LE16 7ST
Near the old Roman road that led to the Roman settlement on which Leicester was built, the 16th-century Old Barn is well worth finding for something from the original bar menu and blackboard specials. Always four ales on draught: Adnams, Shepherd Neame Spitfire, and two guests; also several European bottled beers and a more extensive wine list. Children, on their best behaviour, in eating area of bar. No dogs. Bedrooms.
Open: 12–3, 6.30–11. Sun 12–4, 7.30–10.30. Closed for Mon lunch.

Somerby, Leics
Stilton Cheese ① 01664 454394
High Street, Somerby LE14 2QB
In a pretty village in the north-eastern corner of Leicestershire, between Melton Mowbray and Oakham, this tremendously popular 16th-century pub serves good food, which you can eat in the hop-strung bar or no-smoking restaurant. The changing blackboard menu lists simple dishes, well cooked and presented. Always home-made soup such as Stilton and onion, alongside salmon en croute, braised lamb's liver and bacon in an onion gravy, sausage and mash, steak and kidney pie and daily specials. Marstons Pedigree, Tetleys, the local Grain Store Ten Fifty as well as weekly changing guests from small breweries. Wide-ranging wine list, and a number of malts. Children welcome. No dogs. Wheelchair access.
Open: 12–3, 6–11 (Sun 7–10.30).

Wing, Leics
Kings Arms ① 01572 737634
Top Street, Wing LE15 8SE
South of Oakham and close to Rutland Water, this stone-built 17th-century pub with beams, flagstone floors and huge fires serves reasonably priced bar food: filled baguettes, local sausages with garlic mash, fish stew or pasta in a cream and smoked salmon sauce as well as something from the specials board. The local Batemans and other beers. Children welcome. No dogs. Wheelchair access (not WC). Bedrooms.
Open: 12–12. Closed Sun eve and Mon lunchtime.

Wetherspoon in Leicestershire, Lincolnshire and Nottinghamshire

Leicestershire

Coalville – Monkey Walk, 1 Marlborough Square
① 01530 278950
Hinckley – Baron of Hinckley, 5–7 Regent Street
① 01455 890169
Leicester – High Cross, 103–105 High Street
① 0116 251 9218
Leicester – Last Plantagenet, 107 Granby Street
① 0116 255 5492
Loughborough – Moon & Bell, 6 Wards End
① 01509 241504
Market Harborough – Sugar Loaf, 18 High Street
① 01858 469231
Oadby – Lord Keeper of the Great Seal, 96–100 The Parade
① 0116 2720957
Wigston – William Wygston, 84 Leicester Road
① 0116 288 8397

Lincolnshire

Boston – Moon under Water, 6 High Street
① 01205 311911
Gainsborough – Sweyn Forkbeard, 22–24 Silver Street
① 01427 675000
Grantham – Tollemache Inn, 17 St Peter's Hill
① 01476 594696
Grimsby – Yarborough Hotel, 29 Bethlehem Street
① 01472 268283
Lincoln – Forum, 13–14 Silver Street
① 01522 518630
Lincoln – Ritz, High Street
① 01522 512103
Scunthorpe – Blue Bell Inn, 1–7 Oswald Road
① 01724 863921
Skegness – Red Lion, Roman Banks, Lumley Road
① 01754 612567

Nottinghamshire

Arnold – Ernehale, 149–151 Nottingham Road
① 0115 967 4945
Beeston – Last Post, Foster Avenue/Chilwell Road
① 0115 968 3100
Hucknall – Pilgrim's Oak, 44–46 High Street
① 0115 963 2539
Long Eaton – Twitchel Inn, Clifford Street/Howitt Street
① 0115 972 2197
Mansfield – Court House, Market Place
① 01623 412720

Mansfield – Widow Frost, Leeming Street
🕐 01623 666790
Newark – Sir John Arderne, 1–3 Church Street
🕐 01636 671334
Nottingham – Roebuck Inn, 9–11 St James Street
🕐 0115 979 3400
Nottingham – Wetherspoons, 11–12 South Parade, Market Square
🕐 0115 947 5034
Sutton in Ashfield – Picture House, Fox Street
🕐 01623 554627
Worksop – White Lion, Park Street
🕐 01909 476450

The Midlands

Midlands

Ashton

Chequered Skipper ① 01832 273494
Ashton, Oundle, nr Peterborough, Northants PE8 5LE
Free House. Colin & Ian Campbell, licensees

In a picturesque village surrounded by the rich pastures of the Nene valley, this traditional thatched country pub has an untraditional interior – a surprising, minimalist statement. Rebuilt after a fire, it is now open plan, light and airy, a very 21st-century space. The look might have changed but it is still patronised by the locals, muddy boots, dogs and all. The young staff are helpful and friendly, the food plentiful and inventive. For a starter you could have grilled whole sardines served with a tomato, oregano and garlic sauce; terrine of roasted peppers; wild mushrooms, sweet potato and asparagus with fresh herbs, wrapped in spiced cabbage leaves. For a main course there are some interesting fish dishes – red mullet, lemon sole or halibut steak all prepared in different ways; paupiette of chicken with creamed mango sauce; sautéed venison steak served with a fig sauce and game chips, lots of steaks and grills, vegetarian dishes and delicious puddings to finish. Draught Bass, Oakham JHB and Shepherd Neame Spitfire.

OPEN: 11–3, 6–11. Sat 11.30–11. Sun 12–10.30.
Real Ale.
Children welcome. Dogs yes, but not in dining area.

Baddesley Ensor

Red Lion ① 01827 13009
Keys Hill, The Common, Baddesley Ensor, Atherstone, Warks CV9 2BT
Free House. David Baillie Bell, licensee

A little off the beaten track, just under a mile from the A5 at Grendon near Atherstone (follow the signpost to Boot Hill), this plain little pub, a friendly, one-room local with a good roaring fire, is here for the drinkers among you – those who value an excellent pint without musical accompaniment. Apparently the only musically quiet pub for about ten miles, it doesn't get much in the way of passing trade, but it attracts all the appreciative locals. Marstons Pedigree and Bank's Original are on permanently plus weekly changing guest beers. No food is served, so another crisp and nut place; not so unusual north of London.

OPEN: Mon–Thurs 7–11. Fri–Sun 12–3, 7–11.
Real Ale.
No children. Dogs on leads.

Birmingham

Briar Rose ☺ 0121 634 8100
25 Bennetts Hill, Birmingham, West Midlands B2 5RE
Wetherspoon.

Converted from offices in the centre of the city, decorated with more than a nodding
acquaintance towards Art Deco, this is a Wetherlodge – a new branch on the Wetherspoon
tree. Not only can you eat and drink well but you can stay here too; you really can go out
for the night – all night – and have breakfast in the morning. This Wetherlodge has
bedrooms – 41 of them. Standards are as high, as reliable and as reasonable as you would
expect.

OPEN: Hotel hours.
Real Ale.
Children if staying. No dogs. Wheelchair access. Bedrooms.

Brierley Hill

Vine ☺ 01384 78293
10 Delph Road, Brierley Hill, West Midlands DY5 2TN
Bathams. Melvyn Wood, manager

The locals call it the Bull and Bladder, an old wag's interpretation of the handsome
stained-glass front window which depicts a bull's head and bunch of grapes. Bustling and
full of character, it's a very popular place with a front and back bar and snug. The award-
winning extension has taken in some of the brewery offices next door. Popular, well-made
and reasonably priced lunchtime snacks, freshly filled sandwiches and lots of salads. As
this is the brewery tap, no need to tell you that the beer is just as it should be: Bathams
Bitter and Mild on hand pump, also Delph Strong Ale in winter.

OPEN: 12–11. Food lunchtimes only (not Sun).
Real Ale.
Children in own room. Dogs on leads. Disabled WC but no access into the pub with
wheelchair.

Crick

Red Lion ☺ 01788 822342
52 Main Road, Crick, Northants NN6 7TX
Free House. Tom Marks, MBII, lease

Driving up or down the M1, you might like to know that this pub is only a mile away
from junction 18. Stone built, with a thatched roof, here you can relax by the log fire in
the comfortable low-ceilinged bar or in summer, sit on the terrace at the back of the pub
and admire the floral display. The menu has a wide range of reasonably priced, good-value
lunchtime snacks, and more substantial dishes which can change from day to day:
sandwiches and ploughman's, steaks, chicken Kiev, trout, lamb cutlets, moussaka, and

roast Sunday lunches. Over ten vegetarian dishes are available on the evening menu. Beers change regularly, so what is on today could be off next week. Go and be surprised.

OPEN: 11.30–2.30, 6.30–11. Sun 12–3, 7–10.30. No food Sun eve.
Real Ale.
Children in family room lunchtime only. Dogs on leads. Wheelchair access.
Cards: all except Amex and Diners.

Dorridge

Railway Inn ① 01564 773531
Grange Road, Dorridge, Solihull, West Midlands B93 8QA
Punch Lease. Philip (Joe) Watson, licensee

A friendly and unchanging pub with just public and lounge bars on the edge of the village: village one side, green fields the other. The traditional bar menu ranges from sandwiches (plain and toasted), filled baguettes, ploughman's and salads to smoked salmon, rump steak toasted sandwich (with fried onions) to a mixed grill, chicken Madras, venison steak, beef lasagne, gammon steak, T-bone steak; always vegetarian dishes, home-made pie of the day and specials on the board. Draught Bass, Brew XI, Highgate Mild and a selection of guest beers. There is a choice of wines. Seats in the garden.

OPEN: 12–3, 4.30–11. Sat 11–11. Sun 12–10.30.
Real Ale.
Children at meal times only. Dogs in public bar only.
Cards: MasterCard, Solo, Switch, Visa.

Earlsdon

Royal Oak ① 02476 674140
Earlsdon Street, Earlsdon, Coventry CV5 6EJ
Free House. Ray Evitts, licensee
e-mail: debbie.whyte@barclays.co.uk

In one of the older residential districts of Coventry, this pub is for those who appreciate beer. When you see hanging baskets, you'll find the pub. Immensely popular, they serve well-kept beer in pleasing, unfussy and friendly surroundings. Large wooden communal tables and comfortable chairs. Waiter service in the rear bar. House rules are rigorously applied – no dogs, no music, no rowdy behaviour and no food! Ansells Mild, draught Bass, Tetley Bitter, draught Guinness and guest beers.

OPEN: 5–11. Sun 12–3, 7–10.30.
Real Ale. No food.
No dogs. Wheelchair access (not WC).

Farthingstone

Kings Arms ① 01327 361604
Farthingstone, nr Towcester, Northants NN12 8EZ
Free House. Paul & Denise Egerton, proprietors
e-mail: paul@kingsarms.fsbusiness.co.uk

Handsome, stone-built and Grade II listed, this 18th-century pub is in a quiet village not far from the National Trust's Canons Ashby – a Tudor manor house in a glorious park. The Kings Arms is unusual as, apart from weekends, it is mostly an evening pub and food is served at Saturday and Sunday lunchtimes only. Inside are all the requisites of an old country pub – beams, flagstones, an inglenook fireplace and log fires. On the food side they specialise in using fine regional foods – you can buy these too: Loch Fyne smoked salmon, haggis, Cumberland dry-cured bacon, smoked mussels and a variety of British cheeses – to take away or nibble on, so you can have cheese in a well-filled baguette, a substantial ploughman's or a selection for you to try. Home-made soup is sometimes available in winter. Hook Norton Old Hooky, weekly changing guests and a good selection of wines. Seats on the sheltered terrace.

OPEN: 7–11, closed Mon and Wed. Sat 12–3, 7–11. Sun 12–3, 9–11. Food Sat and Sun lunchtimes only.
Real Ale.
Children welcome. Dogs in garden. Car park.
No cards.

Fiveways

Case is Altered ① 01926 484206
Case Lane, Fiveways, Hatton, nr Warwick CV35 7JD
Free House. Jackie Willacy, licensee

The heart of England – the geographical centre of the country – full of places to see and things to do. It's not far from the nature trail to Hatton locks on the Grand Union canal (with 21 locks the longest flight in England), a great attraction – no wonder this pub is a favourite with walkers and cyclists quenching their thirst. An old-fashioned, centuries-old rural pub with a beamed bar, red tiled floor, old wooden tables and chairs and a good log fire during the winter, it serves liquid refreshment only; no food, except for a crisp or nut. Really well-kept Hook Norton Old Hooky, Greene King IPA, a local beer and one regular guest.

OPEN: 12–2.30, 6–11. Sun 12–2, 7–10.30.
Real Ale.
No children. No dogs. Wheelchair access.

Fotheringhay

Falcon Inn ① 01832 226254
Fotheringhay, nr Oundle, Northants PE8 5HZ
Free House. Ray Smikle, chef/patron
e-mail: huntsbridgefalcon@hotmail.com

Fotheringhay on the River Nene is a village with an interesting early 15th-century church – a shrine to Richard III – and an abiding place in history. It was here in Fotheringhay Castle that Mary Queen of Scots was executed in 1587; a grassy mound and a few stones are all that is left. The Falcon, a busy and informal pub (locals, darts and dominoes in the tap room) has a very stylish conservatory for dining. Here they serve good-value, imaginative food: a bowl of warm olives, selection of crostini, spicy aubergine, coriander and coconut soup, crispy duck spring rolls with spiced Asian coleslaw and sweet and sour dressing, breast of chicken wrapped in parma ham with crushed sauté potatoes, savoy cabbage and rocket and truffle sauce, fillet of salmon with roasted fennel, tomatoes and new potatoes with horseradish and chive cream; to follow, sticky toffee pudding with rum and raisin ice cream and caramel sauce, bitter chocolate pudding with chocolate fudge sauce, ice creams and sorbets gives you some idea of the delights on the menu. Snacks are on the blackboard. You can eat what you like; just a sandwich if the mood takes you, there is no minimum order. Greene King, Adnams, and guest ales. Wide-ranging, inspired wine list, 17 by the glass. Tables in the garden.

OPEN: 11.30–3, 6–11 (winter Mons 7–11). Sun 12–3, 7–10.30.
Real Ale. Restaurant (not Mon lunchtime) and conservatory are no smoking.
Children welcome. No dogs – except guide dogs. Car park. Wheelchair access.
Cards: MasterCard, Switch, Visa.

Ilmington

Howard Arms ① 01608 682226
Lower Green, Ilmington, nr Shipston-on-Stour, Warks CV36 4LT
Free House. R. Greenstock & M. Devereux, licensees
e-mail: info@howardarms.com

South of Stratford, a village of golden-brown stone buildings surrounded by glorious, undulating countryside – and in it a rambling, handsome, flower-bedecked, 16th-century Cotswold pub overlooking the village green. It's well beamed with polished stone floors, a fireplace big enough to burn a tree, comfortable furnishings and a general air of well-being. The weekly changing menus are listed on the blackboard above the fireplace and everything is cooked to order, which means there could be delays, but it is worth the wait. To start with you could have seared scallops, lime, honey and mint dressing and herb salad, Stilton fritters, gooseberry and green peppercorn chutney, Thai fishcakes, coriander and mint yoghurt dip; to follow, pan-fried calves' liver with buttered onions and crisp bacon with balsamic dressing, chargrilled lamb steak with aubergine purée and roast garlic sauce or beef, ale and mustard pie, a couple of vegetarian dishes, and delicious home-made puds to follow. Beers from a local North Cotswold Brewery – Genesis, Everards Tiger and one guest, a short wine list with European and New World wines, 15 served by the glass. There is a delightful garden – and a new dining terrace – and good walks. If your interests lean towards the horticultural, Ilmington is near two of the most famous gardens in the country: Kiftsgate and Hidcote; what's more you can stay here and do a garden a day.

OPEN: 11–2.30. 6–11.
Real Ale. Restaurant.
Children welcome. Guide dogs only. Car park. Wheelchair access (not WC). Bedrooms.
Cards: MasterCard, Switch, Visa.

Kenilworth

Old Bakery Hotel ① 01926 864111
12 The High Street, Kenilworth Warks CV5 1LZ
Free House. Mike Bond, licensee
e-mail: info@theoldbakeryhotel.co.uk

In the old and most picturesque part of this historic town and close to the dramatic ruins of the Norman castle, this really was the old bakery – old shop included. Now looking very smart with dark green woodwork and flowers outside the door. Parts of the building date back to the 17th century; all has been well restored and extended to create the family-run hotel you see today. The bar welcomes locals and visitors alike and serves really well-kept beers: Hook Norton Best Bitter, Timothy Taylors Landlord and Black Sheep Bitter. CAMRA gives it a well-deserved stamp of approval. Bed and breakfast accommodation.

OPEN: 5–11. Sat 12–2, 5–11. Sun 12–2, 7–10.30.
Real Ale. No food.
No children. No dogs. Wheelchair access. Car park. Fourteen bedrooms – all en suite.
Cards: Delta, MasterCard, Switch, Visa.

Lapworth

Navigation Inn ① 01564 783337
Old Warwick Road, Lapworth, Warks B94 1SG
Bass. Andrew Kimber, lease

North of Henley-in-Arden, in a village of cream-washed cottages edging the Stratford-upon-Avon canal, this canalside pub is in a lovely setting; nothing much to look at outside, but inside it is colourful and jolly. Lots of local entertainment at this pub in more ways than one; anything can be going on in the garden, from a barbecue to visiting Morris dancers, even a theatre company bringing a bit of culture. If you just want to sit down and appreciate your surroundings, you can do that too; sitting on the lawn watching the river traffic and the water flow by. They serve generous, appetising bar food: filled rolls, lasagne, a beef, Guinness and mushroom pie, rack of lamb, noisettes of lamb, fresh fish, steaks, curries and some vegetarian dishes. Draught Bass, Brew X1 and Strongbow, Woodpecker and guest ciders. Seats on the lawn which runs down to the water's edge.

OPEN: 11–3, 5.30–11. Sat 11–11. Sun 12–10.30.
Real Ale.
Children in eating area before 9 p.m. Dogs on leads.
Cards: all major cards except Amex and Diners.
Occasional Morris dancing/folk music.

Leamington Spa

Benjamin Satchwell ① 01926 883733
112–114 The Parade, Leamington Spa, Warks CV32 4AQ
Wetherspoon.

The salty, underground springs which led Leamington into becoming a famous spa were discovered in 1586, but Leamington, a town on the River Leam, didn't acquire the Royal prefix until 1838 when it was at the height of its popularity. You can still take the waters at the Royal Pump Room at the far end of The Parade. After that you can wander into the Benjamin Satchwell for a refreshing drink or something from the menu. Always six real ales if you are interested in beer, and anything else you could possibly want if you're not. Good reliable food always available.

OPEN: 11–11.
Real Ale.
No children. No dogs except guide dogs. Full disabled facilities.

Newbold on Stour

White Hart Inn ① 01789 450205
Stratford Road, Newbold on Stour, nr Stratford upon Avon, Warks CV37 8TS
Punch Taverns. Mr & Mrs J. Cruttwell, lease

Dating from the mid-16th century, the White Hart is a popular local serving ample portions of reasonably priced food. Picnic tables and glorious hanging baskets are the first things you see at the front of the pub; you sit amid the flowers. Inside is one spacious main bar and a noisier public bar with jukebox behind, but with luck you may not hear it. From the menu there could be home-made soups, ploughman's, braised lamb in wine and herbs, poached salmon in cream herb sauce and paella, among other dishes. It gets very busy on Friday and Saturday evenings and you should certainly book if you want Sunday lunch. Beers are draught Bass and Adnams Bitter on hand pump.

OPEN: 11–2.30 (Sat 11–3), 6–11.
Real Ale. Restaurant (no food Sun eve).
Children welcome. Dogs on leads.
Cards: MasterCard, Solo, Switch, Visa.

Shustoke

Griffin Inn ① 01675 481205
Nr Coleshill, Birmingham B46 2LB (at Furnace End east of Shustoke)
Free House. Michael Pugh & Sydney Wedge, licensees

Food is good, beer too, but what is basically a 17th-century pub has got caught somewhere in the mid-20th century; the appearance, without ruining the basics, took a seismic leap and landed in the 1960s or thereabouts. The large beamed bar has two fires – one large inglenook – and a roomy conservatory where children are allowed. The traditional choice of bar food ranges from sandwiches, various fish dishes and steak and kidney pie to steaks (large portions) and daily specials on the blackboard. But if you are really into beer, the variety is very tempting. The dozen or so hand pumps allow for a wide choice of ales – the guests change every couple of days; there will be about 10 or more for you to try from small breweries around the country – all in tip-top condition. Seats outside in the garden and on the terrace.

OPEN: 12–2.30, 7–11.
Real Ale. Lunchtime meals and snacks (not Sun).
Children in conservatory. Dogs on leads. Wheelchair access.
No cards.

Stratford upon Avon

Black Swan (Dirty Duck) ① 01789 297312
Waterside, Stratford upon Avon, Warks CV37 6BA
Laurel Pub Co. Sam Jackson, licensee

Overlooking the River Avon, near the theatre, Shakespeare's house and Holy Trinity Church where he is buried, this is the place to go to spot the celebrities. An historic old pub – contemporary with Shakespeare – that caters for the theatre trade, it's a tourist's and theatregoer's heaven; members of the Royal Shakespeare Company regard it as their local. If you dine here, timing is everything. It's a before the performance or after the performance place. Beams and panelling throughout; photos of famous actors decorate the walls. The wide selection of bar food includes a rustic sharing bread for two – herb and garlic bread piled with marinated olives, roasted cherry tomatoes and drizzled with balsamic dressing, salmon and spinach quiche, spicy chicken arrabiatta, creamy four-cheese four-herb risotto, classic Caesar salad, slow-cooked Welsh lamb, steak and ale pie, salmon and dill fish cakes, beer-battered cod and chips, Cumberland sausages with mash and onion gravy, steaks, daily specials and, if you're not very hungry, a sandwich or wrap. Flowers Original, Wadworths 6X and Morlands Old Speckled Hen. Wines by the bottle and glass. No garden, though the terrace, complete with ancient mulberry tree, overlooks the theatre gardens.

OPEN: 11–11. Sun 12–10.30.
Real Ale. Restaurant.
Children in restaurant area only. Dogs in bar. Wheelchair access difficult.

Sulgrave

Star Inn ☽ 01295 760389
Manor Road, Sulgrave, Northants OX17 2SA
Hook Norton Brewery. Jamie & Charlotte King, tenants

In a small village surrounded by largely unspoilt countryside, the Star was originally an old farmhouse and the interior is just as you would expect: heavily beamed with open fireplaces, flagstones and comfortable, traditional furnishings; everyone's ideal of a 17th-century country pub. All the food is freshly cooked: shredded beef, celeriac rémoulade and marinated tomato bruschetta, deep-fried scallops with chilli dipping sauce, smoked eel with warm new potatoes, spring onions and horseradish chantilly, pork tenderloin with Bury black pudding, roast swede, carrots and pickled red cabbage, Gressingham duck breast with buttered spinach, poached celery heart and red wine, pork and herb sausages with spring onion, potato mash and onion gravy, also ham, egg and chips and more. Sunday roasts and good home-made puds. Hook Norton range of ales, a regular guest beer, Stowford Press Cider and good house wines. You can sit in the garden and on the vine-covered terrace. On the border of Oxfordshire and Northamptonshire, you are within walking distance of George Washington's ancestral home – Sulgrave Manor – and not far from Silverstone.

OPEN: 11–2.30, 6–11. Sun 12–3, 7–10.30.
Real Ale. Restaurant.
Children in restaurant. Dogs outside only. Car park. Wheelchair access into bar only. Four en-suite bedrooms.

Wadenhoe

Kings Head ☽ 01832 720024
Church Street, Wadenhoe, Oundle, nr Peterborough PE8 5ST
Free House. Louise Rowell & Richard Spolton, licensees

In a wonderful position by the river Nene; this is an atmospheric old pub in an attractive village. Built in 1662, the Kings Head still has the original quarry-tiled and oak floors, inglenook fireplaces and beams. You can relax and eat in the lounge bar or the no-smoking dining room. The menus change with the seasons but as well as the lunch snack menu, there could be Thai chilli-style crab cakes on leaves with a honey and mustard dressing, venison casserole in Broadside ale and port, roast aubergine with stilton and tomato stuffing or fillet steak strips in brandy and cream, vegetarian dishes, lots of fresh fish and delicious puds too. (They are the proud winners of the 'Best Seafood Pub' and 'Pick of the Pubs' from the AA for the last two years.) Sunday lunch will have a roast as well as fresh fish and casseroles on the menu. Outside are seats in the sheltered courtyard, on the terrace and in the paddock which leads down to the navigable, willow-fringed river Nene – sailors are very welcome. Adnams Southwold, Broadside and guest beers, and a wide-ranging wine list.

OPEN: Summer 12–3, 6.30–11. Sat & Sun 11–11 if sunny. Winter 12–2.30 (Sun 12–4), 7–11. Closed Tues.
Real Ale. Dining room. Evening meals Wed–Sat only.
Children welcome. Dogs on leads. Car park. Wheelchair access.
Cards: all except Amex.

BEST OF THE REST

Alderminster, Warks
Bell ① 01789 450414
Shipston Road, Alderminster CV37 8NY
You're still in the 'Shakespeare triangle' at the Bell, but far from the tourist bustle of Stratford-upon-Avon. South of Stratford, in the Stour Valley, this old coaching inn serves some good, out of the ordinary food. On the monthly changing menu there may be home-made soups and paté, also tomatoes stuffed with prawns, lamb moussaka or lemon and ginger chicken. Lots of other good things to try; wines by the glass and Greene King Abbot and IPA beer. Children welcome. Wheelchair access (not WC). Bedrooms.
Open: 12–2.30, 7–11.

Chapel Brampton, Northants
Brampton Halt ① 01604 842676
Pitsford Road, Chapel Brampton NN6 8BA
This Victorian stationmaster's house turned into a pub is all things to railway buffs: a train ride, a pint and something from the bar menu. Waiting for a train will never be the same. The Northampton steam railway trains stop here at the weekend and while you're waiting you can stoke up with some filling bar food to go with the Adnams, Fullers London Pride, Everards and whatever guest beer is on that week. Decent wines. Note there is no food Sunday. Children – on best behaviour – in the eating area of bar.
Open: 12–2.30, 5.30–11. Sun 12–4, 7–10.30. Summer Sats 12–11.

Wetherspoon in Northamptonshire, Warwickshire and West Midlands

Northamptonshire

Daventry – Saracen's Head, Primrose Hill
① 01327 314800
Kettering – Earl of Dalkeith, 13–15 Dalkeith Place
① 01536 312589
Northampton – Moon on the Square, The Parade, Market Place
① 01604 634062
Northampton – Wetherspoons, 7A St Peter's Way
① 01604 887420
Wellingborough – Red Well, 16 Silver Street
① 01933 440845

Warwickshire

Bedworth – Bear and Ragged Staff, 50 King Street
① 02476 494340
Nuneaton – Felix Holt, Stratford Street
① 01203 347785
Rugby – Rupert Brooke, 8–10 Castle Street
① 01788 576759
Stratford upon Avon – Golden Bee, 41–42 Sheep Street
① 01789 203860

West Midlands

Acocks Green – Spread Eagle, 1146a Warwick Road
① 0121 708 0194
Bilston – Sir Henry Newbolt, 45–47 High Street
① 01902 404636
Birmingham – Briar Rose (also a Wetherspoon Lodge), 25 Bennetts Hill
① 0121 634 8100
Birmingham – Charlie Hall, 49 Barnabas Road, Erdington
① 0121 384 2716
Birmingham – Figure of Eight, 236–239 Broad Street
① 0121 633 0917
Birmingham – Hornet, 991 Alum Rock Road
① 0121 789 5920
Birmingham – Pear Tree, 25–27 Alcester Road South, Kings Heath
① 0121 441 6710
Birmingham – Square Peg, 115 Corporation Street
① 0121 236 6530
Birmingham – Wetherspoons, Unit 31, Paradise Place
① 0121 214 8970
Brierley Hill – Waterfront Inn, 6–7 The Waterfront, Level Street
① 01384 262096
Coventry – City Arms, Earlsdon Street, Earlsdon
① 024 7671 8170
Coventry – Flying Standard, 2–10 Trinity Street
① 024 7655 5723
Cradley Heath – Moon under Water, 164–166 High Street
① 01384 565419
Dudley – Full Moon, 58–60 High Street
① 01384 212294
Halesowen – William Shenstone, 1–5 Queensway
① 0121 585 6246
Moseley – Elizabeth of York, 12a St Mary's Row
① 0121 442 5250
Rowley Regis – Britannia, 124 Halesowen Street
① 0121 559 0010
Sedgley – Clifton, Bull Ring
① 01902 677448
Smethwick – Sampson Lloyd, 24–26 Cape Hill
① 0121 555 4850
Stourbridge – Wetherspoons, Hungary Hill
① 01384 390707
Sutton Coldfield – Bishop Vesey, 63 Boldmere Road
① 0121 355 5077
Sutton Coldfield – Bottle of Sack, 2 Birmingham Road
① 0121 362 8870
Walsall – Imperial, Darwall Street, Walsall
① 01922 640934
Wednesbury – Bellwether, 3–4 Walsall Street
① 0121 502 6404

Wednesfield – Royal Tiger, 41–43 High Street
① 01902 307816
West Bromwich – Billiard Hall, St Michael's Ringway
① 0121 580 2892
West Bromwich – Moon under Water, Kesteven Road
① 0121 588 5839
Willenhall – Malthouse, The Dale, New Road
① 01902 635273
Wolverhampton – Moon under Water, 53–55 Lichfield Street
① 01902 422447
Wolverhampton – Moon under Water, Old Fallings Lane, Low Hill
① 01902 728030

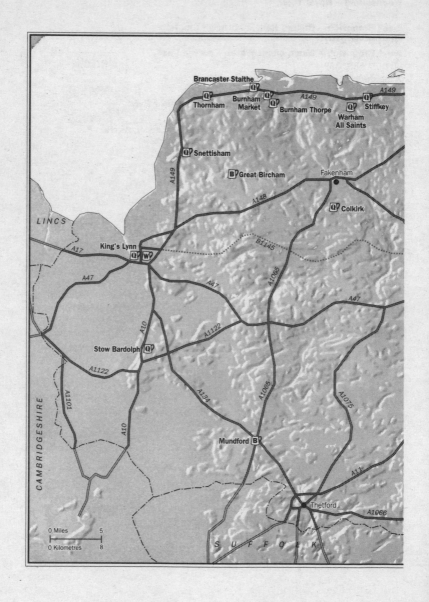

Brancaster Staithe

Thornham

Burnham
Market

Burnham Thorpe

A149

A149

Stiffkey

Warham
All Saints

Snettisham

A149

Great Bircham

Fakenham

A148

Colkirk

LINCS

A17

King's Lynn

B1145

A47

A47

A47

A1066

A47

A1122

A10

Stow Bardolph

A1122

A134

A1065

A1075

CAMBRIDGESHIRE

A1101

A10

Mundford

A11

Thetford

A1066

0 Miles   5
0 Kilometres   8

S U F F O L K

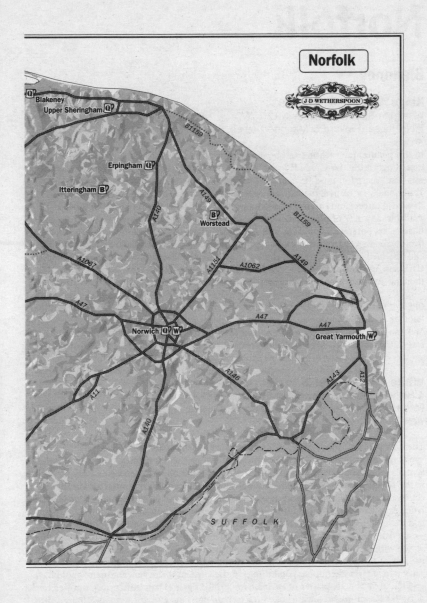

Norfolk

J·D·WETHERSPOON

Blakeney
Upper Sheringham
Erpingham
Itteringham
Worstead
Norwich
Great Yarmouth

B1159
A140
A149
B1159
A1067
A115J
A1062
A149
A47
A47
A47
A146
A143
A12
A11
A140

SUFFOLK

Norfolk

Blakeney

Kings Arms ☎ 01263 740341
Westgate Street, Blakeney NR25 7NQ
Free House. Howard & Marjorie Davies, licensees

In this picturesque yachting and boating centre on the north Norfolk coast is this exceedingly attractive Grade II listed, flint-walled pub. Once three fishermen's cottages, it was first licensed in the 18th century – maybe the date on the roof is relevant. Traditionally furnished, the bars are decorated with photographs of the licensees' theatrical careers and original paintings by local artists. A wide range of bar food is available: a variety of ploughman's, lots of fillings for the sandwiches (plain or toasted), filled jacket potatoes, local crabs in the summer, Blakeney mussels in winter, locally caught fish, steaks, vegetarian dishes and daily specials. Theakstons, Marstons Pedigree, Morland Old Speckled Hen, Adnams plus the local Woodfordes Wherry Bitter. Fosters, Holstein and Carlsberg export lagers. Seats at the front of the pub and in the large garden. There are three no-smoking areas and a separate children's area.

OPEN: 11–11.
Real Ale.
Children welcome. Dogs on leads. All disabled facilities available. Self-catering flatlets. An extension has four en-suite bedrooms and a large dining area which leads into the garden.

White Horse Hotel ☎ 01263 740574 Fax: 01263 741303
4 High Street, Blakeney NR25 7AL
Free House. Daniel Rees, licensee
www.blakeneywhitehorse.co.uk

The high street of flint houses leads to the Quay and the boats in the Blakeney Channel. If you're sailing from here, you are totally dependent on the tides; when the tide is out there is more mud than water. So, if you're waiting for a high tide you can while away the time in the 17th-century White Horse. Originally a coaching inn built around an attractive old courtyard and stables, this handsome, delightful old place was Blakeney's first hotel. The redundant stables, converted into a smart restaurant, overlook the plant-filled courtyard and walled garden. Much more than good sustaining pub fare here: home-made soups (some fishy ones, as you would expect), deep-fried herring roes on toast, cockle chowder served with granary bread, fisherman's pie with a flaky pastry crust, cheese and vegetable pie, lots of salads, freshly made sandwiches and dishes of the day on the bar blackboard. They have a great chef doing good things in the kitchen; the restaurant menu could have cocktail of local crab, platter of Parma ham, grilled figs and balsamic syrup, warmed tartlet of smoked salmon and mascarpone on a tomato dressing, and, for a main course, grilled guinea fowl with wild mushrooms, bacon and Madeira sauce, fillet of hake with crayfish and garlic butter sauce, peppered medallions of beef fillet with chunky chips and spiced fillet of lamb on roasted peppers with mint and yoghurt. Additional seasonal dishes will be on the restaurant blackboard. Vegetarian dishes too. Good home-made puds. Adnams Southwold Bitter, draught Bass, Woodfordes and Guinness; a well-chosen wine list supplied by Adnam's Wine Merchants. Seats in the sunny courtyard.

OPEN: 11–3, 6–11. Bar food all week.
Real Ale. Restaurant 7–9 (last orders) Tues to Sun.
Children in restaurant. No dogs. Car park. Wheelchair access (not WC). Ten en-suite bedrooms.
Cards: Amex, Delta, MasterCard, Switch, Visa.

Brancaster Staithe

Jolly Sailors ① 01485 210314
Brancaster Staithe, Norfolk PE31 8BJ
Free House. Jay Broughton, licensee
www.jollysailors.co.uk

More birdwatching than jolly sailing as, while not quite landlocked, you certainly have to wait for a high tide before you can sail away; at low tide there isn't much more than a narrow channel of water between banks of mud. So it's pluses and minuses; one important plus is that the 200-year-old white-painted Jolly Sailor is just a few hundred yards from the harbour. Inside are a spacious beamed bar and separate restaurant. On the food side there are always filled baguettes or you could choose home-made soup, goat's cheese en croute, deep-fried whitebait, Brie and roasted vegetables, steak and ale pie, at least six fish dishes with the local mussels, crab, lobster and oysters being very much in demand; other goodies from the blackboard. The beers are Woodfordes Wherry, Adnams Bitter, Iceni Fine Soft Day and guests. Very drinkable wines. The other plus is that you are opposite Scolt Head Island nature reserve (you get there by boat), and near Titchwell, the RSPB reserve, which is open daily. If you want to relax at the pub there are seats on the sheltered patio and in the garden.

OPEN: 11–11.
Real Ale. Restaurant – music in here.
Children welcome. Dogs in garden and patio. Car park. Wheelchair access (not WC).
Cards: Delta, MasterCard, Switch, Visa.

Burnham Market

Hoste Arms ① 01328 738777
The Green, Burnham Market PE31 8HD
Free House. Paul Whittome & Jo Race, licensees
e-mail: reception@hostearms.co.uk

Overlooking the green in the prosperous village of Burnham Market, this handsome, 17th-century building, once the manor house of Burnham Westgate, is an elegant hotel with a guest list to die for. Since our last edition a new wing has been built and furnished with African artifacts that reflect the owners' close ties with South Africa. At the front of the hotel the two very welcoming, pubby bars offer excellent lunchtime and evening menus with a combination of British, French and Oriental influences; the menu changes twice a day. Food served in the two panelled dining rooms and the gallery upstairs could include local fish, half a dozen Burnham Creek oysters with crushed ice, red wine and shallot vinegar or spiced lamb meatballs with saffron and onion relish, and for a main course pot-roasted ham hock with green pea purée and parsnip crisps or chargrilled rump steak. To finish, dark chocolate cheesecake, warm blueberry tart with crème fraiche or a selection of British cheeses. The evening restaurant, which is mostly no-smoking, serves an à la carte menu and has a good, reasonably priced wine list. Woodfordes Wherry, Greene King IPA, Abbot and Beamish Red. There is an art gallery to feast your eyes on and you can sit and enjoy your drink in the walled garden or at the front of the hotel among the flower tubs.

OPEN: 11–11.
Real Ale. Restaurant for lunch 12–2, dinner 7–9.
Dogs most welcome. Car park. Wheelchair access. En-suite bedrooms.
Cards: MasterCard, Switch, Visa.

Burnham Thorpe

Lord Nelson ☎ 01328 738241
Walsingham Road, Burnham Thorpe, Kings Lynn PE31 8HN
Greene King. David Thorley, lease

One of the villages known as 'the Seven Burnhams' where, in 1758, Horatio Nelson was born. There was a spirited send off in this pub – then The Plough – when Nelson left to fight for his country in 1794 and a spirited return when his body was brought back in a barrel of brandy after his death in 1805. Soon after, they renamed the pub in his honour. They have a collection of Nelson memorabilia in this charming, unchanging little place which has four rooms – two no smoking – but no bar. The better than usual bar menu has some really good daily changing specials which could be lemon sole, grilled lamb chops in a rosemary and red wine sauce or fresh crab and salmon. The beers, drawn from the barrels in the tap room, are Greene King, Abbot, IPA, Woodfordes Nelson's Revenge and a guest. All the real ales are gravity-fed from the barrel. The parish church of All Saints has some Nelsonian mementoes: the font where he was christened, and a lectern and crucifix made from timbers of his flagship, HMS *Victory*.

OPEN: 11–3, 6–11. Sun 12–3, 7–10.30.
Real Ale.
Children welcome. Dogs on leads. Wheelchair access.
Cards: All major cards over £25. Otherwise Delta, Switch.

Colkirk

Crown ☎ 01328 862172
Crown Road, Colkirk, Fakenham NR21 7AA
Greene King. Roger & Bridget Savell, tenants

A delightful old pub in a quiet village. The bars are homely and welcoming; both have open fires and there is a no-smoking dining room. With a reputation for serving good, interesting food, the menu could include soup, hot herby mushrooms, chef's paté of the day, ham and cheese pancakes, Scotch beef, lots of fresh fish, home-made casseroles, curries and salads. Good puds too. The specials board might have braised steak in cream and garlic sauce, baked cinnamon duck leg with Cumberland sauce, fresh skate-wing provençale and a vegetarian spicy bean casserole. Around 50 wines to choose from, either by the bottle or the glass. Greene King Abbot, IPA and guest ales. Tables outside on the sunny terrace and in the garden.

OPEN: 11–2.30, 6–11.
Real Ale.
Children in lounge & dining area. Dogs on leads. Reasonable wheelchair access.

Erpingham

Saracens Head ① 01263 768909
Wolterton, nr Erpingham NR11 7LX (off A140 near Wolterton Hall)
Free House. Robert Dawson-Smith, licensee
e-mail: racheld@hotmail.com

Publicity from the pub entitled 'Lost in North Norfolk!' assumes you are going to have a little difficulty finding this place, so it's obvious you're not alone – though knowing that delights await will improve your map-reading no end. The secret is to find Wolterton Hall: the pub is close by. It's big and built of brick with an interesting porch, and probably still an eccentric notice directing you to park your camel or helicopter 'at the back, please'. As you would expect, interesting, unusual snacks and a selection of main dishes are on the menu. From Monday to Friday there is a special, very reasonable, two-course lunch with 'no chips, peas or fried scampi'. Also a special 'Two Choice' Sunday supper. Feast nights are held throughout the year: a Mediterranean feast night, for example, or one for Empire Day. You can even organize your own if you are so inclined. The daily changing menu could include parsnip and spring onion soup, a dish of Morston mussels cooked in cider and cream, crispy fried aubergine with garlic mayonnaise; for a main course baked Cromer crab with mushrooms and sherry, grilled salmon with mango and cider, pan-fried breast of chicken with rosemary and cream or wok-sizzled strips of sirloin with olives and tomatoes. Puddings such as a chocolate pot with a rich orange jus or old-fashioned treacle tart. Roast lunch on Sunday. You can even enjoy a special evening menu served in the delightful courtyard or walled garden. Adnams Bitter and Woodfordes Blickling; a good choice of wines from Adnams Wine Merchants.

OPEN: 11–3, 6–11. Sun 12–2, 7–10.30.
Real Ale.
Well-behaved children welcome. No dogs. Wheelchair access possible. En-suite bedrooms.
Cards: All major cards.

King's Lynn

Duke's Head Hotel ① 01553 774996
Tuesday Market Place, King's Lynn PE30 1JS
Free House. David Blair, general manager
e-mail: dukeshead@corushotel.com

Ancient King's Lynn boasts two markets: the 14th-century Tuesday, where you'll find the pink-washed, handsome Duke's Head, and the even older Saturday market which was probably founded when the town was first mentioned in the Domesday Book. In Tuesday Market Place (a car park when there isn't a market) the main entrance to this old coaching inn was originally the carriageway enabling the coaches to drive into the stable yard. The panelled Lynn Bar is where you will find an interesting bar menu and a good selection of beers – Woodfordes Nelson's Revenge, Adnams Best Bitter and Flowers Original. If you want a reasonably priced two-course lunch you will have to listen to music; the bar, lounge and cocktail bar, however, are quiet.

OPEN: 11–3, 6–11. Sun 12–3, 7–10.30.
Real Ale. Two restaurants.
Children to stay. No dogs. Car park. Bedrooms.

Norwich

Bell Hotel ① 01603 630017
5 Orford Hill, Norwich NR1 3QB
Wetherspoon.

It might be called a hotel, but you can't stay the night. Beds have definitely been moved out and beer pumps moved in. However, this is slightly different as they allow children – see below. Wetherspoon took over this old place and gave it a new life, rearranged the inside, installed the mod cons and created two bars – upstairs and downstairs. Full menu available all day – this is standard in all Wetherspoon outlets – changing three times a year. Every day at the Bell you have four different daily specials – no gastronomic fantasies, just good honest fare to go with the cask-conditioned beers. Youngers Scotch Bitter, Courage Directors, Theakston Best, a local regional beer and guest beers from small breweries.

OPEN: 11–11. Sun 12–10.30.
Real Ale.
Children 12–7. Guide dogs only. All wheelchair facilities.

Fat Cat ① 01603 624364
49 West End Street, Norwich NR2 4NA
Free House. Colin Keatley, licensee

A beer lover's paradise. You really are only here for the beer and the like-minded company. Just a traditional ale house with uncomplicated furnishings and filled rolls only at lunchtime. But if it's an excellent, possibly unusual choice of beers you want, this is the place. The customers all thoroughly enjoy tasting lots of different ones – usually about 27 on the go from all over the UK and Ireland. All perfectly kept; what isn't on hand pump will be gravity-served from barrels in a cold room behind the bar. Also lagers, stouts, four draught Belgian beers, country wines and Norfolk cider. A permanent beer festival all year round. Wonderful. National CAMRA pub 1998, 1999 and 2003.

OPEN: 12–11.
Real Ale (lots).
No children. No dogs.

Snettisham

Rose & Crown Inn ① 01485 541382
Old Church Road, Snettisham, King's Lynn PE31 7LX
Free House. Anthony Goodrich, licensee
e-mail: roseandcrown@btclick.com

Inland from the beach and near the church, this 14th-century inn is a lovely old place with beams, big fireplaces, three bars – four including the no-smoking cellar bar – and a garden room. Over the years it has been changed and extended to create the place you see today, pretty as a picture in summer when decked out with colourful hanging baskets. Very popular with families, it is geared up to accommodate children and keep them happy. Well-served, really good bar food in ample proportions: home-made gazpacho soup, locally smoked salmon with cucumber and dill salad, honey and lime crème fraiche, Greek tapas selection served with warm pitta bread, open-flamed rib-eye steak, warm tomato and balsamic salad, breast of Barbary duck served pink, dauphinoise potatoes, black pudding and chocolate jus; even a freshly filled baguette, traditional fish and chips or a choice of vegetarian dishes and grills. There is a specials board, children's menu, a selection of barbecue dishes, also a more extensive evening menu. Adnams, Bass and guest beers on hand pump and a well-chosen wine list. Seats on the terrace and in the walled garden. Family room, and a well-equipped children's play area outside.

OPEN: 11–11.
Real Ale. Restaurant.
Children in own room and eating areas. Well-behaved dogs. Car park. Wheelchair access.
Eleven en-suite bedrooms.
Cards: MasterCard, Switch, Visa.

Stiffkey

Red Lion ① 01328 830552
Wells Road, Stiffkey, Wells-next-the-Sea NR23 1AJ
Free House. Matthew Rees, licensee

A village further from the sea than it originally was; the reclaimed land is now the National Trust's Stiffkey salt marshes, of tremendous interest to birdwatchers and walkers, as is the 16th-century white brick and flint Red Lion where they come for a little recuperation. This straggling village on the north Norfolk coast road has a partly ruined Elizabethan hall, an interesting church with 15th-century brasses and the pub, a busy, jolly place, well used and homely. Three rooms with open fires, furnished with pine tables and settles, and a conservatory serving good, home-cooked food. The blackboard menu is changeable but there are always generously filled sandwiches, a paté, ploughman's, fresh local fish, mussels, lobster, crab and seasonal local game pie. Woodfordes Wherry, Abbot and guest beers, short wine list. Seats on the terraced garden. A track opposite the village church leads to the marshes.

OPEN: 11–3, 6–11.
Real Ale.
Children welcome. Dogs on leads. Car park. Wheelchair access (not WC).
Cards: Delta, MasterCard, Switch, Visa.

Stow Bardolph

Hare Arms ☽ 01366 382229
Stow Bardolph PE34 3HT
Greene King. Trish & David McManus, tenants
e-mail: info@harearms.freeserve.co.uk

This large, Georgian, creeper-covered building at the heart of the village was once the ancestral home of the Hare family. Busy and friendly, it has a spacious bar, no-smoking dining conservatory, and a separate restaurant. They serve a wide variety of food throughout the week. Bar food could include sandwiches and rolls with a choice of fillings, soups and home-made paté; from the daily specials, lemon sole fillets with prawn sauce, salmon fillet with a mushroom, lemon and herb sauce, chunks of tender steak in a black peppercorn, cream and brandy sauce topped with shortcrust pastry, pork steak with orange and sage sauce, local sausages with mash and red wine and onion gravy and lots of steaks. There is a table d'hôte, separate vegetarian menu and an inspired à la carte menu in the restaurant. All the dishes are home-cooked using local seasonal produce, local game, fresh fish, lamb and beef. Imaginative puds too. Greene King ales. Good selection of wines. Tables in the garden among the peacocks and the other feathered residents.

OPEN: 11–2.30, 6–11.
Real Ale. Restaurant (not Sun eves).
Children in conservatory. No dogs. Car park. Wheelchair access (not WC).
Cards: Delta, MasterCard, Switch, Visa.

Thornham

Lifeboat Inn ☽ 01485 512236
Ship Lane, Thornham PE36 6LT
Free House. Charles & Angie Coker, owners & licensees
e-mail: charles.coker@btinternet.com

A delightful, spacious inn with low-beamed ceilings, quarry-tiled floors, old oak furniture, blazing fires in winter and tempting home-cooked food. Keeping the sea from the door is an expanse of marshland; on one side is the RSPB's Titchwell Marsh Reserve, on the other, further to the left and nearer the coast, the Holme Bird Observatory – a birdwatchers' paradise, though in the 16th century this pub and the area, before it was reclaimed for grazing, were the haunt of smugglers and their sinful ways. Unsurprisingly the Lifeboat is big on fish: their own Lifeboat fish pie, fish cakes, Cromer crab salad, Brancaster mussels and whatever fresh fish is available that day. Apart from fish the bar menu ranges from soup, chicken liver paté ploughman's, filled baguettes, pan-fried liver with smoked bacon, roasted vegetables and mash and game pie; daily specials are on the blackboard. The dishes go up a notch on the extensive restaurant menu. Greene King ales, Adnams, Woodfordes Wherry and guest beers. Good range of wines. Seats in the walled garden. Fairly near sandy Thornham beach and lots of wonderful walks.

OPEN: 11–11.
Real Ale. Restaurant.
Children welcome. Dogs too. Car park. Wheelchair access. Bedrooms.
Cards: MasterCard. Switch, Visa.

Upper Sheringham

Red Lion ① 01263 825408
Holt Road, Upper Sheringham NR26 8AD
Free House. Suzanne Prew, licensee

A mile inland from the sandy beaches and the late-Victorian expansion around the old fishing village of Sheringham, Upper Sheringham might be without the sea but there is a fine park surrounding Sheringham Hall, also the flint-built 300-year-old Red Lion. A busy place with two attractive bars where they serve reliable home-cooked food. The blackboard menu changes frequently but there could be home-made soups, hot smoked mackerel fillets and salad, fresh spicy baked Sheringham crab salad, pork with cider, apple and thyme, home-made steak and kidney pie, also lots of fresh fish. Sunday roasts. Greene King IPA and Woodfordes Wherry, Strongbow cider; guest ales change every week in summer. Stella and Guinness on draught and over 30 malts to try. After all that, you can gather yourself together in the sunny walled garden, and later, go and see the old sail-powered Sheringham lifeboat kept in a shed by the shore, or take a trip on the steam train on the North Norfolk Railway. (Great developments are planned: a new kitchen, conservatory, six en-suite bedrooms and disabled loos.)

OPEN: 11.30–3, 6.30–11 (pub quiz Sun eves winter).
Real Ale.
Children in no-smoking eating area. Dogs on leads. Wheelchair access possible, willing helpers on hand. Three bedrooms.

Warham All Saints

Three Horseshoes ① 01328 710547
The Street, Warham All Saints NR23 1NL
Free House. Iain Salmon, licensee

In a pretty village of flint cottages just off the coast road, this very traditional, early 18th-century brick and flint pub still has gas lighting, scrubbed tables on stone floors, good fires, and an early 19th-century grandfather clock which has ticked away the centuries; the interior is from a different age, the atmosphere timeless. But things have moved on in the food front; you'll find a good choice of home-cooked bar food based on fresh, local produce. As well as assorted sandwiches, filled rolls, ploughman's and lots of fillings for the potatoes, there could be a marshman's shellfish bake which includes local mussels, cockles and prawns in a Cheddar sauce grilled until golden, Chalk Hill farm terrine, garden herb and garlic cream mushrooms, a game and wine pie – local game cooked in wine with onions under a shortcrust pastry lid, cod in cheese sauce and a Norfolk beef pie, beef, mushrooms and onions cooked in beer and topped with flaky pastry. A daily selection of dishes on the blackboard complements the printed menu; everything is cooked to order. Half portions too for those with smaller appetites, and no chips with anything. A selection of English cheeses to finish or something from the pudding menu on the board in the main bar. Greene King IPA, Woodfordes Wherry plus guest ales. House wines, a short wine list and eight country wines including a medium-sweet Silver Birch. Tables on the grass outside. Lots of things to see in Warham: St Mary's Church still has its original Georgian box pews and pulpit; Warham Camp, an Iron Age fort, is not far away, and Warham Marsh is one of Europe's largest salt marshes. If you feel energetic, you can join the Norfolk coastal path for a brisk walk.

OPEN: 11.30–2.30, 6–11.
Real Ale. No-smoking restaurant.
Children in eating area. Dogs on leads. Car park. Wheelchair access. Bedrooms in the Old Post Office next door.
Occasional live music Saturday evenings.

BEST OF THE REST

Great Bircham
Kings Head ① 01485 578265
Great Bircham PE31 6RJ
Forget the Great, the locals just call the village 'Bircham'. On the south side of the village, the large, white, imposing building is the King's Head. You really can't miss it. Plenty of room in the lounge bar and you can either eat there or in the restaurant. Always good, the menu ranges from sandwiches, fresh fish and seafood to steak and kidney pudding. Both the bar and restaurant menus have a touch of the Italian – from the licensee; so the pasta will always be just as it should be. Adnams, Bass and Greene King IPA and a decent wine list. Children welcome. Bedrooms.
Open: 11–2.30, 6–11.

Itteringham
Walpole Arms ① 01263 587258
The Common, Itteringham NR11 7AR
An unused farm building was attached to this 18th-century pub and given a new lease of life as the restaurant. Inside the original building is a spacious bar where they serve well-prepared dishes. On the bar snack menu the paté and soups are home made; they home-smoke the salmon and sausages and make delicious puds. Menus change daily so there are always some surprises. Adnams Bitter and Broadside as well as draught Bass, Woodfordes Nelson's Revenge and seasonal beers. Wines by the glass. Children welcome, dogs too – in bar. Wheelchair access.
Open: 12–3, 6–11.

Mundford
Crown Hotel ① 01842 878233
Crown Street, Mundford, Thetford IP26 5HD
Next to the green, this large, white-painted 17th-century inn is in a village on the edge of Breckland. Lightly populated, this part of Norfolk does not have many pubs, so the Crown stands out. Built on a hillside – not many of these in Norfolk either – the kitchens and restaurant are upstairs; the smarter, beamed lounge bar with a big open fire, and the more basic public bar, are on the ground floor. Three menus on virtually all the time; the bar menu, specials board and the à la carte (never on Sundays). From the specials board you could have devilled kidneys in red wine served with saffron rice or Chinese-style chicken – boned whole spring chicken baked in sweet chilli with prawns mixed with a noodle and vegetable stirfry. Good puds too. Woodfordes Wherry, Courage Directors, Nethergate and local Iceni ales. House wines, wide-ranging wine list and over 50 malt whiskies. Woodland walks in Emily's Wood on the road between Mundford and Brandon. Children welcome.

Dogs on leads. Wheelchair access. CD player in bar. Bedrooms. Cards: Amex, Delta, Diners, MasterCard, Switch, Visa.
Open: 11–11. Sun 12–10.30.

Worstead
New Inn ① 01692 536296
Front Street, Worstead NR28 9RW

Difficult to place musically; half and half I suppose, as it is quiet during the morning, not so at night, when they play recorded music or heavily amplified visiting folk groups. So, it's a lunchtime place! An inn at the centre of an attractive conservation village which gave its name to worsted cloth and which holds an annual three-day festival attracting hordes of people. They serve simple, home-cooked food, Greene King, Adnams and Tetleys beers, also a selection of wines. The large garden overlooks fields and the wool church. Children and dogs allowed. Wheelchairs can force their way in. (Large field available for caravans – with prior arrangement.)
Open: 12–3, 7–11.

Wetherspoon in Norfolk

Great Yarmouth – Troll Cart, 7–9 Regent Road
① 01493 332932
Kings Lynn – Lattice House, Chapel Street
① 01553 769585
Norwich – Bell Hotel, 5 Orford Hill
① 01603 630017
Norwich – City Gate, 5–7 Dereham Road
① 01603 661413
Norwich – Glass House, 11–13 Wensum Street
① 01603 877650
Norwich – Whiffler, Boundary Road, Hellesdon
① 01603 424042

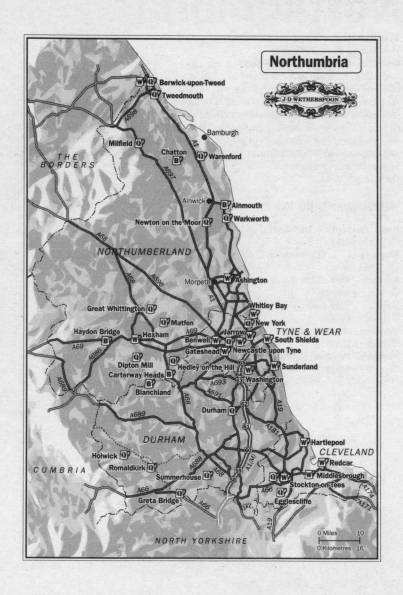

Northumbria

J·D·WETHERSPOON

Berwick-upon-Tweed
Tweedmouth
Bamburgh
Milfield
Chatton
Warenford
THE
BORDERS
Alnwick
Alnmouth
Warkworth
Newton on the Moor
NORTHUMBERLAND
Morpeth
Ashington
Whitley Bay
Great Whittington
Matfen
New York
Haydon Bridge
Hexham
Jarrow
TYNE & WEAR
Benwell
South Shields
Gateshead
Newcastle upon Tyne
Dipton Mill
Hedley on the Hill
Sunderland
Carterway Heads
Washington
Blanchland
Durham
Holwick
Hartlepool
DURHAM
CLEVELAND
Romaldkirk
Redcar
Summerhouse
Middlesbrough
Stockton-on-Tees
Greta Bridge
Egglescliffe
CUMBRIA
NORTH YORKSHIRE

0 Miles 10
0 Kilometres 16

Northumbria

Berwick-upon-Tweed

Free Trade ☎ 01289 306498
75 Castlegate, Berwick-upon-Tweed, Northumberland TD15 1LF
Free House. Brenda Collins, licensee

All that is left of the 12th-century castle in this ancient border town is a section of wall and tower; the Victorians destroyed the rest to build the station. They also built the Free Trade nearby, beyond the Elizabethan walls. This place is for those of you keen on their beer as it's liquid refreshment only; a crisp and nut too perhaps, always biscuits for the dog. An unchanging Victorian drinking pub with an old-fashioned bar. At the moment, the beers are Federation Founders, Smooth, Buchanan and Buchanan Original, maybe Fullers London Pride.

OPEN: 7–11. Sat 12–5.30, 7.30–11. Sun 12–10.30.
Real Ale.
Children if well behaved. Dogs very welcome, biscuits provided.
Jukebox.

Dipton Mill

Dipton Mill Inn ☎ 01434 606577
Dipton Mill Road, nr Hexham, Northumberland NE46 1YA
Free House. Geoff Brooker, licensee
e-mail: diptonmill@supaworld.co.uk

Interesting walks and glorious scenery surround this small pub, converted from a 17th-century farmhouse and adjoining cottages. In a wooded valley two miles from Hexham, by West Dipton Burn, this is a delightfully traditional place, with comfortable, single bar and a room with a bar billiards table. From the freshly prepared menu there could be carrot and celery soup, lots of fillings for the sandwiches, salads, ploughman's, chicken in tarragon sauce, pork fillet with apple, orange and ginger, haddock baked with tomato and basil, tagliatelle with creamy basil sauce and fresh parmesan and steak and kidney pie. A choice of savoury flans, a selection of desirable puddings and some very interesting Northumberland cheeses. Ales are from the very local brewery, Hexamshire (the landlord is the brewer), which produces Devil's Elbow, Shire bitter, Devil's Water, Old Humbug and Whapweasel (named after a burn on the fells). Reasonably priced wine list; four by the glass. Very beautiful countryside, an old mill stream runs through the grounds, and another stream runs alongside the pub. Seats in the attractive garden.

OPEN: 12–2.30, 6–11 (Sun 7–10.30).
Real Ale.
Children welcome. No dogs. Wheelchair access.

Durham

Shakespear Tavern ☎ 0191 3869709
Saddler Street, Durham City DH1 3NU
Newcastle/Courage. Mark Charlton, lease

The original city of Durham was built on a rocky outcrop enclosed by a loop of the river Wear; the view of the cathedral and surrounding buildings high above the river is second to none. The Shakespear, near the town hall, is close to everything that matters in this ancient city: the castle, cathedral, the oldest of the university colleges and the river. Very friendly, popular and full of character. Inside there is a tiny front bar, quiet lounge and snug, still with its original 18th-century panelling. No food at all, a crisp and nut though, to go with the Theakstons, McEwans 80/-, guest beers, Guinness and lagers. Another CAMRA favourite which has an interior of architectural interest.

OPEN: 11–11. Sun 12–10.30.
Real Ale.
Children welcome. Dogs on leads

Egglescliffe

Pot and Glass ☎ 01642 651009
Church Road, Egglescliffe, Cleveland TS16 9DP
Enterprise Inns. Dave Bunyan, tenant

In a setting that couldn't be better: a charming village, an 11th-century church and a 17th-century pub. Next to the church, and looking out over the churchyard, it is all very peaceful. Inside are low beamed ceilings, panelled walls, a public bar, lounge and small side room for meetings and private parties. Menus are constantly changing; lunchtime food is served six days a week: home-made steak pies, lasagne, fish and chips and a scampi or two. Well-kept draught Bass, John Smiths, Guinness, cider and two guest ales. Carling and Stella on pump. Just a small garden where you'll have to sit if you take your dog. They have won CAMRA Pub of the Season award.

OPEN: 12–2.30, 6–11. Sun 12–10.30. No food Mon.
Real Ale.
Children welcome in side room until 9 p.m. Dogs in garden.

Great Whittington

Queen's Head ☎ 01434 672267
Great Whittington, Northumberland NE19 2HP
Free House. Ian Scott, licensee

This 17th-century former coaching inn is near Hadrian's Wall and the Devil's Causeway, in an area popular with cyclists and walkers. This remote stone-built village – more little than great with only about 160 inhabitants – overlooks lovely countryside. Food oriented, the Queen's Head has two comfortable beamed bars, both with log fires, where you can have a tasty sandwich and a drink; or you can choose something from the bistro blackboard menu which could offer lamb's liver with bacon and onion, breast of chicken with broccoli, goujons of fresh haddock or salmon with lemon and dill sauce and really good home-made puds. There is an à la carte menu in the no-smoking restaurant and a choice of over 30 wines to go with the food. Hambleton Bitter and their own Queen's Head Bitter are the beers. Picnic tables in the garden.

OPEN: 12–2.30, 6–11. Sun 12–3. Closed Sun eve and Mon except bank holidays.
Real Ale. Restaurant – music in here.
Well-behaved children at lunchtime only. Dogs in garden. Car park. Wheelchair access.

Greta Bridge

Morritt Arms ① 01833 627232
Greta Bridge, Rokeby, nr Barnard Castle, Co. Durham DL12 9SE
Free House. Barbara Anne Johnston & Peter Phillips, licensees
e-mail: relax@themorritt.co.uk

By the old stone bridge and entrance to Rokeby Park, this appealing 18th-century coaching inn has a strong Dickens connection – the author stayed here in 1834 while researching his novel *Nicholas Nickleby*. They have finished a big refurbishment programme and all is settling in very nicely, having not lost any of its charm. The comfortable, panelled lounges, 'pubby' bar and restaurant were all on the list, but fortunately the bar has kept the very jolly 'Dickensian' murals. The food is fine English cooking with a twist. Good hearty soups, Teesdale terrine with home-made chutney and granary toast, flaked barbecued salmon on a niçoise salad, Finnan smoked haddock omelette glazed with local Wensleydale and chives, local farmhouse sausages, leek and bacon mash with beer-battered shallots, twice-baked Swaledale soufflé, rocket salad and warm pear and saffron compote, home-cured bacon, free-range eggs and hand-cut chips, Morritt pie and mash, daily specials too. Filled baguettes and other dishes from the menu in the lounge bar, an extensive wine list, a dozen or so by the glass. Black Sheep Bitter plus the house beer on hand pump. John Smiths Smooth is the keg beer. Lots of room in the large garden.

OPEN: 11–11. Sun 12–10.30.
Real Ale. Restaurant, music sometimes played in here.
Children welcome. Dogs too. Car park. Wheelchair access. Twenty-three en-suite bedrooms.
Cards: Amex, MasterCard, Switch, Visa.

Hedley on the Hill

Feathers ① 01661 843607
Hedley on the Hill, Stocksfield, Northumberland NE43 7SW
Free House. Marina Atkinson, licensee

A stone-built pub in the middle of a village, high on the hill with views towards the sea. Inside are atmospheric beamed bars, log fires and comfortable furnishings. They serve a tempting selection of dishes: the menus change weekly so there could be home-made soup, Greek salad with balsamic and fresh thyme dressing, Caesar salad with Bywell smoked chicken breast, keema spiced lamb with ginger and fresh coriander with sweetcorn-filled pancake, honey roast ham with mango chutney, Greek beef casserole with tomatoes, red wine and oregano, salmon fillet with lemon and dill butter, several vegetarian dishes and at least one for vegans. Yummy puds and children's meals. Local ales – Mordue's Workie Ticket and Radgie Gadgie, Hadrian Gladiator, Yates Bitter and Big Lamp Bitter could be among the guests. A choice of 30 malt whiskies and a good, short wine list.

OPEN: 6–11. Sat 12–3, 6–11. Sun 12–3, 7–10.30. Daytime opening weekday bank holidays only.
Real Ale. Meals every evening except Mon. Lunch served Sat & Sun.
Children in eating area and family room till 8.30 p.m. No dogs. Car park. Wheelchair access (not WC).
Debit cards only.

Holwick

Strathmore Arms ① 01833 640362
Holwick, Middleton-in-Teesdale, Northumberland DL12 ONJ
Teesdale Traditional Taverns. Helen Osborne & Joseph Cogden, licensees

A quiet, unspoilt pub in beautiful scenery in the hills above Middleton-in-Teesdale, surrounded by waterfalls and the wild landscape above the River Tees. In the middle of the wildness is the Strathmore Arms, on a narrow lane leading nowhere in particular. Inside the pub is an attractive bar, with a roaring log fire on cold days, and behind that, a comfortable snug. The bar menu offers home-made soup, grilled local trout, Cumberland sausages, steak and kidney pie, gammon and eggs – all served with fresh vegetables – vegetarian dishes too. Theakstons Best, Black Bull, Ruddles Best and a guest ale, also Hedgerow wines and mead. The bar has an old but well-kept piano. Plenty of walks, you are very near the Pennine Way.

OPEN: Winter Tues–Fri 7–11. Summer Tues–Fri also 12–2.30. Sat 12–11. Sun 12–10.30. Closed Mon.
Real Ale.
Children welcome until 9 – not in the bar. Dogs on leads. Four en-suite bedrooms.

Matfen

Black Bull ① 01661 886330
Matfen, Newcastle-upon-Tyne NE20 ORD (off B6318 north-east of Corbridge)
Free House. Colin & Michele Scott, licensees

By the green in this remote village, the stone-built, creeper-covered Black Bull is nearly hidden behind the most exuberant summer floral display: hanging baskets and tubs of flowers create an array of colour. Inside you'll find things are a little compact now as part of the pub, including the restaurant, is no more; it has been detached and is now owned by someone else. However, they still serve well-presented lunchtime food: soups, duck liver paté, herb pancake filled with spiced prawns, home-made steak and mushroom pie cooked in ale, honey-glazed chicken with toasted almonds and various salads. Theakstons Black

Bull Bitter only. Seats among the flowers at the front of the pub, overlooking the village green.

OPEN: 11–3, 6–11. Sat 11–11. No food in evening.
Children in eating area. No dogs. Wheelchair access.
N.B. TV is often on in one bar.

Milfield

Red Lion Inn ① 01668 216224
Main Road, Milfield, nr Wooler, Northumberland NE71 6JD
Free House. John Logan, licensee

The 18th-century Red Lion, the oldest building in the village, was, in the heyday of coach travel, a stop for the mail coach from Edinburgh to London via Coldstream and Newcastle; a fresh team of horses was provided, passengers had time for a meal, then they were on their way. Life moves on, but inside the pub the centuries-old fireplace where the locals used to sharpen their knives is still there – the stone pillars are quite worn away. They serve a traditional, changing pub menu: battered mushrooms, deep-fried potato skins, tagliatelle carbonara, filled Yorkshire puddings and vegetarian dishes. There is also a steak menu. A full Northumbrian breakfast sets you up for the day and this is served during opening hours. Draught Bass, Blacksheep and two guests.

OPEN: 12–2, 6–11. Sat 11–11. Sun 12–10.30.
Real Ale.
Children welcome. Dogs on leads. Wheelchair access. One static caravan to sleep four people.
Cards: most accepted.

New York

Shiremoor Farm ① 0191 2576302
Middle Engine Lane, New York, Northshields, Tyne & Wear NE29 8DZ
Free House. C. W. Kerridge, licensee

These well-converted farm buildings have created a delightfully atmospheric pub. Stone walls, flagstone floors, beams, comfortable furniture and good food make this well appointed and popular. They cater for everyone – not only someone wanting a pint and bar snack or a full meal, but also for families in the converted granary. There is a traditional bar menu, also dishes such as roast duck julienne, breast of chicken in garlic and brandy sauce, beef stroganoff, steaks, daily changing specials on the blackboard and home-made puddings. Timothy Taylors Landlord, Theakstons Best, Mordue's Workie Ticket and guests. Wines by the glass. Tables on the grass by the farm courtyard among the flowers.

OPEN: 11–11. Food all day, every day.
Real Ale.
Children in eating areas away from bar. No dogs.
Cards: all major cards.

Newcastle-upon-Tyne

Crown Posada ① 0191 232 1269
33 The Side, Newcastle-upon-Tyne NE1 3JD
Free House. Malcolm McPherson, manager

Near the Tyne Bridge and cathedral, architecturally this old city pub is a gem of a place with magnificent Victorian stained-glass windows, screens, tulip lamps and painted ceilings. Originally just The Crown, it was renamed by the 19th-century owner, a retired sea captain who, in the tradition of his calling, didn't quite have a girl in every port, but certainly a wife in Spain and a girl in his pub. Feeling more at home here than anywhere else he added Posada, the Spanish for inn or place of rest, to the Crown. Inside, the building is long and narrow – known locally as the coffin – with just one bar, and a snug to the side. The only food they serve is lunchtime sandwiches – crisps too of course, probably a nut. The ales are Theakstons Best, Boddingtons Bitter, Butterknowle Conciliation Ale, Jennings and guest beers. If you want to catch up on the day's events, the daily papers are kept in the snug. Hugely popular at the weekend, quieter during the week.

OPEN: 11–11. Sun 11–4, 7–11. Lunchtime snacks (not Sun).
Real Ale.
No children. Dogs on leads if well behaved.

Romaldkirk

Rose & Crown ① 01833 650213
Romaldkirk, Barnard Castle, Co. Durham DL12 9EB
Free House. Christopher & Alison Davy, licensees
e-mail: hotel@rose-and-crown.co.uk

This enchanting Pennine village of lovely houses and cottages surrounds no fewer than three village greens in Upper Teesdale, an unspoilt area of the county. Creeper-covered and handsome, the Rose and Crown, a fine 18th-century coaching inn, overlooks one of the greens – the one with the village stocks. Next to the honey-coloured church, the inn is beamed, panelled, polished and attractive. There is the added bonus of very interesting food served in the bar and the no-smoking restaurant. Monthly changing menus offer lunchtime filled baps and ploughman's – there is a local Cotherstone cheese – or you could choose a smoked salmon soufflé with chive cream sauce, local game terrine with Cumberland sauce, red onion, chicory and Yorkshire Blue cheese salad with sweet pear dressing, or for a main course, smoked haddock kedgeree with prawns, quails eggs and Parmesan, steak, kidney and mushroom pie in Theakstons ale gravy, creamed scrambled eggs with smoked salmon, Mr Peat's pork sausage, black pudding, mustard mash and shallot gravy. The evening bar menu is more extensive. Good-value three-course Sunday lunch in the restaurant. Bread will be home made, as are the chutneys and pickled onions accompanying the ploughman's. Regional cheeses, meat from the local butcher, game from the surrounding moors and fish from the East Coast ports. Blacksheep Bitter and Theakstons Best on hand pump. Wide-ranging wine list – some half bottles, and some by the glass. Barnard Castle is nearby, so is High Force waterfall; you are surrounded by paths to the moors above the village and to the river valley below.

OPEN: 11.30–3, 5.30–11.
Real Ale. No smoking restaurant.
Children welcome. Dogs on leads. Car park. Twelve bedrooms all en suite, two with private sitting rooms.
Cards: MasterCard, Switch, Visa.

Stockton-on-Tees

Masham ① 01642 580414
79 Hartburn Village, Stockton-on-Tees, Cleveland TS18 5DR
Punch Taverns. Dennis & John Eddy, tenant and manager

On the southern outskirts of the town, this small village was once on the edge of a Stockton, but has inevitably been swallowed up and become part of the town. Once you find the Masham, you're in for a friendly welcome in what is a popular local meeting place. It has a bar, bar area, three small rooms and a garden at the back. Well-chosen, traditional bar food from the blackboards is available every day. The Bass and Black Sheep on hand pump are particularly well kept. House entertainment (apart from the customers) is a TV in one of the small rooms for the big sporting events – rugby, cricket, etc. You can't hear the TV anywhere else in the pub – but the customers can get a little enthusiastic! Seats and tables on the paved area in the garden.

OPEN: 11–11. Sun 11–3, 7–10.30.
Real Ale.
Children allowed in beer garden. Dogs on leads.
Cards: all except Amex.

Summerhouse

Raby Hunt Inn ① 01325 374604
Summerhouse, Darlington, Durham DL2 3UD
Free House. Michael Allison, licensee

Near the 14th-century Raby Castle, about seven miles from Darlington, the old Raby Hunt is a refuge from the wild landscape and rugged moors that surround it. Stone built and homely, it has everything you could want. They serve an uncomplicated snack menu of pub favourites: well-filled sandwiches, toasties, burgers and hot beef rolls. Marstons and Banks beers plus a guest from local micro-breweries. Short wine list.

OPEN: 6.30–11. Sun 12–3, 7–10.30.
Real Ale.
Children welcome. Dogs too. Car park. Wheelchair access (not WC).

Tweedmouth

Rob Roy ☎ 01289 306428
Dock Road, Tweedmouth, Berwick-upon-Tweed, Northumberland TD15 2BE
Free House. Keith & Julie Wilson, licensees
e-mail: therobroy@btinternet.com

If you are coming from the Scottish border, you cross the 17th-century Berwick Bridge – the Old Bridge – to Tweedmouth and the Rob Roy. In what was a flourishing port and fishing town, it is not surprising that the Rob Roy is really strong on fish. It's a restaurant and a bar; more somewhere to eat than somewhere to drink, but having said that there is a bar serving keg beers, wine and really good food. The bar menu offers a soup of the day, freshly made sandwiches, salad of sweet pickled herrings, pork and liver paté with toast, smoked Scottish salmon with pickled samphire, baked lemon sole fillets with buttered mushrooms and lemon, grilled crevettes in garlic butter, pasta with seafood and lots more. Sea bass fillet with tomato capsicum salsa from the restaurant menu, also Barbary duck breast sautéed in blackcurrant sauce and grilled North Sea Dover sole with lemon parsley butter. There is a speciality blackboard menu: creamed shellfish soup, salmon Limoux (poached in wine – you drink the rest of the bottle), sirloin steak Rob Roy cooked in a sauce of onions, mushrooms, whisky, and double cream or a chateaubriand for two, also fresh local lobster and a Spanish paella for two – ordered in advance. If you have any room, home-made puds. They serve only wild salmon; fresh during the season, otherwise frozen. The à la carte menu is changed regularly depending on the fish, shellfish and game available; wild Tweed salmon and sea trout during the season and lobsters and crabs if the weather is favourable. A place to be treasured.

OPEN: 11.30–2.30, 6.30–11. Sun 12–2.30, 7–10.30. Closed Tues.
Keg beers and wines only. Restaurant.
No dogs.
Cards: JCB, MasterCard, Switch, Visa.

Warenford

Warenford Lodge ☎ 01668 213453
Warenford, Belford, Northumberland NE70 7HY
Free House. Raymond Matthewman, licensee
e-mail: warenfordlodge@aol.com

Confusingly there is no inn sign to let you know where you are, but if you see what looks like a private house, stone built with mullioned windows and lots of cars parked outside, you know you've arrived. But do look at the opening times as it is closed for lunch during the week and totally closed Mondays and some Tuesdays. When it is open, it is a very popular place – but you do have to book to be sure of a table in the evening. Menus change twice a year, but there are usually lots of fishy dishes, which could include the famous Northumbrian fish soup, or kipper paté, grilled herb mussels and salmon fillet, Italian shank of pork roasted with wine and herbs, seaside fish platter (large portion) or cannelloni with home-cured ham, lean beef and fresh tomato sauce. As they say, 'all main dishes are complete and fairly substantial' – or you could just have a steak or a pair of kippers. Very good cheese. Home-made puddings and a choice of ice creams. John Smiths, Theakstons and McEwans Scottish ales plus a well-chosen, varied wine list.

OPEN: 7–11. Sat & Sun 12–2, 7–11. Closed Mon except bank holidays and winter Tues. Evening restaurant and weekend snacks and meals.
Children in restaurant. No dogs. A few steps for wheelchairs, but there are willing helpers.

Warkworth

Black Bull ① 01665 711367
19 Bridge Street, Warkworth, Alnwick, Northumberland NE65 0XB
Free House. J. Morton, licensee

This area was a stronghold of the Percy family – the Earls of Northumberland; Alnwick castle has been their home since 1309 and it was here, in this impressive, now ruined, castle, that Henry 'Hotspur' Percy was born. The Coquet River serves as a natural moat, protecting both the village and the castle. This is the place to visit in spring when the grassy slopes around the castle walls are covered with daffodils. When you've admired the scenery make your way to the Black Bull, a delightful pub with daily changing menus that are strong on fish, home-made pizzas and with a definite lean towards the Italian. Beers are Black Sheep Bitter, 1744 and a guest, John Smiths Smooth, Carling and Strongbow cider.

OPEN: 11–2.30, 6–11. Sun 12–3, 7–10.30. Closed Mon & Tues lunchtime. Opening hours are more flexible during the tourist season.
Real Ale. Small restaurant.
Children and dogs on leads. Wheelchair access.
No cards.

BEST OF THE REST

Alnmouth, Northumberland
Saddle Hotel ① 01665 830476
24/25 Northumberland Street, Alnmouth NE66 2RA
Sailing and golf: if these are your interests you might like to know that there are two nearby golf courses and a yacht haven in the sheltered estuary of the River Aln. But when you want some shelter from the cold northeasterlies, make your way to the Saddle Hotel, where you can tuck yourself up in the warmth and find well-prepared, unpretentious hearty dishes: ploughman's, Northumberland sausages, Barnsley lamb chops, steak and kidney – that sort of thing. Ruddles Best, Theakstons, Wadworths 6X and a decent wine list. Children and dogs welcome. Wheelchair access (not WC). Bedrooms.
Open: 11–3, 6–11.

Blanchland, County Durham
Lord Crewe Arms ① 01434 675251
Blanchland, nr Consett DH8 9SP
e-mail: lord@crewearms.freeserve.co.uk
One of England's oldest pubs, handsome and haunted. Formerly the home of the abbots of the ruined 13th-century Blanchland Abbey, it's haunted by Dorothy Forster, a heroine

of the Jacobite uprising. On that cheerful note, make your way to the vaulted Crypt Bar for a reviving drink and something from the menu: tagliatelle verde with creamy wild-mushroom sauce and parmesan, tossed salad of Stilton cheese, beans, croutons, bacon, pine nuts and cherry tomatoes, chef's dish of the day; lots of fillings for the rolls, daily specials and Sunday lunches. Upstairs is the Hilyard room – look up the huge chimney to see the priest hole which hid Tom Forster – and a restaurant. Beers are Castle Eden, John Smiths, Boddingtons Bitter and Guinness. Seats in the enclosed garden. Children welcome. Wheelchair access (not WC). Bedrooms.
Open: 11–3, 6–11.

Carterway Heads, Northumberland
Manor House Inn ① 01207 255268
Carterway Heads, Shotley Bridge, Consett DH8 9LX (A68 between Corbridge and Consett)
High above sea level with views over the surrounding moorland, this is a long, stone-built 18th-century converted farmhouse on the edge of the north Pennines. Here the bars have music but the restaurant is quiet, so it is here you'll come to choose something from the imaginative blackboard menu. Dishes could include a leek and courgette soup with French bread, smoked chicken and Brie croissants, moules marinières, baked sea trout, duck breast with orange and coriander and medallions of beef in a madeira sauce. Home-made puddings and a choice of local cheeses. Theakstons Best Bitter, Ruddles County, Westons Beamish and guest ales. Wide-ranging wine list. Seats in the garden (wind permitting!). Well-behaved children welcome. Dogs in small bar only. Car park. Wheelchair access – help always available. Four en-suite bedrooms. Most cards.
Open: 11–3, 6–11.

Chatton, Northumberland
Percy Arms ① 01668 215244
Main Road, Chatton NE66 5PS
In an area known for vigorous walks and fishing, this small, attractive 18th-century hotel offers a good choice of bar food: home-made soups, local fish, salmon in a creamy sauce, seafood platter, steaks and specials on the blackboard. Always one real ale, mainly Theakstons; good wines. If you stay, the Percy Arms has 12 miles of private fishing for you to enjoy. Children welcome. Bedrooms.
Open: 11–3, 6–11.

Haydon Bridge, Northumberland
General Havelock Inn ① 01434 684376
9 Ratcliff Road, Haydon Bridge NE47 6ER
Only yards from the South Tyne river, this roadside inn has tremendous appeal. Family run, the licensee is a first-class chef, so food is really the thing here – the restaurant looks seriously professional. But they haven't forgotten the bar where they serve some exceptional food cooked to perfection and presented with style: there are seasonal menus in the bar – summer Caesar salad with home-smoked chicken or Toulouse sausages in a spicy bean broth; in winter, beef, Guinness and wild mushroom stew, chicken leek and cheddar pie. Important as the bar food is, the emphasis is on the restaurant where they serve a reasonable two-, three- or four-course menu. This menu changes every five to six weeks. Beers are Timothy Taylors Landlord, Adnams Broadside, Mordue's Workie Ticket and Big Lamp Prince Bishop. Wide-ranging wine list, some by the glass. Children welcome. Dogs too. Wheelchair access.
Open: 12–2.30, 7–11. Closed Sun eve and Mon.

Wetherspoon in Northumberland, Cleveland and Tyne and Wear

Northumberland

Ashington – Ronan Kanhai, 1–4 Woodhorn Road
① 01670 857692
Berwick upon Tweed – Leaping Salmon, Golden Square, Bank Hill
① 01289 303184
Hexham – Forum, Market Place
① 01434 609190

Cleveland

Hartlepool – King John's Tavern, 1 South Road
① 01429 274388
Middlesbrough – Isaac Wilson, 61 Wilson Street
① 01642 247708
Redcar – Plimsoll Line, 138–142 High Street East
① 01642 495250
Stockton on Tees – Thomas Sheraton, 4 Bridge Road
① 01642 606134

Tyne & Wear

Benwell – Plaza Tavern, West Road
① 0191 238 6882
Gateshead – Wetherspoons, 85 Russell Way, Metro Centre
① 0191 460 5073
Jarrow – Ben Lomond, Grange Road West
① 0191 483 3839
Newcastle upon Tyne – Union Rooms, 48 Westgate Road
① 0191 261 5718
South Shields – Wouldhave, Mile End Road
① 0191 427 6041
Sunderland – Lambton Worm, Victoria Building
① 0191 568 9910
Sunderland – William Jameson, 30–32 Fawcett Street
① 0191 514 5016
Washington – Sir William de Wessyngton, 2–3 Victoria Road, Concord
① 0191 418 0100
Whitley Bay – Fire Station, 18 York Road
① 0191 293 9030

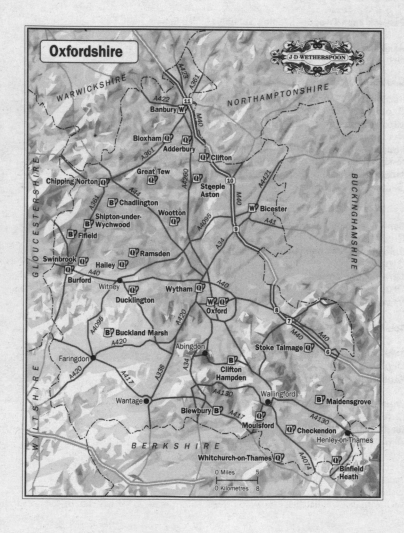

Oxfordshire

Adderbury

The Bell ① 01295 810338
High Street, Adderbury, Banbury OX17 3LS
Hook Norton. Tim Turner, tenant
e-mail: tim@thebelladderbury.com

A tree-fringed village green and an 18th-century pub among 17th-century houses; all built of the warm stone so typical of the area. The pub is the focus for many village activities, including the local bellringers, a theatre workshop and Morris men. Very traditional, beamed, full of atmosphere and friendly, the Bell serves a wide range of reasonably priced food from simple bar snacks to home-made steak pie, local rabbit in juniper and cider, breast of duck in a spicy fruit sauce, fish and chips, daily specials or something from the extensive à la carte menu in the restaurant. They do a very reasonably priced three-course Sunday lunch complete with fresh coffee, fudge and mints. Hook Norton range of beers.

OPEN: 12–3, 6.30–11.
Real Ale.
Children welcome. Dogs too. En-suite double and twin-bedded room. Wheelchair access possible but there are steps – and help.
Cards: Delta, MasterCard, Switch, Visa.
There is a folk club, and occasional live music sessions.

Binfield Heath

Bottle & Glass ① 01491 575755
Harpsden Road, Binfield Heath, Henley-on-Thames RG9 4JT
Brakspears. Jeremy J. Hunt, tenant

On what was an old drovers' road on the edge of Binfield Heath, a village between Henley-on-Thames and Reading – on the scenic route – you'll find this handsome, 15th-century, black and white thatched pub in a lovely garden. The interior of the Bottle & Glass is just as you hope it would be: flagged floors, antique tables, settles, large log fires in winter, a sense of well-being and a friendly ghost. The food is traditional; the portions generous – everything is prepared and cooked 'in house' from fresh ingredients: paté, Cumberland sausages, rump steak, mussels in garlic and fresh fish, also lunchtime sandwiches and other dishes. House specials change from day to day. Outside is a large garden with 24 tables, each with its own thatched canopy to protect you from the noon-day sun. Brakspears Best,

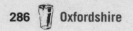

Special and seasonal ales on hand pump, three guests and a good choice of malt whiskies and wines.

OPEN: 11–3, 6–11. No food Sun eves.
Real Ale.
Children and dogs on leads in garden! Wheelchair access (not WC). There is a dining room you can hire for a private lunch or dinner.
Cards: Amex, MasterCard, Switch, Visa.

Bloxham

Elephant & Castle ① 01295 720383
Bloxham, nr Banbury OX15 4LZ
Hook Norton. Charles Finch, tenant
e-mail: elephant.bloxham@btinternet.com

Just a simple public bar, with a rather exceptional old fireplace, and a more comfortable lounge in the stone-built Elephant and Castle. Both have winter log fires and it's where they serve good, straightforward food: smoked haddock and leek chowder, minty lamb pie, Thai chicken, lasagne verde, three-bean chilli, cod in crispy batter and daily specials. In summer there are seats in the flower-filled courtyard. Hook Norton ales and a changing monthly guest beer from a small independent brewery. Good choice of malt whiskies.

OPEN: 11–3, 6–11. Sat 11–11. Sun 12–11.
Real Ale. No bar food evenings or Sunday.
Children in restaurant. Dogs on leads. Wheelchair access (not WC).
Cards: most except Amex and Diners.

Burford

Lamb ① 01993 823155
Sheep Street, Burford OX18 4LR
Free House. Ashley James, licensee
e-mail: info@lambinn-burford.co.uk

This hugely attractive town of honey-coloured stone houses, shops and inns on the river Windrush is the envy of many. You can watch the admiring crowds, glass in hand, from a bench outside the Lamb. You also get delicious food, a classical wine list and well-kept beers. Inside are flagstone floors, log fires, comfortably furnished bars and a pretty pillared restaurant. Since our last edition, new owners have taken over and there is a new, creative kitchen team in place. You can eat in the bar, lounge or restaurant. The lunch menu is seasonal and ranges from traditional to more contemporary dishes: crab and salmon fishcakes, guinea fowl and foie gras terrine with home-made piccalilli, Brixham cod fillet in a Hook Norton beer batter with fries and mushy peas, Oxfordshire beef and mushroom casserole with herb dumplings and creamed mash potatoes, warm rare roast beef salad with red onion and crispy bacon or poached salmon with avocado salsa and anchovy butter. Club sandwiches of smoked salmon with black olive tapenade and lemon dressing, also delicious puds to round off the meal. Wadworths 6X, Hook Norton Best, Badger Brewery Dorset Bitter on hand pump, plus Old Timer in winter. The wine list has many classical marques. Behind the inn is a courtyard and very attractive walled garden with plenty of seats and heaters.

OPEN: 11–2.30, 6–11. Open Christmas and New Year.
Real Ale. Restaurant.
Children welcome. Dogs too. Fifteen bedrooms – all en suite.
Cards: Delta, MasterCard, Switch, Visa.

Checkendon

Black Horse ① 01491 680418
Checkendon, nr Reading RG8 OTE
Free House. Martin & Margaret Morgan, owners/licensees

A traditional pub that has been in the same family for nearly a hundred years – unpretentious, basic, homely and welcoming. Nothing much has changed inside the Black Horse; beer is drawn from barrels in the still room just as it has always been. A good fire keeps you warm; freshly filled rolls keep hunger at bay, fresh coffee and West Berkshire's Good Old Boy, Old Father Thames and one other from this brewery will quench your thirst. You can sit outside in the pleasant garden and appreciate the unchanging quality of the place.

OPEN: 12–2 (Sat 12–3), 7–11 – roughly, flexible closing times.
Real Ale.
Children welcome – under control. Dogs? Yes-ish – do ask first. Car park. Wheelchair access (not WC).
No cards.

Chipping Norton

Chequers ① 01608 644717
Goddards Lane, Chipping Norton OX7 5NP
Fullers. Josh & Kay Reid, tenants

Bigger than it looks; from the outside you wouldn't think there was room for four different drinking areas and a no-smoking restaurant in what was an open courtyard. Next to the Victorian theatre, this is a well-run, friendly, old place with low ceilings, beams and winter log fires. Bar snacks and meals are served every day, the good-value food prepared from fresh, mainly local, ingredients; as well as soup of the day, well-filled sandwiches and ploughman's, there could be home-made vegetable spring rolls with a plum or chilli sauce, smoked chicken and avocado salad with croutons and a basil dressing, chargrilled steaks, braised English lamb shank on concannon mash with rosemary and redcurrant gravy with crispy parsnip shavings or roast salmon fillet on creamed spinach with a Welsh rarebit sauce served with new potatoes. Always a choice of fresh fish, and the excellent home-cooked ham pulls them in from miles around. On Sunday there is a traditional roast. Cask

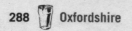

Marque accredited; the award-winning Fullers range of beers is very well kept; they also have a good small wine list, 14 available by the glass.

OPEN: 11–11.
Real Ale. No-smoking restaurant.
No children or dogs. Wheelchair access (not WC).
Cards: Delta, Switch, Visa.

Clifton

Duke of Cumberlands Head ① 018693 38534
Main Street, Clifton, nr Deddington OX15 0PE
Free House. Nick Huntington, licensee

A handsome 17th-century pub of honey-coloured stone. Thatched and beamed with huge fireplaces and a comfortable lounge bar, it's near the county boundary, in an area of considerable activity during the Civil War; tradition has it that some decisions on strategy were discussed in the pub. Now the important decisions centre round what to choose from the tempting, changing blackboard menu in the bar or the daily specials. Dishes vary but there could be a good home-made soup, avocado with prawns, tomato and feta cheese salad, Iverawe smoked trout, baked monkfish with garlic and almonds, Lancashire hotpot, pork Normandie, chicken korma, cottage pie and lots more as well as salads, vegetarian dishes and yummy puds. In the no-smoking restaurant the menu changes monthly. They serve a two- or three-course Sunday lunch. Good range of wines by the glass. Adnams, Hook Norton, Black Sheep and guest ales throughout the summer. Tables in the large garden with views over the surrounding countryside.

OPEN: 12–3, 6.30–11.
Real Ale. Restaurant.
Children until 9 p.m. Dogs on leads. Car park. Disabled facilities. All bedrooms en suite.
Cards: MasterCard, Switch, Visa.

Ducklington

Bell ① 01993 702514
Standlake Road, Ducklington, nr Witney OX8 7UP
Greene King. Danny Patching, tenant

A country pub that specialises in real ales, a wide choice of reasonably priced food and flower displays. They have been placed in the Pub in Bloom contest for many years, winning it too. A stone-built, mostly thatched pub, it has flagstones, stone walls, beams and bells. Obviously no piped music but as the Bell is the headquarters of the local Morris dancers, you may find them doing a practice session. From the daily changing menus a complete range of bar food is available, plus daily and weekly specials; an à la carte menu is served in the restaurant. Roast Sunday lunches – you must book. Always real ales: the Greene King range, Morlands Old Speckled Hen, Charles Wells Bombardier, Abbot Ale,

Triumph Bitter and others; also a full range of wines and spirits. The bedrooms are in a converted brewery and the water source that was used for brewing is still visible in the bar.

OPEN: 12–3, 6–11. Sat 12–11. Sun 12–10.30.
Real Ale. Restaurant.
Children welcome (well behaved and supervised). Dogs too. Car park. Wheelchair access into pub just possible (small steps). Seven en-suite bedrooms.
Cards: Delta, MasterCard, Switch, Visa.
Live folk music nights.

Great Tew

Falkland Arms ① 01608 683653
Great Tew OX7 4DB
Wadworth. Paul Barlow-Heal & S. J. Courage, licensees
e-mail: sjcourage@btconnect.com

Centuries old, the half-thatched, half-tiled, creeper-covered Falkland Arms is in a quiet, attractive village of honey-coloured stone and thatched cottages – mostly built in the 17th century. Inside the pub are shutters at the windows, huge timbers holding up beams, a great inglenook fireplace and more jugs and pots hanging from the beams than you could shake a fist at. Charming inside and out. Lunchtime food is ample and filling, plain and good: soups, shepherds pie, lasagne, filled jacket potatoes and lots of fillings for the baguettes. The evening menu, which changes daily, is more extensive and creative. Plenty of real ales to choose from, about eight on hand pump. Among them Henry's original IPA, Wadworths 6X, guest ales and Inch's cider. About 30 wines to choose from, half of which are English.

OPEN: 11.30–2.30, 6–11. Sun 12–3, 7–10.30. Summer Sat 11.30–11, Sun 12–10.30.
Real Ale. Bar food 12–2. No-smoking dining room.
Children in dining room at lunchtime. Dogs not in dining room! Wheelchair access (not WC). Six bedrooms.
Cards: Amex, Delta, MasterCard, Switch, Visa.
N.B. Evening music in dining room.

Hailey

King William IV ① 01491 681845
Hailey, nr Ipsden, Wallingford OX10 6AD
Brakspears. Neil Frankel, tenant

It's easy to mistake one place for another, especially when there are two Haileys in the same county. The other one is not far from Witney, but this is the one you want. It's a delightful, small, old-fashioned, 16th-century pub with beams and a big log fire in the traditionally furnished bar. Always two menus: the one on the specials board changes daily, depending on what is available from the market; the other on the blackboard stays more or less the same and includes steak pies, lemon sole fillets, poached salmon and sausages – good traditional fare. An extension gives extra dining space and there is a barbecue outside – weather permitting. Brakspears ales drawn from the casks, farm ciders and a new wine list. Wonderful views of the rolling countryside from the terrace.

OPEN: 11–2.30, 6–11.
Real Ale.
Children in eating area at lunchtime. Dogs on leads – they have to wipe their feet first – no muddy paws. Wheelchair access and facilities.

Moulsford

Beetle & Wedge ☉ 01491 651381
Ferry Lane, Moulsford, Oxon OX10 9JF
Free House. Richard & Kate Smith, licensees

A position to die for; a gloriously attractive hotel, wonderfully situated with pretty gardens running down to the water's edge. On the Thames, this exceptional place combines the informal atmosphere of the boathouse bar with the elegance of a well-run hotel. The author of *Three Men in a Boat*, Jerome K. Jerome, lived here and you can row in, and tie up too – the hotel has its own moorings. From there you can make for the beamed, old boathouse bar; in summer, the doors open onto the terrace, feet from the river. Only one ale served, but there is everything else you could possibly want to drink and a menu that's a pleasure to read. Among the delights you could choose home-cured gravadlax with blinis and creamy dill dressing, home-made duck terrine with warm toasted brioche and red onion compote or supreme of sesame chicken with wild mushrooms and creamy curry sauce, or from the charcoal grill fresh scallops with celeriac purée and balsamic vinegar, calves' liver and bacon or rump steak with wild mushroom sauce. Interesting and unusual cheeses, plus amazing puds. More formally you would make a beeline for the elegant dining room where each table has a view of the Thames. If you are looking for a very civilised day by the river, then this is the place to be. Only the finest, freshest, local produce is used in this very appealing riverside hotel. Wadworths 6X on hand pump. Extensive, mainly European wine list. For the truly energetic who want to work up an appetite for lunch, rowing boats are for hire nearby.

OPEN: 11.30–2.30, 6–11. N.B. You must reserve a table if you want to eat – it is very popular.
Restaurants: one no smoking.
Children welcome. No dogs. Wheelchair access. Ten en-suite bedrooms – some with river views.
Cards: Amex, Delta, Diners, MasterCard, Switch, Visa.

Oxford

Kings Arms ① 01865 242369
Holywell Street, Oxford OX1 3SP
Youngs. David Kyffin, manager

Slightly less crowded during the hols when the students are down, but there are always plenty of tourists and locals to keep them on their toes. An old 16th-century coaching inn surrounded by colleges, near the university library buildings and Blackwells bookshop; popular with members of the university, locals and cosmopolitan visitors. Very busy at lunchtime, but service is fast. Food ranges from predictable pub grub – home-made soups, sandwiches, filled rolls and an Oxford ploughman's featuring an award-winning local blue cheese – to a Kings Arms pie made with chicken and mushrooms cooked in Youngs oatmeal stout. Vegetarian dishes too, and specials on the blackboard. Youngs range of ales, Wadworths 6X, over 20 malt whiskies and a choice of over 20 wines by the glass, including champagne. Tables outside in summer so you can enjoy watching Oxford on the move.

OPEN: 10.30–11. Sun 12–10.30.
Real Ale. Dining room is no smoking.
Children and dogs welcome if accompanied by well-behaved people!

Rose and Crown ① 01865 510551
North Parade Avenue, Oxford OX2 6LX
Punch Pub Co. Deborah & Andrew Hall, tenants
e-mail: roseandcrown@ukonline.co.uk

An atmospheric, comfortable, traditional local built towards the end of the 19th century. No slouches though when it comes to the present day: a disapproving eye quickly settles on one of the scourges of the 21st century – the 'portable' phone as it is known here – and they're banned!. Any use or sight of one means a donation to charity, so you have been warned. Inside are three traditional rooms with a bar in two of them, a proper pub piano (in tune) and a friendly, popular landlord who has been here for more than 20 years. A substantial pub menu could list lots and lots of fillings for the baguettes, whole grilled trout, omelettes, gammon or rump steak, filled baked potatoes – all good and sustaining; they also serve a winter Sunday roast. Adnams Southwold Bitter, draught Bass, draught Guinness and draught lagers. Good range of wines and an interesting selection of alcohol-free drinks for all of us who drive. The large courtyard – with grapevine – at the back of the pub has a retractable awning – and big heaters which means it can be used all year.

OPEN: 10–3, 5–11. Sun 12–3, 7–10.30.
Real Ale.
Children: well-behaved, weekend lunchtimes only. No dogs. Most wheelchairs can get in (not WC). Cash machine.

Turf Tavern ① 01865 243235
4 Bath Place, off Holywell Street, Oxford OX1 3SU
Laurel Pub Co. Darren Kent, manager

There are many passageways and courtyards among the dreaming spires. Oxford is full of nooks and crannies, and this is a nook in the guise of an attractive courtyard in which you'll find the Turf – an ancient tavern with an enviable client list stretching over the centuries. Many famous people have crossed the threshold of this old place, among them William Shakespeare, Thomas Hardy, film stars Richard Burton and Elizabeth Taylor, and one American president – Bill Clinton. It was the late Inspector Morse's favourite town pub – and it should be one of yours. The Turf has two comfortable, low-beamed rooms and an ample supply of beer – known for always having five regular and between eight or nine different guest ales on offer. They will get through about 500 different beers in a year. The uncomplicated bar menu lists soup, sandwiches with various fillings, roasts, steak and mushroom and other pies, salads and a vegetarian dish or two. Seats in the courtyards which have heaters to keep you warm. The ales change all the time. Country wines and farm cider are also available. A beer festival is held from time to time.

OPEN: 11–11.
Real Ale.
Children in own room. Guide dogs only.

Ramsden

Royal Oak ① 01993 868213
High Street, Ramsden OX7 3AU
Free House. Jonathan Oldham, FBII, licensee

Here is everything you could wish for; an attractive listed building of honey-coloured Cotswold stone, with beams, comfortable furnishings and open fires, conveniently situated in the centre of the village opposite the war memorial and the village church. Importantly, the 17th-century Royal Oak is known for its first-rate ales and the excellence of its food. The owner and licensee of this unassuming old coaching inn is also a professional chef – a definite plus. The lunchtime bar menu lists sandwiches, ploughman's, smoked Scottish salmon with scrambled egg, baked avocado, cheese and prawn gratinée, fillet of Scottish salmon served with crevettes and lemon and lime velouté, chargrilled haunch of venison steak marinated in red wine served with a redberry sauce, Moroccan chicken tajine cooked with honey, dried fruit and capsicum served with couscous, a vegetarian dish or two, or even a special club sandwich. You can choose a dish from either the printed or blackboard menus and there will always be daily specials. Home-made puds too. Every Thursday they have a fixed-price steak night and on Sunday a three-course Sunday lunch. They use as much local produce as they can in the menus. Three cask-conditioned ales are on all the time: Hook Norton BB and two guests. Wide-ranging wine list. Seats in the sunny courtyard between the pub and four converted holiday cottages.

OPEN: 11.30–2.30, 6.30–11. Sun 12–3, 7–10.30.
Real Ale. Restaurant.
Children welcome. Dogs on leads. Car park. Wheelchair access. Four holiday cottages.
Cards: MasterCard, Switch, Visa.

Steeple Aston

Red Lion ① 018693 40225
South Side, Steeple Aston OX6 3RY
Free House. Colin Mead, licensee

There are two Lions in the village, so don't get confused – the other is of a totally different hue: white. The desirable Red Lion is a pub whose customers have, among other things, a serious interest in crosswords; reference books abound. So, not only a varied collection of books and someone to discuss them with and help with the crossword, but newspapers too, and to round it off, well-kept beer and a decent glass of wine. Bar food is limited to lunchtimes only: home-made soups, ploughman's with local cheeses, sandwiches, winter hotpots and summer salads. There's a more ambitious and creative menu in the evening restaurant. No food at all on Sunday, which makes the Red Lion is a proper pub – a place to go and have a leisurely drink before wending your way home for lunch – just as it should be. Hook Norton Bitter and guest beers only. Over 100 wines are kept; the landlord is very keen on his wines and keeps an interesting, inimitable cellar. Seats on the sunny terrace at the front of the pub among the flowers.

OPEN: 11–3, 6–11. Lunchtime meals & snacks (not Sun).
Real Ale. Evening restaurant (closed Sun & Mon).
Children in restaurant. Dogs on leads.

Swinbrook

Swan Inn ① 01993 822165
Swinbrook, nr Burford OX18 4DY
Free House. Mr & Mrs A. Morris, licensees
e-mail: andy@swaninnox18.freeserve.co.uk

An appealing village with a delightful 15th-century inn close to the bridge over the Windrush river. Soon to disappear under the creeper, this unspoilt and unchanging little pub is traditionally furnished with stone-flagged floors and winter fires. Only a small bar but they seem to have no difficulty in packing in locals and the serious walkers. Home-cooked bar food and a more ambitious evening menu. The home-made steak and kidney pie is very popular at lunchtime. So are the creamy seafood tagliatelle, English lamb cutlets with onions in a mint and cranberry sauce, fish, salads, omlettes and filled baguettes; in the evening there is pork tenderloin pan-fried in butter and onions served with sweet apricot, cider and ginger, or fillet steak served just as you like it. The specials and puddings are on the blackboards. Archers of Swindon, Wadworths 6X, Morlands Bitter and cider from Somerset. Benches outside – muddy boots outside too. There is a lovely walk along a grassy slope of the river valley, from Swinbrook church – Mitford graves here – to the church at Widford which is built over Roman remains.

OPEN: 11.30–3, 6.30–11.
Real Ale.
Children welcome. Dogs on leads. Wheelchair access (not WC). No dirty boots in dining room.
Cards: MasterCard, Switch, Visa.

Whitchurch on Thames

Greyhound ① 01189 842160
High Street, Whitchurch on Thames, nr Reading RG8 7EL
Pubmaster. Stuart Brackley-Pattison, licensee

This pretty, white-painted little town pub, not far from the river, serves good, freshly cooked food in the comfortable bar. Always well-filled sandwiches, ploughman's, Stilton and chestnut paté with hot toast, variety of salads, Cromer crab salad in summer, steak, ale and mushroom pie, pork ribs in barbecue sauce, a pasta dish, cottage pie, pizzas, filled jacket potatoes and comforting puds. Well-kept Flowers Original, Greene King IPA, Marstons Pedigree, Charles Wells Bombardier, Strongbow Cider and three lagers. Pleasant garden to sit in and some good walks.

OPEN: 12–3, 6–11 (Sun 7–10.30).
Real Ale.
Children in garden. Dogs on leads. Wheelchair access.
Cards: Electron, MasterCard, Solo, Switch, Visa.

Wootton by Woodstock

Kings Head Inn ① 01993 811340
Chapel Hill, Wootton OX20 1DX
Free House. Tony & Amanda Fay, licensees
e-mail: t.fay@kings-head.co.uk

There is now a no-smoking policy throughout this 17th-century stone village pub. Inside is well beamed, with a big log fire and comfortable sofas and settles. You can eat in the bar or in the more formal restaurant. Bar snacks – available at lunchtime only – are on a separate slateboard, as are the fresh fish dishes, but from the menu you could choose a home-made soup, paté of fresh marinaded olives wrapped in Waberthwaite ham with an antipasto of roasted peppers, baby artichokes and caperberries with a bramble dressing, warm Gressingham duck salad with a cordon of spicy plum purée sauce and for a main course chargrilled medallions of pork fillet on a bed of red onion marmalade with an orange and juniper-berry sauce or vegetable Mediterraneo – roasted tomatoes, grilled artichokes, olives, peppers and mushrooms served with couscous and creamy goat's cheese. Much more on the dinner menu plus English and Irish cheeses and maybe caramelised citrus tart or icky sticky toffee pudding with vanilla ice cream to finish. Ruddles Best and Wadworths 6X on hand pump, good wine list and a wine board listing 'wines of the month'. Tables in the garden.

OPEN: 12–2.30, 6.45–11. Closed Mon and Sun eve.
Real Ale. Restaurant.
No children under 10. Guide dogs only. Wheelchair access (not WC). Bedrooms.
Cards: MasterCard, Visa.

Wytham

White Hart ① 01865 244372
Wytham, nr Oxford OX2 8QA
Free House. David Peevers, chef/proprietor

Renovated since our last edition; they kept all the best bits and added a touch of the 21st century. In a village of thatched stone houses overlooking the River Thames, this attractive, old creeper-covered pub also featured in *Inspector Morse* episodes, one of his country pubs. Inside is a part-panelled bar with flagstone floors and an open fire. With the renovations has come the great leap forward in the food department; the dishes are modern British with un peu Français and un poco di Italiano. Bar food includes hot foccacia sandwiches with a variety of fillings served with fries and a salad, confit of belly pork salad with tempura of leeks with hoi sin dressing, spinach and Gruyère cheese tart, walnut and radiccio salad, tomato and tarragon dressing, and for a main course wild mushroom risotto with rocket and parmesan biscuit, Aberdeen Angus fillet with fondant potatoes, tapenade, tomato confit, mushroom, crispy bacon and mustard jus; puddings and French and Italian cheeses. Fish and specials are on the slateboards. Most of the food is prepared to order. Adnams Bitter, Morlands Old Speckled Hen, a guest every two weeks and Tetleys Smooth Flow beers – these do change. Seats in the very lovely walled garden. The village is totally owned by Oxford University.

OPEN: 12–3, 6–11. Sat 12–11. Sun 12–10.30. Summer 11.30–11 (Sun 12–10.30).
Real Ale. Food served every day.
Children in own room. Dogs on leads in garden.

BEST OF THE REST

Blewbury
Blewbury Inn ① 01235 850496
London Road, Blewbury OX11 9PD
If you're walking the downs the 17th-century half-timbered Red Lion, on the outskirts of this peaceful downland village, is a good place to start from. If you want to eat well, it is certainly the place to be. From the short, very desirable menu there could be a velouté of leeks with saffron cream and roasted monkfish or traditional French country paté with a salad of green beans tossed with trompet mushrooms and pears flambéed in Armagnac; for a main course, roast fillet of sea bass with oyster mushrooms and sweetcorn risotto, shellfish and basil cream, or supreme of braised chicken wrapped in pancetta on a bed of green asparagus, sun-dried tomato and parmesan risotto in light cider cream – and to finish, home-made tarte tatin with cinnamon ice cream and caramelised passionfruit sauce. Fullers London Pride and Hook Norton beers. Good choice of wine. Seats in the garden. Children in eating areas only. Dogs in the garden. Full wheelchair facilities. Bed and breakfast.
Open: 11–2.30, 6–11 (Sun 7–10.30).

Buckland Marsh

Trout at Tadpole Bridge ① 01387 870382

Buckland Marsh, nr Faringdon SN7 8RF

A tiny hamlet, a bridge over the Thames and the Trout. Find the river and there's the pub. Small, no excesses in the interior decoration line but the beer's well kept: Fullers London Pride and Archers Village Bitter and summer guests, a very comprehensive wine list and some really inventive, worthwhile food: game paté, home-smoked pigeon breast with a celeriac salad, and whole roast partridge served with cherry onions, smoked bacon and almond potato gives you a flavour of what you can expect. Children allowed, dogs too; you can moor your boat, fish – with permission – and you can stay – there are six bedrooms. Open: 11.30–3, 6–11.30. Closed winter Sun eves Sep–Easter.

Chadlington

Tite Inn ① 01608 676475

Mill End, Chadlington OX7 3NY

A 17th-century stone pub, on the very edge of the village, in its own little valley. The unusual name comes from the spring that feeds the trough (in past times the only water supply) at the front of the pub. Past times manifest themselves in the cosy bar and cellars too – the oldest bits of the pub – where a female ghost roams. Otherwise all is warm and friendly, with winter log fires and mulled wine and good food. There are lunch and evening menus. Sandwiches at lunchtime, as well as lamb and apricot pie, caramelised onion and goat's cheese tart. In the evening, possibly a mixed seafood salad or boeuf bourgignon. Well-kept Archers Village, Charles Wells Bombardier, guest beers, draught cider and a wide-ranging wine list. Children, dogs and wheelchairs – all can get in. Open: 12–2.30, 6.30–11. Closed Mon except bank holidays.

Clifton Hampden

Barley Mow ① 01865 407847

Clifton Hampden, nr Abingdon OX14 3EH

Low thatch outside, low beams inside. This is a very old building with origins in the 14th century. Near the river and the old ferry crossing, the inn is the same Barley Mow highly praised in Jerome K. Jerome's book *Three Men in a Boat*, a rambling, cosy old place serving good food. You make your choice from the daily changing boards; fresh fish the speciality. Courage Best and Directors and a good wine list. Seats in the riverside garden. Open: 11–11.

Fifield

Merrymouth ① 01993 831652

Fifield, nr Burford OX7 6HR

Take a right turn off the A424 from Burford, and don't confuse this Fifield with Fyfield just over the border in Gloucestershire. The very ancient stone-built pub – the building was mentioned in the Domesday Book – has a welcoming, beamed bar where they serve freshly made bar food as well as some imaginative dishes and home-made puds – you won't be disappointed. Hook Norton Best, a guest and a small, decent wine list. Children in the eating area, dogs on leads, bedrooms. Open: 12–3, 6–10.30 (Sat 6–11).

Finstock

Plough Inn ① 01993 868333
The Bottom, Finstock OX7 3BY
This is just the place for dogs and their minders; there are entertaining resident dogs
waiting to greet you and lots of good walks from a pub run by very doggy people. This
thatched village pub has a rambling, beamed bar, a log-burning stove in the big inglenook
fireplace, comfortable furnishings, doggy bits and pieces and a no-smoking dining room.
Bar food could include grilled bass, crab and avocado gratin, vegetarian pie, steaks and
home-baked ham. Their speciality is a steak, mushroom and stout pie with a crusty top.
Marstons Pedigree, Hook Norton Best, Morlands Old Speckled Hen, Timothy Taylors
Landlord, Fullers London Pride, Draught Guinness, Scrumpy Jack cider and guest beers.
Farm ciders, choice of wines and a range of malt whiskies. Tables outside in the garden full
of wonderfully scented, old-variety roses. Children welcome. Dogs on leads. One letting
bedroom. Music in public bar, but not in restaurant.
Open: 12–3, 6–11. Sat 11–11. Sun 12–4, 7–10.30.

Maidensgrove

Five Horseshoes ① 01491 641282
Maidensgrove RG9 6EX
Surrounded by glorious Chiltern beechwoods, the Five Horseshoes caters very sensibly for
all serious walkers – who have been given their own bar so they can keep their boots on. In
the rest of the pub they welcome travellers all (as you can see from the bank-notes stuck to
the ceiling). Quite a foody place where you can choose from the printed menu or the daily
changing blackboard specials: home-made soups, stuffed pancakes, warm salad of scampi
and crab, lamb braised in a provençale sauce, delicious puds. Brakspear ales and an
extensive wine list. Children in eating area and dogs on leads.
Open: 11.30–2.30, 6–11.

Shipton-under-Wychwood

Shaven Crown Hotel ① 01993 830330
High Street, Shipton-under-Wychwood OX7 6BA
Full of history, it was built in the 14th century as the hospice for the nearby Bruern Abbey,
later used as a hunting lodge serving the Wychwood. It's built around a medieval
courtyard garden where you can sit enjoying a drink or meal on a summer's day. The
original hall with its double-collar braced roof, still in perfect condition after 600 years, is
worth admiring. In the beamed Monk's bar you'll find a wide choice of bar snacks:
sandwiches, baguettes and wraps, kidneys, bacon and field mushrooms on toast, deep-
fried Camembert with Cumberland sauce, breast of duck with sage and plum sauce, lamb
shank with rosemary and garlic, poached salmon with a prawn and white wine sauce and
much more. Vegetarian dishes and puddings too. Hook Norton beer and a varying wine
list. Children welcome, but none under 5 in evening. No dogs. Wheelchair access. Cards:
all except Diners.
Open 12–2.30, 5–11. Sat 11.30–11. Sun 12–10.30.

Wetherspoon in Oxfordshire

Banbury – Exchange, 49–50 High Street
01295 259035
Bicester – Penny Black, 58 Sheep Street
01869 321535
Oxford – William Morris, 4 Pound Way, Cowley
01865 335950

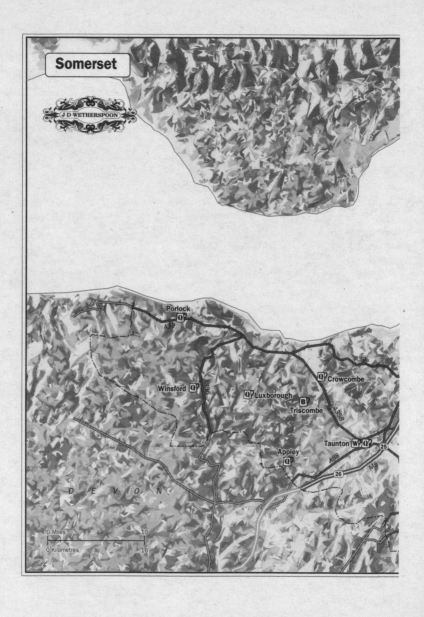

Somerset

J·D·WETHERSPOON

Porlock
A39

Winsford

A396

Luxborough

Crowcombe

A39

Triscombe

A358

Appley

Taunton

25

A38

26

M5

D E V O N

0 Miles 10
0 Kilometres 16

Somerset

Appley

Globe ✆ 01823 672327
Appley, Wellington TA21 0HJ
Free House. A. W. & E. J. Burt, licensees

Near the Somerset/Devon border, the isolated but hugely popular 500-year-old Globe is to be treasured. Drive to the pub along seemingly endless country lanes, through rolling countryside and scattered hamlets and farms. Inside the pub, cosy rooms lead off a brick corridor where there's a serving hatch for the beers. You'll find good home-made food on the bar menu: fish soup with chunks of fresh fish cooked in white wine, saffron and garlic; smoked haddock and bacon chowder, gravadlax served with fresh dill, mustard and brandy dressing, and for the main course a home-made steak and kidney pie cooked in stout with a puff-pastry top. Add to that casseroled venison with bacon, mushrooms, shallots, garlic, tomato and red wine; a vegetarian pasta, seafood pancake and lots more; daily specials and great puds too. Cotleigh Tawny is the main beer with local guests. Local cider too during the summer. Climbing frames, swings and things to keep the little darlings happy. This is a very busy place.

OPEN: 11–3, 6.30–11. Sun 12–3, 7–10.30. Closed Mon except bank holidays.
Real Ale. Restaurant.
Children in eating areas. No dogs.
Cards: MasterCard, Switch, Visa.

Axbridge

Lamb Inn ✆ 01934 732253
The Square, Axbridge BS26 2AP
Free House. Alan Currie, manager

Bypassed by the main road from Wells to the coast, the ancient town of Axbridge is now delightfully quiet. A borough before 1066, the town is full of historic buildings, many in The Square. Opposite the late 15th-century, heavily timbered and jettied King John's Hunting Lodge, which incidentally had nothing to do with King John, is the 15th-century Lamb, disguised by a Georgian frontage. Until the new Town Hall was built in 1830, this was the town's Guildhall; it then became the Holy Lamb Inn – now just the Lamb. Heavily beamed inside with a huge fireplace, the bar is a 'one-off', built entirely of bottles! This is a tremendously popular place where they serve some reasonably priced bar food: filled jacket potatoes, lunchtime baguettes and sandwiches, home-made soup of the day, deep-fried whitebait, smoked trout and prawns with a mixed salad of leaves, home-made beef and Butcombe pie (prime local beef cooked in Butcombe ale under a pastry crust), poached smoked haddock in a butter sauce and daily specials such as pork fillet in cider and apple or chicken breast filled with brie and cranberry. Every Tuesday and Thursday there is a very reasonable two-course senior citizens' lunch. Beers are Butcombe Gold, Bitter and a changing weekly guest. Seats in the small sheltered garden

OPEN: Mon–Wed 11.30–3, 6–11. Thurs–Sat 11.30–11. Sun 12–10.30.
Real Ale. No food Sun eve.
Children welcome, dogs too – in certain areas. Wheelchair access (not WC).
Cards: Amex, MasterCard, Switch, Visa.

Batcombe

Three Horseshoes ① 01749 850359
Batcombe, nr Frome, Somerset BA4 6HE
Silver Haven Group. David Benson, licensee

Giving directions to a sleepy village deep in the countryside is a little difficult when you don't know which direction they're coming from, but if you're heading north-west from Bruton, it's left off the A359. It's easy when you do reach the village: find the church and the pub is next to it. Built in about 1600 of local stone, it's full of atmosphere, and the interior is warm, comfortable and pleasing. Food is good and popular but there is still a welcome for anyone just wanting to lean on the bar for a drink. All dishes are on blackboards and supplemented by daily specials. Butcombe, Adnams and Wadworths 6X are the beers; wines are mainly French with a touch of the New World. Over ten wines by the glass. Tables in the garden where there is a children's play area.

OPEN: 12–3, 6.30–11. Sun 7–10.30.
Real Ale. Restaurant.
Children welcome, dogs too. Car park. Wheelchair access.
Cards: Delta, MasterCard Switch, Visa.

Bath

Old Green Tree ① 01225 448259
12 Green Street, Bath BA1 2JE
Free House. Nick Luke & Tim Bethune, licensees

In the town centre, contemporary with the development of Bath during the 18th century, this small town pub can be traced back to 1752. With a panelled interior, this is a delightful place; very popular, particularly at lunchtime, the only time food is available. A familiar short menu lists well-filled Green Tree rolls, good-sized ploughman's with home-made chutney, home-made soup, paté, curries, sausages and mash, seafood platter, salads and daily specials of freshly cooked seasonal dishes are all listed on blackboards. Breweries – within a radius of 100 miles – supply the six ales, the choice varying considerably. There are also a number of unusual wines. Pimms is served during the summer; hot punch in winter.

OPEN: 11–11. Sun 12–10.30.
Real Ale. Lunchtime meals and snacks.
Children over 10 if eating at lunchtime only. No dogs.
No cards.

Star ① 01225 425072
23 The Vineyards, Bath BA1 5NA
Punch. Terry Langley & Julie Schofield, managers

Now it's recovered from the hiccoughs it had about five years ago – when managers were
in and out like a frantic cuckoo clock – we can bring the Star back into the fold. A classic,
200-year-old town pub near Guinea Lane, off The Paragon, it's an acquired taste; no
unnecessary changes have taken place and it's much the same as it has been for very many
years, which is part of its charm. Inside are small, interconnecting rooms served by one
bar, where you can get a pint of very well-kept beer and a filled roll or two to keep hunger
at bay. They always have excellent Bass from the barrel; the others are Adnams Bitter, Black
Sheep, Charles Wells Bombardier and Abbey Bellringer.

OPEN: 12–2.30, 5.30–11. Sat 12–11. Sun 12–10.30.
Real Ale.
No children. Dogs welcome.

Bristol

Commercial Rooms ① 01179 279681
43–45 Corn Street, Bristol BS1 1HT
Wetherspoon

Sensitively converted and lovingly restored into the place you see today, this impressive
building was a local businessmen's club in the centre of the city. The Grand Coffee Room,
which had been used for coffee auctions, is the main drinking area. Two no-smoking
rooms are at the end of the bar. Six cask-conditioned beers at all times – Youngers Scotch
Bitter, Courage Directors, Theakston Best, XB, Wadworths 6X and a local regional beer.
Guest beers from the smaller breweries. Reliable bar food, with a choice of daily specials, is
served all day.

OPEN: 11–11. Sun 12–10.30.
Real Ale.
No children. No dogs, except guide dogs.

Highbury Vaults ① 01179 733203
164 St Michael's Hill, Kingsdown, Bristol BS2 8DE
Youngs. Bradd Francis, manager

Unsurprisingly, as the university campus backs on to St Michael's Hill, this is a popular
place for students and lecturers to hang out, a Georgian pub with a later interior and a
timeless and appealing atmosphere. The bars you see on the windows are from the years
this old place served time as part of the local jail. Inside is an intimate snug with a bigger,
cosy bar at the back from where you can glimpse the flowery, secluded garden; a favourite
place at all times. Reasonably priced traditional bar food changes daily. All dishes are
freshly cooked and might include a spinach and mushroom lasagne, pork and apples in
cider or a lamb and rosemary casserole. No fried food and no chips with anything. Youngs
range of ales include the seasonal Waggledance or Winterwarmer, Smiles Best, Heritage

and Brains S.A. Seats in the terrace garden which is heated in winter. Blissfully free of jukeboxes and fruit machines.

OPEN: 12–11.
Real Ale. No food Sat or Sun eves.
Children welcome until 9 p.m. Dogs only in the front bar.

Churchill

Crown Inn ➀ 01934 852995
The Batch, Skinners Lane, Churchill BS25 5PP
Free House. Tim Rogers, licensee

A village of stone houses, it takes its name from Churchill Court, a grand ancestral home of the Marlboroughs and of course Winston Churchill. Humbler, but more important to us, is the small, stone, 16th-century Crown Inn; two bars, delightfully unspoilt, with beams, stone and slate floors and open fires – all that you would expect. They serve simple, home-made bar food: soups, ploughman's, sandwiches, seasonal main courses and comforting puddings to go with some unusual beers. Draught Bass and Palmers IPA as well as constantly changing guests. If you're here in summer, you could well be entertained by the local Morris Men. Seats on the attractive front terrace and at the back of the pub. At the base of the Mendip Hills, this is a good walking area.

OPEN: 11–11. Sun 12–10.30.
Real Ale.
Children in eating area. Dogs in garden.

Combe Hay

Wheatsheaf ➀ 01225 833504
Combe Hay, nr Bath BA2 7EG (off the A367 Exeter road out of Bath)
Free House. Richard Allsworth, licensee

Winding, overgrown lanes through wooded valleys lead to the charms of Combe Hay and the Wheatsheaf. A track at the back of the pub takes you on a short, circular walk past farms and back to the village. Inside the black and white 17th-century pub are cosy low-ceilinged rooms, country furnishings, a big log fire in winter and a comprehensive blackboard menu. As well as the familiar bar snacks, there are some interesting dishes; under the new licensee their speciality is vegetarian food, for which they have won The Guardian Award. Home-made puddings and a full à la carte menu. Courage Best and Morlands Old Speckled Hen as the guest beer. Seats in the terraced garden – full of summer colour. Good walks and views over the peaceful valley.

OPEN: 11–3, 6.30–11. Sat & Sun 11–10.30.
Real Ale. Restaurant. Barbecue.
Children welcome. Dogs on leads. Wheelchair access to all parts of pub with a bit of help. Three en-suite bedrooms.

Compton Martin

Ring O' Bells ① 01761 221284
Compton Martin, nr Bath BS18 6JE
Free House. Roger Owen, licensee

There is so much to do and see in the area that this place is popular in all seasons – a rambling, white-painted stone building with a flagstone floor and a big log fire in the bar, carpet in the dining room, toys and a rocking horse in the family room. A traditional menu of pub favourites: sandwiches, ploughman's, filled jacket potatoes, beef in ale, grills and lasagne plus some original specials. Roast lunches on Sundays. Wadworths 6X, Butcombe Bitter and Gold plus a guest. Thatchers local cider on draught and a short list of wines to try. Seats in the garden among the apple trees, and a play area for children. Lots of things to do around here: caves to explore, Blagdon and Chew Valley Lakes to admire, not to mention the Devil's Punchbowl – a significant 'swallet', a hole in the limestone that temporarily swallows up streams.

OPEN: 11–3, 6.30–11. Sun 11.30–3, 6.30–10.30.
Real Ale. Restaurant.
Children in family room. Dogs away from eating areas. Car park. Wheelchair access (not WC).
Cards: all major cards.

Croscombe

Bull Terrier ① 01749 343658
Croscombe, nr Wells BA4 4QJ
Free House. Barry Vidler, licensee
e-mail: barry.vidler@bullterrierpub.co.uk

Thickly wooded hills shelter this unspoilt village and historic pub. At the front is a medieval cross and at the back the village church – an unsurprising religious embrace as this building was originally the priory and home of the Abbot of Glastonbury. The core of the building is late 15th century and the licence was granted in 1612, making it one of the county's oldest pubs. Three bars inside: the inglenook lounge still has its original 16th-century beamed ceiling, and a no-smoking family room. Bar food ranges from ploughman's, filled sandwiches (plain and toasted), home-made paté and vegetarian dishes to fillet steak, chicken and mushrooms in a tarragon sauce, gammon steak, home-made steak and kidney pie, salads and specials such as lemon sole with a crab and seafood sauce. Good puddings. Varying ales, but mainly Bull Terrier Best Bitter brewed for the pub; also Butcombe Bitter, Greene King Abbot, Theakstons XB and Smiles Best. Local cider and a good wine list. The walled garden backs onto the village church and – continuing the ecclesiastical theme – a footpath from the village leads to the Bishop's Palace in Wells.

OPEN: 12–2.30, 7–11. Closed winter Mons.
Real Ale. No food winter Sun eves or all day Mon.
Children in family room. Dogs: if they like the look of them. Wheelchair access (not WC).
Cards: Delta, MasterCard, Solo, Switch, Visa.

Crowcombe

Carew Arms ① 01984 618631
Crowcombe, Taunton TA4 4AD
Free House. R. A. & S. A. Abrose, licensees
e-mail: info@thecarewarms.co.uk

Pastures, moorland and gentle, wooded hills surround this Quantocks pub at the bottom of a very steep incline. Attractive and unspoilt, this 17th-century building, with flagstone floors, old benches and a massive inglenook fireplace, reflects the history of this wonderful old place. Here you will find good food – using much locally grown produce – at sensible prices. All the food is freshly cooked: home-made soup, interesting fillings for the sandwiches, roasted cherry tomato, aubergine bruschetta, eggs Benedict, tortellini of langoustine with lobster sauce, venison sausages, mustard mash and braised onions, salmon fishcakes with lemon butter sauce and tagliatelle, wild mushrooms and pine kernels in a creamy sauce. Exmoor Ale from the barrel is always available, one guest and a local cider. Ales are kept to a very high standard. The old skittle alley is now the garden-room bar and restaurant; a new skittle alley has been created for the keen players. There is a large south-facing garden to enjoy on a warm, sunny day. The whole area is a mecca for walkers, so walkers and their dogs are encouraged – the flagstone floor is muddy feet- and boot-friendly.

OPEN: 11.30–3, 6–11. Sun 12–3, 7–11. Closed Sun eves during the winter. No food Sun eves.
Real Ale.
Well-behaved children. Dogs: yes, encouraged. Car park. Wheelchair access – just. Three reasonably priced bedrooms, all en suite. New skittle alley.
N.B. Live music events, mostly in the evening but also Sun lunchtime.

Doulting Beacon

Waggon & Horses ① 01749 880302
Frome Road, Doulting Beacon, Shepton Mallet BA4 4LA
Ushers. Francisco Cardona, lease
e-mail: e-mail@the-waggon-and-horses.co.uk

This isn't just a pub but a place for events, many of them musical. The walls of the pub are used as a gallery by a number of local artists, works are for sale and the turnover is quite brisk on concert nights. The old beamed meeting room, reached by an outside staircase, has been converted into an art gallery, concert hall – with concert grand – and function room. Señor Cardona is an enthusiast about horses, art, music and of course this wonderful old coaching inn. Inside the pub is a comfortable, rambling beamed bar with big log fires where they serve quite delicious food; a combination of Central European, Mediterranean, Latin American and the best of British – prime Scottish beef and lots of fresh fish and game. You can always order a sandwich or filled baguette or you could start with a salad of smoked ostrich and smoked duck, crab cakes with ginger and chilli or Greek salad, followed by breast of chicken in white wine, cream and tarragon sauce or salmon fishcakes with dill mayonnaise, and a steamed ginger and lemon pudding to finish. As a special treat, if there are four of you, a paella can be ordered in advance. The daily changing specials board reflects the seasons and availability of produce. Two real ales from

Ushers, Blackthorn cider, Murphy's stout and Somerset Royal Cider Brandy. There is a short cocktail list, a modest number of wines including French, local whites, New World, champagne and sparkling. Outside is a delightful, well-planted walled garden, Señor Cardona's pride and joy; also exotic chickens – for the eggs – waiting to be admired. If you want to celebrate in a very special way, they will even arrange a concert just for you. As one of the original 12 pubs chosen to launch the Prince of Wales' 'The Pub is the Hub' initiative, the Waggon and Horses was honoured by a special visit by Prince Charles in July 2003. The Royal Standard was flown above the door and a wonderful time was had by all.

OPEN: 11–3, 6–11. Sun 12–3, 7–10.30.
Real Ale.
Children if very good. Dogs if under control. Big car park to turn a horse box or two.
Wheelchair access.
Cards: MasterCard, Switch, Visa.

East Woodlands

Horse & Groom ① 01373 462802
East Woodlands, nr Frome BA11 5LY
Longleat Estate. Kathy Barrett, licensee
e-mail: horseandgroom@care4free.net

Just two miles from Frome, a country pub in a farming community on the edge of the Longleat estate. Inside is a cosy, flagstoned bar with an open fire and chatty customers, a comfortable lounge and big restaurant/conservatory. All the food is home-cooked and from the bar menu there could be 'Jockey Specials', a tremendous number of fillings for the baguettes, ploughman's and salads or home-made soup of the day, demon prawns, smoked salmon, Yorkshire pudding with roast beef of sausages in onion gravy, savoury spring roll on stir-fried vegetables, omelettes, curry dish of the day, Mediterranean roast vegetable pasta with melted Stilton or battered cod fillet with chips and peas; a favourite is the freshly cooked liver, bacon and onions in a rich gravy. Always inspired vegetarian dishes and daily specials. Beers are Butcombe Bitter, Wadworths 6X, Branscombe Vale Branoc and guests. Wines by the glass. Seats at the front of the pub and in the award-winning garden.

OPEN: 11.30–2.30, 6.30–11. Sun 12–3, 7–10.30. Closed Mon lunch.
Real Ale. No food Sun or Mon eve.
Children under control welcome in lounge and restaurant. Dogs on leads. Wheelchair access.
Cards: all major credit and debit cards.

Faulkland

Tuckers Grave ① 01373 834230
Faulkland, nr Bath BA3 5XF
Free House. Ivan & Glenda Swift, licensees

Only three little rooms in this very traditional cider house; small, unspoilt and basic, but friendly and welcoming, it has been here for centuries serving the local community. Casks of Bass and Butcombe Bitter where you can see them, also Cheddar Valley cider. A fire to keep you warm in winter, a skittle alley for fun, seats in the garden for relaxation and a ploughman's or sandwich at lunchtime.

OPEN: 11–3, 6–11.
Real Ale. No food Sun.
Children welcome. No dogs. Wheelchair access.

Huish Episcopi

Rose & Crown ☎ 01458 250494
Huish Episcopi, Langport TA10 9PU
Free House. Mrs Eileen Pittard, licensee

An unchanging place, this is how the inside of pubs looked for hundreds of years before they created bars to lean on and keep customers a beer pump away. Two small rooms and a flagstoned central still room where they'll take time to draw a perfect pint of beer, cider or stout from the cask and a new games room with a jukebox – well away from the hub of the pub. This is a very welcoming place. Food is good simple fare, all home-made: soup, sandwiches, plain or toasted, ploughman's, steak and ale pie, pork, apple and cider cobbler, vegetable lasagne, Stilton, broccoli and caramelised onion tart, cauliflower cheese and daily specials, delicious home-made puds too. Roast Sunday lunch. Always Teignworthy and three guest ales. Julian Temperley's Burrow Hill Cider (he also makes Somerset Cider Royal Brandy). Tables in the garden; children have a separate play area. Good walks nearby. If you're trying to find the pub, you might have to ask the way to Eli's, after Mrs Pittard's father; the name 'Eli' is in brackets on the inn sign. The pub has been run by the same family for 140 years; even longer if you count the landlady before Mrs Pittard's grandfather, as she was a distant relation.

OPEN: 11.30–2.30, 5.30–11. Fri & Sat 11.30–11. Sun 12–10.30.
Real Ale.
Children welcome. Dogs allowed.

Kelston

Old Crown ☎ 01225 423032
Bath Road, Kelston, nr Bath BA1 9AQ
Butcombe Brewery. Chris Cole, licensee

You'll find the Old Crown a ten-minute car ride – traffic permitting – out of Bath on the busy road to Bristol. A well-run, traditional pub, a favourite with walkers on the Cotswold Way, with four small rooms with polished flagstone floors, hop bines hanging from the beams and good fires. There are two bars and two small attractive dining rooms. Bar food ranges from the usual sandwiches and filled rolls and jacket potatoes to deep-fried crab and coriander cakes, Ardennes paté, Butcombe beef casserole, lasagne al forno, broccoli and brie rösti, country vegetable and cheese cakes; there is also a daily changing specials board. Well-kept ales include Bass, Butcombe Gold, Wadworths 6X and Bath Gem. Tables under the apple trees in the orchard at the back of the building. You have to watch your step when you visit this old pub, as the car park is on the other side of the road.

OPEN: 11.30–2.30, 5–11. Sat 11–11. Sun 12–10.30.
Real Ale. Restaurant (closed Sun and Mon eves).
No children under 14 except in garden. Dogs on leads in pub and garden. Four en-suite bedrooms in an annexe next to, and owned by, the pub.

Litton

Kings Arms ➀ 01761 241301
Litton BA3 4PW
Free House. Alex Meikle, licensee

Bigger than it looks, the rambling, mostly 15th-century Kings Arms is heavily beamed, with polished flagstones, traditional furnishings and a huge fireplace, a picture-book pub filled with affable conversation. There's quite a concentration of food from an extensive menu which lists ploughman's, smoked mackerel, whitebait, garlic crevettes, crispy sweetcorn and lots more for starters; then a choice of fish platters, six different fish dishes, salad snacks and even a slimline platter or sandwiches. The beers are beautifully kept and served at near room temperature: Bass, Courage Best and Wadworths 6X. As well as a large family room there is lots of play equipment in the gardens – everything to keep the children happy and out of the pub.

OPEN: 11–2.30, 6–11.
Real Ale.
Children in own room. Dogs welcome.
Cards: all major cards accepted.

Luxborough

Royal Oak ➀ 01984 640319
Luxborough, nr Dunster, Exmoor National Park TA23 0SH
Free House. James Waller, licensee

This is an area of steep valleys, pastures and heathland. By a stream at the bottom of a valley in the Bredon Hills you'll find the 14th-century Royal Oak, an unspoilt, partly thatched country pub with heavily beamed bars, flagged floors, inglenook fireplaces and an assortment of country furniture as well as two beckoning dining rooms – one no smoking. Bar snacks, all good, hearty cooking, range from home-made soup to a bowl of mussels steamed with lemon grass and black beans, carpaccio of tuna with guacamole and parsley, salad of rocket, quails' eggs and watercress, roast tail of monkfish, steamed fillet of sea bass, loin of lamb baked with mint and yoghurt crust, sirloin of beef or something from the specials board which may have game pies or venison. Home-made puds and local cheeses to follow. Roast lunches on Sunday. Cotleigh Tawny and Thatchers Cheddar Valley are among the ales; also Palmers 200 as a guest beer and Rich's Farmhouse Cider. Good list of wines. Seats outside in the garden. Surrounded as you are by wonderful countryside, you might want to stay – and you can do that too.

OPEN: 12–2.30, 6–11 (Sun 7–10.30).
Real Ale. Restaurant.
Children in dining room and rear bar lunchtime only. Dogs in bar. Car park. Eleven en-suite bedrooms.
Cards: MasterCard, Switch, Visa.
Folk music every second Friday in the month.

Oldbury-on-Severn

Anchor ① 01454 413331
Church Road, Oldbury-on-Severn BS12 1QA
Free House. Michael Dowdeswell & Alex de la Torre, licensees

The Severn is a fascinating river, not only for the huge tides that rush in to cover acres of mudflats, but because it's owned by three different counties: Monmouth, Somerset and Gloucestershire. The Anchor, a very rural pub near the river and the tidal flats, has a cosy beamed bar with window seats, traditional furnishings and big log fires. Using local produce where possible, the bar food – all cooked by the landlord – is as fresh as can be. From an interesting menu, favourite dishes include fettucine pescatore – salmon, prawn, crab and mussels on a bed of pasta covered in a crab sauce – fresh salmon in a white wine and cream sauce, pancakes stuffed with peppers, tomatoes, onions, kidney beans, sweetcorn and onions in a creamy cheese sauce, tender lamb cooked with red wine and rosemary and home-made faggots in onion gravy. Two vegetarian dishes are included in the daily menu and there are lots of other dishes – raspberry crème brûlée to finish or treacle tart. A selection of good cheeses. Plates of rare roast beef always available. The separate no-smoking dining room allows you an extra choice of starters, otherwise the menu is the same throughout the pub. Bass from the cask, Butcombe Bitter, Theakstons Old Peculier and Wickwars Bob Bitter on hand pump. Short wine list, 12 by the glass. If you're a whisky aficionado, there are 75 of them for you to try. Seats outside in the attractive garden. If you want a game of boules they have a large pitch at the end of the back garden and their own boules league.

OPEN: 11.30–2.30, 6.30–11. Sat 11.30–11. Sun 12–10.30.
Real Ale. Restaurant.
Children in restaurant. Dogs welcome. Car park. Wheelchair access.
Cards: MasterCard, Visa.
Occasional live entertainment.

Pitney

Halfway House ① 01458 252513
Pitney, nr Langport TA10 9AB
Free House. Julian & Judy Lichfield, owners/licensees

This is a big plus for those of you who appreciate a fine, well-kept pint, as the Halfway House is on the top of the barrel, so to speak, given a big vote by CAMRA – Somerset branch – and others besides for the excellence of its beer. A very traditional country pub, simply furnished and friendly, with good log fires and newspapers to read. Lots of real ales from the cask, mostly from small local breweries – always Teignworthy Reel Ale, Butcombe Bitter, Hop Back Summer Lightning, Crop Circle and Branscombe Vale Bitter plus five or six that change from day to day. Hearty lunchtime food: home-made soup, well-filled sandwiches, and ploughman's with home-made pickle; in the evenings, they serve the house speciality – really good home-made curries. There is a garden for you to enjoy.

OPEN: 11.30–2.30, 5.30–11.
Real Ale.
Dogs and their walkers welcome. Wheelchair access.
Cards: all major credit and debit cards.

Porlock

Ship Inn ① 01643 862507
High Street, Porlock TA24 8QD
Free House. Mr & Mrs Cottrell, licensees
e-mail: mail@shipinnporlock.co.uk

With views over fields to the sea, this village is set in a natural bowl, flanked by a steep wooded hill. Not to be confused with Porlock Weir, nearer the coast, where they have a pub of the same name, this 13th-century Ship, at the bottom of Porlock Hill, has several literary connections. It was mentioned in *Lorna Doone* and it is said that Southey and Coleridge used to meet here to write their poetry. Still partially thatched, it is heavily beamed, flagstoned and traditionally furnished with good log fires. The well-chosen bar food includes the familiar favourites: soups, ploughman's, paté, mussels in cider, local sausages and game. Daily specials and fresh fish when available. Children's menu too. Regular food festivals; National Seafood Week and an Exmoor Food Festival. Cotleigh Old Buzzard in winter, Barn Owl in summer, Courage Best, a local guest beer and country wines. Steep garden at the back of the pub where there are seats on the covered deck and a children's play area. The prettiest route to the coast is via the delightful village of Bossington; a track then leads to a small car park and a shingle beach.

OPEN: 10.30–11. Sun 12–10.30. Open all year including Christmas.
Real Ale.
Children welcome away from bar. Dogs on leads. Lots of help for wheelchairs. Bedrooms.
Morris dancing and occasional live music. Monthly quiz night.

Rudge

Full Moon ① 01373 830936
Rudge, Frome BA11 2QF
Free House. Patrick Gifford, licensee, Nicky Milland general manager
e-mail: thefullmoon@lineone.net

The Full Moon, a 17th-century drover's pub, is in a quiet hamlet of straggling cottages near the Wiltshire/Somerset border. Attractive, gloriously rambling and well cared for, it has gardens front and back, splendid views and serves good food. The home-made bar food and fresh fish are listed on the daily changing blackboard along with daily specials and vegetarian dishes; carvery on Sundays. You could start with the house special – Arbroath smokies, mushrooms and onions grilled to perfection or red onion tart; for a main course a braised leg of lamb with mint and redcurrants or tenderloin of pork with red onions in a mustard sauce. The fish can be exotic. They bake their own bread and the puds are all home-made. Wadworths 6X, Butcombe Moonshine, cider (including a local rough one), about 10 wines by the glass. Seats in the garden.

OPEN: 12–11.
Real Ale. Restaurant.
Children welcome. Dogs on leads. Car park. Wheelchair access. Bedrooms. Four self-catering cottages next door to the pub.
Cards: MasterCard, Switch, Visa.

Shepton Montague

Montague ① 01749 813213
Shepton Montague BA9 8JW
Free House. Julian & Linda Bear, licensees
e-mail: montagueinn@aol.com

In a peaceful village between Bruton and Castle Cary, the stone-built Montague is in the best tradition of a country pub. Inside are an attractive, comfortable bar with a log fire and a no-smoking restaurant where they serve well-kept ales and creative food in delightful surroundings. Bar snacks and light lunches are served in the bar: French onion soup, country paté, ciabatta with bacon, brie and caramelised peppers, beef and ale pie, ham, egg and chips, luxury fish pie or from the à la carte menu: smoked salmon and prawn cornet, sea bass roasted with garlic, chilli and white wine or a marinated lamb fillet served with couscous, red wine and rosemary sauce. Among the ales you will usually find Greene King IPA, Butcombe Bitter and a guest, all served from the cask. Wines by the glass. There's everything you could wish for here, including seats on the flowery terrace and somewhere to stay. Lots of things to do – visit the gardens at Stourhead or Hadspen, go racing at Wincanton or look at aeroplanes at the Fleet Air Arm Museum, Yeovilton.

OPEN: 11–2.30, 6–11. Sun 12–2.30, 7–10.30.
Real Ale. Restaurant.
Children in restaurant and family room. Dogs on leads in bar. Car park. Wheelchair access. Two double bedrooms and one twin, all en suite.
Cards: Delta, MasterCard, Switch, Visa.

Stanton Wick

Carpenters Arms ① 01761 490202
Stanton Wick, nr Bath BS39 4BX
Free House. Simon Pledge, licensee
e-mail: carpenters@buccaneer.co.uk

A charming pub in a village about 10 miles west of Bath. Very flowery outside, spick and span inside with beams, stripped walls, a big log fire, comfortable settles and good food.

You can eat anywhere you can find a table. Bar food could include a home-made soup of the day with roasted croutons and freshly baked bread, duck liver and pistachio paté with spiced apple chutney and toast, chicken Caesar salad with Parmesan croutons, steak and mushroom pie, tarragon-crusted salmon on steamed pak choi, herb oil and balsamic syrup, cod on lemon-crushed potatoes with a prawn and saffron sauce, tagliatelle with ham, mushrooms and garlic cream, and well-filled sandwiches. More creative dishes find their way on to the specials board. Bass, Butcombe Bitter and Wadworths 6X are on hand pump; they have Addlestones cider and a French-leaning, comprehensive wine list, many by the glass.

OPEN: 11–11. Sun 12–10.30.
Real Ale. Dining room.
Children in dining room. Dogs in bar. Car park. Bedrooms.
Cards: Amex, Delta, Diners, MasterCard, Switch, Visa.

Street

Two Brewers ① 01458 442421
38 Leigh Road, Street BA16 0HB
Free House. Richard & Maggie Pearce, licensees
e-mail: richardwpearce@btinternet.com

Newly 'done up', looking very smart and with a collection of pump clips on the walls to rival any other, this is a comfortable, well-run pub serving traditional favourites: freshly filled sandwiches, giant baps, toasties, jacket potatoes, omelettes, grilled ham, steaks, home-made soup, at least four fish dishes, mixed grill and home-made lasagne; pasta and chicken dishes are listed on the blackboard. No need to tell you about the beers; people travel miles to sample the guest ales. The regulars are Ruddles County, Courage Best and Directors; after that it is anyone's guess – they try lots; 450 since the licensees came here in 1990. Seats in the garden, which has a children's play area and a skittle alley to entertain you.

OPEN: 11–3, 6–11. Sun 12–3, 7–10.30.
Real Ale. Restaurant.
Children welcome. No dogs. Car park. Wheelchair access.
Cards: all except Diners and Amex.

Taunton

Masons Arms ① 01823 288916
Magdalene Street, Taunton TA1 1SG
Free House. Jeremy Leyton, licensee
e-mail: jjmax@jleyton.freeserve.co.uk

Not always a pub; during the first half of the 19th century this was a private house, the home of the local rent collector. Turning it into a public house must have been a very popular move. In the centre of Taunton, in the shadow of St Mary Magdalene Church, the traditional Masons Arms is a friendly, simply furnished, busy town hostelry. The menu is small and well chosen with a good selection of dishes using mainly local produce. The home-made food could include warming soups, various home-made patés, plus daily specials such as beef cooked in local beer, chicken cooked in the local cider, also 'grillstones' – a special stone heated to a very high temperature on which you can cook your own choice of steak. Draught Otter Bitter, two or three local guests, Oakwood and Kingston Black ciders. Somerset CAMRA pub of the year 2002. No garden, but for the energetic among you, a skittle alley awaits.

OPEN: 10.30–3, 5–11. Sat 10.30–11. Sun 12–4.
Real Ale.
Children: rather not. Well-behaved dogs on leads welcome.
Wheelchair access tricky but manageable with help. Self-contained holiday flat for three available to rent.

West Huntspill

Cross Ways Inn ① 01278 783756
Withy Road, West Huntspill, nr Highbridge TA9 3RA (on the A38 and only 3 miles from Exit 22 on the M5)
Free House. Michael Ronca & Tony Eyles, licensees
e-mail: crosswaysinn@virgin.net

On the Somerset levels, facing the westerly breezes, the old Cross Ways Inn, with its low beams, log fires and traditional furnishings, is welcoming, well worn and comfortable. There is an extensive menu with something for everyone – including children: sandwiches or ploughman's, maybe smoked-sausage and bean stew, garlic mushrooms, chicken and ham mornay, chicken breasts stuffed with mushroom paté, lamb shank braised in wine with root vegetables, Thai crab cakes, rack of lamb with redcurrant and rosemary jus, salads, and a vegetable bake. The menu changes regularly. Flowers IPA, Original and Royal Oak plus varying guest ales – could be Smiles Best, Butcombe Bitter, Bass or Oakhill. Choice of malt whiskies, Rich's farmhouse cider and a short wine list. Seats in the large garden among the fruit trees.

OPEN: 12–3, 5.30–11 (Sat 6–11, Sun 7–10.30).
Real Ale. Restaurant Fri and Sat only.
Children welcome (except in main bar). Dogs on leads. Three en-suite bedrooms.
Cards: all except Amex.
Occasional live music.

Winsford

Royal Oak Inn ① 01643 851455
Winsford, Exmoor National Park TA24 7JE
Free House. Charles Steven, licensee
e-mail: enquiries@royaloak-somerset.co.uk

Unrivalled in looks and position, the cream-washed and thatched 12th-century Royal Oak is in a village of stone and thatched cottages on the edge of Exmoor National Park. Well, it was 12th century, but a couple of fires later things have changed a bit. It still has some fine oak beams and panelling but no more open fires. Bar meals include home-made soup, lunchtime sandwiches and ploughman's, and on the menu there could be locally smoked salmon, thinly sliced and served on dressed leaves with a dill dressing, fresh prawns on a bed of shredded lettuce with a fresh lemon and tomato-scented mayonnaise, terrine of pigeon breast, foie gras and chicken liver served with plum and pear chutney, and for a main course, steak and kidney pudding in a rich ale sauce, braised lamb shank in red wine on a rosemary and sweet potato mash and red wine gravy, pan-seared supreme of chicken with a spiced lemon cream sauce and saffron rice, also dishes of the day. These are cooked in small quantities, so when they are sold that's it – there will be something new next day. You know everything is as fresh as can be and all locally sourced. All food is home-cooked, including the bread. Puds too. A full menu is served in the elegant restaurant. Small, select wine cellar. Three barrels of real ale in the bar which change every few weeks, Guinness and Scrumpy Jack cider. The River Winn, on which the Royal Oak has its own beat, runs through the village and fishing can be arranged. Plenty of good walks from the inn.

OPEN: 11–2.30, 6–11.
Real Ale. Restaurant Tues–Sat, very quiet music in here.
Children welcome except in front bar. Dogs on leads.
Eight comfortable en-suite bedrooms in the inn, six more in the annexe. Dogs can be accommodated too.
Cards: Amex, Diners, MasterCard.

Witham Friary

Seymour Arms ① 01749 850742
Witham Friary, Frome BA11 5HF
Free House. Jean Douel, licensee

Solidly Victorian, the Seymour Arms – surrounded by fields – was built as a public house in 1867. An unspoilt old place, seven miles from Frome off the B3092, it has just two rooms, stone flags on the floor, beer from the barrel served through a hatch, and no food. There is a garden where you can sit to enjoy Ushers Best Bitter and Rich's Cider. There are lovely views of the surrounding countryside from the garden and there are good walks nearby. As the name suggests there was indeed a friary here – Carthusian – founded by Henry II as penance for the death of Thomas à Becket in 1170. Dissolved in the 16th century, nothing much remains, but the chapel, much altered, continues to be the parish church.

OPEN: 11–3, 6–11.
Real Ale. Real Cider. No food.
Dogs on leads.

Yarlington

Stags Head Inn ① 01963 440393
Yarlington, Wincanton BA9 8DG
Free House. Steve, Gill & Lucy Culverhouse, licensees
e-mail: steveculverhouse@compuserve.com

It's not immediately obvious that this stone building is a pub as it really does look like somebody's house. However, look on the side of the building and there is the inn sign.

Small, friendly and traditionally run, with no music, pool or TV, it has two bars serving wholesome, varied, bar food: soup of the day, filled baguettes, paté, steak and kidney pie with suet crust, game casserole, luxury fish pie, sausage and mash and always one vegetarian dish. There is a more extensive, imaginative evening menu. Delicious home-made puds too. They also do special Sunday lunches. Always three real ales and a local guest, Greene King IPA, draught Bass, Guinness and draught Grolsch and local organic cider. Seats in the garden.

OPEN: 12–2.30, 5.45–11. Sun 12–3 only. Closed Mon.
Real Ale.
Dogs on leads. Wheelchair access.

BEST OF THE REST

Mells
Talbot ① 01373 812254
Selwood Street, Mells, nr Frome BA11 3PN
Set amongst a glorious group of buildings in a timeless village between Bath and Wells, this is a substantial 15th-century coaching inn with a classy restaurant, unusual public bar – it's in the old tithe barn – lovely garden and seriously good food. The menu – fresh shellfish soup with toasted cheese muffins, hot Brixham crab tartlet with fresh parmesan and mixed leaf salad, roast noisettes of English lamb with a lamb stock, herb and tomato sauce or chargrilled fillet steak with wild mushrooms, bacon and button onions in a shallot and red wine sauce – gives you some idea of the delights you could expect. Butcombe Bitter, Wadworths 6X and Fullers London Pride, eclectic wine list, a few by the glass. A lovely place. Children welcome. No dogs. Bedrooms.
Open: 12–2.30, 6.30–11

Sparkford
Sparkford Inn ① 01963 440218
High Street, Sparkford BA22 7JN
Look for picnic tables and flower tubs in the centre of the village, and behind them is this fine old building. Inside is full of atmosphere; all is well cared for – and so will you be. Efficiently prepared bar food ranges from sandwiches to beef-in-Guinness casserole, pork tenderloin in a port and sage sauce, steaks, also daily specials and a daily carvery. Bass, Butcombe Bitter, Morlands Old Speckled Hen, Sharps Cornish Coaster and other less usual beers. Comprehensive wine list – something for everyone. Children welcome. Bedrooms.
Open: 11–11.

Stoke St Gregory
Rose & Crown ① 01823 490296
Woodhill, Stoke St Gregory TA36 6EW
An attractive, 300-year-old pub in a village near the West Sedgemoor nature reserve, an important woodland and wetland area – birdwatchers to the fore. Delights outside and plenty in. Lots of fresh local produce is used in the cooking: their own eggs, fish from Brixham, local lamb and ducks. Food goes up a gear in the restaurant which has a very reasonably priced menu. Exmoor Ale, Hardy Country and Royal Oak, farm ciders and a good wine list. If you're into baskets of any kind, this is the place to be as, surrounded by willow beds, there are two local basket-makers ready to sell their wares. Children welcome. Bedrooms.
Open: 11–2.30, 7–11.

Triscombe

Blue Ball Inn ☏ 01984 618242
Triscombe TA4 3HE
Between Taunton and Minehead, this long, low, multi-level thatched 18th-century building is on a gently sloping site with nothing quite where you expect it to be. However the food has the right sort of surprises. They have an appealing menu of lunchtime filled baguettes, home-made soup and fish and chips, dishes using locally sourced meat and game on the specials board; also fish from Brixham and home-made puds. Local Cotleigh beers, two guests and farm ciders. The most discerning wine buff will find something on the extensive wine list. Children welcome. Dogs – maybe.
Open: 12–3, 7–11.

Wetherspoon in Bristol and Somerset

Bristol – Commercial Rooms, 43–45 Corn Street
☏ 0117 927 9681
Bristol – Magic Box, 135–137 Cheltenham Road
☏ 0117 970 5140
Bristol – Van Dyck Forum, 748–756 Fishponds Road
☏ 0117 965 1337
Bristol (Bedminster) – Robert Fitz Harding, Cannon Street
☏ 0117 966 2757
Bristol (Clifton) – Berkeley, 15–19 Queens Road
☏ 0117 927 9550
Bristol (Kingswood) – Kingswood Colliers, 94–96 Regent Street
☏ 0117 967 2247
Bristol (Redfield) – St George's Hall, 203 Church Road
☏ 0117 955 1488
Bristol (Staple Hill) – Staple Hill Oak, 84–86 High Street
☏ 0117 956 8544
Bristol (Temple Quay)– Knights Templar, 1 The Square
☏ 0117 930 8710

Somerset

Bridgwater – Carnival Inn, Saint Mary Street
☏ 01278 726180
Chard – Cerdic, Fore Street
☏ 01460 260070
Street – Landokay, 111–113 High Street
☏ 01458 444940
Taunton – Coal Orchard, 30 Bridge Street
☏ 01823 447330
Taunton – Perkin Warbeck, 22–23 East Street
☏ 01823 335830
Weston Super Mare – Dragon Inn, 15 Meadow Street
☏ 01934 621304
Yeovil – William Dampier, 97 Middle Street
☏ 01935 412533

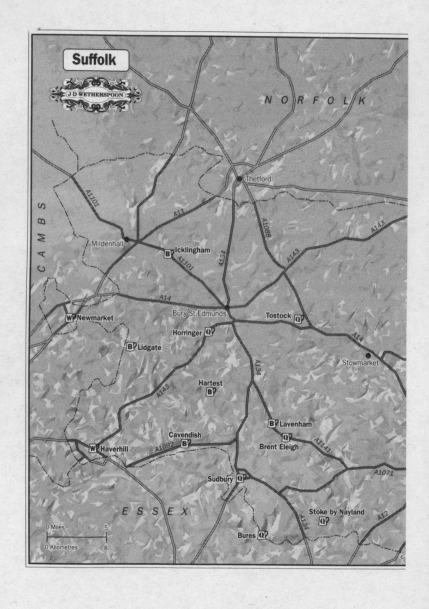

Suffolk

J.D.WETHERSPOON

NORFOLK

CAMBS

A1101

Thetford

A11

A1088

A143

Mildenhall

B Icklingham

A1101

A134

A143

A14

W Newmarket

Bury St Edmunds

Tostock Q

Horringer Q

A14

Stowmarket

B Lidgate

A143

Hartest

B

A134

B Lavenham

Cavendish

Q Brent Eleigh

A1141

W Haverhill

A1092

B

A1071

Sudbury Q

ESSEX

Stoke by Nayland Q

A134

A12

0 Miles   5

Bures Q

0 Kilometres   8

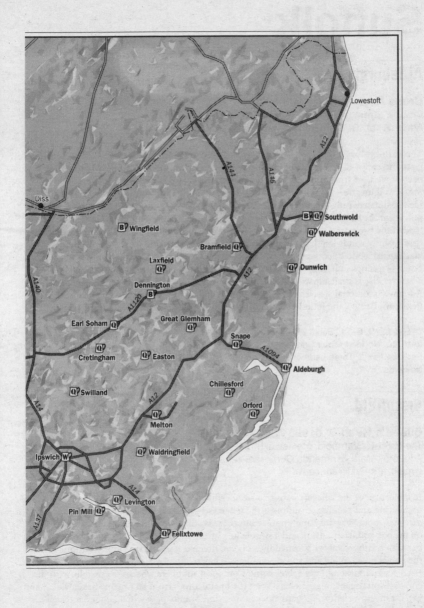

Suffolk

Aldeburgh

Cross Keys ① 01728 452637
Crabbe Street, Aldeburgh IP15 5BN
Adnams. M. G. Clement, licensee

The 16th-century Cross Keys is in the street that commemorates George Crabbe, Georgian poet and rector of St Peter & St Paul's church, in a town that with Snape Maltings has been since 1948 the home of England's largest music festival. Here you can enjoy art, music and theatre – or just the delightful town and bracing winds off the sea. The pub is ideally situated: only the promenade separates the sheltered courtyard at the back of the pub from the beach; you can sit in here, have a drink or a meal and watch the world go by. Inside, the two bars – each with a cosy stove to warm things up – are a refuge from the cold easterly winds that blow in winter. The regularly changing menus are on the blackboard: good open sandwiches, vegetarian dishes and lots of fish – fresh from the beach – scallops in bacon, fisherman's pie, lobster, fresh crab, mussels à la crème and whatever else is available will find its way onto the menu – fish dishes are their speciality. Adnams Traditional ales. The fine John Piper window in the church commemorates Benjamin Britten, the founder of the Aldeburgh Music Festival.

OPEN: 11–3, 6–11. Sun 12–10.30.
Real Ale. No food winter Sun eves.
Dogs on leads. Three bedrooms – all en suite and two with sea views.
No cards.

Bramfield

Queen's Head ① 01986 784214
The Street, Bramfield, Halesworth IP19 9HT
Adnams. Mark & Amanda Corcoran, tenants
e-mail: qhbfield@aol.com

In the centre of the village, opposite a wonderful crinkle-crankle wall – intentionally undulating and peculiar to Suffolk – the Queen's Head has a reputation for serving excellent food. Very busy and popular but there is still a welcome if you just want to lean on the bar and have a drink and a simple lunchtime snack. Inside is a high-beamed lounge bar with scrubbed tables, warmed by a big log fire. No separate restaurant, but one side of the pub is no smoking and you can eat here. They're members of the 'Campaign for Real Food' and all meat and vegetables come from local suppliers whenever possible, with the emphasis on organic ingredients – even the bread comes from an organic baker. The menu will list inventive soups, perhaps chicken liver and brandy paté with Cumberland sauce, hand-dressed Cromer crab with mayonnaise, peppers stuffed with spicy couscous with an apricot and mint sauce, seafood crumble, venison steak with redcurrant, port and orange sauce, steak, kidney and Adnams ale pie and rib-eye steak with mustard and cream sauce, locally made sausages, English cheeses, home-made puds and ice creams. Adnams Bitter, Broadside and seasonal beers, organic cider and a good wine list. Outside, the delightful garden is overlooked by a lovely thatched village church.

OPEN: 11.45–2.30, 6.30–11 Sun 11–3, 7–10.30.
Real Ale.
Children welcome. Dogs: if well behaved. Car park. Wheelchair access (not WC).
Cards: Amex, Diners, MasterCard, Solo, Switch, Visa.

Brent Eleigh

Cock ① 01787 247371
Lavenham Road, Brent Eleigh, Sudbury CO10 9PB
Free House. Charles Lydford, licensee

An unspoilt 15th-century thatched local in a small village near Lavenham, the Cock is well worth a visit for the well-kept beer and local cider with maybe a crisp and pickled egg on the side. A traditional drinking pub with large tables in each bar to take all the beer mugs and coal fires to keep you warm. A firm favourite with those who appreciate Greene King IPA, Abbot, Adnams Bitter – guest beers from time to time – and the regular supply of the organic Castlings Heath cider made a few miles up the road. Seats in the small garden at the front of the pub.

OPEN: 12–3, 6–11 (Sun 7–10.30).
Real Ale. No food.
Children iffy – allowed Sundays in smaller bar. Dogs on leads. Small car parks, front and back. Wheelchairs difficult, but help available. The old wash house has been converted into comfortable letting accommodation.
No cards, or euros!

Bures

Lamarsh Lion ① 01787 227918
Bures, Lamarsh CO8 5EP
Free House. John Sullivan, licensee

Here you really have a foot in both counties as this village straddles the Essex border – and the river Stour. This is Constable country and, overlooking the familiar rolling landscape of his paintings, the 14th-century Lamarsh Lion is a particularly attractive place to be on a summer's evening. Inside is well beamed, flowers decorate the bar and friendly, helpful staff are there to serve you. No fixed menu; the key to culinary creativity depends on what is available, it will however be imaginative and well cooked. The ales could be Adnams The Wherry, Cottage Brewery, John Smiths, Marstons Pedigree, Suffolk Ale and Wadworths 6X, but the beers change regularly. Wines by the glass and a selection of malt whiskies. On

Whit Bank Holiday weekend an annual raft race is held on the river when things can get very exciting and slightly hysterical.

OPEN: 11–3, 6–11. Sun 12–3, 7–10.30.
Real Ale. Restaurant.
Children in eating area. No dogs. Bed and breakfast.
Occasional live music.

Chillesford

The Friars Inn (known as The Froize) ① 01394 450282
The Street, Chillesford, nr Woodbridge IP12 3PU
Free House. David Grimwood, licensee

There's a Suffolk 'burr' in the Froize's name. It doesn't take much imagination to hear rustic locals, over the years, turning the 'Friars' into the 'Froize'. Brick built in the 15th century on the site of Chillesford Friary, this was, until two years ago, a well-known, very popular pub. Then there was a change at the top and it now owned by local chef David Grimwood and the emphasis is more on the restaurant but there is still one heavily beamed bar selling Adnams and other alternating real ales. Menus offer a variety of English and continental dishes, typically honey-roast lamb shanks, venison, ale and mushroom pie or oven-baked salmon with pistachio crust, also a vegetarian menu. There is an all-embracing wine list and a selection of malt whiskies. Great emphasis is placed on no smoking and no music.

OPEN: 11.30–2.30, 6.30–11. Closed Mon.
Real Ale. No lunch in bar – only in restaurant – but dinner served Thurs–Sat from 6.30.
Children welcome. No dogs. Car park. Wheelchair access.

Cretingham

Cretingham Bell ① 01728 685419
The Street, Cretingham, nr Otley, Woodbridge IP3 7BJ
Free House. Vic Llewellyn, licensee

Spacious, beamed and timbered, with a huge log fire in the inglenook, the Cretingham Bell embodies the best of the past centuries with touches of the 21st. Inside are a lively snug, no-smoking lounge bar, restaurant and family room. The delights of the day are written on the blackboards where you will find plenty of choice, either from the traditional menu or the daily specials; vegetarian dishes and children's meals too. Roast on Sunday. Beers from Adnams, Mauldons and Earl Soham; the pub concentrates on local brews. Quite a selection of malt whiskies. Seats at the front of the pub and in the large garden.

OPEN 11–2.30 (Sat 11–3.30), 6–11. Sun 12–2.30, 7–10.30.
Real Ale. Restaurant.
Children welcome. Dogs in the snug. Car park. Wheelchair access. Three en-suite bedrooms.
Cards: Delta, Electron, Eurocard, MasterCard, Solo, Switch, Visa.

Dunwich

Ship Inn ① 01728 648219
St James' Street, Dunwich, nr Saxmundham IP17 3DT
Free House. David Sheldrake, licensee

Old Dunwich was a thriving shipbuilding town in the 12th century but erosion caused by an ever-shifting coastline of sand and shingle closed the way to the sea for ever. Abandoned and washed away over the centuries, a solitary gravestone on the edge of the cliff is all that remains of the medieval town. It is said that the bones of the long dead protrude from the cliff and on stormy nights you can hear the bells of drowned churches tolling away. On a more cheerful note the Dunwich you see today is a charming place and the handsome brick-built Ship, an old smugglers' haunt, is ready to welcome you. Inside are a big comfortable bar with a good fire, a dining room and family conservatory. Fishing and nautical bric-a-brac decorate the pub. The Ship is renowned for its fish and chips and other fish dishes, but at lunchtime you can get soup, sausage and chips, chicken and cider pie, salads, ploughman's and good puddings. During the evening the restaurant menu applies throughout the pub. Adnams ales and Mauldons seasonal ale. Seats on the terrace and in the sheltered garden which has a huge fig tree.

OPEN: 11–11. Sun 12–10.30.
Real Ale. Evening restaurant.
Children not in bar. Dogs on leads. Car park. Wheelchair access (not WC). Bedrooms – some with a sea/marsh view.
Cards: MasterCard, Switch, Visa.

Earl Soham

Victoria ① 01728 685758
Earl Soham IP13 7RL
Free House. Paul Hooper, licensee

A straightforward, unassuming village local where they serve a pint of very local beer. Not quite as local as it once was, as the brewery has moved from the back of the pub to bigger premises further up the road. Nothing much has changed inside the Victoria though, you'll find pine panelling, tiled floors, big open fires and, as a homage to the Victorian era, pictures of Queen Victoria and Victorian life. They serve a good selection of bar food, soups, ploughman's, curries, casseroles, salads, vegetarian dishes plus a Sunday roast. Their beers are Victoria Bitter, Albert – that's the strong one – and Gannet, a mild. Seats at the front of the pub and on the lawn at the back.

OPEN: 11–3, 6–11. Sun 1–3, 6–10.30.
Real Ale.
Dogs welcome.
Cards: all major cards accepted.
Folk music Tues eve.

Easton

White Horse Inn ① 01728 746456
The Street, Easton IP13 OED
Pubmaster. Pip & Sally Smith, licensees

Another village with the remains of a crinkle-crankle wall that surrounded the Easton estate. The White Horse, washed a perfect Suffolk/Essex pink, is an unchanging 16th-century village pub on the edge of the village green. Inside are two bars and a small restaurant. All the food, including their speciality home-made pies – steak and kidney, chicken and game or chicken and leek – is listed on blackboards. There could be garlic mushrooms, king prawns with garlic, ginger and lime, salmon bites in a lemon and dill crumb, mixed grill, fillet steak in a brandy and peppercorn sauce, grilled gammon steak, rack of lamb in rosemary and garlic and pork fillet in mustard or cider apple sauce. Beers are Flowers IPA, Adnams and Greene King IPA. Seats in the garden at the back of the pub.

OPEN: 11–3, 6.30–11.
Real Ale. Restaurant.
Children in eating areas. Dogs in bar only. Wheelchair access (not WC).
Cards: all except Amex.

Felixstowe

Half Moon ① 01394 216009
303 Walton High Street, Felixstowe IP11 9QL
Adnams. Patrick Wroe, tenant
e-mail: patrickpub@aol.com

A mid 18th-century building housing a very friendly drinking pub. As the publican says, 'pickled eggs, that's it!' – and the beer, of course. For those of you who want a good pint or two, this is the only CAMRA pub for about ten miles. Though, as they say, it is more than just an alehouse with lots of blokes swilling pints of beer – they have a wine list and are female-friendly. Go and judge for yourself. Lots of nice quiet games: darts, cribbage, dominoes and backgammon. Certainly no fruit machine or music to annoy, though there is a pub piano.... Adnams Bitter and Broadside and usually two guests.

OPEN: 12–2.30, 5–11. Sat 12–11. Sun 12–3, 7–10.30.
Real Ale.
Children welcome, so are dogs. Car park. Wheelchair access.
No cards.

Great Glemham

Crown ① 01728 663693
The Street, Great Glemham, nr Saxmundham IP17 1DA
Free House. Barry & Susie Coote, licensees

I'm sure you'll be reassured to know that Glemham means happy home. Great Glemham is doubly happy, no doubt; it's certainly an attractive village with a very desirable pub. The old part of the Crown, built early in the 17th century, has a large beamed bar and two huge fireplaces filled with blazing logs during the winter. You eat where you can find a table; the changing menu ranges from well-filled sandwiches to a mushroom and spinach lasagne, home-made steak and kidney pie, large cod fillet with a home-made beer batter, large East Anglian pork chop with apple sauce, vegetarian dishes and a children's menu. Adnams, Greene King IPA, Morlands Old Speckled Hen and guest ales. Choice of wines and a selection of malt whiskies. Tables on the lawn at the corner of the pub during the summer. The village has aristocratic neighbours; Great Glemham Park is the seat of Lord Cranbrook.

OPEN: 12–2.30, 6.30–11. Closed Mon.
Real Ale.
Children welcome, and dogs. Wheelchair facilities.

Horringer

Beehive ① 01284 735260
The Street, Horringer IP29 5SD
Greene King. Gary & Dianne Kingshott, tenants

Horringer means a winding stream, and the Linnet, one of a number of Suffolk's little rivers, rises in Ickworth Park – which shares a boundary with the village – and runs on to Mildenhall, where it loses itself in the watery Fens. The Beehive – and there is one on the grass at the front of the 19th-century flint pub – is a cottagey sort of place with low-beamed, rambling little rooms in which to sit and sample the imaginative food. Menus change daily, so these are just a sample of what you might find on the chalk boards: shellfish chowder with home-made bread, terrine of chicken, coriander and ginger with lime dressing, and for a main course poached haddock on a leek and tomato fondue or braised shank of lamb with a redcurrant reduction, and ginger crème brulée or orange custard tart to follow. Greene King IPA and Abbot ales plus a short, interesting, wine list. Seats on the terrace at the back of the pub and in the garden. The National Trust's Ickworth Park is worth visiting.

OPEN: 11.30–2.30, 7–11.
Real Ale. No food Sun eve.
Children welcome. Dogs – bit iffy, ask first as they have their own. Car park. Wheelchair access (not WC).
Cards: Delta, MasterCard, Switch, Visa.

Laxfield

Kings Head ① 01986 798395
Gormans Lane, Laxfield, nr Woodbridge IP13 8DG
Adnams. George Coleman, tenant

A former market town, Laxfield, with its long wide village street, has an interesting half-timbered Guildhall, and behind the church the thatched, unspoilt, 15th-century Kings Head. No bar at all, the interior is timeless and unchanging; beer is still tapped from casks in the cellar. Food has moved on though, nothing timeless and unchanging about that.

Appetising bar food could include soup, well-filled sandwiches, sausages with mash and onion gravy, a steak and ale pie and puds such as fruit crumble and apple pie. Adnams ales and a guest; country wines and local cider. Seats in the garden around the old bowling green.

OPEN: 12–3, 6–11 (Sun 7–10.30).
Real Ale.
Children in eating area. Dogs on leads in bar. Wheelchair access.
N.B. Possibly live music Tuesday afternoons.

Levington

Ship Inn ① 01473 659573
Church Lane, Levington, nr Ipswich IP10 0LQ
Free House. Mark & Stella Johnson, licensees
e-mail: johnson@theshipinn-levington.co.uk

This is a village close to the Orwell river and very near a large marina – The Suffolk Yacht Harbour. The Ship, near the church, is handsome, white-painted and newly thatched after the fire. This is an idyllic corner of the village. Outside is an exuberant floral display; inside is equally appealing with comfortably furnished, atmospheric rooms decorated with more than a nod towards the nautical: prints, pictures, nets and even a compass under the counter. Popular with locals, townies and visiting yachtsmen. The menu, which changes twice a day, is a mix of traditional and modern European and includes lots of fresh fish dishes; everything from the soup to the puddings is made 'in house'. Adnams Broadside and Greene King IPA drawn from the cask. The wine list includes many from the New World, some by the glass. Seats in front of the pub among the flower tubs look towards fields and the river.

OPEN: 11.30–3, 6–11.
Real Ale. Restaurant.
No children inside, in garden only. No dogs. Wheelchair access.
Cards: Delta, MasterCard, Switch, Visa.

Melton

Wilford Bridge ① 01394 386141
Wilford Bridge Road, Melton, nr Woodbridge IP12 2PA
Free House. Mike Lomas, licensee

Wilford Hollows is the name of this lovely valley, where the river Deben flows silently by, and at the bottom of the hollow is the village of Melton. Unsurprisingly the pub took its name from the old bridge over the river, now modernised and strengthened to take present-day traffic. This inviting, spacious pub, built in 1750, is run by the same family, and on the same lines, as the Butt and Oyster at Pin Mill and the Maybush at Waldringfield. They serve traditional bar food: soups, various ploughman's, sandwiches, lots of fish (fresh lobsters and crabs in summer), steak, Guinness and mushroom pie in winter, vegetarian dishes and steaks to go with the Adnams Best, Broadside and a guest.

Wide-ranging wine list. Walks along the river from the village. The Sutton Hoo burial site is nearby, managed by the National Trust.

OPEN: 11–11.
Real Ale.
Children welcome. No dogs. Car park. Wheelchair access.
Cards: all major credit cards.

Orford

Jolly Sailor ① 01394 450243
Quay Street, Orford, nr Woodbridge IP12 2NU
Adnams. Philip Attwood, tenant
e-mail: info@jollyorf.co.uk

In the middle of the 18th century Orford ceased to be a proper seaport. It was cut off from the sea by a huge shingle spit created by powerful North Sea tides. With no reason for existence it became a backwater, which saved and protected the village leaving it with not much more than a small square and a street of Georgian cottages – and the Elizabethan Jolly Sailor – leading to the quay. An old smugglers' inn, the Jolly Sailor is reputed to be built out of the timbers of ships wrecked nearby. Inside are several small rooms warmed by a big stove in winter and containing smuggling and seafaring mementoes. As you would expect there is local fish and chips on the reasonably priced menu: cod, skate, rock eel, salmon and flounder as well as home-cooked ham, omelettes and sausage, egg and chips to go with Adnams ales. There is a special evening menu at the weekend. The dining room is no smoking and there are tables in the large garden. The 90ft-high Orford castle keep is open every day and there are magnificent views from the battlements. Havergate Island, just below Orford, is an RSPB bird sanctuary. Boats to the island leave from Orford quay.

OPEN: 11.30–2.30, 7–11.
Real Ale.
Dogs on leads in middle bar. Bedrooms.

Pin Mill

Butt & Oyster ① 01473 780764
Pin Mill, nr Chelmondiston, Ipswich IPN 1JW
Deben Inns. Steve & Louise Lomas, tenants

Overlooking the River Orwell, this pub was originally a bargeman's retreat; many famous Thames barges were built in this area. Unfortunately most of the bargemen have gone but other sailors have taken their place. There are two ways to get here, sailing and driving. By road, you reach this favoured spot along a lane from Chelmondiston; if you're sailing, just sail in. A high spring tide gets you really close; then, if you're lucky, you don't even have to leave the yacht to order a drink. A delightful place to visit; a classic 17th-century riverside pub popular with everyone. During July there is the Pin Mill barge match to watch, otherwise you can sit outside, safely anchored to your seat, watching the comings and goings on the busy river. The traditional bar food includes half a pint of prawns, Whitby scampi, fish and chips and crab and lobster in season. A full menu, including vegetarian dishes and blackboard specials, is always available. Well-kept Adnams and Greene King straight from the cask in the back bar. East of Pin Mill, by foot along the river bank, is the National Trust's Cliff Plantation.

OPEN: 11–11. Sun 12–10.30.
Real Ale.
Children and dogs welcome in certain areas.
Cards: most accepted.

Snape

Crown ① 01728 688324
Bridge Road, Snape, nr Saxmundham IP17 1SL
Adnams. Diane Maylott, chef/tenant

At a crossroads in this well-known village not far from Snape Maltings and near everything that goes on during the Aldeburgh Festival. When smuggling was rife along the east coast they chose their favourite inns with care, and the Crown was one of them. A fine, rambling old pub, dating back to the 15th century, with only one small bar and dining room, but full of nooks and crannies, low-beamed ceilings, a big inglenook fireplace and huge settles to settle in. In both the bar and dining room they serve interesting food. No sandwiches, but ploughman's, and from the changing menu there could be lobster and crayfish tart, crayfish tails in Thai mayonnaise served with crisp poppadoms, artichoke, sunblush tomato and olive salad with parmesan shavings, Thai red chicken curry with basmati rice, Turkish lamb sauté with apricots and tomatoes on lemon couscous, a warm tart of Italian vegetables, salad and new potatoes, home-made puds and ice creams; the menu changes every day. Adnams Best Bitter and Adnams seasonal ales. A long and enterprising wine list. A big front garden to sit in.

OPEN: 12–3, 6–11.
Real Ale. Dining room.
No children. No dogs. Lots of car parking space. Wheelchair access. Two double, one twin room, both en suite.
Cards: all major cards accepted.

Golden Key Inn ① 01728 688510
Priory Road, Snape, nr Saxmundham IP17 1SG
Adnams. Max & Susie Kissick-Jones, tenants

A fine old place – a charming, late 15th-century pub with tenants who have been here for over 25 years. For one reason or another the pub has had several identities through the centuries. For its first three hundred years it was 'The Sign of the Cock', then 'The White Lion', only becoming the Golden Key at the turn of the 20th century. Inside is a large main bar divided into public (tiled floor), lounge (carpeted) bars and a dining area; one section is no-smoking. From the changing menu there is ample, sustaining, home-cooked bar food: home-made soups, paté, filled rolls, sausage and onion pie, smoked haddock, quiche, lots of fresh fish and game in season, steaks and roast on Sunday. Adnams ales, local farm ciders and a choice of malt whiskies. Seats at the front of the pub, also in the colourful garden.

OPEN: 11–3, 6–11 (extensions during the Aldeburgh Festival).
Real Ale.
Children in eating area. Dogs on leads. Wheelchair access. Double and twin en-suite rooms.
Cards: all except Amex and Diners.

Plough and Sail ① 01728 688413
Snape Maltings, nr Saxmundham IP17 1SR
Free House. G. J. Gooderham, licensee

The navigable limit of the Alde ends at the Victorian Maltings, built to process barley. This huge space now houses not only the Aldeburgh Festival in summer, but also antique fairs, concerts, shops and the Plough and Sail. Extended to cope with the rush of visitors, the new area surrounds the old, traditionally furnished part of the pub. In the bar and restaurants there is a choice of home-made soups on the blackboard, freshly made sandwiches, smoked salmon or chicken liver paté, grilled sardines, smoked sprats, grilled sea trout with linguini, tomatoes and melted mozzarella, supreme of chicken chasseur and pasta, seared sirloin steak, vegetarian dishes and, as you would expect, plenty more fish dishes plus everything you would find on a good restaurant menu. Adnams Southwold Bitter, Broadside and Barley Mow in summer, Tally Ho in winter, guest beer Wychwood Hobgoblin. Good wine list, some by the glass. Tables in the enclosed, flowery courtyard at the back of the pub.

OPEN: 11–3, 5.30–11. Sun 12–3, 6.30–10.30 (winter 7.30–10.30). Aug 12–11.
Real Ale. Restaurant.
Children in restaurant. No dogs. Wheelchair access (not WC). Disabled facilities at the Maltings.
River trips up (down?) the River Alde.

Southwold

Crown Hotel ① 01502 722275
High Street, Southwold IP18 6DP
Adnams. Michael Bartholomew, manager
e-mail: crown.hotel@adnams.co.uk

Largly rebuilt after a disastrous fire in the late 17th century, this elegant little town is a mix of period houses and Dutch gabled cottages. The Crown, reminiscent of a handsome Georgian town house, combines a pub, wine bar, restaurant and small hotel. It has an extensive wine list, imaginative weekly changing bar food, and a restaurant that serves a good, creative and reasonably priced three-course menu. From the bar you could choose a cream of leek and potato soup, chicken liver parfait with melba toast and plum chutney, Shetland mussels in white wine, garlic and tomato sauce, chargrilled sirloin of beef with a basil and garlic glaze and horseradish relish, salmon fishcakes with a tartare sauce. Lots more, including good puds and cheeses from Neal's Yard. This wonderful hotel is the flagship of the Adnams Brewery nearby. The ales are kept in the very best condition and they have an impressive wine list (Adnams are wine merchants as well). Lots of wines by the glass, including classic vintages selected monthly.

OPEN: 10.30–3, 6–11. Closed first week Jan.
Real Ale. Restaurant.
Children in eating area and restaurant until 7 p.m. Dogs in one bar. Wheelchair access to bar. Bedrooms.
Cards: Amex, Delta, Diners, MasterCard, Switch, Visa.

Lord Nelson ① 01502 722079
East Street, Southwold IP18 6EJ
Adnams. John Illston, tenant

A late-Georgian pub not far from the sea – well, nothing in this town really is, as it's surrounded on three sides by water: sea to the front, Buss creek to the north and the river Blyth to the south. Southwold is virtually an island. A delightful town built around seven open spaces marking the sites of the houses destroyed in a devastating fire in 1659. A prosperous fishing port as far back as the 11th century, its sea-going history abounds, so why not have a pub named after one of Britain's best-known naval commanders – even if he wasn't born in the county? Friendly, well run and popular, the Lord Nelson has a cosy, low-ceilinged bar, panelled walls and an open fire. Freshly prepared, traditional food to go with the range of Adnams beers. Seats in the garden at the back of the pub sheltered from the brisk sea breezes.

OPEN:10.30–11. Sun 12–10.30.
Real Ale.
Children welcome. Dogs if well behaved. Easy wheelchair access (not WC).

Stoke-by-Nayland

Angel Inn ① 01206 263245
Polstead Street, Stoke-by-Nayland, nr Colchester CO6 4SA
Horizon Inns. Mike Everett, licensee
e-mail: theangel@tiscali.co.uk

In the Dedham Vale conservation area, a region of picturesque villages and wide open skies, Stoke-by-Nayland was one of Constable's favourite villages, and the church features in several of his paintings. The Angel, with an enviable ambience, is an attractive 16th-century coaching inn at the main crossroads of the village. The casual drinker is still catered for in the small tiled bar, but on the whole it is a serious, efficient dining pub serving some excellent food. The selection of reasonably priced dishes on the blackboard menus serves both bars and restaurant; these can change daily. A hugely popular place, so if you are eating in the restaurant, called the Well Room – it has a 52ft-deep well – you really do have to book ahead to be sure of a table. A good choice of fish dishes on the menu such as steamed mussels in white wine, smoked trout salad, roasted monkfish wrapped in parma ham on chargrilled field mushrooms; also local game in season, steamed steak and kidney pudding with an onion gravy, a beef and winter vegetable stew with herb dumplings and scrummy home-made puds; on Sunday there's a traditional roast. Greene King Abbot ale, Adnams Bitter, Greene King IPA and a guest bitter;

interesting and varied wine list, some by the glass. Seats outside in the well-planted, very attractive courtyard. You might be interested to know that the church in nearby Nayland houses one of the very few religious paintings by Constable.

OPEN: 11–2.30, 6–11.
Real Ale. Restaurant.
No children in the bar. No dogs. Wheelchair access.
Six en-suite bedrooms.

Sudbury

Angel ① 01787 379038
Friar Street, Sudbury CO10 2AG
Greene King. Brenda Rowe, tenant

Locks built in the 18th century made the River Stour navigable as far as Sudbury, which stands on high ground above a loop of the river. By then, the Angel had been in existence for more than a century. Built on top of 10th-century cellars in the middle of town, it's an attractive, low-ceilinged, beamed building where they serve a good selection of bar snacks: sandwiches, ploughman's or poached salmon, scampi, Cajun chicken, roast chicken, gammon steaks, also a large vegetarian menu. You can eat in the bar or restaurant. Greene King related beers. Outside is a small, pretty patio. Dickens came to the town as a journalist to cover the 1835 general election; he wrote of his experiences in *Pickwick Papers* in which Sudbury became 'Eatenswill' – aptly named, as Sudbury was, politically, tremendously corrupt at that time and later disenfranchised. The painter Thomas Gainsborough was born here; there is a statue to him in the market place and his father's Tudor house is a museum and exhibition centre.

OPEN: 11–11.30. Sun 12–10.30.
Real Ale. Restaurant.
Children welcome. Plenty of dogs.

Swilland

Moon & Mushroom Inn ① 01473 785320
High Road, Swilland, nr Ipswich IP6 9LR
Free House. Clive & Adrienne Goodall, licensees

A very cosy, genuine local in the best possible way. Inside, the quarry-tiled, oak-beamed bar is comfortably furnished with a good winter fire and a homely, no-smoking dining room. The unusual name dates from the owners' takeover during the '80s; what was the Half Moon became the Moon. The addition of Mushroom reflects the owners' interest in exotic fungi, used as often as possible in the cooking. A simply furnished friendly place serving beer as local as you can get and really home-made casseroles: venison with dumplings, pork loin in Stilton sauce or Adrienne's minted lamb, all sitting on a hot plate in the dining area along with freshly cooked vegetables. The contents of the casseroles are constantly changing and there are always fresh fish and vegetarian dishes as an option. The beers, from East Anglian micro-breweries – normally seven or eight – are in the long line of barrels behind the bar. A varied wine list with about nine by the glass. Seats in the garden and on the flowery terrace at the front of the pub.

OPEN: 11–2.30, 6–11. Sun 12–2.30, 7–10.30.
Real Ale. No bar food Sun or Mon.
No children inside. Dogs in bar. Car park. Wheelchair access.
Cards: MasterCard, Solo, Switch, Visa.

Tostock

Gardeners Arms ① 01359 270460
Church Road, Tostock, nr Bury St Edmunds IP30 9PA
Greene King. Reg Ransome, FBII, tenant

Near the village green, this is a jolly, friendly, unspoilt village pub at its best. Two bars, a beamed lounge and a public bar with darts, pool table and games – nothing noisy, only the locals enjoying themselves. They serve well-presented, home-made bar food and well-kept ales. There is the usual selection of bar snacks and more exotic daily specials written on the beams of the pub: a Thai king-prawn curry with stir-fried vegetables on rice, lamb balti, chicken and broccoli bake and various vegetarian dishes. A greater variety of grills and other dishes are available during the evening, when it can get very busy. Greene King Abbot, IPA and seasonal beers. Seats in the attractive garden.

OPEN: 11.30–2.30 (Sat 11–2.30), 7–11.
Real Ale. Restaurant (not Sun lunch). No snacks Mon or Tues eves.
Children in eating area of bar. Dogs on leads.
Cards: most, except Amex.
N.B. Jukebox in public bar.

Walberswick

Bell Inn ① 01502 723109
Ferry Road, Walberswick, Southwold IP18 6TN
Adnams. Sue Ireland-Cutting, tenant
e-mail: bellinn@btinternet.com

This village is at the end of the road so to speak – there's nowhere else to go except the sea. Years ago this was a flourishing port at the mouth of the River Blyth, now it's used mainly by leisure sailors and the seasonal passenger ferry to Southwold just across the river. No distance at all by water but by road a journey of about 8 miles. As a young artist, Philip Wilson Steer discovered the area and painted a series of land and seascapes popularising the village, which become a celebrated artists' colony. The 600-year-old Bell, between the village green, old harbour and the beach was, I'm sure, a favourite place for the artists to meet. It's a charming place with a timeless interior, flagstones, beams, lots of nooks and crannies and winter log fires. Fish and seafood feature largely on the menu: marlin steak with garlic butter, salmon and pesto en croute, sea bass en papillotte with butter, white wine and thyme, as well as tenderloin of pork in green pepper sauce, pan-fried lamb's kidneys in garlic and red wine, vegetarian dishes, daily specials and home-made puds. An à la carte menu features on Friday and Saturday evenings. Menus change frequently but you will find soups, ploughman's, sandwiches and salads if you just want a light snack from the bar. Adnams range of ales includes the seasonal Fisherman (winter) and Regatta (summer); Adnams, with their wine-merchant hat on, supply the wines. Seats in the sheltered, flowery garden.

OPEN: 11–3, 6–11. Sat 11–11. Sun 12–10.30.
Real Ale.
Children welcome. Dogs on leads. Car park. Wheelchair access. Bedrooms – most with river/sea views.
Cards: JCB, MasterCard, Solo, Switch, Visa Delta, Visa.

Waldringfield

Maybush Inn ① 01473 736215
The Quay, Cliff Road, Waldringfield IP12 1QL
Free House. Steve Lomas, licensee

Downriver from Woodbridge, this is an attractive little village on the Deben with a busy sailing centre and ships' chandlers and boat-builders along the foreshore. In a most picturesque position on the bank of the river, the Maybush has views over the yacht masts to a sandy island beyond. Sailing memorabilia decorates this friendly, popular place. Well used to catering for hungry hordes, they serve generous portions of hearty, well-cooked traditional food to go with Adnams and other ales: home-made soup, well-filled sandwiches, deep-fried potato wedges, tiger prawns in filo pastry, mixed grill, gammon steak with egg, pineapple, mushrooms and grilled tomatoes, home-made steak and Guinness pie and other dishes on the blackboard. The river is a popular mooring for yachtsmen, though when the tide is out the beach is muddy shingle, just firm enough to launch your dinghy. From the pub's waterfront position you can watch the nautical activity at high tide, and observe the varied bird life on the mud flats when it's out.

OPEN: 11–11.
Real Ale.
Children welcome. No dogs. Big car park. Wheelchair access.
Cards: all major credit cards.

BEST OF THE REST

Cavendish
Bull ① 01789 280245
High Street, Cavendish CO10 8AX
This pretty village on the upper Stour surrounds a large green. The Bull is one of the Adnams stable, so you'll know the range of beers. As Adnams are also vintners, there will be some good wines to accompany the selection of imaginative dishes on the specials board: lots of fresh fish and there could be crispy duck with Chinese pancakes, salmon stuffed with prawns or baked lamb with herbs and red wine sauce; home-made puds too. Children and dogs welcome. Wheelchair access (not WC). Bedrooms.
Open: 12–3, 6–11 (Sun 6.30–10.30). No bar food Mon.

Dennington

Queens Head ① 01728 638241

The Square, Dennington, nr Woodbridge IP13 8AB

The ancient Queens Head stands on the village green, next to the handsome parish church. Like so many old pubs it has a well-beamed, spacious interior reflecting its great age. As well as soup, sandwiches and ploughman's, there are some imaginative additions to the menu: prawns in filo pastry, braised sausages in red wine or salmon and prawn au gratin. Beers are Adnams Bitter, Morlands Old Speckled Hen and Wadworths 6X. Seats at the side of the pub among the flowers. Older children only allowed in restaurant on Saturday evening.

Open: 11.30–2.30 (Sun 12–3), 6.30–11.

Hartest

Crown ① 01284 830250

The Green, Hartest IP29 4DH

South of Bury St Edmunds, this pink-washed 15th-century pub is on the village green, next to the church. Heavily beamed with a splendid inglenook fireplace, the building had a grander, earlier existence when it was Hartest Hall. Now a popular village pub it serves good-value bar food, but the accent is on fish – lots of creative dishes. Greene King Abbot and IPA beers and a choice of wines. There is a conservatory and seats in the garden and courtyard. Children welcome. Dogs too.

Open: 11–2.30, 6–11.

Icklingham

Red Lion ① 01638 717802

The Street, Icklingham IP28 6PS

Set back from the road with gardens front and back, the Red Lion is in a village, on the edge of the King's Forest near the delightfully named River Lark. An appealing thatched 16th-century pub with rugs on the floor, comfortable chairs around the big fireplace and some tempting dishes on the menu. Usual bar snacks as well as dishes such as chicken breast stuffed with spinach, pork chops in a barbecue sauce, local sausage and mash or mussels in a white wine, garlic and cream sauce. Greene King range of beers, one guest and country wines. Mulled wine in winter. Children welcome. No dogs. Wheelchair access.

Open: 12–3 (Sun 12–2.30), 6–11.

Lavenham

Angel Hotel ① 01787 247388

Market Place, Lavenham CO10 9QZ

Lavenham is full of wonderful medieval buildings, among them the Angel in the Square. It might not look as old as the surrounding buildings but it has held a licence since the early 15th century and inside you see evidence of a building that has been carefully looked after since then. Something for everyone on the daily changing menu: game terrine with Cumberland sauce, smoked salmon and smoked trout with lemon mayonnaise, warm salad of smoked chicken, bacon and red onions, and for a main course, pork medallions with Calvados sauce, fillet of sea bass with saffron and red peppers or steak and ale pie, English cheeses and delicious puds. Adnams, Nethergate, Greene King IPA and Abbot; comprehensive wine list. Seats at the front of the Angel and in the sheltered garden at the back. Lots of things to see in Lavenham – just a wander round is a feast for the eyes. Children welcome. Dogs in bar only. Wheelchair access (not WC).

Open: 11–11. Sun 12–10.30.

Lidgate

Star ① 01638 500275
The Street, Lidgate CB8 9PP

The little river Kennet rises near the village, flowing on before joining the Lark which forms the county boundary. Originally 15th-century cottages, this pink-washed building looks every inch the traditional village pub both inside and out with a difference – some of the decorations have a definite Iberian lean. Not surprising, as you have a Spanish landlady producing some delicious Spanish dishes; the warmth of the Mediterranean is taking the chill off the cold east of England. Greene King beers and some good wines. Children welcome. Dogs too – not in dining room.

Open: 11–3, 5–11. Sun 12–3, 7–11.

Southwold

Sole Bay Inn ① 01502 723736
7 East Green, Southwold IP18 6JN

Pretty and flower bedecked, the Sole Bay Inn is just a short step from the lighthouse that dominates the town, the brewery that provides the beer and the beach. A revamped, more clean-cut interior where they still serve pubby lunchtime food, a range of Adnams beers, decent house wine and good coffee. Seats at the front, where you can soak up the sun, and on a side terrace. Children and dogs welcome.

Open: 11–11. Sun 12–10.30. (It's too late to make this a main entry but it is free of background music, so enjoy!)

Wingfield

De la Pole Arms ① 01379 384545
Church Road, Wingfield IP21 5RA

Next to the church that contains the tomb of Sir John de Wingfield and monuments of the de la Pole family, at first glance the pub could be any age. Inside, parts of the 14th-century priest's building – established to perpetuate Sir John's memory – are still evident. It has been wonderfully restored – the 14th century meets the 21st. Comfortable bars and a delightful no-smoking dining room. Food is inventive and plentiful. Over 30 wines on the list including one from the local vineyard at Fressingfield. On draught are St Peter's Bitter, Strong Ale and Wheat Beer in the summer. Dogs and children welcome. Wheelchair access.

Open: 11–3, 6–11. Sun 12–3, 7–10.30.

Wetherspoon in Suffolk

Haverhill – Drabbet Smock, 5–6 Peas Hill, Market Square
① 01440 713070
Ipswich – Cricketers, 51 Crown Street
① 01473 225910
Ipswich – Wetherspoons, 10 Corn Hill
① 01473 210334
Newmarket – Golden Lion, 44 High Street
① 01638 672040

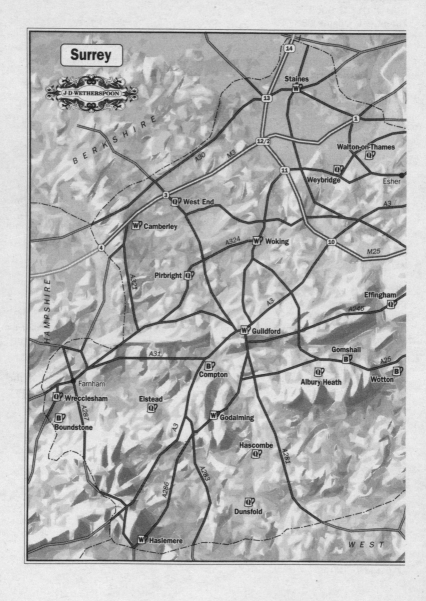

Surrey

J·D·WETHERSPOON

BERKSHIRE

HAMPSHIRE

WEST

14

Staines W

13

1

12/2

Walton-on-Thames Q

A30   M3   Weybridge Q   Esher

11

A3

3 Q West End

W Camberley

4   A324   W Woking   10   M25

A321   Pirbright Q   A3   Effingham Q

A246

W Guildford

A31   Gomshall B

Compton B   A25

Albury Heath Q   Wotton B

Farnham

Q Wrecclesham   Elstead Q

B Boundstone   W Godalming

A287   Hascombe Q

A281

A3   A283

A286   Dunsfold Q

W Haslemere

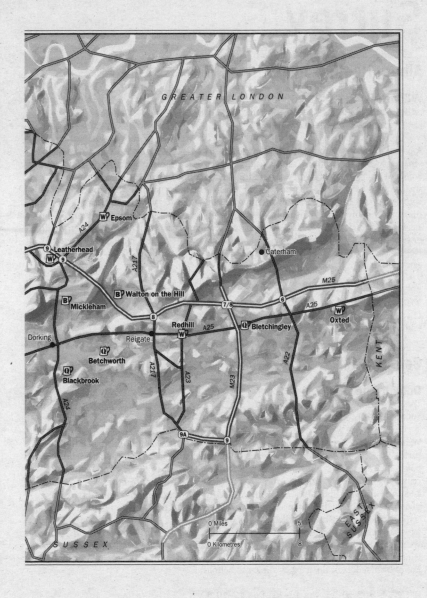

GREATER LONDON

A24 W Epsom

A217

9 Leatherhead
W 9

M25

● Caterham

B Walton on the Hill

B Mickleham

7/8

6

A25

Dorking

8

Redhill
W

Reigate

A25

Q Bletchingley

W Oxted

KENT

Q Betchworth

A217

A23

M23

A22

Q Blackbrook

A24

9A

9

0 Miles   5

0 Kilometres   8

S U S S E X

E A S T
S U S S E X

Surrey

Albury Heath

William IV ☎ 01483 202685
Little London, Albury Heath, nr Guildford GU5 9DG
Free House. Giles Madge, licensee

A popular walkers' pub in an area as varied as the walks; here the Tillingbourne valley separates woods, commons, sandy heaths and the many footpaths that cross the Downs. South of Shere, the William IV is a traditional, uncomplicated, 16th-century pub. The small rooms have beams, flagstone floors and in one there is a huge inglenook fireplace with an equally huge log fire in winter; go up a few steps to the carpeted dining area. The short, reasonably priced bar menu lists a good selection of sandwiches, home-made pies, stews, fish and chips on Friday, steaks, pasta, a Sunday roast and always a vegetarian dish or two. Five real ales; four regulars and one occasional guest among them: Flowers IPA, Hogs Back TEA, Hop Garden Gold, Greene King Abbot and Bass. Seats in the pretty front garden.

OPEN: 11–3, 5.30–11 (Sun 7–10.30).
Réal Ale.
Children and dogs on leads. Car park. Wheelchair access.
Cards: MasterCard, Visa.

Betchworth

Dolphin Inn ☎ 01737 842288
The Street, Betchworth RH3 7DW
Youngs. George Campbell, manager

Walks abound; there are wonderful views from Betchworth Clump, north-west of the parish, and a short walk along the bank of the River Mole takes you to Brockham, which boasts the most charming village green in the country. Opposite the church, the 18th-century Dolphin – though an earlier Dolphin was here in the 16th century – is popular and unspoilt, with open fires, flagstones in the front bar, carpets and panelling in the saloon. Always busy, they cope admirably with the rush. The bar menu lists sandwiches, six varieties of ploughman's, filled baked potatoes, mussels in garlic butter, potato waffles with bacon and cheese, honey-roast ham, steak and mushroom pie, salads, grills, daily specials and filling puddings. Youngs range of ales, including the seasonal Winter Warmer; wines by the glass. Seats at the front, side and back of the pub. Our spies tell us there are lots of birdfeeders in the garden – 'a joy to behold'.

OPEN: 11–3, 5.30–11. Sat 11–11. Sun 12–10.30.
Real Ale.
No children. Dogs on leads. Car park. Wheelchair access.
Cards: most major cards.

Blackbrook

Plough ① 01306 886603
Blackbrook Road, Blackbrook, Dorking RH5 4DS
Hall & Woodhouse. Robin & Christine Squire, tenants

Close to Holmwood Common, surrounded by some of the best Surrey countryside, the white-painted Plough has been done up and looks particularly welcoming. All very jolly inside with red walls, touches of green and gold, and fresh flowers on the tables. No restaurant, so you eat in the bars – the saloon is no-smoking. There is a lunchtime snack menu of ploughman's, filled jacket potatoes, toasted 'deli' bagels, coarse garlic paté, deep-fried breaded scampi, steak sandwich in ciabatta bread with tomato, onion, relish and fries, local sausages, lasagne and chicken curry. Three boards in the pub list the specials and other dishes. It is planned to introduce local cheeses on the lunchtime snack menu. Beers are Fursty Ferret, Badger, Tanglefoot and Sussex. Good choice of wine. Seats in the attractive cottagey garden.

OPEN: 11–2.30 (summer and Sat 11–3), 6–11. Sun 12–3, 7–10.30.
Real Ale.
Children and dogs welcome. Car park. Wheelchair access.
Cards: MasterCard, Visa.

Bletchingley

William IV ① 01883 743278
Little Common Lane, Bletchingley RH1 4QF
Lease. Su, James & Robert Saunders, licensees
e-mail: william1v@freeserve.com

Along a leafy country lane just outside this village on the edge of the North Downs, the William IV, a welcoming, well-run country pub, was originally a pair of mid-Victorian cottages. Weatherboarded and half tile-hung, it has charming small rooms and a separate no-smoking dining room. New licensees have taken over; new hands in the kitchen. The full menu is available in both the bar and dining room. The generous bar food could include whitebait with farmhouse bread, fresh mushrooms in garlic butter, game and port paté, pork escalopes with peppers, mushrooms in a tarragon and white wine sauce, lamb chops in a redcurrant and rosemary sauce, home-made steak and kidney pie, macaroni cheese, meatballs in a basil sauce with pasta, grills, fish, pizzas and vegetarian dishes. Friday is fish day – lunch and evening. Beers are Harveys Best, Adnams Best, Youngs and Fullers London Pride. Seats in the sheltered garden. From the village, a short, easterly walk will take you to Tilburstow Hill which looks over the valleys of the River Mole and Eden towards Ashdown forest.

OPEN: 12–3, 6–11. Sun 12–10.30.
Real Ale.
Children welcome in dining room and garden. Dogs on leads. Reasonable wheelchair access.
Cards: all major cards.

Dunsfold

Sun Inn ① 01483 200242
The Common, Dunsfold GU8 4LE
Punch Pub Co. Chris Lindesay, licensee

The three 'Fold' villages in the area – Alfold, Chiddingfold and Dunsfold – all have a
history of smuggling wines, spirits and cloth. In Dunsfold there is more than meets the
eye, and when you know that down the lane from the 13th-century church there's a holy
well containing water high in chloride (like Lourdes) which is good for the eyes, you
should appreciate the pun. The Sun, an attractive double-fronted, brick-built 18th-century
coaching inn, overlooks the common. The comfortable, beamed interior has three open
fires and a cottage restaurant with both table d'hôte and à la carte menus. Everything is
freshly cooked: home-made soups, well-filled sandwiches, ploughman's, the speciality of
the house – local Dunsfold quail – other game in season, fresh fish and good puds. Daily
specials on the blackboard; roasts on Sunday. Harveys Sussex, Adnams Bitter, Courage
Best, Youngs and the occasional guest beer. Range of malt whiskies. Decent wine list. Seats
at the front of the pub overlook the green.

OPEN: 11–3, 5–11. Fri & Sat 11–11. Sun 11–10.30.
Real Ale. Restaurant.
Children welcome. Dogs on leads. Car park. Wheelchair access (not WC).
Cards: Delta, MasterCard, Switch, Visa.
N. B. Music in one bar.

Effingham

Plough ① 01372 458121
Orestan Lane, Effingham KT24 5SW
Youngs. Jason Buttery, tenant

Between Leatherhead and Guildford, in the best of the Surrey countryside, the Plough is
an attractive rural pub with a comfortable bar, lounge, no-smoking area and winter fires.
Cooking is a mix of traditional and modern. The menus change once a month but there
could be freshly prepared chorizo and black olive salad and garlic aioli, beetroot gravadlax
with mixed leaves, shredded chilli beef and crispy noodles, and for a main course, mixed
game casserole, roasted root vegetables and herb dumplings, bangers, spring onion mash
and gravy or pan-fried duck breast, rösti potato, broccoli purée and berry jus, perhaps an
apple and sultana crumble and custard to finish. Youngs Bitter, Special and a good
selection of wine. There is a newly developed garden to sit in.

OPEN: 11–3, 5.30–11. Sun 12–3, 7–10.30.
Real Ale.
Children only if eating. No dogs. Car park. Wheelchair access.
Cards: all except Amex and Diners.

Elstead

Woolpack ① 01252 703106
The Green, Elstead GU8 6HD
Punch. Sally Macready, lease

By the small green in this thriving village, the name of the pub is a reminder that this area was a centre for the processing of wool. Early in its life this 18th-century building was used to store the wool bales after shearing; only later was it licensed, eventually becoming the pub you see today. Inside, the long main bar – with a fireplace at each end – is decorated with a number of artifacts relating to its woollier past. On the blackboard menus you'll find some real favourites: king prawns in filo pastry with a sweet chilli sauce, deep-fried whitebait, smoked trout with horseradish sauce, pork medallions with mango, brandy and a touch of chilli, beef in ale casserole, grills, home-made pies and a duck and spicy sausage cassoulet, daily specials and Sunday lunches. The menu is constantly changing – it depends on what is available and what inspires the chef. The puddings are another inspiration – all home-made. Children's portions available. Greene King Abbot ale and one other from the cask. A selection of wines by the bottle and by the glass. A family room opens onto the garden and a children's play area. Seats in the garden for the grown-ups.

OPEN: 11–2.30, 6–11. Sun 12–3, 7–10.30.
Real Ale. Restaurant.
Children in family room and restaurant. Dogs on leads. Wheelchair access (not WC).
Cards: all major cards except Amex and Diners.

Hascombe

White Horse ① 01483 208258
Hascombe, nr Godalming GU8 4JA
Punch. Susan Barnett, lease
e-mail: thewhitehorse-1@hotmail.com

In this area of winding lanes and attractive villages tucked under the summit of the greensand ridge, Hascombe has some very handsome houses – a number built by Lutyens early in his career. On the edge of the village is the popular, well-run 16th-century White Horse. This old coaching inn, with very friendly staff, serves really good food ranging from well-filled sandwiches and ploughman's to Thai-style fishcakes, home-made chicken pie, burgers, grilled steaks, a fresh fish board and daily specials. Fresh dressed crab with mayonnaise, filo-wrapped prawns deep fried and served with a sweet chilli dip, grilled whole Dover sole, or Scotch fillet steak au poivre from the full à la carte menu in the restaurant. All the food is freshly cooked to order, so you have to be patient. Beers are Adnams Bitter, Directors Bitter, Harveys and a comprehensive wine list. Lots of walks around here, the nearest of note is the Greensand Way. If you're interested in trees, Winkworth Arboretum is nearby. Seats in the large garden.

OPEN: 11–3, 5.30–11. Sat 11–11. Sun 12–10.30.
Real Ale.
Children welcome, dogs too. Wheelchair access difficult but staff willing to help.
Cards: Amex, MasterCard, Visa.

Pirbright

Royal Oak ① 01483 232466
Aldershot Road, Pirbright, Aldershot GU24 0D4
Laurel Pub Co. Geoff Middleton, manager

Surrounded by the military – the names of the barracks and camps in this area are so well known they trip off the tongue. South of the village, away from the urban sprawl, the 16th-century Royal Oak is a delightful, rural pub set back off the road in its own big garden. At the height of summer you'll see why it is so frequently placed in the Guildford in Bloom competition. On the menu you'll find a good selection of bar food: herb and garlic bread piled with marinated olives and roasted cherry tomatoes drizzled with balsamic dressing – for two to share, Brie and bacon quiche, spinach and mushroom cannelloni, slow-cooked Welsh lamb, salmon and dill fishcakes, Cumberland sausages and mash, beer-battered cod, seasonal salads, well-filled sandwiches and daily specials. A CAMRA pub so you know the beers are kept as they should be: currently Hogsback Traditional English Ale, Flowers IPA, Original, Bass, Wadsworths 6X, Ringwood Best, Fortyniner, St Austell Tribute and three guests. Seats among the flowers at the front, or away from the traffic noise in the quieter garden at the back. Good walking country.

OPEN: 11–11. Sun 12–10.30.
Real Ale.
Children to dine only if room is available in no-smoking area. No dogs. Car park. Full disabled facilities.

Walton on Thames

Regent ① 01932 243980
19 Church Street, Walton on Thames KT12 2QP
Wetherspoon.

Cinemas always look like cinemas irrespective of what has changed inside. So it is with this building, but it knocks spots off the original – a successful total rebuild. Just off the High Street, this is one big space with a very long bar, always with a no-smoking area. They serve about eight real ales – one is competitively priced, as well as good, reliable food and daily specials.

OPEN: 11–11. Sun 12–10.30.
Real Ale.
No children. No dogs. Disabled facilities.

West End

Inn at West End ① 01276 858652
42 Guildford Road, West End GU24 9PW
Free House. Gerry & Ann Price, licensees
e-mail: greatfood@the-inn.co.uk

A Rugosa rose hedge and hanging baskets bloom in summer around the inn. Inside is everything you could wish for: an attractive redesigned interior, bare boards, light oak tables, comfortable seats in the bar, newspapers and magazines to read while you wait, a wood-burning stove to keep you warm in winter, a jolly landlord to talk to and more importantly, some really good food. With eating in mind, there is a more formal dining area, a conservatory and terrace with dining tables. Many of the ingredients that find their way into the kitchen are locally sourced; game from local shoots, meat from local farmers and fish brought up from the coast in the inn's own chiller van. All is as fresh as fresh can be – they have their own veg garden too. From the bar snack menu, home-made leek and potato soup, Welsh rarebit with grilled tomato, Worcestershire sauce and dressed leaves, smoked salmon salad with walnuts and capers or a mixed plate of Mediterranean hors d'oeuvres; for a main course, a selection of fresh fish with a herb and fennel dressing, pot-roast quail flavoured with a wild mushroom mousse on a tarragon and truffle risotto, or Cumberland sausages with spinach, mash and gravy. There is a reasonable two- or three-course set lunch menu. Fullers London Pride and Courage Best are the beers. The wine list is rather special. The licensees run a small wine business and this is reflected in the variety and quality of their list, which has over 150 to choose from. Plenty of seats in the garden.

OPEN: 12–3, 5–11. Sat 12–11. Sun 12–10.30.
Real Ale.
No children. Dogs allowed in bar. Car park.
Cards: Most, except Diners.

Weybridge

Old Crown ① 01932 842844
83 Thames Street, Weybridge KT13 8LP
Free House. Mark Redknap, licensee
e-mail: markredknap@aol.com

Very much an old-fashioned, well-run pub. The same family have been here for over 40 years and they look after you well. A smart white, 16th-century, long, low – well most of it – partly weatherboarded, Grade II listed building, it has three bars inside, a snug and an air-conditioned no-smoking conservatory. A short menu: sandwiches – hot or cold, plain or toasted – filled jacket potatoes, quiche, steaks, lamb lasagne, gammon steak, ham, egg and chips, steak burgers – traditional, sustaining pub fare. The specials board will always

have a choice of fish. Courage Best, Directors and revolving guest ales. Seats on the patio
and in the riverside garden.

OPEN: 10–11. Sun 12–10.30.
Real Ale.
Children in lounge bar and conservatory only. Dogs on leads. Car park.
Cards: all major credit/debit cards.

Woking

Wetherspoons ① 01483 722818
Chertsey Road, Woking GU21 5AJ
Wetherspoon.

There isn't ever anything very much that is new about a Wetherspoon establishment. Beers
change, the menu changes with the seasons and there are daily specials, otherwise they
exist for you and me. This one is in a converted Woolworth store, but it does have a
theme – H. G. Wells and his book *War of the Worlds*. A model of a time-machine is
attached to the ceiling! At ground level three ales are on permanently and at least three
regional ales are guests. They hold regular beer festivals.

OPEN: 11–11. Sun 12–10.30.
Real Ale.
No children. No dogs. Always a big no-smoking area and disabled facilities.

Wrecclesham

Sandrock ① 01252 715865
Sandrock Hill, Wrecclesham, Farnham TU10 4NS
Free House. David Walton, manager and licensee

Paradise for the beer aficionado in more ways than one. Not only a choice of eight beers –
which change weekly – but if you hit the pub at the right time in March, there seems to be
an endless beer festival for you to enjoy. The Sandrock is well known for serving the more
unusual beers; they squeeze you into one large and one small bar, the latter is also used as
the games room – for bar billiards – and leads into the garden. A straightforward bar
menu is served at lunchtime – sandwiches, a club sandwich, ploughman's, ham and eggs,
chilli – that sort of thing. Filled rolls only in the evening to go with the range of well-kept
ales, maybe Enville and Bathams Best, both small breweries in the Midlands, also eight
constantly changing beers from micro-breweries on hand pump. Lots of chairs and tables
in the garden to cope with the keen customers.

OPEN: 11–11. Sun 12–10.30.
Real Ale. No food Sun lunchtime.
Children welcome. Dogs on leads. Wheelchair access (not WC). Small car park.

BEST OF THE REST

Boundstone

Bat & Ball ☎ 01252 792108

Bat and Ball Lane, Boundstone, Farnham GU10 4SA

In the Bourne valley, in an attractive area of residential Farnham and surrounded by footpaths that meander through the valley, the mid-Victorian Bat & Ball has a garden running down to the Bourne stream. Substantially refurbished by the owners who for over 18 years were licensees at the Woolpack in Elsted. Because it's hard to find, mainly because Bat and Ball lane is on the 'wrong' side of the stream, it's called Farnham's best-kept secret. You need Sandrock Hill Road and then Upper Bourne Lane to reach the pub. Food is good-value 'old English and Colonial': home-made chicken liver paté, smoked trout, deep-fried whitebait with home-made tartar sauce, and for a main course tandoori chicken with rice and pitta bread, pork medallions in apricot, schnapps and thyme sauce, locally made sausages, salads, a choice of ploughman's and lots more. The menu changes regularly and there are specials on the blackboard and salads in the cold cabinet. Six cask ales on at any one time. Wines are mostly New World; eight by the glass. Children welcome but not in main bar. Dogs on leads. Wheelchair access. Cards: all except Amex and Diners.
Open: 11–3, 5.30–11. Fri, Sat & Sun 11–11.

Compton

Withies Inn ☎ 01483 421158

Withies Lane, Compton GU3 1JA

Not far from the impressive Tudor mansion at Losely, the Withies is a popular rendezvous – full of atmosphere and beautifully kept. Low beams and a huge fire in the small bar. Here they serve an uncomplicated snack menu: fisherman's broth, ploughman's, quiche, Cumberland sausages with mashed potato, onions and gravy, seafood platter, sandwiches and filled jacket potatoes. If you want to push the boat out they have an interesting, more extensive restaurant menu. Fullers London Pride, Bass, King & Barnes Sussex and Greene King IPA are the beers. A comprehensive wine list. Children welcome. No dogs.
Open: 11–3, 6–11.

Gomshall

Compasses Inn ☎ 01483 202506

Station Road, Gomshall GU5 9LA

Originally known as 'God Encompasses', this was such a mouthful that it eventually evolved into the 'Goat and Compasses', now just The Compasses. In pretty surroundings on the Guildford to Dorking road – the pub is separated from its garden by the Tillingbourne stream and its ghost. It's a good place to stop. The no-smoking restaurant is a delightful symphony in yellow, all very cheery and happy. Reasonably priced food is served in generous portions, the ingredients are fresh and all the dishes are cooked 'in pub', as are the bar snacks. Adnams, Morlands, Hop Back Summer Lightning, Fullers London Pride – two beers change monthly. Plenty of tables in the riverside garden. Children welcome. Bedrooms. Cards: Delta, MasterCard, Switch, Visa.
Open: 11–11. Sun 12–10.30.

Mickleham

King William IV ① 01372 372590

Byttom Hill, Mickleham, nr Dorking RH5 6EL

Once an alehouse for Lord Beaverbrook's staff, the King William IV, a mix of Georgian and Victorian architecture, is high on the hill with wonderful views from its own colourful garden towards the Mole valley and Norbury Park. An appreciative public flock here to sample well-known favourites as well as more creative dishes, including fish and vegetarian specials. Adnams, Badger Best Bitter, Hogs Back and a monthly changing guest beer. Short wine list, some by the glass. You are very near White Hill and Box Hill; surrounded by lots of walks. Children over 12, no dogs.

Open: 11–3, 6–11. Sun 12–3, 7–10.30.

Walton-on-the-Hill

Chequers ① 01737 812364

Chequers Lane, Walton-on-the-Hill KT20 7SF

The bars are at the front and the Chequers' front door seems to be at the back. You reach the bars from the car park through an enclosed garden and the garden bar. There is a traditional bar menu: sausage, mash and onion gravy, grilled Mediterranean vegetables, fresh cod fillet, several salads, sandwiches, ploughman's and filled paninis. Weather permitting, the barbecue will be going full pelt from the end of April to the end of September. Full Youngs range of ales plus seasonal ales and guests from Smiles brewery. Plenty of room in the garden for you and the barbecue. Children in the play area and garden. Dogs on leads. Wheelchair access.

Open: 11–3, 5.30–11. Fri & Sat 11–11. Sun 12–10.30.

Wotton

Wotton Hatch ① 01306 732931

Guildford Road, Wotton, Dorking RH5 6QQ

Not to be missed, though it could be, as this old place is on a bend on the Dorking–Guildford road. Basically a 17th-century pub with additions. The reliable bar food changes with the seasons, but there will always be a good, varied choice. The evening menu is more extensive. Bass, Fullers London Pride, a guest beer and wines by the glass. You can see the Surrey countryside at its best from the pub garden. Children in eating area of bar. No dogs.

Open: 11–11.

Wetherspoon in Surrey

Camberley – Claude du Vall, 77–81 High Street
☎ 01276 672910
Godalming – Jack Philips, 48–56 High Street
☎ 01483 521750
Guildford – Rodboro Buildings, 1–10 Bridge Street
☎ 01483 306366
Haslemere – Swan Inn, High Street
☎ 01428 641747
Leatherhead – Edmund Tylney, 30–34 High Street
☎ 01372 362715
Oxted – Oxted Inn, 1–4 Station Road West
☎ 01883 723440
Redhill – Sun, 17–21 London Road
☎ 01737 766886
Woking – Wetherspoons, 51–57 Chertsey Road
☎ 01483 722818

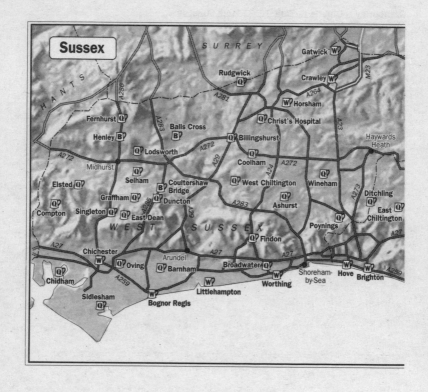

East Grinstead

Wadhurst

Ticehurst

KENT

Burwash

Danehill

A265

Fletching

Blackboys

Heathfield

Rye

EAST SUSSEX

Udimore

Barcombe

Battle

Chiddingly

Wartling

Lewes

Hastings

Kingston

Alciston

A259

Berwick

Alfriston

Eastbourne

East Dean

0 Miles 10

0 Kilometres 16

J·D·WETHERSPOON

Sussex

Alfriston

Smugglers Inn ① 01323 870241
Market Cross, Alfriston, Polegate, E. Sussex BN26 5UE
Leased, free of tie. Mrs Maureen Ney, licensee

Alfriston, on the meandering Cuckmere river, was an important smuggling centre during the 18th century, the river giving the smugglers an easy route to and from quiet Cuckmere Haven on the coast. This old pub – once owned by one of the most notorious smugglers – is by the market cross in a delightful village, hugely popular with visitors and walkers. Here you can relax in the low-beamed, hop-hung bar and enjoy something from the menu. Always a soup of the day, a countryman's, huntsman's or ploughman's lunch, several double-decker sandwiches, lots of smuggler's sandwiches or a choice of toasted ones, rump-steak platters, Albert's sausages, gammon steak with pineapple, fresh grilled trout, spinach and mushroom lasagne, cod in batter or a wholemeal-base vegetarian flan. Courage Directors, Harveys Best Bitter and local seasonal ales. Beyond the lounge bar is a conservatory which in turn leads to a brick courtyard and garden.

OPEN: 11–2.30 (Sat 11–3), 6.30–11. Sun 12–3, 7–10.30.
Real Ale.
Children welcome, but not in bar. Dogs on leads. Wheelchair access.

Ashurst

Fountain Inn ① 01403 710219
Ashurst, nr Steyning, W. Sussex BN44 3AP (north of Steyning on B2135)
Free House. Mark & Christopher White, licensees

Now that all the building work has finished you can appreciate the changes – inside and out – that have been made over the last few years. The alterations of previous owners have been stripped away to reveal the original 16th-century building which had been hidden away for too long. Now there is a beamed snug with flagstones and a huge inglenook fireplace to match the one in the tap room. Very popular, therefore very busy, serving a wide variety of interesting food listed on both the printed and the blackboard menus. From the printed menu there is the usual choice of bar food – soup, freshly made sandwiches, ploughman's, steak, ale and mushroom pie, chargrilled steaks, caramelised onion, goat's cheese and cranberry tart, Sussex smokie (smoked haddock and prawns in a cheese sauce), chargrilled fillet of seabass with roasted pepper, lemon and dill dressing and more. On the specials board will be fresh fish such as lemon sole, grilled halibut and black bream. Seats on the terrace and in the pretty garden which has had an improving makeover. Six ales usually available, among which could be Harveys Best, Shepherd Neame

Masterbrew, Youngs Best, Kings Horsham Best and one changing guest served from the barrel on the bar. If you are feeling energetic there is a skittle alley in the stables.

OPEN: 11–2.30, 6–11.
Real Ale. No food Sun or Mon eves except sandwiches.
Children over 10 in restaurant. Dogs welcome.
No cards.

Barcombe

Anchor Inn ☎ 01273 400414
Anchor Lane, Barcombe, nr Lewes, E. Sussex BN8 5BS
Free House. Peter & Michael Harris, licensees

Just the place to be on a summer's day; the pub garden goes down to the river from where you can take boat trips up the river and boats are for hire. There has always been a watery connection at the Anchor – apart from the closeness of the river. In the 18th century it was built as a convenient stopping place for the bargees travelling up the River Ouse from the coast at Newhaven – a little light refreshment then off they would float! An excess of rain and you can float in too. The approach road has been known to flood, but the kind landlords tend to leave a boat somewhere so they don't miss any custom. Two cosy little bars inside, and a separate restaurant. They are willing to cater for every eventuality and function; you can get married here too (plenty of room outside for a marquee). There is an à la carte menu in the restaurant and a range of freshly made bar food such as home-made soups, filled baguettes and baked potatoes, steak and kidney pie, sausages in an onion gravy and daily specials. Harveys Best, Badgers Best and Tanglefoot are the beers; they also have a good, short wine list. Seats in the garden.

OPEN: 11–3, 6–11. Sun 12–10.30.
Real Ale.
Children – preferably in summer only. Dogs on leads. Wheelchair access (not WC). Four bedrooms.

Barnham

Murrell Arms ☎ 01243 553320
Yapton Road, Barnham, Bognor, W. Sussex PO22 0AS
Gales. Mervyn Cutten, tenant

Unspoilt, unchanging and a devil to dust. Inside this delightful old place you could be forgiven for thinking you have stumbled into a bric-a-brac collector's heaven that also sells beer. Here is an eclectic assortment of all those bits and pieces someone couldn't resist buying; little treasures that help to make the pub friendly and welcoming. Only two small bars, both with open fires, where they serve proper bar food. Just a simple, short menu so you know everything is freshly prepared: ploughman's, sausages – that sort of thing, and a couple of daily specials such as a boiled bacon hock, chicken curry, or a rabbit and pork casserole – good, honest pub food. No puddings. They know what they can do and they do it well. Barrels of Gales ales and a guest are kept in the still room on the ground floor,

English country wines and French wines by the glass. Outside is a flower-filled courtyard and seats in the enclosed garden; swings in the garden for the children.

OPEN: 11–3, 6–11. Sat 11–11. Sun 12–10.30.
Real Ale.
Children if controlled. Dogs on leads. Car park. Wheelchair access possible.
No cards.

Berwick

Cricketers Arms ➀ 01323 870469
Lower Road, Berwick, Polegate, E. Sussex BN26 6SP
Harveys. Peter Brown, tenant
www.cricketersberwick.co.uk

This village, at the foot of a glorious sweep of the South Downs, is close to that walkers' paradise, the South Downs Way. Four hundred years old, the Cricketers Arms is an interesting, unspoilt country pub that was once two flint-built cottages, becoming an ale house about 200 years ago. Friendly, busy and well loved, it has comfortable furnishings, tiled floors, heavily beamed bars and good winter log fires. Cricket is celebrated in the pub with the collection of cricket bats and old related photographs, past and present. Home-made pub food: soup, garlic mushrooms, oak-smoked salmon, local cod in batter, locally cured ham with eggs and chips, filled jacket potatoes, various ploughman's, vegetarian dishes and daily specials on the blackboard. Fresh fish comes in daily and there is always a vegetarian special on the blackboard. Harveys Bitter and seasonal ales from the cask. A wine of the month – guest wines from around the world. Plenty of seats in the attractive gardens at the front and back of the pub.

OPEN: Apr–Sep 11–11 (Sun 12–10.30). Winter weekdays 11–3, 6–11. Sat 11–11. Sun 12–10.30.
Real Ale.
Children allowed in certain areas. Dogs welcome with well-behaved owners. Car park. Wheelchair access.
Cards: Amex, Delta, MasterCard, Switch, Visa.

Billingshurst

Blue Ship ➀ 01403 822709
The Haven, nr Billingshurst, W. Sussex RH14 9BS
Hall & Woodhouse. J. R. Davie, tenant

An 'out-with-the-map' pub, as the unspoilt Blue Ship is well away from the main road; look for the signpost to The Haven after the junction of the A264 and A29. Built in the 15th century – with Victorian additions – in a hamlet surrounded by the lovely Sussex countryside; a charming, unchanging place, particularly popular at weekends. One front bar and two small rooms – one for children – they serve a good choice of traditional bar food: ploughman's, sandwiches, home-made soups, a fish dish or two, cottage pie, macaroni or cauliflower cheese, steak and onion pie, mushroom broccoli and pasta bake and good puds. Hall & Woodhouse Badger Beers from the barrel and Stopford Press Cider. Tables in the garden and in front of the pub by the honeysuckle.

OPEN: 11–3, 6–11.
Real Ale. No food Sun or Mon eves.
Children in rooms without bar. Dogs on leads.
N.B. Warning: £1 fine if you use your mobile phone!

Blackboys

Blackboys Inn ① 01825 890283
Lewes Road, Blackboys, nr Uckfield, E. Sussex TN22 5LG
Harveys. Edward Molesworth, tenant

Seats by the pond, or in the shade of the spreading chestnut tree; in summer this is a lovely place to be. Set back from the main road through the village, the pub is a large, sociable place. Old, rambling, full of fascinating bits and pieces, with antique furniture and big winter log fires in the inglenook. The interesting choice of bar food is listed on the blackboard; sometimes there is home-made fish soup with croutons and aioli, mushrooms baked in a port and Stilton sauce, scallop of seafood gratinée, fillet of cod in prawn, mussel and scallop sauce, pheasant braised with red wine and sweet chestnuts, fillet steak in a mushroom, cream and brandy sauce or a green peppercorn and garlic sauce, even a steak butty, sausage, egg and chips, ploughman's or a filled baked potato. Fantastic puds, real ice cream or fresh fruit sorbets. Harveys ales, usually a choice of three.

OPEN: 11–3, 6–11. Sun 12–3, 7–10.30.
Real Ale. Restaurant (no smoking).
Children in restaurant. Dogs on leads. Car park. Wheelchair access (not WC).
Cards: Delta, MasterCard, Switch, Visa.
N.B. There is a jukebox.

Broadwater

Cricketers ① 01903 233369
66 Broadwater St West, nr Worthing, W. Sussex BN14 9DE
Punch Taverns. Mr J. A. Sinsbury, licensee

This Saxon parish has been engulfed by its big neighbour. As you would expect from the name, very much the cricket team's local. It was originally called the Brewers Arms, but they changed it in 1878 as cricket had been played on the green since early in the 18th century and was no longer thought a passing fancy. Always a popular meeting place, especially for the home-cooked bar food, table d'hôte and à la carte menus – they specialise in seafood. Greene King IPA, Youngs Special, Bass, Fullers London Pride, Harveys and Bass Worthington are the beers.

OPEN: 11–3, 6–11. Sun 11–10.30.
Real Ale. Restaurant every lunchtime and Thurs to Sat eves.
Children in family room. Dogs on leads.
Cards: all major cards accepted.

Chiddingly

Six Bells ① 01825 872227
Chiddingly, nr Lewes, E. Sussex BN8 6HE (off A22 Uckfield–Hailsham)
Free House. Paul Newman, licensee

Something seems to be going on here all the time; if it's not, they're preparing for it. A meeting place for vintage car enthusiasts – once a month – live folk and jazz – three evenings a week and Sunday lunchtime. In between it's for those of us who want a quiet life; so now you know when to be there or when not. As you might gather, this is rather a fun place, jolly and unassuming. Opposite the church, it's an 18th-century pub serving the best of pub grub – all good, home-made and very reasonable: French onion soup, tuna pasta bake, chicken and mushroom pie, spare ribs in barbecue sauce, rack of ribs, steak and kidney pie, lasagne, filled potatoes, etc. Puddings too. John Smiths, Harveys Best and Courage Best Bitter on hand pump. Seats out in the large garden which has a fish pond. Good long walks nearby.

OPEN: 11–3, 6–11.
Real Ale.
Children in family room. Dogs on leads. Car park. Wheelchair access.
Cards: Delta, MasterCard, Switch, Visa, but not Amex.
There is live music Tues, Fri & Sat eves and Sun lunchtimes – in a separate building admittedly, but it does reverberate. Folk & blues evening every other Tues. Live jazz etc. Fri, Sat & Sun eves. The Sunbeam M.C.C. meet the first Thurs of every month.

Chidham

Old House at Home ① 01243 572477
Cot Lane, Chidham, nr Chichester, W. Sussex PO18 8SU
Punch Taverns. Mike Burchett, licensee

Things have shifted a bit here. New people have taken over since the last edition and the emphasis now is more on food. That said you can still lean on the bar in this old pub and enjoy a glass of wine or a pint of beer. Chidham, a village on a promontory between two tidal creeks, the Bosham and Thorney Channels, is surrounded by tidal flats, water, small boats and lots of birds. A little out of the way but worth finding if you want to enjoy good home cooking. It has a fairly straightforward bar menu on the blackboard ranging from home-made soups, filled baguettes, ploughman's, steak and kidney pie to chef's specials; there is always lots of fresh fish, steaks and other dishes, also a separate à la carte and pudding menu. Keeping a well-stocked cellar, they also have Bass, Fullers London Pride, Greene King Abbott and a guest. Seats on the terrace and in the garden. The pub can get extremely busy, so to be sure of a table you should book, particularly in the evenings.

OPEN: 11–3, 6–11. Sat 11–11. Sun 12–10.30.
Real Ale. No-smoking restaurant.
Children welcome. Dogs on leads. Wheelchair access.
Cards: all accepted.

Christ's Hospital

Bax Castle ① 01403 730369
Two Mile Ash Road, Southwater, Horsham, W. Sussex RH13 7LA (on the
Christ's Hospital–Southwater road)
English Country Inns. Mike Porteous, licensee

Close to the pub, the disused railway track between Guildford and Shoreham is now the
Downs link which joins the South Downs Way. So, walking or cycling, or however you
arrive, the Bax Castle is an ideal place to stop. Behind the old railway bridge, this small,
white-painted country pub has its own big, tree-fringed garden. The outside gives you no
idea that the building was originally a 15th-century weaver's cottage, but inside there is a
big inglenook and age-old beams; the bar leads into a dining area and the converted old
cowshed serves as a function room. Plenty of choice on the menu: soup, deep-fried
whitebait, Greek salad, gammon steak, fresh cod fillet in real-ale batter, steak and kidney
pie with a shortcrust pastry top (these last two are currently the most popular dishes),
fisherman's platter, lots of fish: halibut, trout, salmon, tuna and swordfish; or you could
have a mixed grill, fillet steak or half a shoulder of lamb, perhaps a daily special or two
from the blackboard, such as a minted lamb casserole. Harveys Sussex Bitter, Kings Red
River, Horsham Bitter and a guest beer.

OPEN: 12–2.30, 6–11. Sun 12–3, 6.30–10.30.
Real Ale. Restaurant.
Children welcome. Dogs in bar. Car park. Wheelchair access. Children's play area.

Compton

Coach & Horses ① 02392 631228
Compton, nr Chichester, W. Sussex PO18 9HA
Free House. David Butler, licensee

South of Petersfield, in a Sussex downland village of flint-built houses not far from
Uppark, a delightful 17th-century house high on the downs, now owned by the National
Trust. The contemporary Coach and Horses – with a Victorian extension – has a large
pine-panelled main bar with the original pine window shutters and two open fires; a
beamed smaller bar and restaurant. From the interesting menu there could be local game
in season, pigeon, black pudding and bacon on leek mash, chicken, mushroom and
tarragon pie, scallops and mussels with coriander on pasta ribbons, fish pie with cod,
salmon, mussels, smoked haddock and saffron. There's also their own icky sticky toffee
pudding or bread and butter pudding made with brioche, apricots and raisins soaked in
brandy to finish. Home-made soup, sandwiches and well-filled baguettes too. Always
between four and six real ales, among them Fullers ESB, Brewsters Hophead, Darkstar
from the Darkstar brewery, Moondance from Triple fff and Ballards Best. Wide-ranging
wine list. Tables at the front of the pub.

OPEN: 11.30–2.30, 6–11. Sun 12–3, 7–10.30.
Real Ale.
Children and dogs welcome. Wheelchair access.
Cards: MasterCard, Solo, Visa.

Coolham

George & Dragon ① 01403 741320
Dragons Green, nr Coolham, W. Sussex RH13 7JE
Hall & Woodhouse. R. Fisher & Nigel Tideswell, licensees

Knowing that you are probably having difficulty finding the pub, they have sensibly put a signpost for the George and Dragon on the main road. An attractive, low, brick-built cottagey place, it has a low-ceilinged, dimly lit bar. The beams are massive and the fireplace is huge. Tremendously popular at weekends; there is plenty of room in the big garden but on a wet day it would be quite a squash inside. They serve good traditional pub food which is much appreciated: home-made soups, ploughman's, steak and kidney pie. They cook their own ham and also make proper chips with real potatoes – rarer than you think. Sunday roasts. On hand pump they have King and Barnes Sussex (Old in winter), Hall and Woodhouse Badger, Tanglefoot and Champion beers. An interesting, atmospheric place with a spacious garden.

OPEN: 11–3, 6–11 (winter 6.30–11). Sat 11–11. Sun 12–10.30.
Real Ale.
Children and dogs welcome if under control. Car park. Good wheelchair access.
No credit cards.

Danehill

Coach & Horses ① 01825 740369
Danehill, nr Forest Row, E. Sussex RH17 7JF
Free House. Ian Philpots, licensee

To get to this early 19th-century pub on the outskirts of the village, turn off the A275 at School Lane and head for Chelwood. Inside this favourite local are stone walls with some half-panelling, polished floor boards and a general air of well-being. Plenty of room to spread out in the main bar, a smaller, cosy bar with a log-burning stove or the dining area. Well-liked bar snacks include soup of the day, sandwiches, grilled ciabatta and focaccia bread with different toppings. From the à la carte menu: warm shredded ham hock with puy lentil salad and grain mustard, spaghetti with cherry tomatoes, black olives and baby courgettes, roasted Mediterranean vegetable panini with basil oil, pork and leek sausages with mashed potato, onion marmalade and red wine jus are examples of the style of cooking; always fish, daily specials and home-made puddings such as bakewell tart with vanilla cream. There is an evening menu too. Harveys Best and a two-weekly changing guest beer. Champagne by the glass and Champagne-method cider in summer. A choice of 30 wines, 5 by the glass. There is an enclosed children's play area and wonderful views towards the South Downs from the pub garden.

OPEN: 11–3, 6–11. Sun 12–4, 7–10.30.
Real Ale.
Children welcome. Dogs on leads away from dining area.
Most cards.

Ditchling

Bull Inn ① 01273 843147
2 High Street, Ditchling, E. Sussex BN6 8TA
Free House. Dominic Worrall, licensee

As with many old buildings this one has had a diverse past. What you see now is a popular, cheerful place that had a darker former life. This 16th-century building was the local courthouse, responsible for sending many condemned men to the gallows on Ditchling Common. It later became a coaching inn with a happier future. Inside the Bull are two well-beamed bars, some fine old furniture, good winter log fires and a no-smoking area. Wholesome bar food is served as well as specials from the daily changing blackboard. From the menu there are sandwiches and baguettes, ploughman's, filled baked potatoes, traditional steak, kidney and Guinness pie, chef's fish pie, cauliflower cheese, bangers and mash – always steaks and vegetarian dishes; Sunday roasts. Harveys Sussex Bitter with two or three guests and a short wine list. Seats outside on the terrace and in the large, pretty garden with fine views towards Ditchling Beacon.

OPEN: 11–11. Sun 12–10.30.
Real Ale. No-smoking area.
Children welcome. Dogs on leads. Three doubles and one twin bedroom, all en suite.
Cards: all accepted.

Duncton

Cricketers ① 01798 342473
Main Road, Duncton, nr Petworth, W. Sussex GU28 0LB
Free House. Jonathan O'Reilly, manager and licensee

Set back from the road behind the summer flowers, this attractive old pub has been changed around a bit over the last couple of years. The former skittle alley has been transformed – it's now a dining room, with kitchen attached – big enough to feed 150 people with the 'added attraction', but not to us, of wall-to-wall music. However, all is not lost in this 15th-century pub; away from the dining room you'll find a big winter log fire in the musically quiet bar and, naturally enough, cricketing memorabilia decorating the pub to remind you of glorious summer days. The bar food ranges from filled baguettes and ploughman's to freshly prepared chicken, local game and fish dishes from the full menu; simple ingredients put together to create something interesting and worthwhile. Good puds too. Youngs IPA and guest ales, a number of malt whiskies and a reliable selection of wines. Seats in the attractive garden.

OPEN: 11–2.30, 6–11. Sun 12–3, 7–10.30.
Real Ale.
Children in restaurant. Well-behaved dogs. Car park. Wheelchair access to all parts of the pub.
Cards: Delta, MasterCard, Switch, Visa.

Eastbourne

Lamb ① 01323 720545
36 High Street, Old Town, Eastbourne, E. Sussex BN21 1HH
Harvey & Son. Steve Hume, tenant & licensee

The lovely old Lamb was licensed as an inn in 1603 but the cellars are even older, dating from the 12th century. It also had an underground passage connecting the pub to the Old Parsonage, reputed to have been used by the local smugglers, now unfortunately closed. In the old quarter, less than a mile from what is now the centre of the Victorian expansion of the town, there are two low-beamed bars in this well-run, friendly inn, which is furnished with some interesting old pieces, also an upstairs dining room. Sandwiches or ploughman's are served in the bar, or you can have a light meal of Indian savouries or deep-fried salmon and prawn delights, pasta dishes, fish, grills, steak and kidney pie, braised breast of duck and vegetarian dishes. Daily specials on the blackboard; puddings too. There is also a restaurant now. Harveys Best Bitter, Pale and their seasonal ales. No garden, but tables on the adjoining terrace.

OPEN: 10.30–3, 5.30–11. Fri & Sat 10.30–11. Sun 12–4, 7–10.30.
Real Ale. Restaurant.
Children in lower bar. Dogs on leads. Small car park.
Cards: all accepted.

East Chiltington

Jolly Sportsman ① 01273 890400
Chapel Lane, East Chiltington, E. Sussex BN7 3BA
Free House. Bruce Wass, proprietor
e-mail: jollysportsman@mistral.co.uk

The Jolly Sportsman is about 10 minutes west of Lewes with its own signpost along a 'no through road'. This quiet lane, and the pub, are within the boundary of the proposed South Downs National Park. Part tiled and weatherboarded, the building was originally an ale house and village shop – now the place to be for some seriously good food. Inside is a small public bar and restaurant; you can eat in the bar, or choose from a constantly changing à la carte menu which serves both bar and restaurant or even take advantage of the reasonably priced two-course lunch. Bruce Wass is the able chef responsible for the delights on the menu: more-ish home-baked bread and seasonal soups, roast scallops with wild mushroom salad, six Irish oysters, pumpkin risotto, herbed roast rump of Sussex lamb with ratatouille, poached john dory, with salmon caviar, chives and baby leeks, roast free-range chicken breast with ceps, chanterelles and wood blewits, roast young grouse in juniper and port, vegetarian menu and delicious puds. The constantly changing barrels of ale are mostly from micro-breweries. Eight wines by the glass and a fine wine list. The garden – with a climbing frame – has some rather fetching rustic garden seats – made by the farmer opposite the pub in his spare (spare?!) time – from where you can admire the view towards the South Downs.

OPEN: 12–2.30, 6–11. Sun 12–4. Closed Sun eve and Mon (except bank holiday Mondays).
Real Ale. Restaurant.
Children and dogs welcome. Car park. Wheelchair access.
Cards: MasterCard, Switch, Visa.

East Dean

Tiger Inn ① 01323 423209
The Green, East Dean, Eastbourne, E. Sussex BN20 0DA
(village off A259 Eastbourne–Seaford)
Free House. Nicholas Denyer, licensee

This is a serious walking area. Not only is there a really big car park in the village for the walkers' cars but there seems to be a constant movement of people wearing proper walking boots and studying folded maps. A delightful, white-painted old pub among cottages bordering the green in East Dean, a village in the hollow of the South Downs. The picnic tables at the front of the pub fill up quickly in summer, and the Tiger has a comfortable, low-beamed bar with good winter fires and a family room upstairs. The ingredients for the menu are as locally sourced as can be to create interesting, ever-changing dishes. These could include venison casserole, garlic mushrooms, macaroni cheese with tomatoes or ploughman's; local fish, cheeses, vegetables and fresh game will feature too. Beers do change but could include Flowers Original, Harveys Best, Adnams Best and Timothy Taylors landlord as a guest. There is also a good choice of bin-ends of wine on the blackboard and seven or eight wines by the glass. From here there are some invigorating walks to Birling Gap, the lighthouse at Belle Tout and Beachy Head.

OPEN: 11–3, 6–11. Sat 11–11. Sun 12–10.30.
Real Ale.
No children. Dogs on leads.
No cards.
Bank holiday Morris Dancers.

Elsted

Three Horseshoes ① 01730 825746
Elsted, Midhurst, W. Sussex GU29 0JX (west of Midhurst, off A272)
Free House. Sue Beavis, licensee

West of Midhurst, this old drovers' pub on the South Downs just happens to be in the right place for refuge, or encouragement – depending on whether you are coming or going – to anyone out for an invigorating walk. The pub serves generous quantities of changing bar food to help keep up the energy levels of the walkers and cyclists who drop in. This is a very traditional 16th-century pub with cosy, low-beamed rooms, full of old furniture and big fireplaces, blazing with logs in winter. A changing blackboard menu could offer home-made soups, a choice of ploughman's, casseroles, steak pies, fresh fish and filling puddings. Ales, which are kept behind the bar, could include Ballards Best, Fullers London Pride and Cheriton Pots Ale. They often have beers from smaller independent breweries. Seats in the pretty garden which has a marvellous view of the South Downs.

OPEN: 11–3 (winter 11–2.30), 6–11. Closed winter Sun eves.
Real Ale. Restaurant.
Well-behaved children in eating areas. Dogs on leads.
Cards: most accepted.

Fernhurst

Kings Arms ① 01428 652005
Midhurst Road, Fernhurst, W. Sussex GU27 3HA
Free House. Michael Hirst, licensee

Surrounded by Sussex farmland, south of the village, this small, early 17th-century stone building has tremendous appeal. Not only for the really good food they served but, on a totally different level, the beer festivals – and other functions – that go on in the wisteria-clad barn; everyone is happy. Licensed for nearly all its long life, there is just a small bar, with mind-your-head low beams and a big inglenook fireplace. The bar is definitely a bar; bar food is served here at lunchtime, but no crumbs allowed during the evening – then you eat in the restaurant. Family run, with a very friendly atmosphere, the good traditional bar food has a touch of the cosmopolitan about it: modern British is how they describe it. The menu leaps from grilled steak sandwich and three-cheese ploughman's to English onion soup with garlic and parmesan croutons, salmon and crab fishcakes with herb salad and mild horseradish mayonnaise, smoked salmon and scrambled eggs on toast, beer-battered cod and handcut chips, chicken breast with dauphinoise potatoes and wild mushroom and Madeira jus, seared salmon fillet with garlic pommes purée and mussel and tomato velouté and delicious puds. Fish is bought fresh from the coast so there are at least four fish dishes a day. Menus change monthly and dishes depend on what is available and in season. Everything is home-made including salad dressings, pasta, ice creams and sorbets. Five real ales change regularly; one beer is brewed especially for the pub by the Ventnor Brewery in the IOW. Real Guinness, still with a Dublin accent, and a comprehensive wine list that includes half bottles and bin ends.

OPEN: 11.30–3, 5.30–11. Closed Sun eve.
Real Ale.
Children welcome – but no children under 14 after 7 – dogs too. Car park. Wheelchair access (not WC).
Cards: Electron, MasterCard, Solo, Switch, Visa.

Findon

Gun Inn ① 01903 873206
The Square, Findon, W. Sussex BN14 0TA
Free House. Nick Georgiou, licensee

This old timber-framed building is in a charming, unspoilt downland village surrounded by woods and rolling hills. The Gun has been much changed over the years, but at least it now has a more settled future since it moved from tied to free house. All smartened up, the pub is now a welcoming place to be. The beams in the low-ceilinged lounge are reputed to be from old sailing ships broken up on the coast. They serve generous helpings of home-cooked food in both the bar and restaurant. Menus change with the seasons but there could be Peking duck, spring onions, cucumber, hoi sin sauce and pancakes, wild boar and foie gras terrine with plum pickle, oriental beef on a Thai mango pickle, chicken, mushroom and tarragon pie, peppered fillet steak with roasted vine tomatoes and mangetout, griddled lamb steak with rosemary and anchovy dressing and herb salad, as well as daily specials. Up to five real ales, among them Adnams, Fullers London Pride, Summer Lightning and Harveys HSB, Adnams Broadside as a guest. Forty wines on the list. Seats in the sheltered garden.

OPEN: 11–11.
Real Ale. Restaurant – music in here.
Children in family room. Dogs on leads. Wheelchair access (not WC).
Cards: Diners, MasterCard, Visa.

Fletching

Rose & Crown ① 01825 722039
High Street, Fletching, E. Sussex TN22 3ST
Free House. Roger & Sheila Haywood, licensees
e-mail: rose.and.crown@talk21.com

An ancient pub in a very old village that represents virtually every architectural milestone through the ages. The village is Saxon in origin, the 13th-century church has a Norman tower, the 15th-century Rose and Crown is built on the remains of a 12th-century building – a piece of the daub and wattle, circa 1150, is on display inside the pub – and the rest of the village has evolved over the centuries. Inside, the pub is full of atmosphere with a comfortable, heavily beamed bar and splendid inglenook fireplace. From the good bar snacks menu there could be home-made soup, grilled jumbo prawns in garlic butter, cream and spinach log, leek and mushroom puff, omelettes, macaroni cheese, ploughman's, toasted sandwiches and several vegetarian dishes. Daily specials, home-made puddings and ice-creams. The à la carte menu in the restaurant changes to reflect availability and the seasons. Harveys Ales and Ind Coope Burton. Choice of wines, some by the glass and half bottle. Seats in the garden.

OPEN: 11–2.30, 6–11. Sun 12–2, 7–10.30.
Real Ale. Restaurant.
Children in restaurant only. Dogs in bar only. Wheelchair access. Bed and breakfast accommodation.

Graffham

Foresters Arms ① 01798 867202
Graffham, nr Petworth, W. Sussex GU28 0QA
Free House. Lloyd F. Pocock, licensee

Originally built in 1607, but fiddled around with by the Victorians, this is an attractive old place. A steady, horticultural hand is at work here as the pub looks wonderfully flowery during the summer when the opulent hanging baskets are at their best. Close to the South Downs Way, it is a favourite with walkers and ramblers. You'll find a warm, friendly atmosphere in the heavily beamed bar; literally warm in winter when there will be a good log fire in the inglenook. Bar snacks such as large baguettes filled with cheese, bacon, lettuce, tomato and egg mayonnaise, or brown baguettes with smoked salmon are served in the bar; an à la carte menu of English country cooking, with game a speciality, in the restaurant. The well-kept beers are Timothy Taylors Landlord, Hop Back Summer Lightning and guests. They keep a good wine list. Seats in the particularly attractive garden.

OPEN: 11–2.30, 5.30–11. Sun 12–3, 7–10.30.
Real Ale. Restaurant.
Children at landlord's discretion. Dogs on leads. Wheelchair access.
Cards: MasterCard, Switch, Visa.

Kingston

Juggs ① 01273 472523
Kingston, nr Lewes, E. Sussex BN7 3NT (off A27 west of Lewes).
Shepherd Neame. Simon Wood & Nicola Tester, licensees

There is a walk over the downs from Lewes to this small, charming 15th-century pub where you'll see a wonderful sweep of tiled roof, roses climbing up the walls and tables on the sunny terrace. Inside, there's a rambling, beamed main bar with winter log fire; two no-smoking areas and a family room. One menu is shared by all; food includes a variety of sandwiches, locally made sausages, always vegetarian dish, steak and kidney pie, fresh fish, daily specials and a children's menu. Shepherd Neame cask ales – Spitfire, MasterBrew and seasonal ales. More tables outside in the courtyard and on the lawn.

OPEN: 11–11. Sun 12–10.30.
Real Ale.
Children in dining area. Dogs on leads in the bar. Wheelchairs have one step into pub.
Cards: most cards accepted.

Lewes

Lewes Arms ① 01273 473152
Mount Place, Lewes, E. Sussex BN7 1YH
Greene King. Clair Murray, licensee
e-mail: 1618@greeneking.co.uk

Remains of a Norman castle overlook this town that was built on a steep hill above the River Ouse, and just off the main street, tucked under the Castle Mound, is the historic Lewes Arms. Built in the 17th century, this is a charming, old-fashioned town pub with small bars and a cosy snug. Daily papers to read while you wait for something from the traditional bar menu: well-filled baguettes, ploughman's, jacket potatoes, fresh seasonal salads, lasagne, gammon, egg and chips or a filling 'brunch' of sausage, bacon, egg, baked beans, mushrooms and sauté potatoes which should keep the wolf from the door.

Well-kept Harveys Best, Old, Greene King Abbot and IPA, plus seasonal beers. For a breath of fresh air there is a very small terrace up a few steps, otherwise it's the pavement outside.

OPEN: 11–11. Sun 12–10.30.
Real Ale. Lunchtime food only.
Children in games room. Dogs on leads. Limited access for wheelchairs. No mobile phones.
Cards: all accepted.

Shelley's Hotel Bar ① 01273 472361
137 High Street, Lewes, E. Sussex BN7 1XS
Free House. Gary Coles, licensee

Unmissable: an elegant, cream-washed building among the Georgian shops and houses in Lewes High Street. Georgian from the outside, but this is an enlarged and remodelled 17th-century building. In its less grand days is was an inn called the Vine, then gentrified and extended to create a fine manor house by the 4th Earl of Dorset, later sold to the Shelley family who lived in it for some years before selling it to become an inn yet again, only this time it was on a far grander scale. Now a smart hotel with a Victorian bar, where they serve a selection of interesting bar snacks – home-made soup, a seasonal fish stew, seafood platter, moules marinière, grilled goat's cheese salad, chargrilled chicken, Hungarian goulash, tortellini filled with cream cheese with a tomato and basil sauce, interesting continental salads, sandwiches, filled baguettes and toasted sandwiches. Menus change on a regular basis. One real ale – the local Harveys; all other beers are bottled. Choice of wines. Seats in the lovely garden where they also serve tea.

OPEN: 11–3, 6–11.
Real Ale. Lunchtime snacks only.
Children: not in bar. No dogs. Wheelchair access to bar.

Lodsworth

Halfway Bridge Inn ① 01798 861281
Lodsworth, nr Petworth, W. Sussex GU28 9BP
Free House. Sheila, Simon & James Hawkins, licensees
e-mail: mail@thesussexpub.co.uk

Slightly confusing if you follow the address. Do not turn off the Midhurst to Petworth road – you want the pub, not the village; the pub is well marked. You see the car park first, but behind the foliage there is an 18th-century coaching inn which you reach up a garden path. Some seriously good food is served here in delightful surroundings. Several small rooms; many of the tables will be laid up for meals, but there is always room and a welcome in the bar for you to enjoy a pint and something from the bar menu. The blackboard could list dishes ranging from warm salad of scallops and bacon, fish soup, Gruyère cheese, rouille and croutons, calves' liver and bacon, steak, kidney, mushroom and Guinness pudding, fish pie with mangetout, niçoise salad with grilled fresh tuna steak to the daily changing specials and home-made puds. Sunday roasts. Cheriton Brewhouse Pots Ale, Fullers London Pride and Gales HSB on hand pump. Also changing guest beers, a porter, old or stout in winter and something from one of local independent breweries in summer. Farm cider and impressive list of wine by the glass. Lots of traditional pub games played – shut-the-box, bagatelle, backgammon, dominoes and more. Tables in the garden and on the sheltered terrace at the back of the pub.

OPEN: 11–3, 6–11.
Real Ale. Restaurant.
Children over 10 in restaurant. Dogs on leads. Wheelchair access (not WC). Eight bedrooms in the converted barn, one with disabled access.

Oving

Gribble Inn ① 01243 786893
Oving, Chichester, W. Sussex PO20 6BP (east of Chichester)
Woodhouse Inns. Microbrewery. Cyn Elderfield, manager, Rob Cooper, brewer
e-mail: brianelderfield@hotmail.com

A complete experience, with everything created under one roof so to speak. They brew their own beer in the brewery next to the skittle alley by the car park, virtually all the dishes on the menu are home-made, and happily, this is a mobile phone-free zone. All that, and the attractive thatched pub completes the picture; a delightful, rose-covered 16th-century building, once two cottages, in a lovely cottage garden. Inside is a heavily beamed bar with a big log fire, a dining area and a no-smoking family room; you eat wherever you can find the room. They serve a familiar, traditional menu of home-cooked food: soups, ploughman's, sandwiches, salads, ham and eggs, steak, also Sunday lunches. Specialities are fisherman's pie and home-made steak and kidney puddings. Fish dishes and a fish of the day from the blackboard such as fresh cod with a watercress sauce, also 'Old Favourites' and vegetarian dishes. The specials board changes at least once a day. Once a month there are themed culinary evenings. Seats outside among the apple trees. The pub's own skittle alley, along with the brewery (tours can be arranged), is on the other side of the car park. Own brew Pig's Ear, Gribble Ale, Oving Bitter, Black Adder II and the 'new' Fursty Ferret are the beers.

OPEN: July–Sep: Mon–Thurs 11–3, 5.30–11, Fri & Sat 11–11, Sun 12–10.30. Rest of the year 11–3, 5.30–11. Sun 12–3.30, 7–10.30.
Real Ale – brewed on the premises.
Children in family room. Dogs on leads in garden and bar. Wheelchair access and to ladies WC.
Cards: Delta, MasterCard, Switch, Visa.

Poynings

Royal Oak ① 01273 857389
The Street, Poynings, W. Sussex BN45 7AQ
Free House. Paul Day, licensee

Always a welcome at the Royal Oak for walkers and their dogs where, depending on the time of year, there will be either a welcoming log fire in the large beamed bar or plenty of seats in the attractive garden that has far-reaching views of the South Downs. There is a popular walk along the nearby Devil's Dyke. This deep hollow in the downs above

Brighton is the largest dry valley in southern England; you reach the car park at the top of the Dyke from the village. In the pub they serve generous portions from a well-chosen menu: home-made soup, grilled red snapper, pan-fried duck breast with a honey and orange glaze, traditional steak and kidney pie or locally made bangers and mash. Prime Sussex beef and lamb are sourced whenever possible from nearby Poynings Grange Farm. Always ploughman's, with a choice of interesting cheeses – some local – chunky, hearty sandwiches and a daily changing specials board. The beers are Harveys Sussex and others that could include Abbott Ale, Old Speckled Hen; also Harveys Old in winter. There is a comprehensive wine list which includes wine from a local vineyard. You are surrounded by good walks.

OPEN: 11–11. Sun 12–10.30.
Real Ale. No-smoking area.
Children welcome. Dogs on leads. Car park. Wheelchair access.
Cards: all except Diners.

Rudgwick

Blue Ship ① 01403 822709
The Haven, Rudgwick, Horsham, W. Sussex RH14 9BS
King & Barnes. John Davie, tenant

Rather remote, in a small hamlet between Rudgwick and Five Oaks, the Blue Ship from the outside is definitely a Victorian villa; inside, a surprise. The main bar harks back to its 15th-century origins, with several small connecting rooms. The public bar hasn't changed much over the years: flagstone floors, scrubbed deal tables, in winter a roaring fire in the big inglenook fireplace and farm dogs waiting patiently under the benches – wonderfully unspoilt. No bar as such in the Blue Ship; your drinks are served through a hatch, just as they used to be. The really good food is all home-cooked and the blackboard menu changes constantly – ploughman's, steak and onion pie, macaroni cheese, chilli con carne; ham, egg and chips is a speciality. Everything they serve is very wholesome. King and Barnes Broadwood and Sussex ales; Old is available during the winter. Tables at the front of the pub; views over the surrounding countryside from the garden. This is a very popular place and you should know that mobile phones are banned; use one, and you'll get fined.

OPEN: 11–3, 6–11. Sun 12–3, 7–10.30.
Real Ale.
Children welcome. Dogs on leads.

Rye

Mermaid Inn ① 01797 223065
Mermaid Street, Rye, E. Sussex TN31 7EU
Free House. Robert Pinwill, licensee
e-mail: mermaidinnrye@btclick.com

Rebuilt during the late 15th century, the Mermaid is the largest medieval building in a town that has an overwhelming number of architectural milestones representing every period through the centuries. A steep cobbled street leads to the heavily timbered, slightly leaning building whose cellars are probably a couple of centuries older, maybe 13th century. A famous smuggling inn; during the Georgian period the local smugglers used to drink in the inn with their pistols on the table, ready to defy the law. Inside is wonderfully beamed and panelled with a really vast inglenook fireplace, two very comfortable lounges, a bar and restaurant. One lounge and the restaurant are no smoking. Traditional bar food of freshly filled baguettes, baked fish pie, 'Mermaid' steak and kidney pudding, seafood platter or chicken, ham, leek and mushroom pie as well as an interestingly creative restaurant menu. Courage Best and Morlands Old Speckled Hen on hand pump. House wines and sherries. Brass-band concerts and enthusiastic Morris Men occasionally in the car park during summer.

OPEN: 11–11.
Real Ale. Restaurant.
Children welcome. No dogs. Car park. Bedrooms.
Cards: all except Diners.
N.B. Classical music in one bar. Lounges and restaurant quiet.

Selham

Three Moles ① 01798 861303
Selham, nr Petworth, W. Sussex GU28 0PN
Free House. Mrs Val Wingate, licensee
e-mail: val@thethreemoles.co.uk

You can ride in – there is a hitching rail – drive, walk or cycle, take your own picnic and even move in with your barbie if you give fair notice by telephoning first. Standing above the road, built as the Railway Inn but soon renamed the Three Moles – after the three moles on the coat of arms of the Mitford family who have always owned the pub. The station has long gone, so has the railway, but the Moles' popularity continues. Friendly and successful, it's a solid and unpretentious country pub between Petworth and Midhurst. Unmissable, but no food, just a range of crisps and nuts. But when you know how many awards it's won in the past – including National Runner-up in CAMRA's Pub of the Year – you know you can be sure of an excellent pint. No chance of driving straight past this place, sitting as it does high on the bank with a distinctive white porch; the very positive inn sign is detached and on the edge of the road. The ever-changing ales are from West Country and Southern micro-breweries; always a strong ale and a seasonal one from an unusual micro-brewery. You know that a new experience will be waiting for you from the beer pumps on every visit. There is also the popular Betty Stogs real cider. You can eat your picnic, or set up the barbecue (don't forget to telephone) in the garden or on the covered terrace – and there is no hamper charge! Lots of old and new pub games and an old-fashioned sing-song, with accordion, on the first Saturday of the month – either to be avoided like the plague or a fixed date in your diary. Another date for the diary is the annual beer festival that takes place every June.

OPEN: 12–2, 5.30–11. Sat 11.30–11. Sun 12–10.30.
Real Ale.
No children in the bar. Dogs, yes, but beware of the pub cat. If you're on horseback, the hitching rail is under the tree in the car park.
No cards.

Sidlesham

Crab & Lobster ☎ 01243 641233
Mill Lane, Sidlesham, Chichester, W. Sussex PO20 7NB
Free House. Brian Cross, licensee

A working harbour until the middle of the 19th century, old Sidlesham is now just an attractive backwater. Walkers, cyclists and ornithologists all flock here; there is a path around Pagham harbour which is a famous nature reserve for many birds and plants. Backing onto the harbour tidal flats, this old local has two beamed bars, both with log fires and a no-smoking dining area. Bar food includes a variety of the usual bar snacks. During the summer the menu includes crab, lobster and prawns, also a lasagne and two vegetarian dishes; in winter, steak and kidney pie, beef in Guinness and fish pie plus home-made puddings. Seats in the very pretty garden at the back of the pub overlooking the old harbour. Cheriton Pots, Arundel 1999, Ballards Best and Itchen Valley Fagin beers on hand pump.

OPEN: 11–3, 6–11. Sun 12–3. Closed Sun eve.
Real Ale.
Children in the garden. Dogs on leads. Wheelchair access.
Cards: MasterCard, Switch, Visa.

Singleton

Fox & Hounds ☎ 01243 811251
Singleton, Chichester, W Sussex PO18 0EY
Enterprise Inns. Tony Simpson, lease

In a village off the Midhurst to Chichester road, this is an attractive, well-cared for, white-painted 16th-century pub. Part of the Arundel estate and later owned by the Duke of Richmond, it was probably used as a hunting lodge during the 18th century, opening as a beer house during 1840. By all accounts a bad-mannered sort of place then, a bit of a nuisance in the village. All has changed; it's now a perfectly behaved, very welcoming, popular pub. Inside are low beams, traditional furnishings and wonderful log fires to sit by. As well as 'ramblers' soup from the bar menu, there is a great choice of toppings for the open sandwiches, also open toasties, a cheese platter, smoked salmon with prawns, chef's paté, whitebait, or king prawns wrapped in filo pastry with salad and oyster sauce and filling puddings such as spotted dick or apple and blackberry crumble. Always something interesting on the specials board; also a fuller, main menu. Roast on Sunday. Beers are Ringwood Best, Greene King IPA and Fullers London Pride. There is also something for everyone on the wine list. Outside is a glorious walled garden for you to enjoy. Singleton is not far from Goodwood or West Dean Gardens, and the famous Weald and Downland Museum is just outside the village.

OPEN: 11.30–3, 6–11.
Real Ale. Restaurant.
Children and dogs welcome. Car park. Wheelchair access.

Ticehurst

Bell Hotel ① 01580 200234
High Street, Ticehurst, E. Sussex TN5 7AS
Free House. Mrs Pamela Tate, licensee

There are bells everywhere in the Bell. The family who have been running this 14th-century inn for nearly 50 years have been collecting all the bells they could possibly lay their hands on, and among the ancient timbers in the lounge bar there are nearly 400 of them on show. An atmospheric old place full of beams and with a huge inglenook fireplace ablaze with logs in winter, where all you'll hear is friendly chatter and the clink of glasses. Bar snacks and meals are always freshly cooked to order from the menu. Harveys and Whitbread ales. Seats in the garden.

OPEN: 11–3, 6–11.
No food Sun eves.
Children welcome. Dogs on leads. Wheelchair access. Bedrooms.

Udimore

Kings Head ① 01424 882349
The Street, Udimore, E. Sussex
Free House. Trevor & Anita Jones, licensees

Outside Rye, on the B2089, this old-fashioned pub is in a wonderful position overlooking the Brede valley towards Hastings. Inside is better than it looks from the outside; no gardeners here to give it kerb appeal. Nevertheless, cosy in winter as the long bar has fires at either end. Food is hearty, traditional pub food: lamb with all the trimmings, steak and ale pie, egg and chips, salads and curries, roasts at the weekend – that sort of thing. The beers are well kept; always Harveys, as well as Fullers and Batemans beers, scrumpy jack and a selection of wines. Seats at the front of the pub on the edge of the car park; those at the back overlook orchards.

OPEN: 11–2.30, 6–11.
Real Ale.
Children welcome. Dogs on leads at one end of bar.

Wadhurst

Greyhound ① 01892 783224
St James' Square, Wadhurst, E. Sussex TN5 6AP
Free House. Jonathan & Emma Harrold, licensees

Set back from the road in the middle of the village; the seats at the front of the pub give you a perfect view of Wadhurst on the move. You kept your head down during the 18th century though as, along with other Sussex pubs, it was a favourite with smugglers – the infamous Hawkhurst gang used it as one of their safe houses. Life is less fraught now in the well-kept Greyhound, all beamed, polished and panelled with a huge inglenook fireplace and an equally huge log fire in winter. From the daily changing menus, food is served in the bar or the restaurant; a good choice of bar snacks, including tapas-style finger food, as well as an à la carte menu and daily specials: garlic prawn kebabs with chilli and lime dipping sauce, chicken liver and peppercorn paté, braised lamb neck with cranberry mash, Cajun chicken filled with brie and sun-dried tomatoes, pork fillet with spicy plum sauce and mash, battered fish and chips, steaks, pie of the day – or you can have a full English breakfast. The back section of the bar is for games: bar billiards, darts and in one corner ring the bull's nose, a game apparently brought over by the Romans. The only other pub with this particular game is a pub in Kent. Harveys Sussex, Bass, Morlands Old Speckled Hen and a guest. About eight house wines by the glass and about 30 on the wine list. There is an upstairs meeting room for hire, regularly used by the Art and Yoga classes, and a sheltered back garden.

OPEN: 11–11. Sun 12–3, 7–10.30.
Real Ale. Restaurant.
Children welcome. Dogs on leads. Car park. Wheelchair access. Five en-suite bedrooms.
Cards: all except Amex.

West Chiltington

Five Bells ① 01798 812143
Smock Alley, West Chiltington, W. Sussex RH20 2QX
Free House. Bill Edwards, licensee

A busy, friendly pub built in the 1930s on the site of a much older inn. A much-appreciated local where contented customers come to appreciate the friendly welcome, really well-kept ale and good, reasonably priced food cooked by the landlady. Inside is a spacious bar area, a fire to warm you and your dog and a dining conservatory. According to one of our well-informed readers, the beer aficionados will want to know that among the local ales and guest beers will be one bitter, two best bitters, one premium bitter and one mild. The rest of us might like to know that Biddenden cider is served from the barrel. Outside is a quiet, sunny garden.

OPEN: 12–3, 6–11. Sun 12–3, 7–10.30.
Real Ale.
No children. Dogs welcome. Car park. Five en-suite bedrooms.

Wineham

Royal Oak ① 01444 881252
Wineham Lane, Wineham, nr Henfield, W. Sussex BN5 9AY
Inn Business. Tim Peacock, tenant

No pretentions here, they wisely continue to keep the emphasis on liquid refreshment only, with just the simplest of bar food to keep the hunger pangs at bay. Luckily nothing much changes at this charming black and white old pub; it has tremendous 'kerb' appeal so it's not surprising that it is hugely popular. A well-cared-for, 14th-century family pub with low beams, huge inglenook fireplace – with equally huge log fires – and a cosy back snug. Food is limited to a good range of freshly made sandwiches, plain or toasted, ploughman's and home-made soups in winter. Ales straight from the cask in the still room – Wadworths 6X and Harveys BB. Tables on the lawn at the front of the pub next to the old well.

OPEN: 11–2.30, 5.30–11 (Sat 6–11).
Real Ale.
Children in family room. Dogs on leads. Wheelchair access.

BEST OF THE REST

Alciston
Rose Cottage ☎ 01323 870377
Alciston BN26 6UW
Off the Polegate to Lewis Road, this is an appealing, 17th-century, cottagey pub, as the name suggests. Full of village life, past and present, quite a lot of it attached to the walls! Way above average bar snacks and changing specials on the blackboard. Locally caught fish, locally grown vegetables and very local eggs – their own. The menu could feature lamb cooked in red wine, rosemary and garlic, pork in cider or Thai-style curries. Harveys Best and Rother Valley Best, good wines, some by the glass and proper cider. Children in restaurant and eating area of bar.
Open: 11.30–3, 6.30–11.

Balls Cross
Stag ☎ 01403 820241
Balls Cross, Petworth, W. Sussex GU28 9JP
This should really be with the 'no music' pubs but we didn't get enough information to do it justice, so for this edition it stays here. An unspoilt 16th-century village pub north of Petworth, it has the original flagstones and a wonderful log fire in the inglenook. By all accounts the landlord is quite a character and runs it well, serving a good choice of traditional pub food and an excellent pint of Badger Bitter, Tanglefoot and seasonal beer. Seats in the attractive garden.
Open: 11–3, 6–11. Sun 12–3, 7–10.30.

Burwash
Bell ☎ 01435 882304
Burwash, E. Sussex TN19 7EH
Surrounded by outstanding countryside, this attractive village of mainly 16th- and 17th-century houses spreads along a ridge between two rivers, the Rother and Dudwell. Opposite the church, this popular pub looks its flowery best in the summer. There is something for everyone on the menu, from sandwiches to steak in a peppercorn sauce. Local Arundel, Batemans and Harveys as well as Greene King IPA beers. Children and dogs welcome.
Open: 11–3.30, 6–11.

Coultershaw Bridge
Badgers ☎ 01798 342651
Coultershaw Bridge, nr Petworth GU28 0JF
The emphasis here is more towards eating than drinking, though you can still join a local or two leaning on the bar. Known for their imaginative bar snacks and restaurant menu, these change regularly but from the bar there could be sausages and bubble and squeak,

Caesar salad, pasta with scallops, prawns and basil, tapas or a shellfish stew. Badger and Theakstons Best beers and a good list of wines. No very young children.
Open: 11–3, 5.30–11 (Sat 7–11). Closed winter Sun eves.

Fletching
Griffin ➀ 01825 722890
Fletching, E. Sussex TN22 3SS
Inside, the 16th-century Griffin reflects its age; a heavily beamed main bar, creaking floors defying the horizontal, big log fires and an attractively decorated restaurant which expands onto the terrace during the summer. The good, imaginative bar food menu changes daily and could include home-made soups, warm chicken and bacon salad, marinated herring and warm potato salad, Italian sausages with beans and polenta, salmon fishcakes or grilled fish. Harveys, Hall & Woodhouse Tanglefoot, Rother Valleys Spirit Level, also Kronenbourg 1664 lager, and a very good wine list. Splendid views towards Sheffield Park from the two acres of garden. Children welcome, and dogs. Wheelchair access. Bedrooms. Cards: all major cards. Piano Fri/Sat eves & Sun lunchtime.
Open: 12–3, 6–11.

Henley
Duke of Cumberland Arms ➀ 01428 652280
Henley, W. Sussex GU27 3HQ
North of Midhurst, this is a charming, creeper-covered small country pub in a large, fascinating, garden – with views – which slopes off towards a stream and ponds. Inside are two, simple beamed rooms where they serve very desirable food including some very fresh fish – including trout from the ponds. Gales, Ballards, Hop Back and Adnams ales from the cask; farm ciders. Children welcome, but none under 5 in evening.
Open: 11–3, 6–11.

Old Heathfield
Star ➀ 01435 863570
Old Heathfield, E Sussex TN21 9AH
In the attractive old part of town, first find the church – the pub is tucked behind it. A wonderful old building dating back to the mid 14th century, full of beams, panelling, low ceilings, an inglenook fire and upstairs a restaurant with a fine 'barrel ceiling'. From the menu, lunchtime ploughman's and filled jacket potatoes as well as fresh home-made soup, chicken liver and brandy paté with Cumberland sauce and hot toast, Scottish smoked salmon dressed with olive oil and cracked black pepper, cold meats, bubble and squeak and beetroot, home-made English beef, ale and potato pie served with seasonal vegetables, real Cumberland sausages with mashed potatoes and red wine and onion gravy or free-range duckling served with a tangy honey and orange sauce. Harveys Best, Shepherd Neame Masterbrew and Hopback Summer Lightening are the beers; some fine wines and farm cider. Outside is a lovely garden with a view immortalised by Turner. Children and dogs welcome. Car park. Wheelchair access. Cards: all except Amex and Diners.
Open: 11.30–3, 5.30–11.

Rye
Ypres Castle ➀ 01797 223248
Gun Garden, Rye TN31 7HH
Reached either up steps from the road around Rye, or from the aptly named Ypres Tower. As you gather, it's high in Rye – well, Rye is on a hill and so is the pub, with views over the muddy River Rother, the fishing boats and out to sea. A very straightforward town pub

with some interesting dishes on the menu. Delicious ways with fish, much of it local and some very local lamb. Daily specials too such as grilled sardines or chicken in a white wine sauce. Badger Tanglefoot, Harveys Best, Charles Wells and Youngs beers; wines by the bottle and glass, also proper cider. Children welcome.
Open: 11–11.

Wartling
Lamb Inn ☎ 01323 832116
Wartling, E. Sussex BN27 1RY
On the right, just after the church on the road to Herstmonceaux, a traditional Sussex pub with two beamed bars with open fires, a lounge and dining room. Plenty of experience on the culinary front as the licensees ran a restaurant in Seaford. The 'small plates' in the bar could include a fresh crab and cheddar tartlet with sweet chilli dipping sauce, or locally smoked salmon with fresh prawns and tomato mayonnaise, and for a main course, wellington of asparagus, spinach, potato and mushrooms with a port and mushroom sauce or braised shank of lamb with a mint and redcurrant gravy. Rother Valley Level Best, Horsham Red River and Cuckmere Haven Guv'nor on draught. There are 21 wines on the list. Children welcome. No dogs. Car park. All cards.
Open: 11–3, 6–11. Closed Sun eve and Mon.

Wetherspoon in Sussex

Bognor Regis – Hatters Inn, 2–10 Queensway
☎ 01243 840206

Brighton – Wetherspoons, 20–22a West Street
☎ 01273 224690

Chichester – Dolphin and Anchor Hotel, West Street
☎ 01243 790280

Crawley – Jubilee Oak, 6 Grand Parade, High Street
☎ 01293 565335

Eastbourne – Wetherspoons, 21–23 Cornfield Road
☎ 01323 419670

East Grinstead – Wetherspoons, The Antrium, Little King Street
☎ 01342 335130

Hastings – John Logie Baird, 29–31 Havelock Road
☎ 01424 448110

Horsham – Lynd Cross, St John's House, Springfield Road
☎ 01403 272393

Hove – Cliftonville Inn, 98–101 George Street
☎ 01273 726969

Littlehampton – George Inn, 14 Surrey Street
☎ 01903 739863

Worthing – Sir Timothy Shelley, 47–49 Chapel Road
☎ 01903 228070

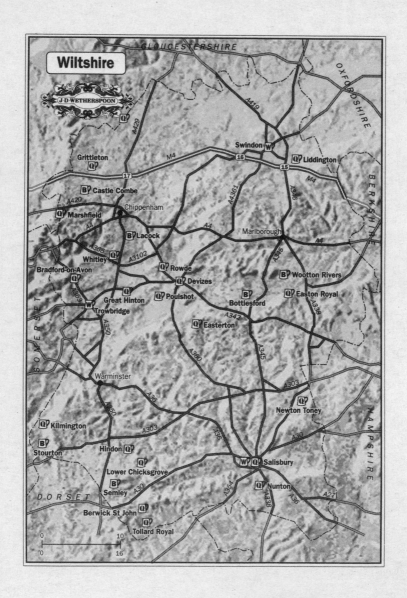

Wiltshire

J·D·WETHERSPOON

Grittleton

Castle Combe

Chippenham

Marshfield

Lacock

Whitley

Bradford-on-Avon

Great Hinton

Trowbridge

Rowde

Devizes

Poulshot

Easterton

Warminster

Kilmington

Stourton

Hindon

Lower Chicksgrove

Semley

Berwick St John

Tollard Royal

GLOUCESTERSHIRE

OXFORDSHIRE

Swindon

Liddington

BERKSHIRE

Marlborough

Wootton Rivers

Bottlesford

Easton Royal

Newton Toney

Salisbury

Nunton

HAMPSHIRE

DORSET

SOMERSET

Wiltshire

Berwick St John

Talbot Inn ① 01747 828222
The Cross, Berwick St John, Shaftesbury SP7 OHA
Free House. Marilyn & Peter Hawkins, licensees

East of Shaftesbury, close to the Dorset border and in an area of unspoilt, sweeping landscapes, Berwick village is tucked in a hollow at the western end of the Chalke Valley. The lovely old Talbot has just one heavily beamed bar with an impressive inglenook fireplace – a roaring fire in winter – and separate dining room. They serve a simple, traditional pub menu of sandwiches, ploughman's, ham, egg and chips, sausage and mash and a few daily specials. Bass and Wadworths 6X, guest beers and a local cider. Good selection of wine available by the bottle, carafe or glass; mulled wine in winter. Tables in the garden. Good walks nearby.

OPEN: 12–2.30, 6.30–11. Sun 12–5. Closed Sun eves and Mon except bank holidays.
Real Ale.
Children, with adult, in eating area at lunchtime. Well-behaved dogs on leads in main bar.
Cards: all major cards except Amex.

Bradford-on-Avon

Beehive ① 01225 863620
263 Trowbridge Road, Bradford-on-Avon BA15 1UA
Free House. Mrs C. Crocker, licensee

A lifetime of popularity; location is all. Near the Kennet and Avon canal and Widbrook Bridge, this is a lively, busy pub, a favourite with canal users, towpath walkers, locals and everyone else who appreciates a welcoming, friendly pub serving exceptionally well-kept beer and really good, straightforward, home-made food. It was built during the early years of the 19th century to accommodate the navvies building the canal and all home comforts were provided, in more ways than one – Mrs Kelly also ran a very successful brothel here! Less exotic comforts are on offer now: chairs to match the scrubbed wooden tables in the bar and log fires in the stone fireplace – if you want to, you can sponsor a log, it saves on the fuel bills. Most of the food on the daily changing menu is home-cooked: winter soups served with crusty bread, the ever-popular traditional steak and kidney pie, cheese and onion pie, the Beehive's acclaimed cold beef and home-cooked hams, a selection of vegetarian dishes and for the really hungry, huge portions of sausages, egg and chips. Always Butcombe and a minimum of five well-kept real ales from a changing selection on hand pump or gravity fed. A well-chosen list of reasonably priced wines and champagnes.

On Wednesday summer evenings the boules team practise their skills – you can join in too. The large garden has a children's play area.

OPEN. 12–2.30, 7–11. Sun 12–3, 7–10.30.
Real Ale. No food Sun eve, Mon or Tues lunchtime.
Children welcome. Dogs on leads. Car park.

Devizes

Bear ① 01380 722444
The Market Place, Devizes SN10 1HS
Wadworth. Andrew Maclachlan MBII, tenant
e-mail: info@thebearhotel.net

A solid, prosperous-looking hotel in the centre of Devizes, with an Edwardian frontage to a much older, 16th-century building; local records show that the Bear was first mentioned in 1559. Inside is a comfortable, carpeted bar serving traditional bar food: hot sausage sandwiches, French bread toasties, filled jacket potatoes, all-day breakfasts, omelettes, ploughman's and daily specials too. Also a panelled and polished Lawrence Room named after the painter Sir Thomas Lawrence, whose father ran this old coaching inn in the 18th century – buffet meals in here – and the more formal Master Lambton restaurant where they serve a two- or three-course table d'hôte dinner menu. Interesting wine list. Wadworths ales, which are brewed very locally, and a guest. Morning coffee. Tables in the courtyard.

OPEN: 10–11.
Real Ale. Restaurant (closed Sun eve).
Children in eating area. Dogs on leads. Wheelchair access into bar and restaurant; new lift should be installed by now. Bedrooms all en suite.
Cards: Amex, MasterCard, Visa.

Easterton

Royal Oak ① 01380 812343
11 High Street, Easterton, Wilts SN10 4PE
Wadworth. Wayne Nicholas, licensee

High praise all round for the thatched Royal Oak, their interesting menus and well-kept beer. In a village on the edge of the huge expanse of Salisbury Plain: miles of undulating chalk downland, a large area farmed but some taken over by the military – it is not unusual to see a tank or two crossing the road in front of you – the little Royal Oak, built in 1595 in an age of pikes and cannon, has only two rooms but manages to pack them in. Here you can sample the reasonably priced, imaginative home-made food which is taking a southerly turn towards the Mediterranean, so there will be tapas now and more fish dishes on the menu. Wadworths range of beers and some guests. Good wine list. Seats in the small, gated front garden.

OPEN: 12–3, 5.30–11. Sun 12–10.30.
Real Ale.
Children over five allowed. Dogs in public bar only. Car park. All disabled facilities.
Cards: all major cards except Amex.

Easton Royal

Bruce Arms ① 01672 810 216
Easton Royal, nr Pewsey SN9 5LR
Free House. Jackie & John Butler, licensees

Truly isolated, all alone but certainly not forgotten. An unchanging early Victorian country pub just off the Pewsey road, old-fashioned, charming and unspoilt. The last major upheaval was when they put the bar in during the 1930s and rebuilt the fireplace. A games room and skittle alley (jukebox on here after 8 p.m.) have been added but nothing else has altered much. Still with a brick floor and the old wooden benches and long tables; none of the good things about the pub has been changed. Limited food, only well-filled cheese and onion rolls and home-pickled eggs to go with the Wadworth 6X, Henrys IPA and a guest ale. Seats in the garden and cricket on their own cricket pitch opposite the pub.

OPEN: 12–2.30, 6–11. Sun 12–3, 7–10.30.
Real Ale.
Children welcome, not in the bar. Dogs on leads. Car park and you can park your caravan in the field behind the pub.
No cards.

Great Hinton

Linnet ① 01380 870354
Great Hinton, Trowbridge BA14 6BU
Wadworth. Jonathan Furby, landlord/chef

Candlelight, wonderful flowers, and cooking far more ambitious than the usual pub food. Inside this old place is a comfortable little bar, books to read in the snug and a more formal dining room where they serve a very reasonable two- or three-course lunch. Pushing the boat out, you could go à la carte and create your own delights: lots of different salads with a variety of dressings, roast salmon with prawn sauce, chicken casserole, grilled rib-eye steak with a rosemary sauce or medallions of monkfish on a prawn and lemon risotto with a saffron sauce – and more. Wadworths range of ales and a full wine list.

OPEN: 11–2.30, 6–11. Closed Mon.
Real Ale. No smoking restaurant
Children welcome, dogs too. Car park. Wheelchair access.

Grittleton

Neeld Arms ☎ 01249 782470
The Street, Grittleton, nr Chippenham SN14 6AP
Free House. Charlie West, licensee
e-mail: neeldarms@zeronet.co.uk

A popular place for many reasons. Being next to the village church they do a very good trade in calming pre-wedding nerves, and it also seems to be a favourite venue for stag parties. And talk about nurturing them when young, Grittleton House School is just across the road so pub lunches are just the thing for parents and hungry pupils. Back to the nitty gritty. This is a delightful 17th-century pub in a convivial village where you are welcomed by an enthusiastic owner. Fairly traditional lunchtime menu, always 'sausages of the week', a choice of fish, game in season and different ways with steak. The blackboard menu moves up a notch in the evening. Wadworths 6X, Buckleys Best, Hop Back, Brakspear and Coopers beers and a comprehensive wine list.

OPEN: 12–3, 5.30–11.30.
Real Ale.
Children welcome, dogs too. Car park. Wheelchair access. Bedrooms.
Most cards accepted.

Hindon

Angel Inn ☎ 01747 820696 Fax: 01747 820869
High Street, Hindon, Salisbury SP3 6DJ
Free House. Penny Simpson, licensee

Renamed too late for us to do anything for our last edition; so if you were frantically looking for the Grosvenor Arms, you now know why you couldn't find it. Behind the classic Georgian frontage of the Angel is a pub, restaurant and hotel run by friendly, welcoming staff. Beams, some flagstones, lovely fires and jolly red walls in the bars, more muted colours in the sitting room and restaurant. The emphasis is on food, but it is still a pub and the locals pile in to lean on the bar to enjoy a beer or glass of wine – 14 by the glass – or warm themselves by the log fires. Bar snacks and meals are served in the bars and lovely courtyard garden; there is also full restaurant service. The food is as fresh as fresh can be and all cooked to order. Fish arrives daily. From the changing menu there could be home-made soup, lemon and thyme-marinated chicken Caesar salad with anchovy dressing, duck rillette with salad of smoked duck breast, orange and coriander with toasted brioche or mussels marinière, and for a main course roast topside of beef with Yorkshire pudding, wild mushroom risotto with rocket and parmesan or seared fillet of salmon with rice vermicelli, langoustine, crab and ginger consommé; a number of fish dishes and yummy puds; cheeses are from Neal's Yard. Beers are Bass, Wadworths 6X and Henry's IPA; the wine list is mainly French with a touch of the New World.

OPEN: 11–3, 6–11. Closed Sun eve.
Real Ale. Restaurant.
Children welcome. Dogs in bar and they can bring their suitcases. Car park. 10 en-suite bedrooms.
Cards: Amex, Delta, MasterCard, Switch, Visa.

Lamb Inn ① 01747 820573
Hindon, Salisbury SP3 6DP
Youngs. Nick James, licensee

There is a small colourful garden outside this lovely old inn which takes up a corner site in this quiet village; a building that has changed with the centuries. The oldest part of the present inn was built in the 17th century on the site of a 15th-century structure and was used for a time as a courthouse for the local assizes. Over time the old area of the Lamb has been added to and altered, becoming the place you see today. For years it was a busy posting inn and used by a notorious Wiltshire smuggling gang as a centre for its activities. A little less exciting now – but more law abiding – they serve a seasonally changing, well-chosen menu written on the blackboard in the big, beamed bar. There is a no-smoking restaurant with an evening table d'hôte menu; an à la carte menu is available at lunchtime. Ales from the Youngs range. Picnic tables outside in an attractive courtyard.

OPEN: 11–11. Sun 12–10.30.
Real Ale. Restaurant.
Children welcome. Dogs on leads. Wheelchair access. Fourteen bedrooms.
Cards: Amex, Delta, MasterCard, Switch, Visa.

Kilmington

Red Lion ① 01985 844263
Kilmington, Warminster BA12 6RP (on the B3092, 3 miles north of Mere (A303))
Free House. Chris Gibbs, FBII, licensee

What was once just a simple farm cottage is now an unassuming, creeper-covered old pub with a cosy, low-ceilinged, appealing bar and winter log fires. On the National Trust's Stourhead Estate, the Red Lion is in a lovely part of Wiltshire, undulating and well-wooded. The pub serves simple but satisfying lunchtime bar food and this could include home-made soups, the Red Lion's home-cooked ham, ploughman's, filled baked potatoes, popular toasted sandwiches, game, chicken casserole, steak and kidney, cottage pie in the winter, maybe a creamy fish pie and a vegetarian dish or two; daily specials are on the blackboard. The dining area is no-smoking. Butcombe Bitter and Butts Jester, changing guest beers and farm ciders. Seats in the large garden. Only a half a mile from the gardens at Stourhead – one of the finest 18th-century landscapes in the country. Lots of good walks.

OPEN: 11.30–2.30, 6.30–11. Sun 12–3, 7–10.30.
Real Ale.
Children in eating area until 9 p.m. Dogs on leads. Wheelchair access (not WC).
Bedrooms.

Liddington

Village Inn ① 01793 790314
Bell Lane, Liddington, Swindon SN4 0HE
Arkells Brewery Ltd. Vince & Donna Jones, licensees

Nearly hidden by enthusiastic creeper – but at least you can still see the door! Everyone seems to find their way into this welcoming little inn in the middle of the village. Renamed in the 1980s, it was the Bell in Bell Lane years ago, a replacement for the old inn, now demolished, that stood on the other side of the road. Originally built as four cottages, the pub is in two and the other two are used for staff. Well cared for, there is an extensive blackboard menu with reasonably priced dishes ranging from home-made soup, game pie with melba toast and oriental prawn rolls to home-made steak and ale pie, roast loin of pork with apple and apricot stuffing, lamb fillet braised in garlic and rosemary and a mixed grill. Everything is prepared and cooked on the premises. Sunday roasts – must book – all washed down with Arkells Best Bitter, 3B, Kingsdown and guest ales. Seats in the small, quiet garden.

OPEN: 12–2.30, 6.30–11 (Sun 7–10.30).
Real Ale.
No children. No dogs. All disabled facilities. Prize-winning loos.
Cards: all cards.

Lower Chicksgrove

Compasses Inn ① 01722 714318
Lower Chicksgrove, Tisbury, nr Salisbury SP3 6NB
Free House. Alan & Susie Stoneham, licensees
e-mail: thecompasses@aol.com

Drive along narrow country lanes to reach this charming thatched pub in a tiny hamlet in the Nadder valley off the A30 between Swallowfield and Fovant. A popular 16th-century inn with a spacious, unspoilt, beamed main bar and a decor to suit its rural surroundings – country and farming bits and pieces hang from the beams and walls. The imaginative menus are written on the blackboard; specials above the wood-burning stove in the inglenook. From the menu there could be mussels cooked in bacon, cream, garlic and white wine, smoked duck and red onion tartlet, baked red pepper stuffed with garlic and anchovies and for a main dish, shoulder of lamb roasted with red wine, molasses and soy, steak and kidney pie with suet crust, grilled lemon sole, a selection of vegetarian and fish dishes as well as filled jacket potatoes, salads and fillings for the onion loaves. Everything is home-cooked to go with a good selection of beers: Bass, Wadworth 6X plus two guest and a comprehensive wine list. Seats in the garden and courtyard – there is a children's play area.

OPEN: 12–3, 6–11. Closed Mon except bank holidays (then closed the Tues following a bank holiday Mon).
Real Ale.
Well-behaved children in certain areas. Dogs under the table on leads. Bedrooms.
Cards: Delta, MasterCard, Solo, Switch, Visa.

Marshfield

Catherine Wheel ① 01225 892220
High Street, Marshfield SN14 8LR
Free House. David Field, licensee

Looking nothing like the usual image of a pub, this stately, solid stone-fronted building is indeed the old Catherine Wheel. The original Elizabethan building has been well hidden behind an 18th-century frontage. The inside has been remodelled too, particularly the dining room, which reflects the Georgian more than the Elizabethan period. However, there is a welcoming beamed main bar with a big fireplace, pine tables and country chairs where they serve traditional bar food, as well as fresh fish and imaginative specials, all cooked to order. Courage Best, Abbey's Bellringer, Buckleys Best, Stowford Press cider and a good wine list.

OPEN: 11–3, 6–11. Closed Mon lunch except bank holidays.
Real Ale. Restaurant. No meals Sun eve.
Children in eating area until 8.30 p.m. Dogs on leads. Three en-suite bedrooms.

Newton Tony

Malet Arms ① 01980 629279
Newton Tony, Salisbury SP4 0HF
Free House. Noel & Annie Cardew, licensees

At first glance, if you ignore the pub sign, this looks like a desirable piece of real estate with a small front garden and path leading to the front door. Actually, it's a popular local with a growing reputation for serving some inspired food to go with an interesting range of ales. The pub is 17th century and it's in the middle of this village on the banks of the River Bourne, which you have to ford on the way to the pub – although there is an alternative approach, highly recommended at a time of high rainfall! Inside are low beams, a large fireplace, comfortable furnishings, prints, paintings and photographs to admire. Menus are chalked on boards and from the bar menu you could have a warm salad of pigeon and bacon with spinach and croutons, rump steak sandwich with fried onions, salad and chips, stew of pheasant, pigeon, duck and hare with orange and juniper, or crêpes filled with cod and shrimps served with fresh vegetables. Many of the ingredients are local: all the smoked foods, game and venison comes from Wilbury Park. Always four ales, Wadworths 6X, Stonehenge Heelstone, Butts Barbus Barbus, Palmers IPA and Ringwoods. Real scrumpy and a wide-ranging wine list. Energetic lot here: it's home to the local football and cricket teams which get a great deal of support from the cricket-mad landlord.

OPEN: 11–3, 6–11.
Real Ale.
Children and dogs welcome. Car park. Wheelchair access.
Cards: MasterCard, Visa.

Nunton

Radnor Arms ① 01722 329722
Nunton, nr Salisbury SP5 4HS
Free House. Mr & Mrs Jelfs, licensees

Busy and popular, a pretty, creeper-covered pub in a quiet village overlooking water meadows. Built as a cottage in the 18th century, it became a pub in the middle of the Victorian era. There is plenty of room in the low-ceilinged, beamed bars where they serve an extensive, daily changing, home-cooked menu which is also available in the more formal restaurant. Badger Tanglefoot, Dorset Best and draught Guinness. A decent wine list and a good selection of malt whiskies. The extensive garden at the back of the pub has plenty of tables and country views.

OPEN: 11–3, 6–11.30.
Real Ale.
Children welcome. Dogs on leads. Large car park. Wheelchair access.

Poulshot

Raven ① 01380 828271
Poulshot, nr Devizes SN10 1RW (take a left turn off the A361, Devizes–Seend road)
Wadworth. Susan & Philip Henshaw, tenants

Smartly whitewashed, this small, well-kept and charming pub is opposite the village green. A delightful place with two comfortable well-beamed bars and a separate, no-smoking dining room. The inventive menu is far more interesting than usual in a pub and chosen with considerable care. The menu leans towards the European, with risotto, goulash, stroganoff, tagliatelle, lamb in red wine and hotpot: a little something from everywhere including a home-made soup, salmon paté, Somerset pork (grilled pork steak with a cider, leek, apple and herb sauce), vegetable curry, home-made fresh salmon fishcakes served with lemon butter sauce, Burgundy beef, daily specials too. Exceptionally well-kept Wadworths ales served from the wood, a home-brew and other guests. Outside is a large walled garden.

OPEN: 11–2.30, 6.30–11. Sun 12–3, 7–10.30 Sun.
Real Ale.
Children in dining room only. Dogs on leads. Wheelchair access difficult but possible.
Cards: all except Amex and Diners.

Rowde

George and Dragon ① 01380 723053
High Street, Rowde, nr Devizes SN10 2PN
Free House. Tim Withers, licensee
e-mail: gd-rowde@kiscali.co.uk

A well-established dining pub with a limited number of tables, so if you're thinking of doing any serious eating, you really must book. Not a tremendous looker from outside, but very handsome inside, beamed and full of charm. It has a small bar with a log fire in a lovely old fireplace, and a larger dining room. The inventive cooking makes this old place very appealing. The bar and restaurant menus are the same: fishy hors-d'oeuvres, salad of marinated anchovies, chargrilled peppers and quail eggs, cheese soufflé baked with parmesan and cream, fillet steak topped with gorgonzola, loin of venison with butternut squash mash and red onion compote, home-made puddings too – lemon cheesecake with poached nectarine and raspberry coulis or bread and butter pudding should fill any remaining gap. Small in size it may be, but the George and Dragon is 'big on fish'; fish dishes on the blackboard are based on deliveries fresh from Newlyn, so there could be Cornish crab salad, fillet of John Dory with crab sauce, roast hake with peppers and aioli, warm salad of scallops and bacon or monkfish with green peppercorns, brandy and cream. Well-kept beers too: Stonehenge ales, one from Butcombe and Hopback, also Nicks from the Milk Street Brewery in Frome. A glass of wine or two, and port to finish. Small garden and small car park.

OPEN: 12–3, 7–11. Closed Mon lunchtime.
Real Ale. Restaurant. No food Sun or Mon.
Children welcome. Dogs on leads in bar.
Cards: Delta, MasterCard, Switch, Visa.

Salisbury

Haunch of Venison ① 01722 322024
1 Minster Street, Salisbury SP1 1TB
Courage. Arnaud Rochette, manager
e-mail: haunchven@aol.com

In the historic heart of this beautiful cathedral city built in the 13th century at the meeting point of four river valleys, the ancient Haunch of Venison, near Poultry Cross, is an outstanding black and white building of jettied construction, most of it more than 600 years old. Over the years it has inevitably gathered its very own 'Grey Lady' who wanders the pub at night. Next to the fireplace – dating back to the pub's very early days – is a man's mummified hand, discovered earlier last century, holding some 18th-century playing cards. There is no mention of the rest of him but could it be his spirit that is wandering the pub searching for his lost hand? Several small bars inside the Haunch, all heavily beamed with timbered and panelled walls and open fires, where they serve a good choice of bar food: sandwiches – doorsteps – home-made soup, calves' liver parfait with red onion marmalade, pavé of venison with swede mash and red wine sauce, and the very popular Haunch of Venison platter (venison sausage, potted venison, cobbler and black pudding, with garnish and apple sauce) served with a free glass of wine or a pint of

Courage Best. Delicious puds too. Lunch and dinner menus are quite separate. Over 80 malt whiskies. Courage Best and Directors ales from a pewter bar counter. Comprehensive wine list. A charming, historic pub: not to be missed.

OPEN: 11–11.
Real Ale. Restaurant. No meals/snacks Sun eves Jan–March.
Children away from bar. Dogs on leads. Wheelchair access (not WC).
Cards: all cards except Amex and Diners.
Jazz evening every other Thursday.

Tollard Royal

King John Inn ① 01725 516207
Tollard Royal, nr Salisbury SP5 5PS
Free House. Tim & Michelle Birks, licensees

An attractive creeper-covered building hung about with flowering baskets and surrounded by tubs of flowers in spring and summer, the King John is in an area of outstanding natural beauty, in a delightful village full of thatched cottages tucked into a wooded hollow on the edge of Cranborne Chase. Opened in the middle of the 19th century as a working man's pub to quench the thirst of the locals labouring at the Tollard Royal iron foundry, it still refreshes the locals and everyone else, but they feed you too now. You will find a good choice of food; bar snacks and a full menu, all prepared from fresh ingredients. Smiles Best, Fullers London Pride as well as two or three guest ales, usually from a local brewery, wines by the glass and local cider. Lots of picnic tables outside. There are many paths through the surrounding woodland.

OPEN: 12–2.30, 6–11.
Real Ale. Restaurant.
No children. Dogs welcome. Car park. Wheelchair access difficult. Three bedrooms – all en suite.

Whitley

Pear Tree ① 01225 709131
Top Lane, Whitley, nr Melksham SN12 8HB
Free House. Martin & Debbie Still, licensees
e-mail: sales@peartreeinn.co.uk

The perfect Pear Tree brings together under one roof the very desirable combination of a successful pub and a notable restaurant. Found along a wandering country lane, it has the appearance of an appealing, stone-built 18th-century farmhouse, but whatever it might have been, a transformation has taken place. Still with the right amount of informality, the pub has become a very successful restaurant without forgetting the essentials of a pub: a bar where you can relax and just have a drink or a light lunch to set you up for the day. The same menu is available throughout the pub; cooking style moves from open sandwiches to Cornish crab spring roll with sprouting beans, Chinese cabbage and chilli jam, ham hock and leek terrine, risotto of oyster mushrooms and asparagus with courgette fries and guacamole, pork and herb sausages, grilled sea bass with red pesto crushed potatoes, shaved fennel and rocket salad or rump of lamb with garlic mash, ratatouille and rosemary jus vinaigrette. That's not all: how about a chocolate, rum and raisin cheesecake with crème fraiche sauce to finish? Fine cheeses too and bread made in their own bakery. Wadworths 6X, the local Oakhill Best Bitter and Gem, also Barnstormer from Bath Ales. The comprehensive wine list includes wines from local vineyards, ten by the glass. Delightful gardens for you to enjoy.

OPEN: 11–3, 6–11.30.
Real Ale. No-smoking restaurant.
Children welcome. Dogs, other than guide dogs, only in bar. Car park. Wheelchair access.
Cards: Delta, MasterCard, Switch, Visa.

BEST OF THE REST

Bottlesford
Seven Stars ① 01672 851325
Bottlesford SN9 6LU
Between Pewsey and Woodborough, watch for the sign to Bottlesford. In the Vale of Pewsey, this old thatched pub, with an interior to match its age, is a little bit of France in Wiltshire. The cooking has a definite Gallic influence – not surprising as the landlord is French. Good relaxed atmosphere where you can appreciate the imaginative cooking: French onion soup, boeuf bourguignon, filled baguettes. Mostly French wine on the list but they don't forget the beer. Usually something from Badger, Fullers, Wadworths 6X and a guest. Children welcome if dining. Dogs – must ask first. Wheelchair access (not WC). Open: 11–3, 6–11. Sun 12–3. Open for lunch on Bank Holiday Mondays but closed Tues following.

Castle Combe
White Hart ① 01249 782295
Market Place, Castle Combe, nr Chippenham SN14 7HS
According to one of our readers, this is the only pub in Castle Combe that offers a little peace and tranquility – notwithstanding the occasional background music. A cosy, friendly place attracting visitors and locals, it serves an inexpensive, traditional pub menu of home-made soup, freshly made sandwiches, filled jacket potatoes, ploughman's, steaks, pies and daily specials. Wadworths 6X and Henrys IPA and two guests from the four hand pumps. Short wine list and some excellent coffee. Children welcome, dogs too. Wheelchair access. Cards: all main cards.
Open: 11–11.

Holt
Tollgate Inn ① 01225 782326
Ham Green, Holt BA14 6PX
If you're a bit of a foodie and want to sample some adventurous dishes, this is the place to be. There are very interesting things going on in the food department in this sprawling old stone inn. Holt is a tiny village between Melksham and Bradford-on-Avon and the Tollgate has a cosily pubby bar with sofas and a big fire and a restaurant on the first floor. On both the bar and restaurant menus you'll experience some very good English cooking – with an imaginative edge – from a first-class chef. Weekly changing ales, maybe farm ciders and a

short wine list, four by the glass. Children welcome Sunday lunchtime only. No dogs.
Wheelchair access.
Open: 11.30–3, 6.30–11.30. Closed Sun eve and Mon.

Lacock

George Inn ① 01249 730263
4 West Street, Lacock SN15 2LH
Lacock Abbey is one of the reasons to come to this village; the other is the George, a pub
that has held a beer licence since the time of the Civil War. Full of horizontal and vertical
timbers, plenty of cosy corners and a huge inglenook fireplace with a dog wheel – which
turned the roasting spit – still in situ. Traditional bar food includes a good choice of fish:
salmon and seaweed roulade with a herb and pesto sauce, marlin steak with a creamy wine
and pernod sauce as well as beef medallions pan-fried in red wine, onions and garlic are
just a few of the dishes on the menu. Wadworths range of beers and wines from around
the world. Children in eating areas.
Open: 11–2.30, 5–11. Sat 10–11. Sun 12–10.30.

Semley

Benett Arms ① 01747 830221
Semley, Shaftesbury, Dorset SP7 9AS
Large and white, and that's the pub. In a lovely position opposite the big village green –
which had a new pond built to celebrate the millennium – and looking towards the
church, this popular place has a flagstone-floored bar with log fire, a room for the children
and spacious restaurant. The well-liked food is served in both the bar and restaurant as
well as on the village green during the summer season. From the changing menu there
could be soup of the day, ploughman's and various sandwiches, leek and cheese bake,
omelettes, Wiltshire ham served with either salad or chips, scampi royale, avocado and
seafood salad, venison pie, grills, steaks and occasionally bouillabaisse; also interesting
daily specials from the blackboard. Table d'hôte Sunday lunch. Home-made puddings.
Brakspear, Adnams Bitter and Youngs Special ales. Good extensive wine list – the landlord
is agent for wine shippers. Lots of liqueurs and Inchs ciders. Seats in the small garden and
on the village green. Children in upper bar. Dogs under control. Wheelchair access (not
WC). Five en-suite bedrooms. Cards: Amex, Diners, MasterCard, Visa.
Open: 11–3, 6–11.

Stourton

Spread Eagle ① 01747 840587
Church Lawn, Stourton BA12 6HQ
In an unrivalled position near Stourhead – an early 18th-century Palladian house in the
most beautifully landscaped grounds, now owned by the National Trust – the Spread Eagle
is in an elegant and spacious building at the head of a lake. Tastefully and comfortably
furnished, the food on offer is excellent and ranges from sandwiches, ploughman's, steak
and kidney pie and specials on the board to three-course meals. Beers are Courage Best
and Wadworth 6X from the cask and John Smith's keg. Children welcome. Bedrooms.
Open: 11–11. Sun 12–10.30.

Wootton Rivers

Royal Oak ① 01672 810322
Wootton Rivers, nr Marlborough SN8 4NQ
Handsome, half-timbered and thatched, the Royal Oak is in a delightful village near the
Kennet and Avon canal. Inside are a wealth of timbers holding up the walls and ceilings,

polished tables, flowers and a general feeling of well-being. Four different eating areas, so you can be sure you'll find somewhere to rest your plate. Freshly made sandwiches and several different ploughman's – even seasonal ones – available at lunchtime only. Otherwise you could order home-made soup, pan-fried sardines with tomato and basil sauce, prawn and quail egg mayonnaise with lumpfish caviar, chicken liver and brandy paté, roast rack of English lamb and a great deal of fish, changing daily specials and lots of good puds. Whitbread Best, Wadworth 6X and guest ales. Comprehensive wine list. Small sitting-out area near the car park. Children welcome, dogs too. Bed and breakfast in adjoining house.

Open: 11–3.30, 6.30–11. Sun 12–10.30.

N.B. Jukebox can occasionally be heard throughout the pub.

Wetherspoon in Wiltshire

Salisbury – King's Head Inn, 1 Bridge Street
➲ 01722 342050
Swindon – Groves Company Inn, 22–23 Fleet Street
➲ 01793 402040
Swindon – Savoy, 38–40 Regent Street
➲ 01793 533970
Trowbridge – Sir Isaac Pitman, Market Place
➲ 01225 763287

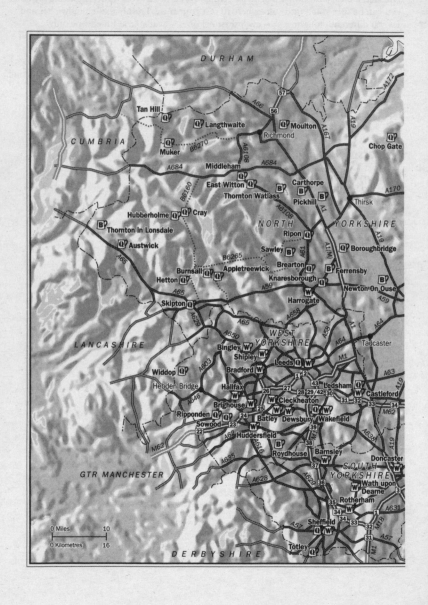

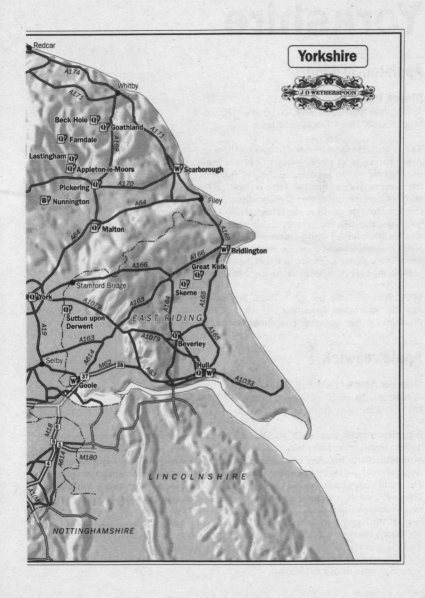

Yorkshire

J·D·WETHERSPOON

Redcar
A174
A171
Whitby
Beck Hole
Goathland
A171
Farndale
A169
Lastingham
Appleton-le-Moors
Pickering
A170
Scarborough
Nunnington
A64
Filey
A464
Malton
A166
A165
Bridlington
A166
A166
Great Kelk
Stamford Bridge
Skerne
York
A1079
A163
A164
A165
Sutton upon Derwent
EAST RIDING
A19
A163
A1079
Beverley
A165
Selby
A614
M62
38
A63
Hull
Goole
37
A1033
M18
6
5
1
A614
M180
LINCOLNSHIRE
NOTTINGHAMSHIRE

Yorkshire

Appleton-le-Moors

Moors Inn ☺ 01751 417435
Appleton-le-Moors, nr York, N. Yorks YO62 6TF
Free House. Janet Frank, licensee

This one-street village of stone houses on the edge of the North York moors is not the most picturesque of places, but as one of our readers says, 'this is a plus, as the village has not been overrun by tourists and the pub still feels like a village local'. Both the reports that came to us agree that this place is good, and comes 'well recommended'. Refurbished and looking very smart, the main bar, divided into two distinct areas, has an old range that's put to good use in winter. There is also a separate restaurant and a pool room, where you can smoke. The food comes highly praised: tomato and tarragon soup, garlic and herb chicken breast served with a cream and wine sauce, pheasant casserole, pork medallions in a ginger sauce, broccoli pancake, celeriac and blue cheese pie. Always a choice of fish and a home-made ginger ice cream to finish. Sunday roast. Beers are Black Sheep and Tetleys. Seats in the big garden from where there are far-reaching views.

OPEN: Tues–Fri 7–11. Sat 12–3, 7–11. Sun 12–3, 7–10.30. Closed Mon.
Real Ale. No-smoking throughout the pub.
Children and dogs welcome. En-suite bedrooms. No cards.

Appletreewick

Craven Arms ☺ 01756 720270
Appletreewick, nr Skipton, N. Yorks BD23 6DA
Free House. Keith Rose, licensee

A creeper-covered, stone-built, traditional Dales pub. Popular with everyone, including walkers enjoying the Dales Way, the footpaths along the lovely River Wharfe and the wonderful North Yorkshire countryside. Between the Wharfdale Valley and the moors, Appletreewick is as pretty as its name, full of handsome houses and attractive cottages. The traditionally furnished old Craven Arms has cosy beamed rooms with winter fires. They serve ample portions of pub food in the bar or the no-smoking dining room: soups, sandwiches, ploughman's, Cumberland sausages with onion gravy, steak and kidney pie, lasagne, fish, vegetarian dishes and daily specials on the blackboard. Black Sheep Special and Bitter, Theakstons Best and a guest beer, lagers, stouts and ciders. Choice of wines and a selection of malt whiskies. Seats at the front of the pub to admire the view. Just beyond the village is the 17th-century Parcevall Hall, which has 16 acres of terraced gardens and woodland open during the season.

OPEN: 11.30–3, 6.30–11. Sat 11.30–11. Sun 12–10.30.
Real Ale. Food served 11.30–9 (Sun 12–9).
Children welcome. Dogs and their walkers welcome. Wheelchair access. Cards: all major cards accepted.

Austwick

Game Cock ① 01524 251226
The Green, Austwick, nr Settle, N. Yorks LA2 8BB
Thwaites. Richard Lord, tenant

Austwick is surrounded by dramatic countryside: high moorlands, steep-sided valleys and rushing mountain streams. In the main street the old stone Game Cock has a beamed, simply furnished, very welcoming bar, separate dining room, family room and, at the front, a glassed-in veranda for cooler days. A tremendous favourite with visitors, walkers and villagers alike. All the food is made 'in pub', including the bread. As well as sandwiches and bar snacks served only in the bar there could be Brittany mussels, a smoked salmon platter, king prawns in filo pastry on a bed of French leaf salad and for a main course, steak cooked slowly with mushrooms and onions in red wine under a puff pastry crust, pork fillet in black bean sauce, tandoori lamb and game cock pie – tender pieces of venison, rabbit, pheasant and snipe cooked in red wine gravy with a puff pastry lid; also lamb shank in a red wine sauce and last, but not least, more-ish puddings. The changing specials board always has a few culinary surprises. Very well-kept Thwaites range of ales. There is a play area for children in the garden.

OPEN: 11.30–3, 6–11.
Real Ale. No-smoking dining room.
Children in restaurant. No dogs.
Cards: all major cards except Amex.

Beck Hole

Birch Hall Inn ① 01947 896245
Beck Hole, Goathland, Whitby, N. Yorks YO22 5LE
Free House. Colin Jackson, licensee
e-mail: birchhallinn@beckhole.freeserve.co.uk

In an enviable setting – a small hamlet of a few cottages and a couple of farms – the Birch Hall Inn is tucked into a hilly landscape with open rolling pastures, woodland and a meandering river. The inn provides all the essentials for the travelling tourist; it wears two hats, pub and village shop. Inside the 17th-century inn are two small bars, one of them with a serving hatch and open fire and between the bars a shop selling postcards, sweets, ices and soft drinks. The food served in the pub is more sustaining: local pork, turkey and ham pies, Beck Hole butties with generous fillings of ham, cheese, paté or corned beef. Home-baked scones and their famous beer cake for tea. Theakstons Bitter, Black Sheep, local beers and guests – all from the cask. Family room and seats in the steep garden. A delightful hamlet in a naturally wooded valley in a lovely part of Yorkshire. Good walking country.

OPEN: May–Aug 11–11. Sep–Apr 11–3, 7.30–10.30. Closed Mon eves in winter.
Real Ale.
Children in small bar and garden. Dogs on leads. Limited car parking.

Beverley

White Horse Inn ① 01482 861973
22 Hengate, Beverley, E. Yorks HU17 8BP
Sam Smiths. Anna, manager
e-mail: anname@talk21.com

An old inn in an historic town. Only North Gate at North Bar, one of the original medieval gates of the walled town, remains; nearby is the ancient, 12th-century church of St Mary, which has a stunning medieval interior and near the church is the White Horse, known as 'Nellies' after a memorable landlady. There was certainly an inn on the site during the mid-17th century, which over the years has developed to become the place you see today – much of it very late Victorian. Spacious, rambling even, with lots of areas to get lost in, flagstones on the floor, coal fires to keep you warm and gas lights to see by, the pub has a timeless quality which is much appreciated. Reasonably priced traditional bar food which includes interesting fillings for the sandwiches or toasties, among which are Ostlers Bag (chicken and fried mushrooms), Mail Coach (ham, Stilton, onion, mustard and horseradish), Saddler (cheddar, mushrooms and garlic) or Nellie's Fancy (brie, grilled bacon with mango and salad), a seasonal soup, bangers and mash with a rich beef gravy, ploughman's, steak 'n' ale pie and a roast on Sundays. There is a no-smoking room behind the bar. Well-kept Sam Smiths Ales, no guest beer. Seats in the old stable yard behind the inn.

OPEN: 11–11. Sun 12–10.30.
Real Ale.
Children welcome (not in main bar or pool room). Dogs on leads.
N.B. Music in pool room.

Boroughbridge

Black Bull ① 01423 322413
6 St James' Square, Boroughbridge, N. Yorks YO51 9AR
Free House. Tony Burgess, licensee

From the evidence of the ancient monoliths – Devil's Arrows alongside the A1 – it is obvious that Boroughbridge has been a settlement since prehistoric times. On the edge of Wensleydale, once a busy staging post on the Great North Road, everyone from the Romans to present-day travellers has passed through this place. But still here, in the centre of the town, is the black and white, well-run 13th-century Black Bull which has a comfortable beamed bar, inglenook fireplace, cosy snug and a very popular restaurant serving good, interesting food. From the bar menu you could choose cold or hot fillings for the sandwiches or pasta with smoked ham, mushrooms in a white wine, garlic and Dijon mustard sauce glazed with double cheese melt, Scottish smoked salmon and scrambled eggs served on toasted brioche, chargrilled steaks, chicken, tuna, lamb and pork, pork and chive sausages with creamy mashed potato and a number of dishes with a Thai influence. Fresh seafood and seasonal specials are on the blackboard; there is an à la carte menu in the restaurant. Ales – all on hand pump – are John Smiths, Black Sheep and one regular guest; over 50 wines on the list, 10 of them by the glass.

OPEN: 11–11. Sun 12–10.30.
Real Ale. Restaurant (classical music here).
Children in eating area. Dogs welcome. Bedrooms in the modern bit.
Cards: all except Amex.

Brearton

Malt Shovel ① 01423 862929
Brearton, Harrogate, N. Yorks HG3 3BX
Free House. Les & Charlotte Mitchell, licensees

This pub is a tremendously popular meeting place, full of character with a reputation for serving well-chosen, well-cooked food, and an attention to detail that lifts it above the ordinary. East of Ripley, the Malt Shovel is an unspoilt 16th-century pub in a small remote village on a road that eventually peters out, so if you suddenly find yourself on the moor, you know you've missed it – you were going in the right direction though, so turn around and go back the way you came. Inside is cosy, heavily beamed, with panelled rooms and good winter fires. The blackboard menus change daily but could include the favourites: liver, bacon and black pudding with mash with red wine gravy, warm chicken salad, also beef lasagne, lamb shanks braised in white wine with garlic and preserved lemons, mussels steamed in white wine with garlic, herbs and tomatoes, a seafood gratin and a cold seafood platter; usually seven meat, fish and vegetarian choices on the menu – something for everyone. All the puddings – seven or more – are home-made. Three regular beers, Theakstons Bitter, Daleside Nightjar, Blacksheep Bitter, two others from any micro-brewery – Durham Magus, Roosters Special or Rudgate Battleaxe. Interesting wine list and wines by the glass. Farm ciders. Seats on the terrace – which has heaters – at the back of the pub.

OPEN: 12–3, 6.45–11. Closed Mon. No food Sun eve.
Real Ale.
Children welcome. Dogs on leads. Wheelchair access (not WC).

Burnsall

Red Lion ① 01756 720204
Burnsall, Skipton, N. Yorks BD23 6BU Fax: 01756 720292
Free House. Elizabeth Grayshon, licensee
e-mail: redlion@daelnet.co.uk

The perfect setting for a village and an inn. One of the prettiest villages in the Wharfe valley sits on a loop of the river, crossed by a most attractive 17th-century bridge. The village green borders the river and the 16th-century Red Lion, once a ferryman's inn, is on the bank. This favoured place has a low-ceilinged, panelled main bar, a no-smoking lounge bar, where they serve good, interesting bar food, a more formal restaurant and a recent extension that includes a new dining room that leads out onto the terrace, an extended function room and extra bedrooms. On the bar menu will be soups and lunchtime sandwiches, hot Stilton rarebit and home-made chutney – with or without bacon – salmon and coriander fishcakes with mango and chilli relish, a plate of northern cheeses, pickles and chutneys, foie gras and duck liver terrine, fresh Whitby crab and avocado, and for a main course, loin of suckling pig, chargrilled chicken and red lentils braised with bacon and garlic, spinach, leek and Gambozola cannelloni, roasted duck breast, sticky onion tartlet with blackcurrant relish and free-range calves' liver with bubble and squeak. Lots of other goodies to choose from including some really yummy puds. All the dishes will be freshly prepared and nearly all the meat – beef, lamb and pork – is local, some raised by the family, the rest from farms across the river; this is a place that believes in supporting local farmers. Theakstons Best, Black Bull, Old Peculier, Morlands Old Speckled Hen, Black Sheep and a guest beer. At least 12 wines by the glass, a further 90 bins by the bottle. Choice of malt whiskies. Seats outside at the front and at the back of the pub.

OPEN: 11.30–11. Sun 12–10.30.
Real Ale. Restaurant.
Children welcome. Dogs on leads. (No dogs in hotel rooms.) Wheelchair access. Fifteen en-suite bedrooms. Three holiday cottages to rent or as serviced accommodation.
Cards: all credit cards.

Chop Gate

Sun Inn ① 01439 798206
Chop Gate, nr Fangdale Beck, Middlesbrough, N. Yorks TS9 7LQ
Free House. William Ainsley, licensee

The postal address may lead you to think you are in a village, but the Sun stands alone about four miles south of Chop Gate and half a mile south of Fangdale Beck church. Part pub, part farm, it has been in the Ainsley family since the early 19th century and is known locally as Spout House from the water spout – still there – behind the old building. The present Sun is early 20th century and has just a simple room with settles, a coal fire and walls decorated with old photographs of village bands and cricket teams. No food but you can bring your own sandwiches and enjoy them with beer from Black Sheep.

OPEN: 11–11. Sun 12–10.30.
Real Ale.
Children – yes-ish. Dogs allowed. Car park. Wheelchair access difficult.

Cray

White Lion ① 01756 760262
Cray, Buckden, Upper Wharfedale, N. Yorks BD23 5JB
Free House. Kevin Roe, licensee
e-mail: admin@whitelioncray.com

Sitting on the sunny terrace at the front of the White Lion you can watch the water tumbling over limestone slabs on the other side of the road. The 17th-century White Lion, a welcoming, traditional Dales pub, is at the centre of a small hamlet in wonderful country between Wharfedale and Bishopdale. At the foot of Buckden Pike, this old drovers' pub is the highest in the dale; a welcome resting place to refresh the parts your walking boots have tired out. Flagstone floors, beams, an open fire and filling home-cooked meals including soups, chicken liver paté with toast and salad garnish, warm peppered fillet of mackerel with a lime mayonnaise and salad, home-made steak and mushroom pie in rich beer gravy, diced venison casserole with root vegetables in a red wine and pimento gravy, also filled Yorkshire puddings and jacket potatoes. A children's menu, vegetarian dishes and puddings on the blackboard. There is a separate evening menu. Moorhouses Pendle Witches Brew and Premier, Timothy Taylors Landlord and guest beers. Seats on the sunny terrace.

OPEN: 11–11. Sun 12–10.30.
Real Ale.
Children in specific areas. Dogs on leads. En-suite bedrooms.
Cards: Delta, MasterCard, Switch, Visa.

East Witton

Blue Lion ① 01969 624273
East Witton, nr Leyburn, N. Yorks DL8 4SN
Free House. Paul Klein, lease
e-mail: bluelion@breathemail.net

You can stay, eat well or just drop in for a drink at this old stone Dales inn. Outwardly nothing much has changed; built at the end of the 18th century this village pub, in one of the most lovely wooded areas of the Dales, has been brought bang up to date without losing an ounce of its charm. The two bars are full of interesting bits and pieces, comfortable chairs, high backed settles on stone floors and big log-filled fireplaces. It takes quite a time to read the delights on offer on the numerous blackboards, but you can be sure the home-made food is seriously good: roasted king scallops with lemon risotto and Gruyère cheese, sliced figs with Parma ham, Caesar salad with pancetta and chargrilled chicken, warm salad of sautéed wood pigeon and smoked foie gras with a grain mustard and beetroot dressing, warm onion and blue Wensleydale tart with tomato chutney, fillet of beef with red wine and braised oxtail and lamb shank with spring onion mash are just a few of the dishes on the menu – lots more to choose from, all with a dash of imagination – fish and a vegetarian menu too. The same menu is available in the elegant, candle-lit restaurant. Theakstons Best, Black Sheep Bitter and John Smiths on hand pump. There is an extensive wine list which includes half bottles – some by the glass – and old English liqueurs. Seats outside the front of the pub and in the big attractive garden at the rear.

OPEN: 11–11.
Real Ale. Restaurant (closed Sun eve).
Children welcome. Dogs on leads. Car park. Disabled facilities. Bedrooms in the pub and the converted stables.
Cards: MasterCard, Switch, Visa.

Cover Bridge Inn ① 01969 623250
East Witton, nr Leyburn, N. Yorks DL8 4SQ
Free House. Mr & Mrs N. Harrington, licensees
e-mail: enquiries@thecoverbridgeinn.co.uk

Downhill from the village, near to where the River Cover is joined by the River Ure, this solid, substantial building is next to the old packhorse bridge across the Cover. A very ancient place that is known to have been in existence before the nearby Jervaulx Abbey was destroyed in 1536. When you get inside – everyone admits that getting past the door handle seems to be a challenge! – you'll find a well-beamed bar, a large log fire and wooden settles to settle in – the changes made over the years have helped to keep that timeless atmosphere. A range of home-made snacks and meals are available in both the bar and the dining room: traditional ham and eggs, home-made steak pie, chicken, ham and mushroom pie, lasagne or a mixed grill are the favourites. If you're a vegetarian, vegetarian lasagne. All washed down with Theakstons Old Peculier from the wood, John Smiths, Black Sheep and Timothy Taylors Best Bitters. Lots of room in the beer garden from where you can watch the river flow by. Walks along the river and to the historic Jervaulx Abbey. From here you are within easy reach of Ripon and Harrogate, remains of the castles at Richmond, Middleham and Bolton, racing, fishing on the Cover and golf – there are lots of things to keep you out of mischief and bring you here to stay.

OPEN: 11–11. Food served 12–2, 6.30–9 every day.
Real Ale. Restaurant.
Children welcome. Dogs too. Car park. Wheelchair access (not WC). Three en-suite bedrooms. Day fishing permits can be obtained at the inn.
Cards: all major cards except Amex and Diners.

Farndale

Feversham Arms ① 01751 433206
Church Houses, Farndale, nr Kirkby Moorside, N. Yorks YO6 6LF
Free House. Fran Debenham, licensee

Such an attraction in spring: field after field in this little Farndale valley turns yellow with early wild daffodils. Ideally placed next to the nature reserve, the Feversham Arms, a delightful, well-kept old pub, has two flagstone-floored rooms with coal fires and a smart restaurant in the converted barn. Hearty appetites are a necessity as the portions are generous in both the restaurant and the bar. A house speciality is fillet of pork en croute stuffed with garlic and shallots, also the tournedos Rossini. Sunday lunches (must book). Full Yorkshire breakfast if you stay. Tetleys ales, also stouts and lagers. Seats in the garden. The path, along the loveliest section of the River Dove, runs for one and a half miles between Church Houses and Low Mill. The wonderful, golden wave of miniature daffodils in April is thought to be the inspiration behind 'the host of golden daffodils' in Wordsworth's well-known poem.

OPEN: Summer 11–3, 5.30–11. Winter 12–2.30, 7–11. Closed Mon in Jan, Feb and March.
Real Ale. Restaurant.
Children welcome. Dogs on leads. Three en-suite bedrooms. One holiday cottage.
Cards: all credit cards.

Goathland

Mallyan Spout Hotel ① 01947 896486
Goathland, Whitby, N. Yorks YO22 5AN
Free House. Michael Bell & Stuart Knight, licensees

Named after a local waterfall, this very handsome, creeper-covered hotel is on the edge of a common kept short by efficient four-legged woolly lawn-mowers – the local sheep. Inside are three comfortable lounges with good winter fires and views past the garden to the moors beyond, a bar serving well-kept ales and an attractive restaurant. With a change of licensees the bar food is more traditional and includes home-made lasagne, home-cooked Yorkshire ham, giant Yorkshire puddings, traditional ploughman's, minute steak ciabatta, rib-eye steak, cod and chips and a Mallyan mixed grill. Beers are Theakstons Best, Tetley Smoothflow and weekly guest beers. They have an extensive wine list and choice of malt whiskies. Starting at the hotel, a 20-minute walk down a steep track will bring you to the Mallyan Spout, a 70ft waterfall tumbling over mossy cliffs into the Esk Valley below. Not far away, a lane leads to Beck Hole. This is a wonderful area for walks. If you're a fan of the TV series *Heartbeat* you might like to know that the cast hang out here.

OPEN: 10–11. Daily bar snacks 12–2.30, 6–8.30.
Real Ale. Restaurant (eves and Sunday lunch; music in here). Afternoon teas.
Children welcome until 8.30. Dogs on leads. Disabled facilities. Twenty four en-suite bedrooms.
Cards: Amex, MasterCard, Solo, Switch, Visa.

Great Kelk

Chestnut Horse ① 01262 488263
Main Street, Great Kelk, Driffield, E. Yorks YO25 8HN
Free House. Jon Allan & Julie Costello, licensees
e-mail: thechestnuthorse_greatkelk@yahoo.co.uk

Between Great and Little Kelk, the late 18th-century Chestnut Horse is in a rural hamlet equidistant from both villages. Originally called 'The Board', this charming pub, which had a short life as a Coroners' Court, is a popular place serving some enjoyable food. Inside is a log fire, drinks-only bar, lounge bar where food is served and a no-smoking restaurant. From the menu you could start with home-made soup of the day, chicken liver and pork paté, crab fritters, or sautéed lamb kidneys in brandy and pink peppercorns on steamed noodles and fresh herbs, and for a main course, haggis and black pudding Wellington, tarragon and smoked chicken, liver and onions, pan-fried pork fillet with cream, mushrooms, leeks and tarragon, also steaks and grills, a fish menu and vegetarian dishes, as well as a weekly changing specials board. A range of guest beers and a good wine list with special additions on offer from the local wine dealer. Outside is a large, walled beer garden where you can bring your dog and tie up your horse.

OPEN: Mon–Fri 6–11. Sat & Sun 12–3, 6–11.
Real Ale.
Children welcome. No dogs inside. Car park. Wheelchair access.
No cards.

Hetton

Angel Inn ① 01756 730263
Hetton, nr Skipton, N. Yorks BD23 6LT
Free House. Denis Watkins, licensee
e-mail: info@angelhetton.co.uk

It might have started out as a humble crofter's cottage, but several hundred years later this attractive building is one very desirable place, a perfect merger under one roof of well-known, fantastically good restaurant and relaxed, informal and welcoming bars. If you're doing some serious eating you need to get here early to beat the queues. Inside, separate rooms have beams, panelling and open fires; the lounge bar and snug are no-smoking. You can eat in the informal bar brasserie, or in the elegant restaurant which has a greater choice of dishes on its fixed-price menu. Food here is an experience: seafood filo parcels in a lobster sauce, Angel fish soup, tomato and basil risotto, pappardelli with spicy meatballs, sweet pepper sauce and pecorino shavings, slowly cooked shoulder of lamb on buttered spring cabbage with a rosemary and garlic fritter, lamb jus and pesto, chargrilled fillet of beef with pomme purée, button onions, bacon lardons, wood mushrooms in a red wine sauce gives you some idea of the delights on the menu. Friday is fish day; yummy puds all the time – and advice on what dessert wine to drink with them – also English cheeses. Special gourmet evenings are organized throughout the year. Black Sheep, Timothy Taylors Landlord and Copper Dragon beer. Quite an impressive wine list – over 20 by the glass, a couple of champagnes for when you want to celebrate and a choice of malt whiskies. Seats outside on the terrace.

OPEN: 12–2.30, 6–10.30 (Sat 6–11).
Real Ale. Restaurant (closed Sun eve).
Well-behaved children welcome. Dogs outside only. Car park. Wheelchair access (not WC).
Cards: Amex, MasterCard, Switch, Visa.

Hubberholme

George Inn ① 01756 760223
Kirk Gill, Hubberholme, nr Skipton, N. Yorks BD23 5JE
Free House. Barry Roberts, licensee
e-mail: thegeorge.inn@virgin.net

A tiny, pretty little hamlet on the River Wharfe, and just across the bridge from the very old church of St Michael and all Angels is the George. The hamlet of Hubberholme; just a few cottages, farms, a church and the pub, takes its name from a marauding Viking king – Hubba the Berserker! – who established a community here a thousand years ago. This is walking country; along the Dales Way or beside the river to Buckden and Cray, and the George, a solid, stone building is in just the right place to sustain the traveller. In the traditional, beamed, stone-walled bars they serve home-made soup, garlic bread, Ardennes paté with Cumberland sauce and salad, filled rolls, ploughman's, filled Yorkshire puddings, rump steak and fried onions in a toasted panini, steak and kidney pie, Black Sheep casserole – lamb in ale, fish lasagne and daily specials. More specials and vegetarian dishes are available during the evening. The breakfast room is no smoking. Tetleys Bitter, Blacksheep Bitter and Special. Twenty malt whiskies and a choice of nearly 40 wines. Seats outside for the view and for gazing at the river.

OPEN: 11.30–3 (Sat 11–3), 6–11.
Real Ale.
Children in eating area. Dogs on leads. Car park. Wheelchair access (not WC). Six letting rooms.
Cards: MasterCard, Solo, Switch, Visa.

Hull

Ye Olde White Harte ① 01482 326363
25 Silver Street, Hull, E.Yorks HU1 1JG
Scottish Courage. Gerry Drew, licensee

Ye Olde Harte, reached along an alley between Silver Street and Bowl Alley Lane, is part of the heritage of Hull, a building that is practically in the folk memory of everyone in the city. Hugely atmospheric, this 16th-century courtyard pub has ancient beams, panelling, two huge sit-in fireplaces, lots of nooks and crannies and all the architectural features you would expect of a building that has been here for over 500 years. Upstairs in 'Ye Plotting Parlour', now part of the restaurant, the decision was made by the then Governor of Hull, Sir John Hotham, to lock the gates of the city against Charles I. Not a good move: he was beheaded by the Parliamentarians soon after. Food is available only during the day and this includes all the traditional dishes including sandwiches, paté, pies, salads, chicken and ham pie, beef in ale pie and changing specials. The dining area is up a fine old staircase. McEwans 80/-, Theakstons XB, Old Peculier and Courage Directors plus a weekly changing guest beer. Selection of malt whiskies. There is an 'all weather garden' – with heaters. That sorts out the cold: what about the rain?

OPEN: 11–11.
Real Ale. Lunchtime restaurant (music in here).
Children in eating areas. Dogs welcome. Disabled facilities.

Knaresborough

Blind Jacks ① 01423 869148
19 Market Place, Knaresborough, N. Yorks HG5 8AL
North Bay Ltd. Paul Holden-Ridgway, manager & licensee

Open evenings only, this is for the beer aficionados among you, only here for the atmosphere and a taste of some unusual beers. A cosy three-storey town pub in an 18th-century building at the heart of this market town full of Georgian buildings, steep steps and alleyways leading down to the River Nidd. This is a charming, friendly place, lots of small rooms, one no-smoking, where they serve a good selection of unusual beers including the Village Brewer White Boar Bitter, Dalesides Greengrass as well as Timothy

Taylors Landlord, Black Sheep Bitter, Gales fruit wines and four changing guest ales, but alas, no food.

OPEN: Mon 5.30–11. Tues–Thurs 4–11. Fri & Sat 12–11. Sun 12–10.30.
Real Ale. No food.
Children welcome. Dogs on leads.

Langthwaite

Red Lion ① 01748 884218
Langthwaite, Arkengarthdale, Richmond, N. Yorks DL11 6RE
Free House. Mrs Rowena Hutchinson, FBII, licensee
e-mail: rlionlangthwaite@aol.com

Together Langthwaite, the main village in Arkengarthdale, and the Red Lion are gathering up a formidable list of television and film credits. All that and running a successful pub too. The humpback bridge is very photogenic and the beamed bar has been the location for both TV and film – signed photos of the stars and where they filmed adorn the walls. So, not just a delightful pub but a pub with a very glamorous life and a great atmosphere. Small, entirely unspoilt with a bar and tiny snug. They serve very reasonably priced sustaining food to go with the beer. There is a selection of sandwiches, Cornish pasties, hot or cold cheese and onion pasties, sausage rolls and pork pies to go with the Black Sheep Bitter and Riggwelter on hand pump, also Worthington Smooth, John Smiths, Guinness, Bulmers Original cider, Carling lager. Now a magnet for film location enthusiasts, the pub sells local preserves, honey and small gifts, also books, stamps, postcards and maps for the intrepid walker.

OPEN: 11–3, 7–11. Sun 12–3, 7–10.30. These times are extended when very busy.
Real Ale.
Children at lunchtime. No dogs. Wheelchair access (not WC).
Cards: Delta, Solo, Switch, Visa (cashback available)

Lastingham

Blacksmiths Arms ① 01751 417247
Front Street, Lastingham, N. Yorks YO62 6TL
Free House. C. R. & M. Miller, licensees

A very attractive village in a fold of the North York Moors. Here is a church of note with an ancient Norman crypt, and in prime position opposite this gem is the Blacksmiths Arms. This very pleasant, friendly stone-built inn has a cosy, beamed bar with a large collection of pewter mugs to admire and a fire to sit by. You'll find a good choice of food on the menu: home-made soup, spicy chicken wings, garlic bread topped with melted cheese, Yorkshire puddings with onion gravy, salmon and broccoli bake topped with sliced potato and melted cheese, roast topside of beef with Yorkshire pudding, pork and apple sausages with cider gravy in a giant Yorkshire pudding, steak and ale pie, using Black Bull Bitter, under a short pastry crust; daily specials too. Beers are Theakstons Best, Black Bull and Marstons Pedigree. Also a comprehensive wine list. Seats in the garden at the back of the pub. You are surrounded by wonderful walking country.

OPEN: 12–2.30, 7–11.
Real Ale. Restaurant.
Children welcome. No dogs. No car park. Wheelchair access.
Cards: all accepted except Amex and Diners.

Ledsham

Chequers Inn ☎ 01977 683135
Claypit Lane, Ledsham, nr South Milford, W. Yorks LS25 5LP (turn left where the A63 joins the A1)
Free House. Chris Wraith, licensee

The Chequers is quite unique: the only pub in England subject to its own licensing law. One Sunday, early in the 19th century, a drunken workman shouted abuse at the local magistrate as he walked home from church. Blaming the pub for the drunken disorderliness, the magistrate used his influence to restrict the Chequers licence to six days – never on a Sunday. However, this stone-built, well-kept village local, with beams, a bit of panelling, log fires and a nice old-fashioned air doesn't seem to suffer. Familiar, reliable bar food: home-made soup, filled baguettes, ploughman's, wild boar terrine, scrambled eggs and smoked salmon, sausage and mash, grilled lemon sole, home-baked hams – that sort of thing – and several daily specials. Beers are Brown Cow Bitter and Simpsons No. 4, Theakstons Best and John Smiths. Outside is a flowery, two-level beer garden.

OPEN: 11–3, 5–11. Sat 11–11. Closed Sun.
Real Ale. Restaurant.
Children in own room. Dogs welcome.

Leeds

Whitelocks ☎ 01132 453950
Turks Head Yard, off Briggate, Leeds LS1 6HB
Youngers. Nick James, manager

Whitelocks is as well known as the city it is part of. The Victorians did such an exciting, over-the-top modernisation of the building that you can forgive them for ruining what was probably a perfectly good, very classical, certainly very early Georgian, structure. Look down this alley off the main shopping centre and you'll see the Victorian lamps, hanging baskets, the seats and converted barrels that are used as tables. Here you can enjoy a drink in fine weather, or if you're really desperate, sit and wait for the doors to open. Inside is a celebration of Victorian pub architecture at its best: stained-glass windows, fine mirrors, red banquettes, marble tiles on the bars and a panelled dining room at the back of the pub. Good choice of traditional bar food: sandwiches, pies, sausages, filled Yorkshire puddings, Scotch eggs, deep-fried whitebait, Yorkshire pudding with onion gravy, Whitelocks fish pie, farmhouse mixed grill, roast lamb, grilled gammon or beefsteak pie. Home-made roly-poly or fruit pie to finish. Wallow in nostalgia by reading the pre-war

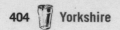

prices which are still etched on the mirrors. Hand-pulled Theakstons Bitter and Old Peculier, John Smiths and guests. A selection of wines. Summer cider. Seats in the narrow beer garden.

OPEN: 11–11.
Real Ale. Restaurant (not Sun eve).
No children. Guide dogs only. Wheelchair access.
Cards: Amex, MasterCard, Switch, Visa.

Malton

Crown Hotel (Suddaby's Ltd) ☎ 01653 692038
12 Wheelgate, Malton, N. Yorks YO17 7HP
Free House. Neil Suddaby, licensee
e-mail: enquiries@suddabys.co.uk

A handsome, listed, Georgian-fronted building that replaced the original coaching inn which sadly burnt down. In the main shopping area of this old market town, which grew up on the site of a Roman fort, the present Crown has been in the same family since 1879. Many changes have been made but its Georgian past has not been forgotten. Only sandwiches are served during the week; full menu on Saturday. Food is served in either the bar or the conservatory – the menu gives you a choice of eight home-made soups, among which could be carrot and coriander, tomato and roasted peppers, Tuscan minestrone or fish chowder, also a home-made lasagne, filled Yorkshire puddings, shepherd's pie, home-made chilli, ploughman's, salads and specials. The family are brewers too; Malton Brewery in the courtyard is where they brew Malton Golden Chance, Double Chance, Pickwicks Porter, Auld Bob and Ryedale Champion. When the spirit takes them they produce some special brews. They also have John Smiths and some guest beers. Jazz and piano recitals in the conservatory, also seasonal beer festivals.

OPEN: 11–11. Sun 12–10.30.
Real Ale.
Children welcome. Dogs on leads. Wheelchair access. Six bedrooms in the hotel; two in the annexe.
Cards: Delta, MasterCard, Switch, Visa.

Middleham

White Swan Hotel ☎ 01969 622093
Market Place, Middleham, nr Leyburn, N. Yorks DL8 4PE
Free House. Andrew Holmes, manager

This attractive small town, with a cobbled market square full of Georgian buildings, is overlooked by the massive ruins of the castle which Richard III acquired in 1471. Just past the market square is the White Swan, an old coaching inn dating back to Tudor times which has grown over the years into the smart place you see today. At the front there are seats among the flowers, and inside are four rooms, including a main flagstoned bar with beams and open fire and an elegant restaurant. For a starter you could choose crispy duck and bacon salad with plum sauce, black pudding and bacon risotto in a red wine sauce or finely sliced smoked salmon with spring onions; for a main course local sausages with a grain mustard mash, fish and chips with mushy peas, fricassee of lamb with seasonal vegetables and braised pilau rice or home-made steak and kidney or chicken pie. Always fresh fish of the day, vegetarian dishes and maybe queen scallops in a bacon and shallot cream sauce or a 'White Swan' bouillabaisse with rouille, or fillet of beef stuffed with black pudding and wrapped in smoked bacon in a forestière sauce. Yorkshire cheeses and more-ish puds to finish. Four hand-pulled ales: Black Sheep Best, Special, Riggwelter and John Smiths cask. Twenty-eight wines on the list – something for everyone. At the back of the hotel is an open courtyard and from the rooms there are views towards the market square, the castle and the country beyond. Known as the Newmarket of the north, you will hear the clatter of horses' hooves as they make their way through the town to the gallops on Low Moor.

OPEN: 11–11. Sun 12–10.30.
Real Ale. Restaurant.
Children welcome, as are dogs. Car park. Wheelchair access. Eleven en-suite bedrooms.
Cards: Delta, EuroCard, MasterCard, Switch, Visa.

Moulton

Black Bull Inn ☎ 01325 377289
Moulton, nr Richmond, N. Yorks DL10 6QJ
Free House. Audrey & Sarah Pagendam, licensees
e-mail: sarah@blackbullinn.demon.co.uk

Very handy if you're passing Scotch Corner. Only a mile away, the Black Bull is an exceptional place. Behind the long, low cottagey front you'll find lots of intimate, connecting rooms: beyond the bar – all red plush, velvet curtains and lovely log fire where they serve hot and cold snacks – is a panelled seafood restaurant which opens in the evenings – no booking necessary. In the garden there is a 1932 Pullman carriage from the Brighton Belle with just eight tables for two; and for small parties there is a flowery conservatory complete with grape vine. The menu leans heavily towards fish: oysters, home-made soups, smoked salmon paté, dressed crab and avocado cake with quails' eggs, mixed leaves and herb vinaigrette, seafood pancake Thermidor, egg Florentine with smoked haddock, chicken liver, smoked bacon and wild mushroom crostini, spinach and cheddar soufflé; maybe a peppered fillet steak with cream and wine sauce or roast rack of lamb with leek and potato crumble, rosemary and Madeira sauce. Monday to Friday lunchtimes you'll find an impressive, very reasonable three-course prix-fixe menu (£16.50). Lots more on offer in the restaurant, a quite wonderful selection of fish and some well-chosen meat dishes. The evening menu is served in all the restaurants. Bookings essential except in the fish bar. Theakstons and John Smiths ales. Good choice of wines and sherries. Seats outside in the courtyard.

OPEN: 12–2.30, 6–10.30 (Sat 6–11). Closed Sun eve.
Restaurant. No meals Sun.
No children under seven in restaurant. No dogs. Wheelchair access.
Cards: Amex, Connect, MasterCard, Switch, Visa.

Muker

Farmers Arms ① 01748 886297
Muker, nr Richmond, N. Yorks DL11 6QG
Free House. David & Sheil Alderson, licensees

Writing about a walk from Thwaite to Muker, the author of a book on Yorkshire probably meant this pub when he wrote, 'go down farm track into Muker – pub nearby'. It's an unspoilt place with just one big room, traditionally furnished with a welcoming fire and flagstone floors, which means your walking boots are allowed in – and you too. An ancient, popular and busy village and old pub in the heart of Swaledale – convenient for walkers on the Pennine Way or those of you exploring the Yorkshire Dales. The pub serves excellent-value bar food lunchtime and evenings including soups, filled baps, baked potatoes, home-made steak pie, gammon and egg, other home-made dishes and a children's menu. John Smiths, Theakstons and Black Sheep ales on hand pump.

OPEN: Summer 11–11. Winter 11–3, 6–11.
Real Ale.
Children in eating area. Dogs on leads. Self-catering flat for two available all year.
Cards: all major cards accepted.

Pickering

White Swan Hotel ① 01751 472288
Market Place, Pickering, N. Yorks YO18 7AA
Free House. Victor Buchanan, licensee
e-mail: welcome@white-swan.co.uk

There are many attractions in the vicinity of this old market town at the southern edge of the North York Moors, so it's not surprising the delightful town is so popular and the 16th century White Swan an attraction. Originally a coaching inn, now a classy hotel in the very centre of town. The small panelled bar, with a big log fire, is a popular meeting place. For lunch there is quite a variety of dishes on the menu: chicken liver paté with home-made tomato chutney and oatcakes, fish soup with toast, Gruyère cheese and rouille, pink pigeon breast with red wine risotto and sage, dressed Portland crab with watercress salad, herb roasted Harome chicken with bubble and squeak, roast garlic and thyme, 'real' fish and chips with posh mushy peas, also lunchtime sandwiches, including a club sandwich, and ploughman's. Vegetarian dishes too. Also a set-price lunch menu in the elegant restaurant. There is a greater selection of dishes on the evening menu. All the pickles, chutneys and ketchups are made 'in house' and can be purchased. Black Sheep Best Bitter and Nick Stafford's Stallion are the beers, plus a guest. Wines by the glass and a considerable wine list, mostly Bordeaux from the St Emilion region of France.

OPEN: Tues–Fri 11–3, 5.30–11. Mon & Sat 11–11. Sun 12–3, 7–10.30).
Real Ale. Restaurant. You must book for Sunday lunch. They have an AA rosette for food.
Children's room. Dogs on leads. Car park. Wheelchairs – one step from the street. En-suite bedrooms.
Cards: Amex, Delta, MasterCard, Switch, Visa.

Ripon

One Eyed Rat ① 01765 607704
51 Allhallowgate, Ripon, N. Yorks HG4 1LQ
Free House. Les Moon, licensee
e-mail: lesmoon1@aol.com

Take the sign away and this small pub devoted to beer would be just another charming cottage among its neighbours in one of the oldest streets in the city. Inside is a long room with open fires piled high with logs and usually a few local characters guaranteed to give a good verbal account of themselves, all enjoying either the well-kept British beers – Timothy Taylors Landlord, Black Sheep Bitter and daily changing guests – or German draught beers and the strong cider. Outside is a surprisingly large garden, part of which is home to the outdoor pool table – there's probably nowhere else to put it. No food; crisps and nuts only.

OPEN: Mon–Wed 6–11.Thurs 12–3.30, 6–11. Fri 12–3.30, 5.30–11. Sat 12–11. Sun 12–3.30, 7–10.30.
Children welcome, as are dogs. Wheelchair access.
Annual German beer festival.

Ripponden

Old Bridge Inn ① 01422 822595
Priest Lane, Ripponden, W. Yorks HX6 4DF
Free House. Timothy Walker, licensee

This whitewashed, 14th-century cruck-framed building, reputedly the oldest in Yorkshire – 1380 they think – is opposite the village church and next to the packhorse bridge over the Ryburn river. The three split-level rooms inside are full of antique tables, rush chairs and pictures, prints and interesting artifacts hung on the thick stone walls. On weekdays they do a reasonably priced buffet luncheon of home-made soup and cold, rare roast beef, Virginia ham, home-made scotch eggs, quiche, other goodies and salads; very popular, and very good – you simply must book if you want to sit and eat. Blackboard specials on weekday evenings and weekend lunchtimes. Service is first class, everything is excellent value for money. Beers are all from independent brewers: Black Sheep, Timothy Taylors. and one weekly guest. Bottled beers include White Shield Worthington, others from around the world, and several imported lagers. Over 30 malt whiskies, six wines by the glass and a well-chosen wine list. Seats on a paved area at the front of the inn. About five miles west of Ripponden, off the A68 and beyond Batings reservoir, is Blackstone Edge and one of the best-preserved sections of paved Roman road in Britain.

OPEN: 12–3, 5.30–11. Sat 12–11. Sun 12–10.30.
Real Ale. No food Sat or Sun eves.
Children in limited area. No dogs. Car park. Wheelchair access (not WC).
Cards: MasterCard, Switch, Visa.

Sheffield

Cask & Cutler ① 0114 2492295
1 Henry Street, off Infirmary Road, Sheffield S3 7EQ
Free House. Sheila Clarke, owner/licensee

No problems about drinking and driving if you patronise this suburban ale house, which was last seriously refurbished in the 1940s, as it's conveniently located next to the Shalemoor tram stop in north Sheffield. Two rooms, a bar and a no-smoking lounge – with winter fire. This is a serious drinking establishment. No food at all. A crisp and a nut perhaps; that's your lot. Beer is the thing. They even have their own micro-brewery at the back of the pub – the Port Mahon Brewery; always 7 to 9 hand-pulled ales, mainly from micro-breweries. These will include a mild, a stout, also a hand-pulled scrumpy cider. Thirty Belgian bottled beers too. They hold an annual beer festival in mid-November when you can try over 40 beers in four days. A CAMRA favourite, a past Sheffield Pub of the Year and Yorkshire Pub of the Year, so you know everything is as it should be. Seats in the beer garden so you can enjoy your summer pint.

OPEN: Mon 5.30–11. Tues–Fri 12–2, 5.30–11. Fri & Sat 12–11. Sun 12–2, 7–10.30.
Real Ale.
Children in garden. Quiet dogs admitted – ask first, they have their own, and a cat!
Wheelchair access with assistance (not WC).

Fat Cat ① 0114 2494801
23 Alma Street, Sheffield S3 8SA
Own Brew. Steven Fearn, licensee

Years ago this used to be The Alma, a commercial hotel in the cutlery-producing area of the city, tied to one of the big brewers. It was rescued over 20 years ago to become Sheffield's first real ale house – a saviour for a city that was awash with keg beer. Not only did they bring in beers from small independent brewers, but in 1990 they started brewing their own Kelham Island beer in premises next door to the pub. So successful were they that they now have a new, purpose-built brewery at Kelham Island. Once you would probably have come only for the beer but now you can eat too. They serve very reasonably priced food; the full menu is available Monday to Friday evening as well as every lunchtime – filling home-made soups, steak and onion pie, tikka mushrooms and rice (for vegans), sausage and tomato casserole and rice, not forgetting a ploughman's. Good English puddings – crumbles and pies with cream or custard. Roast Sunday lunch which also has vegan and gluten-free dishes. Ten draught ales always available: Timothy Taylors Landlord, four from Kelham Island and six guest beers. Draught Belgian beers are kept together with Belgian fruit jenevers and draught cider. Country fruit wines and small barrels of Kelham Island Beer can be ordered in advance to take away. Seats in the courtyard at the back of the pub. The Fat Cat was the CAMRA South Yorkshire Pub of the Year 2003, so you know the beer is excellent.

OPEN: 12–3, 5.30–11 (Sun 7–10.30).
Real Ale.
Children in beer garden. the no-smoking lounge and upstairs room. Half the pub is no smoking. Dogs on leads. Wheelchair access. The old brewery is now a visitor centre.

Skerne

Eagle ① 01377 252178
Wansford Road, Skerne, Driffield, E. Yorks YO25 9HS
Free House. R. Edmond, licensee

A weekend pub for those travelling through, as the old Eagle is an evening-only pub; closed during the day Monday to Friday. This is a pub for those of you who appreciate a bit of nostalgia – and a good pint. The Eagle hasn't changed for years. An original: small, unspoilt, and still without a bar, this village pub has two small rooms, a public one and a more comfortable lounge – both with coal fires – and a friendly landlord who delivers the drinks to your table. One beer, Cameron Bitter, perfectly kept in the cellar near the entrance. The only food is a possible crisp or nut.

OPEN: Mon–Fri 7–11. Sat 12–3, 7–11. Sun 12–3, 7–10.30.
Real Ale. No food.
No children. Car park.

Skipton

Narrow Boat ① 01756 797922
38 Victoria Street, Skipton, N. Yorks BD23 1JE
Market Town Taverns. Ian Reid, manager

The main Leeds to Liverpool canal skirts Skipton but a cut, called the Springs Branch, serves the town; this lovely, wide stretch of the canal in the centre of Skipton is a hive of activity, home to pleasure craft and narrow boats. Very close to the canal basin, on firm ground, is the Narrow Boat. Quiet and cool in summer with bare wooden floors, wooden tables and padded church pews, the whole of the ground floor is no-smoking – upstairs to the mezzanine if you want a quick puff! You'll find a good traditional bar menu of well-filled sandwiches, jacket potatoes, ciabatta melts with different toppings, Black Sheep pie – steak and mushrooms in ale – Cumberland sausages and home-made Irish stew; there is a changing specials board. They feature a steak night every Wednesday; curry on Thursday. Always 8 cask ales on the go, including a mild and stout, as well as over 30 continental beers.

OPEN: 12–11.
Real Ale.
Children and dogs welcome. Wheelchair access.
Cards: most accepted.

Sowood

Dog & Partridge Inn ① 01422 374249
Forest Hill Road, Sowood, Holywell Green, W. Yorks HX4 9LB
Free House. Frank Collins, owner/licensee

In a totally rural area, virtually equidistant from Halifax and Huddersfield, the inn was once an overnight stop for drovers moving sheep from the Dales to Derbyshire via

Marsden. Built during the Georgian period, on the site of a 17th-century inn, it was a centre of activity. Not only was there an inn, a barn, a quarry and 25 acres but also an abbatoir and farm, making it totally self-sufficient. Only the barn, two and a half acres and a few cottages remain. Known locally as Mabel's after widow Mabel who ran the pub until her death aged 95 in April 2001; her son Frank is now the landlord. A small, friendly place; last updated during the '50s, when they put in water and electricity, it has a bar lounge and 'best room'. Customers come from miles around, which is just as well as there are only six neighbours to enjoy the general bonhomie and the landlord's sense of humour! A popular walkers' pub; television companies like it too, and so will you. No food, just a crisp, nut to go with Timothy Taylors Landlord, Black Sheep Bitter and guest. Come at the right time and you may see the ghost of a black sheepdog searching for his flock.

OPEN: 7–11. Sun 12–4, 7–10.30.
Real Ale.
Children welcome. No dogs, except guide dogs. Car park. Wheelchair access.

Sutton-upon-Derwent

St Vincent Arms ① 01904 608349
Main Street, Sutton-upon-Derwent, N. Yorks YO4 5BN
Free House. P. W., A. & S. Hopwood, licensees

This really is a family-run business: they all have a hand in making the old place run well. Lots of room in the comfortable panelled bar which has an open fire; there is also a no-smoking restaurant and small no-smoking dining room. Just one menu for the bar and restaurant, but there are always a number of specials on the board which could feature peppered steak, fillet steak with wild mushrooms, steak and kidney pie, half a chicken or scampi, freshly made sandwiches too. Always nine or ten beers on the go. Among them John Smiths, Timothy Taylors Landlord, Fullers London Pride, Chiswick and ESB, Yorkshire Terrier from the York Brewery, Old Mill Bitter from Suffolk and Charles Wells Bombardier. Well-chosen wine list. Seats in the pleasant garden.

OPEN: 11.30–3, 6–11. Sun 12–3, 7–10.30.
Real Ale. Restaurant.
Children welcome. Dogs in garden only. Car park.

Tan Hill

Tan Hill Inn ① 01833 628246
Tan Hill, Keld, nr Richmond, N. Yorks BL11 6ED
Theakstons. Margaret Baines, licensee

Hugely popular and extended in 1990 to cope with the rush, the Tan Inn, at the head of Swaledale, is on what was once an important drovers' route, now just a lane next to a disused mine. Undeterred, everyone seems to find this isolated place – grateful walkers, cars and the occasional coach. From the inn, 1732ft above sea level, there are sweeping views of the wild landscape towards Durham. A minor moorland road from Keld – your nearest civilization – brings you to this, England's highest inn – cold and bracing in winter, just bracing in summer, one of the few pubs to keep a fire burning all year round.

The drovers might have long gone but the Pennine Way passes the door, so many tired walkers have gratefully found the shortest way across the flagstones to the welcoming bar. They have to be super-efficient as the nearest corner shop is eleven miles away. Also, local services are a bit thin on the ground so they have their own water and electricity supply, freezers full of food and parking for the snow plough to help them through the year. No need for extra ice, they have plenty of that! Hearty, energy-giving food is provided, from sandwiches to giant Yorkshire puddings filled with Tan Hill sausages and gravy. Theakstons XB, Best and Old Peculier. Hugely popular place in summer. In the depths of winter, the odd lonely traveller finds a very welcome refuge in its rarefied air. Hundreds of acres of moorland to get lost in.

OPEN: 11–11. Sun 12–10.30.
Real Ale.
Children welcome. Dogs – yes-ish: you have to keep an eye on the resident canine. Seven en-suite bedrooms. You can get married here too.

Totley

Crown Inn ① 01142 360789
Hillfoot Road, Totley, Sheffield S17 3AX.
Punch Taverns. John Hicklin, licensee

Very near the Derbyshire border, a small stone-built 16th-century pub. Low doors into the one room with a good fire and central bar, all very quaint, very warm and very welcoming. From a blackboard menu, all the dishes are freshly cooked, not bought in. Tetleys, Marstons Pedigree, Fullers London Pride on hand pump and a weekly changing guest beer.

OPEN: 12–3, 5.30–11 (Sun 7–10.30).
Real Ale. No food Sun or Mon eves.
No children. Dogs on leads. Wheelchair access into pub only.
Cards: all credit cards.

Wakefield

The Redoubt ① 01924 377085
28 Horbury Road, Wakefield, W. Yorks WF2 8TS
Punch Taverns. M. Grady, lease
e-mail: jillian.grady@btopenworld.com

A smart, whitewashed corner pub; one of the oldest in the city. The unspoilt Redoubt, next to St Michael's Church, has four rooms off a central corridor, one of which, the lounge, occasionally has music. Called The Redoubt since the late 19th century, nothing much has changed; it still has the atmosphere of a prosperous Victorian pub. The comfortable rooms are decorated with sporting photographs, cricket, football and Rugby League – keen supporters all. Plenty of beer but no food, but if you want to come to enjoy the pub, you can bring your own – and there's no hamper charge. The beers are Tetleys Traditional

Bitter and Mild, Timothy Taylors Landlord and they stock a good selection of malt whiskies. There is a beer garden so you can sup your pint in the fresh air.

OPEN: 12–11.
Real Ale. No food – but you can bring your own.
Children until 7 in one room and beer garden. Dogs in the tap room. Wheelchair access. No cards.

Widdop

Pack Horse Inn ① 01422 842803
The Ridge, Widdop, Hebden Bridge, W. Yorks HX7 7AT
Free House. Andrew Hollinrake, licensee

The old packhorse trail crossed Widdop Moor from Burnley to Halifax and this was the tiny inn that gave them shelter. This is a remote area, a moorland road between Hebden Bridge and Colne, near Slack Top, Widdop reservoir and 300 yards from the Pennine Way. Below the inn, Hebden water leads you into a lovely wooded valley. This area is a haven for walkers throughout the summer; the route can be difficult in winter, though when you arrive you'll find a warm welcome (if they're open) in this sturdily built 17th-century converted farmhouse, with fires in the grate, cosy seats in the window and good sustaining food on the menu: soup, filled baguettes, ploughman's, gammon and eggs – hearty and sustaining. Draught Thwaites Traditional Bitter, Black Sheep Bitter, Morlands Old Speckled Hen and Theakstons XB. Good range of wines, with New World additions. Over a hundred single malts for you to try.

OPEN: 12–2, 7–10. Closed Mon–Fri lunchtimes, and all day Mon Oct–Easter.
Real Ale.
Children until 8 p.m. – under control. Dogs on leads. Car park. Disabled facilities.
Cards: all major cards accepted.

York

Ackhorne ① 01904 671421
9 St Martins Lane, York YO1 6LN
Enterprise Inns. Jack Merry, licensee
www.ackhorne.com

Tucked away in a quiet alleyway leading off Micklegate and near St Martin's church, this has been a beer drinkers' haven for more than 240 years. There has been a building on the site for over 250 years with first mention of a licence nine years later. Behind the handsome stained-glass windows is a big main bar and a cosier back room with a fire. The pub usually has about six beers on the go from various parts of the country: Caledonian and Rooster's of Harrogate are permanent, Wychwood Ales from Witney, Orkney Brewery and Brown Cow from Selby are frequently on – all well kept and knowledgeably served.

Food is served at lunchtime only. Unusually for a city pub there is a small, sunny outside drinking area.

OPEN: 12–11.
Real Ale. No food Sun.
Children allowed, so are dogs. Wheelchair access (not WC).

BEST OF THE REST

Carthorpe, N. Yorks
Fox & Hounds ① 01845 567433
Carthorpe DL8 2LG
A tiny village off the A1 north of Ripon and a friendly village pub serving some really good food. You can still get sandwiches, home-made soup and paté but from the specials board there could be halibut steak with a lobster and prawn sauce or lamb's liver with bacon and parsley mash. Puds are inventive too. Only John Smiths beer but there will be something to tempt you from the extensive wine list. Children welcome. No dogs. Wheelchair access.
Open: 12–3, 7–11. Closed Mon.

Ferrensby, N. Yorks
General Tarleton ① 01423 340284
Boroughbridge Road, Ferrensby HG5 0QB
Eighteenth century and handsome. Inside this comfortable, well-polished old coaching inn, they serve interesting and imaginative dishes in the brasserie-style bar. There is also a more formal restaurant. Think of this as a dining pub, but still a place where you can have a sandwich or bowl of soup – Provençale fish – and a pint of Black Sheep or Tetley beers. As you would expect – they do have their own wine importing company – there is a very good choice of wines. Seats in the sheltered garden and in the no-smoking courtyard. Children and dogs welcome. Wheelchair access (not WC). Bedrooms (14).
Open: 12–3, 6–11. (Shorter hours in winter.)

Newton on Ouse, N. Yorks
Dawnay Arms ① 01347 848345
Newton on Ouse, nr York YO30 2BR
Off the A1, north of the city, in the glorious Vale of York, very near the fine 18th-century Beningbrough Hall. Of similar age, this riverside pub has gardens running down to the water's edge. A comfortable old place, beamed and spacious, serving good, varied bar food. As well as the bar favourites you could have beef bourguignon, lamb's liver in a red wine sauce, grilled fish or rack of lamb. Home-made puds too. Boddingtons, Flowers Original Morlands and Tetleys beers. Children welcome. No dogs.
Open: 11–3, 7–11.

Nunnington, N Yorks
Royal Oak ① 01439 748271
Church Street, Nunnington YO62 5US
On the edge of the North York moors, between the bridge over the river and the church, you'll find a welcoming landlord and a solid, stone pub where they serve classic pub favourites: home-made soup, ploughman's, stuffed mushrooms, chicken liver paté with home-made chutney, steak and kidney casserole with herb dumplings, lasagne and sweet

and sour vegetables with rice. Fish too, something for everyone. Tetley Bitter, Theakstons Best and Old Peculier on handpump. A few wines by the glass. Our intrepid researcher praised the pub but said it brought to mind the words of Flanders and Swann: 'I've an opera here that you shan't escape/·On miles and miles of recording tape!' Children in family room. No dogs. Car park. Wheelchair access. Cards: Delta, MasterCard, Switch, Visa.
Open: 12–2.30, 6.30–11 (Sun 7–10.30)

Pickhill, N. Yorks
Nags Head ☉ 01845 567391
Pickhill YO7 4JG
At the centre of the village, primped, polished and comfortable, a hotel, pub and restaurant all rolled into one and rolling along very nicely too. On the food side you can get all the dishes you would expect from a bar menu as well as smoked salmon and scrambled egg, rack of lamb with honey and rosemary and perhaps steak, mushroom and oyster pie. Beers are Black Sheep, Theakstons, Hambletons, John Smiths and one guest. Decent wines, some by the glass. Children and dogs welcome. Wheelchair access. Bedrooms.
Open: 11–11.

Roydhouse, W. Yorks
Three Acres ☉ 01484 602606
Roydhouse HD8 8LR
Time for a good map: not that the pub is remote, more that Roydhouse doesn't seem to be on a signpost. Look for Shelley and a left turning to Elmley Moor – or ask a local – it is very worthwhile. Something for everyone at this old coaching inn. You can stay, eat extraordinarily well and stock up with goodies from their own delicatessen. Here you will get imaginatively filled sandwiches, maybe French onion soup or moules marinière, steak, kidney and mushroom pie and a wide choice of fish from the fish bar. There will be a greater variety of dishes on the evening menu. Maybe Adnams, Mansfield, Morlands and Timothy Taylors Landlord beers; also a good list of wines. Children in eating areas. Bedrooms.
Open: 12–3, 6–11.

Sawley, N. Yorks
Sawley Arms ☉ 01765 620642
Sawley HG4 3EQ
You'll know you are where you want to be when you see the most glorious summer floral display. Behind it is the old stone pub; inside are small rooms with comfortable chairs and log fires. Here is served English food at its best: home-made soups, paté, salmon mousse, roast duck and apple pie with cream could be·on the menu. Theakstons and John Smiths beers and of course, house wines. Near the remains of Fountains Abbey. Children over 9 – on best behaviour. Bedrooms.
Open: 11.30–3, 6.30–10.30.

Thornton-in-Lonsdale, N. Yorks.
Marton Arms ☉ 01524 241281
Thornton-in-Lonsdale, Carnforth LA6 3PB
In a small hamlet on the old road between Skipton and Kendal, the Marton Arms is surrounded by rolling countryside crossed with tracks and paths. The stone pub is a tremendous attraction not only for the selection of 15 hand-pulled, cask-conditioned,

constantly changing beers and 300 malts for the whisky aficionados, but consistently good pub food: home-made soup, burgers, pizzas, well-filled sandwiches, steak and ale pie, Cumberland sausages and daily specials. Children welcome. No dogs. Car park. Wheelchair access – two bedrooms on ground floor. Ten other en-suite bedrooms. Cards: Amex, MasterCard, Switch, Visa.
Open: 11–11. Sun 12–10.30.

Thornton Watlass, N. Yorks
Buck Inn ① 01677 422461
Thornton Watlass HG4 4AH
In a pretty village in the Ure Valley between Bedale and Masham, the Buck Inn is so close to the cricket pitch that netting has been erected to prevent straight-driven sixes breaking the pub windows. The blackboard menu for both bar and dining room lists well-presented and interesting pub cooking. Beers are Theakstons, Black Sheep Bitter, John Smiths and guests. Children welcome. No dogs. Wheelchair access. Bedrooms.
Open: 11–11. Sun 12–10.30.

Wetherspoon in Yorkshire

Barnsley – Courthouse Station, 24 Regent Street
① 01226 779056
Batley – Union Rooms, 4 Hick Lane
① 01924 448990
Bingley – Myrtle Grove, 141 Main Street
① 01274 568637
Bradford – Sir Titus Salt, Unit B, Windsor Baths
① 01274 732853
Bridlington – Prior John, 34–36 Promenade
① 01262 674256
Brighouse – Richard Ostler, Bethal Street
① 01484 401756
Castleford – Glass Blower, 15 Bank Street
① 01977 520390
Cleckheaton – Obediah Brooke, 19 Bradford Road
① 01274 860700
Dewsbury – Time Piece, 11–15 Northgate
① 01924 460051
Doncaster – Gate House, Priory Walk, High Street
① 01302 554540
Doncaster – Red Lion, 37–38 Market Place
① 01302 732120
Goole – City and County, Market Square
① 01405 772600
Halifax – Barnum Top Inn, Rawson Street
① 01422 300488
Harrogate – Winter Gardens, Unit 4, Royal Baths
① 01423 877010
Huddersfield – Cherry Tree, Pearl Assurance House
① 01484 448190
Kingston upon Hull – Admiral of the Humber, Analby Road
① 01482 381850

Kingston upon Hull – Zachariah Pearson, 386 Beverley Road
① 01482 474181
Leeds – Beckett's Bank, 28–30 Park Row
① 0113 394 5900
Leeds – Stick or Twist, Merrion Way
① 0113 234 9748
Leeds – Three Hulats, 13 Harrogate Road, Chapel Allerton
① 0113 262 0524
Leeds – Wetherspoons, Unit 6, Wellington Quarter, Leeds City Station
① 0113 247 1676
Rotherham – Blue Coat, The Crofts
① 01709 539500
Rotherham – Rhinoceros, 35–37 Bridgegate
① 01709 361422
Scarborough – Lord Roseberry, 85–87 Westborough
① 01723 361191
Sheffield – Bankers Draft, 1–3 Market Place
① 01142 756609
Sheffield – Wetherspoons, 6–7 Cambridge Street
① 0114 263 9500
Shipley – Sun Hotel, 3 Kirkgate
① 01274 530757
Wakefield – Moon under Water, 2 Batley Road
① 01924 239033
Wakefield – Six Chimneys, 41–43 Kirkgate
① 01924 239449
Wath upon Dearne – Church House, Montgomery Square
① 01709 879518

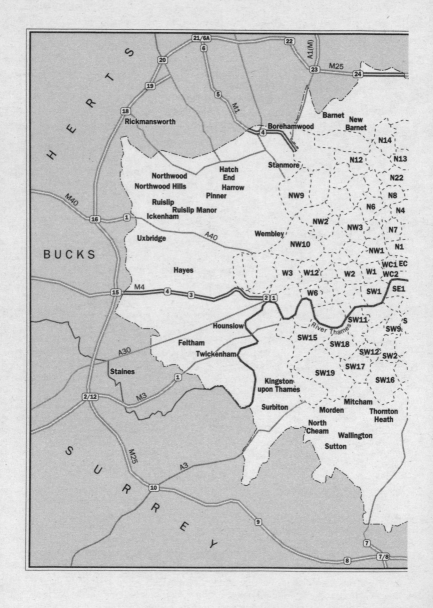

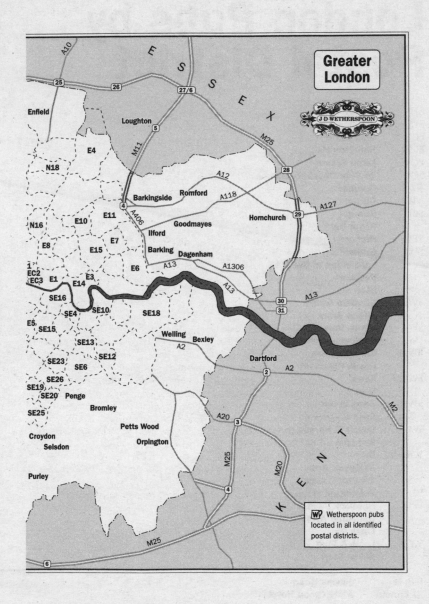

Greater London

J·D·WETHERSPOON

Enfield

A10

ESSEX

Loughton

E4

N18

M11

Barkingside
Romford

A12

M25

Hornchurch

A118

A127

N16
E10
E11
A406
Goodmayes
Ilford
E8
E7
Barking
Dagenham
E15
A13
A1306
EC2
E1
E3
EC3
E14
SE16
A13
SE4
SE10
SE18
E5
SE15
Welling
Bexley
SE13
A2
Dartford
SE23
SE12
A2
SE6
SE26
SE19
SE20
Penge
Bromley
A20
SE25
Petts Wood
Croydon
Orpington
Selsdon
M25
M20
K E N T
Purley
M2

M25

WP Wetherspoon pubs
located in all identified
postal districts.

London Pubs by Postal District

E11	**George**
E15	**Goldengrove**
EC1	**Olde Mitre**
EC2	**Hamilton Hall**
EC3	**Lamb Tavern**
EC4	**Ye Olde Cheshire Cheese**
N7	**Coronet**
NW8	**Clifton**
SE1	**George**
	Royal Oak
SE10	**Richard I**
SW1	**Grenadier**
	Lord Moon of the Mall
	Red Lion
	Star
SW3	**Coopers Arms**
	Phene Arms
SW6	**White Horse**
SW7	**Anglesea Arms**
SW10	**Chelsea Ram**
	Fox & Pheasant
SW18	**Alma**
	Ship
SW19	**Hand in Hand**
	Rose & Crown
W1	**Coach & Horses**
	Red Lion
W6	**Dove**
	Anglesea Arms
W8	**Windsor Castle**
W9	**Warrington Hotel**
W14	**Havelock Tavern**
WC1	**Calthorpe Arms**
	Lamb
WC2	**Lamb & Flag**
	Seven Stars
Pinner	**Queens Head**
Richmond	**White Cross Hotel**

BEST OF THE REST

E14	**Grapes**
EC1	**Bishops Finger**
N1	**Duke of Cambridge**
SE1	**Horniman**
SW1	**Fox and Hounds**
	Westminster Arms
SW11	**Castle**
SW13	**Bulls Head**
W11	**Ladbroke Arms**

If the pubs indicated on the map are not fully described in the main section, you will find them in the Wetherspoon list at the end of the chapter.

London

(within the M25)

London SW18

Alma ☏ 020 8870 2537
499 Old York Road, Wandsworth SW18 1FT
Youngs. Charles Gotto, MBII, tenant, Stuart Day, manager

A handsome mid-Victorian pub – all shiny tiles outside and well-restored Victorian decor inside, with opulent mirrors, touches of gold, plaster friezes and a fire in the art deco fireplace. Opposite Wandsworth Town railway station, after match days this is a favourite with ardent rugby followers, boisterous and enthusiastic but well behaved. During TV coverage of the match itself there will be enthusiastic support – or otherwise – from the customers. At quieter times you'll have room to appreciate this prosperous-looking Victorian pub. Here you get friendly service in attractive surroundings. The morning papers are there for you to read while waiting for something from the 'light lunches' menu: a toasted muffin with field mushrooms, crab blini hollandaise and poached egg or a 'Gado-Gado' Indonesian vegetable salad with peanut sauce. Otherwise, grilled pepper and aubergine soup, chicken liver risotto, spicy salmon fishcake on warm potato salad, marinated beef stirfry, noodles and mangetout or steak frites, garlic and green peppercorn butter, fresh fish, salads, daily specials and desirable puds. Whenever possible all of the meat is sourced from their own farm in Surrey; if not, they always know where it has come from. Youngs range of ales and a good choice of wines by the bottle or glass. Both espresso and ordinary coffee.

OPEN: 11–11.
Real Ale. Restaurant.
Children in eating areas. Dogs on leads. Wheelchair access.
Cards: all credit cards

London SW7

Anglesea Arms ☏ 020 7373 7960
15 Selwood Terrace, South Kensington SW7 3QG
Free House. Jenny Podmore & Jodie Brennan, licensees
e-mail: enquiries@angleseaarms.com

You know you're in the right place when you see a jolly crowd on the forecourt – the pub's very own outside space. This is a well-loved, very atmospheric, early Victorian pub in affluent South Kensington. Inside, space is always at a premium; the comfortable armchairs and settles, all plumped and polished, are taken early, but there are counters to lean on, or if it gets too crowded, the party can continue outside. Service is very efficient, even with all those al fresco drinkers. Bar food is good pub grub – filled baguettes, sausage and mash, home-baked ham, steak and kidney pie, fish and chips and daily specials – that sort of thing. An à la carte menu is offered in the evening dining room seven days a week, and there is a Sunday roast in both the bar and dining room. A good range of ales: Fullers London Pride, Adnams Broadside, Youngs Bitter – all on hand pump – and one guest. A selection of fine wines.

OPEN: 11–11. Sun 12–10.30.
Real Ale.
Children welcome. Dogs in bar.
Cards: all except Amex, Diners and JCB.

London W6

Anglesea Arms ① 020 8749 1291
35 Wingate Road, Shepherds Bush W6 0UR
Free House. Fiona Evans, licensee
e-mail: fiona.evans@bt.connect.com

Beyond Shepherds Bush and off the Goldhawk Road, this is one of a growing number of pubs where the emphasis is on serving some exciting, exceptional food. This is a tremendously popular neighbourhood pub where you can experience the best of all worlds. Have a drink in the cosy, panelled bar with a roaring winter log fire or eat extremely well in the more modern-feel restaurant. They don't take bookings, so unless you get there early to grab a table, just be patient and have a drink while you wait for one to come free. If the weather is suitable you can eat outside – there are tables at the front of the pub. Enjoy the wait. It is, after all, still a pub. The clever, inventive menus change twice a day and there could be an asparagus and broad bean soup, duck, quail and foie gras terrine, home-cured gravadlax, potato blini, pickled cucumber, dill and mustard, half a dozen Irish rock oysters, Guinness bread, shallot relish, lamb tagine, couscous, spiced vegetables and tzatziki or monkfish brochette, ratatouille, white wine sauce, and to drink there is Morlands Old Speckled Hen, Fullers London Pride, or something from the reasonably priced, wide-ranging wine list – a choice of about 15 by the glass.

OPEN: 11–11.
Restaurant.
Children welcome. Dogs too. Wheelchair access (not WC).
Cards: Delta, MasterCard, Switch, Visa.

London WC1

Calthorpe Arms ① 020 7278 4732
252 Gray's Inn Road WC1X 8JR
Youngs. A. Larner, tenant
e-mail: adeboss@hotmail.com

Just a straightforward, single-bar, corner pub with a busy lunchtime trade. At one time a temporary magistrates' court convened here after an historic first – the murder of an on-duty policeman in 1830. Still with an important part in the scheme of things, it is now a favourite with office workers and television news staff catching up with the local gossip in between keeping an eye on world events; low-volume TV is on most of the time. Simple lunchtime food is served in the bar or the upstairs restaurant. A past CAMRA pub of the year so you know the beer is tip-top. Youngs Bitter, Special and Winter Warmer. A few seats on the pavement.

OPEN: 11–11. Sun 12–10.30.
Real Ale.
No children. Dogs – maybe the odd one!
Cards: all except Amex and Diners.

London SW10

Chelsea Ram ① 020 7351 4008
32 Burnaby Street, off Lots Road SW10 0PL
The Establishment Ltd. James Symington, licensee

An Edwardian pub, built when the surrounding streets were being developed. The only problem was that the new residents thought a pub on the corner would lower the tone of their area, so it was refused a licence, and until one was granted in 1984 it led a somewhat chequered existence. Now, after the initial struggle – it took time to gain popularity – it is very fashionable – a bright, cheerful place with pine tables and chairs and a good fire. A pub-cum-restaurant, known for the quality of the imaginative, well-presented food. The menus change daily but they do have vegetarian dishes, pasta, chicken in different delicious sauces and several fish dishes. On Sunday they do a very popular roast lunch. All Youngs beers. About 25 wines and three champagnes.

OPEN: 11–11. Sun 12–10.30.
Real Ale.
Children welcome. Dogs on leads. Wheelchair access (not WC).

London NW8

Clifton ① 020 7372 3627
96 Clifton Hill, St John's Wood NW8 0JT
Mitchell & Butler. Russell Danby, manager

What was once a straightforward, substantial Georgian villa has, over the years, become a homage to the Edwardian era. There are several stories told about the Clifton. One that could explain why it took the leap from private house to public house in the early 19th century is that the original owner, fed up with so many of his friends turning up and drinking him dry, started charging them. Realizing he was onto a good wheeze, he progressed from there. The other is that Edward VII met his mistress Lillie Langtry here in a private bar. The pub's owners preferred the Edwardian theory, so it was restored and redecorated to create that atmosphere: panelling, polished floors and rugs, pictures of Edward VII, Lillie Langtry, and Edward's wife, Queen Alexandra. Inside, the U-shaped bar serves three attractively decorated rooms. The restaurant – which seats about 25 – is in the conservatory. One menu serves both the bar and restaurant. Ales are Tetleys, Fullers

London Pride, Bass and possibly two changing guest beers. Seats on the leafy terrace at the front of the pub and on the sunny terrace at the back.

OPEN: 11–11. Sun 12–10.30.
Real Ale. Restaurant.
Children welcome. Dogs on leads.
Slightly borderline, and certainly different; low-level music during the day, quiet at night.

London W1

Coach & Horses ☎ 020 7437 5920
29 Greek Street, Soho W1V 5LL
Taylor Walker. Norman Balon, MBII, tenant

Not so much a pub, the Coach & Horses is more an institution – a star on the literary tourist trail. We have film stars but this is a stage star. On the corner of Romilly Street and Greek Street, it has become synonymous with its tenant and is called 'Norman's' by the regulars. When the play *Jeffrey Bernard Is Unwell* is staged, the Coach & Horses is the main set; the strong personality of Norman Balon, the landlord, making his presence felt offstage. It has also been immortalised as 'The Regulars' in the satirical magazine *Private Eye*. Do not be put off by any rumour that the landlord here is the rudest in the capital – he probably is – but he is also one of the most famous. This is a serious drinking pub and one of London's most well known. All-day sandwiches – ham, cheese, etc – to go with the Burton Ale, Fullers London Pride and Marstons Pedigree.

OPEN: 11–11. Sun 12–10.30.
Real Ale.
No children. No dogs. Wheelchair access (not WC).
Cards: all except Amex and Diners.

London SW3

Coopers Arms ☎ 020 7376 3120
87 Flood Street, Chelsea SW3 5TB
Youngs. Mr & Mrs S. Lee, managers

A corner pub off the King's Road, very near all the excitement and activity just up the road. This is a favourite lunchtime meeting place for shoppers, professionals and frequently, as it is close to Chelsea Register Office, jollifications, as the bride and groom, plus guests celebrate the happy day. Inside this civilized place is a spacious bar, an upstairs dining room and reception room with one of the biggest tables ever seen – all 17ft of it – a draughtman's table from a redundant shipyard. Framed drawings by the cartoonist Jak to amuse you, and a selection of daily newspapers to let you know what is happening in the big wide world. The interesting, imaginative menu changes daily, but there could be Thai hot and sour prawn soup, Japanese teriyaki chicken salad with sesame seeds, seared king scallops in crème fraiche and sweet chilli, garlic and chilli tiger prawns served on spaghetti of lemon balsamic chicken with coriander and olive mash, desirable desserts too. Youngs range of ales. Also a good selection of New World, French, Italian, Spanish and other wines listed on the blackboard.

OPEN: 11–11. Sun 12–10.30.
Real Ale.
Children welcome. Dogs on leads. Wheelchair access into pub and gents' WC.
Cards: Amex, Electron, MasterCard, Solo, Switch, Visa.

London N7

Coronet ① 020 7609 5014
338–346 Holloway Road N7 6NJ
Wetherspoon.

Wetherspoon don't do anything by halves. We have here a big, big drinking area, a sort of 6000-square-foot translocated 'Bier Keller'. You can fit a lot of pint pots into that. This was yet another redundant cinema – originally the Savoy, then the ABC, finally the Coronet, before being converted in 1996 into this popular Wetherspoon outlet. Instead of the stalls, there is a huge bar kept busy all the time. Keeping an eye on things are lifesize statues of stars of the silver screen. Between five and six real ales, one guest and an extensive, reliable menu served all day. Always a big no-smoking area.

OPEN: 11–11.
Real Ale.
No children. No dogs. Wheelchair facilities.

London W6

Dove ① 020 8748 5405
19 Upper Mall, Hammersmith W6 9TA
Fullers. Alison Juliff, manager

Just above Hammersmith Bridge, this is one of the most perfect riverside pubs, complete with a terrace overlooking the river. Entering the pub from a narrow alley you follow in the footsteps of some literary giants: Ernest Hemingway, Graham Greene, Charles Kingsley and the designer William Morris – they all knew the place well. The 17th-century Dove has, according to the *Guinness Book of Records*, the smallest bar in England. On the right as you go in, it measures just over four foot by seven foot ten inches – five people, elbows well tucked in, are a crowd, and it seems to be permanently full! There is a much bigger, beamed and panelled bar with much old charm and character. Lunchtime is quiet-ish, but come evening, space is at a premium, not only in the Dove but, depending on the weather, on the terrace overlooking the river. Well-cooked lunchtime bar food of a starter Greek salad, duck and apricot paté with toasted ciabatta, fruit chutney and roquette leaves, warm chicken salad with crispy bacon avocado, garlic croutons and mustard dressing, home-made beef lasagne, home-made steak and ale pie or pan fried fillet steak with potato gratin, French beans in a wild mushroom sauce. Fullers London Pride, ESB and a seasonal guest beer. The patriotically minded among you might like to know that a copy of the score of *Rule Britannia* is on a wall of the bar. James Thompson, who wrote it, had a room here.

OPEN: 11–11. Sun 12–10.30.
Real Ale.
Children until 9 p.m. Dogs on leads. Wheelchair access (not WC).

London SW10

Fox and Pheasant ✆ 020 7352 2943
1 Billing Road, off the Fulham Road SW10 9UJ
Greene King. Lyn & Ben Asher, tenants

In a smart enclave – a private side road off the Fulham Road – the area backs onto peaceful Brompton cemetery, which contrasts with its noisier neighbour, Chelsea football ground, and the roar of the crowd on match days. Apart from that slight inconvenience, this little 'country pub', originally two 18th-century cottages, is a delight. Very pretty outside, with flourishing hanging baskets, it's beamed inside with traditional furnishings and a big fireplace. A central bar separates the two rooms. Not much difference between them except that the saloon bar has a square of carpet and the public bar a dartboard. Another tremendous plus is that this lucky place has its own walled garden; hugely popular on warm summer evenings. In colder months all is not lost as there is a covered – and heated – outside drinking area. The lunchtime menu changes daily and list hot and cold dishes as well as sandwiches and filled jacket potatoes. Ales are Greene King IPA and Abbots. Water for the dog. (On match days the pub is sometimes closed to avoid over-enthusiastic football supporters.)

OPEN: 11–11. Sun 12–10.30.
Real Ale. Food served lunchtimes only, 12–2.30.
Children in garden. Dogs on leads.
Cards: all except Diners.

London E11

George ✆ 020 8989 2921
159 High Street, Wanstead E11 2RL
Wetherspoon.

There's no point in wasting space, and Wetherspoon really believe in packing them in. Before conversion, this was a furniture showroom. Now it's a large, friendly, comfortable pub. All the usual Wetherspoon attributes: a no-smoking area, food served all day and the attraction of between one and two thousand books on display which anyone can read. Full menu, the usual drinks and Theakstons XB, Best, Courage Directors, Youngers Scotch Bitter and a guest.

OPEN: 11–11.
Real Ale.
No children. No dogs. Wheelchair facilities.

London SE1

George ① 020 7407 2056
77 Borough High Street, Southwark SE1 1NH
Laurel Pub Co. George Cunningham, manager
e-mail: info@georgeinn-southwark.co.uk

If you are looking in the right direction, ignoring the modern surroundings, you are swept back in time to a place that looks familiar. A film, a Christmas card, you will have seen it all before. This wonderful old coaching inn has been in many films depicting London's past, with stagecoaches coming in and out and skulduggery in dark corners. Rebuilt three times since the original was built circa 1542, what remains of the magnificent 17th-century George was given to the National Trust by London & North Eastern Railway in 1937. Early in the 19th century it had become one of the most important inns in Southwark, with huge stables and yards. It was these that attracted the LNER's predecessor, the Great Northern Railway, to buy the George in 1874 to use as a depot. Sadly, by 1937 they had pulled down or sold off many of the old buildings, leaving the inn, a couple of houses within the structure, and only one of the magnificent galleries to posterity. Today the George caters for a totally different traveller. The remaining galleries of the south range look over the courtyard where you can sit and enjoy your food and drink, occasionally entertained by visiting Morris men or players from the nearby Globe Theatre. There is a simple bar menu of soup, filled baguettes, filled jacket potatoes, roasted vegetable lasagne, steak, mushroom and Guinness pie, sausage and mash with onion gravy, omelettes, fish, salads and a cheese platter. The menu goes up a notch in the Coaching Room restaurant. Boddingtons, Fullers London Pride, Morlands Old Speckled Hen, Flowers Original, Greene King Abbot, Adnams Bitter, Marstons Pedigree and a guest beer. If you don't know the pub, search it out, as it is not clearly visible behind the huge gates on Borough High Street.

OPEN: 11–11. Sun 12–10.30.
Real Ale. Restaurant (not Sun); lunchtime meals and snacks.
Children in eating area. No dogs.

London E15

Goldengrove ① 020 8519 0750
146–148 The Grove, Stratford E15 1NS
Wetherspoon.

The name 'Goldengrove' is taken from one of Gerard Manley Hopkins' poems: 'Margaret are you grieving/Over Goldengrove unleaving?' Hopkins was born in Stratford Grove in 1844 and lived there for the first eight years of his life. The family house, in a Georgian terrace, was bombed in the last war; the buildings that replaced the terrace are not worth a mention. Some of his poems, some more obscure than others, hang framed on the walls. Less poetically, before being converted into the place you see today, this site housed London's largest discount jeans store. Big, open-plan, with a bar at the front and ample seating, a full menu is served all day: good, satisfying fare and daily specials. They also have a Curry Club on Thursday evenings featuring eight different curries. Shepherd

Neame Spitfire, Courage Directors, Theakstons Best and Greene King Abbott ale plus a guest beer. Outside, a lovely large garden overlooks the nearby Theatre Royal.

OPEN: 11–11.
Real Ale.
No children. No dogs. Wheelchair facilities.

London SW1

Grenadier ① 020 7235 3074
18 Old Barrack Yard, Wilton Row SW1X 7NR
Scottish Courage. Patricia Ann Smardon, manageress

All spick and span as befits the military connection – especially the pewter bar counter, which has been cleaned and polished regularly since the place was built in 1827. During the 18th century the Duke of Wellington's officers used it as their mess; it has lost none of its charm or character over the years. Adding to its appeal, or maybe not, the pub has gained a ghost, an officer, they say, beaten to death for cheating at cards. You have to walk here – no parking in the mews these days – either from Wilton Crescent or Old Barrack Yard. You can't miss it when you do turn the corner as it is painted patriotically in the colours of the Union Flag and a sentry box stands next to the front door. Just a small bar and small candlelit dining room where, naturally enough, you can order beef Wellington. Good hearty bar food: soup, ploughman's, fish and chips, sausage and mash, scampi and chips and a vegetarian dish or two. The beers change frequently; there is always a guest beer and they stock quite a range of lagers, cider, bottled beer and Guinness. The Grenadier has its own very special 'Bloody Mary', which wins awards; the recipe for it is passed on from landlord to landlord. When possible, the mews becomes the outside drinking area.

OPEN: 12–11.
Real Ale. Restaurant.
Children in restaurant. Dogs on leads.
Cards: all major credit cards.

London EC2

Hamilton Hall ① 020 7247 3579
Liverpool Street Station EC2M 7PY
Wetherspoon.

One of the glories of Wetherspoon pubs is that they are usually just where you want one to be, and Hamilton Hall certainly is. It also has the added bonus of something spectacular to look at. So, if you're waiting for a train, wanting something to drink with a sandwich or a full meal, waiting for a friend – this is the place to be. On the station concourse, it was built at the turn of the 19th century as the grand ballroom of the Great Eastern Hotel, with splendid, soaring, Baroque decor, and it is still grand. It was closed at the outbreak of war in 1939, and Wetherspoon then converted it to create a huge space with a comfortably furnished mezzanine floor, a great part of which is no smoking. Reliable bar food, with a choice of daily specials and puddings, is served from 11 a.m. to 10 p.m. every day. Beers in

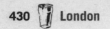

this chain are frequently cheaper than elsewhere. Courage Directors, Theakstons Best, Fullers London Pride, Shepherd Neame Spitfire and a guest beer are all on hand pump.

OPEN: 11–11.
Real Ale.
No children. No dogs. Wheelchair facilities.

London SW19

Hand in Hand ① 020 8946 5720
6 Crooked Billet, Wimbledon SW19 4RQ
Youngs. Sally Marley, licensee

Beer has been sold here since the mid 19th century when the building was owned by the founder of Watney's brewery. Crooked Billet is a very old and tiny hamlet on the edge of Wimbledon Common. The Hand in Hand was just an ale house until 30 years ago, and it's now a popular family pub A cottagey sort of place, hung about with flowering baskets and window boxes, its sunny front courtyard looks over a small green, much used during the summer. Traditional pub menu features burgers, pizzas and pasta dishes. Youngs range of beers. Wide selection of wines from many countries of the world.

OPEN: 11–11.
Real Ale.
Children in no-smoking family room. Dogs on leads. Wheelchair access (not WC).

London W14

Havelock Tavern ① 020 7603 5374
57 Masbro Road, Brook Green W14 0LS
Free House. Peter Richnell, licensee

Nothing too exciting from the outside, but this building, on the corner of Masbro and Irving roads, houses the ideal combination of a proper pub with real ale that serves really good food. Inside is an L-shaped bar and beyond that a small room leading to a terrace. The menus change twice a day. At lunchtime they are geared up to serving a one-course meal for those on the run; evenings they cater for more relaxed diners with time to appreciate two or three courses. From the changing menu there could be chicken liver parfait, gherkins, toast and apple chutney, deep-fried monkfish with lemon and herb mayonnaise, rocket and tomato salad, spaghetti with clams, white wine, tomato, parsley and garlic, rabbit stew with leeks and cream with new potatoes and savoy cabbage or chargrilled leg of lamb steak, puy lentils, green beans, smoked bacon, white wine and cream, scrummy puds and interesting, specialist cheeses. Everything is freshly cooked, so a popular dish may run out if you're a bit late. Beers are Marstons Pedigree, Fullers London Pride, Brakspear Bitter, Guinness and draught lagers. There is a selection of wines to suit every palate: 12 red, 12 white, four of each by the glass – also a 'monthly special' on the wine board – red and white – available by the glass.

OPEN: 11–11. Sun 12–10.30.
Real Ale.
Children and dogs welcome. Wheelchair access.
No cards.

London WC1

Lamb ① 020 7405 0713
94 Lamb's Conduit Street, WC1N 3LZ
Youngs. Michael Hehir, manager

You wouldn't think that the Lamb was part of old Georgian London. Built in 1720, it was 'improved' within an inch of its life by the Victorians, who seemed to hate the simple, classical lines of 18th-century architecture. Forgetting its origins – and thinking Victorian – the Lamb is a wonderful example of a Victorian pub with fine etched windows and inside, some original 19th-century fittings and comfortable leather seats. The U-shaped bar and glass snob screens are worth noting, also the photographs of the old Holborn Empire, a famous music hall bombed in the last war. The odd street name commemorates a very philanthropic gesture by an Elizabethan engineer, William Lamb, who paid for a conduit to be built to carry water to, but not into, all the houses in the street – he provided some buckets too, so the poor could carry the water home – a charitable act forever remembered. Traditional bar food is served every day except Sunday evening. On the menu will be traditional smoked salmon, old-fashioned ploughman's lunch, traditional fish and chips, sausage and mash, vegetable curry and steaks and gammon from the griddle. During the week the most popular dishes are the home-cooked 'Celebration 1729 Pie', steak, mushroom and Youngs ale pie topped with puff pastry and lamb's liver with bacon and onions. For Sunday lunch the specials board will include a choice of roasts. There is a small no-smoking room where you can enjoy your pint without a fug and a small, outside drinking area. Youngs Bitter, Special, the seasonal Waggledance and Winter Warmer, also Smiles guest beer.

OPEN: 11–11. Sun 12–4, 7–10.30.
Real Ale. No food Sun eve.
Children in eating area. No dogs. Wheelchair access (not WC).
Cards: Amex, MasterCard, Visa and debit cards.

London EC3

Lamb Tavern ① 020 7626 2454
Leadenhall Market EC3V 1LR
Youngs. David & Linda Morris, managers

At the entrance to the grandest of the Victorian markets is the late Georgian Lamb. A tall narrow building, the Lamb became so busy that an extra floor was squeezed into the high saloon bar to accompany the original three. The fine, tiled wine bar and smoking room in the basement stayed as it was, as did the top floor no-smoking bar that overlooks the market. During the week it is full of city workers drinking gallons of beer – draught bitter mostly – and enjoying slices cut off the roast ribs of beef, slapped between two pieces of French bread. Four large joints of beef are consumed each day. Youngs range of beers and some lagers to accompany the hearty food. Note that both the market and the pub are closed at the weekends. But if you are in the area you could go by and see what is happening, as film crews have been known to move in and take over this wonderfully photogenic place. There are tables to sit at in the market.

OPEN: 11–9.30 Mon–Fri only.
Real Ale.
No children. Dogs on leads. Wheelchair access (not WC).

London WC2

Lamb & Flag ✆ 020 7497 9504
33 Rose Street, Covent Garden WC2E 9EB
Free House. Terry Archer & Adrian Zimmerman, licensees

In a 17th-century alley between Floral and Garrick Streets, the Lamb and Flag is the oldest tavern in Covent Garden. The first mention of the pub, on this particular site, was in 1772 – when it was known as the Coopers Arms. Dickens knew this place when he was working in nearby Catherine Street and it retains much of the character and atmosphere of that time: low ceilings, panelled walls and the original built-in benches. Frequently crowded in early evening, you'll find the customers spilling out onto the pavement, sometimes so many it can be difficult to see the pub! Bar food, served in the upstairs bar, includes soup, roast-beef-filled baps, roast pork or lamb with the trimmings, quiche, Thai lemon chicken with salad and daily changing hot dishes. Courage Best and Directors, Youngs PA Bitter and Special, Greene King Abbot, Marstons Pedigree and various guest beers. They have a selection of malt whiskies.

OPEN: Mon–Thurs 11–11. Fri & Sat 11–10.45. Sun 12–10.30.
Real Ale. Lunchtime meals only but snacks 11–5.
No dogs. Wheelchair access (not WC).
Live jazz Sunday eves.

London SW1

Lord Moon of the Mall ✆ 020 7839 7701
16–18 Whitehall, SW1A 2DY
Wetherspoon.

You're right in the middle of things here – sights to see and places to visit surround you. Before Wetherspoon took it out of banking, this was a branch of Barclays; before that, a less commonplace Martin's and even earlier one of the 'grander' banks: Cocks, Biddulfs and Co., bankers to the good, the famous and Edward VII. Built by Sir Giles Gilbert Scott's pupil in the 1870s, a huge amount of money was spent converting it into a spacious, elegant, drinking house retaining the original soaring ceilings, arched windows and exit onto the Mall (emergencies only) but now with granite counters, comfortable chairs, books, a big no-smoking area and the usual Wetherspoon attractions: well-run, reasonably priced beer, food all day and a happy atmosphere. Always five beers and a weekly changing guest.

OPEN: 11–11.
Real Ale.
Unusually for Wetherspoon, they allow children. No dogs. Wheelchair facilities.

___

London EC4

Olde Cheshire Cheese ① 020 7353 6170
Wine Office Court (off Fleet Street) EC4A 2BU
Sam Smiths. Gordon Garrity, licensee

Things have changed so much around here over the last few years. The whole of the newspaper industry has decamped and left a huge void. Though it's been filled by others, that very individual atmosphere has gone. But not in Ye Olde Cheshire Cheese, one of the most famous places in London, and probably 200 years old when it had to be rebuilt in 1668 on the foundations of the original building burnt to the ground in the great fire of London in 1666. Still very much a typical 17th-century chop house, with cosy rooms, open fires, settles and sawdust on the floor. There are a formidable number of dining rooms, four ground-floor bars and the original panelled chop room which has famous literary connections. Anybody who was anybody in the literary world crossed the threshold of this charming, timeless old pub. Only sandwiches are available in the cellar bars (these are the original cellars where they do have loud music): elsewhere in the pub it's quiet with quite a choice of places to sit and eat. Good hearty English fare on offer: soups, Ye famous steak, kidney, mushroom and game pudding, chef's speciality sausage, vegetarian crêpes filled with mushrooms, onions and courgettes served on a tomato and basil sauce, fish and chips and various puddings. Sam Smiths beers on hand pump.

OPEN: 11.30–11. Sat 11.30–3, 5.30–11. Sun 12–4. Closed Sun eve.
Real Ale. Restaurant (closed Sun eve).
Children welcome. No dogs.

___

London EC1

Olde Mitre ① 020 7405 4751
Ely Court, off Ely Place EC1N 6SJ
Punch. Don O'Sullivan, manager

The 13th-century St Etheldreda's Church off Hatton Garden and the Olde Mitre are a sort of pair. The church came within the jurisdiction of the Bishop of Ely and the pub was built to provide refreshment for the Bishop's staff. In a very narrow alley off Hatton Garden, rebuilt during the mid-18th century and named after an earlier 16th-century tavern, it's a picturesque, delightful pub near the Bishop's church. The small panelled rooms are crowded during weekday lunchtimes – closed at weekends – when they serve simple bar snacks and a variety of toasted sandwiches – simple but good. Ind Coope

Burton, Adnams and Tetleys on hand pump. There are wooden casks for tables in the pretty small yard between the pub and the church.

OPEN: 11–11. Closed Sat, Sun & bank hols.
Real Ale.
No children. No dogs.

London SW3

Phene Arms ① 020 7352 3294
9 Phene Street, Chelsea SW3 5NY
Free House. Joakim Haegset, manager; Carmen Davis, licensee

On the corner of Phene Street and Margaretta Terrace, the pub was named after Dr John Phene, who in the 19th century developed this area, built the pub, lined the streets with trees and created one of the most delightful and desirable areas in Chelsea. The pub has had a huge make-over in recent years, which is not universally admired; the character of the old place has changed for ever. Now there is a padded leather bar, poufs to perch on, candles on the table and a new trendy menu. If you didn't know it before then it's probably fine, if you did, then make your own mind up. However the lucky Phene still has its own leafy front garden, hugely popular on a balmy summer evening. Bistro-like cooking and a good selection of wines. Roast lunch on Sundays. Fullers London Pride, Adnams Best and Broadside and Morlands Old Speckled Hen.

OPEN: 11–11.
Real Ale.
Children welcome. Dogs on leads. Wheelchair access (not WC).
Cards: most cards accepted.

London, Pinner

Queen's Head ① 020 8385 6475
31 High Street, Pinner HA5 5PJ
Spirit Group. Jill & James Tindall, licensees

A Grade II listed building, Pinner's oldest inn was built on the site of a 14th-century ale house. Parts of the present inn are fairly ancient, dating back to the 16th century. The Crown, as it was known, changed its name soon after George I ascended the throne in 1715 – probably to honour its most illustrious customer, the late Queen Anne, who would change horses here on the way from Hatfield to Windsor. Inside is beamed and panelled with an open fire – just as you would expect. Well run and very atmospheric, it is the focal point of the village. Good-value bar snacks: breakfast in bread – a bacon and fried egg sandwich – steak and twelve other fillings on the sandwich menu, filled jacket potatoes, ploughman's, fillet steak, bangers and mash and daily specials. Beers are Tetleys, Youngs,

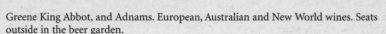

Greene King Abbot, and Adnams. European, Australian and New World wines. Seats outside in the beer garden.

OPEN: 11–11. Sun 12–10.30.
Real Ale.
No children. Dogs, except 12–3 when food is served. Car park.
Cards: Amex, Diners, MasterCard, Switch, Visa.

London SW1

Red Lion ➀ 020 7321 0782
2 Duke of York Street, Piccadilly SW1Y 6JP
Mitchell & Butler. Michael Brown, FBII, manager

This little pub is a bit small for a gin palace, but that's what it is – a Victorian gem. Outside, the cut-glass windows twinkle away in the sunlight. Inside are mirrors, polished mahogany counters, decorative plasterwork and usually a lot of people who have managed to force their way into this very small, popular, delightful pub. Only limited bar snacks are on offer weekday lunchtimes, except Friday and Saturday when they serve home-made fish and chips – a tremendous favourite with tourists. A huge amount of beer is sold, the range is constantly changing; most of the beers are guests from the smaller breweries and some are especially brought in for the regulars. As someone said, 'to get inside and admire the interior is worth the price of a pint'.

OPEN: 11.30–11. Closed Sun.
Real Ale.
No children. No dogs.
No cards.

London W1

Red Lion ➀ 020 7499 1307
1 Waverton Street, Mayfair W1J 5QN
Scottish Courage. Greg Peck, manager
e-mail: redlionmayfair.co.uk

When the Red Lion was built on a muddy lane in the 17th century it had the very grand Chesterfield House as a neighbour. The muddy lane has long been paved, the surrounding fields have gone and the neighbours are as grand as ever. The humble little ale house has become a very smart Red Lion in what is now, and has been for a long time, an exclusive area of London. A charming pub in a quiet, delightful corner, quite unspoilt. In summer the customers will be out on the forecourt enjoying themselves; in winter, cosying up by the fire in the small panelled bars where they serve food all day: Cumberland sausages and mash with onion gravy, chargrilled burgers, Cajun chicken, well-filled sandwiches, also salads and hot daily specials. The food in the restaurant goes up a notch; from the à la carte menu you could have Dover sole, grilled Scotch salmon, half a roast duck, shoulder of lamb or fillet of beef Wellington. Greene King IPA, Fullers London Pride, Youngs

Ordinary and Scottish Courage Directors. There is of course the house special, the Red Lion's very own Bloody Mary.

OPEN: 11.30–11. Sat 6–11. Sun 12–3, 6–10.30.
Real Ale. Restaurant.
Children in eating area. Only guide dogs. Wheelchair access.
Cards: Amex, Delta, MasterCard, Switch, Visa.

London SE10

Richard I ① 020 8692 2996
52–54 Royal Hill, Greenwich SE10 8RT
Youngs. Bill Wood, manager

The Richard I has a wonderfully grand address in an area steeped in naval history. It's an unspoilt, attractive local in a delightful street – mainly residential but with a few interesting shops. Inside, bare boards on the floor, panelled walls and books to read if you're kept waiting. The menu lists hearty pub fare, the current favourite being hot toasted paninis with a variety of fillings. At weekends, if the weather is fine, you can enjoy a barbecue in the decent-sized garden – with heaters if it gets a bit chilly. A brisk walk and there are lots of things to see. In a dry dock near the pier is the Victorian clipper ship *Cutty Sark*. On the banks of the river is the Royal Naval College, known as Greenwich Hospital, which was designed by Sir Christopher Wren; behind that is the National Maritime Museum, the oldest part of which is the Queen's House, built by Inigo Jones in 1633, and to crown it all, 130 acres of glorious park laid out by Le Nôtre for Charles II. The pub stocks the full range of Youngs beers: Bitter, Special and Ramrod plus the seasonal Wheat Beer and an extensive range of Young's speciality bottled beers and lagers. Lots of seats in the walled garden.

OPEN: 11–11. Sun 12–10.30.
Real Ale.
Children in garden. Dogs on leads.

London SW19

Rose & Crown ① 020 8947 4713
55 High Street, Wimbledon SW19 5BA
Youngs. Karen & Jeff Messitt, managers

An elegant, wonderfully proportioned early 17th-century building, this lovely place was here when Charles I was on the throne and has flourished since then. During the coaching era some coaches started and finished here – and this was one of Young's first properties. The ailing poet Walter Swinburne, who died in 1909, used to walk across Putney Heath and the common to the Rose & Crown which he regarded as his local; the chair he sat in is still in the pub. Brought up to date without losing any of its charm, it is a comfortable place with open fires; maps of old Wimbledon and Hogarth engravings decorate the walls of the bar, there is a small no-smoking area and an open fire in the conservatory. On the food side you will find a varied menu – all home-made – and a roast on Sunday. They have the full range of Youngs beers. Seats in the paved, walled coachyard.

OPEN: for breakfast Mon–Fri 7–9.30, Sat & Sun 8–10. Bar hours 11–11. Sun 12–10.30.
Real Ale.
Children welcome in conservatory. Dogs on lead. Thirteen bedrooms.
Cards: all accepted.

London SE1

Royal Oak ☎ 020 7357 7173
44 Tabard Street SE1 4JU
Harvey & Son (Lewes) Ltd. John Porteous & Frank Taylor, tenants

You might think that Tabard Street had something to do with the ancient Tabard Inn where Chaucer's pilgrims started their journey to Canterbury in his Canterbury Tales. But no, the famous inn was in the nearby Talbot Yard and burnt down in the 17th century; not a beam is left. However, this is still an historically interesting area; behind Charles Dickens' 'Little Dorrit Church', St George the Martyr on Borough High Street, and near the wonderful, galleried George Inn, is this well-restored, friendly and welcoming, Victorian Royal Oak. With just two bars and a private dining room for pre-booked lunch or dinner, they serve some reasonably priced, good home-cooked food. From the bar menu are sandwiches, ploughman's, sausage and mash, steak and ale pie, steak and kidney pudding, cod and chips, Lancashire hotpot and from the specials board there could be rabbit casserole, pork in cider, as well as grills, steaks and roasts. This is Harvey's only London pub and they keep Harveys range of ales: Mild, Pale, Best, Armada and seasonal ales in tip-top condition, also a comprehensive list of European and South African wines.

OPEN: Mon–Fri 11–11. Weekends by arrangement.
Real Ale. Private dining room.
No children. Dogs welcome.
Cards: most accepted.

London WC2

Seven Stars ☎ 020 7242 8521
53 Carey Street, Holborn WC2A 2JB
Adnams. Roxy Beaujolais & Nathan Silver, free tie lease
e-mail: nathan.silver@ntlworld.com

Delightfully unchanging – a little 'refurbishment' has been going on inside, but nothing that takes away the unique atmosphere of this Grade II building. Not only one of the smallest, but one of very few early 17th-century pubs in London. Built in 1602, facing the back of the Royal Courts of Justice, it was and is just the place for a bit of Dutch courage if you have to face the realities of life. To cheer you up it is all flowery outside – opulent hanging baskets – and snugly intimate inside – just two small rooms. They all come here; litigants – they could be the ones staring into their beer, lawyers happily thinking of their fees, reporters listening out for a good story and musicians appreciating the musical quiet – all enjoying the good food. The landlady, author of *Home from the Inn Contented* keeps an experienced hand on the food front. Hand-fried potato chips, olives and pistachios as an appetiser and a small changing menu: charcuterie with sourdough bread, club sandwich, cured herrings in dill with potato salad, Napoli sausages with sliced pork belly and cauliflower purée; also two or three specials which could include lamb steak with barley, baked sea bream and 'country scramble' – scrambled eggs, smoked ham, chives, sliced potato, parsley and thyme with sourdough bread. Adnams range of ales, Guinness and Bitburger and guest ales including Harveys. Bottled lagers, decent house wines and celebratory cigars. The law courts' stone balustrade provides an extra bar and beer garden – weather permitting. The loos are a talking point here – they are up extremely narrow Elizabethan stairs.

OPEN: 11–11. Closed Sun.
Real Ale.
No children. Well-behaved dogs welcome – there is a pub cat – Tom Paine.
Cards: Amex, MasterCard, Switch, Visa.

London SW18

Ship ① 020 8870 9667
41 Jews Row, Wandsworth SW18 1TB
Youngs. Charles Gotto, MBII, licensee

If you don't know the area, it can be difficult to find the Ship but Wandsworth Bridge is a good landmark to make for; you reach Jews Row from a little slip road just before you cross the river. You can of course get there clutching your A-Z. Once you've arrived there is nothing nicer on a summer's day than to sit on the terrace amid the floral display, enjoy a barbecued lunch, a pint, and watch the Thames slip by – along with hundreds of others who've had no trouble finding it! A pavilion outside bar has been built to give you easier access to the beer. Weather permitting, anything that can be barbecued will be; if the barbecue is off, it's back inside for the bar menu. This features soups, baguettes, steak sandwiches, chargrilled chicken, Caesar salad, fishcakes with pecan sauce, ploughman's with a choice of British cheeses, and daily specials from the blackboard. All the pork is free-range and, along with the lamb, comes from the Gotto farm. Good puds too. Youngs range of well-kept ales, a guest beer and a good selection of wines, many by the glass. Fantastic evening celebrations for the Last Night of the Proms; a huge television screen gives an opportunity for everyone to join in the singing and for all budding conductors to practise like mad. Even though it has a car park, walk if you can, as parking can be a bit of a problem.

OPEN: 11–11.
Real Ale. Restaurant.
Children in eating area. Dogs on leads. Wheelchair access (not WC).

London SW1

Star ① 020 7235 3019
Belgrave Mews West SW1X 8HT
Fullers. Christine & T. J. Connell, managers

Lucky Belgrave Square has three mews, north, south and west; west is the one you want, just off Chesham Place. The Star, with an outstanding display of colourful window boxes, hanging baskets and flowering tubs, was built at the same time as the surrounding squares for the staff of the very grand houses nearby. They all knew their place and who went where in the pub; things have changed a lot since then. This lovely mews is always a haven from the noisy, frenetic life of London just a few yards away. Smart, comfortable and well kept the Star has three rooms downstairs with open fires and an upstairs room if it gets too crowded. Bar food includes lunchtime sandwiches, salads and favourite hot dishes such as fish and chips and steak pie. There is a greater choice on the evening menu. Well-kept Fullers Chiswick, London Pride, ESB and seasonal ales. On summer evenings everyone spreads out into the mews.

OPEN: 11.30–3, 5–11 (Sat 6.30–11). 11.30–11 Fri & daily for two weeks before Christmas.
Real Ale.
Children if eating. Dogs on leads. Wheelchair access (not WC).

London W9

Warrington Hotel ① 020 7286 2929
93 Warrington Crescent, W9 1EH
Free House. John Brandon, licensee

A gem of a place. Listed Grade II, the ceramic pillars at the entrance, mosaic steps, wrought iron lamps, semi-circular marble bar, sweeping staircase, high ceilings, cherubs and Art Nouveau decoration created what they used to call a gin palace. This particular gin palace was just that little bit different – a wonderful relic of the Victorian Very Naughty Nineties. It was owned by the Church of England, who happily – for the church – didn't know that at its naughtiest it was a successful brothel, which accounts for the risqué murals upstairs. Today it's still lively and popular; they serve Thai bar meals at lunchtime and there is a Thai restaurant upstairs – you have to book a table. Ales are Fullers London Pride, ESB, Brakspears Special, Youngs Special Bitter and guests. The Warrington is lucky to have a garden with 20 tables. Arrive early if you want one on a summer's day.

OPEN: 11–11. Sun 12–10.30.
Real Ale.
No children. Dogs on leads.
Cards: MasterCard, Switch, Visa.

London, Richmond

White Cross Hotel ① 020 8940 6844
Water Lane, Richmond TW9 1TH
Youngs. Mr & Mrs Heggie, licensee/managers

You can't get much nearer the river. A very high tide and the steps into the pub stop the river joining you in the bar. The early 19th-century White Cross was once a hotel. It's just a pub now, but a pub in a super setting with a garden overlooking the Thames. Inside is one large bar with two fireplaces, one of which is directly under the picture window overlooking Richmond Bridge, which always makes one wonder: 'where's the chimney?' Also a room on the mezzanine floor with a balcony overlooking the river. Occasionally during the summer there is live music in the garden which is now partly covered and heated. Food is all self-service from a buffet in the bar; no surprises, sandwiches, sausages, salads, vegetarian options and a daily special. Seasonal game dishes at the weekend. Youngs Bitter, seasonal ales and 30 wines by the glass or bottle. Their motto is 'real ale, real food and real fires'. From Richmond you can have a day out on the Thames; a little lunch beforehand and a leisurely trip – there is no better way to see the wonderful gardens, parks, riverside inns and villages than from the river. Just watch where you park your car though – study the tides carefully or you could find it floating past you.

OPEN: 11–11. Sun 12–10.30. Food served over an extended lunchtime – not evenings.
Real Ale.
Children in garden, but no under 18s allowed into pub. Dogs very welcome.

London SW6

White Horse ① 020 7736 2115
1–3 Parsons Green, Fulham SW6 4UL
Six Continents. Mark Dorber, manager
e-mail: inn@whitehorsesw6.com

Regular beer festivals, a wine list of note and some inspired cooking add up to a very desirable pub. Once a coaching inn on a corner site on the edge of Parsons Green, it was the last stop before facing the rigours of the road to the West. A Victorian gin palace later, it is now a hugely popular pub from which there's no hurry to go anywhere else. Inside, wood and flagstone floors, a big comfortable bar with winter fires and a no-smoking restaurant in the old coach house at the back of the pub. This is a lively, busy place, so arrive in good time if you want a meal and somewhere to put the plate. The creative food is a mile away from your usual pub menu – they even have waitress service with drinks brought to your table. An à la carte menu features during the evening. The upstairs gallery, where they serve Sunday lunch, can be used for private meetings and dinner parties. Outside there is a wonderfully sunny terrace – just the place for lunch, weekend brunches and relaxation in the early evening. Towards the end of November they hold an annual Old Ale Festival, so that is worth putting in your diary. They are very into beer; there is always a good selection of ales in tip-top condition: Adnams Broadside, Harveys Sussex, Roosters Yankee, Oakhams JHB and two guest beers, including one from the Rooster

Brewery: 15 Trappist beers, 75 Belgian, Dutch, German and US beers and 80 different wines.

OPEN: 11–11.
Real Ale.
Children in eating area. Dogs on leads.
Occasional jazz nights. Wheelchair access (not WC).

London W8

Windsor Castle ① 020 7243 9551
114 Campden Hill Road, Holland Park W8 7AR
Six Continents. Sally Hemingway, manager

Appealing throughout the year, this early 19th-century pub was built high on the hill before the area was developed. Then, surrounded by farmland, it led a very bucolic existence and had far-reaching views, from upstairs, towards Windsor Castle nearly 20 miles away to the west. The view might have changed to very smart, expensive real estate, but this old pub hasn't lost any of its charm. Inside are three panelled bars – each with its own entrance and customers – and a small dining room. The pub fills up rapidly on summer evenings when the attractive, shady walled garden comes into its own. Interesting pub grub is served all day: sandwiches on foccacia herb bread, chicken Caesar, oysters and mussels, Mediterranean lamb with roasted vegetables, linguini with tomatoes, olives and capers, steamed mussels, sausage and mash and a tremendously popular roast beef and Yorkshire pudding or roast lamb shank for lunch on Sunday. Ales are Adnams, Fullers London Pride and a guest. There are also house wines, a very reasonable champagne and various malt whiskies.

OPEN: 12–11.
Real Ale.
No children. Dogs on leads (not in garden!). Wheelchair access to garden.

BEST OF THE REST

London EC1
Bishops Finger ① 0207 2482341
9/10 West Smithfield EC1A 9JR
Close to everything of any importance in the City of London: St Paul's Cathedral, St Bart's hospital, Museum of London, Barbican Arts Centre and the now stabilised Millenium Bridge. Opposite a small park next to Smithfield Market this small pub has pretty hanging baskets outside, inside uplifting decor, comfortable furniture, fresh flowers on tables and bars, candles at night to add to the atmosphere, interesting food and very well-kept beer. Thirteen different sausages available every day with creamed potato, home-made chutney and onion gravy; the favourites are Scotch beef with wholegrain mustard, pheasant and tarragon, wild boar and apple and guinea fowl and ginger. Their very own butcher is opposite – Smithfield market – and there is always a choice of fresh fish. A Shepherd Neame pub, so tip-top Shepherd Neame beers including seasonal specials. Good choice of

wine. Children welcome. No dogs. Wheelchair access. Cards: Amex, Diners, MasterCard, Visa.
Open: Mon–Fri 11–11.

London SW13

Bulls Head ① 020 8876 5241
373 Lonsdale Road, Barnes SW13 9PY
This very well-run pub – they have been voted Inn Keepers of the Year – is a haven for modern jazz groupies. Weekday lunchtimes are blissfully silent – musically – whilst they gird themselves for another jazz session. You pay an admission charge to hear the top jazz groups perform in their own wonderfully equipped music studio, but if you want a lower decibel rate you can still get some idea of what you're missing from the lounge bar. Lunchtime bar food is all home-made; there is a popular carvery and a selection of other hot dishes. In the evening they have some wonderful Thai food, freshly cooked to order. Youngs Bitter, Special, and over 80 malt whiskies. A very comprehensive wine list – over 220 bottles, 34 by the glass. Weekday lunches are quiet. The rest of the time you either like jazz or wear your ear plugs. Live jazz every Sunday lunchtime and evening in own room with bar. Children welcome in daytime.
Open: 11–11.

London SW11

Castle ① 0207 228 8181
115 Battersea High Street SW11 9HS
No kerb appeal here, but ignore the rather dreary 1960s exterior – architecture at its lowest – and go through to the rather rustic interior. Here are bare boards, a collection of unmatched tables and chairs, a huge fireplace – but without a fire – and beyond the bar, a conservatory and attractive garden. A popular, well-liked place that attracts the locals. Food wavers in quality, so we are told, which usually means there is a different pair of hands wielding the cooking pots on the off days. The menu is fairly traditional, sausage and mash, barbecued pork steak, poached salmon etc. with the usual puds. Youngs range of ales and a good selection of wines. The background music is a bit like the food, sometimes on, sometimes not; totally inconsistent, but always played at low volume. As our informant says, 'music seems to be played solely by and for the benefit of bar staff'. How often have we heard that! Children welcome.
Open: 12–11.

London N1

Duke of Cambridge ① 020 7359 3066
30 St Peter's Street, Islington N1 8JT
Certainly different. When this old pub re-opened at the end of last century the owners decided to run it along environmentally friendly lines and this includes the beer. One of London's new gastro-pubs, the interior has been opened up to create one spacious bar and there are separate, atmospheric dining areas. The interesting, creative blackboard menus served in the bar and dining rooms change twice a day. They try their hardest to make sure all the ingredients used to create the menus are organic but with game and fish that is a bit difficult. Beers are a certainty though, Pitfield Eco Warrior and St Peters Best Bitter are accredited by the Soil Association. Organic lagers, ciders, wines, spirits, coffee and tea etc are all listed on the blackboard. The exclusivity is reflected in the price. Children welcome.
Open: 12–11.

London SW1
Fox and Hounds ① 020 7730 6367
29 Passmore Street, (corner of Graham Terrace) SW1W 8HR
When this small place opened for business it was only licensed to sell beer, cider and wine – the result of Victorian thinking that the working man should be kept away from the temptation of spirits. Now they have a spirit licence – well, for limited spirits, as they confine themselves to one gin, one vodka, two whiskies, one rum and one brandy – all classy brands. Anyway, how many do you need? The Fox and Hounds is just a tiny corner pub, with two small panelled rooms, at the end of an early 19th-century terrace on the edge of the Grosvenor Estate. The menu, which changes weekly, usually has home-made soup, a risotto, something with pasta, salads, chicken in various guises, something fishy and whatever else they think the customers would like. A choice of five red and six white wines, four of each by the glass, also Youngs range of ales. Children welcome, dogs too.
Open: 11–3, 5.30–11 (Sat 6–11, Sun 6.30–10.30).

London E14
Grapes ① 020 7987 4396
76 Narrow Street , Limehouse E14 8BP
If you have read Dickens' *Our Mutual Friend*, this is the pub that features. A watery, 16th-century pub with some gruesome stories to tell. Not the easiest place to find; feet are better than wheels, or if the tide is right you could probably still row in as there are steps leading up from the shore. Parts of the pub are older than others but there is not a right angle in the place; old and leaning, this is a place to come to soak in the atmosphere. Good, simple bar food; a fish restaurant upstairs, roast lunch on Sunday. Adnams, Tetleys, Ind Coope Burton and a changing guest beer. Children over 14 only.
Open: 12–3, 5.30–11. Closed Sat lunch, otherwise 7–11. Sun 12–3, 7–10.30.

London SE1
Horniman ① 020 7407 3611
Hays Galleria, nr London Bridge SE1 2BA
Spacious and comfortable, this is the place to be for wonderful views over the Thames and Tower Bridge. Tea, rather than ale, is what the name of this pub conveys, as Hornimans have been tea merchants since 1826. It has a set of clocks made for the founder, Frederick, that show the time in various places around the world, and a frieze illustrating tea from bush to pot. Two beers, Adnams and Fullers London Pride; teas and coffee, the usual bar food and daily changing dishes. No children.
Open: 11–11.

London W11
Ladbroke Arms ① 020 7727 6648
54 Ladbroke Road W11 3NW
A pub with lots of things going for it: it's a free house – a rare thing in this area – and they serve some interesting home-made food; there are about four beers for you to enjoy, Courage Directors, Greene King Abbot and two guests and, lastly, on a balmy evening you can sit outside on their own terrace to enjoy your drink. No children.
Open: 11–3, 5.30–11. Sat 11–11. Sun 12–10.30.

London SW1

Westminster Arms ☽ 020 7222 8520
Storey's Gate SW1P 3AT
You are in Division Bell area, so if the bell rings the place could suddenly empty, depending who's propping up the bar. This is as close to the seat of government most of us will get – fraternising with government staff and researchers while they down a few well-deserved drinks in the small panelled bar. Five beers on the go here, plus a guest; these include Westminster Best brewed by Charringtons. They also have a decent wine list. Food is served in the downstairs bar – steak and kidney pie, fish and chips – that sort of thing; also in the restaurant upstairs. Children welcome in restaurant.
Open: 11–11. Sat 11–6. Sun 12–6.

Wetherspoon within the M25

Barking & Dagenham

Barking – Barking Dog, 51 Station Parade
☽ 020 8507 9109
Dagenham – Lord Denham, 270–272 Heathway
☽ 020 8984 8590

Barnet

Barnet – Moon under the Water, 148 High Street
☽ 020 8441 9476
Colindale – Moon under the Water, 10 Varley Parade
☽ 020 8200 7611
New Barnet – Railway Bell, 13 East Barnet Road
☽ 020 8449 1369
North Finchley N12 – Tally Ho, 749 High Road
☽ 020 8445 4390

Brent

Harlesden NW10 – Coliseum, 26 Manor Park Road
☽ 020 8961 6570
Kingsbury NW9 – J. J. Moons, 553 Kingsbury Road
☽ 020 8204 9675
Neasden NW10 – Outside Inn, 312–314 Neasden Lane
☽ 020 8452 3140
Wembley – J. J. Moons, 397 High Road
☽ 020 8903 4923

Bexley

Bexley – Wrong 'Un, 234–236 The Broadway
☽ 020 8298 0439
Welling – New Cross Turnpike, 55 Bellgrove Road
☽ 020 8304 1600

Bromley, Kent

Bromley – Wetherspoons, Unit 23, Westmoreland Place
☽ 020 8464 1586

Orpington – Harvest Moon, 141–143 High Street
☎ 01689 876931
Penge SE20 – Moon and Stars, 164–166 High Street
☎ 020 8776 5680
Petts Wood - Sovereign of the Seas, 109–111 Queensway
☎ 01689 891606

Camden

Camden NW1 – Man in the Moon, 40–42 Chalk Farm Road
☎ 020 7482 2054
Cricklewood NW2 – Beaten Docket, 50–56 Cricklewood Broadway
☎ 020 8450 2972
Hampstead NW3 – Three Horseshoes, 28 Heath Street
☎ 020 7431 7206
Swiss Cottage NW3 – Wetherspoons, O2 Centre, 255 Finchley Road
☎ 020 7433 0920

City of London

EC1 – Masque Haunt, 168–172 Old Street
☎ 020 7251 4195
EC1 – Sir John Oldcastle, 29–35 Farringdon Road
☎ 020 7242 1013
EC2 – Green Man, 1 Poultry
☎ 020 7248 3529
EC2 – Hamilton Hall, Unit 32, The Broadgate Centre, Liverpool Street Station
☎ 020 7247 3579
EC3 – Crosse Keys, 9 Gracechurch Street
☎ 020 7623 4824
EC3 – Liberty Bounds, 15 Trinity Square
☎ 020 7481 0513
SE1 – Pommelers Rest, 196–198 Tower Bridge Road
☎ 020 7378 1399
WC1 – Penderels Oak, 283–288 High Holborn
☎ 020 7242 5669
WC2 – Knights Templar, 95 Chancery Lane
☎ 020 7831 2660
WC2 – Shakespeare's Head, Africa House, 64–68 Kingsway
☎ 020 7404 8846

Croydon

Croydon – George, 17–21 George Street
☎ 020 8649 9077
Croydon – Ship of Fools, 9–11 London Road
☎ 020 8681 2835
Croydon – Skylark, 34–36 Southend
☎ 020 8649 9909
Crystal Palace SE19 – Postal Order, 33 Westow Street
☎ 020 8771 3303
Norbury SW16 – Moon under Water, 1327 London Road
☎ 020 8765 1235

Purley – Foxley Hatch, 8–9 Russell Hill Road
Ⓓ 020 8763 9307
Selsdon – Sir Julian Huxley, 152–154 Addington Road
Ⓓ 020 8657 9457
South Norwood SE25 – William Stanley, 7–8 High Street
Ⓓ 020 8653 0678
Thornton Heath – Wetherspoons, 2–4 Ambassador House
Ⓓ 020 8689 6277

Ealing

Acton W3 – Red Lion and Pineapple, 281 High Street
Ⓓ 020 8896 2248

Enfield

Enfield – Moon under Water, 116–117 Chase Side
Ⓓ 020 8366 9855
Enfield – Picture Palace, Howard's Hall, Ponders End
Ⓓ 020 8344 9690
Palmers Green N13 – Whole Hog, 430–434 Green Lane
Ⓓ 020 8882 3597
Southgate N14 – New Crown, 80–84 Chase Side
Ⓓ 020 8882 8758
Upper Edmonton N18 – Gilpin's Bell, 50–54 Fore Street
Ⓓ 020 8884 2744

Greenwich

Eltham SE10 – Banker's Draft, 80 High Street
Ⓓ 020 8294 2578
Greenwich SE10 – Gate Clock, Cutty Sark Station, Creek Road
Ⓓ 020 8269 2000
Woolwich SE18 – Great Harry, 7–9 Wellington Street
Ⓓ 020 8317 4813

Hackney

Hackney E8 – Baxter's Court, 282 Mare Street
Ⓓ 020 8525 9010
Stoke Newington N16 – Rochester Castle, High Street
Ⓓ 020 7249 6016

Hammersmith

Hammersmith W6 – Plough & Harrow, 120–124 King Street
Ⓓ 020 8725 6020
Hammersmith W6 – William Morris, 2–4 King Street
Ⓓ 020 8741 7175
Shepherds Bush W12 – Central Bar, Unit 1, West 12 Shopping Centre
Ⓓ 020 8746 4290

Haringey

Highgate N6 – Gatehouse, 1 North Road
Ⓓ 020 8340 8054

Hornsey N8 – Tollgate, 26–30 Turnpike Lane
℗ 020 8889 9085
Wood Green N22 – Wetherspoons, 5 Spouters Corner, High Road
℗ 020 8881 3891

Harrow

Harrow – Moon on the Hill, 373–375 Station Road
℗ 020 8863 3670
Harrow – New Moon, 25–26 Kenton Park Parade, Kenton Road
℗ 020 8909 1103
Hatch End – Moon and Sixpence, 250 Uxbridge Road
℗ 020 420 1074
Pinner – Village Inn, 402–408 Rayners Lane
℗ 020 8868 8551
Stanmore – Man in the Moon, Buckingham Parade
℗ 020 8954 6119

Havering

Hornchurch – J. J. Moons, 46–62 High Street
℗ 01708 478410
Romford – Colley Rowe Inn, 54–56 Collier Row Road
℗ 01708 760633
Romford – Eva Hart, 1128 High Street, Chadwell Heath
℗ 020 8597 1069
Romford – Moon and Stars, 99–103 South Street
℗ 01708 730117

Hertfordshire

Borehamwood – Hart & Spool, 148 Shenley Road
℗ 020 8953 1883
Rickmansworth – Pennsylvanian, 115–117 High Street
℗ 01923 720348
Watford – Moon under the Water, 44 High Street
℗ 01923 223559
Watford – Wetherspoons, 4 Bridlington Road, South Oxhey
℗ 020 8421 7580

Hillingdon

Hayes – Botwell Inn, 25–29 Coldharbour Lane
℗ 020 8893 7506
Ickenham – Titchenham Inn, 11 Swakeleys Road
℗ 01895 678916
Northwood – Sylvan Moon, 27 Green Lane
℗ 01923 820760
Northwood Hills – William Jolle, 53 Joel Street
℗ 01923 842240
Ruislip Manor – J. J. Moons, 12 Victoria Road
℗ 01895 239852
Uxbridge – Good Yarn, 132 High Street
℗ 01895 239852

Hounslow

Feltham – Moon on the Square, Unit 30, The Centre
℗ 020 8893 1293
Hounslow – Moon under Water, 84–86 Staines Road
℗ 020 8572 7506

Islington

Holloway N7 – Coronet, 338–346 Holloway Road
℗ 020 7609 5014
Islington N1 – Angel, 3–5 High Street
℗ 020 7837 2218
Islington N1 – White Swan, 255–256 Upper Street
℗ 020 7251 4195
Stroud Green N4 – White Lion of Mortimer, 125–127 Stroud Green Road, nr Finsbury Park
℗ 020 7281 4773

Kent

Dartford – Paper Moon, 55 High Street
℗ 01322 281127

Kingston upon Thames

Kingston upon Thames – Kings Tun, 153–157 Clarence Street
℗ 020 8547 3827
Surbiton – Cap in Hand, 174 Hook Rise
℗ 020 8397 3790
Surbiton – Coronation Hall, St Marks Hill
℗ 020 8390 6164

Lambeth

Brixton SW9 – Beehive, 407–409 Brixton Road
℗ 020 7738 3643
Streatham SW2 – Crown & Sceptre, Streatham Hill
℗ 020 8671 0843
Streatham SW16 – Holland Tringham, 107–109 High Road
℗ 020 8769 3062

Lewisham

Brockley SE4 – Brockley Barge, 184 Brockley Road
℗ 020 8694 7690
Catford SE6 – London & Rye, 109 Rushey Green
℗ 020 8697 5028
Catford SE6 – Tiger's Head, 350 Bromley Road
℗ 020 8698 8645
Forest Hill SE23 – Capitol, 11–21 London Road
℗ 020 8291 8920
Lee Green SE12 – Edmund Halley, 25–27 Leegate Centre
℗ 020 8318 7475
Lewisham SE13 – Watch House, 198–204 High Street
℗ 020 8318 3136

Sydenham SE26 – Windmill, 125–131 Kirakdale
℡ 020 8291 8670

Loughton

Loughton – Last Post, 227 High Road
℡ 020 8532 0751

Merton

Mitcham – White Lion of Mortimer, 223 London Road
℡ 020 8646 7332
Morden – Lady St Helier, 33 Aberconway Road
℡ 020 8540 2818
Wimbledon SW19 – Wibbas Down Inn, 6–12 Gladstone Road
℡ 020 8540 6788

Middlesex

Staines – George, 2–8 High Street
℡ 01784 462181

Newham

East Ham E6 – Miller's Well, 419–421 Barking Road
℡ 020 8471 8404
Forest Gate E7 – Hudson Bay, 1–5 Upton Lane
℡ 020 8471 7702
Stratford E15 – Golden Grove, 145–148 The Grove
℡ 020 8519 0750

Redbridge

Barkingside – New Fairlop Oak, Fencepiece Road
℡ 020 8500 2217
Goodmayes – Standard Bearer, 7–13 Goodmayes Road
℡ 020 8597 7624
Ilford – Great Spoon of Ilford, 114–116 Cranbrook Road
℡ 020 8518 0535
Wanstead E11 – George, 159 High Street
℡ 020 8989 2921

Richmond upon Thames

Twickenham – Moon under Water, 53–57 London Road
℡ 020 8744 0080

Southwark

Camberwell SE5 – Fox on the Hill, 149 Denmark Hill
℡ 020 7738 4756
Elephant & Castle SE1 – Wetherspoons, Metro Central Heights, Newington Causeway
℡ 020 7940 0890
Peckham – Kentish Drovers, 71–79 Peckham High Street
℡ 020 7277 4283
Rotherhithe – Surrey Docks, 185 Lower Road
℡ 020 7394 2832

Surrey

Epsom – Assembly Rooms, 147–154 High Street
① 01372 737290
Walton on Thames – Regent, 19 Church Street
① 01932 243980

Sutton

North Cheam – Wetherspoons, 552–556 London Road
① 020 8644 1808
Sutton – Moon on the Hill, 5–9 Hill Road
① 020 8643 1202
Wallington – Whispering Moon, 25 Ross Parade
① 020 8647 7020

Tower Hamlets

Bethnal Green E2 – Camden's Head, 456 Bethnal Green Road
① 020 7613 4263
Bow E3 – Matchmaker, 580–586 Roman Road
① 020 8709 9760
Docklands E14 – Ledger Building, 4 Hertsmere Road
① 020 7536 7770
Mile End E1 – Half Moon, 213–233 Mile End Road
① 020 7790 6810
Whitechapel E1 – Goodman's Field, Mansell St
① 020 7680 2850

Waltham Forest

Chingford E4 – King's Ford, 250–252 Chingford Mount Road
① 020 8523 9365
Leyton E10 – Drum, 557–559 Lea Bridge Road
① 020 8539 9845
Leytonstone E11 – Walnut Tree, 857–861 High Road
① 020 8539 2526

Wandsworth

Balham SW12 – Moon under Water, 194 Balham High Street
① 020 8673 0535
Battersea SW11 – Asparagus, 1–13 Falcon Road
① 020 7801 0046
Putney SW15 – Railway, 202 Upper Richmond Road
① 020 8788 8190
Southfields SW18 – Grid Inn, 22 Replingham Road
① 020 88874 8460
Tooting SW17 – J. J. Moons, 56a High Street
① 020 8672 4726
Wandsworth SW18 – Rose & Crown,134 Wandsworth High Street
① 020 8871 4497

Westminster

Marble Arch – Tyburn, 18–20 Edgware Road
① 020 7723 4731
Marylebone – Metropolitan Bar, 7 Station Approach
① 020 7486 3489
Victoria – Willow Walk, 25 Wilton Row
① 020 7828 2953
Victoria Station – Wetherspoons, Unit 5, Victoria Island
① 020 7931 0445
Westminster – Lord Moon of the Mall, 16–18 Whitehall
① 020 7839 7701
West End – Moon and Sixpence, 183–185 Wardour Street
① 020 7734 0037
West End – Moon under Water, 105–107 Charing Cross Road
① 020 7287 6039
West End – Moon under Water, 28 Leicester Square
① 020 7839 2837

Scotland

Aberdeen

Prince of Wales ① 01224 640597
7–11 St Nicholas Lane, Aberdeen AB10 1HE
Free House. Kenny Gordon, licensee

The Prince of Wales, surrounded by solid, handsome, Victorian contemporaries, is in a cobbled lane just off Union Street. This mid-Victorian pub reputedly has the longest bar in the city, all 60ft of it, and at busy times every inch is taken. It has a comfortable lounge and a flagstone-floored bar area beyond. Eight hand pumps on the go, so it's hugely popular, not only for a pint of well-kept ale but a generous lunchtime snack: home-made soup, steak and ale pie, chicken Kiev, oven-roasted vegetables and rice, breaded haddock, cold meats from the salad bar, filled baguettes, baked potatoes and various sandwiches. The menu listing the home-cooked food changes daily. No distractions from a jukebox or TV; so you can chat to your neighbour and enjoy either the Caledonian 80/-, Orkney Dark Island or Isle of Skye beers; other Scottish beers are regularly promoted. Fresh coffee too.

OPEN: 11–12.
Real Ale.
Children in eating area. No dogs. Wheelchair access (not WC).
Live music Sunday afternoons.

St Machar's Bar ① 01224 483079
High Street, Old Aberdeen AB24 3EH
Free House. James Alexander, owner/licensee

North of the main city, Old Aberdeen was once a separate community near the River Don. It's very atmospheric, with cobbled streets, small cottages, the oldest inhabited house in the old city (Chaplains Court, built in 1519), the medieval Kings College in the High Street and St Machar's Bar – named after, but nothing to do with the twin-towered, 14th-century St Machar's Cathedral. Called the best licensed corridor in the world, the bar is surrounded by the university and can on occasion be overrun by students. When the university is not in session, you can spend an idyllic few hours relaxing with a pint of McEwan's 70/- and one of the generously sized sandwiches that cross the bar for extremely reasonable prices. McEwans Export 70/-, 80/-, John Smiths, Guinness and Theakstons.

OPEN: 11–11. Sun 12.30–10.30.
No children. No dogs. No car park. Wheelchair access.

Applecross

Applecross Inn ① 01520 7442620
Shore Street, Applecross, Highland IV54 8LR
Free House. Judith Fish, licensee

Until the 1970s when a single-track road was built to Applecross from Sheildag, this was one of the most inaccessible communities in Britain. A monastery was established here in the seventh century – but the monks, very sensibly, probably arrived by sea. For centuries the only other route was a scary journey along the old cattle track negotiating dizzy hairpin bends, climbing over 2000ft, edging along precipices, eventually joining the road to Ardarroch. Suitably terrified and relieved, you would have arrived at this whitewashed inn close to the shore. The modern, easier route follows the coast, less breathtaking but more relaxing. In the Applecross there is a true communal atmosphere with lively repartee between locals, staff and visitors. The bar is very well stocked with bottled beers from the Skye Brewery and over 50 single malts. Food served is ample and excellent. Fish and seafood take first place on the menu: as well as soup and sandwiches there could be local oysters, prawns, smoked salmon, crabs, scallops in a creamy sauce, haggis, steak pie, or a chicken dish if you're not wanting fish. Short wine list. Outside is a beer garden for those sultry summer days.

OPEN: 11.30–11.30. Winter 12–11.
Children before 8.30 p.m. Dogs in bar. Car park. Wheelchair access. Bedrooms.
Cards: MasterCard, Switch, Visa.

Arduaine

Loch Melfort Hotel and Restaurant ① 01852 200233
Arduaine, By-Oban, Argyll PA34 4XE
Free House. Nigel & Kylie Schofield, licensees

Someone once said that this part of Scotland looks as though it was dropped from a great height, shattering into islands, sea lochs, headlands and islets. The hotel and the National Trust's Arduaine Gardens share the view and a wonderful position on the edge of Loch Melfort. You can walk down to the shore – where the hotel has its own pots and nets – and you might see what the sea has provided for supper; you'll know the fish is as fresh as can be. Also on the menu will be venison sausages served with caramelised onions, fillet of salmon en croute, a home-made soup, sandwiches, ploughman's and some interesting specials. Comprehensive wine list (they have won the Scottish Wine Award of the Year) and a good selection of malt whiskies. Mooring facilities if you are bringing your yacht, showers for sailors, a drying room too if you need it, plenty of walks and wonderful views from the terrace of Loch Melfort and Luing, one of the 'Slate Islands' – islands whose slate quarries had been worked for hundreds of years – now abandoned.

OPEN: 9.30–11. Two AA Rosettes.
Restaurant (no-smoking).
Children welcome. No dogs in the main hotel but they are allowed in the extension. Car park. Mooring. Wheelchair access. Bedrooms.

Balerno

Johnsburn House ① 0131 449 3847
Johnsburn Road, Balerno, Lothian EH14 7BB
Free House. Martin & Linda Mitchell, licensees

Built in 1760 in a village at the foot of the Pentland Hills, this listed baronial mansion is now a favoured country pub and Martin Mitchell the most decorated of licensees; 86 awards so far, among them Master Chef, Master Cellarman and Master Restaurateur. There is a cosy, beamed bar, a panelled dining lounge and other, more formal, dining rooms; some of Scotland's best food is produced in these kitchens. From the bar menu, poached egg Florentine, crayfish cocktail, bangers and mash, seared salmon with lemon hollandaise, steak pie, seafood risotto, Mongolian spicy beef, filled crêpes, toasted sandwiches, omelettes, salads, more-ish puds too. There is a very reasonable four-course dinner served in the restaurant – must book. Five changing cask ales; Caledonian Deuchars IPA and guests. Among the many awards are two silver medals for 'Wine Pub of the Year' – so, an interesting wine list.

OPEN: Tues–Fri 12–3, 5–11. Sat 12–12. Sun 12–11. Closed Mon.
Real Ale. Restaurant.
Children and dogs welcome. Wheelchair access.

Banff

Ship Inn ① 01261 812620
8 Deveronside, Banff, Grampian AB45 1HP
Free House. Moire MacLellan, owner/licensee

An unspoilt, historic inn overlooking the harbour, which, having largely silted up in the 19th century, is mainly used as a sailing centre. This area of coastline is known as the 'garden of the north' as, surprisingly, the climate is on the whole dry and mild. Banff, built at the mouth of the River Deveron, boasts some fine Georgian architecture, built when it was a favourite winter resort. You would come here for the view over the Bay and the beer in the Ship; no food, only a crisp and a nut. Courage Directors, Murphys, occasionally McEwans 80/- and various guest ales.

OPEN: Mon–Thurs 11–12. Fri & Sat 11–12.30. Sun 7–12 during the summer.
Real Ale.
Children in the lounge bar. Dogs on leads. Wheelchair access.

Broughty Ferry

Fishermans Tavern Hotel ① 01382 775941
10–14 Fort Street, Broughty Ferry, Dundee, Tayside DD5 2AD
Free House. Jonathan Stewart, licensee

Yards from the shore of the Tay estuary, an old, extended, fisherman's cottage in what was once a fishing village on the eastern side of Dundee. There is still a harbour, so if you are coming by sea you can tie up here. Inside the attractive, rambling, Fishermans Tavern is a cosy snug, lounge bar – with fire – and back bar used as a dining area. The family room is no-smoking. The hotel is known for its very well-kept ales, excellent wine list and good traditional bar food, which could include a home-made soup of the day, beefsteak roll with onions, toasted sandwiches, steak or chicken and mushroom pie, filled jacket potatoes and daily specials. Belhavens 60/-, 80/- and St Andrew's, Maclays 80/- and a daily changing guest beer. There is a small garden and tables at the front. They hold a beer festival during early summer for the RNLI.

OPEN: Mon–Wed 11–12. Thurs–Sat 11–1 a.m. Sun 12.30–12.
Real Ale.
Children in eating area. Dogs on leads. Wheelchair access. Bedrooms.
Folk music Thurs eves.

Crinan

Crinan Hotel ① 01546 830261
Crinan, By Lochgilphead, Argyll PA31 8SR
Free House. Nicholas Ryan, licensee
www.crinanhotel.com

On a small inlet off Jura Sound, this hotel is in a spectacular position tucked under the wooded cliffs where the Crinan Canal meets the sea. This very busy canal is a short cut between Loch Fyne and the sea; negotiating fifteen locks is preferable to the long haul around the Mull of Kintyre. Nothing much else here; just this splendid hotel, quays, a few cottages and Argyll's rugged coastline. From the picture windows upstairs you can see the entrance to the canal and spend a happy time watching the seemingly endless procession of boats negotiating the locks. If it's a very light lunch you're after, you can eat in either the public bar or the coffee shop/bakery by the fishing-boat dock. Lots of fresh and locally smoked fish included in the bar menu: local mussels, whole Loch Crinan jumbo prawns, Loch Fyne undyed kippers, trout, princess clams, seafood stew; also honey-roast ham, local butcher's sausages with mashed potatoes and black pudding and chicken stuffed with leeks and mushrooms. Lots of salads and daily specials. Tennants 70/-, 80/-, Belhaven Best and Worthington Cream Flow. A choice of malt whiskies and a good wine list. During the evenings, when there is a shift of emphasis towards the restaurant, the atmosphere does become more formal. Seats outside on the terrace from where you can enjoy the view.

OPEN: 11–11. Winter 11–2.30, 5–11.
Restaurant. Bar meals lunchtimes.
Children in eating area of cocktail bar. Dogs on leads. Car park. Wheelchair access.
Bedrooms.
Cards: Amex, MasterCard, Switch, Visa.

Earlsferry

Golf Tavern ① 01333 330610
5 Links Road, Earlsferry, Fife KY9 1AW
Free House. Douglas Duncanson, licensee
www.the19th.freeola.com

Facing south with sheltered beaches – and two golf courses – the old fishing port of Elie and the ancient market town of Earlsferry are as one. The Golf Tavern, a low, whitewashed old Victorian-style pub is on the southern edge of the course at Elie, near the 19th hole. The atmosphere and the furniture in the panelled bar are very club-like, with a fire in the grate, gas lighting and a gas cigar lighter on the bar. Golfers, locals and land-bound travellers all flock here. Home-made soups in the bar, also steak sandwiches with a side salad, toasties – that sort of thing. Caledonian Deuchars IPA, 80/-, Guinness and a summer guest beer; all in tip-top condition. No garden but you can admire the golf course.

OPEN: Mon–Thurs 11–12. Fri & Sat 11–1 a.m. Sun 12.30–1 a.m. Oct–Easter Mon–Fri 11–2.30, 5.30–12.
Real Ale.
Children and dogs welcome.
N.B. Sometimes music in lounge but not in bar.

Edinburgh

Bow Bar ① 0131 226 7667
80 West Bow, Edinburgh EH1 2HS
Free House. Helen McLoughlin, licensee

Off Grassmarket, this is a one-room, very traditional drinkers' bar representing the heyday of the late 19th century – all glass mirrors, mahogany panelling, gas fires, and barmen in long white aprons; even the beer pumps are well over 90 years old. Always Deuchars IPA, Belhaven 80/- and Timothy Taylors Landlord, but eight well-kept ales at any one time during the season, chosen from the 400 which are tried during the year. Well over 145 malt whiskies and a choice of gins, rums and vodkas. Cheap and cheerful bar snacks of the filled rolls and pies variety.

OPEN: 12–11.30.
Real Ale. Lunchtime snacks.
No children. Dogs on leads. Wheelchair access possible – one small step.
Cards: most accepted but not Amex and Diners.

Starbank ① 0131 552 4141
64 Laverockbank Road, Edinburgh EH5 3BZ
Free House. Valerie West, licensee

An elegant little stone building on a corner site with wonderful views over the Firth of Forth, this is a friendly, straightforward place serving some of the best regional beers, and of course whisky. Ales change all the time but the Starbank keeps about eight on hand pump, so you can always be assured of a well-chosen range; four regulars – Belhaven 80/- and Sandy Hunter's Ale, Timothy Taylors Landlord and Deuchars IPA; four guests from different English and Scottish brewers. There is also a choice of appealing bar food: home-made soup, paté, roll-mop herring salad, steak and ale pie, home-cooked gammon salad, ploughman's lunch, a vegetarian dish of the day and daily specials. Wines by the glass and a selection of malt whiskies. Seats on the terrace, out of the prevailing wind.

OPEN: Mon–Wed 11–11. Thurs–Sat 11–12. Sun 12.30–11.
Real Ale. No-smoking restaurant.
Children welcome. Dogs on leads. Wheelchair access.
Cards: MasterCard, Visa.
N.B. TV sometimes on.

Elie

Ship Inn ① 01333 330246
The Toft, Elie, Fife KY9 1DT
Free House. Richard & Jill Philip, licensees
e-mail: shipinnelie@aol.com

On a glorious summer day you will probably see the crowd before you see the inn; they will be sitting on the harbour wall encouraging some sporting event that will be taking place on the sand or in the sea below. The hard, sandy beach replaces the village green, though having a cricket match dependent on the tide could be a problem – unique too. Immensely popular, the Ship is a jolly, 'gung-ho' place, not for the fainthearted, though you don't have to join in – you can watch and admire. Every watersport you can think of seems to go on here: windsurfing, water-skiing and sailing in the bay. On a dryer note, the pub organizes its own cricket fixtures and even rugby matches on the sandy beach beyond the beer garden. Licensed since 1838, the Ship has perfected the art of catering for the traveller – and sportsman. Inside is a big downstairs bar, three dining areas – one upstairs – where they serve lunchtime and evening bar food, also a three-course lunch, à la carte dinner and a children's menu. In July and August the beer garden is covered with a marquee in which they have a bar and barbecue and hold occasional beer and jazz festivals. The menu could include Maryland crab cakes, mussels cooked as you like them, devilled mushroom crumble, Ship Inn seafood pie, grilled sea bass, Thai green chicken curry with spicy rice, steak and Guinness pie, pork fillet with peppercorns, steaks, vegetarian and children's dishes. There is also a roast Sunday lunch. Belhaven 80/-, Belhaven Best, Theakstons Best Bitter, draught Guinness, Blackthorn Cider, Tartan Special and a draught lager. Comprehensive wine list and a choice of malt whiskies. The big beer garden overlooks a sandy bay, any cricket or rugby match taking place, and the Firth of Forth.

OPEN: 11–12. Sun 12.30–11.
Real Ale. Restaurant (not Sun eve).
Children in restaurant and lounge bar. Dogs on leads. Wheelchair access.
Cards: Delta, MasterCard, Switch, Visa.
Occasional jazz outside.

Glasgow

Babbity Bowster ① 0141 552 5055
16/18 Blackfriars Street, Glasgow G1 1PE
Free House. Fraser Laurie, licensee

Luckily some of the city escaped 'modernisation' during Victorian times and the 18th-century Babbity Bowster was one of the lucky ones. This elegant renovated Adam town house is in a quiet pedestrianised street in the city's old merchant quarter. With a lively pub-type atmosphere it is tremendously popular with everyone: journalists, businessmen, students, or anyone wanting a refreshing drink from a cup of tea to a glass of the Babbity Bowster's very own beer. They seem to be permanently on the go; really it's more a café/bar with a restaurant and hotel attached than a pub. Breakfast is served at 8.30 and bar snacks from 12 noon until 9 at night. Bar food includes filled baguettes, spicy chicken, haggis, neeps and tatties. Specials from the blackboard include lots of fish dishes: langoustines, oysters, prawns, fresh fish – all with home-baked bread. Barbecued dishes in the summer. The upstairs restaurant has its own menu. Maclays 80/- and a guest beer. This is the only pub in the city centre which has an outside drinking area with seats and tables on a small, flowery terrace.

OPEN: 8–12.
Real Ale. Restaurant.
Children in restaurant. No dogs. Bedrooms.

Counting House ① 0141 225 0160
2 St Vincent Place, Glasgow G2 1EG
Wetherspoon.

From 80ft up, Sir Walter Scott keeps a weather eye over George Square; a square with a statue at every corner, more than any other square in Scotland. The solid and prosperous-looking Counting House was converted from a redundant Royal Bank of Scotland. Out went the safes, in came the beer pumps and they have hardly stopped pumping since. As always, the conversion was sensitively done; it all looks solid and prosperous – just as an ex-bank should. Popular for all the right reasons: efficient, reasonably priced and open, ready to serve you, when others are closed. All the usual Wetherspoon attributes: a selection of local real ales and a reliable, inexpensive, something-for-everyone menu, plus daily specials.

OPEN: 11–12.
Real Ale.
No children. No dogs. All wheelchair facilities.

Three Judges ① 0141 337 3055
141 Dumbarton Road, Partick Cross, Glasgow G11 6PR
Maclay-Alloa. Helen McCarroll, manager

If you're looking for somewhere to taste the best beers brewed in Scotland and the north-east then this is the pub to make for. So many beers have been brought in over the years that they have lost count. Nothing has changed much in the pub though – except the beer. Very much a no-nonsense sort of corner local where Gaelic seems to be the first language. But you wouldn't be here for the language lessons, and possibly not the simple bar snacks – toasties, pork pies – that sort of thing – but for the beer. Nine beers plus a draught farm cider and a good range of whiskies: they feature a 'malt of the month'. Very near the university and the Kelvingrove Art Gallery; the Botanical Gardens are 200 yards away and the Transport Museum just 100 yards along the road. CAMRA award winners since 1992, so you know the beers are in tip-top condition.

OPEN: 11–11. Fri & Sat 11–12. Sun 12.30–11.
Real Ale.
No children. Dogs on leads.
Cards: all accepted.

Ubiquitous Chip ① 0141 334 5007 Fax: 0141 337 1302
12 Ashton Lane, Hillhead, Glasgow G12 8SJ
Free House. Ronnie Clydesdale, licensee
e-mail: ubiquitouschip.co.uk

Going great guns on the ground floor of this old Victorian coach house is the 'Wee Pub at the Chip', where they serve something from a wine selection – reputed to be the best in Scotland – or their choice of 120 malt whiskies or, if you're being abstemious, a cup of excellent coffee. Upstairs is a bigger bar and well-known brasserie-style restaurant where you are served some memorable food. Frequented by university lecturers, students and anyone else who knows a good thing when they find it, the Ubiquitous Chip is in a cobbled lane in the very heart of Glasgow. There is a daily changing menu but there could be home-made soup, oak-smoked fillet of mackerel, chicken and ham paté with Cumberland sauce, honey-roast ham, Aberdeen Angus steak, vegetarian haggis with neeps and tatties, roast chicken piri piri, a fish dish, red onion and tomato salad and yummy puds. A two-or three-course lunch is served in the dining room next to the pretty courtyard. Last but not least, real ales: Caledonian 80/- and Deuchars IPA. Draught Guinness, Addlestone Cask cider and Furstenberg lager.

OPEN: 11–12. Sun 12.30–12.
Real Ale. Restaurant.
No children. Dogs on leads in bar. Wheelchair access to WC.
Cards: Amex, Diners, MasterCard, Switch, Visa.

Killiecrankie

Killiecrankie Hotel ① 01796 473220 Fax: 01796 472451
Killiecrankie, nr Pitlochry, Tayside PH16 5LG
Free House. Colin & Carole Anderson, licensees
e-mail: enquiries@killiecrankiehotel.co.uk

Overlooking the impressive Pass of Killiecrankie where the River Garry rushes past woodlands and steep granite sides, this handsome, early-Victorian hotel is in a beautiful area of Perthshire, midway between Pitlochry and Blair Atholl. In four acres of grounds, it was built as a manse for the local vicar, becoming an hotel in 1939 – not the best timing!

Inside the hotel they provide bar lunches and suppers in the attractive panelled bar and a noted, creative, table d'hôte menu in the elegant dining room. Bar food includes soups, sweet-cured herrings with salad, chicken liver parfait with Cumberland sauce and toast, tapas, home-made chicken goujons served with curried mayonnaise, chargrilled leg of lamb steak with garlic butter, rib-eye steak with garlic and peppercorn butter, Cumberland sausage with onion chutney, ploughman's, honey-roast ham with salad, smoked salmon and prawn open sandwiches, good puddings and cheese to follow. A good, varied wine list and a selection of malt whiskies. You are surrounded by lovely countryside with lots of things to see. The 17th-century mill at Blair Atholl is still working and the smallest distillery in Scotland is north-east of Pitlochry, which also has a theatre festival every year. Go at the right time of the year and you can watch the salmon struggle up a 'fish ladder' at the southern end of Loch Faskally.

OPEN: 11–2.30, 6–11. Closed 3 Jan to mid-February.
No-smoking evening restaurant.
Children welcome. No dogs where food is served. Wheelchair access (not WC). Ten en-suite bedrooms.
Cards: Delta, MasterCard, Switch, Visa.

Kippen

Cross Keys Hotel ① 01786 870293
Main Street, Kippen, Stirlingshire FK8 3DN
Free House. Marjorie Scoular & Gordon Scott, licensees
e-mail: crosskeys@kippen70.fsnet.co.uk

West of Stirling on the road to Loch Lomond, an early 18th-century inn at the centre of a south-facing village. Roses around the door and, inside, a comfortable lounge bar, public bar, family room and small function room. The highly praised, home-cooked food from the daily changing menu could include home-made soup, creamy mousse of Arbroath smokies, Orkney herring fillet marinated in sherry, casserole of hill lamb with tomato and fresh rosemary, home-made lasagne, their own-recipe steak and mushroom pie, smoked salmon omelette, plus specials, vegetarian dishes and a choice of puddings. Children's portions. The real ales change on a rota system; there are lots of malt whiskies and an inclusive wine list. Seats in the garden.

OPEN: 12–2.30, 5.30–11. Sat 12–12. Sun 12.30–11.
Real Ale. Choice of dining areas including no-smoking area.
Children welcome. Dogs in bar, and can stay. Wheelchair access into hotel and ladies' WC. Bedrooms.
Cards: Delta, MasterCard, Switch, Visa.
N.B. Music in public bar.

Melrose

Burts Hotel ① 01896 822285
Market Square, Melrose, Borders TD6 9PL
Free House. Graham Henderson, licensee
e-mail: burtshotel@aol.com

In the very heart of border country, the small town of Melrose on the banks of the River Tweed is the centre of Sir Walter Scott country and surrounded by wonderful countryside. The early 18th-century Burts Hotel, originally a private house, is among other contemporary buildings in the attractive Market Square. This listed building, has been carefully extended to create this well-run hotel where you have the best of both worlds: a relaxing, informal lounge bar where they serve lunch and supper and a more formal, elegant restaurant. Consistently good, creative menus feature the 'best of Scottish': Loch Fyne mussels in garlic cream, venison and game paté, local lamb and haggis in various guises, escalopes of Scottish smoked salmon with a dill and wine cream sauce, Aberdeen Angus steak and other dishes with a more cosmopolitan touch. Deuchars IPA and Caledonian 80/- are the regular beers. They have enough varieties of whisky to keep you happy for a very long time and an extensive wine list.

OPEN: 11–2, 5–11. Sun 12–2, 6–11.
Real Ale. Restaurant.
Children welcome. Dogs in bar. Car park. Bedrooms.
Cards: Amex, Delta, MasterCard, Switch, Visa.

Netherley

Lairhillock Inn ① 01569 730001
Netherley, nr Stonehaven AB39 3QS
Free House. Roger and Angela Thorne, licensees
www.lairhillock.co.uk

The smart yet traditional Lairhillock is a 200-year-old coaching inn surrounded by miles of gentle, undulating countryside off the B979, midway between Aberdeen and Stonehaven. Inside is a snug bar and lounge, both with good fires, a no-smoking conservatory with a view and an adjoining restaurant – the 'Crynoch', which, like the pub, serves some really exceptional food. They take full advantage of the fact that they are in the midst of plenty: Aberdeen Angus beef, mussels from Shetland, scallops from Orkney, wild boar and venison from the Highlands, wild salmon from the Dee and Don and langoustines from Gourdon. So from the bar there will always be chef's soup of the day, ploughman's with cheese from their selection of British cheeses, terrine or paté, maybe smoked salmon salad, Cullen skink – a traditional smoked-fish soup – spicy spare ribs, Aberdeen Angus steaks and home-made sausages as well as daily specials. Beers are Timothy Taylors Landlord, Hebridean Gold from the Isle of Skye, something from the

Inveralmond brewery in Perth and from Belhaven. The wine list in the restaurant is exceptional; a shorter version is available in the bar.

OPEN: 11–2.30, 5–11. Sat 11–12. Sun 11–11. Winter: 12–2, 6.30–9.30 (Sat 6.30–10, Sun 5.30–9).
Real Ale. Restaurant.
Children in eating areas. Dogs in snug bar. Car park. Wheelchair access.
Cards: most cards accepted.

Pitlochry

Moulin Hotel ① 01796 472196
11–13 Kirkmichael Road, Moulin, nr Pitlochry, Tayside PH16 5EW
Free House. Heather Reeves, licensee
e-mail: hotel@moulin.u-net.com

Here you are in what is claimed to be the geographical centre of Scotland – the Highlands, surrounded by mountains, lochs, rivers and woodland. The village of Moulin, on the outskirts of Pitlochry, is at the foot of the 2760ft-high Ben Vrackie. Tourists and walkers abound. The Moulin, originally a coaching inn, is warm, friendly and popular. The oldest part of the hotel was here in the late 17th century, well established when Bonnie Prince Charlie passed through Moulin on his way to the battlefield of Culloden in 1746. Extended over the years, the bar in the old area is very 'pub-like', traditionally furnished and with log fires. They serve good, reasonably priced food: home-made soups, sandwiches and filled baked potatoes, tomato and aubergine tartlet, Skye mussels, grilled salmon, Angus steaks, haggis, neeps and tatties of course, lasagne, game casserole McDuff, vegetarian dishes, specials and comfort puds. From their own microbrewery – in the old coach house – a Light Ale, Old Remedial, Moulin Ale of Atholl, Braveheart, and maybe a guest beer. Folk music on Friday evenings, but apart from that – music-free. Seats outside among the tubs of flowers.

OPEN: 11–11. Sun 12–11.
Real Ale. Restaurant.
Children welcome. Dogs too. Car park. Wheelchair access. Bedrooms in the new part of the hotel.
Cards: MasterCard, Visa.

St Mary's Loch

Tibbie Shiels Inn ① 01750 42231
St Mary's Loch, Selkirk, Borders TD7 5NE
Free House. Jill Brown, licensee
e-mail: tibbies@faxvia.net

Built on the finger of land separating St Mary's Loch and the Loch of the Lowes, this inn was named after Isabella Shiel, a redoubtable 19th-century landlady. St Mary's Loch is a very popular sailing and fishing centre and the whitewashed inn a welcoming sight for walkers on the long-distance Southern Upland Way, which conveniently passes the door. This is a lonely spot, only the inn, the loch and rolling, treeless hills. Over the years the inn has been extended since those heady days when Mrs Sheil managed to find space for 35 chaps during the shooting season, many of them on the floor! Meals are served in either the bar or no-smoking dining room; the menu includes soups, ploughman's, Holy Mole chilli salad and garlic bread and a spicy chicken. The fresh local Yarrow trout, salmon, escalope of pork with ginger wine sauce, queen scallops with a bacon and cream sauce are among the favourites. Some vegetarian dishes and a variety of puddings. Broughton Green Mantle and Belhaven 80/- on hand pump. Selection of wines and over 50 malt whiskies. Lots of sailing and fishing on St Mary's Loch; walks too.

OPEN: 11–11. Sat 11–12. Sun 12.30–11. Closed Mon–Wed Nov–Easter.
Real Ale. Restaurant.
Children welcome. No dogs. Wheelchair access throughout the inn. Bedrooms, all en suite.
Cards: Delta MasterCard, Solo, Switch, Visa.

St Monance

Seafood Restaurant & Bar ① 01333 730327
16 West End, St Monance, Fife KY10 2BY
Free House. Tim Butler, licensee

Stone walls and pantiles on the roofs make this fishing village typical of the area. This restaurant overlooks the small working harbour, busy with boat building and repairs, the Isle of May and the Firth of Forth. There is a definite lean towards the nautical here, the local mariners feel very much at home in the cosy, woodlined, windowless bar – very cabin-like – behind which is an excellent seafood restaurant – with windows. As you have gathered, the emphasis is on seafood: home-made soup, oysters, smoked fish, langoustines, and, well, just lots and lots of fish. Duck, chicken and pork in various guises feature too. Justly very popular. Food is served only in the restaurant and on the terrace in summer. If you want a beer, they have Belhaven 80/-, St Andrews and a changing guest. Modest wine list and a good selection of malt whiskies. Tables on the terrace; you eat with a view.

OPEN: 12–3, 6–11. Sun 12.30–11. Closed Mon and three weeks in January.
Real Ale.
Children in restaurant. Dogs on leads in bar.

Shieldaig

Shieldaig Bar ① 01520 755251
Shieldaig on Loch Torridon, Ross-shire IV54 8XN
Free House. Mr & Mrs C. Field, owners/licensees
e-mail: tighaneileanhotel@shieldag.fsnet.co.uk

A small, unassuming hotel on the edge of Loch Shieldaig, off Loch Torridon; spectacular scenery surrounds this small village of whitewashed, slate-roofed cottages and its hotel. The huge sandstone mountains on the far side of the loch are over 750 million years old. The village of Shieldaig, however, was only created by the Admiralty in 1800 to train seamen at the height of the Napoleonic wars; the windows in the locals' bar looks out to the sea. In the bar, the well-chosen, daily changing menu ranges from sandwiches, soups, salmon and seafood to daily specials which could include Shieldaig crab bisque, marinated Orkney herring, Shieldaig bar seafood stew, oxtail stew with fresh vegetables, Hebridean scallop mornay, creamy vegetable crumble, always a choice of fresh fish and good puddings. The fish dishes depend on what is available that day. There is also an evening restaurant in the adjacent Tigh an Eilean hotel, and comprehensive wine list. Tables and chairs in a front courtyard overlook the loch. Excellent walking country.

OPEN: 11–11. Sun 11–10. Winter: 11–2.30, 5–11.Sat 11–11. Sun 12.30–10.
Evening restaurant April–October. Bar food all year.
Children until 8 p.m. No dogs. Wheelchair access. Bedrooms.
Cards: MasterCard, Visa.

Strachur

Creggans Inn ① 01369 860279
Strachur, Argyll PA27 8BX
Free House. Robertson family, owners
e-mail: info@creggans-inn.co.uk

Painted white, with a slate roof and touches of dark-green wood, the Creggans looks a typical Scottish inn. On the shore of Loch Fyne, just feet from the water's edge, it has the most wonderful views over the loch to the hills beyond. Being so close to the water they can provide five yacht moorings for those of you who prefer to sail in, and a perfectly ample car park for the more traditional arrival. Built early in the 19th century, the Creggans has grown from a small coaching inn into the quietly elegant, accommodating place you see today. In the smart panelled bar (fire in here), there is a wonderful variety of dishes to choose from. From the daily changing menu there could be a soup of the day, cullen skink – smoked haddock soup – haggis timbale, oysters from Loch Fyne, cod in crisp beer batter, grilled lamb cutlets with red onion marmalade and dauphinoise potatoes, steak pie, venison sausages, always the freshest of seafood from the loch, Loch Fyne smoked salmon and sirloin steak with a pepper sauce. The dinner menu will be more creative and extensive. Delicious puds and Scottish cheeses. The ales are Belhaven Best, St Andrews ale and two revolving guests which could include beers from the local Fyne Brewery. A choice of malt whiskies and an interesting wine list. Woodland walks on the surrounding MacLean estate.

OPEN: 11–1 a.m.
Real Ale. Restaurant.
Children welcome, dogs too (only in the bar). Car park. Yacht mooring. Fourteen bedrooms, all en suite.
Cards: Delta, MasterCard, Switch, Visa.
N.B. Jukebox in public bar but the rest of the hotel is music-free.

Strathtummel

Loch Tummel Inn ① 01882 634272
Strathtummel, by Pitlochry, Perthshire PH16 5RP
Free House. Michael & Liz Marsden, owners/licensees

When you arrive here you are in a gentle, intimate landscape around the beautiful, tree-fringed shores of Loch Tummel and only three miles from the famous 'Queen's View' – named after, and much favoured by, Queen Victoria. There are also wonderful views over the loch from the inn. Not only can you admire the scenery but you can explore the Perthshire countryside, fish in the loch, attend the festival theatre at Pitlochry, visit Blair Atholl or just have a good, long walk. Family run, this is a handsome, comfortable, stone-built old coaching inn. The bar, in the old stables, serves informal meals, Braveheart Ale – from the brewery at Moulin – Guinness and anything else you want to drink. A more formal restaurant is in the old hay-loft. Whatever you've been doing, you are bound to have an appetite for the freshly prepared dishes: soup of the day with home-made bread, oak-smoked salmon with brown bread, chicken-liver paté with oatcakes, haggis with creamed turnip, baked Arbroath smokie with bacon, game pie or griddled Angus rib-eye steak with mushrooms and onions. Vegetarian dishes are available and the specials and puddings are on the blackboard. Well-balanced wine list. Fantastic views from most of the rooms.

OPEN: 11–11. Sun 12.30–11. Closed from end October–Easter.
Real Ale. Restaurant.
Children welcome. Dogs on leads. Car park. Wheelchair access (not WC). Six bedrooms, some with log fires.

Tayvallich

Tayvallich Inn ① 01546 870282
Tayvallich by Lochgilphead, Strathclyde PA31 8PL
Free House. Roddy Anderson, licensee
e-mail: tayvallich.inn@virgin.net

Tucked into a sheltered, wooded inlet off Loch Sween, this small 18th-century fishing village now concentrates on the energetic holiday-maker who appreciates walks in Knapdale forest, along the loch, swimming off the safe beaches and sailing in the sheltered waters. The Tayvallich is not a conventional inn, more a successful restaurant and bar on the edge of a perfect, natural harbour off Loch Sween. In good weather the glass doors in the conservatory are opened onto the terrace so you can sit and admire the view and any yachts at anchor. The bar and restaurant menus offer a wonderful variety of shellfish. They specialise in seafood, so there could be Loch Sween moules marinière, Loch Sween oysters, pickled herring with a dill and mustard mayonnaise, pan-fried Sound of Jura scallops, whole jumbo prawn salad with lime mayonnaise, seafood platter and, of course, smoked salmon. Not forgotten, though, is the grilled prime Scottish sirloin or fillet steak, vegetarian dishes and, last but not least, scrummy home-made puddings on the

blackboard and Scottish blue cheese to finish. Choice of wines and malt whiskies plus: Tennents Velvet Ember, Deuchars IPA, Stella Artois, Strongbow cider and Guinness.

OPEN: 11–12. Sat 11–1 a.m. Closed Mon Nov–March.
Restaurant.
Children in eating areas. Dogs on leads after food has been served. Car park. Wheelchair access difficult.
Cards: all cards accepted.

BEST OF THE REST

Aboyne, Grampian
Boat Inn ① 01339 886137
Charleston Road, Aboyne AB34 5EL
On the north bank of the river Dee, near the bridge, this is a tremendously popular riverside pub with an unusual attraction: a model train occasionally chuffing around the bar above head height, to the amusement of many. At ground level they run a normal pub serving some really good food, a wide range of vegetarian dishes and very well-kept beers. Draught Bass and beers from Scottish independent breweries. Children welcome, dogs too – in bar. Wheelchair access. Self catering flat.
Open: 11–2.30, 5–11. Sat 11–12. Sun 11–11.

Brig o'Turk, Stirling
Byre Inn ① 01877 376292
Brig o' Turk FK17 8HT
What was a Victorian cow byre is now a small, cosy inn with stone walls, beams and a fine open fire. Leading a quiet, local life during the winter, it becomes hugely popular during the summer months with tourists and walkers. Simple lunchtime menus, otherwise good, generous, home-cooked dishes using lots of local produce helping to create a varied menu: mussels in garlic and white wine, game pie, maybe chicken, bacon with a whisky and mustard sauce or venison with port and redcurrant sauce, also dishes with a touch of the exotic. Maclays 70/- and Wallace IPA, also Guinness and good choice of malt whiskies. Children welcome. No dogs. Wheelchair access.
Open: 12–3, 6–11. Sun 12–11. Closed Mon.

Carbost, Skye
Old Inn ① 01478 640245
Carbost IV47 8SE
Slightly tricky to find and a map isn't going to be much good – it might point you in the right direction, but as there is no obvious sign saying 'Old Inn', it's a bit of a guess to know if you've actually arrived. When you do, there are several things to attract you. Firstly it is on the shores of Loch Harport, making it a good place for refreshment if you plan to walk, climb or sail; secondly they serve good filling bar food, including home-made soup and some fine Scottish cheeses, and last but not least, they are very near Talisker malt whisky distillery – summer guided tours available complete with samples. Children in eating area. Bedrooms.
Open: 11–12. Sun 12.30–11. Winter 11–2.30, 5–11. Closed Mon–Wed Jan & Feb.

Edinburgh
Guildford Arms ☺ 0131 556 4312
West Register Street, Edinburgh EH2 2AA
There are lots of reasons to make your way to this hugely popular city pub. They always have a tremendous range of beers for you to try – eleven usually, mostly from Scottish breweries -, but you are also here to appreciate your surroundings – an exuberant Victorian pub interior at its best: painted plasterwork and ceilings, mahogany fittings, huge mirrors and swagged velvet. Filling bar food of the chargrilled beefburger, fish and steak pie variety, but it is always busy – one of the most popular in Edinburgh. No children.
Open: 11–11.

Fort Augustus, Highland
Lock Inn ☺ 01320 366302
Canalside PH32 4AU
A village stretching along the six locks that bring the Caledonian canal from Loch Oich into Loch Ness. Find the first lock and you'll find the Lock Inn. Stone walls, beams and open fire, this old post office is a popular, welcoming place. The good, interesting menu could include Loch Fyne mussels, grilled trout, venison casserole, seafood stew or something from the specials board. Always very fresh fish; the beers are from Scottish breweries and there are about 100 malts for you to work through. Children welcome.
Open: 11–11.

Glendevon, Perth & Kinross
Tormaukin Hotel ☺ 01259 781252
Glendevon FK14 7JY
An extended 18th-century drovers' inn where you will be well looked after and very well fed. Home-made soup, pâté and ploughman's and there could be a fish casserole, pork and pineapple, steaks, or a beef and Guinness pie. Daily specials too. Harviestoun beers, a decent wine list and several malts. Lots of places to walk. Bedrooms.
Open: all day.

Inverarnan, Stirling
Inverarnan Inn ☺ 01301 704234
Inverarnan
Atmospheric 16th-century building – faded grandeur sums it up but there's certainly no mistaking which country you're in when you go through the door: tartan, kilts, bagpipes, deerskins and a golden eagle – dead and stuffed. No identity crisis here. Hearty bar food: Scotch broth, toasted sandwiches, steak pie – that sort of thing – and they can put their hands on over 100 malts for you to try. Children in eating areas. Bedrooms.
Open: 11–11.

Kilberry, Argyll
Kilberry Inn ☺ 01880 770223
Kilberry PA29 6YD
A red phone box and a low, traditional, white-painted re-roofed inn 16 winding miles around the single-track road from Tarbert (overlooked by the stronghold of Robert the Bruce) and Lochgilphead (B8024), giving you plenty of time to work up an appetite for the delights on offer at the Kilberry Inn and appreciate the spectacular views across the

loch to Gigha. Given an award for 'bar meal of the year', favourites can always be found
but the menu is constantly changing. Scottish bottled beers, a choice of malt whiskies.
Children in family room. No dogs. Wheelchair access. Bedrooms.
Open: 11–11. Sun 12–6. Closed Sun eve late Oct–end March.

Kilmahog, Stirling
Lade Inn ① 01877 330152
Kilmahog FK17 8HD
Not far from Callender and, if you're interested, the Rob Roy and Trossachs visitor centre.
In the glorious Pass of Leny, Kilmahog and The Lade is where the A821 meets the A84.
When you've finished admiring the scenery you will find some really good, freshly home-
made food here. Always soups, lunchtime sandwiches and daily specials. On the menu
there could be vegetable pancakes, game casserole and grilled trout. Heather Froach (when
available), Broughton Greenmantle and Orkney Red MacGregor beers and a good wine
list. Children in eating area of bar. Dogs welcome.
Open: 12–3, 5.30–11. Sat 12–12. Sun 12.30–11.

Minnigaff, Dumfries & Galloway
Creebridge House Hotel ① 01671 402121
Minnigaff DG8 6NP
Built in the mid 18th century for the Earl of Galloway, this is a handsome place
surrounded by acres of glorious gardens and woodland. There's much to admire, and they
do pretty well on the food front too. An interesting menu lists the bar usuals and could
include a crispy duck salad, fillet of sea bass or beef stroganoff with wild mushrooms and
brandy, daily specials and good puds. Orkney Dark Island, Tetley and Marstons Pedigree
beers as well as a very good selection of malts. Children and dogs welcome. Wheelchair
access (not WC). Bedrooms.
Open: 12–2.30, 6–11.

Mountbenger, Selkirk
Gordon Arms Hotel ① 01750 82232
Yarrow Valley, Mountbenger TD7 5LE
When you land on the doorstep of the Gordon Arms you find a very welcome retreat from
the bleak and rugged moorland that surrounds you. This is serious walking country; the
village is remote, in rolling border hills. With a new regime things have changed, moving
away from the hearty sustaining food of the past towards French and Italian cooking.
Changes too, with the introduction of background jazz, so they have been demoted. But if
it's a case of any port in a storm, it is friendly and accommodating with open fires in the
bars to warm you up in cold weather and a choice of malts. Particularly geared up to the
walker/cyclist/bird-watcher, it has a cleverly converted bunkhouse which offers clean,
warm, basic accommodation. Broughtons Greenmantle Ghillie is the beer. Over 50 malt
whiskies. Trout and salmon fishing can be arranged. Fantastic, wild scenery. Children in
eating area.
Open: 11–11. Sat 11–12.

Portpatrick, Dumfries & Galloway
Crown ① 01776 810261
North Crescent, Portpatrick DG9 8SX
In an attractive fishing village and a short step from the harbour, so if you pick the right
moment you can watch your fish sail in on the boat that caught it. A busy, friendly old
place that will have a good choice of the usual bar favourites, as well as very local prawns,

scallops, lobster and so on. No beer to speak of, but they have over 200 malts and a decent wine list. Children welcome. Bedrooms.
Open: 12–11.30.

Swinton, Borders

Wheatsheaf Hotel ① 01890 860257
Main Street, Swinton, Duns TD11 3JJ
Rooms have shifted around a bit since our last edition. There has been 'an element of refurbishment', as one unforgettable American Ambassador said to the Queen years ago. Everywhere is looking very smart and the old public bar is now the lounge bar with a piscatorial theme – well, there's a lot of fishing on the Tweed only a few miles away. This handsome stone building faces the green in a village tucked in the gentle, wooded border landscape. Warm, friendly and tremendously popular with everyone: locals, tourists and fishermen. Deuchars IPA, Caledonian 70/- and one guest beer. Extensive wine list, six house wines and choice of malt whiskies. This is a very touristy area, with lots of things to do and see: Abbotsford, Sir Walter Scott's home, is nearby, racing at Kelso, fishing on the River Tweed and you're not far from the historic city of Berwick-on-Tweed or Coldstream (Battle of Flodden Field, 1513). Children welcome. Dogs on leads. Car park. Six en-suite bedrooms. Cards: Delta, MasterCard, Switch, Visa.
Open: 11.30–11. Closed Sun eve.

Wetherspoon in Scotland

Aberdeen – Archibald Simpson, Castle Street
① 01224 621365
Airdrie – Robert Hamilton, 12–14 Bank Street
① 01236 771110
Arbroath – Corn Exchange, Market Place
① 01241 432430
Ayr – West Kirk, 58a Sandgate
① 01292 880416
Bathgate – James Young, 32 Hopetoun Street
① 01506 651600
Coatbridge – Vulcan, 181 Main Street
① 01236 437972
Dumfries – Robert the Bruce, 81–83 Buccleuch Street
① 01387 270320
Dundee – Counting House, 67–71 Reform Street
① 01382 225251
Edinburgh – Standing Order, George Street, Edinburgh
① 0131 225 4460
Elgin – Muckle Cross, 34 High Street
① 01343 559030
Falkirk – Carron Works, Bank Street
① 01324 673020
Galashiels – Hunter's Hall, 56–58 High Street
① 01896 759795
Glasgow – Counting House, 2 St Vincents Place
① 0141 248 9568
Glasgow – Crystal Palace, 36 Jamaica Street
① 0141 221 2624

Glasgow – Edward Wylie, 103–107 Bothwell Street
① 0141 229 5480

Glasgow – Esquire House, 1487 Great Western Road
① 0141 341 1130

Glasgow – Hengler's Circus, 351–363 Sauchiehall Street
① 0141 331 9810

Glasgow – Kirky Puffer, 1 Townhead, Kirkintilloch
① 0141 222 1780

Glasgow – Sir John Moore, Argyle Street
① 0141 222 1780

Glasgow – Sir John Stirling Maxwell, 140 Kilmarnock Road
① 0141 636 9024

Glenrothes – Golden Acorn (also a Wetherspoon Lodge), 1 North Street
① 01592 755252

Greenock – James Watt, 80–92 Cathcart Street
① 01475 722640

Inverness – King's Highway (also a Wetherspoon Lodge), 72–74 Church Street
① 01463 251830

Kilmarnock – Wheatsheaf Inn, Unit 5, Portland Gate
① 01563 572483

Kirkcaldy – Robert Nairn, 6 Kirk Wynd
① 01592 205049

Lanark – Clydesdale Inn, 15 Bloomgate
① 01555 678740

Leith – Foot of the Walk, 183 Constitution Street
① 0131 553 0120

Livingstone – Wetherspoons, Almondvale Boulevard
① 01506 424190

Motherwell – Brandon Works, 45–61 Merry Street
① 01698 358806

Paisley – Last Post, County Square
① 0141 848 0353

Perth – Capital Asset, 26 Tay Street
① 01738 580457

Saltcoats – Salt Cot, 7 Hamilton Street
① 01294 465924

Wick – Alexander Bain, Market Place
① 01955 609920

Wishaw – Wishaw Malt, 62–66 Kirk Road
① 01698 358806

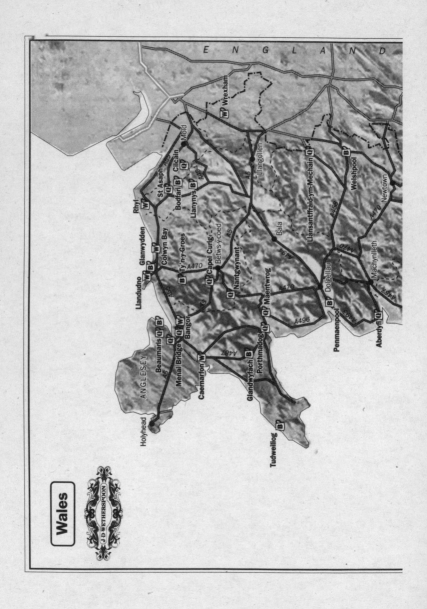

Wales

J D WETHERSPOON

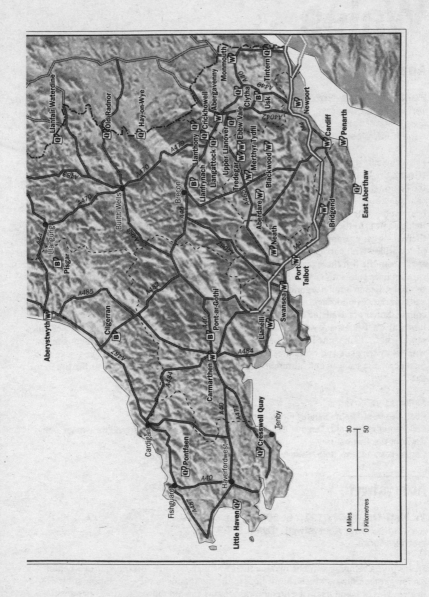

Wales

Aberdyfi

Penhelig Arms Hotel ① 01654 767215
Terrace Road, Aberdyfi, Gwynedd LL35 OLT
Free House. Robert & Sally Hughes, licensees
e-mail: info@penheligarms.com

In an enviable position in this attractive seaside resort on the beautiful, wooded Dyfi estuary, the 18th-century cream-painted Penhelig Arms looks across the estuary towards the National Nature Reserve on the other side. On the edge of the busy harbour, this charming hotel has above-average accommodation, an excellent restaurant and small beamed bar where they serve imaginative lunchtime and more extensive evening menus. Being so near to the sea, they are really big on fish. There are fresh deliveries every day so there is always a considerable variety to choose from: steamed fillet of salmon with salad; plaice grilled with parsley and lemon; chargrilled tuna with aioli. Menus change daily and apart from the fish there could be linguini with tomato and basil sauce, fresh dressed crab, chicken liver paté with crostini, grilled lamb's liver and bacon with onion gravy, lamb shank braised in a red burgundy sauce with winter vegetables, English and Welsh cheeses and a variety of puddings. An inventive, reasonably priced two-course lunch and three-course dinner are available in the no-smoking restaurant; also a three-course Sunday lunch. If it's just a snack you're after there will always be a home-made soup and well-filled sandwiches. Champagne by the glass if you want to be indulgent. A well-chosen wine list with 30 by the glass and beers that change every two weeks. In warm weather you can sit outside by the sea wall and admire the view; in winter tuck yourself up near the fire in the bar.

OPEN: 11–3, 6–11.
Real Ale. Restaurant. Sunday lunch in bar or restaurant.
Children in restaurant. Dogs in bar. Bedrooms – all with private bathrooms – most with views of the Dyfi estuary.
Cards: MasterCard, Solo, Switch, Visa.

Aberystwyth

Yr Hen Orsaf ① 01970 636080
Alexandra Road, Aberystwyth, Dyfed SY23 1LN
Wetherspoon.

Steam train enthusiasts will be making their way here for a trip on the Vale of Rheidol narrow-gauge railway, which climbs high in the mountains to the tiny station at Devil's Bridge. The Yr Hen Orsaf (the literal translation is 'the old railway station') has a very civilized covered terrace where you can wait for your train or just watch all the comings and goings with a good pint and a snack in hand. As with all Wetherspoon places you will find something for everyone: salads, light bites, filled baps and jacket potatoes, curries, vegetarian dishes, and traditional main dishes – bangers and mash, Aberdeen angus pie, fish and chips – all well cooked and enjoyable. Always reasonably priced beer, a short wine list, champagne and almost anything else you might fancy.

OPEN: 11–11.
Real Ale.
No children. No dogs. Wheelchair access.

Bangor

Union Hotel ① 01248 362462
Garth Road, Bangor, Gwynedd LL57 2SF
Burtonwood. John Duggan, tenant

Near the pier and next to the local boatyard and yacht basin, this spacious pub, known as the Union Garth, is full of bits and pieces – all with a distinctly nautical theme; even the view of Snowdonia from the small garden at the back of the pub is seen through a forest of yacht masts. The Menai Strait and the wide sweep of Conwy Bay are favourite sailing areas. The Union serves a traditional, generous bar menu of soups, ploughman's, paté, smoked mussels and salads, omelettes, grilled gammon, steaks, filled baked potatoes, home-made steak and kidney pie throughout the year; seafood salads in summer. Burtonwood Ales and a guest beer. Seats in the small garden. You might like to know that the Bishop's Garden in Bangor has a collection of all the plants mentioned in the Bible – well, those that survive a Welsh winter – well worth a visit.

OPEN: All permitted hours. No food Tues eve.
Real Ale.
Quiet children welcome, but not in bar. Dogs on leads.
Bedrooms. Wheelchair access (not WC).

Beaumaris

Ye Olde Bulls Head ① 01248 810329 Fax: 01248 811294
Castle Street, Beaumaris, Anglesey LL58 8AP
Free House. David Robertson, licensee
e-mail: info@bullsheadinn.co.uk
www.bullsheadinn.co.uk

A very historic building in an ancient, elegant town dominated by Edward I's huge, impressive moated castle; the last in a series of fortresses built in an effort to control the troublesome Welsh. Nearby, the imposing Grade II-listed Bulls Head has its own place in history: in 1645 one of Cromwell's generals moved in and used it as his base whilst his troops laid siege to the castle. The plain, timeless exterior hides a building that is part 15th but mostly early 17th century. The inside reflects its long history: oak beams, open fires and interesting artifacts collected over the years including the town's original ducking stool – kept in reserve! The bar is for drinking only; you eat in the brasserie (music played here in the evening), or the restaurant. Brasserie menus change every two months but there are always specials on the blackboard – and the food here really is special. You could choose a home-made soup, carpaccio of beef with a roquette salad, walnut oil and parmesan, bruschetta of chargrilled chicken with roquette, tapenade, peppers and pesto, cassolette of seafood in a cream, saffron and dill sauce, braised Welsh lamb with vegetables and mint gravy or chargrilled rib-eye steak with garlic mash and black peppercorn sauce, pasta, salads, vegetarian dishes and freshly filled sandwiches. Delicious puds too. There is a very good, inventive restaurant menu too – the Bulls Head has become *the* place to eat in Beaumaris. Bass, Worthington and a guest beer. Broad selection of wines, some by the glass.

OPEN: 11–11.
Real Ale. Restaurant (not Sun). Brasserie open seven days a week for lunch and dinner. Children until 8 p.m. (none under seven in restaurant). No dogs. Car park. Wheelchair access to brasserie only. Bedrooms.
Cards: Amex, Delta, JCB, MasterCard, Switch, Visa.

Caernarvon

Tafarn Y Porth ① 01286 662920
5–9 Eastgate Street, Caernarvon, Gwynedd LL55 1AG
Wetherspoon

Narrow streets, medieval houses and inns shelter under the impressive walls of the old town, the ceremonial capital of Wales. Edward I built the imposing castle and his son, born here in 1284, was the first Prince of Wales. Next to the castle, this place has some very ancient roots: the foundations of the building rest on the remains of the original bridge leading to the castle entrance. As you would expect from Wetherspoon, everything else is firmly in the 21st century. The menu lets you choose from a filled bap to a curry or a mixed grill. Always reasonably priced beer and a choice of wines. Outside is a spacious terrace and garden.

OPEN: 11–11.
Real Ale.
No children. No dogs. Wheelchair access.

Capel Curig

Bryn Tyrch Hotel ① 01690 720 223
Capel Curig, Betws-y-Coed, Conwy LL24 0EL
Free House. Rita Davis, licensee

Snowdonia National Park is a wild and varied landscape of tremendous importance to both climbers and walkers. Equally important is this welcoming country pub, truly in a league of its own. For over a hundred years it has been a base for visitors to this area – huge fires, appealing menus, good beer and fruit wines for you to try. One thing makes this place stand out from the rest: it specializes in vegetarian and vegan cooking, though if you insist, they do cater for the rest of us. The changing menus are inventive and use wholefoods, seasonal fruit and vegetables and fresh herbs. All the puddings, including the vegan, are freshly made. Flowers IPA, Bass and Castle Eden are the beers, and they have a balanced wine list. Outside there is a steep little garden.

OPEN: Mon–Thurs 5–11. Fri–Sun 12–11.
Real Ale.
Children and dogs welcome. Car park. Bedrooms.
Cards: all except Amex.

Cilcain

White Horse ① 01352 740142
The Square, Cilcain, Flintshire CH7 5NN
Free House. Peter Jeory, licensee
e-mail: christine.jeory@btopenworld.com

In a glorious area, tucked into the foothills of the Clwydian Range, near Offa's Dyke Path and close to Loggerheads Country Park, the old White Horse has several low-beamed bars with big fires and settles. Dogs – with their minders – and walkers with muddy boots have to use the quarry-tiled public bar. They serve good, hearty, home-made food, using mostly local produce (including free-range eggs and organically grown vegetables): filled baps, ploughman's, three-egg omelettes, grilled steaks, breaded fillets of haddock, vegetarian dishes and a variety of puddings. Their very own steak and kidney pies – highly praised – are made with their own butter shortcrust pastry. The home-made specials on the blackboard change daily. Banks Ale plus two weekly changing guests; CAMRA pub of the year, so you know the beers are well kept; a selection of wines and farm ciders. Seats at the side of the pub.

OPEN: 12–3, 6.30–11. Sat 12–11. Sun 12–10.30.
Real Ale.
No children inside pub. Dogs on leads. Wheelchair access (not WC).
Cards: MasterCard, Solo, Switch, Visa.

Clytha

Clytha Arms ①/Fax: 01873 840206
Clytha, nr Abergavenny, Monmouthshire NP7 9BW
Free House. Andrew, Sarah & Beverley Canning, licensees

In its own lovely gardens, the delightful Clytha is in country off the old Abergavenny/Raglan road. Inside, the Clytha has a good-sized country bar – with a dartboard – favoured by the locals, a smaller lounge bar with log fires and a restaurant. They serve good, reasonably priced country dishes on the bar menu: the usual sandwiches and ploughman's, faggots and peas with beer and onion gravy, smoked salmon and scrambled egg, liver, bacon and onions, wild boar sausages with potato pancakes, grilled queen scallops, dish of cockles, as well as specials from the blackboard. The no-smoking, more formal restaurant has a separate, more expensive menu featuring regional specialities, including Welsh beef and local lamb. Excellent three-course Sunday lunch. Felinfoel Double Dragon, Bass and Bullmastiff Gold Brew ales, plus an interesting selection of three guest beers, Old Rosie Scrumpy cider and a guest cider. An extensive wine list includes some Welsh wines and ten house wines. Attractive gardens and wonderful walks along the banks of the River Usk – not too far away – and through the grounds of Clytha Castle.

OPEN: 11.30–3.30, 6–11. Sat 11–11. Closed Mon lunchtimes except bank holidays.
Real Ale. No bar snacks or restaurant Sun or Mon eves.
Children welcome. No dogs. Car park.
Cards: Amex, Delta, MasterCard, Switch, Visa.

Cresswell Quay

Cresselly Arms ① 01646 651210
Cresswell Quay, Kilgetty, Dyfed SA68 OTE
Free House. Maurice & Janet Cole, licensees

The timeless, creeper-covered Cresselly Arms is little changed since early last century. It's on the edge of the Cresswell river, so you can sail right in if the tide is right. Three little rooms inside, one with an open fire. No bar as such: your pint is still served from the cask into large jugs. A jolly, friendly, traditional pub serving good beer as well as a crisp or a nut. Worthington BB, a local ale, also Guinness, Two Cannons Xtra or Heineken. Seats outside to watch the watery coming and goings. Not too far from Carew, its ruined 13th-century castle (open most days), and the only 19th-century Welsh tidal mill on the Carew River (restored, and open daily during the summer).

OPEN: 11–3, 5–11. Sat 11–11.
Real Ale. No food.
No children. No dogs.

Crickhowell

Nantyffin Cider Mill ① 01873 810775 (also fax)
Brecon Road, Crickhowell NP8 1SG
Free House. Glyn Bridgeman & Sean Gerrard, licensees

Outside Crickhowell in a glorious area at the foot of the Black Mountains, the large and appealing Nantyffin is more a restaurant than a pub. Converted from a 16th-century cider mill, it now has a main bar, an informal eating area and a no-smoking restaurant in the barn which still contains the old cider press. Well known for its excellent way of using mostly local produce. You could have a bowl of home-made soup, an open prawn sandwich, a delicious omelette, fishcakes such as you have never had before, oak-smoked salmon or something more substantial – such as roast rack of Welsh lamb. Always three real ales – Buckley IPA and two guests – and always three draught ciders. About 90 wines on the list – mostly New World vintages. Views towards the River Usk – on the other side of the road – from the garden.

OPEN: 12–2.30, 6–11. Sun 12–3, 7–10.30. Closed Mon and Tues in winter.
Real Ale. Restaurant – music in here.
Children welcome. Dogs in the bar only – do ask first. Big car park. Wheelchair access.
Bedrooms.
Cards: Amex, Delta, MasterCard, Switch, Visa.

East Aberthaw

Blue Anchor Inn ① 01446 750329
East Aberthaw, South Glamorgan, CF62 3DD
Free House. Jeremy Coleman, owner/licensee

On the road between St Athan and Barry, this very old, creeper-covered, stone thatched pub has a racy past. Aberthaw was, for centuries, a flourishing port and local smugglers centred their activities on this place; rumour has it that a secret tunnel connects the Blue Anchor to the shore. In the main bar are low beams, flagstones, a huge fireplace and two other fireplaces in the small interconnecting rooms. Run by the same family for over 60 years, this extremely popular place has evolved from a CAMRA flagship late last century into a thriving dining pub. People flock from miles around to sample something from the menu. They take food very seriously here. Specializing in local produce and vegetables – many of those grown on their own two acres by Mr Coleman senior – the reasonably priced bar menu could offer chef's home-made soup of the day, spinach and cream cheese mousse, steamed Penclawdd cockles, Cajun salmon brochettes and as a main course, prime Welsh Black fillet or sirloin steak, or chargrilled pork loin stuffed with walnut and spinach over caramelised apples, delicious home-made puds and a selection of Welsh cheeses. Local steak, lamb and pheasant on the well thought-out restaurant menu; the rabbits probably have a Welsh accent too. Marstons Pedigree, Wadworths 6X, Buckleys Best and Theakstons Old Peculier beers. A well-balanced wine list. Seats at the front of the pub and in the garden. Walks towards the estuary.

OPEN: 11–11. Sun 12–10.30.
Real Ale. Restaurant – very quiet music in here.
Children and dogs welcome. Car park. Wheelchair access.
Cards: MasterCard, Switch, Visa.

Hay-on-Wye

Old Black Lion ① 01497 820841
Lion Street, Hay-on-Wye, Hereford HR3 5AD
Free House. Vanessa King, resident proprietor
e-mail: info@oldblacklion.co.uk

Built on the southern bank of the River Wye, the town grew up around the now ruined Norman castle. Near the old Lion Gate, one of the entrances to the old walled town, and putting on a good show of appearing to be a 17th-century coaching inn, is the 13th-century, white-painted, Old Black Lion – a convivial, comfortable hotel. Inside is an attractive beamed bar with a big fireplace serving anything from light bar snacks and lunchtime bar meals to dishes from the more extensive evening menu. There is a creative à la carte menu in the Cromwell restaurant – yes, he was here too. From the menu there could be a wild mushroom and leek soup, Caesar salad with silver anchovies or spiced guinea fowl terrine, coleslaw of celeriac, baby chard and harissa dressing, and for a main course, herb-crusted rack of local lamb with Mediterranean vegetable tart and rosemary lamb jus, goose breast with a honey and five-spice glaze served on braised red cabbage, apples and sultanas, beef Wellington prime fillet steak with paté and duxelle and red wine sauce, loin of pan-fried venison on a parsnip purée tart with blackberry and gin sauce and very more-ish puds to finish. Three-course Sunday lunches. Wye Valley's Cask ales and an interesting choice of wines. Chairs and tables on the terrace during the summer. You have to focus on books when you think of Hay, the capital of Britain's secondhand book trade. There are more than a million books here – all waiting to be bought.

OPEN: 11–11. Sun 12–10.30.
Real Ale. Restaurant.
Children over five restricted to eating areas. No dogs. Car park. En-suite bedrooms. If you're staying, they can arrange fishing for you on the Wye.
Cards: MasterCard, Switch, Visa.

Little Haven

Swan Inn ① 01437 781256
Point Road, Little Haven, Haverfordwest, Pembrokeshire SA62 3UL
Free House. Glyn & Beryl Davies, licensees

The small, attractive harbour at Little Haven was built in the mid 19th century for the sole purpose of shipping coal from local colleries to other areas of the country. The Swan, in a delightful location by the sea wall, has views over the beach – sandy at low tide – and along St Brides Bay. Good fires warm the unspoilt, traditional rooms and the food is a cut above the usual. From the bar menu: traditional Welsh lamb and vegetable soup, ploughman's, sandwiches, crab bake (a hot snack of crab, mayonnaise, herbs and cheese), Swan Upper (sardines, spinach and egg topped with mozzarella and grilled), all served with wholemeal bread and a side salad, fresh, locally caught crab, rolled cured salmon in a mustard and dill mayonnaise dressing, chicken liver, brandy and garlic paté, and for a main course, home-made chicken korma, ham salad or locally smoked salmon. More formal dishes in the restaurant include roast rack of Welsh lamb, grilled fillet of Welsh beef or scampi provençale. Shepherd Neame Spitfire, Greene King Abbot, Morlands Old Speckled Hen, Brains Reverend James, Worthington Best and wines by the glass. Invigorating walks; the Pembrokeshire Coastal Path passes through Little Haven.

OPEN: 11.30–2.30, 6.30–11.
Real Ale. Restaurant – open Wed–Sat eves.
No children. No dogs. Wheelchair access (not WC).
No cards.

Llanfair Waterdine

The Waterdine ① 01547 528214
Llanfair Waterdine, nr Knighton, Powys LD7 1TU
Free House. Mr K. H. Adams, licensee

It is so close to the Shropshire border that the Waterdine gets moved from place to place. We're putting it where the owners say it is – in Wales. Not that it matters; it's a delight wherever you put it. The black and white Waterdine, opposite the church in this small hamlet in the Teme Valley, is a 16th-century Welsh long-house built as a drovers' pub. Very food-orientated, the pub still has a comfortable lounge bar with a log-burning stove – where you can get a drink – and a bistro for lunch. The conservatory and the stone-floored, beamed taproom – the oldest part of the building – both have the most fantastic views and are used for dining. The cooking here is expert and clever and based on the freshest, locally grown organic produce, including eggs from their own hens. Every lunchtime there is a blackboard menu which includes filled home-made baguettes and bread, chutneys for the ploughman's, otherwise pan-fried foie gras on caramelised onion tart tatin, roast chicken and almond soup, mushroom and vegetable ragoût, partridge roasted with herbs, fillet of brill, spinach, shallots and beurre blanc, scrummy seasonal puds and British cheeses. Sunday has a very good value prix-fixe three-course lunch, and there is an equally good value Saturday dinner. Woods Parish Bitter, others from Woods range of ales and Westons traditional cider. Wide-ranging wine list. Very close to Offa's Dyke, so plenty of invigorating walks nearby.

OPEN: 12–2.30, 7–11. Closed all day Mon and Sun eve.
Real Ale. Bistro and restaurant.
Children welcome. No dogs. Car park. Wheelchair access. Bedrooms.
Cards: MasterCard, Switch, Visa.

Llangattock

Vine Tree Inn ① 01873 810514
The Legar, Llangattock, Crickhowell, Powys NP8 1HG
Free House. Andrew Lennox, licensee

The Vine Tree, just outside this hillside village in the mountains surrounding Crickhowell, is opposite the medieval bridge across the Usk. Several cottages have been knocked through to create this efficient pub where food is all important. Stone walled and comfortable, it's cosy inside and a large blackboard in the bar lists an extensive, enterprising menu; everything freshly cooked using local produce where possible and fish from Cornwall. For a starter, hot curried prawns, tuna and tomato salad, smoked trout, egg mayonnaise, and for a main course, rabbit in a wine and celery sauce, supreme of chicken stuffed with prawns wrapped with bacon on a bed of seafood sauce, pork loin stuffed with marinated apricots in an orange sauce, venison in a red berry casserole, chicken cymru in a creamy white wine, tomato and mushroom sauce, steak and ale pie, home-boiled ham, steaks, a variety of vegetarian dishes, Sunday roasts and delicious puds – even the bread is home-made. Fresh fish and seafood on the specials board. The regularly changing beers are from the Coors range and local brewers. The wine list has expanded to reflect the changes of menu. Seats outside overlook the river. Wonderful walks along the Newport/Brecon Canal, River Usk and the old tramway into the mountains.

OPEN: 12–3, 6–11.
Real Ale. Restaurant.
Children welcome. No dogs. Willing hands for the wheelchairs.

Llanthony

Abbey Hotel ① 01873 890487
Llanthony, nr Abergavenny, Monmouthshire NP7 7NN
Free House. Ivor Prentice, licensee

Remains of the old priory are scattered around the site; all the useable buildings have become part of this very atmospheric hotel. Historically fascinating, the hotel contains part of the Norman church, the prior's house and a Norman staircase. Llanthony Priory, an ecclesiastical ruin of a late 12th-century Augustinian priory, which itself was built on the site of a Norman knight's hermitage, is in an unrivalled setting; a wonderfully wooded landscape in the Brecon Beacons. The dining room in the Abbey was originally the prior's outer parlour and meeting room, and the cellar is now the vaulted crypt bar. In the simply furnished flagstoned main bar, you can find a menu of hearty food: home-made soups, garlic mushrooms, jalapeno bean dip, pork tenderloin with mango and cream sauce, seafood risotto, Moroccan chicken spiced with cumin, coriander, chilli and lemon, spicy bean goulash. Evening dishes include casseroles, local lamb with garlic, wine and mushrooms – or, for the vegetarians among you, a nut roast. Draught Bass, Felinfoel Double Dragon and guests such as Ashvine Hop and Glory, Brains Rev James and Shepherd Neame Bishops Finger. Glorious setting; wonderful walking and riding country.

OPEN: 11–3, 6–11. Sat and summer hols 11–11. Open Christmas & New Year week.
Closed weekdays early Nov–end March.
Real Ale.
Children welcome. No dogs. Bedrooms.
Cards: all major cards accepted, 5% added to all credit cards.

Maentwrog

Grapes ① 01766 590365
Maentwrog, Blaenau Ffestiniog, Gwynedd LL14 4HN
Nelson Williams Leisure Group. Gruff Jones, licensee
e-mail: grapesmaen@aol.com

A spacious old stone coaching inn, set in a Grade II-listed 19th-century building over a 13th-century cellar. Solidly comfortable, well-polished pine-panelled bars, settles, pews with an ecclesiastical history and big fires. The public bar has a jukebox and there is a musical ghost that has been heard playing a piano on the hotel landing so, if you're staying and you hear a little night music, you know what it is. In the bar they serve good-value, well-presented bar food. This could include lunchtime soups – changing daily – filled jacket potatoes, their very own proper beefburgers, French bread filled with steak and mushrooms or onions, smoked bacon or veggie sausage, steak and mushroom pies, salads, the 'Grapes' famous pork ribs, lamb steak marinated in red wine, redcurrant and rosemary sauce, seafood lasagne and vegetarian dishes. There are lots of fishy specials; everything is cooked to order. Roast on Sunday. The restaurant is no smoking and there is a children's menu. Bass, John Smiths, Marstons Pedigree and Morlands Old Speckled Hen, about four guest beers from a total of 30 or 40 rotating throughout the year. Seats on the verandah which look over the extensive garden to the railway and the mountains beyond. Using

1860 locomotives, the Ffestiniog Railway travels through 14 miles of breathtaking scenery and is well worth a ride.

OPEN: 11–11.
Real Ale. Restaurant.
Children in family room, on the verandah and there is a play area. Dogs on leads. Wheelchair-access. En-suite bedrooms.

Menai Bridge

Liverpool Arms ① 01248 712453
St George's Pier, Menai Bridge, Anglesey, North Wales LL59 5EY
Free House. Glynwen Thickett, licensee

The town might share its name with the graceful suspension bridge built in 1826 to link the Welsh mainland with the island of Anglesey, but it is very much older. There is a regatta in the town every August and a huge fair every October that has been held for over 400 years. Newly extended to provide extra accommodation, the friendly, welcoming stone-built early 19th-century Liverpool Arms is full of nautical artifacts, prints and pictures. There are two comfortable bars, a dining room and west-facing conservatory. The dishes on the menu in the restaurant and the bar are all home-made and could include soup of the day, ploughman's platter, assiette of seafood, leek and ham mornay, baked ham salad, steak, mushroom and potato pie, gammon, egg and chips, salmon, prawn and fresh local crab salads, sirloin and fillet steaks and changing daily specials. The beers are Flowers Original, IPA, Morlands Old Speckled Hen, Courage Directors, Marstons Pedigree and various guests during the week. No garden, just a patio.

OPEN: 11–11. Sun 12–3, 7–10.30.
Real Ale.
Children welcome. No dogs, except guide dogs. Wheelchair access (not WC). Twelve en-suite rooms in annexe.

Nantgwynant

Pen-y-Gwryd Hotel ① 01286 870211
Nantgwynant, Gwynedd LL55 4NT (at junction of A498 and A4086)
Free House. Jane Pullee, licensee

The Vale of Nantgwynant is wooded, beautiful and peaceful; Llanberis Pass more rocky and determined. The jolly, well-run Pen-y-Gwryd Hotel, in the wooded area of the Snowdonia National Park, is a favourite base for keen climbers who feel at home in the climbers' bar, which has an interesting collection of boots that have made famous climbs, and where they serve hearty, energy-giving, home-made food: special pies – a different pie a day, casseroles in winter, soups, sandwiches, home-made bread to go with the home-made paté and local cheeses for the ploughman's. No bar food in the evening, just meals in the no-smoking restaurant. Bass and Boddingtons ales. There are several routes to the top of Mount Snowdon for every level of experience. Among the better known, Watkin's Path on the south side near the village of Nantgwynant, initially picturesque, gradually become really difficult. The other well-known route is the easier Pyg Track. If you do make it to

the summit, 3560ft later, and the visibility is good, you can see both the Derbyshire peaks and the Wicklow Mountains in Ireland.

OPEN: 11–11. Closed Nov–New Year. Open weekends only Jan–Feb.
Real Ale. Filling restaurant.
Well-behaved children welcome, not in residents' bar. Dogs on leads. Wheelchair access.
Bedrooms.
No cards.

Old Radnor

Harp Inn ① 01544 350655
Old Radnor, Presteigne, Powys LD8 2RH
Free House. Heather Price & Erfyl Protheroe, licensees

The church and the Harp Inn are contemporaries, both built during the 15th century. St Stephen's church is particularly fine with some Tudor panelling, a notable rood screen and a 6th- or 7th-century stone font. Next to the church, on the village green with the most wonderful, panoramic views over the Welsh Marches, the ancient Harp has a cosy old-fashioned feel provided by beams, slate floors, some nice pieces of antique furniture and log fires in both public and lounge bars. Menus change regularly and everything is home-cooked, but the bar menu will have soup, filled baguettes, ploughman's, faggots, mash, peas and gravy, steak and kidney pie, pork and leek sausages with onion gravy, fish and chips – good filling food. In the restaurant Hereford rump steak, lamb shank braised in red wine and rosemary, pork Valentine – pork steak with a wholegrain mustard sauce – and at least two vegetarian dishes. Beers change too, Timothy Taylors Landlord is a permanent; the weekly guest is a local brew. Range of malts and some organic wines. There are lots of seats outside so you can admire the view. Plenty of good walks.

OPEN: Tues–Fri 7–11. Sat 12–3, 7–11. Sun 12–3, 7–10.30. Closed Mon except lunch on bank holidays.
Real Ale. Restaurant.
Children welcome. No dogs. Five en-suite bedrooms.
Cards: all debit cards, MasterCard, Switch, Visa.

Pontfaen

Dyffryn Arms ① 01348 881305
Pontfaen, Dyfed SA65 9SE
Free House. Bessie Davis, licensee

In the timeless, glorious Gwaun valley, the Dyffryn Arms – and the landlady – are part of this unchanging countryside between Preseli and Fishguard. Pontfaen seems very remote but is actually only a mile or so off the B4314. Surrounded by woodland and lots of rushing water, this tiny, unspoilt place, with just two rooms, has been in Bessie Davis's family for over 150 years. Very well-kept draught Bass or Burtons still served from the jug and a very occasional guest. Only one real beer kept at a time, the rest are bottled or canned. To eat? Well, crisps, nuts and a pickled egg!

OPEN: 12–11.
Real Ale.
Children in the garden. Dogs on leads. Car park.

Porthmadog

Ship ① 01766 512990
Lombard Street, Porthmadog, Gwynedd LL49 9AP
Free House. Georgina Adams, licensee

The town and the Ship are as one, both built in the 19th century on land reclaimed from the Glaslyn estuary. This little harbour town was created to serve the slate quarries of Blaenau Festiniog and the narrow-gauge railway that brought the slate down from the mountains is working again. The Ship, a popular local near the harbour has, as befits its position, a decidedly nautical decor. Two rooms, traditionally furnished with good fires; the lounge is no smoking. There is a varied, changing menu of home-made soup, casseroles, lots of seafood, including sea bass, maybe gammon hock with a white bean sauce, braised shoulder of lamb provençale, chicken in a smoky barbecue sauce, salmon and spinach in a tarragon sauce and at least five vegetarian dishes. At lunchtime they suggest a two-for-one main course – the cheaper main dish is free; that sounds like an offer you can't refuse. Roast lunch on Sunday. Six different cask beers: Timothy Taylors Landlord, Greene King IPA, Morlands Old Speckled Hen, Tetleys Bitter and M&B cask Mild and lots of malt whiskies. They have a beer festival in March. Don't forget a trip on the railway that takes you into some dramatic country.

OPEN: 11–11. Sun 12–4. Closed Sun out of season.
Real Ale.
Children, lunchtime only. Dogs when food not served. Wheelchair access.
Cards: all cards accepted.

St Asaph

Farmers Arms ① 01745 582190
The Waen, nr St Asaph, Clwyd LL17 ODY (on the B5429 between the A55 expressway and Tremeirchion)
Free House. R. & A. Sibeon, licensees

A delightful country pub in the Vale of Clwyd, an area that has been inhabited since prehistoric times; everyone came – the Romans built a road, the Normans started to build the cathedral in St Asaph – the smallest in Britain – and in the caves at Cefn, south-west of St Asaph, are prehistoric bones of bears, bison and reindeer. When you've done the sights, you can make your way to the Farmers Arms, where you can always get a drink and something to eat from the well-thought-out menu. The home-cooked food is available in the bar and there could be soup of the day, chicken liver and brandy paté with melba toa savoury crêpe filled with honey-roast ham, asparagus and topped with a cheese sauce, home-made fishcakes, steak, onion and ale pie, roast Welsh lamb with a piquant sauce, escalope of pork in Calvados, chicken Véronique, as well as fresh fish, steaks, salads and vegetarian dishes. The public bar does have music but is well away from the main lounge. The real ales vary.

OPEN: Mon & Tues 7–11. Wed–Fri 5–11. Sat & Sun 12–11.
Real Ale.
Children and dogs welcome. Wheelchair access.
Cards: all accepted.

Tintern

Cherry Tree Inn ① 01291 689292
Devauden Road, Tintern, nr Monmouth NP16 6TH
Free House. Steve Pocock, licensee
e-mail: steve@thecherry.co.uk

Outside the busy village, up a little alley, nothing has changed to ruin the atmosphere of this charming, little pub. The beer is still brought by hand from the cellar but after years of just crisps and nuts they do feed you now. The 16th-century Cherry Tree has just one beamed room with a small bar and fire where they serve generous, uncomplicated food – sandwiches, ploughman's, sausage and mash, gammon and egg and specials on the blackboard. The Cherry Tree's own water feature doesn't compare with the river down the road, but they do have a little tumbling stream and a pretty, sunny garden. Only Hancocks HB, a guest beer and a draught cider – all in tip-top condition. Situated west of the main village of Tintern, the River Wye and the glories of ruined Tintern Abbey.

OPEN: 11–11. Sun 12–10.30.
Real Ale.
Children: under control, until 8 p.m. Dogs in garden only.
Cards: all cards accepted.

Upper Llanover

Goose & Cuckoo Inn ① 01873 880277
Upper Llanover, Abergavenny NP7 9ER
Free House. Michael & Carol Langley, licensees

By all accounts a 'stunner'. Mind you, you've got to find it first. South of Abergavenny, along a lane off the A4042, keep going and watch out for a sign. In the Brecon Beacons National Park, on the 'Marches Way' and not far from the Monmouth/Brecon canal, it looks very like a traditional Welsh farmhouse, with a low wall at the front and surrounded by gently rolling fields. Inside is a warm and friendly bar, with a wood-burning stove, and a small no-smoking dining room with a view. They specialize in traditional home cooking and have a snack menu of soup, filled rolls – freshly baked every day – ploughman's and jacket potatoes. They don't run to a large menu but there is always something from the family recipe book served with fresh vegetables and salads – including pies, perhaps liver and bacon casserole, pheasant and rabbit dishes and to finish, their very own ice cream using seasonal fruits. For Sunday lunch you must book. Bullmastiff beer brewed in Cardiff and maybe something from Shepherd Neame, Wadworths, Brakspears or Charles Wells.

No fewer than 75 single malts to warm you after your brisk walk, and for the locals, Dortmunder lager, which seems to be their favourite tipple. Outside is a large beer garden – sheep, goats, geese, ducks and chickens to admire and a view to appreciate. If you're that way inclined, there is room to pitch your tent and a cooked breakfast is available in the pub.

OPEN: Tues–Thurs 11.30–3, 7–11. Fri–Sun 11–11. Closed Mon except bank holidays.
Real Ale.
Children welcome, dogs too. Car park. Wheelchair access. One en-suite bedroom.
No cards.

BEST OF THE REST

Beaumaris
Sailors Return ☺ 01248 811314
Church Street, Anglesey LL58 8AB
Comfortable and popular, with open fires and naval memorabilia. Any returning sailor would be happy in this friendly, jolly town pub as they look after you very well. They serve traditional bar food: soup, sandwiches, filled baguettes, gammon and pineapple as well as daily specials to go with the Bass and guest beers. Children welcome in eating area of bar. Bedrooms.
Open: 11.30–3, 6–11.

Bodfari, Clywd
Dinorben Arms ☺ 01745 710309
Bodfari LL16 4DA
In the well bar is a glassed-over Roman well which is supposed to have magical qualities; legend is a wonderful thing. Several things make this pub stand out from the rest, though when I tell you they have the full range of McCallan's malts as well as over 250 others for you to try, stand is perhaps not the word to use. Whisky aside, here is a delightful old pub in a wonderful position – clinging to the side of a mountain – where they serve familiar bar food; daily specials too. If it's a beer you want, they have Tetleys, Batemans and a changing guest. Children in eating areas.
Open: 12–3.30, 6–11. Sat & Sun 12–11.

Cilgerran
Pendre Inn ☺ 01239 614223
Cilgerran, nr Cardigan, Dyfed SA43 2SL
One of the oldest pubs in Wales in one of the loveliest areas. The village is set in a wooded gorge overlooked by the remains of the 13th-century castle – only about 100 years older than the Pendre – built on a bluff high above the River Teifi. This ancient whitewashed pub has low beams, polished slate and flagstone floors, medieval stone walls and lots of atmosphere. They serve a varied menu to go with something from Tomos Watkins' brewery in Llandeilo. There are seats outside in the big garden. There are coracle races on the river in mid-August; the coracles are built further up the river at Cenarth. Children welcome, and dogs. Bedrooms. No cards.
Open: 11.30–3, 6–12 (Sun 6–10.30).

Glanwydden, Conwy
Queens Head ① 01492 546570
Glanwydden LL31 9JP
Between Colwyn Bay and Llandudno. A plain, modest-looking pub outside, but looks belie. Exciting things happen on the food front, so – more of a place to eat than to stop for a quick pint. You can do that too, but you should really be here to appreciate something from the weekly changing menu. Bar snacks such as home-made soups, chicken liver pâté and stuffed pancakes as well as mussels in garlic butter, potted local crab, seafood platter, loin of pork with a whisky, leek and cream sauce and good puddings. There is a list of over 40 wines as well as beer: Tetleys, Ind Coope Burton and a guest. No children under 7. No dogs. Wheelchair access (not WC).
Open: 11.30–3, 6–11. Sun 11.30–10.30.

Glandwyfach, Gwynedd
Goat Inn ① 01766 530237
Glandwyfach, Brynar LL51 9LT
A quiet country pub with lots of character, friendly staff and a pleasant atmosphere, halfway between Caernafon and Portmadog, on the A487. Here they serve generous portions of home-cooked food: traditional bar snacks, hot roast beef sandwiches, and from the restaurant menu: pot-roast lamb in redcurrant gravy, salmon with a white wine and tarragon sauce, braised steak in a red wine and mushroom sauce, and much more. Well-kept Robinsons range of ales and a comprehensive wine list. Children welcome. No dogs. Wheelchair access (not WC).
Open: 11–11. Winter 12–2.30, 6–11.

Llanfrynach, Monmouthshire
White Swan ① 01874 665276
Llanfrynach LD3 7BZ
If you're looking for a friendly village pub, south-east of Brecon, where you can eat well, here it is. Flagstone floors, open fires and plenty of room so you can enjoy the beef and mushroom pie, lasagne, fisherman's pie, steaks, grilled trout and much more. Flowers and Brains beer. Children welcome.
Open: 12–3, 7–11. Closed Mon & Tues and most of Jan.

Llanynys, Clywd
Cerrigllwydion Arms ① 01745 890247
Llanynys LL16 4PA
Next to a very early, 7th-century church which has some interesting medieval wall paintings, this pub was apparently built for the benefit of the church congregation during the 15th century. But, if you're driving from north Wales to Ruthin on the country roads, making for this impossibly named pub, you need to know not to turn up on a Monday or Tuesday; it's closed. This old, rambling, village pub serves the usual reliable bar menu: filled baguettes, steak and ale pie, mixed grill and varied dishes. Bass and Tetleys and a fair choice of wine. Children if eating.
Open: 12–3, 7–11. Closed Mon & Tues.

Penmaenpool, Gwynedd
George III ① 01341 422525
Penmaenpool LL40 1YD
...ow Cader Idris and overlooking the wooded Mawddach Estuary, one of the loveliest ...sh estuaries, this hotel is just about the linchpin of the village. Fantastic views, walks

and a wildlife centre in the old signal box of the disused railway line (now a footpath). All this means the hotel bar is a popular place. Always good things on the menu – quite a lot of fish – with the addition of daily specials. Ruddles Best, John Smiths and a changing guest. Children allowed. Bedrooms.
Open: 11–11.

Pisgar, nr Aberystwyth
Halfway Inn ① 01970 880631
Pisgar SY23 4NE
West of Aberystwyth towards Devil's Bridge. Depending on what you can stand listening to in the way of inoffensive music, you need to know that it's classical at lunchtime and country and folk in the evening. In the Rheidol valley and in a wonderful position to take full advantage of the glorious views, this is a nice old-fashioned place serving filling, familiar bar food. About four real ales and the same number of ciders to quench your thirst. Family orientated; you can camp if you're a customer and it is a well-known stop on the pony-trekking circuit. No lunchtime food during winter months. Children in eating area. Bedrooms.
Open: 12–2.30, 6.30–11. Closed lunchtimes Jan & Feb.

Pont-ar-gothi
Salutation Inn ① 01267 290336
Pont-ar-gothi, Carmarthenshire SA32 7NH
A black and white roadside inn between Carmarthen and Llandeilo. More geared to dining than drinking, but there is still a bar where they will welcome you and serve a pint of local beer. The beamed bar and open fire in the Salutation gives the pub a homely atmosphere and the blackboard menu gives you some idea of the delights that await. You will experience something really worthwhile – traditional cooking with a twist. Felinfoel Dragon and Double Dragon ales, and a comprehensive wine list, some by the glass. Children welcome. No dogs. Car park. Cards: most accepted.
Open: 12–3, 6–11.

Ty'n y Groes, Gwynedd
Groes ① 01492 650545
Ty'n y Groes LL32 8TN
Spectacular views of the Conwy estuary on one side and Snowdon on the other. An early 16th-century building, thought to be one of the oldest licensed houses in Wales; certainly it's on the old bit of road the Romans used on their way to Anglesey. A classy, rambling old place where they feed you well. Lots of local produce, imaginatively cooked: Welsh lamb, local fish, Welsh cheeses, delicious puds. Tetleys and Ind Coope Burton, as well as a choice of wines. Children in family room. No dogs. Wheelchair access. Bedrooms.
Open: 12–3, 6–11.

Usk, Monmouthshire
Nags Head ① 01291 672820
Twyn Square, Usk NP5 1BH
A 500-year-old coaching inn in a delightful small market town with a 12th-century castle. A comfortable, well-kept old place filled with interesting bric-a-brac, serving some good, home-made food, much of it local, but with a few imported touches. The bar menu lists soup, also seasonal game, local rabbits made into a pie and, of course, salmon. Brains range of beers. Built into the courtyard and open during the tourist season is a small

coffee bar and tea room. You are very near the river Usk, surrounded by some wonderful scenery and good walks. Children welcome.
Open: 11–3, 5.30–11.

Welshpool
Royal Oak Hotel ☎ 01938 552217
Severn Street, Welshpool SY21 7DG
An historic border town with a 13th-century castle, full of medieval and elegant Georgian houses. Once the home of the Earls of Powis, the handsome, Georgian-pillared Royal Oak has been a hostelry for over 350 years. The bar menu and specials board offer an excellent variety, including vegetarian dishes and a full three-course traditional Sunday lunch. Worthington Best always available, along with two weekly changing guest beers and a wide selection of wines and bottled beers. Children welcome. No dogs. Wheelchair access. Bedrooms. N.B. The two bars – musical Ostler and quiet Oak – have different opening times – the Oak is only open during the evening.
Open: 11–3, 5.30–11.

Wetherspoon in Wales

Aberdare – Y Iuean Ap Iago, High Street
☎ 01685 880080
Abergavenny – Coliseum, Lion Street
☎ 01873 736960
Aberystwyth – Yr Hen Orsaf, Alexandra Road
☎ 01970 636080
Bangor – Black Bull Inn, High Street
☎ 01248 387900
Blackwood – Sirhowy, 61–63 High Street
☎ 01495 226374
Bridgend – Wyndham Arms, Dunraven Place
☎ 01656 663608
Caernarfon – Tafarn Y Porth, 5–9 Eastgate Street
☎ 01286 662920
Carmarthen – Yr Hen Dderwen, 47–48 King Street
☎ 01267 242050
Cardiff – Central Bar, 39 Windsor Place
☎ 029 2078 0260
Cardiff – Ernest Willows, 2–12 City Road
☎ 029 2048 6235
Cardiff – Gatekeeper, 9–10 Westgate Street
☎ 029 2064 6020
Cardiff – Ivor Davis, 243–249 Cowbridge Road East
☎ 029 2066 7615
Cardiff – Prince of Wales, St Mary Street
☎ 029 2064 4449
Colwyn Bay – Picture House, 24–26 Princes Drive
☎ 01492 535286
Ebbw Vale – Picture House, Market Street
☎ 01495 352382
Llandudno – Palladium, 7 Gloddaeth Street
☎ 01492 863920

Llaneli – York Palace, 51 Stepney Street
① 01554 758609
Merthyr Tydfil – Y Dic Penderyn, 102–103 High Street
① 01685 385786
Monmouth – King's Head (also a Wetherspoon Lodge), 8 Agincourt Square
① 01600 713417
Neath – David Protheroe, 7 Windsor Road
① 01639 622130
Newport – Godfrey Morgan, 158 Chepstow Road
① 01633 221928
Newport – Tom Toya Lewis, 108–112 Commercial Street
① 01633 245030
Newport – Wetherspoons, Units 10–12 The Cambrian Centre
① 01633 251752
Penarth – Bear's Head, 37–39 Windsor Road
① 029 2070 6424
Port Talbot – Lord Caradoc, 63–73 Station Road
① 01639 896007
Rhyl – Sussex, 20–26 Sussex Street
① 01745 362910
Swansea – Bank Statement, 57–58 Wind Street
① 01792 455477
Swansea – Potters Wheel, 86 The Kingsway
① 01792 465113
Tredegar – Olympia, Morgan Street
① 01495 712910
Wrexham – Elihu Yale, 44–46 Regent Street
① 01978 366646

Wetherspoon in Northern Ireland

Ballymena – Spinning Mill, 17–21 Broughshane Street
Tel. 028 2563 8965
Belfast – Wetherspoons, 35–37 Bedford Street
Tel. 028 9023 8238
Carrickfergus – Central Bar, 13–15 High Strret
Tel. 028 9335 7840
Coleraine – Old Court House, Castlerock Road
Te. 028 7032 5820
Derry City– Diamond, 23–24 The Diamond
Tel. 028 7127 2880
Lisburn – Tuesday Bell, Unit 1 & 2 Lisburn Square
Tel. 028 9262 7390
Newtownards – Spirit Merchant, 54–56 Regent Street
Tel. 028 9182 4270

Wetherspoon at the airports

Edinburgh

Wetherspoons, Airside
☽ 0131 344 3032
Wetherspoons, Landside
☽ 0131 344 3030

Gatwick

Red Lion, North Terminal International, Departure Lounge
☽ 01293 569874
Village Inn, South Terminal, Landside
☽ 01293 579800

Heathrow

Skylark, Terminal 1, Landside
☽ 020 8607 5650
Wetherspoons, Terminal 2, Airside
☽ 020 8564 7856
Wetherspoons, Terminal 2, Landside
☽ 020 8607 5900
Wetherspoons, Terminal 4, Airside
☽ 020 8759 0355
Wetherspoons, Terminal 4, Landside
☽ 020 8759 2906

Stansted

Windmill, Airside
☽ 01279 682210

Nomination form

There are now two categories of pub listed in *The Quiet Pint*:

- **Music-free**, in which no piped music is played
- **Best of the Rest**, where music does not intrude upon conversation

Before you nominate a pub in the first category, please confirm with the licensees that they **DO NOT** play any background music, i.e. tapes, CDs, radio.

To qualify for the second category, music should be of the **hardly-hear-it** variety and definitely **NOT POP**.

Return your nomination form to The Quiet Pint, c/o Aurum Press Ltd, 25 Bedford Avenue, London WC1B 3AT, or e-mail your nomination to: derek.dempster@virgin.net

Pub name . . . .

☐ Music-free ☐ Best of the rest (*tick appropriate box*)

Publican's name (*it's usually above the entrance*) . . . .

Address . . . .

. . . .

. . . .

Telephone number . . . .

E-mail (if applicable) . . . .

Please use the space overleaf to describe in your own words the pub and its surroundings, the standard of cooking (if applicable), and the range of ales on offer. *The Quiet Pint* is full of examples to follow. If the pub has a brochure or menu, please enclose them along with this form. Don't forget to give us your:

Name . . . .

Address . . . .

. . . .

. . . .

E-mail (if applicable) . . . .

Index

Abbey Hotel, Llanthony, Monmouthshire
Ackhorne, York
Acorn Inn, Evershot, Dorset
Albion, Chester
Alma, London SW18
Anchor, High Offley, Staffordshire
Anchor, Oldbury-on-Severn, Somerset
Anchor Inn, Barcombe, East Sussex
Anchor Inn, Oldbury-on-Severn,
    Gloucestershire
Anchor Inn, Sutton Gault, Cambridgeshire
Ancient Shepherds, Fen Ditton,
    Cambridgeshire
Angel, Hindon, Wiltshire
Angel, Sudbury, Suffolk
Angel Hotel, Lavenham, Suffolk
Angel Inn, Hetton, North Yorkshire
Angel Inn, Stoke-by-Nayland, Suffolk
Angelsea Arms, London SW7
Angelsea Arms, London W6
Applecross Inn, Applecross, Highlands
Axe & Compasses, Arkesden, Essex

Babbity Bowster, Glasgow
Badgers, Coultershaw Bridge, West Sussex
Bakers Arms, Broad Campden,
    Gloucestershire
Bakers Arms, Thorpe Langton, Leicestershire
Barley Mow, Clifton Hampden, Oxfordshire
Barley Mow, Kirk Ireton, Derbyshire
Barnsdale Lodge Hotel, Rutland Water
Bat & Ball, Boundstone, Surrey
Bax Castle, Christ's Hospital, West Sussex
Beacon, Tunbridge Wells, Kent
Bear, Devizes, Wiltshire
Bear Inn, Bisley, Gloucestershire
Beehive, Bradford-on-Avon, Wiltshire
Beehive, Horringer, Suffolk
Beer Engine, New St Cyres, Devon
Beetle & Wedge, Moulsford, Oxfordshire
Belgian Arms, Holyport, Berkshire
Bell, Adderbury, Oxfordshire
Bell, Alderminster, Warwickshire
Bell, Aldworth, Berkshire
Bell, Burwash, East Sussex
Bell, Coleby, Lincolnshire
Bell, Ducklington, Oxfordshire
Bell, Purleigh, Essex
Bell, Waltham St Lawrence, Berkshire
Bell Hotel, Norwich
Bell Hotel, Ticehurst, East Sussex

Bell Inn, Halton Holegate, Lincolnshire
Bell Inn, Horndon on the Hill, Essex
Bell Inn, Sapperton, Gloucestershire
Bell Inn, Walberswick, Suffolk
Benett Arms, Semley, Wilts
Benjamin Satchwell, Leamington Spa,
    Warwickshire
Birch Hall Inn, Beck Hole, North Yorkshire
Bird in Hand, Earls Colne, Essex
Bishops Finger, London EC1
Black Bull, Boroughbridge, North Yorkshire
Black Bull, Matfen, Northumberland
Black Bull, Warkworth, Northumberland
Black Bull Inn, Moulton, North Yorkshire
Black Dog, Belmont, Lancashire
Black Horse, Amberley, Gloucestershire
Black Horse, Checkendon, Oxfordshire
Black Horse, Elton, Cambridgeshire
Black Horse, Hose, Leicestershire
Black Horse, Stansted, Kent
Black Swan, Stratford-upon-Avon,
    Warwickshire
Blackboys Inn, Blackboys, East Sussex
Blacksmiths Arms, Broughton Mills, Cumbria
Blacksmiths Arms, Lastingham, North
    Yorkshire
Blewbury Inn, Blewbury, Oxfordshire
Blind Jacks, Knaresborough, North Yorkshire
Blue Anchor, Helston, Cornwall
Blue Anchor Inn, East Aberthaw, South
    Glamorgan
Blue Ball, Sidford, Devon
Blue Ball Inn, Triscombe, Somerset
Blue Bell Inn, Smallwood, Cheshire
Blue Boar, Chieveley, Berkshire
Blue Lion, East Witton, North Yorkshire
Blue Ship, Billingshurst, West Sussex
Blue Ship, Rudgwick, West Sussex
Boat Inn, Aboyne, Grampian
Boat Inn, Ashleworth Quay, Gloucestershire
Boat Inn, Penallt, Gloucestershire
Bonchurch Inn, Bonchurch, Isle of Wight
Boot Inn, Willington, Cheshire
Bottle & Glass, Binfield Heath, Oxfordshire
Bottle House Inn, Smarts Hill, Kent
Bow Bar, Edinburgh
Brace of Pheasants, Plush, Dorset
Brampton Halt, Chapel Brampton,
    Northamptonshire
Briar Rose, Birmingham
Bricklayers Arms, Flaunden, Hertfordshi

Bricklayers Arms, Thornton, Leicestershire
Bridge Hotel, Buttermere, Cumbria
Bridge Inn, Topsham, Devon
Britannia Inn, Elterwater, Cumbria
Brocket Arms, Ayot St Lawrence, Hertfordshire
Brown Jug, Dumpton Park, Broadstairs, Kent
Bruce Arms, Easton Royal, Wiltshire
Brushmakers Arms, Upham, Hampshire
Bryn Tyrch Hotel, Capel Curig, Conwy
Buck Inn, Thornton Watlass, North Yorkshire
Bull, Blackmore End, Essex
Bull, Cavendish, Suffolk
Bull, Stanford Dingley, Berkshire
Bull Inn, Ditchling, East Sussex
Bull Terrier, Croscombe, Somerset
Bulls Head, London SW13
Burlton Inn, Burlton, Shropshire
Burton Bridge Inn, Burton-on-Trent,
    Staffordshire
Burts Hotel, Melrose, Borders
Bush Inn, Morwenstow, Cornwall
Bush Inn, Ovington, Hampshire
Butcher's Arms, Sheepscombe,
    Gloucestershire
Butcher's Arms, Oakridge Lynch,
    Gloucestershire
Butt & Oyster, Pin Mill, Suffolk
Byre Inn, Brig O'Turk, Stirling

Calthorpe Arms, London WC1
Cambridge Blue, Cambridge
Carew Arms, Crowcombe, Somerset
Carpenter's Arms, Miserden, Gloucestershire
Carpenters Arms, Stanton Wick, Somerset
Carrington Arms, Moulsoe, Buckinghamshire
Cartwheel, Whitsbury, Hampshire
Case is Altered, Five Ways, Warwickshire
Cask & Cutler, Sheffield, South Yorkshire
Castle, Chiddingstone, Kent
Castle, London SW11
Castle Inn & Hotel, Lydford, Devon
Cat & Custard Pot, Shipton Moynes,
    Gloucestershire
Catherine Wheel, Marshfield, Wiltshire
Caunton Beck, Caunton, Nottinghamshire
Cavendish, Baslow, Derbyshire
Cerrigllwydion Arms, Llanynys, Clywd
Chafford Arms, Fordcombe, Kent
Champion of the Thames, Cambridge
Chelsea Ram, London SW10
Chequered Skipper, Ashton, Northamptonshire
Chequers, Fowlmere, Cambridgeshire
Chequers, Chipping Norton, Oxfordshire
Chequers, Smarden, Kent
Chequers, Wheeler End, Buckinghamshire
Chequers, Walton-on-the-Hill, Surrey
Chequers Inn, Ledsham, West Yorkshire

Chequers Inn, Well, Hampshire
Cherry Tree Inn, Tintern, Monmouthshire
Chestnut Horse, Great Kelk, East Yorkshire
Cholmondeley Arms, Cholmondeley, Cheshire
Church House, Holne, Devon
Church House, Rattery, Devon
Church House, Stokeinteignhead, Devon
Church House Inn, Harberton, Devon
Church Inn, Uppermill, Lancashire
Churchill Arms, Paxford, Gloucestershire
Cider House, Defford, Worcestershire
Circus Tavern, Manchester
Cleave, Lustleigh, Devon
Clifton, St John's Wood, London NW8
Clytha Arms, Clytha, Monmouthshire
Coach & Horses, Compton, Sussex
Coach & Horses, Danehill, East Sussex
Coach & Horses, London W1
Cock, Brent Eleigh, Suffolk
Cock & Bottle, East Morden, Dorset
Commercial Rooms, Bristol
Compasses Inn, Damerham, Hampshire
Compasses Inn, Lower Chicksgrove, Wiltshire
Compasses Inn, Gomshall, Surrey
Coopers Arms, London SW3
Coronet, London N7
Corse Lawn Hotel, Corse Lawn,
    Gloucestershire
Cott Inn, Dartington, Devon
Counting House, Glasgow
Cover Bridge Inn, East Witton, North Yorkshire
Crab & Lobster, Sidlesham, West Sussex
Craven Arms, Appletreewick, North Yorkshire
Craven Arms, Brockhampton, Gloucestershire
Creebridge House Hotel, Minnigaff, Dumfries
    & Galloway
Creggans Inn, Strachur, Argyll
Cresselly Arms, Cresswell Quay, Dyfed
Cretingham Bell, Cretingham, Suffolk
Cricketers, Broadwater, West Sussex
Cricketers, Duncton, West Sussex
Cricketers Arms, Berwick, East Sussex
Cricketers Arms, Tangley, Hampshire
Crinan Hotel, Crinan, Argyll
Crispin Inn, Ashover, Derbyshire
Crooked Billet, Leigh-on-Sea, Essex
Crooked Billet, Newton Longville,
    Buckinghamshire
Crooket Billet, Wokingham Without, Berkshire
Cross Keys, Aldeburgh, Suffolk
Cross Keys, Pulloxhill, Bedfordshire
Cross Keys Hotel, Kippen, Stirlingshire
Cross Ways Inn, West Huntspill, Somerset
Crow's Nest, Crosby, Liverpool
Crown, Burchetts Green, Berkshire
Crown, Colkirk, Norfolk
Crown, Great Glenham, Suffolk

Crown, Groombridge, Kent
Crown, Hartest, Suffolk
Crown, Ibberton, Dorset
Crown, Little Missenden, Buckinghamshire
Crown, Old Dalby, Leicestershire
Crown, Portpatrick, Dumfries & Galloway
Crown, Snape, Suffolk
Crown Hotel, Malton, North Yorkshire
Crown Hotel, Mundford, Norfolk
Crown Hotel, Southwold, Suffolk
Crown Inn, Churchill, Somerset
Crown Inn, Lanlivery, Cornwall
Crown Inn, Pucknowle, Dorset
Crown Inn, Totley, South Yorkshire
Crown & Anchor, Lugwardine, Herefordshire
Crown & Sceptre, Torquay, Devon
Crown Posada, Newcastle-upon-Tyne

Daneway Inn, Sapperton, Gloucestershire
Darnley Arms, Cobham, Kent
Dartmoor Inn at Lydford, Devon
Dawnay Arms, Newton-on-Ouse, North Yorkshire
De la Pole Arms, Wingfield, Suffolk
Dering Arms, Pluckley, Kent
Devonshire Arms, Beeley, Derbyshire
Devonshire Arms, Mellor, Gtr Manchester
Devonshire Inn, Sticklepath, Devon
Diggers Rest, Woodbury Salterton, Devon
Dinorben Arms, Bodfari, Clywd
Dipton Mill Inn, Dipton Mill, Northumberland
Dog & Gun Inn, Aughton, Lancashire
Dog & Patridge Inn, Sowood, West Yorkshire
Dolphin Inn, Betchworth, Surrey
Dolphin Inn, Kingston, Devon
Dove, Dargate, Kent
Dove, Hammersmith, London W6
Dove & Olive Branch, Grasmere, Cumbria
Drake Manor Inn, Buckland Monachorum, Devon
Drewe Arms, Broadhembury, Devon
Drewe Arms, Drewsteignton, Devon
Druid Inn, Birchover, Derbyshire
Drunken Duck, Barngates, Cumbria
Duke of Cumberland Arms, Henley, West Sussex
Duke of Cumberlands Head, Clifton, Oxfordshire
Duke's Head Hotel, King's Lynn, Norfolk
Duke of Cambridge, London N1
Duke of York, Iddesleigh, Devon
Duke William, Ickham, Kent
Dundas Arms, Kintbury, Berkshire
Dyffryn Arms, Pontfaen, Dyfed
Dysart Arms, Bunbury, Cheshire

Eagle, Cambridge
Eagle, Skerne, East Yorkshire

Eagle & Child, Stow-on-the-Wold, Gloucestershire
Ebrington Arms, Ebrington, Gloucestershire
Eight Bells, Dover, Kent
Elephant & Castle, Bloxham, Oxfordshire
Evesham Hotel, Evesham, Worcs
Eyre Arms, Hassop, Derbyshire

Falcon, St Mawgan, Cornwall
Falcon Inn, Fotheringhay, Northamptonshire
Falkland Arms, Great Tew, Oxfordshire
Farmers Arms, Birstmorton, Worcestershire
Farmers Arms, Muker, North Yorkshire
Farmers Arms, St Asaph, The Waen, Clwyd
Fat Cat, Norwich
Fat Cat, Sheffield
Fat Lamb Country Inn, Ravenstonedale, Cumbria
Feathers, Hedley on the Hill, Northumberland
Feathers Hotel, Ledbury, Herefordshire
Feversham Arms, Farndale, North Yorkshire
Fishermans Rest, Tichfield, Hampshire
Fishermans Tavern Hotel, Broughty Ferry, Dundee
Five Arrows, Waddesdon, Buckinghamshire
Five Bells, Smock Alley, West Chiltington, West Sussex
Five Horseshoes, Maidensgrove, Oxfordshire
Five Mile House, Duntisbourne Abbots, Gloucestershire
Fleece, Bretforton, Worcestershire
Flower Pot, Derby
Flower Pots, Cheriton, Hampshire
Forest, Fence, Lancashire
Forest Gate Inn, Bell Common, Essex
Foresters Arms, Graffham, West Sussex
Fountain Head, Branscombe, Devon
Fountain Inn, Ashurst, West Sussex
Fox, Lower Oddington, Gloucestershire
Fox and Barrel, Cotebrook, Cheshire
Fox Inn, Corfe Castle, Dorset
Fox Inn, Corscombe, Dorset
Fox & Goose, Illston on the Hill, Leicestershire
Fox & Hounds, Barnston Village, Merseyside
Fox & Hounds, Carthorpe, North Yorkshire
Fox & Hounds, London SW1
Fox & Hounds, Riseley, Bedfordshire
Fox & Hounds, Singleton, West Sussex
Fox & Pheasant, London SW10
Frampton Arms, Moreton, Dorset
Free Press, Cambridge
Free Trade, Berwick-upon-Tweed, Northumberland
Friars Inn, Chillesford, Suffolk
Full Moon, Rudge, Somerset

Game Cock, Austwick, North Yorkshire

Gardeners Arms, Tostock, Suffolk
Gate Inn, Marshside, Kent
General Havelock Inn, Haydon Bridge, Northumberland
General Tarleton, Ferrensby, North Yorkshire
George, Alstonefield, Derbyshire
George, Bridport, Dorset
George, London E11
George, Shalford, Essex
George, Southwark, London SE1
George Inn, Blackawton, Devon
George Inn, Hubberholme, North Yorkshire
George Inn, Lacock, Wiltshire
George & Dragon, nr Coolham, West Sussex
George & Dragon, Elsworth, Cambridgeshire
George & Dragon, Rowde, Wiltshire
George & Dragon, Watton at Stone, Hertfordshire
George & Dragon, West Wycombe, Buckinghamshire
George of Stamford, Stamford, Lincolnshire
George III, Penmaenpool, Gwynedd
Globe, Appley, Somerset
Globe on the Lake, Alresford, Hampshire
Goat Inn, Glan Dwyfach, Gwynedd
Golden Cross Hotel, Bromsgrove, Worcestershire
Golden Heart, Brimpsfield, Gloucestershire
Golden Key, Snape, Suffolk
Golden Rule, Ambleside, Cumbria
Goldengrove, London E15
Golf Tavern, Earlsferry, Fife
Goose & Cuckoo, Upper Llanover, Monmouthshire
Gordon Arms Hotel, Mountbenger, Selkirk
Grain Store, Oakham, Leicestershire
Grapes, London E14
Grapes, Maentwrog, Gwynedd
Grapes Hotel, Gee Cross, Cheshire
Grape Vaults, Leominster, Hereford
Green Dragon, Young's End, Essex
Green Man, Gosfield, Essex
Green Man, Thriplow, Bedfordshire
Grenadier, London SW1
Greyhound, Beaconsfield, Buckinghamshire
Greyhound, St Ippollitts, Hertfordshire
Greyhound, Wadhurst, East Sussex
Greyhound, Whitchurch on Thames, Oxfordshire
Gribble Inn, Oving, West Sussex
Griffin, Fletching, East Sussex
Griffin Inn, Shustoke, West Midlands
Griffins Head, Chillenden, Kent
Groes, Ty'n y Groes, Gwynedd
Grosvenor Arms, Aldford, Cheshire
Guildford Arms, Edinburgh
Gun Inn, Findon, West Sussex

Gurnard's Head Hotel, Treen, Cornwall

Half Moon, Felixstowe, Suffolk
Half Moon, Sheepwash, North Devon
Halfway Bridge, Lodsworth, West Sussex
Halfway House, Kingsand, Cornwall
Halfway House, Pitney, Somerset
Halfway Inn, Pisgar, nr Aberystwyth
Halzephron, Gunwalloe, Cornwall
Hambro Arms, Milton Abbas, Dorset
Hamilton Hall, London EC2
Hampden Arms, Great Hampden, Buckinghamshire
Hampshire Bowman, Dundridge, Hampshire
Hand in Hand, Wimbledon, London SW19
Hare Arms, Stow Bardolph, Norfolk
Hare & Hounds, Foss Cross, Gloucestershire
Hare & Hounds, Levens, Cumbria
Harp Inn, Old Radnor, Presteigne
Harrow Inn, Steep, Hampshire
Haunch of Venison, Salisbury, Wiltshire
Havelock Tavern, London W14
Highbury Vaults, Bristol
Holly Bush, Potters Crouch, Hertfordshire
Holly Bush Inn, Makeney, Derbyshire
Hoop, Stock, Essex
Hornimans, London SE13
Horns, Crazies Hill, Berkshire
Horse & Groom, East Woodlands, Somerset
Hoste Arms, Burnham Market, Norfolk
Howard Arms, Ilmington, Warwickshire
Howtown Hotel, Howtown, Cumbria
Hunters Hall, Kingscote, Gloucestershire

Imperial, Exeter, Devon
Inn at West End, West End, Surrey
Inn at Whitewell, Whitewell, Lancashire
Inn for All Seasons, Little Barrington, Gloucestershire
Inverarnan Inn, Inverarnan, Stirlingshire

John O'Gaunt Inn, Sutton, Bedfordshire
Johnsburn House, Balerno, Lothian
Jolly Farmer, Cookham Dean, Berkshire
Jolly Sailor, Orford, Suffolk
Jolly Sailor, Ramsey, Cambridgeshire
Jolly Sailors, Brancaster Staithe, Norfolk
Jolly Sportsman, East Chiltington, East Sussex
Juggs, Kingston, East Sussex

Kentish Horse, Markbeech, Kent
Kilberry Inn, Kilberry, Argyll
Killiecrankie Hotel, Killiecrankie, Perth & Kinross
King William IV, Hailey, Oxfordshire
King William IV, Mickleham, Surrey

King John Inn, Tollard Royal, Wiltshire
Kingfisher, Colyton, Devon
Kings Arms, Blakeney, Norfolk
Kings Arms, Cleobury Mortimer, Shropshire
Kings Arms, Didmarton, Gloucestershire
Kings Arms, Emsworth, Hampshire
Kings Arms, Farthingstone, Northamptonshire
Kings Arms, Fernhurst, West Sussex
Kings Arms, Litton, Somerset
Kings Arms, Old Amersham, Buckinghamshire
Kings Arms, Ombersley, Worcestershire
Kings Arms, Oxford
Kings Arms, Stockland, Devon
Kings Arms, Tring, Herts
Kings Arms, Wing, Leicestershire
Kings Head, Great Bircham, Norfolk
Kings Head, Laxfield, Suffolk
Kings Head, Ruan Lanihorne, Cornwall
Kings Head, Udimore, East Sussex
Kings Head, Wadenhoe, Northamptonshire
Kings Head Inn, Wootton by Woodstock,
    Oxfordshire
Kirkstile Inn, Loweswater, Cumbria
Knife & Cleaver, Houghton Conquest,
    Bedfordshire

Ladbroke Arms, London W11
Lade Inn, Kilmahog, Stirlingshire
Lairhillock, Netherley, Grampian
Lamarsh Lion, Bures, Suffolk
Lamb, Burford, Oxfordshire
Lamb, Eastbourne, East Sussex
Lamb, Great Rissington, Gloucestershire
Lamb, London WC1
Lamb Inn, Axbridge, Somerset
Lamb Inn, Hindon, Wiltshire
Lamb Inn, Wartling, East Sussex
Lamb & Flag, London WC2
Lamb Tavern, Leadenhall Market, London EC3
Langstrath Country Inn, Stonethwaite,
    Cumbria
Langton Arms, Tarrant Monkton, Dorset
Leathers Smithy, Langley, Cheshire
Lewes Arms, Lewes, East Sussex
Lifeboat Inn, Thornham, Norfolk
Linnet, Great Hinton, Wiltshire
Lions of Bledlow, Bledlow, Buckinghamshire
Little Pack Horse, Bewdley, Worcestershire
Liverpool Arms, Menai Bridge, Anglesey
Loch Tummel Inn, Strathtummel, Perthshire
Loch Melfort Hotel, Arduaine, Argyll
Lock Inn, Fort Augustus, Highland
Loders Arms, Loders, Dorset
London Inn, Molland, Devon
Lone Tree, Thornborough, Buckinghamshire
Lord Crewe Arms, Blanchland, Co Durham
Lord Denman, Dagenham, Essex

Lord Nelson, Burnham Thorpe, Norfolk
Lord Nelson, Southwold, Suffolk
Lord Raglan, Staplehurst, Kent
Lord Moon of the Mall, London SW1
Lough Pool, Sellack, Herefordshire
Lower Red Lion, St Albans, Hertfordshire

Magazine Hotel, Wallasey, Merseyside
Mallyan Spout Hotel, Goatland, North
    Yorkshire
Malet Arms, Newton Tony, Wiltshire
Malsters Arms, Tuckenhay, Devon
Malt Shovel, Brearton, North Yorkshire
Manor Arms, Broughton-in-Furness, Cumbria
Manor House Inn, Carterway Heads,
    Northumberland
Manor Inn, Lower Ashton, Devon
Marisco Tavern, Lundy Island, Devon
Marquis of Lorne, Nettlecombe, Dorset
Martins Arms, Colston Bassett,
    Nottinghamshire
Marton Arms, Thornton-in-Lonsdale, North
    Yorkshire
Masham, Stockton-on-Tees, Cleveland
Masons Arms, Branscombe, Devon
Masons Arms, Taunton, Somerset
Maybush Inn, Waldringfield, Suffolk
Mermaid Inn, Rye, East Sussex
Merry Harriers, Clayhidon, Devon
Merrymouth, Fifield, Oxfordshire
Mildmay Colours, Holbeton, Devon
Mill Brook, Southpool, Devon
Mill Inn, Withington, Gloucestershire
Miners Arms, Eyam, Derbyshire
Miners Arms, Hemerdon, Devon
Miners Arms, Milltown, Derbyshire
Mole & Chicken, Easington, Buckinghamshire
Montague, Shepton Montague, Somerset
Moon & Mushroom Inn, Swilland, Suffolk
Moon & Spoon, Slough, Berkshire
Moon in the Square, Bournemouth, Dorset
Moon under Water, Manchester
Moors Inn, Appleton-le-Moors, North Yorkshire
Morritt Arms, Greta Bridge, Co Durham
Moulin, Moulin, Perthshire
Mountain Inn, Lutton, Devon
Murrel Arms, Barnham, West Sussex
Museum Inn, Farnham, Dorset
Myerscough Hotel, Balderstone, Lancashire

Nags Head, Pickhill, North Yorkshire
Nags Head, Usk, Monmouthshire
Nags Head Inn, Castle Donington,
    Leicestershire
Nantyffin Cider Mill, Crickhowell, Powys
Narrow Boat, Skipton, North Yorkshire
Navigation, Buxworth, Derbyshire

Navigation Inn, Lapworth, Warwickshire
Neeld Arms, Grittleton, Wiltshire
New Fountain Inn, Whimple, Devon
New Inn, Manaccan, Cornwall
New Inn, Pembridge, Herefordshire
New Inn, Tywardreath, Cornwall
New Inn At Coln, Coln St Aldwyns,
    Gloucestershire
New Inn, Worstead, Norfolk
Newfield Inn, Seathwaite, Cumbria
Nobody Inn, Doddiscombsleigh, Devon

Oddfellows Arms, Mellor, Gtr Manchester
Old Bakery, Kenilworth, Warwickshire
Old Barn, Glooston, Leicestershire
Old Black Lion, Hay-on-Wye, Herefordshire
Old Bridge Hotel, Huntingdon
Old Bridge Inn, Ripponden, West Yorkshire
Old Boot Inn, Stanford Dingley, Berkshire
Old Chequers, Crowle, Worcestershire
Old Crown, Cavendish Bridge, Leicestershire
Old Crown, Kelston, Somerset
Old Crown, Weybridge, Surrey
Old Dungeon Ghyll, Great Langdale, Cumbria
Old Green Tree, Bath
Old Harker's Arms, Chester
Old House at Home, Chidham, West Sussex
Old Inn, Carbost, Isle of Skye
Old Manor, Bracknell, Berkshire
Old Swan at Swan Bottom, Buckinghamshire
Old Three Pigeons, Nesscliffe, Shropshire
Old Yew Tree Inn, South Wingfield, Derbyshire
Olde Cheshire Cheese, London EC4
Olde Mitre, London EC1
Olde White Harte, Burnham-on-Crouch, Essex
Olde White Harte, Hull
Oddfellows Arms, Mellor, Cheshire
Olive Branch, Clipsham, Rutland
One Eyed Rat, Ripon, North Yorkshire
Opera House, Tunbridge Wells, Kent

Pack Horse Inn, Widdop, West Yorkshire
Pandora, Restronguet Creek, Cornwall
Pandy, Dorstone, Herefordshire
Panniers, Barnstaple, Devon
Pear Tree, Whiteley, Wiltshire
Peat Spade, Longstock, Hampshire
Peldon Rose, Peldon, Essex
Pen-y-Gwryd Hotel, Nantgwynant, Gwynedd
Pendre Inn, Cilgerran, Dyfed
Penhelig Arms Hotel, Aberdovey, Gwynedd
ercy Arms, Chatton, Northumberland
easant, Bassenthwaite Lake, Cumbria
asant, Keyston, Cambridgeshire
e Arms, London SW3
e House, Stafford
    Ashmansworth, Hampshire

Plough, Blackbrook, Surrey
Plough, Effingham, Surrey
Plough Inn, Finstock, Oxfordshire
Plough Inn, Radwinter, Essex
Plough & Sail, Paglesham Eastend, Essex
Plough & Sail, Snape Maltings, Suffolk
Plume of Feathers, Crondall, Hampshire
Polecat Inn, Prestwood, Buckinghamshire
Port Gaverne Inn, Port Gaverne, Cornwall
Pot Kiln, Frilsham, Berkshire
Pot & Glass, Egglescliffe, Cleveland
Preston Gate Inn, Poughill, Cornwall
Prince Albert, Ely, Cambridgeshire
Prince Albert, Freith, Buckinghamshire
Prince of Wales, Aberdeen
Prince of Wales, Stow Maries, Essex
Punch Bowl Inn, Crosthwaite, Cumbria
Pyewipe Inn, Fossebank, Lincolnshire

Quarryman, Edmonston, Cornwall
Queens Head, Bramfield, Suffolk
Queens Head, Dennington, Suffolk
Queens Head, Glanwydden, Conwy
Queens Head, Great Whittington,
    Northumberland
Queens Head, Lichfield, Staffordshire
Queens Head, Milbourne Port, Dorset
Queens Head, Newton, Cambridgeshire
Queens Head, Pinner
Quiet Woman, Earl Sterndale, Derbyshire

Raby Hunt Inn, Summerhouse, Durham
Radnor Arms, Nunton, Wiltshire
Railway Inn, Dorridge, West Midlands
Ram Inn, South Woodchester, Gloucestershire
Ramblers Rest, Chislehurst, Kent
Rashleigh, Polkerris, Cornwall
Raven, Poulshot, Wiltshire
Red Lion, Baddesley Ensor, Warwickshire
Red Lion, Boldre, Hampshire
Red Lion, Broadclyst, Devon
Red Lion, Burnsall, North Yorkshire
Red Lion, Chenies, Buckinghamshire
Red Lion, Coleshill, Buckinghamshire
Red Lion, Crick, Northamptonshire
Red Lion, Freshwater, Isle of Wight
Red Lion, Great Kingshill, Buckinghamshire
Red Lion, Hinxton, Cambridgeshire
Red Lion, Icklingham, Suffolk
Red Lion, Kilmington, Wiltshire
Red Lion, Langthwaite, North Yorkshire
Red Lion, London SW1
Red Lion, London W1
Red Lion, Marsworth, Hertfordshire
Red Lion, Nottingham Fee, Oxfordshire
Red Lion, Snargate, Kent
Red Lion, Steeple Aston, Oxfordshire

Red Lion, Stevington, Bedfordshire
Red Lion, Stiffkey, Norfolk
Red Lion, Stodmarsh, Kent
Red Lion, Upper Sheringham, Norfolk
Red Lion, Westbury-on-Severn,
    Gloucestershire
Red Lion Country Inn, Clanville, Hampshire
Red Lion Inn, Litton, Derbyshire
Red Lion Inn, Milfield, Northumberland
Redoubt, Wakefield, West Yorkshire
Regent, Walton-on-Thames, Surrey
Richard I, Greenwich, London SE10
Ring O'Bells, Chagford, Devon
Ring O'Bells, Compton Martin, Somerset
Rising Sun, High Wych, Hertfordshire
Rising Sun, St Mawes, Cornwall
Rising Sun, Tarporley, Cheshire
Rising Sun, Woodland, Devon
Riverside Inn at Cound, Cressage, Shropshire
Rob Roy, Tweedmouth, Berwick-upon-Tweed,
    Northumberland
Robin Hood, Elkesley, Nottinghamshire
Rock, Haytor Vale, Devon
Roebuck, Brimfield, Shropshire
Romping Cat, Old Woods, Shropshire
Roscoe Head, Liverpool
Rose Cottage, Alciston, East Sussex
Rose and Crown, Elham, Kent
Rose & Crown, Fletching, East Sussex
Rose & Crown, Huish Episcopi, Somerset
Rose and Crown, Oxford
Rose & Crown, Perry Wood, Kent
Rose & Crown, Ridgmont, Bedfordshire
Rose & Crown, Romaldkirk, Co. Durham
Rose & Crown, St Albans, Hertfordshire
Rose & Crown, Stoke St Gregory, Somerset
Rose & Crown, Trent, Dorset
Rose & Crown, Wimbledon, London SW19
Rose & Crown, Wivenhoe, Essex
Rose & Crown Inn, Snettisham, Norfolk
Rose & Thistle, Rockbourne, Hampshire
Roseland, Philleigh-in-Roseland, Cornwall
Royal Oak, Bovingdon Green, Hertfordshire
Royal Oak, Cardington, Shropshire
Royal Oak, Didsbury, Gtr Manchester
Royal Oak, Earlsdon, Warwickshire
Royal Oak, Easterton, Wiltshire
Royal Oak, Langstone, Hampshire
Royal Oak, London SE1
Royal Oak, Luxborough, Somerset
Royal Oak, Millthorpe, Derbyshire
Royal Oak, Nunnington, North Yorkshire
Royal Oak, Pirbright, Surrey
Royal Oak, Poynings, West Sussex
Royal Oak, Ramsden, Oxfordshire
Royal Oak, Riley Green, Lancashire
Royal Oak, Wineham, West Sussex

Royal Oak, Wootton Rivers, Wiltshire
Royal Oak Hotel, Welshpool, Powys
Royal Oak Inn, Bongate, Cumbria
Royal Oak Inn, Lostwithiel, Cornwall
Royal Oak Inn, Painswick, Gloucestershire
Royal Oak Inn, Winsford, Somerset
Royal Standard of England, Forty Green,
    Buckinghamshire
Rugglestone Inn, Widecombe-in-the-Moor,
    Devon
Rydespence Inn, Whitney-on-Wye,
    Herefordshire

S. Fowler & Co, Ryde, Isle of Wight
Saddle Hotel, Alnmouth, Northumberland
Sailors Return, Beaumaris, Anglesea
St Kew Inn, St Kew, Cornwall
St Machar's Bar, Old Aberdeen
St Vincent Arms, Sutton-upon-Derwent, North
    Yorkshire
Salutation Inn, Pontargothi, Carmarthenshire
Salutation Inn, Weobley, Herefordshire
Sandrock, Wrecclesham, Surrey
Saracens Head, Erpingham, Norfolk
Sawley Arms, Sawley, North Yorkshire
Scotch Piper, Lydiate, Merseyside
Seafood Restaurant & Bar, St Monance, Fife
Seven Stars, Bottlesford, Wiltshire
Seven Stars, Falmouth, Cornwall
Seven Stars, London WC2
Seven Tuns, Chedworth, Gloucestershire
Seymour Arms, Witham Friary, Somerset
Shakespear Tavern, Durham City
Shaven Crown Hotel, Shipton-under-
    Wychwood, Oxfordshire
Shelley's Hotel, Lewes, East Sussex
Shieldag Bar, Sheieldag, Ross-shire
Ship, Porthmadog, Gwynedd
Ship, Wandsworth, London SW18
Ship, Wincle, Cheshire
Ship Inn, Banff, Grampian
Ship Inn, Barnoldby-le-Beck, Lincolnshire
Ship Inn, Dunwich, Suffolk
Ship Inn, Elie, Fife
Ship Inn, Levington, Suffolk
Ship Inn, Noss Mayo, Devon
Ship Inn, Porlock, Somerset
Shiremoor Farm, New York, Tyne & Wear
Shrewsbury Arms, Little Budworth, Cheshire
Six Bells, Chiddingly, East Sussex
Sloop Inn, Bantham, Devon
Smithfield, Derby
Smugglers Inn, Alfriston, East Sussex
Snooty Fox, Kirkby Lonsdale, Cumbria
Sole Bay Inn, Southwold, Suffolk
Sow & Pigs, Toddington, Bedfordshire
Spaniards Inn, London NW3

Sparkford Inn, Sparkford, Somerset
Spread Eagle, Stourton, Wiltshire
Springer Spaniel, Treburley, Cornwall
Spyway Inn, Askerwell, Dorset
Stag, Ballscross, West Sussex
Stag, Mentmore, Buckinghamshire
Stagg Inn, Titley, Herefordshire
Stags Head Inn, Yarlington, Somerset
Stalybridge Station Buffet Bar, Stalybridge,
   Cheshire
Star, Bath, Somerset
Star, Cop Mere End, Staffordshire
Star, Heathfield, East Sussex
Star, Lidgate, Suffolk
Star, London SW1
Star, St Just In Penwith, Cornwall
Star Inn, East Tytherley, Hampshire
Star Inn, Sulgrave, Northants
Star Inn, West Leake, Leicestershire
Starbank, Edinburgh
Stilton Cheese, Somerby, Rutland
Strathmore Arms, Holwick, Northumberland
Sun Inn, Bentworth, Hampshire
Sun Inn, Chop Gate, nr Fangdale Beck, North
   Yorkshire
Sun Inn, Clun, Shropshire
Sun Inn, Corfton, Shropshire
Sun Inn, Dent, Cumbria
Sun Inn, Dunsfold, Surrey
Sun Inn, Feering, Essex
Sun Inn, Winforton, Herefordshire
Swan at Swan Bottom, Buckinghamshire
Swan Inn, Little Haven, Haverfordwest
Swan Inn, Swinbrook, Oxfordshire
Swan in the Rushes, Loughborough,
   Leicestershire
Sweeney Todd, Reading, Berkshire
Sydney Arms, Chislehurst, Kent

Tafarn Y Porth, Caernarvon, Gwynedd
Talbot, Mells, Somerset
Talbot Inn, Berwick St John, Wiltshire
Talbot Inn, Knightwick, Worcestershire
Tally Ho! Aswarby, Lincolnshire
Tally Ho! Broughton, Hampshire
Tan Hill Inn, Tan Hill, North Yorkshire
Taps, Lytham, Lancashire
Tayvallich Inn, Tayvallich, Strathclyde
Thatched Public House, Poulton-le-Fylde,
   Lancashire
Thatched Tavern, Cheapside, Ascot, Berkshire
Theydon Oak, Coopersale Common, Essex
Thomas Ingoldsby, Canterbury, Kent
Three Acres, Roydhouse, West Yorkshire
Three Compasses, Deal, Kent
Three Chimneys, Biddenden, Kent
Three Crowns Inn, Ullingswick, Herefordshire

Three Horseshoes, Batcombe, Somerset
Three Horseshoes, Elsted, West Sussex
Three Horseshoes, Madingley, Cambridgeshire
Three Horseshoes, Powerstock, Dorset
Three Horseshoes, Warham All Saints, Norfolk
Three Kings, Hanley Castle, Worcestershire
Three Judges, Partick Cross, Glasgow
Three Moles, Selham, West Sussex
Three Shires Inn, Little Langdale, Cumbria
Three Stags Heads, Wardlow Mires,
   Derbyshire
Three Tuns, Biddenham, Bedfordshire
Three Tuns, Bishop's Castle, Shropshire
Three Tuns, Bransgore, Hampshire
Tibbie Shiels Inn, St Mary's Loch, Borders
Tiger Inn, East Dean, East Sussex
Tinners Arms, Zennor, Cornwall
Tite Inn, Chadlington, Oxfordshire
Tollemache Arms, Mossley, Lancashire
Tollgate Inn, Holt, Wiltshire
Tormaukin Hotel, Glendevon, Perth & Kinross
Tower Bank Arms, Near Sawrey, Cumbria
Tradesman's Arms, Stokenham, Devon
Travellers Rest, Grasmere, Cumbria
Tregilly Wartha, Nancenoy Constantine,
   Cornwall
Trooper Inn, Stourton Caundle, Dorset
Trout at Tadpole Bridge, Buckland Marsh,
   Oxfordshire
Trout, Barlow, Derbyshire
Trout Inn, Lechlade-on-Thames,
   Gloucestershire
Tuckers Grave, Faulkland, Somerset
Turf Tavern, Oxford
Two Brewers, Street, Somerset

Ubiquitous Chip, Glasgow
Unicorn, Ludlow, Shropshire
Union Hotel, Bangor, Gwynedd

Valiant Trooper, Aldbury, Hertfordshire
Verzons, Trumpet, Herefordshire
Victoria, Earl Soham, Suffolk
Victoria, Lincoln
Village Inn, Liddington, Wiltshire
Vine, Brierley Hill, West Midlands
Vine, Hambledon, Hampshire
Vine Tree Inn, Llangattock, Powys
Viper, Mill Green, Essex

Waggon & Horses, Doulting Beacon, Somerset
Walpole Arms, Itteringham, Norfolk
Walter de Cantelupe Inn, Kempsey,
   Worcestershire
Waltzing Weasel, Birch Vale, Derbyshire
Warenford Lodge, Warenford, Northumberland
Warrington Hotel, London W9

Wasdale Head Inn, Wasdale Head, Cumbria
Waterdine, Llanfair Waterdine, Powys
Watermill Inn, Ings, Cumbria
Weighbridge Inn, Nailsworth, Minchinhampton, Gloucestershire
Wenlock Edge Inn, Wenlock Edge, Shropshire
Westminster Arms, London SW1
Wetherspoons, Woking, Surrey
Wheatsheaf, Combe Hay, Somerset
Wheatsheaf Hotel, Swinton, Borders
Wheatsheaf Inn, Raby, Merseyside
White Cross Hotel, Richmond
White Hart, Bythorn, Cambridgeshire
White Hart, Castle Combe, Wiltshire
White Hart, Great Yeldham, Essex
White Hart, Littleton-on-Severn, Gloucestershire
White Hart, Ludgvan, Cornwall
White Hart, Wytham, Oxfordshire
White Hart Inn, Newbold on Stour, Warwickshire
White Horse, Bridge, Kent
White Horse, Cilcain, Flintshire
White Horse, Frampton Mansell, Gloucestershire
White Horse, Fulham, London SW6
White Horse, Hascombe, Surrey
White Horse, Hedgerley Village, Buckinghamshire
White Horse, Hertford
White Horse, Pleshey, Essex
White Horse, Woolley Moor, Derbyshire
White Horse Hotel, Blakeney, Norfolk
White Horse Inn, Beverley, East Yorkshire
White Horse Inn, Droxford, Hampshire
White Horse Inn, Easton, Suffolk
White Horse Inn, Priors Dean, Hampshire

White House, Blackstone Edge, Lancashire
White Lion, Barthomley, Cheshire
White Lion, Cray, North Yorkshire
White Swan, Llanfrynach, Monmouthshire
White Swan, Sileby, Leicestershire
White Swan, Stow cum Quy, Cambridgeshire
White Swan Hotel, Middleham, North Yorkshire
White Swan Hotel, Pickering, North Yorkshire
Whitelocks, Leeds
Wig & Mitre, Lincoln
Wilford Bridge, Melton, Suffolk
William IV, Albury Heath, Surrey
William IV, Bletchingly, Surrey
Windjammer, Dartmouth, Devon
Windsor Castle, London W8
Withies Inn, Compton, Surrey
Woodman, Nuthampstead, Hertfordshire
Woolpack, Elstead, Surrey
Woolpack, Slad, Gloucestershire
Wotton Hatch, Wotton, Surrey
Wykeham Arms, Winchester, Hampshire
Wyndham Arms, Clearwell, Gloucestershire

Ye Olde Bulls Head, Beaumaris, Anglesey
Ye Olde Bulls Head, Little Hucklow, Derbyshire
Ye Olde Dolphin, Derby
Ye Olde Gate, Brassington, Derbyshire
Ye Olde Smugglers Inn, Alfriston, East Sussex
Ye Olde Trip to Jerusalem, Nottingham
Ye Olde Two Brewers, Shaftesbury, Dorset
Ye Olde White Harte, Hull, East Yorkshire
Ypres Castle, Rye, East Sussex
Yr Hen Orsaf, Aberystwyth, Dyfed

Zetland Arms, Kingsdown, Kent